Advances in Knowledge Discovery and Data Mining

Advances in Knowledge Discovery and Data Mining

Edited by

Usama M. Fayyad
Jet Propulsion Laboratory, California Institute of Technology

Gregory Piatetsky-Shapiro
GTE Laboratories Incorporated

Padhraic Smyth
Jet Propulsion Laboratory, California Institute of Technology

& Ramasamy Uthurusamy
General Motors R & D Center

AAAI Press / The MIT Press
Menlo Park, California • Cambridge, Massachusetts • London, England

Copublished and distributed by The MIT Press,
Massachusetts Institute of Technology,
Cambridge, Massachusetts, and London, England.
ISBN 0-262-56097-6

Library of Congress Cataloging-in-Publication Data

Advances in knowledge discovery and data mining / Usama M. Fayyad
    ... [et al.] eds.
        p.   cm.
    Includes bibliographical references and index.
    1. Knowledge acquisition (Expert systems)   2. Databases.
3. Knowledge, Theory of.   4. Artificial intelligence.   I. Fayyad,
Usama M.
QA76.76.E95A38   1996
001.4'225'028563—dc20   95-45329
                                                                CIP

This book was set in Computer Modern
by The AAAI Press and manufactured in the United States of America

Fifth printing

Contents

Foreword
On the Barriers and Future of Knowledge Discovery

Gio Wiederhold
Stanford University

Knowledge discovery is the most desirable end-product of computing. Finding new phenomena or enhancing our knowledge about them has a greater long-range value than optimizing production processes or inventories, and is second only to tasks that help preserve our world and our environment. It is not surprising that it is also one of the most difficult computing challenges to do well.

A number of complementary approaches exist. They all have advantages and problems. Knowledge acquisition from experts often includes discovery as a byproduct, since the formalization often uncovers new linkages, but that discovery also depends on human recognition of unexpected phenomena. Such discoveries must often be validated with broader tests, since a single expert typically has a narrow view of the world, and hence a bias which should be eliminated, or at least circumscribed. One of the hardest tasks has been the formalization of common knowledge, which is nearly transparent in human reasoning, but crucial if obvious tautologies or errors are to be avoided (Lenat and Guha 1991). Discovering knowledge from data, or data-mining, can help in turn in overcoming the limitations of these alternatives.

When acquiring knowledge from data the problems of understanding capabilities and barriers must be dealt with so that the emerging knowledge discovery discipline can avoid the ups and downs that arise if great expectations are put forward, and then remain unfulfilled. Such roller-coaster rides have characterized other disciplines within computer science, and the parent disciplines *of knowledge discovery,* artificial intelligence and statistics, are not trusted widely. We don't want to add knowledge discovery to the trio of 'Lies, Damned Lies, and Statistics' (Huff 1954).

The major barrier in obtaining high-quality knowledge from data is due to the limitations of the data itself. The data are *rarely* collected for the mining of knowledge, but *usually as* a byproduct of other tasks.

The data may have limited breadth or coverage, say they only cover the population that has a certain credit card, and hence do not represent all of the market for a product. Such limitations can be circumscribed, and extrapolations can take the difference in population into account.

The data may have limited depth, and essential variables may be missing. In most clinical studies no data on diet is available, although for many medical problems food and drink are significant factors. Careful clinical trials try to eliminate such bias by careful study design, selection of participants, and randomization of treatments. Such controls are absent in data mining. Data mining based on correlation can lead to non-sensical results, as pointed out by Piero Bonissone: "Drinking diet drinks leads to obesity." If causality is to be shown, then access to historical data can be crucial. The RX system used the straightforward heuristic: Causality requires that for any patient event C *(cause)* had to precede E *(effect),* i.e., the effect of a drug has to follow its administration. A strong correlation without consistent precedence at most implies the existence of a third variable, say an injury I for which C is the drug of choice and E is a secondary effect of the injury (Blum 1982). Often the real cause I is not recorded and data mining is futile. That is a danger in many market studies, when having sufficient income and making a purchase is correlated, but the desire for the purchase is caused by other factors.

Having a good model which lists and links all the candidate variables, including those that are not available in any databases helps in establishing sound knowledge acquisition schemes, although it cannot resolve problems of missing data (Walker 1987). An important criterion is completeness of sets and subsets, for instance that all drug types suitable for a type of injury are listed, so that one can determine that the injury was diagnosed and treated. The knowledge base used by CARNOT provided a model of common knowledge, but completeness can not be claimed (Collet 1991). Completeness was attempted for a very limited domain of immunological diseases and treatments in the RX system by adopting and encoding the hierarchical structure from a medical textbook, at least in the branches that were ancestors of the data used in the study. Without completeness, the closed world assumption cannot be used, and 'negation-by-failure', an essential feature of PROLOG and similar deductive methods, is invalid (Reiter 1978).

A model can also be used to collect known relationships, so that computing is not wasted on the obvious. Actually, sometimes the obvious is not initially obvious to the human expert. In the RX system one of the first unknown causal relationships discovered was that being registered in the immunology clinic led to prescriptions of aspirin: true, but hardly exciting. Since in RX all discovered knowledge had the same represcntation as the controlling knowledge, initial and discovered knowledge could be merged and the system can focus on assessing yet unknown relationships.

To increase the basis for knowledge discovery multiple databases may be combined, say databases that have cost and sales data. Database integration, however, is still a problematic area, especially where the source domains differ. The product designators are likely to differ, say internal product identifiers versus the Universal Product Codes used by point-of-sales scanners. Even after the matching rules for the join variables have been obtained the scope of the actual data must be inspected with care, since their coverage may not match. Cost may cover a company's manufactured products, but sales may include accessories added by vendors, and exclude spoilage and goods traded for market development or for goodwill. Again, having good models of the processes that link the data help, but such expertise has to cover domain intersections and there may be few knowledgeable people. At the same time, knowledge acquisition techniques may be used to discover unexpected differences or similarities, and those can trigger the development of better models.

Better models are crucial to making sense out of the complexities in large scientific databases. Large volumes of data are being gathered in molecular biology, by earth-observing satellites, and in ecological monitoring. But all of this data is of little use unless it can be analyzed, and here knowledge discovery and model building go hand-in-hand. For instance, the structure of DNA determines the structure of proteins to be generated in cells, but knowledge about promotors and inhibitors is needed to determine how and when these proteins are created (Oliver 1994).

Model-driven knowledge acquisition will compare well with browsing, which has become the must popular method of gathering information. Through tools such as Mosaic we can follow links in the world wide web, and gathering specific topic information is aided by tools as HARVEST (Bowman et al 1994, Hardy 1994) and ALIWEB (Koster 1994). Discovery based on these approaches is quite incomplete, and biases are great due to the differences in information submission from different sources and the conflicts that arise when valuable material is copyrighted for publication. However, the success of these browsing tools encourages improvements, and may blur the distinctions with knowledge discovery based on artificial intelligence techniques.

Results from browsing *do* provide references to sites of new resources for data and information. Data are the ore for data mining, and much unpublished data can be located via on-line world wide web references. Information found in retrieved documents can help in model building. Models are also important in database integration, and in querying and analyzing data. Research in managing heterogeneous systems is starting to deal formally with the terminology used in their domains (Wiederhold 1994). Active databases can notify mining programs that new data are available.

It is clear that there is much related activity in the world of information systems. Sharing models and technology with related disciplines will make knowledge discovery an integral part of the information system enterprise.

References

R. L. Blum, 1982. *Discovery and Representation of Causal Relationships from a Large Time-Oriented Clinical Database: The RX Project.* Lecture Notes in Medical Informatics, no.19, Lindberg and Reichertz, (eds.). New York: Springer-Verlag.

Bowman, C. Mic.; Danzig, Peter B.; Manber, Udi; and Schwartz, Michael F. 1994. Scalable Internet Resource Discovery: Research Problems and Approaches. *Communications of the ACM,* 37(8):98–107, August.

Collet, C.; Huhns, M.; and Shen, W-M. 1991. Resource Integration Using a Large Knowledge Base in Carnot. *IEEE Computer,* 24(12): 55–63, Dec.

Oliver, D. E.; and Altman, R. B. 1994. Extraction of SNOMED Concepts from Medical Record Texts. Tech. Rep. KSL-94-33, Knowledge Systems Laboratory, Medical Computer Science, Stanford Univ.

Huff, D. 1954. *How to Lie With Statistics.* New York: W. W. Norton. & Company.

Koster, M. 1994. *On Information Discovery.* http://web.nexor.co.uk/users/ mak/doc/robots/robots.html

Lenat, D.; and Guha, R. 1991. *Building Large Knowledge-Based Systems.* Reading, Mass: Addison-Wesley.

xi

Hardy, D. R.; and Schwartz, M. F. 1994. *Harvest User Manual.* http:// harvest.cs.colorado.edu, Oct.

Reiter, R. 1978. On Closed World Data Bases. In *Logic and Data Bases,* ed. Gallaire and Minker. New York: Plenum Press.

Walker, M. G. 1987. How Feasible Is Automated Discovery? *IEEE Expert* 2(1):78–82.

Wiederhold, G. 1994. Interoperation, Mediation, and Ontologies. FGCS / ICOT Workshop, Tokyo, Dec.

Preface

The decade of the 1990s has brought a growing data glut problem to the worlds of science, business, and government. Our capabilities for collecting and storing data of all kinds have far outpaced our abilities to analyze, summarize, and extract "knowledge" from this data. Traditional methods of data analysis, based mainly on the human dealing directly with the data, simply do not scale to handling voluminous data sets. While database technology has provided us with the basic tools for the efficient storage and lookup of large data sets, the issue of how to help humans understand and analyze large bodies of data remains a difficult and unsolved problem. To deal with the data glut, a new generation of intelligent tools for automated data mining and knowledge discovery is needed. This need has been recognized by researchers in different areas, including artificial intelligence, statistics, data warehousing, on-line analysis processing, expert systems, and data visualization.

Growing interest in data mining and discovery in databases, coupled with the realization that the specialists in these areas were not always aware of the state of the art in other areas, led us to organize a series of workshops on Knowledge Discovery in Databases (KDD) in 1989, 1991, 1993, and 1994.[1]

The success of the first volume, *Knowledge Discovery in Databases* (AAAI/MIT Press, 1991), and the significant research progress since then, have motivated us to present an updated view of the state-of-the-art of the field.

This collection is composed of a carefully selected set of papers from the 1994 KDD Workshop as well as a set of invited survey chapters. The 1994 workshop papers have been expanded and rewritten to provide a uniform treatment of certain key issues, such as the use of *domain knowledge* in discovery, the *process* of knowledge discovery, the treatment of *uncertainty*, perspectives from *statistics*, and coverage of several successful *applications* of KDD systems. The introductory chapter gives a broad coverage of the areas of knowledge discovery and data mining.

---

[1]The continuing growth of interest in KDD culminated in the conversion of 1995 KDD workshop into the First International Conference on Knowledge Discovery and Data Mining, that was held along with the Fourteenth International Joint Conference on Artificial Intelligence (IJCAI-95) in Montreal, Canada in August of 1995.

The remaining chapters focus on particular issues and methods. We believe this collection gives a broad overview of the state of the art in the research and application of knowledge discovery and data mining in the context of large databases.

Putting together a book on an exciting and rapidly evolving area of new technology is not an easy matter. The KDD workshops have served to bring together researchers interested in this area from many fields and many countries. That only established our base community for sampling the chapters to include in this book. This collection is the result of the outstanding cooperation of almost a hundred people on several continents. First and foremost we thank the authors of the chapters of this book who performed multiple revisions under tight time constraints, and who put up with our demands and suggested changes. We are also grateful to the the members of the program committee of the 1994 AAAI Workshop on KDD.

We thank Mike Hamilton, who ably coordinated the typesetting and timely production of this volume. For encouraging this effort throughout the last two years, we are grateful to our management at our respective institutions: NASA and the Jet Propulsion Laboratory—California Institute of Technology, GTE Laboratories, and General Motors Research and Development Center. Finally, this work would not have been possible without the patience and understanding of our families.

– Usama Fayyad, Gregory Piatetsky-Shapiro,
Padhraic Smyth, & Ramasamy Uthurusamy.

1 From Data Mining to Knowledge Discovery: An Overview

Usama M. Fayyad
Jet Propulsion Laboratory
California Institute of Technology

Gregory Piatetsky-Shapiro
GTE Laboratories

Padhraic Smyth
Jet Propulsion Laboratory
California Institute of Technology

We are drowning in information,
but starving for knowledge
– *John Naisbett*

Abstract

The explosive growth of many business, government, and scientific databases has far outpaced our ability to interpret and digest this data, creating a need for a new generation of tools and techniques for automated and intelligent database analysis. These tools and techniques are the subject of the rapidly emerging field of knowledge discovery in databases (KDD) and are the subject of this book. This chapter presents an overview of the state of the art in this field. We first clarify our view of the relation between knowledge discovery and data mining. We begin with a definition of the KDD process and basic data mining methods. We proceed to cover application issues in KDD including guidelines for selecting an application and current challenges facing practitioners in the field. The discussion relates methods and problems to applicable chapters in the book, with the goal of providing a unifying vision of the common overall goals shared by the chapters.

1.1 What Is this Book About?

In the last decade, we have seen an explosive growth in our capabilities to both generate and collect data. Advances in scientific data collection (e.g. from remote sensors or from space satellites), the widespread introduction of bar codes for almost all commercial products, and the computerization of many business (e.g. credit card purchases) and government transactions (e.g. tax returns) have generated a flood of data. Advances in data storage technology, such as faster, higher capacity, and cheaper storage devices (e.g. magnetic disks, CD-ROMS), better database management systems, and data warehousing technology, have allowed us to transform this data deluge into "mountains" of stored data.

Representative examples are easy to find. In the business world, one of the largest databases in the world was created by Wal-Mart (a U.S. retailer) which handles over 20 million transactions a day (Babcock 1994). Most health-care transactions in the U.S. are being stored in computers, yielding multi-gigabyte databases, which many large companies are beginning to analyze in order to control costs and improve quality (e.g. see Matheus, Piatetsky-Shapiro, & McNeill, this volume). Mobil Oil Corporation, is developing a data warehouse capable of storing over 100 terabytes of data related to oil exploration (Harrison 1993).

There are huge scientific databases as well. The human genome database project (Fasman, Cuticchia, & Kingsbury 1994) has collected gigabytes of data on the human genetic code and much more is expected. A database housing a sky object catalog from a major astronomy sky survey (e.g. see Fayyad, Djorgovski, & Weir, this volume) consists of billions of entries with raw image data sizes measured in terabytes. The NASA Earth Observing System (EOS) of orbiting satellites and other spaceborne instruments is projected to generate on the order of 50 gigabytes of remotely sensed image data per *hour* when operational in the late 1990s and early in the next century (Way & Smith 1991).

Such volumes of data clearly overwhelm the traditional manual methods of data analysis such as spreadsheets and ad-hoc queries. Those methods can create informative reports from data, but cannot analyze the contents of those reports to focus on important knowledge. A significant need exists for a new generation of techniques and tools with the ability to *intelligently* and *automatically* assist humans in analyzing the mountains of data for nuggets of useful knowledge. These techniques and tools are the subject of the emerging field of knowledge discovery in databases (KDD).

The interest in KDD has been increasing, as evidenced by the number of recent workshops (Piatetsky-Shapiro 1991, Piatetsky-Shapiro 1993, Ziarko 1994, Fayyad & Uthurusamy 1994), which culminated in the

First International Conference on Knowledge Discovery and Data Mining (Fayyad & Uthurusamy 1995). A growing number of publications have been devoted to the topic, including (Inmon & Osterfelt 1991, Piatetsky-Shapiro 1992, Parsaye & Chignell 1993, Cercone & Tsuchiya 1993, Piatetsky-Shapiro et al 1994, Piatetsky-Shapiro 1995). These various publications and special issues document some of the many KDD applications which have been reported across diverse fields in business, government, medicine, and science (see Section 1.6). This book brings together the most recent relevant research in the field, continuing in the tradition of the first *Knowledge Discovery in Databases* book (Piatetsky-Shapiro and Frawley 1991).

The chapter begins by discussing the historical context of KDD and data mining and the choice of title for this book. We begin by explaining the distinction between the terms *data mining* and *knowledge discovery*, and explain how they fit together. The basic view we adopt is one where data mining refers to a class of methods that are used in some of the steps comprising the overall KDD process. We then provide a definition of KDD in Section 1.2. The typical steps involved in the KDD process are outlined and discussed in Section 1.3. We then focus in particular on data mining methods in the context of the overall KDD process. Section 1.4 covers the general issues involved in data mining while Section 1.5 discusses specific data mining methods. Having defined the basic terms and introduced some of the methods, we turn our attention to the practical application issues of KDD in Section 1.6. Section 1.7 concludes the chapter with a preview of the rest of the chapters in this volume. Throughout, we relate the discussion of particular methods and techniques to applicable chapters with the goal of providing a unifying vision of the common overall goals shared by the chapters constituting this book.

1.1.1 About this Book's Title

Historically the notion of finding useful patterns (or nuggets of knowledge) in raw data has been given various names, including knowledge discovery in databases, data mining, knowledge extraction, information discovery, information harvesting, data archaeology, and data pattern processing. The term *knowledge discovery in databases*, or KDD for short, was coined in 1989 to refer to the broad process of finding knowledge in data, and to emphasize the "high-level" application of particular *data mining* methods. The term *data mining* has been commonly used by statisticians, data analysts and the MIS (Management Information Systems) community, while KDD has been mostly used by artificial intelligence and machine learning researchers.

In this overview chapter we adopt the view that KDD refers to the overall *process* of discovering useful knowledge from data while *data mining* refers to the application of algorithms for extracting patterns from data without the additional steps of the KDD process (such as incorporating appropriate prior knowledge and proper interpretation of the results). These additional steps are essential to ensure that useful information (knowledge) is derived from the data. Blind application of data mining methods (rightly criticised as "fishing" or "dredging," and sometimes a "mining," in the statistical literature) can be a dangerous activity in that invalid patterns can be discovered without proper interpretation.

Thus, the overall *process* of finding and interpreting patterns from data is referred to as the KDD *process*, typically interactive and iterative, involving the repeated application of specific *data mining* methods or algorithms and the interpretation of the patterns generated by these algorithms. In sections to follow we will provide a more detailed definition of the overall KDD process and a more detailed look at specific data mining methods.

In combining the two terms "data mining" and "knowledge discovery" in the title of the book, we are attempting to build bridges between the statistical, database, and machine learning communities and appeal to a wider audience of information systems developers. The dual nature of the title reflects the contents of the book and the direction of the field, namely a focus on both types of issues: (i) the overall knowledge discovery process which includes preprocessing and postprocessing of data as well as interpretation of the discovered patterns as knowledge, and (ii) particular data mining methods and algorithms aimed solely at extracting patterns from raw data.

1.1.2   Links Between KDD and Related Fields

KDD is of interest to researchers in machine learning, pattern recognition, databases, statistics, artificial intelligence, knowledge acquisition for expert systems, and data visualization. KDD systems typically draw upon methods, algorithms, and techniques from these diverse fields. The unifying goal is extracting knowledge from data in the context of large databases.

In the fields of machine learning and pattern recognition, overlap with KDD lies in the study of theories and algorithms for systems which extract patterns and models from data (mainly data mining methods). KDD focuses on the extension of these theories and algorithms to the problem of finding special patterns (ones that may be interpreted as *useful or interesting knowledge*, see the next section) in large sets of real-world data. KDD also has much in common with statistics, particularly exploratory data analysis (EDA). KDD systems often embed particular statistical procedures for modeling data and handling noise within an overall knowledge discovery framework.

Machine discovery which targets the discovery of empirical laws from observation and experimentation (Shrager & Langley 1990), and *causal modeling* for the inference of causal models from data (Spirtes, Glymour, & Scheines 1993) are related research areas. Kloesgen & Zytkow (this volume) provide a glossary of terms common to KDD and machine discovery.

Another related area is *data warehousing*, which refers to the recently popular MIS trend for collecting and cleaning transactional data and making them available for on-line retrieval. A popular approach for analysis of data warehouses has been called OLAP (*on-line analytical processing*), after a new set of principles proposed by Codd (1993). OLAP tools focus on providing multi-dimensional data analysis, which is superior to SQL (standard query language) in computing summaries and breakdowns along many dimensions. We view both knowledge discovery and OLAP as related facets of a new generation of intelligent information extraction and management tools.

1.1.3   A Simple Illustrative Example

In the discussion of KDD and data mining methods in this chapter, we shall make use of a simple example to make some of the notions more concrete. Figure 1.1 shows a simple two-dimensional artificial data set consisting of 23 cases. Each point on the graph represents a person who has been given a loan by a particular bank at some time in the past. The horizontal axis represents the income of the person, the vertical axis represents the total personal debt of the person (mortgage, car payments, etc.). The data has been classified into 2 classes: the x's represent persons who have defaulted on their loans, the o's represent persons whose loans are in good status with the bank. Thus, this simple artificial data set could represent a historical data set which may contain useful knowledge from the point of view of the bank making the loans. Note that in actual KDD applications there are typically many more dimensions (up to several hundreds) and many more data points (many thousands or even millions). The purpose here is to illustrate basic ideas on a small problem in 2-dimensional space.

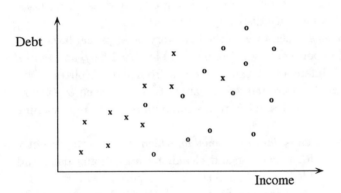

Figure 1.1
A simple data set with 2 classes used for illustrative purposes.

1.2   A Definition of Knowledge Discovery in Databases

To reflect the recent developments and growth in KDD, we have revised the definition of KDD given in (Frawley, Piatetsky-Shapiro, & Matheus 1991). We first start with a general statement of this definition in words:

> *Knowledge discovery in databases* is the non-trivial process of identifying valid, novel, potentially useful, and ultimately understandable patterns in data.

Let us examine these terms in more detail.

- *Data* is a set of facts F (e.g., cases in a database). In our simple example of Figure 1.1, F is the collection of 23 cases with three fields each containing the values of *debt*, *income*, and *loan status*.

- *Pattern* is an expression E in a language L describing facts in a subset F_E of F. E is called a pattern if it is simpler (in some sense, see below) than the enumeration of all facts in F_E. For example, the pattern: "If income $<$ \$$t$, then person has defaulted on the loan" would be one such pattern for an appropriate choice of t. This pattern is illustrated graphically in Figure 1.2.

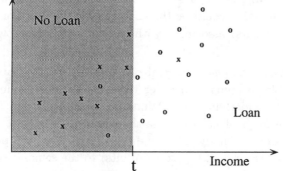

Figure 1.2
Using a single threshold on the income variable to try to classify the loan data set.

- *Process:* Usually in KDD process is a multi-step process, which involves data preparation, search for patterns, knowledge evaluation, and refinement involving iteration after modification. The process is assumed to be non-trivial—that is, to have some degree of search autonomy. For example, computing the mean income of persons in the loan example, while producing a useful result, does not qualify as discovery.

- *Validity:* The discovered patterns should be valid on new data with some degree of certainty. A measure of certainty is a function C mapping expressions in L to a partially or totally ordered measurement space M_C. An expression E in L about a subset $F_E \subset F$ can be assigned a certainty measure $c = C(E, F)$. For example, if the boundary for the pattern shown in Figure 1.2 is moved to the right, its certainty measure would drop since more good loans would be admitted into the shaded region (no loan).

- *Novel:* The patterns are novel (at least to the system). Novelty can be measured with respect to changes in data (by comparing current values to previous or expected values) or knowledge (how a new finding is related to old ones). In general, we assume this can be measured by a function $N(E, F)$, which can be a boolean function or a measure of degree of novelty or unexpectedness.

- *Potentially Useful:* The patterns should potentially lead to some useful actions, as measured by some utility function. Such a function U maps expressions in L to a partially or totally ordered measure space M_U: hence, $u = U(E, F)$. For example, in the loan data set this function could be the expected increase in profits to the bank (in dollars) associated with the decision rule shown in Figure 1.2.

- *Ultimately Understandable:* A goal of KDD is to make patterns understandable to humans in order to facilitate a better understanding of the underlying data. While this is difficult to measure precisely, one frequent substitute is the simplicity measure. Several measures of simplicity exist, and they range from the purely syntactic (e.g., the size of a pattern in bits) to the semantic (e.g., easy for humans to comprehend in some setting). We assume this is measured, if possible, by a function S mapping expressions E in L to a partially or totally ordered measure space M_S: hence, $s = S(E, F)$.

An important notion, called *interestingness*, is usually taken as an overall measure of pattern value, combining validity, novelty, usefulness, and simplicity. Some KDD systems have an explicit interestingness function $i = I(E, F, C, N, U, S)$ which maps expressions in L to a measure space M_I. Other systems define interestingness indirectly via an ordering of the discovered patterns.

Given the notions listed above, we may state our definition of knowledge as viewed from the narrow perspective of KDD as used in this book. This is by no means an attempt to define "knowledge" in the philosophical or even the popular view. The purpose of this definition is specify what an algorithm used in a KDD process may consider knowledge.

- *Knowledge:* A pattern $E \in L$ is called knowledge if for some user-specified threshold $i \in M_I$, $I(E, F, C, N, U, S) > i$.

Note that this definition of knowledge is by no means absolute. As a matter of fact, it is purely user-oriented, and determined by whatever functions and thresholds the user chooses. For example, one instantiation of this definition is to select some thresholds $c \in M_C$, $s \in M_S$, and $u \in M_u$, and calling a pattern E knowledge if and only if

$$C(E, F) > c \text{ and } S(E, F) > s \text{ and } U(S, F) > u.$$

By appropriate settings of thresholds, one can emphasize accurate predictors or useful (by some cost measure) patterns over others. Clearly, there is an infinite space of how the mapping I can be defined. Such decisions are left to the user and the specifics of the domain.

> *Data Mining* is a step in the KDD process consisting of particular data mining algorithms that, under some acceptable computational efficiency limitations, produces a particular enumeration of patterns E_j over F (see Sections 1.4 and 1.5 for more details)

Note that the space of patterns is often infinite, and the enumeration of patterns involves some form of search in this space. The computational efficiency constraints place severe limits on the subspace that can be explored by the algorithm.

> *KDD Process* is the process of using data mining methods (algorithms) to extract (identify) what is deemed knowledge according to the specifications of measures and thresholds, using the database F along with any required preprocessing, subsampling, and transformations of F.

The data mining component of the KDD process is mainly concerned with means by which patterns are extracted and enumerated from the data. Knowledge discovery involves the *evaluation* and possibly *interpretation* of the patterns to make the decision of what constitutes knowledge and what does not. It also includes the choice of encoding schemes, preprocessing, sampling, and projections of the data prior to the data mining step.

1.3   The KDD Process

The KDD process is interactive and iterative, involving numerous steps with many decisions being made by the user. Brachman & Anand (this

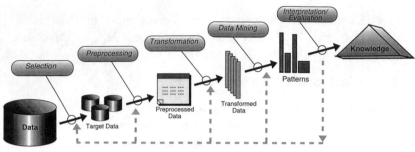

Figure 1.3
An overview of the steps comprising the KDD process.

volume) give a practical view of the KDD process emphasizing the interactive nature of the process. Here we broadly outline some of its basic
steps:

1. Developing an understanding of the application domain, the relevant prior knowledge, and the goals of the end-user.

2. Creating a target data set: selecting a data set, or focusing on a
   subset of variables or data samples, on which discovery is to be
   performed.

3. Data cleaning and preprocessing: basic operations such as the removal of noise or outliers if appropriate, collecting the necessary
   information to model or account for noise, deciding on strategies
   for handling missing data fields, accounting for time sequence information and known changes.

4. Data reduction and projection: finding useful features to represent
   the data depending on the goal of the task. Using dimensionality reduction or transformation methods to reduce the effective
   number of variables under consideration or to find invariant representations for the data.

5. Choosing the data mining task: deciding whether the goal of the
   KDD process is classification, regression, clustering, etc. The various possible *tasks* of a data mining algorithm are described in more
   detail in Section 1.4.1.

6. Choosing the data mining algorithm(s): selecting method(s) to be
   used for searching for patterns in the data. This includes deciding
   which models and parameters may be appropriate (e.g. models

for categorical data are different than models on vectors over the reals) and matching a particular data mining method with the overall criteria of the KDD process (e.g. the end-user may be more interested in understanding the model than its predictive capabilities—see Section 1.4.2).

7. Data mining: searching for patterns of interest in a particular representational form or a set of such representations: classification rules or trees, regression, clustering, and so forth (see Section 1.5 for details). The user can significantly aid the data mining method by correctly performing the preceding steps.

8. Interpreting mined patterns, possible return to any of steps 1–7 for further iteration.

9. Consolidating discovered knowledge: incorporating this knowledge into the performance system, or simply documenting it and reporting it to interested parties. This also includes checking for and resolving potential conflicts with previously believed (or extracted) knowledge.

The KDD process can involve significant iteration and may contain loops between any two steps. The basic flow of steps (although not the potential multitude of iterations and loops) are illustrated in Figure 1.3. Most previous work on KDD has focused on step 7—the data mining. However, the other steps are of considerable importance for the successful application of KDD in practice. See the chapter by Brachman & Anand, this volume, for a more elaborate account of this aspect.

Having defined the basic notions and introduced the KDD process, we now focus on the data mining component, which has by far received the most attention in the literature.

1.4   An Overview of Data Mining Methods

The data mining component of the KDD process often involves repeated iterative application of particular data mining methods. The objective of this section is to present a unified overview of some of the most popular data mining methods in current use. We use the terms *patterns* and *models* loosely throughout this chapter: a pattern can be thought of as instantiation of a model, e.g., $f(x) = 3x^2 + x$ is a pattern whereas $f(x) = \alpha x^2 + \beta x$ is considered a model.

Data mining involves fitting models to, or determining patterns from, observed data. The fitted models play the role of inferred knowledge: whether or not the models reflect *useful* or *interesting* knowledge is part of the overall, interactive KDD process where subjective human judgment is usually required. There are two primary mathematical formalisms used in model fitting: the *statistical* approach allows for non-deterministic effects in the model (for example, $f(x) = \alpha x + e$ where e could be a Gaussian random variable), whereas a *logical* model is purely deterministic ($f(x) = \alpha x$) and does not admit the possibility of uncertainty in the modeling process. We will focus primarily on the statistical/probabilistic approach to data mining: this tends to be the most widely-used basis for practical data mining applications given the typical uncertainty about the exact nature of real-world data-generating processes. See the chapter by Elder & Pregibon (this volume) for a perspective from the field of statistics.

Most data mining methods are based on concepts from machine learning, pattern recognition and statistics: classification, clustering, graphical models, and so forth. The array of different algorithms for solving each of these problems can often be quite bewildering to both the experienced data analyst and the novice. In this section we offer a brief overview of data mining methods and in particular try to convey the notion that most (if not all) methods can be viewed as extensions or hybrids of a few basic techniques and principles.

The section begins by discussing the primary tasks of data mining and then shows that the data mining methods to address these tasks consist of three primary algorithmic components: *model representation*, *model evaluation*, and *search*. The section concludes by discussing particular data mining algorithms within this framework.

1.4.1 The Primary Tasks of Data Mining

The two "high-level" primary goals of data mining in practice tend to be *prediction* and *description*. Prediction involves using some variables or fields in the database to predict unknown or future values of other variables of interest. Description focuses on finding human-interpretable patterns describing the data. The relative importance of prediction and description for particular data mining applications can vary considerably. However, in the context of KDD, description tends to be more important than prediction. This is in contrast to pattern recognition and machine learning applications (such as speech recognition) where prediction is often the primary goal (see Lehmann 1990, for a discussion from a statistical perspective).

The goals of prediction and description are achieved by using the following primary data mining tasks.

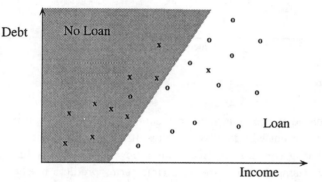

Figure 1.4
A simple linear classification boundary for the loan data set: shaded region denotes class "no loan."

- *Classification* is learning a function that maps (classifies) a data item into one of several predefined classes (Hand 1981; Weiss & Kulikowski 1991; McLachlan 1992). Examples of classification methods used as part of knowledge discovery applications include classifying trends in financial markets (Apte & Hong, this volume) and automated identification of objects of interest in large image databases (Fayyad, Djorgovski, & Weir, this volume). Figure 1.4 shows a simple partitioning of the loan data into two class regions—note that it is not possible to separate the classes perfectly using a linear decision boundary. The bank might wish to use the classification regions to automatically decide whether future loan applicants will be given a loan or not.

- *Regression* is learning a function which maps a data item to a real-valued prediction variable. Regression applications are many, e.g., predicting the amount of biomass present in a forest given

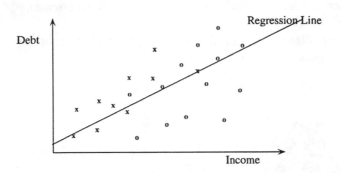

Figure 1.5
A simple linear regression for the loan data set.

remotely-sensed microwave measurements, estimating the probability that a patient will die given the results of a set of diagnostic tests, predicting consumer demand for a new product as a function of advertising expenditure, and time series prediction where the input variables can be time-lagged versions of the prediction variable. Figure 1.5 shows the result of simple linear regression where "total debt" is fitted as a linear function of "income": the fit is poor since there is only a weak correlation between the two variables.

- *Clustering* is a common descriptive task where one seeks to identify a finite set of categories or clusters to describe the data (Titterington, Smith & Makov 1985: Jain & Dubes 1988). The categories may be mutually exclusive and exhaustive, or consist of a richer representation such as hierarchical or overlapping categories. Examples of clustering applications in a knowledge discovery context include discovering homogeneous sub-populations for consumers in marketing databases and identification of sub-categories of spectra from infra-red sky measurements (Cheeseman & Stutz, this volume). Figure 1.6 shows a possible clustering of the loan data set into 3 clusters: note that the clusters overlap allowing data points to belong to more than one cluster. The original class labels (denoted by x's and o's in the previous figures) have been replaced by +'s to indicate that the class membership is no longer assumed known. Closely related to clustering is the task of *probability density estimation* which consists of techniques for estimating from data the joint multi-variate probability density function of all of the variables/fields in the database (Silverman 1986).

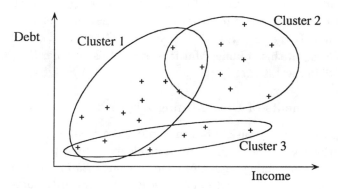

Figure 1.6
A simple clustering of the loan data set into 3 clusters. Note that original labels are replaced by +'s.

- *Summarization* involves methods for finding a compact description for a subset of data. A simple example would be tabulating the mean and standard deviations for all fields. More sophisticated methods involve the derivation of summary rules (Agrawal et al., this volume), multivariate visualization techniques, and the discovery of functional relationships between variables (Zembowicz & Zytkow, this volume). Summarization techniques are often applied to interactive exploratory data analysis and automated report generation.

- *Dependency Modeling* consists of finding a model which describes significant *dependencies* between variables. Dependency models exist at two levels: the *structural* level of the model specifies (often in graphical form) which variables are locally dependent on each other, whereas the *quantitative* level of the model specifies the strengths of the dependencies using some numerical scale. For example, probabilistic dependency networks use conditional independence to specify the structural aspect of the model and probabilities or correlations to specify the strengths of the dependencies (Heckerman, this volume; Glymour et al., 1987). Probabilistic dependency networks are increasingly finding applications in areas as diverse as the development of probabilistic medical expert systems from databases, information retrieval, and modeling of the human genome.

- *Change and Deviation Detection* focuses on discovering the most significant changes in the data from previously measured or normative values (Berndt & Clifford, this volume; Guyon et al., this volume; Kloesgen, this volume; Matheus et al., this volume; Basseville & Nikiforov 1993).

1.4.2   The Components of Data Mining Algorithms

Having outlined the primary tasks of data mining, the next step is to construct algorithms to solve them. One can identify three primary components in any data mining algorithm: *model representation, model evaluation,* and *search.* This reductionist view is not necessarily complete or fully encompassing: rather, it is a convenient way to express the key concepts of data mining algorithms in a relatively unified and compact manner (Cheeseman (1990) outlines a similar structure).

- *Model Representation* is the language L for describing discoverable patterns. If the representation is too limited, then no amount of training time or examples will produce an accurate model for the data. For example, a decision tree representation, using univariate (single-field) node-splits, partitions the input space into hyperplanes which are parallel to the attribute axes. Such a decision-tree method cannot discover from data the formula $x = y$ no matter how much training data it is given. Thus, it is important that a data analyst fully comprehend the representational assumptions which may be inherent to a particular method. It is equally important that an algorithm designer clearly state which representational assumptions are being made by a particular algorithm. Note that more powerful representational power for models increases the danger of overfitting the training data resulting in reduced prediction accuracy on unseen data. In addition the search becomes much more complex and interpretation of the model is typically more difficult.

- *Model Evaluation* estimates how well a particular pattern (a model and its parameters) meet the criteria of the KDD process. Evaluation of predictive accuracy (validity) is based on cross validation. Evaluation of descriptive quality involves predictive accuracy, novelty, utility, and understandability of the fitted model. Both logical and statistical criteria can be used for model evaluation. For example, the maximum likelihood principle chooses the parameters for the model which yield the best fit to the training data.

- *Search Method* consists of two components: *Parameter Search* and *Model Search*. In *parameter search* the algorithm must search for the parameters which optimize the model evaluation criteria given observed data and a fixed model representation. For relatively simple problems there is no search: the optimal parameter estimates can be obtained in closed form. Typically, for more general models, a closed form solution is not available: greedy iterative methods are commonly used, e.g., the gradient descent method of backpropagation for neural networks. *Model Search* occurs as a loop over the parameter search method: the model representation is changed so that a family of models are considered. For each specific model representation, the parameter search method is instantiated to evaluate the quality of that particular model. Implementations of model search methods tend to use heuristic search techniques since the size of the space of possible models often prohibits exhaustive search and closed form solutions are not easily obtainable.

1.5   A Discussion of Popular Data Mining Methods

There exist a wide variety of data mining methods: here we only focus on a subset of popular techniques. Each method is discussed in the context of model representation, model evaluation, and search.

1.5.1   Decision Trees and Rules

Decision trees and rules that use univariate splits have a simple representational form, making the inferred model relatively easy to comprehend by the user. However, the restriction to a particular tree or rule representation can significantly restrict the functional form (and thus the approximation power) of the model. For example, Figure 1.2 illustrates the effect of a threshold "split" applied to the income variable for loan data set: it is clear that using such simple threshold splits (parallel to the feature axes) severely limit the type of classification boundaries which can be induced. If one enlarges the model space to allow more general expressions (such as multivariate hyperplanes at arbitrary angles), then the model is more powerful for prediction but may be much more difficult to comprehend. There are a large number of decision tree and rule induction algorithms described in the machine learning and applied statistics literature (Breiman et al 1984; Quinlan 1992).

To a large extent they are based on likelihood-based model evaluation methods with varying degrees of sophistication in terms of penalizing model complexity. Greedy search methods, which involve growing and pruning rule and tree structures, are typically employed to explore the super-exponential space of possible models. Trees and rules are primarily used for predictive modeling, both for classification (Apte & Hong, this volume; Fayyad, Djorgovski, & Weir, this volume) and regression, although they can also be applied to summary descriptive modeling (Agrawal et al., this volume).

1.5.2   Nonlinear Regression and Classification Methods

These methods consist of a family of techniques for prediction which fit linear and non-linear combinations of basis functions (sigmoids, splines, polynomials) to combinations of the input variables. Examples include feedforward neural networks, adaptive spline methods, projection pursuit regression, and so forth (see Friedman (1989), Cheng & Titterington (1994), and Elder & Pregibon (this volume) for more detailed discussions). Consider neural networks, for example. Figure 1.7 illustrates the type of non-linear decision boundary which a neural network might find for the loan data set. In terms of model evaluation, while networks of the appropriate size can universally approximate any smooth function to any desired degree of accuracy, relatively little is known about the representation properties of *fixed* size networks estimated from *finite* data sets. In terms of model evaluation, the standard squared error and cross entropy loss functions used to train neural networks can be viewed as log-likelihood functions for regression and classification respectively (Geman, Bienenstock & Doursat 1992; Ripley 1994). Backpropagation is a parameter search method which performs gradient descent in parameter (weight) space to find a local maximum of the likelihood function starting from random initial conditions. Nonlinear regression methods, though powerful in representational power, can be very difficult to interpret. For example, while the classification boundaries of Figure 1.7 may be more accurate than the simple threshold boundary of Figure 1.2, the threshold boundary has the advantage that the model can be expressed as a simple rule of the form "if income is greater than threshold t then loan will have good status" to some degree of certainty.

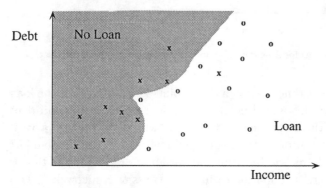

Figure 1.7
An example of classification boundaries learned by a non-linear classifier (such as a neural network) for the loan data set.

1.5.3   Example-based Methods

The representation is simple: use representative examples from the database to approximate a model, i.e., predictions on new examples are derived from the properties of "similar" examples in the model whose prediction is known. Techniques include nearest-neighbor classification and regression algorithms (Dasarathy 1991) and case-based reasoning systems (Kolodner, 1993). Figure 1.8 illustrates the use of a nearest neighbor classifier for the loan data set: the class at any new point in the 2-dimensional space is the same as the class of the closest point in the original training data set.

A potential disadvantage of example-based methods (compared with tree-based methods for example) is that a well-defined distance metric

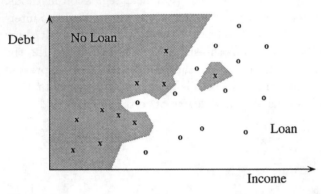

Figure 1.8
Classification boundaries for a nearest neighbor classifier for the loan data set.

for evaluating the distance between data points is required. For the loan data in Figure 1.8 this would not be a problem since income and debt are measured in the same units: but if one wished to include a variable such as the duration of the loan, then it would require more effort to define a sensible metric between the variables. Model evaluation is usually based on cross-validation estimates (Weiss & Kulikowski, 1991) of a prediction error: "parameters" of the model to be estimated can include the number of neighbors to use for prediction and the distance metric itself. Like non-linear regression methods, example-based methods are often asymptotically quite powerful in terms of approximation properties, but conversely can be difficult to interpret since the model is implicit in the data and not explicitly formulated. Related techniques include kernel density estimation (Silverman 1986) and mixture modeling (Titterington, Smith, & Makov 1985).

1.5.4   Probabilistic Graphical Dependency Models

Graphical models specify the probabilistic dependencies which underlie a particular model using a graph structure (Pearl 1988; Whittaker, 1990). In its simplest form, the model specifies which variables are directly dependent on each other. Typically these models are used with categorical or discrete-valued variables, but extensions to special cases, such as Gaussian densities, for real-valued variables are also possible.

Within the artificial intelligence and statistical communities these models were initially developed within the framework of probabilistic expert systems: the structure of the model and the parameters (the conditional probabilities attached to the links of the graph) were elicited from experts. More recently there has been significant work in both the AI and statistical communities on methods whereby both the structure and parameters of graphical models can be learned from databases directly (Buntine, this volume; Heckerman, this volume). Model evaluation criteria are typically Bayesian in form and parameter estimation can be a mixture of closed form estimates and iterative methods depending on whether a variable is directly observed or hidden. Model search can consist of greedy hill-climbing methods over various graph structures. Prior knowledge, such as a partial ordering of the variables based on causal relations, can be quite useful in terms of reducing the model search space. Although still primarily at the research phase, graphical model induction methods are of particular interest to KDD since the graphical form of the model lends itself easily to human interpretation.

1.5.5   Relational Learning Models

While decision-trees and rules have a representation restricted to propositional logic, relational learning (also known as inductive logic programming) uses the more flexible pattern language of first-order logic. A relational learner can easily find formulas such as X=Y. Most research so far on model evaluation methods for relational learning are logical in nature. The extra representational power of relational models comes at the price of significant computational demands in terms of search. See Dzeroski (this volume) for a more detailed discussion.

Given the broad spectrum of data mining methods and algorithms, our brief overview is inevitably limited in scope: there are many data mining techniques, particularly specialized methods for particular types of data and domains, which were not mentioned specifically in the discussion. We believe the general discussion on data mining tasks and components has general relevance to a variety of methods. For example, consider time series prediction: traditionally this has been cast as a predictive regression task (autoregressive models and so forth). Recently, more general models have been developed for time series applications such as non-linear basis function, example-based, and kernel methods. Furthermore, there has been significant interest in *descriptive* graphical and local data modeling of time series rather than purely *predictive* modeling (Weigend & Gershenfeld 1993). Thus, although different algorithms and applications may appear quite different on the surface, it is not uncommon to find that they share many common components. Understanding data mining and model induction at this component level clarifies the task of any data mining algorithm and makes it easier for the user to understand its overall contribution and applicability to the KDD process.

We would like to remind the reader that our discussion and overview of data mining methods has been both cursory and brief. There are two important points we would like to make clear:

1. *Automated Search:* Our brief overview has focused mainly on automated methods for extracting patterns and/or models from data. While this is consistent with the definition we gave earlier, it does not necessarily represent what other communities might refer to as *data mining*. For example, some use the term to designate any manual search of the data, or search assisted by queries to a DBMS or humans visualizing patterns in data as data mining. In other communities, it is used to refer to the automated correlation of data from transactions or the automated generation of transaction reports. We choose to focus only on methods that contain certain degrees of search autonomy.

2. *Beware the Hype:* The state-of-the-art in automated methods in data mining is still in a fairly early stage of development. There are no established criteria for deciding which methods to use in which circumstances, and many of the approaches are based on crude heuristic approximations to avoid the expensive search required to find optimal or even good solutions. hence, the reader should be careful when confronted with overstated claims about the great ability of a system to mine useful information from large (or even small) databases.

1.6   Application Issues

In the business world, the most successful and widespread application of KDD is "Database Marketing," which is a method of analyzing customer databases, looking for patterns among existing customer preferences and using those patterns for more targeted selection of future customers. Business Week, a popular business magazine in the United States, carried a cover story on Database Marketing (Berry 1994) that estimated that over 50% of all retailers are using or planning to use database marketing. The reason is simple—significant results can be obtained using this approach: e.g. a 15-20% percent increase in credit-card purchases reported by American Express (Berry 1994).

Another major business use of data mining methods is the analysis and selection of stocks and other financial instruments. There are already numerous investment companies (Barr and Mani 1994) which pick stocks using a variety of advanced data mining methods.

Several successful applications have been developed for analysis and reporting on change in data. These include Coverstory from IRI (Schmitz, Armstrong, & Little 1990), Spotlight from A.C. Nielsen (Anand & Kahn 1992) for supermarket sales data, and KEFIR from GTE, for health care databases (Matheus, Piatetsky-Shapiro, & McNeil, this volume)

Fraud detection and prevention is another area where KDD plays a role. While there have been many applications, published information is, for obvious reasons, not readily available. Here we mention just a few noteworthy examples. A system for detecting healthcare provider fraud in electronically submitted claims, has been developed at Travelers Insurance by Major and Riedinger (1992). The Internal Revenue Service has developed a pilot system for selecting tax returns for audits. Neural network based tools, such as Nestor FDS (Blanchard 1994) have been developed for detecting credit-card fraud and are reportedly watching millions of accounts.

A number of interesting and important scientific applications of KDD have also been developed. Example application areas in science include

- *Astronomy:* The SKICAT system from JPL/Caltech is used by astronomers to automatically identify stars and galaxies in a large-scale sky survey for cataloging and scientific analysis (see Fayyad, Djorgovski, & Weir, this volume).

- *Molecular Biology:* Systems have been developed for finding patterns in molecular structures (Conklin, Fortier, and Glasgow 1993) and in genetic data (Holder, Cook, and Djoko 1994).

- *Global Climate Change Modeling:* Spatio-temporal patterns such as cyclones are automatically found from large simulated and observational datasets (Stolorz et al. 1994).

Other recent applications are described in (Fayyad & Uthurusamy 1994–1995, Piatetsky-Shapiro 1993).

1.6.1 Guidelines for Selecting a Potential KDD Application

The criteria for selecting applications can be divided into practical and technical. The practical criteria for KDD projects are similar to those for other application of advanced technology, while the technical ones are more specific to KDD.

Practical criteria include consideration of the **potential for significant impact of an application**. For business applications this could be measured by criteria such as greater revenue, lower costs, higher quality, or savings in time. For scientific applications the impact can be measured by the novelty and quality of the discovered knowledge and by increased access to data via automating manual analysis processes. Another important practical consideration is that **no good alternatives exist**: the solution is not easily obtainable by other standard means. Hence the ultimate user has a strong vested interest in insuring the success of the KDD venture. **Organizational support** is another consideration: there should be a champion for using new technology; e.g. a domain expert who can define a proper interestingness measure for that domain as well as participate in the KDD process. Finally, an important practical consideration is the **potential for privacy/legal issues**. This applies primarily to databases on people where one needs to guard against the discovered patterns raising legal or ethical issues of invasion of privacy.

Technical criteria include considerations such as the **availability of sufficient data (cases)**. The number of examples (cases) required for reliable inference of useful patterns from data varies a great deal with each particular application. In general, the more fields there are and the more complex are the patterns being sought, the more data are needed. However, strong prior knowledge (see below) can reduce the number of needed cases significantly. Another consideration is the **relevance of attributes.** It is important to have data attributes relevant to the discovery task: no amount of data will allow prediction based on attributes that do not capture the required information.

Furthermore, **low noise levels (few data errors)** is another consideration. High amounts of noise make it hard to identify patterns unless a large number of cases can mitigate random noise and help clarify the aggregate patterns. A related consideration is whether one can attach **confidence intervals** to extracted knowledge. In some applications, it is crucial to attach confidence intervals to predictions produced by the KDD system. This allows the user to calibrate actions appropriately.

Finally, and perhaps one of the most important considerations is **prior knowledge**. It is very useful to know something about the domain— what are the important fields, what are the likely relationships, what is the user utility function, what patterns are already known, and so forth. Prior knowledge can significantly reduce the search in the data mining step and all the other steps in the KDD process.

1.6.2   Privacy and Knowledge Discovery

When dealing with databases of personal information, governments and businesses have to be careful to adequately address the legal and ethical issues of invasion of privacy. Ignoring this issue can be dangerous, as Lotus found in 1990, when they were planning to introduce a CD-ROM with data on about 100 million American households. The stormy protest led to the withdrawal of that product (Rosenberg 1992).

Current discussion centers around guidelines for what constitutes a proper discovery. The Organization for Economic Cooperation and Development (OECD) guidelines for data privacy (O'Leary 1995), which have been adopted by most European Union countries, suggest that data about specific living individuals should not be analyzed without their consent. They also suggest that the data should only be collected for a specific purpose. Use for other purposes is possible only with the consent of the data subject or by authority of the law.

In the U.S. there is ongoing work on draft principles for fair information use related to the National Information Infrastructure (NII), commonly known as the "information superhighway." These principles permit the use of "transactional records," such as phone numbers called, credit card payments, etc., as long as such use is compatible with the original notice. The use of transactional records can be seen to also include discovery of patterns.

In many cases (e.g. medical research, socio-economic studies) the goal is to discover patterns about groups, not individuals. While group pattern discovery appears not to violate the restrictions on personal data retrieval, an ingenious combination of several group patterns, especially in small datasets, may allow identification of specific personal information. Solutions which allow group pattern discovery while avoiding the potential invasion of privacy include removal or replacement of identifying fields, performing queries on random subsets of data, and combining individuals into groups and allowing only queries on groups. These and related issues are further discussed in (Piatetsky-Shapiro 1995b).

1.6.3   Research and Application Challenges for KDD

We outline some of the current primary research and application challenges for knowledge discovery. This list is by no means exhaustive. The goal is to give the reader a feel for the types of problems that KDD practitioners wrestle with. We point to chapters in this book that are of relevance to the challenges we list.

- *Larger databases.* Databases with hundreds of fields and tables, millions of records, and multi-gigabyte size are quite commonplace, and terabyte (10^{12} bytes) databases are beginning to appear. For example, Agrawal et al (this volume) present efficient algorithms for enumerating all association rules exceeding given confidence thresholds over large databases. Other possible solutions include sampling, approximation methods, and massively parallel processing (Holsheimer et al, this volume).

- *High dimensionality.* Not only is there often a very large number of records in the database, but there can also be a very large number of fields (attributes, variables) so that the dimensionality of the problem is high. A high dimensional data set creates problems in terms of increasing the size of the search space for model induction in a combinatorially explosive manner. In addition, it increases the chances that a data mining algorithm will find spurious patterns that are not valid in general. Approaches to this problem include methods to reduce the effective dimensionality of the problem and the use of prior knowledge to identify irrelevant variables.

- *Overfitting.* When the algorithm searches for the best parameters for one particular model using a limited set of data, it may overfit the data, resulting in poor performance of the model on test data. Possible solutions include cross-validation, regularization, and other sophisticated statistical strategies (Elder & Pregibon, this volume).

- *Assessing statistical significance.* A problem (related to overfitting) occurs when the system is searching over many possible models. For example, if a system tests N models at the 0.001 significance level, then on average, with purely random data, $N/1000$ of these models will be accepted as significant. This point is frequently missed by many initial attempts at KDD. One way to deal with this problem is to use methods which adjust the test statistic as a function of the search, e.g., Bonferroni adjustments for independent tests.

- *Changing data and knowledge.* Rapidly changing (non-stationary) data may make previously discovered patterns invalid. In addition, the variables measured in a given application database may be modified, deleted, or augmented with new measurements over time. Possible solutions include incremental methods for updating the patterns and treating change as an opportunity for discovery by using it to cue the search for patterns of change only (Matheus et al, this volume).

- *Missing and noisy data.* This problem is especially acute in business databases. U.S. census data reportedly has error rates of up to 20%. Important attributes may be missing if the database was not designed with discovery in mind. Possible solutions include more sophisticated statistical strategies to identify hidden variables and dependencies (Heckerman, this volume; Smyth et al., this volume).

- *Complex relationships between fields.* Hierarchically structured attributes or values, relations between attributes, and more sophisticated means for representing knowledge about the contents of a database will require algorithms that can effectively utilize such information. Historically, data mining algorithms have been developed for simple attribute-value records, although new techniques for deriving relations between variables are being developed (Dzeroski, this volume; Han and Fu, this volume).

- *Understandability of patterns.* In many applications it is important to make the discoveries more understandable by humans. Possible solutions include graphical representations (Buntine, this volume; Heckerman, this volume), rule structuring with directed acyclic graphs (Gaines, this volume), natural language generation (Matheus et al., this volume), and techniques for visualization of data and knowledge. Rule refinement strategies (e.g. Major 1993; Kloesgen 1993) can be used to address a related problem: the discovered knowledge may be implicitly or explicitly redundant.

- *User interaction and prior knowledge.* Many current KDD methods and tools are not truly *interactive* and cannot easily incorporate prior knowledge about a problem except in simple ways. The use of domain knowledge is important in all of the steps of the KDD process as outlined in Section 1.3. Bayesian approaches (e.g. Cheeseman & Stutz, this volume) use prior probabilities over data and distributions as one form of encoding prior knowledge. Simoudis et al (this volume) make use of deductive databases to discover knowledge that is then used to guide the data mining search.

- *Integration with other systems.* A stand-alone discovery system may not be very useful. Typical integration issues include integration with a DBMS (e.g. via a query interface), integration with spreadsheets and visualization tools, and accommodating real-time sensor readings. Examples of integrated KDD systems are described by Simoudis et al (this volume) and Shen et al (this volume).

1.7   Organization of this Book

The chapters of this book span fundamental issues of knowledge discovery, classification and clustering, trend and deviation analysis, dependency derivation, integrated discovery systems, augmented database systems, and application case studies. The contributing authors include researchers and practitioners in academia, government laboratories, and private industry, indicating the breadth of interest in the field. We have organized the book into seven parts and an appendix.

Part I deals with fundamental issues in discovery. Brachman and Anand outline the state-of-the-practice of the KDD process. Buntine presents a unifying view of various data mining techniques under the broad area of graphical models. Elder and Pregibon provide the reader a general statistical perspective on knowledge discovery and data mining.

Part II deals with specific techniques for data mining. Dzeroski presents an overview of recent developments relevant to KDD in inductive logic programming (ILP). Cheeseman and Stutz present a Bayesian approach to clustering and discuss the details of the AutoClass system. AutoClass attempts to infer the most likely number of classes in the data, and the most likely parameterization of the probability distributions chosen to model the data. Guyon, Matic, and Vapnik present a novel approach for discovering informative patterns within a supervised learning framework and describe the application of their techniques to "data cleaning" of large optical character recognition databases. Gaines discusses the use of exception directed acyclic graphs (EDAGs) for efficient representation of induced knowledge.

Part III presents methods for dealing with trend and deviation analysis. Berndt and Clifford show how to adapt dynamic time warping (a dynamic programming technique used in speech recognition) to finding patterns in time series data. Kloesgen describes Explora, a multi-strategy discovery assistant, and examines the options for discovering different types of deviations and other patterns.

Part IV focuses on data mining techniques for deriving dependencies. Heckerman provides a survey of current research in the field of learning graphical models (also known as Bayesian networks) from data: graphical models provide an efficient framework for representing and reasoning with joint probability distributions over multiple variables. Agrawal, Mannila, Srikant, Toivonen and Verkamo introduce a variety of novel extensions of earlier work on deriving association rules from transaction data: empirical results demonstrate that the new algorithms are much more efficient than previous versions. Zembowicz and Zytkow show how to use contingency tables to discover different types of knowledge, including dependencies and taxonomies.

Part V focuses on integrated discovery systems which include multiple components, employ several data mining techniques, and generally address issues in solving some real-world problems. Simoudis, Livezey, and Kerber discuss how rule induction, deductive databases, and data visualization can be used cooperatively to create high quality, rule-based models by mining data stored in relational databases. Shen, Mitbander, Ong, and Zaniolo present a framework that uses metaqueries to integrate inductive learning methods with deductive database technologies in the context of knowledge discovery from databases, and illustrate this with three case studies. Han and Fu show how to use attribute-oriented induction (which generalizes the relevant subset of data attribute-by-attribute) to find patterns of different types, including characteristic and classification rules.

Part VI includes two chapters on approaches for next generation database systems. Hsu and Knoblock show how learning can be used to generate rules for semantic query optimization. Holsheimer, Kersten, and Siebes present a parallel DBMS engine, called Data Surveyor, which has special features for optimizing various types of data mining.

Part VII presents several real and successful applications. Fayyad, Djorgovski, and Weir present SKICAT, a system which automatically detects and classifies sky objects from image data resulting from a major astronomical sky survey. The data mining techniques used in SKICAT enabled solving a difficult, scientifically significant problem, and resulted in a system that can outperform astronomers in its accuracy in classifying faint sky objects. It is now used to automatically catalog an estimated two billion objects. Matheus, Piatetsky-Shapiro, and McNeill present a framework for determining the interestingness of deviations from normative and previous values and show its implementation in the KEFIR system for the analysis of Healthcare data. Smyth, Burl, Fayyad, and Perona address the inconsistencies of human classifications in automating the catalog of a million small volcanoes in the 30,000 Venus images returned by the Magellan spacecraft. Apte and Hong show how to use minimal rule generation and contextual feature analysis techniques for extracting useful information from securities data to predict equity returns.

We conclude the book with an epilogue by Uthurusamy. The appendix provides a list of terms used in the KDD literature and their equivalents in other related fields. The goal of Appendix A by Kloesgen and Zytkow, is to provide the seeds for a common terminology in the rapidly growing KDD field. Appendix B by Piatetsky-Shapiro provides pointers to the many resources for Knowledge Discovery and Data Mining, including software, datasets, and publications that are available via the Internet and the World-Wide Web.

Acknowledgments

The authors would like to thank Evangelos Simoudis, R. Uthurusamy, and Chris Matheus for their comments and insights on an earlier draft of this chapter. GPS thanks Shri Goyal for his encouragement and support. Part of the writing of this chapter was performed at the Jet Propulsion Laboratory, California Institute of Technology, under a contract with the National Aeronautics and Space Administration and was supported in part by ARPA and ONR under grant number N00014-92-J-1860.

References

Anand, T.; and Kahn, G. 1992. SPOTLIGHT: A Data Explanation System. In *Proceedings of the Eighth IEEE Conference on Applied AI*, 2–8. Washington, D.C.: IEEE Press.

Babcock, C. 1994. Parallel Processing Mines Retail Data. *ComputerWorld*, 6, September 26, 1994.

Barr, D.; and Mani, G. 1994. Using Neural Nets to Manage Investments. *AI Expert*, 16–21, February.

Basseville, M.; and Nikiforov, I. V. 1993. *Detection of Abrupt Changes: Theory and Application*. Englewood Cliffs, NJ: Prentice Hall.

Berry, J. 1994. Database Marketing. *Business Week*, 56–62, September 5.

Blanchard, D. 1994. News Watch. *AI Expert*, 7, December.

Breiman, L.; Friedman, J. H.; Olshen, R. A.; and Stone, C. J. 1984.*Classification and Regression Trees*. Belmont, Calif.: Wadsworth.

Cercone, N.; and Tsuchiya, M. 1993. Special Issue on Learning and Discovery in Databases, *IEEE Transactions on Knowledge and Data Engineering*, 5(6), Dec.

Cheeseman, P. 1990.On Finding the Most Probable Model. In *Computational Models of Scientific Discovery and Theory Formation*, ed. J. Shrager and P. Langley. San Francisco: Morgan Kaufmann, 73–95.

Cheng, B.; and Titterington, D. M. 1994. Neural Networks—a Review from a Statistical Perspective. *Statistical Science*, 9(1): 2–30.

Codd, E.F. 1993. *Providing OLAP (On-line Analytical Processing) to User-Analysts: An IT Mandate*. E.F. Codd and Associates.

Conklin, D.; Fortier, S.; and Glasgow, J. 1993. Knowledge Discovery in Molecular Databases. *IEEE Transactions on Knowledge and Data Engineering*, 5(6): 985–987, Dec.

Dasarathy, B. V. 1991. *Nearest Neighbor (NN) Norms: NN Pattern Classification Techniques.* Los Alamitos, Calif.: IEEE Computer Society Press.

Fasman, K. H.; Cuticchia, A. J.; and Kingsbury, D. T. 1994. The GDB (TM) Human Genome Database Anno 1994. *Nucl. Acid. R.,* 22(17): 3462–3469.

Fayyad, U. M.; and Uthurusamy, R. 1994. Proceedings of KDD-94: the AAAI-94 Workshop on Knowledge Discovery in Databases, AAAI Technical Report WS-94-03. Menlo Park, Calif.: The AAAI Press.

Fayyad, U. M.; and Uthurusamy, R. 1995. Proceedings, First International Conference on Knowledge Discovery and Data Mining. Menlo Park, Calif.: The AAAI Press.

Frawley, W. J.; Piatetsky-Shapiro, G.; and Matheus, C. J. 1991. Knowledge Discovery in Databases: An Overview. In *Knowledge Discovery in Databases,* ed. G. Piatetsky-Shapiro and B. Frawley. Cambridge, Mass: AAAI/MIT Press, 1–27.

Friedman, J. H. 1989. Multivariate Adaptive Regression Splines. *Annals of Statistics,* 19: 1–141.

Geman, S.; Bienenstock, E.; and Doursat, R. 1992. Neural Networks and the Bias/Variance Dilemma. *Neural Computation,* 4: 1–58.

Glymour, C.; Scheines, R.; Spirtes, P.; and Kelly, K. 1987. *Discovering Causal Structure.* New York: Academic Press.

Hand, D. J. 1981. *Discrimination and Classification.* Chichester, U.K.: John Wiley and Sons.

Harrison, D. 1993. Backing Up. *Network Computing,* October 15, 98–104.

Holder, L.; Cook, D.; and Djoko, S. 1994. Substructure Discovery in the SUBDUE system. In Proceedings of KDD-94: the AAAI-94 Workshop on Knowledge Discovery in Databases, 169–180. AAAI Technical Report WS-94-03. Menlo Park, Calif.: The AAAI Press.

Inmon, W. H.; and Osterfelt, S. 1991. *Understanding Data Pattern Processing: The Key to Competitive Advantage.* Wellesley, Mass.: QED Technical Publishing Group.

Jain, A. K.; and Dubes; R. C. 1988. *Algorithms for Clustering Data.* Englewood Cliffs, NJ: Prentice-Hall.

Kloesgen, W. 1993. Some Implementation Aspects of a Discovery System. In Proceedings of KDD-94: the AAAI-94 Workshop on Knowledge Discovery in Databases, 212–226. AAAI Technical Report WS-94-03. Menlo Park, Calif.: The AAAI Press.

Kolodner, J. 1993. *Case-Based Reasoning.* San Francisco: Morgan Kaufmann.

Lehmann, E. L. 1990. Model Specification: the Views of Fisher and Neyman, and Later Developments. *Statistical Science,* 5(2), 160–168.

Major, J. 1993. Selecting Among Rules Induced from a Hurricane Database. In Proceedings of KDD-94: the AAAI-94 Workshop on Knowledge Discovery in Databases, 28–44. AAAI Technical Report WS-94-03. Menlo Park, Calif.: The AAAI Press.

Major, J.; and Riedinger, D. 1992. EFD: A Hybrid Knowledge/Statistical-Based System for the Detection of Fraud. *International Journal of Intelligent Systems,* 7(7): 687–703.

Matheus, C.; Chan, P.; and Piatetsky-Shapiro, G. 1993. Systems for Knowledge Discovery. *IEEE Trans. on Knowledge and Data Engineering,* 5(6): 903–913.

McLachlan, G. 1992. *Discriminant Analysis and Statistical Pattern Recognition.* New York: Wiley.

O'Leary, D. 1995. Some Privacy Issues in Knowledge Discovery: OECD Personal Privacy Guidelines. *IEEE Expert.* Forthcoming.

Parsaye, K.; and Chignell, M. 1993. *Intelligent Database Tools & Applications.* New York: John Wiley.

Pearl, J. 1988. *Probabilistic Reasoning in Intelligent Systems.* San Francisco: Morgan Kaufmann.

Piatetsky-Shapiro, G.; and Frawley, W. 1991. *Knowledge Discovery in Databases.* Menlo Park, Calif.: AAAI Press.

Piatetsky-Shapiro, G. 1991. Report on the AAAI-91 Workshop on Knowledge Discovery in Databases. *IEEE Expert,* 6(5): 74–76.

Piatetsky-Shapiro, G. 1992. Editor, Special issue on Knowledge Discovery in Databases and Knowledgebases. *International Journal of Intelligent Systems* 7:7, September.

Piatetsky-Shapiro, G.; Matheus, C.; Smyth, P.; and Uthurusamy, R. 1994. KDD-93: Progress and Challenges in Knowledge Discovery in Databases. *AI Magazine,* 15(3): 77–87.

Piatetsky-Shapiro, G. 1995b. Knowledge Discovery in Personal Data Versus Privacy: A Mini-Symposium. *IEEE Expert.* Forthcoming.

Quinlan, J. 1992. *C4.5: Programs for Machine Learning.* San Francisco: Morgan Kaufmann.

Ripley, B. D. 1994. Neural Networks and Related Methods for Classification. *Journal of the Royal. Stat. Society,* 56(3): 409-437.

Rosenberg, M. 1992. Protecting Privacy, Inside Risks Column. *Communications of ACM,* 35(4): 164.

Schmitz, J.; Armstrong, G.; and Little, J. D. C. 1990. CoverStory—Automated News Finding in Marketing. In *DSS Transactions,* ed. L. Volino, 46–54. Providence, R.I.: Institute of Management Sciences.

Shrager, J.; and Langley, P., eds. 1990. *Computational Models of Scientific Discovery and Theory Formation.* San Francisco, Calif.: Morgan Kaufmann.

Silverman, B. 1986. *Density Estimation for Statistics and Data Analysis.* New York: Chapman and Hall.

Spirtes, P.; Glymour, C.; and Scheines, R. 1993. *Causation, Prediction, and Search,* New York: Springer-Verlag.

Stolorz, P. et al. 1994. Data Analysis and Knowledge Discovery in Geophysical Databases. *Concurrent Supercomputing Consortium Annual Report,* California Institute of Technology, 12–14.

Titterington, D. M.; Smith, A. F. M.; and Makov, U. E. 1985. *Statistical Analysis of Finite Mixture Distributions.* Chichester, U.K.: John Wiley and Sons.

Way, J.; and Smith, E. A. 1991. The Evolution of Synthetic Aperture Radar Systems and their Progression to the EOS SAR. *IEEE Transactions on Geoscience and Remote Sensing,* 29(6): 962–985.

Whittaker, J. 1990. *Graphical Models in Applied Multivariate Statistics.* New York: Wiley.

Weigend, A.; and Gershenfeld, N., eds. 1993. *Predicting the Future and Understanding the Past.* Redwood City, Calif: Addison-Wesley.

Weiss, S. I.; and Kulikowski, C. 1991. *Computer Systems that Learn: Classification and Prediction Methods from Statistics, Neural Networks, Machine Learning, and Expert Systems.* San Francisco, Calif.: Morgan Kaufmann.

Ziarko, W. 1994. *Rough Sets, Fuzzy Sets and Knowledge Discovery.* Berlin: Springer Verlag.

I FOUNDATIONS

2 The Process of Knowledge Discovery in Databases

Ronald J. Brachman
AT&T Bell Laboratories

Tej Anand
AT&T Global Information Solutions

Abstract

The general idea of discovering knowledge in large amounts of data is both appealing and intuitive. Typically we focus our attention on learning algorithms, which provide the core capability of generalizing from large numbers of specific facts to useful high-level rules; these learning techniques seem to hold the most excitement and perhaps the most substantive scientific content in the knowledge discovery in databases (KDD) enterprise. However, when we engage in real-world discovery tasks, we find that they can be extremely complex, and that low-level data mining is only one small part of the overall process. While others have written overviews of the concept of KDD, and even provided block diagrams for "knowledge discovery systems," no one has begun to identify all of the building blocks in a realistic KDD process. This is what we attempt to do here. In this chapter, we bring into the discussion several parts of the process that have received inadequate attention in the KDD community. Besides providing opportunities for new technologies and tools, a careful elucidation of the steps in a realistic knowledge discovery process can provide a framework for comparison of different systems that are almost impossible to compare without a clean model.

2.1 Focusing on the User and the Process

The general idea of discovering "knowledge" in large amounts of data is both appealing and intuitive, but technically it is significantly challenging and difficult. Generally speaking, knowledge discovery in databases (KDD) is considered to be the non-trivial extraction of implicit, previously unknown, and potentially useful information from data (Frawley *et al.* 1992). Definers of KDD have also added further conditions on the discovered knowledge in an attempt to fine-tune the term and clarify its scope.[1] But while reasonable for starters, this kind of definition

---

[1] For example, the discovered information should not be obvious; the information extracted should be simpler than the data itself, implying that there should

tends to focus only on features of the resultant information. Above all, knowledge discovery is a *process*; limiting our attention to the data may keep us from seeing and addressing the complexity of real-world instances of extraction, organization, and presentation of discovered information. Further, many advocates have implied that systems for doing KDD should be autonomous. While perhaps desirable in the long run, this approach tends to underemphasize the key role played by humans in all current-day knowledge discovery. Overall, then, we see a clear need for more emphasis on a human-centered, process-oriented analysis of KDD. When articulated, the KDD process should help us better understand how to do knowledge discovery, and how best to support the human analysts without whom there simply would be no KDD.

2.1.1   Who is the User? Knowledge Discovery Support Versus Business Applications

On the technology side, as we see it, a "knowledge discovery system" would be an integrated environment that somehow assisted a user in carrying out the complex knowledge discovery process. Contrary to the more common notion that the output of a knowledge discovery system is simply some fragment of "knowledge," the output of the knowledge discovery process in a commercial setting, at least, would more typically be the specification for a knowledge discovery *application*. Such an application could then be built and installed in a business environment to provide analysis and action recommendations on an ongoing basis, using, for example, incoming business data. Its user would be a business person (product manager, etc.) watching for important events in business data, rather than a data analyst looking in an exploratory manner for general underlying trends and patterns in a domain.[2] In this sense "a program that monitors the set of facts in a database and produces patterns" (Frawley *et al.* 1992) is more a knowledge discovery application than a general KDD system.

Research and development in the rapidly emerging area of KDD has led to a number of successful knowledge discovery applications (Anand 1995; Anand and Kahn 1992; Fayyad *et al.* 1993; Uthurasamy *et al.*

---

be a high level language for expressing such information; the information should be "interesting"; etc. (Frawley *et al.* 1992).

[2]In this chapter, we use "business" to represent a wide class of enterprises, including those tackled by scientific, government, and commercial business people.

1993).   The development process for each of these applications can be characterized by (1) an initial laborious discovery of knowledge by someone who understands the domain as well as specific data analysis techniques, (2) encoding of the discovered knowledge within a specific problem-solving architecture, and finally (3) application of the discovered knowledge in the context of a real world task by a well-understood class of end-users (this always involves the design of output that conveys to the user the import of applying the knowledge to the data). Note that there was ultimately a single task supported in each of these applications, and the end-users were not data analysts but business people (e.g., managers, and not statisticians).

In contrast, most existing systems that label themselves "knowledge discovery systems" (Klosgen 1992; Piatetsky-Shapiro and Matheus 1992; Simoudis *et al.* 1995; Ziarko *et al.* 1993; Zytkow and Baker 1991) provide one or more data-mining techniques, such as decision-tree induction, clustering, linear regression, etc. These support discovery of knowledge by a user who has to understand the various discovery techniques themselves, the data elements within the database, and the task for which knowledge is sought. The task being performed, the style of work, and the type of user here are all quite different than their counterparts in the more end-user-directed applications mentioned above. Once we acknowledge this distinction, it appears that instead of using one overly general term—"knowledge discovery system"—we would be better off differentiating between "knowledge discovery *support environments*" and "knowledge discovery *applications*."[3]

2.1.2   A Human-Centered Process

The laboriousness of the development of realistic KDD applications, previously reported examples of knowledge discovery in the literature (Major and Mangano 1993), and our own experience in real-world knowledge discovery situations all lead us to believe that

> knowledge discovery is a *knowledge-intensive* task consisting of *complex interactions*, *protracted over time*, between a *human* and a (large) database, possibly supported by a

---

[3]There is probably some merit in referring to the latter as "business applications," but here we focus on the fact that such applications arise from knowledge discovery expeditions.

heterogeneous suite of tools.

Most existing "knowledge discovery systems" reported in the literature have been motivated by one or more novel data-mining techniques rather than concern for the data analyst's overall task. As a result, these have met with mixed or minimal commercial success. For more successful development of knowledge discovery support tools, it is critical to understand the exact nature of the interactions between a human and data that leads to the discovery of knowledge. We characterize the overall interaction as the *knowledge discovery process* and we believe that a more user- and task-centered view of the problem is essential. Our goal is to lay out each of the major phases in this process.

In our own previously reported work on IMACS (Interactive Marketing Analysis and Classification System) (Brachman *et al.* 1993), we tried to take a user-centered approach. IMACS is a prototype system that provides integrated knowledge representation support for interactive knowledge discovery (especially segmentation and classification). In its development, we worked continually with a data analyst who performed knowledge discovery on a regular basis as part of her job. Working with the analyst for more than a year, we eventually came to realize that almost all of her most important concerns had little to do with particular knowledge discovery techniques or tools. Rather, the critical issues had to do with the support of her *task*, which was *iterative*; *protracted over time*; and involved *keeping track* of numerous files, tables, queries, programs, and unintegrated systems, not to mention a plethora of subproblems that needed to be solved before the main problem could be addressed. In other words, the structure of her task was complex, and she had to deal constantly with data conversions, messy data, repeated activities with small twists and turns, and computer subsystems that were not built to work together. As a result, the principal contributions of the IMACS work were in its support for this iterative discovery and analysis task and its tight integration of segmentation, classification, analysis, output templates, monitoring for changes, and several other subtasks and their work objects.

Besides what we learned from IMACS, our understanding has been bolstered by conversations with numerous data analysts who are involved in tasks such as the development of statistical and operations research models, development of coherent visualizations of large data sets, and the (manual) interrogation of large databases to find key business information. In spite of their varying backgrounds and their use of different tools and techniques, these analysts all echo the same general themes regarding the processes they follow, the most important of which is that the knowledge discovery task is much more complex than simply the discovery of interesting patterns. It involves, among other things, negotiating with the owners of the data; struggling interactively with the data to see what it reveals; constantly wrestling with dirty, flawed data; wrangling with large SQL queries with little debugging help; etc. It is our hope that by taking more seriously this messy, complex process, we will begin to develop a better understanding of the capabilities that are required in a realistic knowledge discovery support system. We also hope to focus attention on some key aspects of knowledge discovery that have received little attention to date. Finally, the careful elucidation of the steps in a realistic knowledge discovery process can provide a framework for comparison of different technologies and tools that are almost impossible to compare without a general model.

In the rest of this brief introduction to the human-centered process of discovering knowledge in data, we first focus on the central, most basic ingredients of almost any knowledge discovery process. These include basic data analysis, data-driven model selection and refinement, and the generation of output. We then outline some of the more complex aspects of the KDD process, including the up-front step of acquiring requirements, getting to know the data, data cleaning, and the inclusion of background knowledge. We conclude by examining the need for an integrating workspace based on knowledge representation principles, and a few additional requirements for handling a realistic discovery scenario.

2.2   Basic Ingredients of the KDD Process

As we have emphasized, a key premise of our framework for understanding knowledge discovery is that the human user is always close at hand, intimately involved with many, if not all steps of the process. It is critical to understand exactly who that user is and exactly what his or her task is. In our analysis of the knowledge discovery enterprise, we assume that our customer is not a business end-user interested in business applications, but someone who might ultimately supply such an application,

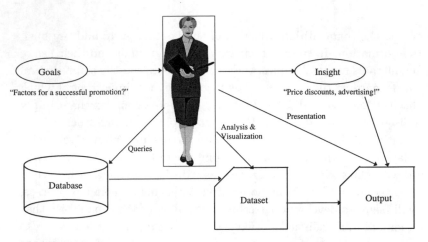

Figure 2.1
Overview of the analyst's task.

once he or she has understood what the data has had to say. We will thus usually refer to our canonical user here as "the analyst," and it is the analyst's needs and subtasks that consume our attention throughout the discussion.

2.2.1 Process Overview

Figure 2.1 shows the tasks that a data analyst involved in KDD has to contend with. At a very high level, the data analyst, in response to a goal, queries a database to extract data relevant to the goal. The analyst then "analyzes" the data using data analysis and/or visualization tools. This analysis leads the analyst to some sort of "insight" about the data. The analyst then uses presentation tools to disseminate this insight to a broader audience, e.g., the parties that generated the original goal of the analysis.

For example, let us consider an analyst working for a retail company who has the goal of determining, "What are the factors that lead to a successful Father's Day promotion?" In response to this goal the analyst would extract data such as sales volume of products sold during a specific Father's Day sale for the week prior to the promotion and for the week during the promotion; characteristics of these products such as their category, brand, manufacturer, etc.; and characteristics of the promotion itself, such as price discount, amount of in-store support, and amount of advertising support in media such as newspapers and television.

The analyst might then set up a formal analysis by first defining a measure that could be used to quantify achievement of the goal of a successful promotion, such as "percentage increase in sales." The analyst could then decide to segment the products based on this percentage sales increase measure. This would allow her to investigate the characteristics of products with relatively higher sales increases, and to contrast their attributes with those with relatively lower sales increases.

Visualizing the data in each segment the analyst might notice that the products were evenly distributed across the segments, and that characteristics of products within a segment varied significantly. This would indicate that it was probably not something intrinsic about the type of product that made it a successful seller (although such a hypothesis would bear further investigation). This insight would in turn lead to a conjecture concerning some extrinsic properties of the products as contributing to their sales increases. An analysis of the correlation of some specific attributes with the percentage sales increase could lead to the discovery that price discount, in-store promotional support, and advertising support were all higher in the segments with higher percentage sales increases.

At this stage the analyst could decide to prepare a report that described the insights she had gleaned, using presentation tools such as a word processor or graphical presentation program. In the report the analyst might include a table describing the segmentation analysis, line graphs showing the relationships between the percentage sales increases and promotion characteristics, and a textual description of her findings. If the analyst felt comfortable with this analysis she might distribute an application that let a business user generate the same kind of report for future Father's Day promotions.

In the example above the analyst was involved in three main tasks: (1) *model selection and evolution*, (2) *data analysis*, and (3) *output generation*. (1) and (2) are in general anchored by analysis and visualization methods and supported by tools for querying the database. Output generation is usually supported by a variety of presentation and data transformation tools. In the subsequent subsections, we spend a little time investigating these three core phases of the knowledge discovery process, starting with the cornerstone step of data analysis.

2.2.2 Data Analysis

As illustrated in the example, the analyst in a knowledge discovery task goes through a number of steps, but at its core the process looks like *confirmatory data analysis*: the analyst has a hypothesis about the data (e.g., that it is the type of product that dictates its sales increase around Father's Day; or that it is a promotional factor like price discount that has the primary effect), and some type of analysis tool is used to build a model from the data (the kinds of models used here are mostly classification and regression models). In general, the idea is to understand why certain groups of entities behave the way they do, e.g., determine what rules govern the behavior of a previously deemed interesting segment of the population, such as "products that were promoted for Father's Day." One starts with a labeled population, that is, one where the interesting subclasses have already been identified.

Among the key sub-processes in data analysis are (1) *model specification*, wherein a specific model is written down in a formal way (the initial model can be derived by many different means—see Section 2.2.3); (2) *model fitting*, wherein, when necessary, some specific parameters of a model are determined based on the data (in some cases, the model is constructed independent of the data, while in others it is fitted to "training" data); (3) *evaluation*, wherein the model is evaluated against the data (in some cases, all the data; in others, just "test" data); and (4) *model refinement*, wherein the initial model may be iteratively refined, depending on what the evaluation shows. There are several types of tools that exist to support these subprocesses; we will characterize these analysis tools as algorithm-based or visualization-based.

In algorithm-based analysis tools a model is specified by means of associating an outcome (dependent) variable with the independent variables that the outcome depends on. In certain cases, the data set is subdivided into a training data set and a test data set. The training data set is then used to fit the parameters of the model to the data. The model is then evaluated by applying it to the test data set, and, if necessary, subsequently refined. In some cases, the population to which the model is being applied will be refined, as will the parameters considered (see Section 2.2.3).

Algorithm-based data-mining tools include statistical packages like S, SAS, etc., certain machine learning tools (e.g., decision-tree induction and other supervised learning techniques), neural networks, case-based reasoning platforms, and classification tools.

In visualization-based analysis tools, the hypothesis is specified by means of a visualization metaphor (for example a specific type of graph) and the selection of the data elements to be rendered in the metaphor. The visualization produced is by itself a model, and the user can examine the visualization to determine its explanatory power. In a realistic knowledge discovery task, visualization is a key ingredient for all three core phases of the process (model development, data analysis, and output generation). Appropriate display of data points and their relationships can give the analyst insight that is virtually impossible to get from looking at tables of output or simple summary statistics. In fact, for some tasks, appropriate visualization is the *only* thing needed to solve a problem or confirm a hypothesis, even though we do not usually think of picture-drawing as a kind of analysis.

Visualization techniques that might be appropriate for knowledge discovery tasks are quite wide-ranging, although there is a standard cadre of graph- and chart-drawing facilities that is common amongst almost all commercial discovery-oriented tools. Statistical packages like S and SAS provide extremely useful visualizations to complement their algorithmic analysis capabilities; these include matrices of coordinated scatter-plots, multi-dimensional "point cloud rotation," etc. Further, *interactive* visualizations, such as "brushing,"[4] provide a powerful complement to conventional algorithmic analysis techniques.

In any real-world KDD task the analyst needs to use algorithm-based and visualization-based analysis tools iteratively. The output from one tool helps refine the input to another tool. From a technology standpoint this integration is lacking in most KDD systems and is the cause of extreme frustration for data analysts.

2.2.3 Model Development

Rarely, if ever, does the analyst simply start with a formally-specified hypothesis to be confirmed or disconfirmed. In many discovery applica-

---

[4]Brushing is a technique where the mouse controls a (typically rectangular) region that behaves like a paint brush, changing the color of data points (typically on a scatterplot). Brushing can be used to display identification for data points and is often used in conjunction with linking, where points in one view are linked to points in another view; brushing on one view causes highlighting of the points in the linked views.

tions (for example, marketing data analysis), a key operation is to find *subsets* of the population that behave enough alike to be worthy of focused analysis. In other words, in many cases, the whole population may be too diverse to understand, but details about subsets of the population are more manageable. Similarly, even when we know what subpopulation we want to analyze, we may need to *restrict the parameters* used to do the analysis—not all variables will be of utility in an analysis, there may be correlation relationships amongst them that we need to correct for, and the sheer amount of data may be too overwhelming to deal with.

All of this implies that there is a key phase in the knowledge discovery process that must precede the actual analysis of the data. Initially, the data must lead the way. In fact, a number of the real world analysts we have interviewed strongly emphasize the fact that interaction with the data leads to the formation of hypotheses. In this regard, we see the overall activity of KDD as more akin to what an archaeologist does than what a miner or dredger might do (IMACS (Brachman *et al.* 1993) directly addresses this key aspect of interactive knowledge discovery). In this early phase, the data archaeologist looks at the data landscape, and decides where to dig based in part on what he or she sees and in part on his or her experience and background knowledge. Once "at the site," he or she brushes away the dust (but see below for more on this "data cleaning" activity), pieces fragments together that seem to fit, and decides what to do next in order to confirm an evolving hypothesis about the creator and meaning of the "artifacts." The data archaeologist also decides what is worthy of further exploration and what should be ignored in later analysis.

Among the key sub-processes in this part of the KDD process are (1) *data segmentation*, (2) *model selection*, and (3) *parameter selection*. Among the more common aids to data segmentation are unsupervised learning techniques (clustering).[5] As for model selection, there are a wide variety of analysis models that could be used on large amounts of data, including regression, decision trees, neural nets, and case-based reasoning. The analyst has to choose the best type of model before invoking any particular analysis tool; usually she explores different types of models before deciding which appears best to use. This kind of model

---

[5]But note, as we implied earlier, that proper visualization can have a hugely salutary effect on segmentation.

exploration often involves data analysis as a substep, highlighting the fact that in realistic KDD, data analysis and model development are highly intertwined. Finally, within the chosen model, it must be determined which parameters one needs to focus on.

One key thing to note about model development is that it implicitly involves the analyst's *background knowledge* about the domain. A novice archaeologist may have no idea how to piece together small bits of artifacts, may have no idea where to look next, and may even break or lose things by not treating them appropriately. When doing the kind of knowledge engineering one does in choosing a particular model, the background knowledge of the domain expert is crucial. Further, some analysis tools can actually take advantage of explicitly represented background knowledge. For example, ReMind (1992), a commercial product for case-based reasoning, allows the user to represent a qualitative model of the relationships of the independent variables to the dependent variable. This qualitative model is then used to bias the decision tree generated by ReMind. In the Father's Day example the analyst used background knowledge to decide which data elements to extract and to select percentage increase in sales as a measure to evaluate the promotion. Domain knowledge such as the differences between in-store support and advertising support could also be used to provide better insight into the promotion. The engineering of background knowledge for input to an intelligent analysis tool is also part of this model development process (see Section 2.3.4).

It is also clear from looking at real KDD tasks that the analysis and model development phases complement one another, and that the analyst can bounce back and forth between them repeatedly. This cycle is the very heart of the discovery process. But, as we have begun to see, it is by no means the whole story.

2.2.4   Output Generation

In the simplest possible scenario, an analysis results in a report of some sort (this might include statistical measures of the goodness of fit of the model, data about outliers, etc.). But in realistic scenarios the outputs can be much more varied and complicated. A textual description of a trend, or an elaborate graph capturing the relationships in the model might be appropriate. It is also potentially desirable to have action descriptions as outputs—these might tell the user what to do given what was found in the data. In fact, in the right kind of integrated ("information factory") setting, one could imagine actions being taken directly as the output of a data analysis. Finally, a useful kind of output might be a *monitor* to be placed back in the database, which would trigger an alarm or action when a certain condition was detected. In the Father's Day example the analyst might want to be notified if the percentage increase in sales for a product was below a certain threshold in some future Father's Day promotion. Or the analyst might create a segment of products labeled "High Performers," for those with a 50% increase in sales, and would like to be notified if a product were to fall out of the "High Performers" segment in a future Father's Day promotion. IMACS (Brachman *et al.* 1993) allows monitors that trigger a notification when there is a migration of members into or out of a particular segment or between two segments.

One issue to be considered in designing an output module for a KDD support system is when exactly an output should be triggered. This is especially relevant for monitors, but can make sense for other types of output as well.

Finally, as we mentioned earlier, it is also appropriate to think of the output of a KDD process as the specification for an application to be built, which will, on a continuous basis, answer a key business question for the customer. This would usually come in the form of a model that would be used as the core specification for an application.

2.3   More Complex Aspects of the KDD Process

2.3.1   Task Discovery

One truism about realistic KDD expeditions is that the client will state the problem or goal as if it were clear and focused, but further investigation is always warranted. In other words, the requirements for the task—and thus, for any application that might result once the basic KDD task is completed—must be engineered by spending time with the customer and various parts of the customer's organization.

Only as one digs deeper into the questions initially raised, and as one spends time sifting through the raw data and understanding its form, content, organizational role, and sources, will the real goal of the discovery emerge. While occasionally the person or organization who needs the discovery done will have the right questions ready at the beginning, more often than not, what was initially considered the goal is only a starting point.

This dialectic, up-front process can be very time-consuming and difficult, but without it, it is all too easy to spend time answering the wrong questions.

2.3.2 Data Discovery

As a complement to spending time with the client in understanding the need for a discovery application, analysts inevitably need to spend time sifting through the raw data, just getting a feel for what the data looks like and what ground it covers (and importantly, what it does *not* cover). While the main goal of the KDD enterprise comes from the task discovery subprocess just described, it cannot be pinned down completely without a detailed understanding of the structure, coverage, and quality of the data. For example, even if discussion with the client makes it clear that he is looking for the effect on sales of products from Father's Day advertising, if there is no data collected anywhere on the advertising to complement the sales data, the goal is ill-formed and cannot be satisfied (unless new data is collected or found).

2.3.3 Data Cleaning

Another truism about real-world KDD is that the client's data virtually always has problems. Data may have been collected in an *ad hoc* manner, unfilled fields in records will invariably be found, mistakes in data entry may have been made, etc. As a result, a KDD process cannot succeed without a serious effort to "clean" the data. Without the data discovery phase just discussed, the analyst will have no idea if the data quality can support the task at all; once the quality and details are assessed, serious work is usually needed to get the data in shape for analysis.

For the Father's Day example some of the data quality issues the analyst might have to grapple with include incorrect recording of price discounts and incorrect capture of sales data due to a high percentage of manual recording of sales (instead of scanning) by check-out clerks. For some products, data about their characteristics could be missing.

In our interviews with data analysts, we find that the most common method used to verify the accuracy of data is to extract (if possible) the same data element from multiple sources and compare the results. The analyst's background knowledge plays a crucial role in the data cleaning resulting from such comparisons. In some situations it is also possible to implement automated "data-edit" procedures that clean the data before it is loaded into the database. An example of a data-edit procedure might be a correction applied to the sales figures for a product from a particular store based on the average scan rate (fraction of the time a product is scanned vs. entered manually without recording the proper product code) for that product in that store: we might have general statistics on how regularly certain types of items are scanned rather than entered manually (some bulky products are more difficult than others to scan), and we can use those statistics to increase the figures in our database and make them more realistic. For example, if one type of bulk diapers in one store is scanned only two-thirds of the time, we should increase the diaper sales figure transmitted from point-of-sale terminals in that store by 50%.

Data cleaning is a double-edged sword. It is almost always necessary because of inevitably poor data quality, but occasionally what looks like an anomaly to be scrubbed away is in reality a crucial indicator of an interesting domain phenomenon. In other words, what look like outliers to be dismissed can actually be the key data points worth focusing on. For example, while analyzing retail sales of a product, we might eliminate a store with apparently zero sales because all other stores have high sales, since we might attribute the zero figure to a data quality problem. In most cases this might be a correct cleansing of the data, but in some instances the store with zero sales might provide us knowledge about conditions leading to out-of-stocks. Or, we might be tempted to remove all transaction voids from a retail database, but voids are crucial to measuring cashier productivity, and sometimes help in detecting fraud.

Data cleaning is also a matter of dealing with symptoms that could reoccur if some base process for collecting data is faulty. If the data is static and will not be updated, a one-shot cleaning process will work. But if it is updated in the same way that the initial database was created, continual data quality problems will occur. As a result, what looks like a simple data-mining exercise on the surface could really be the impetus for a major organizational and infrastructure overhaul to produce data that can be collected and analyzed reliably. Readers are referred to (Redman 1992) for a comprehensive review of the dimensions of data

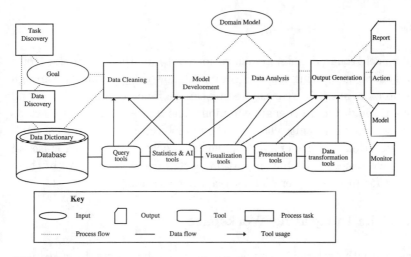

Figure 2.2
The complete KDD process.

quality and processes for monitoring and improving data quality.

2.3.4   Background Knowledge

Finally, it is important to include the role of background knowledge and
a mental model of the domain in the KDD process. Much of that is resident only in the mind of the expert, but some analysis techniques can
take advantage of formally-represented knowledge in the course of fitting
data to a model. As mentioned, ReMind uses a qualitative model in generating a decision tree. Similarly, some time-series forecasting techniques
can take advantage of explicit representation of seasonality (Stellwagen
and Goodrich 1994). Some of the theory-guided machine-learning techniques, such as explanation-based learning, can be integrated with inductive learning techniques to "fill gaps" in domain knowledge (Danyluk
1989).

In some sense, we could also consider a data dictionary, integrity constraints, and various forms of metadata from the DBMS as contributing
background knowledge to the process, even if they are used just informally by the analyst. Sometimes just having the ability to represent
metadata, or abstract concept descriptions (as in IMACS), or abstract
data elements (as in ReMind, using formula fields), gives users the ability
to provide richer inputs to the data analysis methods.

Figure 2.2 illustrates the entire KDD process as we have described it.
It includes inputs to the process, such as the raw data, data dictionary,

and a background domain model; various outputs; the key process steps; and generic supporting tools. The arrows show the general flow through the process, but it is clear that steps can be repeated many times, and loops through the process are common. The figure is also missing steps such as a *post hoc* sanity check on the model/rules induced during analysis, iteration of parts or even the entire process over long expanses of time, and other subtle but important parts of the process. All of these remain for further exploration and characterization.

2.4   The Integrating Workspace

Even with the relatively simple set of subprocesses we have defined, it is clear that a KDD enterprise can be extremely complicated and convoluted. While there may be a nominal canonical order for the above phases (e.g., it is important to clean the data before analyzing it), the entire process is iterative and the analyst can move from almost any phase to almost any other at any time. Work products derived from one phase may serve as input to others. Further, the process may be repeated at different intervals, either with updated data (e.g., each month when the remote retail outlet reports come in) or with new data in similar form to that analyzed before (e.g., sales to businesses vs. sales to consumers).

All this implies that a missing component in our process model (and noticeably in the KDD literature itself) is an *integrating workspace and intelligent bookkeeping platform* that supports work that has a long time-course and that would benefit from reuse of previous work. In the IMACS system we addressed this issue, providing a common form for objects shared in the workspace, including queries, abstracted queries, outputs of queries, graphs, and domain model (schema) concepts.[6] We also provided a template mechanism for constructing output reports (the templates can be shared and reused), and the ability to name and reuse queries. Finally, we provided a way to specify changes that should be monitored in the database over time, in a high-level way that integrates smoothly with the rest of the analysis environment. The key to this integration—and much more could be done to really address the analyst's total task—was our use of a formal, well-founded knowledge representation system (CLASSIC [Brachman *et al.* 1991]). While not as

---

[6]Recon (Simoudis *et al.* 1995) also has an integrating environment.

powerful as a full first-order logic reasoner, CLASSIC provides enough representational power to enhance a relational schema in an interesting (object-oriented) way, and sufficient inferential power to provide key features like automatic classification of new entities.

There are many different approaches that could be taken to this integration task, but it is important to note how central a role the integrating workspace should play in any KDD environment.

2.5   Some Additional Requirements

We wrap up by suggesting some consequences of the above discussion. Clearly, besides providing tools to support each of the above-mentioned phases, we need technology to support the integration of the workspace, reuse of work, etc. Further, some other requirements for a knowledge discovery support environment (KDSE) come to mind:

- Tight coupling of the KDSE with the database. Based on the database schema and the data dictionary, it should be possible to create a more natural representation of the data for the user to view and interact with. This will support the expression of relations that the user knows to be true. This requirement is similar to the functionality available in deductive databases. For example, Recon incorporates a deductive database component that supports rule-based user views of the data. IMACS can populate a pre-specified user-created object-oriented domain model from a database;

- Data structures that can be shared between the various phases of the knowledge discovery process, e.g., representations of interactively-defined subpopulations and the queries that produced them;

- The ability to suggest to the user the most appropriate discovery technique based on the outcome variable and the distributions of the independent variables;

- The ability to suggest the most appropriate graph for relationships that are being viewed;

- The ability to use relationships expressed by the user during discovery;

- The user should be able to interrogate the discovered knowledge to understand the rationale for the discovery.

There are, of course, many other key requirements for a KDSE, but these at least highlight some of the concerns that arise when looking seriously at the process of KDD, as well as looking at the problem from the point of view of the user.

2.6   Comparing KDD Systems

The knowledge discovery framework that we have presented can provide the basis for comparing different KDD systems. With it, we can begin to ask some key questions whose answers could lead to a wide variety of possibly incomparable systems. Among the questions we are led to are the following:

- Who is the intended user? Is it a data analyst doing exploratory, iterative discovery, or a business user looking for specific patterns in business data?
- What tasks within the KDD process does the system support?
- What tools are used to support each of the tasks?
- How integrated are the tools? Is there a shared workspace? Can outputs of some steps be used as inputs to others?
- Does the system support the inclusion of background knowledge, ranging from data dictionaries to full formal domain models?
- What kinds of outputs are possible? Does the system support the generation of actions? Does it support the placement of monitors in the database?
- Does the system support the generation of applications from the models it produces? How?

In our future work, we plan to tackle several of the known knowledge discovery support systems to see how they address the above types of questions, as well as how those attempting to tackle the same task stack up against one another.

2.7   Conclusions

Knowledge discovery is a complex process, and it fundamentally—for the foreseeable future, at least—requires human participation. As a result, it is paramount to try to understand what a human who carries out this process actually *does*, and to consider supporting each of the phases in the process as well as their integration. The KDD process includes at least front-end requirements engineering, data cleaning, model development, analysis, visualization, background knowledge, and output. Further study of analysts at work and related processes in other data-intensive areas is still needed, but this chapter begins to sketch the skeleton of a process that seems to be quite common in real-world KDD situations.

We have also proposed that it is valuable to consider knowledge discovery *support environments* as very different from KDD *applications*. A KDSE facilitates the creation of a knowledge discovery application, and supports the work of someone who understands not only the domain, but also data analysis techniques. A KDSE also needs to support wideranging, somewhat unpredictable exploratory interaction ("data archaeology"). The resulting application, on the other hand, is expected to solve a narrow business problem, and will be used by someone not familiar with analytic techniques. Even if the application monitors data streams looking for patterns, its goals and structure are likely to be quite different from those of a general KDSE.

It is our hope that our experience with commercially significant KDD tasks and the resulting articulation of a more realistic process model will help provide a context for understanding the true complexity of knowledge discovery and the true contribution of KDD support systems. As we further refine our model, we hope to begin to use it to analyze and compare the various KDD systems that have been built or proposed, a task that is still in search of some real progress.

References

Anand, T. 1995. Opportunity Explorer: Navigating Large Databases Using Knowledge Discovery Templates. *Journal of Intelligent Information Systems* 5(1): 23–35.

Anand, T.; and Kahn, G. 1992. Making Sense of Gigabytes: A System for Knowledge Based Market Analysis. In Proceedings of the Fourth of Innovative Applications of Artificial Intelligence, 57–69. Menlo Park, Calif.: AAAI Press.

Brachman, R. J.; Borgida, A.; McGuinness, D. L.; Patel-Schneider, P. F.; and Resnick, L. A. 1991. Living with CLASSIC: When and How to Use a KL-One-Like Language. In *Principles of Semantic Networks, ed.* J. Sowa, 401–456. San Mateo, Calif.: Morgan Kaufmann Publishers, Inc.

Brachman, R.; Selfridge, P.; Terveen, L.; Altman, B.; Halper, F.; Kirk, T.; Lazar, A.; McGuinness, D.; Resnick, L.; and Borgida, A. 1993. Integrated Support for Data Archaeology. *International Journal of Intelligent and Cooperative Information Systems* 2(2):159–185.

Danyluk, A. 1989. Finding New Rules for Incomplete Theories: Induction with Explicit Biases in Varying Contexts. In Proceedings of the Sixth International Machine Learning Workshop, 34–36. Menlo Park, Calif.: AAAI Press.

Fayyad, U.; Weir, N.; and Djorgovski, S. 1993. Automated Analysis of a Large-Scale Sky Survey: The SKICAT System. In Working Notes of the Workshop on Knowledge Discovery in Databases, 1–13. Seattle, Wash.: American Association for Artificial Intelligence.

Frawley, W.; Piatetsky-Shapiro, G.; and Matheus, C. 1992. Knowledge Discovery in Databases: An Overview. *AI Magazine* 14(3): 57–70.

Klosgen, W. 1992. Problems for Knowledge Discovery in Databases and Their Treatment in the Statistics Interpreter Explora. *International Journal of Intelligent Systems* 7(7): 649–673.

Major, J.; and Mangano, J. 1993. Selecting Among Rules Induced From a Hurricane Database. In Working Notes of the Workshop on Knowledge Discovery in Databases, 28–44. Seattle, Wash.: American Association for Artificial Intelligence.

Norman, D.; and Draper, S. 1986. *User-Centered System Design.* Hillsdale, New Jersey: Lawrence Erlbaum Associates.

Piatetsky-Shapiro, G.; and Matheus, C. 1992. Knowledge Discovery Workbench for Exploring Business Databases. *International Journal of Intelligent Systems* 7(7): 675–686.

Redman, T. 1992. *Data Quality: Management and Technology.* New York: Bantam Books.

ReMind 1992. *ReMind Developer's Reference Manual.* Boston, Mass.: Cognitive Systems, Inc.

Simoudis, E.; Livezey, B.; and Kerber, R. 1995. Integrating Inductive and Deductive Reasoning for Data Mining.

Stellwagen, E.; and Goodrich, R. 1994. *Forecast Pro for Windows.* Belmont, Mass.: Business Forecast Systems, Inc.

Uthurasamy, R.; Means, L.; and Godden, K. 1993. Extracting Knowledge from Diagnostic Databases. *IEEE Expert* 8(6): 27–38.

Ziarko, R.; Golan, R.; and Edwards, D. 1993. An Application of Datalogic/R Knowledge Discovery Tool to Identify Strong Predictive Rules in Stock Market Data. In Working Notes of the Workshop on Knowledge Discovery in Databases, 89–101. Seattle, Wash.: American Association for Artificial Intelligence.

Zytkow, J.; and Baker, J. 1991. Interactive Mining of Regularities in Databases. In *Knowledge Discovery in Databases*. ed. G. Piatetsky-Shapiro and W. J. Frawley, 31–53. Menlo Park, Calif.: AAAI Press.

3 Graphical Models for Discovering Knowledge

Wray Buntine
Thinkbank, Inc.

Abstract

There are many different ways of representing knowledge, and for each of these ways there are many different discovery algorithms. How can we compare different representations? How can we mix, match and merge representations and algorithms on new problems with their own unique requirements? This chapter introduces probabilistic modeling as a philosophy for addressing these questions and presents graphical models for representing probabilistic models. Probabilistic graphical models are a unified qualitative and quantitative framework for representing and reasoning with probabilities and independencies.

3.1 Introduction

Perhaps one common element of the discovery systems described in this and previous books on knowledge discovery is that they are all different. Since the class of discovery problems is a challenging one, we cannot write a single program to address all of knowledge discovery. The KEFIR discovery system applied to health care by Matheus, Piatetsky-Shapiro, and McNeill (1995), for instance, is carefully tailored for a particular class of situations and could not have been easily used on theSKICAT application (Fayyad, Djorgovski, and Weir 1996). I do not know of a universal learning or discovery algorithm (Buntine 1990), and a universal problem description for discovery is arguably too broad to be used as a program specification.

As a consequence, the power to perform in an application lies in the way knowledge about the application is obtained, used, represented and modified. Unfortunately with today's technology, it is not possible to dump data into a discovery system and later read off the dollar savings. Rather one has to work closely with the experts involved, for instance in selecting and customizing tools. See the chapter by Brachman and Anand (1996) in this book for an account of the interactive aspects of knowledge discovery.

It is important then to have knowledge discovery techniques that allow flexibility in the way knowledge can be encoded, represented and discovered. Probabilistic graphical models offer such a technique. Probabilistic graphical models are a framework for structuring, representing and decomposing a problem using the notion of conditional independence. They have special cases and variations including Bayesian networks, influence diagrams, Markov networks, and causal probabilistic networks. These models are useful for the same reason that constraint satisfaction graphs are used in scheduling, data flow diagrams are used in scientific modeling, and fault trees are used in systems health management. They allow access to the structure of the problem without getting bogged down in the mathematical detail. Probabilistic graphical models do this by representing the variables in a problem and the relationships between them. Associated with graphical models themselves are the mathematical details such as the equations linking variables in the model, and algorithms for performing exact and approximate inference on the model.

Probabilistic graphical models are an attractive modeling tool for knowledge discovery because:

1. They are a lucid representation for a variety of problems, allowing key dependencies within a problem to be expressed and irrelevancies to be ignored. They are flexible enough to represent supervised and unsupervised learning systems, neural networks, and many hybrids.

2. They come with well understood techniques for key tasks in the discovery process:

   - problem formulation and decomposition,
   - designing a learning algorithm (Buntine 1994),
   - identification of valuable knowledge (using decision theory), and
   - generation of explanations (Madigan, Mosurski, and Almond 1995).

Only a simple form of graphical model is considered in this chapter, the Bayesian network. Reasoning about the value of knowledge on Bayesian networks can be done by adding "value" nodes, and using the tools of influence diagrams and utility theory (Shachter 1986), part of modern decision theory. This is not covered in this chapter. Bayesian networks are introduced in Section 3.2, problem decomposition is discussed in Section 3.3, knowledge refinement is discussed in Section 3.4, and relationships to a variety of learning representations are discussed in Section 3.5. Implications to discovery are given in the conclusion.

3.2   Introduction to Graphical Models

Graphs are used to represent *models*. A model in general is some proposed representation of the problem at hand showing the different variables involved, data and parameters, and the probabilistic or deterministic relationships between them. The basic model we consider consists of nodes representing variables, and arcs that indicate dependencies between variables (or, no arcs indicating independencies). The *variables* represented may be real valued or discrete, and may be

- variables whose values are given in the data,
- "hidden" variables believed to exist such as medical syndromes or hypothesized classes in a data base of stars, or
- *parameters* used to specify a model such as the weights in a neural network, the standard deviation of a Gaussian, the radius of diffusion in an instrument, or the error rate along a transmission channel.

These are all variables but often considered different from data. Their difference being that some might have their values currently known, some might be revealed to us in the future, some we might reasonably measure indirectly, and some we only hypothesize they exist and use the calculus of probability to estimate.

Below we introduce the basic kind of graphical model, a Bayesian network, and give a brief insight into its interpretation. This brief tour is necessary before applying graphical models to discovery and learning. A Bayesian network is a graphical model that uses directed arcs exclusively to form an directed acyclic graph (i.e., a directed graph without directed cycles). Figure 3.1, adapted from Shachter and Heckerman (1987), shows a simple Bayesian network for a simplified medical problem. This graph represents a *domain model* for the problem. This organizes variables in the way the medical specialist would usually like to understand the problem, and arcs in the graph intuitively correspond to the notion *can cause* or *influence*. For instance, it may be thought that disease causes symptoms, and that age, occupation and climate causes disease. Under no stretch of the imagination could a disease be said to be caused by its symptoms[1]. The graph of Figure 3.1 can also be called a *causal model*. Other graphical models might represent the variables in a different ordering depending on whether the graph is being used to represent the domain model, a *computational model* for use by a program, or a particular view representative of some user. Graphical models can be manipulated to represent all these different views of a probabilistic knowledge base.

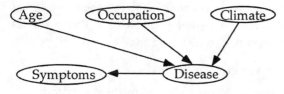

Figure 3.1
A simplified medical problem.

Graphical models are a language for expressing problem decomposition. They show how to decompose a problem into simpler subproblems. For a directed acyclic graph, this is done by a conditional decomposition of the joint probability (see, for instance, Lauritzen *et al.* [1990], and Pearl [1988] for more detail including other interpretations). This is as follows (full variable names have been abbreviated). M here represents the context. All probability statements are relative to context (context is dropped in later discussions for brevity).

$$p(Age, Occ, Clim, Dis, Symp|M) =$$
$$p(Age|M)\, p(Occ|M)\, p(Clim|M)\, p(Dis|Age, Occ, Clim, M)$$
$$p(Symp|Dis, M) \, . \tag{3.2.1}$$

Each variable is written down conditioned on its *parents*, where *parents(x)* is the set of variables with a directed arc into x. The general form for this for a set of variables X is

---

[1]Unless there was some kind of time delay and feedback involved.

$$p(X|M) = \prod_{x \in X} p(x|parents(x), M) \ . \tag{3.2.2}$$

Compare Equation (3.2.1) with one way of writing the *complete* joint probability:

$$p(Age, Occ, Clim, Dis, Symp|M) = p(Age|M)\,p(Occ|Age, M)$$
$$p(Clim|Age, Occ, M)\,p(Dis|Age, Occ, Clim, M)$$
$$p(Symp|Age, Occ, Clim, Dis, M) \ . \tag{3.2.3}$$

This complete joint is an identity of probability theory, and makes no independence assumptions about the problem. Probability models such as these are used primarily for performing *inference* on new problems. Graphical models are useful here because many kinds of inference can be performed on them. Basic inference involves calculating probabilities for arbitrary sets of variables (Shachter, Andersen and Szolovits 1994). Graphical models have been used in domains such as diagnosis, probabilistic expert systems, in planning and control (Dean and Wellman 1991; Chan and Shachter 1992), and in statistical analysis of data (Gilks, Thomas, and Spiegelhalter 1993), which is often more goal directed than typical knowledge discovery. Graphical models also generalize some aspects of Kalman filters (Poland 1994) used in control and hidden Markov models, the basic tool used in speech recognition (Rabiner and Juang 1986) and fault diagnosis (Smyth and Mellstrom 1992). Therefore graphical models are also used for dynamic systems and forecasting (Kjæruff 1992; Dagum *et al.* 1995). Various methods for learning simple kinds of graphical models from data also exist (Heckerman 1995). More extensive introductions to probabilistic graphical models can be found in (Henrion, Breese, and Horvitz 1991; Whittaker 1990; Pearl 1988; Spiegelhalter *et al.* 1993), and to learning in graphical models can be found in (Spiegelhalter *et al.* 1993; Buntine 1994; Heckerman 1995).

3.3   Problem Decomposition

Learning and discovery problems rarely come neatly packaged and labeled according to their type. It is common for the practitioner to spend some time analyzing a problem as to how and where data analysis should be applied. This analysis and decomposition of a problem is routinely done for knowledge acquisition and software development, but has not attracted as much attention in the data analysis, discovery and learning literature. This section introduces the technique of problem decomposition using graphical models. The reasons for doing decomposition are two-fold. First and clearly, simplifying a problem is good in itself. Second and more importantly, a simpler model is easier to learn from data because it has less parameters. This makes discovery feasible and more reliable. Graphical models are a convenient way of making the structure of the decomposition apparent without going into the precise mathematical detail.

This section illustrates the process of problem decomposition by working through an example of topic spotting. Several other examples could equally well have illustrated this process. The topic spotting example addresses two common problems in supervised learning: a large input space and a multi-class decision problem.

Associated Press produces short newswires at a rate of tens of thousands per year. These come in approximately 90 broad topics and contain in all some 11,000 different words. Although a single newswire may only be 400 words long. A typical newswire is given below.

> **Precious Metals Climate Improving, Says Montagu**
> LONDON, April 1 – The climate for precious metals is improving with prices benefiting from renewed inflation fears and the switching of funds from dollar and stock markets ... Silver prices in March gained some 15 pct in dollar terms due to a weak dollar and silver is felt to be fairly cheap relative to gold ... The report said the firmness in oil prices was likely to continue in the short term ...

The topics for this newswire are gold, silver and precious metals. The topics for any given newswire are often given in the subject line, as written by the author of the newswire. However, we ignore this for the purposes of illustration.

Suppose we wish to predict the topics from the text of the newswire, ignoring the subject line. The naive approach is to attempt to predict the 90 topics from the 400 words using a monolithic classifier with 11,000 inputs. Instead, this problem can be readily decomposed: The 90 or so topics can be broken down into sub-topics and co-topics because the topic space has a rich structure. Moreover, the space of input words has structure itself: Suppose a newswire is known to have the topic

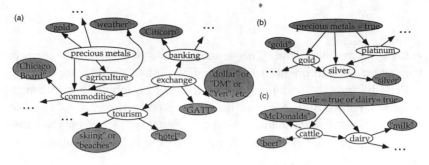

Figure 3.2
Three components of a topics-subtopics model (shaded nodes have known values).

"precious metals." The presence of the word "beef" is irrelevant when trying to determine whether the sub-topic is gold or silver. However, the word "beef" would be relevant if the topic were known to be relevant to agriculture.

A partial decomposition for this problem is given in Figure 3.2. These three Bayesian networks are different to the previous in that some nodes are shaded and some are not. By convention, shaded nodes have their values known at the time of inference, and unshaded nodes do not. The partial decomposition goes as follows: First, we break the 90 topics up into groups. In Figure 3.2(a) these are the boolean variables *agriculture*, *precious-metals*, *tourism* and so forth. These topic variables can be recognized as the unshaded nodes in the graph. This graph is a model for these topics conditioned on the presence of various words in the newswire text. Variables consisting of quoted words indicate whether the word appears in the text. For instance, the variable *"gold"* in Figure 3.2(a) will be true if the word gold appears in the text, and false otherwise. Note this is different to whether the topic of the text is gold. In practice, word frequency counts are used and there are many more hundreds of words. Ignore this complication for the purposes of illustration. Also, all these quoted variables appear in shaded nodes. This indicates that we have the text before us, so we know the value of each of these word variables, whereas we do not know the topics.

Each topic now has its own graph to predict subtopics, and perhaps sub-subtopics. For instance, Figure 3.2(b) shows a sample subtopic graph for precious metals. Notice this graph has the top boolean variable *precious-metals* whose value is known to be true. This notation is used to indicate that this subgraph is contingent on *precious-metals* being a true topic. Likewise, Figure 3.2(c) shows a graph contingent on either *cattle* or *dairy* being true. This graph assumes at least one of them is true and is used to predict whether one, the other, or both are true.

Probability is the unifying framework used to combine these different graphical models into a global model to predict the complete set of topics. This is done as follows: Adapting Equation (3.2.2) for the three graphs of Figure 3.2 yield three formulae for the following probabilities:

- $p(precious\text{-}metals, banking, exchange, commodities,$
$$agriculture, tourism | \text{``}ChicagoBoard\text{''},$$
$$\text{``}gold\text{''}, \text{``}weather\text{''}, \text{``}Citicorp\text{''}, etc.)$$
- $p(gold, silver, platinum | precious\text{-}metals = true, \text{``}gold\text{''}, etc.)$
- $p(dairy, cattle | dairy = true \; OR \; cattle = true,$
$$\text{``}beef\text{''}, \text{``}McDonald's\text{''}, etc.)$$

Likewise, corresponding formulae are obtained for the other graphs not depicted here. These probabilities can then be manipulated and combined to yield individual probabilities. For instance, suppose we wish to evaluate the probability $p(silver | newswire)$, where *newswire* indicates the contents of the newswire is given and so all the words like *"beef"* are also given. This can be computed using the two probability identities:

$p(silver | newswire) \; =$

$\quad p(silver | precious\text{-}metals = true, newswire)$

$\quad p(precious\text{-}metals = true | newswire)$

$p(silver | precious\text{-}metals = true, newswire) \; =$

$$\sum_{gold \in \{T,F\}} \; \sum_{platinum \in \{T,F\}} p(gold, silver, platinum | precious\text{-}metals =$$
$$true, newswire)$$

where $p(precious\text{-}metals = true | newswire)$ is computed similarly by summing out the other topic variables in Figure 3.2(a). Methods for combining probabilities from multiple networks can involve more complex schemes. A method developed for medical diagnosis that is suitable to the topic spotting problem considered here is similarity networks (Heckerman 1990). This is based on many graphs of the form of Figure 3.2(c) used to distinguish pairs of topics.

There are a number of interesting questions for this decomposition approach. How do we develop such a decomposition? In diagnosis domains such as medicine, this kind of decomposition has been done manually in the development of probabilistic expert systems. It is found that experts are able to explain their own decompositions of a problem. Second, how can the decomposition be done automatically? While this is an open research question, standard techniques for learning should adapt to the task.

3.4   Knowledge Refinement

Unsupervised learning is a standard tool in statistics and pattern recognition. A well known example in discovery is the Autoclass application to the IRAS star database (Cheeseman and Stutz 1996). While these applications of unsupervised learning sometimes proceed routinely, it is more often the case that discovery is an iterative process. Initial exploration reveals some details and the discovery algorithm is modified as a result. Here, the discovery process parallels the iterative refinement strategies popular in software engineering. These strategies are made possible by rapid prototyping software such as Tcl/Tk used for developing interfaces (Ousterhout 1994). This aspect of discovery is discussed further by Brachman and Anand (1996). The application of iterative refinement to knowledge discovery and knowledge acquisition is one way of viewing knowledge refinement (Ginsberg, Weiss, and Politakis 1988; Towell, Shavlik, and Noordewier 1990).

An application where this kind of refinement was required is the analysis of aviation safety data given by Kraft and Buntine (1993). The task was to discover classes of aircraft incidents. In this case, standard unsupervised learning revealed incident classes that the domain expert believed were confounded by basic relationships expected in the data. A graphical model illustrating and simplifying the standard unsupervised learning is given in Figure 3.3.

The algorithm used in this initial investigation was an algorithm called SNOB (Boulton and Wallace 1970), related to Autoclass. This algorithm builds a classification model as represented in the figure. For a given aircraft incident, details are recorded on the pilot, the controller, the kind of aircraft, its mission, and other information. Figure 3.3 indicates that if a set of aircraft is of the same hidden incident class, then the details recorded are rendered independent. That is, the joint probability

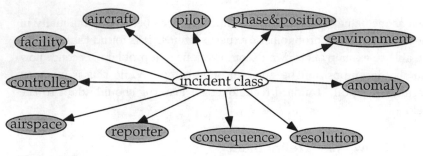

Figure 3.3
Simple unsupervised model of the aircraft incident domain.

of the recorded details and the hidden incident class read from the graph is

$$p(incident\text{-}class)\, p(airspace|incident\text{-}class)$$
$$p(controller|incident\text{-}class)$$
$$p(facility|incident\text{-}class)\, p(aircraft|incident\text{-}class) \ldots$$

Each of these probabilities is evaluated using parameters set by the learning algorithm. For instance, a particular hidden incident class might have predominantly wide-body aircraft, experienced pilots, and have equipment failure, but otherwise the details are similar to the general population of incidents. The occurrence of wide-body aircraft, experienced pilots, and equipment failure would occur independently in this class, as indicated by the figure.

Aviation psychologists experienced in this domain expected relationships, for instance, between the pilot's qualifications and the type of aircraft, the type of aircraft and the phase of flight: for instance, wide-body aircraft do not go on joy rides. In some cases, these relationships were encoded as requirements of the Federal Aviation Authority, and in other cases they were well understood causal relationships. The discovered classes of aircraft incidents tended to be confounded by these known relationships. A way around this problem is to construct a hybrid model as given in Figure 3.4.

The expected relationships are encoded into the model. For instance, that the pilot's qualifications are influenced by the aircraft, and that the facility tracking the aircraft depends on the type of aircraft and which airspace it is in (commercial, private and military aircraft have different behaviors) are encoded. This leaves the hidden *incident class* to explain

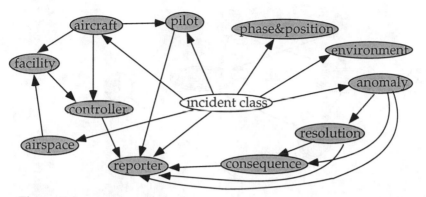

Figure 3.4
Hybrid unsupervised model of the aircraft incident domain.

the remaining regularity in the domain. That is, probability tables would be elicited from the aviation psychologists for the understood probability relations such as $p(controller|facility, aircraft)$ and these fixed in the model. The learning system now needs to refine the model by filling in the remaining parts of the model that are left unspecified by this knowledge elicitation.

Again, there are a number of interesting questions about this refinement approach. How can the refinement algorithm proceed with some parts of the model fixed? This is not a difficult problem in the sense that standard algorithmic schemes like the expectation maximization (EM) algorithm used in SNOB and Autoclass are known to handle learning in this context (Buntine 1994). Software suited to this exact task is not currently available, however. So on this problem the iterative refinement process of knowledge discovery stops after one iteration, due to lack of available software.

3.5   Models for Learning and Discovery

This section outlines how various learning and discovery representations can be modeled with probabilistic graphical models. A characteristic problem is given along with the graphical model. The intention is to illustrate the rich variety of discovery tasks that can be represented with graphical models. Given the generality of the language, it should be clear that many hybrid models are represented as well, such as the

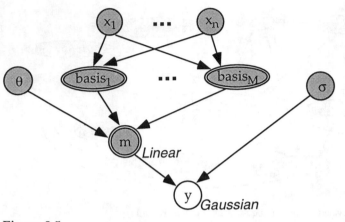

Figure 3.5
Linear regression with Gaussian error.

hybrid unsupervised model of Figure 3.4.

The graphical models given here have their model parameters as well as the problem inputs marked as known. Of course, in the practice of data analysis, the model parameters are unknown and need to be learned from the data, and the training set or sample will usually have both problem inputs and outputs known for each case in the set. However, this represents the subsequent inference task underlying the problem, not the learning problem itself. In some cases, the functional form is also given for the probabilistic model implied by the graphical model.

3.5.1   Linear Regression

Linear regression is the classic method in statistics for doing curve fitting, that is, predicting a real valued variable from input variables, real or discrete. See Casella and Berger (1990), for instance, for a standard undergraduate introduction. Linear regression, in its most general form, fits non-linear curves as well because the term "linear" implies that the mean prediction for the variable is a linear function of the parameters of the model, but can be a non-linear function of the input variables. In the standard model, a Gaussian error function with constant standard deviation is used. This is shown in Figure 3.5.

This is an instance of a generalized linear model (McCullagh and Nelder 1989), so has a linear node at its core. The M basis functions $basis_1, \ldots, basis_M$ are known deterministic functions of the input variables $x_1, \ldots, x_n$. Variables that are deterministic functions of their inputs are represented with *deterministic nodes* that have double ellipses. These deterministic functions would typically be non-linear orthogonal functions such as Legendre polynomials. The linear node combines these linearly with the parameters θ to produce the mean m for the Gaussian.

$$m = \sum_{i=1}^{M} \theta_i basis_i(x) .$$

The graphical model of Figure 3.5 implies the above equation (each deterministic node implies an equality holds) and the conditional probability

$$p(y|x_1, \ldots, x_n, \theta, \sigma) = \frac{1}{\sqrt{2\pi}\sigma} e^{-(y-m)^2/2\sigma^2} ,$$

the standard normal density with mean m and standard deviation σ. This graph also shows that the inputs x_1 to x_n are given, and so there is no particular distribution for them.

3.5.2   Weighted Rule-Based Systems

Weighted rule-based systems are an interesting representation because they have been independently suggested in artificial intelligence, neural networks, and statistics, with each community using their own notation. The system, given in Figure 3.6, is the discrete version of the linear regression network given in Figure 3.5. Like linear regression, this is also an instance of a generalized linear model, so has the linear construction of Figure 3.5 at its core. Each of the deterministic nodes for variables $rule_1, \ldots, rule_m$ represents a rule, an indicator function with the value 1 if the rule fires, and the value 0 otherwise. Those rules that fire cause weights (θ) to be added up, and consequently a prediction to be made.

   In the binary classification case ($c \in \{0,1\}$), when multiple rules fire, the probability that the class $c = 1$ is given by the transformation

$$p(c = 1|x_1, \ldots, x_n, \theta) = Logistic^{-1}\left(\sum_{i=1}^{m} rule_i\theta_i\right)$$

The functional type for the Logistic node is the function,

$$p(c = 1|u) = \frac{e^u}{1 + e^u} = 1 - Sigmoid(u) = Logistic^{-1}(u) , \qquad (3.5.4)$$

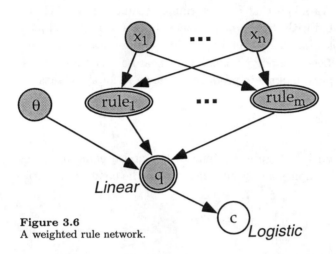

Figure 3.6
A weighted rule network.

which maps a real value u onto a probability for the binary variable c. This function is the inverse of the logistic or logit function used in generalized linear models, and is also related to the sigmoid function used in feed-forward neural networks.

According to this weighting scheme, if a rule $rule_i$ fires in isolation, the probability that class $c = 1$ becomes $Logistic^{-1}(\theta_i)$. Hence θ_i can be interpreted as the log odds of p_i ($Logistic(p_i)$), where p_i is the probability that c will be 1 when only the single rule i fires. If multiple rules fire then this formula corresponds to combining the probabilities p_i using the original Prospector combining formula (Duda, Hart, and Nilsson 1976; Berka and Ivánek 1994)

$$Combine(p_i, p_j) = \frac{p_i \cdot p_j}{p_i \cdot p_j + (1 - p_i) \cdot (1 - p_j)} .$$

This combining formula is associative and commutative so the order of combination is irrelevant.

This approach thus implements a weighted rule-based system for classification using the Prospector combining formula. The model can also be interpreted as a neural network since the output node corresponds to a sigmoid, and the intermediate deterministic nodes can be interpreted as unparameterized hidden nodes. By using other combination rules different effects can be achieved; even for instance, fuzzy-style combinations.

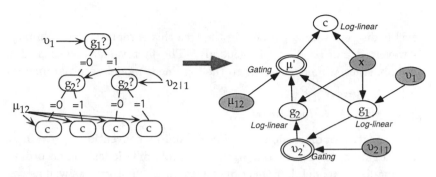

Figure 3.7
A two level mixture of "experts."

3.5.3   Hierarchical Mixtures of Experts

Jordan and Jacobs (1993) have developed a classification approach based on the notion of a "mixture of experts." Like the weighted rule-based system, this model predicts a class c from a vector of inputs x. It does so, however, by combining a number of linear models to form a more complex classifier.

The decision tree representation and the DAG for this mixture model are given in the left and right of Figure 3.7 respectively. The decision tree is presented here for the case of discrete variables. In general both inputs and outputs can be real valued or discrete. Traversing the tree in the left of the figure down to a leaf node leads one to the leaf, which represents an "expert." These experts then combine to make the prediction for the class c. The prediction is done with a log-linear model, using the parameters $\mu' = \mu_{g_1 g_2}$, for the two "gates" g_1, g_2. Suppose the class is C-valued, so $c \in \{1, 2, \ldots, C\}$. The class prediction is:

$$p(c = i | x, \mu') \;=\; \textit{log-linear}(i, x, \mu') \;=\; \frac{e^{x \cdot \mu'_i}}{\sum_{j=1}^{C} e^{x \cdot \mu'_i}} \; .$$

This is similar to the weighted rule-based system described in Section 3.5.2, where the rules correspond to the vector x. μ' is a matrix of dimension $C \times dim(x)$, and by convention $\mu'_C = 0$. For c binary, this is equivalent to the logistic node used in Section 3.5.2.

The decision tree also has two variables denoting "gates," g_1 at the first node and g_2 at the two second level nodes, however, these are not present in the data. The values for the gates g_1 and g_2 are predicted using the data and the parameters v_1 and $v_{2|g_1}$ respectively. At the first level is discrete valued gate g_1 (in the tree this is represented as binary, however, it can be N-ary in general). The first value is chosen in a probabilistic fashion according to the log-linear model with parameters v_1.

$$p(g_1 = i | x, v_1) \; = \; log\text{-}linear(i, x, v_1) \; .$$

v_1 is a matrix of dimension $C \times dim(x)$, and by convention $v_{1,C} = 0$. A second gate g_2 is then chosen, again in a probabilistic fashion according to a log-linear model, but this time based on the first gate as well as the input x. The final probabilities for c are generated by another log-linear model as given by the first formula above.

In the graphical model this goes as follows. There are three log-linear models, two for the gates g_1 and g_2 and one for the final class probability. Gating nodes (which do matrix lookup) select the parameters for the log-linear nodes based on the values of other variables.

The graphical model of Figure 3.7 therefore yields the following conditional probability:

$$p(c | x, v_1, v_{2|1}, \mu_{12}) =$$
$$\textstyle\sum_{g_1} log\text{-}lin(g_1, x, v_1) \sum_{g_2} log\text{-}lin(g_2, x, v_{2|g_1}) \, log\text{-}lin(c, x, \mu_{g_1 g_2}) \; .$$

This is a *mixture* model (Titterington, Smith, and Makov 1985), in the sense that it sums over hidden variables g_1 and g_2, where the basic joint probability $p(c, g_1, g_2 | x, v_1, v_{2|1}, \mu_{12})$ is in a standard form. If only one layer were used (so g_2 and associated gates were deleted), then this model corresponds to a supervised version of the unsupervised Autoclass system described next in Section 3.5.4.

3.5.4   Unsupervised Learning

There are a range of unsupervised learning systems in statistics, neural networks, and artificial intelligence. Many of these can be represented as graphical models with hidden nodes that are used to represent hidden classes. In a sense, the learning of Bayesian networks from data can be called unsupervised learning as well, however, it is more accurately termed model discovery. This is described by Heckerman (1995). The aviation safety model given in Figure 3.4 is a hybrid of these different kinds of models.

Consider Autoclass III and the probabilistic unsupervised learning systems it is based on. For instance, a simple Autoclass III classification

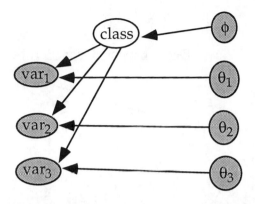

Figure 3.8
Explicit parameters for a simple Autoclass model.

for three boolean variables var_1, var_2 and var_3 has the parameterization ϕ, θ_1, θ_2 and θ_3 given in Figure 3.8.

The *class* is unobserved or "hidden." If the class assignment were known, then the variables var_1, var_2 and var_3 would be rendered statistically independent, or "explained" in some sense. More complex models allow correlations between variables, but Autoclass III does not introduce this. The parameter ϕ (a vector of class probabilities) here gives the proportions for the hidden classes, and the three parameters θ_1, θ_2 and θ_3 give how the variables are distributed within each hidden class. For instance, if there are 10 classes, then ϕ is a vector of 10 class probabilities such that the prior probability for a case being in class c is ϕ_c. If var_1 is a binary variable, then θ_1 would be 10 probabilities, one for each class, such that if the case is known to be in class c, then the probability var_1 is true is given by $\theta_{1,c}$ and the probability var_1 is false is given by $1 - \theta_{1,c}$.

There are many other models for unsupervised learning that can be similarly represented with probabilistic graphs. Sometimes this includes undirected graphs or mixtures of directed and undirected graphs (Buntine 1994). This includes the stochastic networks used in Hopfield models and others in neural networks (Hertz, Krogh, and Palmer, 1991), more complex unsupervised learning systems such as Autoclass IV which has a variety of covariances (Hanson, Stutz, and Cheeseman 1991), and systems with multiple classes.

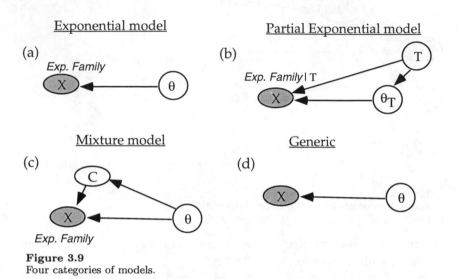

Figure 3.9
Four categories of models.

3.6   Learning Algorithms

Methods have been developed for learning simple discrete and Gaussian Bayesian networks from data, and for learning simple unsupervised models such as those mentioned in Section 3.5.4. Given that all the previous models such as linear regression and weighted rule-based systems can also be represented as Bayesian networks, will these same learning algorithms apply? Unfortunately not. However, there are general categories of algorithm schemes for learning that can be mixed and matched to these various problems. Four categories considered here are represented by the models they address, given in Figure 3.9.

This section briefly explains these categories. Algorithms for learning them are described in (Buntine 1994), and references therein.

The simplest category of learning models have exact, closed form solutions to the learning problem. This category is the exponential family of distributions, which includes the Gaussian, the multinomial, and other basic distributions (Bernardo and Smith 1994), but also the decision tree or Gaussian Bayesian network of known fixed structure, and linear regression with Gaussian error described in Section 3.5.1. These exponential family distributions all have closed form solutions to the learning problem which are linear in the sample size (Bernardo and Smith 1994; Buntine 1994). For instance, if X has a univariate Gaussian distribution, then we estimate its unknown mean and standard deviation from the sample mean and sample standard deviation (usually along with some adjustment to make the estimate unbiased). No search or numerical optimization is involved. The exponential family category is represented by the *exponential model* in Figure 3.9(a). The probability model for the data given the parameters, $p(X|\theta)$ is shown in this figure to be in the exponential family.

Two important categories of learning models are based on the exponential family category. The second category of learning models is where a useful subset of the model does fall into the exponential family. This is represented by the *partial exponential model* in Figure 3.9(b). The part of the problem that is exponential family can be solved in closed form, as mentioned above. The remaining part of the problem is typically handled approximately. Decision trees and Bayesian networks over multinomial or Gaussian variables fall into the second category (Buntine 1991a; Buntine 1991b; Spiegelhalter *et al.* 1993) when the structure of the tree or network is *not* known, as does linear regression with subset selection of relevant variables. In the figure, this is represented as follows. If we know the structure T, then the model is in the exponential family with parameters θ_T. So the probability model $p(X|\theta_T, T)$ is in the exponential family if we hold T fixed.

The third category of learning models is where, if some hidden variables are introduced into the data, the problem becomes exponential family if the hidden values were known. This is represented by the *mixture model* in Figure 3.9(c). In general, this family of models has that $p(X|C, \theta)$ is in the exponential family where C is the hidden variable (or variables) and θ are the model parameters. C does not occur in the data so this yields a probability model for X given by:

$$p(X|\theta) = \sum_C p(X|C, \theta)\, p(C|\theta) \ .$$

Two examples of this category are the mixture of experts model of Section 3.5.3, and the unsupervised learning models mentioned in Section 3.5.4. This category of models is used to model unsupervised learning, incomplete data in the classification problems, robust regression, and general density estimation (Titterington *et al.* 1985). The mixture model category can often be learned using the EM algorithm. The EM algorithm has an inner loop using the closed form solution found for the underlying exponential family model.

The final category of problems is a catch-all represented by the *generic model* in Figure 3.9(d). In this case the data X has the unconstrained probability model $p(X|\theta)$, and we assume nothing about its form. This includes feed-forward neural networks and the weighted rule-based model of Section 3.5.2. These models can be learned by algorithms such as the maximum *a posteriori* (MAP) algorithm and other general error minimization schemes. Notice that in general the other three categories of learning models can be cast into this form by ignoring some structural detail of the model. Hence the algorithms like the MAP algorithm can be applied to all the other categories of learning models as well.

3.7   Conclusion

The graphical component of the probabilistic models presented here is only relevant as a visual aid for describing models. However, the graphs provide a structural view of a probability model without getting lost in the mathematical detail. This is invaluable in the same way that a qualitative physical model can be invaluable for explaining behavior without recourse to the numeric detail. So what of probabilistic modeling? What does all this buy you?

First, probabilistic models provide a language for performing problem decomposition and recomposition, illustrated in Section 3.3, and knowledge refinement, illustrated in Section 3.4. Inference on the probabilistic models developed can be performed using a variety of probabilistic inference schemes, as listed in Section 3.2.

Second, because of the flexibility of probabilistic graphical models, they are a suitable language to represent a wide variety of learning models. Of course, the same can be said of C++. However, probabilistic models allow probability theory to be applied directly to derive inference algorithms via principles such as maximum likelihood, maximum *a posteriori*, and other probabilistic schemes. Some relevant algorithms are discussed in Section 3.6. This offers a unifying conceptual framework for the developer, with, for instance, smooth transitions into other modes of probabilistic reasoning such as diagnosis, explanation, and information

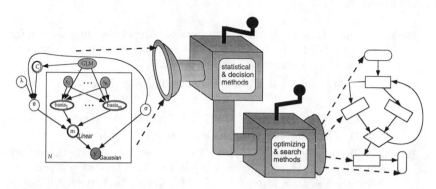

Figure 3.10
A software generator.

gathering.

Third, this probabilistic framework offers a computational approach to developing learning and discovery algorithms. The conceptual framework for this is given in Figure 3.10. Probability and decision theory are used to decompose a problem into a computational prescription, and then search and optimization techniques are used to fill the prescription. A software tool exists that implements a special case of this conceptual framework using Gibbs sampling as the computational scheme (Gilks *et al.* 1993). The Gibbs sampler is but one family of algorithms, and many more can be fit into this general framework. As explained by Buntine (1994), the framework of Figure 3.10 can use the categories of learning models described in Section 3.6 as its basis.

The real gain from the scheme of Figure 3.10 does not arise from the potential re-implementation of existing software, but from understanding gained by putting different models for learning and discovery in a common language, the ability to create novel hybrid algorithms, and the ability to tailor special purpose algorithms for specific problems. For instance, by recognizing the connection between logistic regression, neural networks and Prospector rules, done in Section 3.5.2, we are able to borrow algorithms from other fields to address the task. The scheme of Figure 3.10 supports the problem decomposition and iterative knowledge refinement processes described in Sections 3.3 and 3.4.

References

Berka, P.; and Ivánek, J. 1994. Automated Knowledge Acquisition for PROSPECTOR-Like Expert Systems. In *Proceedings of the European Conference on Machine Learning*, 339–342.

Bernardo, J. M.; and Smith, A. F .M. 1994. *Bayesian Theory*. Chichester: John Wiley.

Boulton, D. M., and Wallace, C. S. 1970. A Program for Numerical Classification. *The Computer Journal*, 13(1):63–69.

Brachman, R. J.; and Anand, T. 1996. The Process of Knowledge Discovery in Databases: A Human-Centered Approach. In *Advances in Knowledge Discovery and Data Mining*, ed. U. M. Fayyad, G. Piatetsky-Shapiro, P. Smyth, and R. S. Uthurasamy. Menlo Park, Calif.: The AAAI Press.

Buntine, W. L. 1994. Operations for Learning with Graphical Models. *Journal of Artificial Intelligence Research*, 2:159–225.

Buntine, W. L. 1991a. Learning Classification Trees. In *Artificial Intelligence Frontiers in Statistics*, ed. D. J. Hand, 182–201. London: Chapman & Hall.

Buntine, W. L. 1991b. Theory Refinement of Bayesian Networks. In *Uncertainty in Artificial Intelligence: Proceedings of the Seventh Conference*, ed. B. D. D'Ambrosio, P. Smets, and P. P. Bonissone, 52–60. San Mateo, Calif.: Morgan Kaufmann.

Buntine, W.L., 1990. Myths and Legends in Learning Classification Rules. In *Eighth National Conference on Artificial Intelligence*, 736–742. Boston, Massachusetts: AAAI Press.

Casella G.; and Berger, R. L. 1990. *Statistical Inference*. Belmont, Calif.: Wadsworth & Brooks/Cole.

Chan, B. Y.; and Shachter, R. D. 1992. Structural Controllability and Observability in Influence Diagrams. In *Uncertainty in Artificial Intelligence: Proceedings of the Eighth Conference*, ed. D. Dubois, M. P. Wellman, B. D. D'Ambrosio and P. Smets, 25–32. San Francisco: Morgan Kaufmann.

Cheeseman, P., and Stutz, J. 1996. Bayesian Classification (AutoClass): Theory and Results. In *Advances in Knowledge Discovery and Data Mining*, ed. U. M. Fayyad, G. Piatetsky-Shapiro, P. Smyth, and R. S. Uthurasamy. Menlo Park, Calif.: The AAAI Press.

Dagum, P., Galper, A., Horvitz, E., and Seiver, A. 1995. Uncertain reasoning and forecasting. *International Journal of Forecasting*. Forthcoming.

Dean T. L.; and Wellman, M. P. 1991. *Planning and Control*. San Mateo, Calif.: Morgan Kaufmann.

Duda, R. O.; Hart, P. E.; and Nilsson, N.J. 1976. Subjective Bayesian Methods for Rule-based Inference Systems. In *National Computer Conference (AFIPS Conference Proceedings, Vol. 45)*, 1075–1082.

Fayyad, U. M., Djorgovski, S., and Weir, N. 1996. Automating the Analysis and Cataloging of Sky Surveys. In *Advances in Knowledge Discovery and Data Mining,* ed. U. M. Fayyad, G. Piatetsky-Shapiro, P. Smyth, and R. S. Uthurasamy. Menlo Park, Calif.: The AAAI Press.

Gilks, W. R.; Thomas, A.; and Spiegelhalter, D. J. 1993. A Language and Program for Complex Bayesian Modeling. *The Statistician,* 43:169–178.

Ginsberg, A.; Weiss, S. M.; and Politakis, P. 1988. Automatic Knowledgebase Refinement for Classification Systems. *Artificial Intelligence,* 35(2):197–226.

Hanson, R., Stutz, J., and Cheeseman, P. 1991. Bayesian Classification with Correlation and Inheritance. In *International Joint Conference on Artificial Intelligence,* 692–698. San Mateo, Calif.: Morgan Kaufmann.

Heckerman, D. 1996. Bayesian Networks for Knowledge Discovery. In *Advances in Knowledge Discovery and Data Mining,* ed. U. M. Fayyad, G. Piatetsky-Shapiro, P. Smyth, and R. S. Uthurasamy. Menlo Park, Calif.: AAAI Press.

Heckerman, D. 1990. Probabilistic Similarity Networks.*Networks,* 20:607–636.

Henrion, M.; Breese, J. S.; and Horvitz, E. J. 1991. Decision Analysis and Expert Systems. *AI Magazine,* 12(4): 64–91.

Hertz, J. A.; Krogh, A. S.; and Palmer, R. G. 1991. *Introduction to the Theory of Neural Computation.* Reading, Mass.: Addison-Wesley.

Jordan, M. I.; and Jacobs, R. I. 1993. Supervised Learning and Divide-and-Conquer: A Statistical Approach. In *Machine Learning: Proceedings of the Tenth International Conference,* 159–166. San Mateo, Calif.: Morgan Kaufmann.

Kjæruff, U. 1992. A Computational Scheme for Reasoning in Dynamic Probabilistic Networks. In *Uncertainty in Artificial Intelligence: Proceedings of the Eighth Conference,* ed. D. Dubois, M. P. Wellman, B. D. D'Ambrosio and P. Smets, 121–129. San Mateo, Calif.: Morgan Kaufmann.

Kraft, P.; and Buntine, W. L. 1993. Initial Exploration of the ASRS Database. In *Seventh International Symposium on Aviation Psychology.* Columbus, Ohio.

Lauritzen, S. L., Dawid, A. P., Larsen, B. N., and Leimer, H.-G. 1990. Independence Properties of Directed Markov Fields. *Networks,* 20:491–505.

McCullagh, P.; and Nelder; J. A. 1989.*Generalized Linear Models.* London: Chapman and Hall.

Madigan, D.; Mosurski, K.; and Almond, R. G. 1995. Explanation in Belief Networks. StatSci Research Report 33, StatSci/Mathsoft, Seattle, Washington.

Matheus, C., Piatetsky-Shapiro, G., and McNeill, D. 1995. Key Findings Reporter for the Analysis of Healthcare Information. In *Advances in Knowledge Discovery and Data Mining,* ed. U. M. Fayyad, G. Piatetsky-Shapiro, P. Smyth, and R. S. Uthurasamy. Cambridge, Mass.: The MIT Press.

Ousterhout, J.K. 1994. *Tcl and the Tk Toolkit.* Reading, Mass.: Addison-Wesley.

Pearl, J. 1988. *Probabilistic Reasoning in Intelligent Systems.* San Francisco: Morgan Kaufmann.

Poland, W. B. 1994.*Decision Analysis with Continuous and Discrete Variables: A Mixture Distribution Approach.* Ph.D. diss., Dept. of Engineering Economic Systems, Stanford Univ.

Rabiner, L. R.; and Juang, B. H. 1986. An Introduction to Hidden Markov Models.*IEEE ASSP Magazine,* January: 4–16, 1986.

Shachter, R. D.; Andersen, S. K.; and Szolovits, P. 1994. Global Conditioning for Probabilistic Inference in Belief Networks. In *Uncertainty in Artificial Intelligence: Proceedings of the Tenth Conference,* ed. R. Lopez de Mantaras and D. Poole, 514–522. San Mateo, Calif.: Morgan Kaufmann.

Shachter, R. D.; and Heckerman, D. 1987. Thinking Backwards for Knowledge Acquisition. *AI Magazine,* 8 (Fall): 55–61.

Shachter, R. D. 1986. Evaluating Influence Diagrams.*Operations Research,* 34(6): 871–882.

Smyth, P.; and Mellstrom, J. 1992. Detecting Novel Classes with Applications to Fault Diagnosis. In *Ninth International Conference on Machine Learning.* San Mateo, Calif.: Morgan Kaufmann.

Spiegelhalter, D. J.; Dawid, A. P.; Lauritzen, S. L.; and Cowell, R .G. 1993. Bayesian Analysis in Expert Systems. *Statistical Science,* 8(3):219–283.

Titterington, D. M.; Smith, A. F. M.; and Makov, U. E. 1985. *Statistical Analysis of Finite Mixture Distributions.* Chichester: John Wiley & Sons.

Towell, G. G.; Shavlik, J. W.; and Noordewier, M. O. 1990. Refinement of Approximate Domain Theories by Knowledge-based Neural Networks. In Proceedings, Eighth National Conference on Artificial Intelligence, 861–866. Menlo Park, Calif.: AAAI Press.

Whittaker, J. 1990. *Graphical Models in Applied Multivariate Statistics.* New York: John Wiley.

4 A Statistical Perspective on Knowledge Discovery in Databases

John F. Elder IV
Rice University

Daryl Pregibon
AT&T Bell Laboratories

Abstract

The quest to find models usefully characterizing data is a process central to the scientific method, and has been carried out on many fronts. Researchers from an expanding number of fields have designed algorithms to discover rules or equations that capture key relationships between variables in a database. The task of this chapter is to provide a perspective on statistical techniques applicable to KDD; accordingly, we review below some major advances in statistics in the last few decades. We next highlight some distinctives of what may be called a "statistical viewpoint." Finally we overview some influential classical and modern statistical methods for practical model induction.

4.1 Recent Statistical Contributions

It would be unfortunate if the KDD community dismissed statistical methods on the basis of courses that they took on statistics several to many years ago. The following provides a rough chronology of "recent" significant contributions in statistics that are relevant to the KDD community. The noteworthy fact is that this time period coincides with the significant increases in computing horsepower and memory, powerful and expressive programming languages, and general accessibility to computing that has propelled us into the Information Age. In effect, this started a slow but deliberate shift in the statistical community, whereby important influences and enablers were to come from computing rather than mathematics.

4.1.1 The 1960s

This was the era of *robust* and *resistant* statistical methods. Following ideas of G. E. P. Box and J. W. Tukey, Huber (1964) and Hampel (1974) formalized the notion that the usual estimators of location and regression coefficients were very sensitive to "outliers," "leverage values," and otherwise unreasonably small amounts of contamination. Key concepts are the

- *influence* function of Hampel (essentially the derivative of an estimator with respect to the data)

- *M*-estimators of Huber, so-called because they generalize maximum likelihood estimators (which require a probability distribution) to a closely related class of estimating equations

- *diagnostics*, where implicit downweighting of observations afforded by robust estimators is replaced by empirical derivatives that quantify the effects of small changes in the data on important aspects of regression-like models (see for example, Belsley, Kuh, and Welsch, 1980)

The theory supporting these ideas is elegant and important as it unifies many seemingly unrelated concepts (*e.g.* trimmed means and medians) and more so because it reflects the realism that data does not usually obey assumptions as required by (mathematical) theorems. Thus the robustness era freed statisticians of the shackles of narrow models depending on unrealistic assumptions (*e.g.* normality).

The only downside of the era was that too much effort was placed on deriving new estimators that deviated only slightly from each other both qualitatively and quantitatively.[1] What was needed instead, was the leadership and direction in *using* these methods in practice and dealing with the plethora of alternatives available. Partly because of this misguided effort, many of the techniques of the era never made it into commercial software and therefore never made it into the mainstream of methods used by nonstatisticians.

4.1.2   The Early 1970s

The term exploratory data analysis (EDA) characterizes the notion that statistical insights and modeling are driven by data. John Tukey (1977; Mosteller and Tukey, 1977) reinforced these notions in the early 70's using a battery of ultra-simple methods, *e.g.* what could be done with pencil and paper. But the deeper message was to dispel the traditional dogma stating that one was not allowed to "look at the data prior to

---

[1]Basically reflecting R. A. Fisher's insight (*Statistical Methods for Researchers*, 1924) that there is nothing easier than inventing a new statistical estimator.

modeling." On the one side the argument was that hypotheses and the like must not be biased by choosing them on the basis of what the data seem to be indicating. On the other side was the belief that pictures and numerical summaries of data are necessary in order to understand how rich a model the data can support.

A key notion in this era characterized statistical modeling as decomposing the data into structure and noise,

$$data = fit + residual \tag{4.1.1}$$

and then examining residuals to identify and move additional structure into the fit. The fitting process would then be repeated and followed by subsequent residual analyses.

The iterative process described above has its roots in the general statistical paradigm of partitioning variability into distinct parts (*e.g.*, explained and unexplained variation; or, in classification, within-group and between-group variation). The EDA notion simply uses the observed scale of the response rather than the somewhat unnatural squared units of "variability." While this might seem like a trivial distinction, the difference is critical since it is only on the observed scale that diagnosis *and* treatment is possible. For example, a component of variance can indicate that nonlinearity is present but cannot prescribe how to accommodate it.

Graphical methods (not to be confused with graphical *models* in Bayes nets) enjoyed a renaissance during this period as statisticians (re-) discovered that nothing outperforms human visual capabilities in pattern recognition. Specifically, statistical tests and models focus on *expected* values, and in many cases, it is the *un*expected that upsets or invalidates a model (*e.g.*, outliers). Tukey argued that (good) graphical methods should allow *un*expected values to present themselves—once highlighted, models can be expanded or changed to account for them.

Another important contribution was to make data *description* respectable once more. Statistics has its roots in earlier times when descriptive statistics reigned and mathematical statistics was only a gleam in the eye. Data description is concerned with simplicity and accuracy, while not being overly formal about quantifying these terms (though an important area of research tries to do just that; *e.g.*, Mallows (1973), Akaike (1973), and Rissanen (1978)). A key notion popularized in this era was that there is seldom a single *right* answer—in nearly all situations there are many answers. Effective data description highlights those that are simple, concise, and reasonably accurate. Simple transformations of a dataset are used to effect such descriptions, the two most common ones being *data reexpression, e.g.* using log(*age*) instead of *age*, and *data splitting, e.g.* setting aside outliers to simplify the description of the bulk of the data.

4.1.3 The Late 1970s

To an outsider much of the statistical literature would seem fragmented and disjoint. But the fact of the matter is that much is closely related, but that specific details of individual contributions hide the real similarities. In the late 70's, two review papers and one book elegantly captured the essence of numerous prior publications. The first of these, *Generalized Linear Models* (Nelder and Wedderburn, 1974; McCullagh and Nelder, 1989) extended the usual normal theory linear model to a much wider class of models that included probability models other than the normal distribution, and structural models that were nonlinear. The theory accomplished this by decomposing the variation in a response variable into systematic and random components, and allowed the former to capture covariate effects through a strictly monotone *link* function, $g(\mu) = \sum x_j \beta_j$, and allowing the latter to be a member of the exponential family of distributions, $\mathcal{E}(\mu, \sigma)$. In so doing, these models provided a unifying theory for regression-like models for binary and count data, as well as continuous data from asymmetric distributions. The second major review paper is well known outside of statistics as the *EM* algorithm (Dempster, Laird, and Rubin, 1977). This paper neatly pulled together numerous ways of solving estimation problems with incomplete data. But the beauty of their general treatment was to instill the concept that even if data are complete, it is often useful to treat it as a missing value problem for computational purposes. Finally, the analysis of nominal or discrete data, specifically counts, had several disconnected streams in the literature and inconsistent ways to describe relationships. Bishop, Fienberg, and Holland (1975) pulled this material together into the class of *loglinear* models. The associated theory allowed researchers to draw analogies to models for continuous data (for example, analysis of variance ideas) and further provided computational strategies for estimation and hypothesis testing. It is also noteworthy that this work anticipated current work in so-called *graphical models*, a subset of the class of loglinear models for nominal data.

4.1.4   The Early 1980s

Resampling methods had been around since the late 1950s under the moniker *jackknife*, so-named by Tukey because it was a "trusty general purpose tool" for eliminating low-order bias from an estimator (Schreuder, 1986). The essence of the procedure is to replace the original n observations by n or more (possibly) correlated estimates of the quantity of interest (called *pseudovalues*). These are obtained by systematically leaving out one or more observations and recomputing the estimator. More precisely, if θ is the parameter of interest, the ith pseudovalue is defined by

$$p_i = n\hat{\theta}_{all} - (n - k)\hat{\theta}_{-i} \qquad (4.1.2)$$

where the last quantity is the estimator $\hat{\theta}$ based on leaving out the ith subset (of size k). The jackknife estimate of θ is the arithmetic mean of the pseudovalues, $\bar{p} = \sum p_i/n$.

While the jackknife was originally proposed as a bias reduction tool, it was quickly recognized that the ordinary standard deviation of the pseudovalues provides an honest estimate of the error in the estimate. Thus an empirical means of deriving a measure of uncertainty for virtually *any* statistical estimator was available. One interpretation of the procedure is that the construction of pseudovalues is based on repeatedly and systematically sampling *without* replacement from the data at hand. This led Efron (1979) to generalize the concept to repeated sampling *with* replacement, the so-called *bootstrap* (since it allowed one to "pick oneself up by the bootstraps" in constructing a confidence interval or standard error). This seemingly trivial insight opened the veritable flood gates for comprehensive analytic study and understanding of resampling methods. The focus on estimating precision of estimators rather than bias removal coupled with the advance of computing resources, allowed standard errors of highly nonlinear estimators to be routinely considered.

Unfortunately, as with robustness, the bulk of the research effort was directed at theoretical study of resampling ideas in what KDD researchers would regard as uninteresting situations. The most nonlinear procedures, such as those resulting from combining model identification and model estimation (see Section 4.1.6), received only cursory effort (*e.g.* Efron and Gong, 1983; Faraway, 1991).

4.1.5   The Late 1980s

One might characterize classical statistical methods as being "globally" linear whereby the explanatory/prediction/classification variables affect the distribution of the response variable via linear combinations. Thus the effect of x_j on y is summarized by a single regression coefficient β_j. Nonlinear relationships could only be modeled by specifically including the appropriate nonlinear terms in the model, *e.g.* x_j^2 or $\log x_j$. Cleveland (1979) helped seed the notion that globally linear procedures could be replaced with locally linear ones by employing scatterplot smoothers in interesting ways. A scatterplot smoother $s(x)$ is a data-dependent curve defined pointwise over the range of x. For example, the *moving average* smoother is defined at each unique x, as the mean $\bar{y}(x) = \sum y_i / k$ of the k (symmetric) nearest neighbors of x. The ordered sequence of these pointwise estimates traces out a "smooth" curve through the scatter of (x, y) points. Originally smoothers were used simply to enhance scatterplots where clutter or changing density of plotted points hindered visual interpretation of trends and nonlinear features. But by interpreting a scatterplot smoother as an estimate of the conditional mean $E(y|x)$, one obtains an adaptive, nonlinear estimate of the effect of x on the distribution of y. Moreover, this nonlinearity could be tamed while simultaneously reducing bias caused by end-effects, by enforcing "local" linearity in the smoothing procedure (as opposed to local constants as provided by moving averages or medians). Thus by moving a *window* across the data and fitting linear regressions within the window, a globally nonlinear fit is obtained, *i.e.* the sequence of predictions at each point x_i, $s_i(x) = a_i + b_i x$, where the coefficients a_i and b_i are determined by the least squares regression of y on x for all points in the window centered on x_i.

This notion has been applied now in many contexts (*e.g.* regression, classification, discrimination) and across many "error" distributions (*e.g.* the generalized additive model of Hastie and Tibshirani, 1990). While this work reduced the emphasis on strict linearity of the explanatory variables in such models, it did not ameliorate the need for having previously identified the relevant variables to begin with.

4.1.6 The Early 1990s

Within the statistics community, Friedman and Tukey (1974) pioneered the notion of allowing a model to adapt even more nonlinearly by letting the data determine the interesting structure present with "projection pursuit" methods (Section 4.4.3). These are less restrictive than related nonlinear methods such as neural networks (Section 4.4.4), supposing a model of the form

$$\mu(y|x) = \sum_{k=1}^{K} g_k \left(\sum_{j=1}^{J} x_j \beta_{jk} \right) \tag{4.1.3}$$

where both the regression coefficients β_{jk} and the *squashing* functions $g_k()$ are unknown.

Important algorithmic developments and theory resulted from these models even though they failed to achieve widespread use within the statistics community. Part of the reason was that these models were regarded as *too* flexible in the sense that arbitrarily complex functions could be provably recovered (with big enough K). The community instead retreated back to additive models that had limited flexibility but afforded much greater interpretability. Indeed, interpretability was the focus of much of the work in this area as alternative formulations of the locally linear model were derived, *e.g.*, penalized likelihood and Bayesian formulations (O'Sullivan *et al.* 1986).

Still, these ambitious methods helped to nudge the community from focusing on model estimation to model selection; for modern methods (see Sections 4.4.3 to 4.4.7) the modeling search is over structure space as well as parameter space. It is not uncommon now for many thousands of candidate structures to be considered in a modeling run—which forces one to be even more conservative when judging whether improvements are significant, since any measure of model quality optimized by a search is likely to be over-optimistic (see *e.g.*, Miller, 1990 in the context of regression subset selection). When considering a plethora of candidates it usually becomes clear that a wide variety of models, with different structures and even inputs, score nearly as well as the single "best." Therefore, following the ancient statistical adage that "in many counselors there is safety"[2] some researchers are now explicitly *blending* the outputs from

---

[2]Proverbs 24:6b

several viable models to obtain estimates with reduced variance and (almost always) better accuracy on new data (*e.g.*, Wolpert, 1992; Breiman, 1994b). Such techniques are especially promising when the models being merged are from completely different families (for example, trees, polynomials, kernels, and splines), and if the local influence of each is a function of its estimated accuracy in that region of design space.

4.2   Distinctives of a Statistical Viewpoint

4.2.1   Interpretability

Researchers from different fields seem to emphasize different qualities in the models they seek. For example, Breiman (1994a) noted that the "neural network community" appears not to be wedded to variations on that approach, but may experiment with a wide variety of techniques under the overriding goal of developing a model minimally misclassifying new data. Statisticians, on the other hand, are usually interested in interpreting their models, and may sacrifice some performance to be able to extract meaning from the model structure. If the accuracy is acceptable they reason that a model which can be decomposed into revealing parts is often more useful than a "black box" system, especially during early stages of the investigation and design cycle.

4.2.2   Characterizing Uncertainty

The randomness in sampled data is inherited by estimated model parameters since these are functions of the data. Statisticians summarize the induced randomness by so-called *sampling distributions* of estimators. By judicious assumptions, exact sampling distributions are analytically tractable; more typically asymptotic arguments are invoked. The net result is often the same, the estimated parameters are approximately normally distributed. This distribution characterizes the uncertainty in the estimated parameters, and owing to normality, the uncertainty is succinctly captured in the standard deviation of the sampling distribution, termed the *standard error* of the estimate. Standard statistical practice requires stating the standard errors of estimated model parameters. Parameters associated with estimates that are small in comparison to their standard errors, ($e.g.$, $t = \hat{\beta}/s.e.(\hat{\beta}) < 2$) are not likely to be part of the "true" underlying process generating the data, and it is often prudent to drop such parameters from the model. A term by term analysis such as this breaks down in the presence of collinear variables and is weakened also by nonlinear models that stretch the applicability of the asymptotic normal sampling theory. Yet, the basic insight is very useful: estimates should be accompanied by uncertainty measures (*e.g.*, error bars) to be useful.

The Bayesian paradigm provides a different though related perspective. Here one treats the parameter itself as a random variable and merges prior beliefs about the parameter together with observed data. The resulting *posterior* distribution, $p(\theta|data)$, can often itself be approximated by a normal distribution, and thereby a single number summary of parameter uncertainty is available. Of course, recent computational advances and ingenious algorithms (*e.g.* Markov chain monte carlo) obviate the need for analytically derived normal approximations. But lacking a picture of the posterior distribution, the second moment is often used to summarize the spread of the induced posterior distribution.

Other disciplines also deal with unavoidable variation. For instance, electrical engineers design circuits to filter noisy signals using components with inexact values themselves (*e.g.*, resistors with 15% tolerances). Similarly, financial analysts know that potential investments need to be evaluated not only on their expected return, but on their risk—usually, the standard deviation of those returns. Investments with higher historical or implied deviations make sense only if they are accompanied by an appropriate "risk premium" (higher expected return). On the other hand, logicians and computer scientists have been slow to appreciate the importance of explicitly handling uncertainty. Arguably, Statistics has had a head start on this problem and seems to have the natural language, the *probability* calculus, to propagate and characterize uncertainty in models. The "certainty factors" in early expert systems and the "fuzzy logic" of later ones, are weak attempts to do what probability has done for centuries.

In some modeling contexts, emphasis is on prediction rather than estimation (of model parameters). This change in emphasis does not reduce the need to characterize and report uncertainty. Properly formulated models provide not only the prediction at each point in the design space, $E(y|x)$), but also the associated variance, $var(y|x)$. Monitoring local variance is useful for more than confidence estimates. For example, Cox and John (1993) and Elder (1993a) employ conditional variances of a response surface to guide global search algorithms very efficiently in low dimensions. Unfortunately, only a few nonlinear inductive modeling techniques (see Section 4.4) explicitly incorporate conditional variance into their estimates—a clear area for potential improvement.

4.2.3   Borrowing Strength

It is often the case in statistical problems that inferences are desired but data is sparse. Consider an example from retail marketing. An SKU (stock keeping unit) is a unique label assigned to a retail product, for example, men's size 12 blue socks. Predictions of SKUs are required at a store level in a large chain of department stores to build up sufficient inventory for promotions and seasonal demand or other "predictable" events. The problem is that detailed historical data on individual SKU sales at each and every store in the chain is not available; for example, it may be that no men's size 12 blue socks sold in the Florida store since last November. The concept of *borrowing strength* allows us to build forecasts at the site-SKU level by exploiting hierarchies in the problem, possibly in more ways than one. By aggregating across stores, sufficient information is available to build a site-independent prediction for each SKU. This prediction can be used to add stability to predictions of SKUs in each of several regions, which can in turn be used to add stability at the site level. Similar types of decompositions could allow us to borrow strength by looking at sales of, say, all blue socks independent of size, then all socks, then men's undergarments, then menswear overall. Such "hierarchical models" have their origins in *empirical Bayes* models, so-called because inferences are not truly Bayesian, as maximum likelihood estimates are used in place of "hyperparameters" (the parameters in prior distributions) at the highest levels of the hierarchy where data is most numerous. This typically results in estimates of the form $\hat{y}_i = \alpha \bar{y}_i + (1 - \alpha)\bar{y}$ where $\bar{y}_i$ is the estimate specific to the ith level of the hierarchy and $\bar{y}$ to that of its parent (where data is more abundant). The mixing parameter, α, captures the similarity of the individual estimate to its parent relative to the tightness of the distribution of the $\bar{y}_i$'s.

4.2.4   Explicit Assumptions

Statisticians are typically very aware of the explicit and implicit assumptions associated with their models. Though some of the appeal of non-traditional models and methods undoubtedly stems from their apparent ability to bypass statistical analysis stages many see as cumbersome, it is clear that matching the assumptions of a method with the characteristics of a problem is beneficial to its solution. Statistical analysts usually take the useful step of checking those assumptions; chiefly, by examining:

1. Residuals (model errors)

2. Diagnostics (model sensitivity to perturbations)

3. Parameter covariances (redundancy)

Not all violations of assumptions are equally bad. For example, assumptions about stochastic behavior of the data are typically less important than the structural behavior; the former might lead to inefficient estimates or inaccurate standard errors, but the later could result in biased estimates. Within these two broad classes, normality and independence assumptions are typically less important than constancy (homogeneity) of variance (e.g., $var(y|x) = constant$ for all x). A single outlier from the structural model can bias the fit everywhere else. Likewise, leverage values are those observations that have undue influence on the fit, for example if deleting the ith observation resulted in a large change in the estimate of a key parameter. An important distinction is that leverage values need not correspond to large residuals—indeed by virtue of their "leverage," they bias the fit toward themselves resulting in small or negligible residuals. Colinearity among the predictor variables confuses the interpretation of the associated parameters, but can also be harmful to prediction; the new data must strictly abide by the interrelationships reflected in the training data or the model will be extrapolating beyond the confines of the training space, rather than interpolating within it.

4.2.5 Regularization

The aim of statistical inference and inductive modeling is to infer general laws from specific cases—to summarize observations about a phenomenon into a coherent model of the "underlying data-generating mechanism" which can be tested for explanatory power on new cases. To perform well on data not seen during "training," models need appropriate structure and complexity; they must be powerful enough to approximate the known data, but constrained enough to generalize successfully.

"Ockham's razor" is often invoked as a guiding principle in model selection, which suggests one select for use, from competing hypotheses with similar explanatory power, the simplest one. In many cases the simpler, less accurate model will generalize better to new data arising from the process that generated the training set.

In statistical terms, the tradeoff is between model "underfit" (bias) and "overfit" (variance), and the imposition of modeling restraint is called "regularization." If data are plentiful, model overfit can be avoided by reserving representative subsets of the data for testing as the model is constructed. When performance on the test set systematically worsens, model growth is curtailed. In the more common scenario in which the design space is less densely populated with data, all the cases can be employed for training, and model complexity (e.g., number of parameters) or roughness (e.g., integrated squared slope of its response surface) is used to constrain the fit. The criterion to be minimized is then a weighted sum of the training error and the measure of model complexity or roughness. Note that nonlinear and adaptively-selected parameters can have more influence on a model than is typical for linear terms, so their inclusion must be accompanied by a correspondingly greater increase in training accuracy to "pay their way."

Two other regularization methods are employed, the first in statistics and the other in nonstatistical communities. The first method, parameter *shrinkage*, uses all the variables but constrains their overall influence to make the models more robust. For example, with collinear variables, there can be infinite solutions to a linear estimation problem. Even with nearly collinear variables, the estimated "optimal" parameters may have huge variances—a clear type of overfit. By shrinking the parameters, e.g., through a singular value decomposition of the ill-conditioned design matrix, a relatively robust weight solution is selected more near the origin (where all parameters are zeroed out). Likewise, ridge regression pushes unstable solutions in the direction of smaller values, effectively reducing the complexity of the model. Shrinkage can also be performed on trees (Hastie and Pregibon, 1990) and neural networks (known as "optimal weight decay"). Most shrinkage procedures have a Bayesian interpretation whereby the user-defined prior guides the direction and degree of regularization.

The second method, which applies to iterative procedures (and is considered a relatively crude approach by many statisticians), is to halt the adjustment procedure some time before convergence. This has been the primary means by which artificial neural network training (weight modification) is halted but has also been reported in other contexts such as taming the EM algorithm in positron emission tomography.

To summarize, it is a hallmark of the statistical approach to *regularize* models; *i.e.,* to employ simplifying constraints alongside accuracy measures during model formulation in order to best generalize to new cases—the true goal of most empirical modeling activities.

4.3   Reservations to Automatic Modeling in Statistics

The experienced statistician, perhaps the most capable of guiding the development of automated tools for data analysis, may also be the most acutely aware of all the difficulties that can arise when dealing with real data. This hesitation has bred skepticism of what automated procedures can offer and has contributed to the strong focus by the statistical community on model *estimation* to the neglect of the logical predecessor to this step, namely model *identification*. Another culprit underlying this benign neglect is the close historical connection between mathematics and statistics whereby statisticians tend to work on problems where theorems and other analytical solutions are attainable (*e.g.* sampling distributions and asymptotics). Such solutions are necessarily conditional on the underlying model being specified up to a small number of identifiable parameters that summarize the relationship of the predictor variables to the response variable through the first few moments of the conditional distribution, $f(y|x)$. For example the common regression model takes the form:

$$\mu(y|x) = \sum_{j=1}^{J} x_j \beta_j \qquad (4.3.4)$$

$$\sigma(y|x) = constant \qquad (4.3.5)$$

The implicit parameter J is not part of the explicit formulation nor is the precise specification of which x_j's define the model for the mean parameter μ. Traditional statistics provides very useful information on the sampling distribution of the estimates $\hat{\beta}_j$ for a fixed set of x_j's but no formalism for saying which x's are needed.

The relatively small effort by the statistical community in model identification has focused on marrying computing horsepower with human judgment (as opposed to fully automated procedures). The general problem is deciding how large or complex a model the available data will support. By directly and explicitly focusing on mean squared prediction error, statisticians have long understood the basic tradeoff between bias (too small a model) and variance (too large a model) in model selection. Algorithms (Furnival and Wilson, 1978) and methods (Mallows, 1973) have been used extensively in identifying candidate models summarized by model accuracy and model size. The primary reason that human judgment is crucial in this process is that algorithmic optimality does not and cannot include qualitative distinctions between competing models of similar size—for example, if the accuracy/availability/cost of the variables differ. So it is largely human expertise that is used to select (or validate) a model, or a few models, from the potentially large pools of candidate models.

The statistician's tendency to avoid complete automation out of respect for the challenges of the data, and the historical emphasis on models with interpretable structure, has led that community to focus on problems with a more manageable number of variables (a dozen, say) and cases (several hundred typically) than may be encountered in KDD problems, which can be orders of magnitude larger at the outset.[3] With increasingly huge and amorphous databases, it is clear that methods for automatically hunting down possible patterns worthy of fuller, interactive attention, are required. The existence of such tools can free one up to, for instance, posit a wider range of candidate data features and basis functions (building blocks) than one would wish to deal with, if one were specifying a model structure "by hand."

This obvious need is gaining sympathy but precious little has resulted. The subsections below highlight some of the areas that further underlie the hesitation of automating model identification by the statistical community.

---

[3]Final models are often of similar complexity; it's the magnitude of the initial candidate set of variables and cases that is usually larger in KDD.

4.3.1   Statistical Significance Versus Practical Significance

A common approach to addressing the complexity and size of *model space* is to limit model growth in the model fitting/learning stage. This is almost always accomplished using a statistical test of significance at each step in the incremental model building stage. Thus for example, one could use a standard χ^2 test of independence between two nominal variables as a means to limit growth of a model that searches for "significant" association. The main problem with this approach is that significance levels depend critically on n, the sample size, such that as n increases, even trivial differences attain statistical significance. Statisticians ameliorate this problem by introducing context to better qualify findings as "significant."

4.3.2   Simpson's Paradox

A related problem with automated search procedures is that they can often be completely fooled by anomalous association patterns, even for small datasets. An accessible and easily understood example (Freedman, Pisani, and Purves, 1978) concerns admission to graduate school at UC Berkeley in 1973. Across major departments, 30% of 1835 female applicants were admitted while 44% of 2691 male applicants were admitted. Do these disparate fractions indicate sex bias? On the face yes, but if the applicants and admissions are broken down by department, then the fractions of the two sexes admitted shows a very different story, where one might even argue that "reverse" sex bias is present! The "paradox" here is that the choice of major is *confounded* with sex—namely that females tend to apply to majors that are harder to get into while males apply to "easy" majors.

The implication of this paradox is that KDD tools which attack large databases looking for "interesting" associations between pairs of variables must also contain methods to search for potential confounders. Computationally, this changes the problem from an n^2 to an n^3 operation (or higher if one considers more confounders). The computational burden can only be avoided by providing knowledge about potential confounders to the discovery algorithm. While this is in principle possible, it is unlikely to be sufficient since common sense knowledge often suggests what confounders might be operating. Statisticians have long brought these common sense insights to the problem rather than delegate them to automata.

4.3.3   Selection Bias

Automated knowledge discovery systems are applied to databases with the expectation of translating *data* into *information*. The bad news is that often the available data is not representative of the population of interest and the worse news is that the data itself contains no hint that there is a potential bias present. Namely, it's more an issue of what is *not* in a data set rather than what information it contains. For example,[4] suppose that the White House Press Secretary is using a KDD (*e.g.* information retrieval) tool to browse through email messages to president@whitehouse.gov for those that concern health care reform. Suppose that she finds a 10:1 ratio of pro-reform to anti-reform messages, leading her to assert that "Americans favor reform by a 10:1 ratio" followed by the worrisome rejoinder "and Government can fix it." But it may well be that people dissatisfied with the health care system are *more likely* to "sound off" about their views than those who are satisfied. Thus even if the true distribution of views on health care reform has mean "score" of zero, self-selected samples that are heavily biased towards one of the tails of this distribution will give a very misleading estimate of the true situation. It is not realistic to expect automated tools to identify such instances. It is probably even less realistic to expect users (*e.g.* lawyers) of such systems to critically question such interesting "facts."

4.3.4   Quantifying Visual Capabilities

Today's data analyst is very dependent on interactive analysis where numerical and graphical summaries are computed or displayed "on the fly." Successful instances of data mining by statisticians are often sprinkled with cries of "aha" whereby some subject matter (context) information, or unexpected behavior in a plot, is discovered in the course of the interaction with the data. This discovery can change the intended course of subsequent analysis steps in quite unpredictable ways. Assuming that it is a very hard problem to include common sense and context information

---

[4]A less modern but more realistic situation occurred in US politics when three major polls overwhelmingly projected Dewey over Truman in the 1948 presidential election—too bad for Dewey (the Republican) that there was a discrepancy between the voting public and those with phone service.

in automated modeling systems, this leaves automated interpretation of plots as a promising area to explore. There are two problems that have served as a barrier to statisticians in this regard:

1. it is hard to quantify a procedure to capture the *unexpected* in plots.

2. even if this could be accomplished, one would need to describe how this maps into the next analysis step in the automated procedure.

What is sorely needed in the statisticians armory is a way to represent meta-knowledge about the problem at hand and about the procedures commonly used. This suggests an opportunity where the KDD and statistical communities can complement their skills and work together to provide an acceptable and powerful solution.

4.4   Statistical Methods

In this section we review some classical and more recent methods that are used in knowledge discovery problems where interest centers on a single response variable, y, and a collection of predictors, $\mathbf{x} = (x_1, x_2, ..., x_J)$. All the models assume the availability of training data, and the goal is to find a model to predict y from $\mathbf{x}$ that performs well on new data. This problem had a well-defined solution (least squares) for many decades until computing advances made it possible to relax classical assumptions. Statisticians have since been on a feeding frenzy devising new estimation methods (*e.g.*, M-estimates) and models (*e.g.*, additive models) to exploit the less restricted formulation.

Others have been caught up in the race to develop increasingly flexible models, perhaps encouraged by the famous result of Kolmogorov (1957) that *all* multi-dimensional functions can be represented by a composition of one-dimensional functions. But statisticians are not comforted by this result as any such class of models has far too much flexibility to be useful in practice where finite and noisy data prevail. We need models that scale up to real data, which due to its size and complexity (*e.g.*, missing values) beguiles all but the simplest of analyses.

Following discussion of classical linear methods and nonparametric techniques, we briefly describe five modeling algorithms selected to span "statistical method space": projection pursuit, neural networks, polynomial networks, decision trees, and adaptive splines.[5] While each can be treated as a "black box" (with a few "knobs" to set) that performs variable selection and feature extraction from a set of candidate inputs, we do not recommend such reckless abandon. Rather, careful modeling and familiarity with the subject matter domain can lead to greatly improved performance.

Several recent references are recommended for further information on this subject. Friedman (1995) provides an excellent overview of the major issues involved in building models from data, applicable to all induction techniques. Weiss and Kulikowski (1991) describe, in a very accessible manner, the basics of major inductive or "machine learning" classification techniques, including linear discriminant analysis, decision trees, neural networks, and expert systems. Useful (and more advanced) recent surveys focusing on neural networks and their statistical properties include those by Ripley (1993) and Cheng and Titterington (1994). Barron and Barron (1988) provide a unifying view of many methods as "statistical learning networks." A comparison of approximately twenty public-domain classification algorithms is summarized on a number of diverse applications in the European StatLog project (Michie, Spiegelhalter, and Taylor, 1994). Lastly, modern developments in statistical density estimation and data visualization are effectively presented by Scott (1992).

4.4.1   Linear Models

The classical models for prediction and classification are linear regression and linear discriminant analysis, respectively. The term "linear" in these models pertains primarily to the fact that the regression or classification surface is a plane—a linear combination of the available predictors (equations 4.3.4-5) (which may be nonlinear functions of the original data). The flexibility and straightforward computation involved in linear regression leads to its wide use within other techniques. For example, *radial basis function* networks are merely the linear regression of a set of *kernel* features—nonlinear functions of the separation of each

---

[5] Clearly, tree methods dominate work in the KDD, machine learning, and expert system communities—and not without reason. Trees can be mapped into rules, can more easily handle categorical data and missing values, and are usually far more interpretable. However, the "smooth" methods deserve consideration where applicable, as their basis functions can often be more appropriate for the data, and thus lead to improved performance.

case from several (potentially adaptively-selected) data centroids (next Section). Lowe and Webb (1991) employ a neural network architecture (Section 4.4.4) to compute nonlinear data features which feed into a final linear regression stage, and polynomial networks (Section 4.4.5) use linear regression in every node to combine previous (nonlinear) polynomial data transformations. Even linear discriminant analysis, with appropriate pre- and post- processing, can be formulated as a problem with a linear regression stage (Hastie, Tibshirani, and Buja, 1994). This allows one to replace the linear regression module with an advanced nonlinear/nonparametric estimation method, greatly increasing the types of patterns that can be handled by such classification techniques.

The models are also linear in a second important respect; namely, that the estimated parameters in the model are linear in the response variable, y. For example, in the usual linear regression model,

$$\hat{\beta}_j = \sum_{i=1}^{n} c_{ij} y_i. \tag{4.4.6}$$

This type of linearity enables an exact sampling theory for estimated model parameters (Section 4.2.2), unless the x's were selected during the course of the analysis (in which case a hard to untangle nonlinearity is involved).

4.4.2   Nonparametric Methods

Linear models are parametric methods; they replace sample data with a model representing a global "consensus" of the pattern the data represents (to the degree to which the patterns can be captured by the particular building blocks used; typically, lines or quadratic curves). Nonparametric, "model-free," or "code book" methods instead keep the data around and refer to it when estimating the response or the class of a new point. The simplest such method is *nearest neighbors*, which returns the response of the closest known point (as measured in the input-variable, or design, space according to some distance metric, *e.g.*, Euclidean). The resulting estimation surface or discrimination boundaries are thus extremely responsive to local variations. To smooth these somewhat, the data set can be pared of unusual points, or the responses of the nearest K neighbors can be averaged. This simple method is often quite competitive in performance and asymptotically, as the data density increases, results in no worse than twice the Bayes optimal error (Cover and Hart, 1967).

Kernel estimation (*e.g.*, Parzen, 1962) provides a smoothed, generalized weighting of near-neighbors. A density function (*e.g.*, uniform, triangular, or normal) is centered over each point to be predicted.[6] The prediction is the kernel-weighted average of all the data. A single parameter representing the spread of the kernel can be adjusted to govern the roughness (local responsivity) of the prediction.

While such methods appear to be model-free, a type of model is implicit in the choice of distance function. Even if one considers Mahalanobis distance between two points i and j,

$$d_{ij} = (\mathbf{x_i} - \mathbf{x_j})^{\mathbf{T}} \Sigma^{-1} (\mathbf{x_i} - \mathbf{x_j}) \qquad (4.4.7)$$

there is considerable latitude in deciding which x's should enter into the distance calculation, and in what form (*e.g.*, x or $\log x$). Scaling issues, as reflected in Σ, can make or break the resulting prediction. As with all modeling methods, such issues need to be carefully considered and experimented with on the training data.

More so than parametric methods, nonparametric techniques are essentially constrained to operate in low dimensions; they depend heavily on *local* structure, and high-dimensional data is so sparse that "local neighborhoods are empty and non-empty neighborhoods are not local" (Scott, 1992). For example, for data uniformly distributed throughout a 10-dimensional unit cube, $U^{10}[0,1]$, only 0.1% of the data is in a histogram bin of width 0.5—not a very local neighborhood! Also, as dimension grows, nearly every point both views itself as an outlier with respect to the rest of the training data, and becomes closer to an outer boundary of the space than to its next nearest neighbor (Friedman, 1995). Thus, methodological intuition gained from experience in low dimensions is thoroughly out of place in high-D spaces—a phenomenon known as the "curse of dimensionality."

Still, when intelligently selecting variables to reduce the dimensionality to where samples can reasonably densely populate predictor space, these simple methods can work very well, often outperforming parametric methods. Accordingly, even when automated induction methods

---

[6]A rectangular kernel leads to a type of histogram with flexible bin edges.

(described below) are employed, it is useful to examine the performance of simple- or kernel-weighted nearest neighbors on the subset of variables selected for use by the adaptive algorithms.

4.4.3   Projection Pursuit

In low dimensions, the human ability to recognize patterns is unlikely to be matched by automata. Straightforward visual examination of data using histograms, scatterplots, and rotating 3-D plots, can often reveal structure which is missed by automated induction algorithms (Elder 1993b). Under the "grand tour" strategy (Asimov 1985) the data is rotated smoothly through all (or most) 2-D views, allowing one to discover interesting perspectives. However, the number of different views explodes exponentially with dimension, limiting such visual coverage methods to problems with a moderate number of candidate predictor variables. Accordingly, statisticians have sought to quantify measures of "interestingness" which can be optimized by the computer to identify revealing views in high-D.

In a procedure known as Exploratory Projection Pursuit (Friedman and Tukey, 1974), one searches for 1-D projections that maximally deviate from normality, robustly smoothes the data along that projection, and subtracts the smooth from the response. This process is repeated, projection by projection, until the error reduction cannot justify the added complexity. The anti-normal projection index is a reasonable one to employ since, regardless of the true density, most random projections of high-D data are normal (Diaconis and Freedman, 1984). Other exploratory projection indices are designed to seek holes or clusters. Projection Pursuit Regression (Friedman and Stuetzle, 1981) utilizes a maximal correlation index while maximal class separation is used for building a classifier.

However, it is very difficult to capture "interestingness" in a single criterion; structure which would be obvious to an analyst can be missed (see, *e.g.*, Elder 1994). Even if a particular quality could be well-quantified in an index, an analyst employing visualization has the advantage of "multiple end-points"; that is, of recognizing any of a wide variety of patterns encountered without explicitly choosing them as a goal beforehand. This weakness is shared by all automated modeling techniques to varying degrees, so to maximize performance, the automated search for structure in high-D space must be complemented by visualization of the lower-D manifolds discovered. (In practice therefore, techniques producing models with interpretable components have the additional advantage of speeding up the "design cycle" or entire iterative process of model development.)

4.4.4   Neural Networks

Artificial neural networks (ANNs) are a useful class of models consisting of layers of nodes, each implementing a linearly-weighted sum of its inputs with an adjustable sigmoidal (S-shaped) output transformation as the bounded squashing function. The outputs of every node on a layer feed into each node on subsequent layers as their inputs. With the backpropagation weight adjustment procedure (e.g., Werbos, 1974), cases are fed through one at a time, and errors are used to adjust the weights of the final output node to a degree proportional to their contribution (magnitude). Then, weights for nodes which feed into it are similarly adjusted, and so forth, back to the first layer. Initial weights are typically set randomly.

Statisticians have been suspicious of ANNs due to their overzealous promotion, but also because they appear so over-parameterized, and the weight adjustment procedure is a local gradient method (missing global optima), sequential (allowing early cases to have too much influence), and interminable (leading to a crude type of regularization wherein moderating the runtime becomes the principle way to avoid overfit). However, these weaknesses cancel somewhat, as the slow, local search doesn't allow the excess of parameters to be overfit easily. Note also that the true degrees of freedom employed by an ANN are usually fewer than at first glance. The danger of overfit can depend on the training duration, since many random node weights lead to essentially linear functions (nodes operating in either the middle or an extreme of the sigmoid) and such linear functions are absorbed by subsequent layers. Only as nodes get pushed into the curved part of the sigmoids during training do many parameters become active. (This may explain the common observation that the performance of an ANN on a problem is often surprisingly robust with respect to changes in its network structure.)

4.4.5   Polynomial Networks

Regression terms are often adaptively selected from a candidate pool in a forward stepwise (greedy) manner: choose the single best term, add the term which best combines with it, add the third term which works best with the pair, and so forth (occasionally deleting a term which is not useful enough) until the accuracy improvement is too small to justify the increment in complexity. The first polynomial network algorithm, the Group Method of Data Handling (GMDH) (Ivakhnenko, 1968; see also Farlow, 1984), expanded this idea by considering "chunks" of terms simultaneously. The GMDH uses linear regression to fit quadratic polynomial nodes to an output variable using all input variable pairs in turn. The best M nodes are retained as the first layer, and their outputs are the candidate inputs for the next layer, and so on, until complexity impairs performance on a checking set of data (whence the name). The best node on the final layer, and all nodes feeding into it, become the model, thereby forming a hierarchical composition of functions (a feed-forward network).

Considerable improvements to the GMDH approach were introduced in the 1970s and 1980's with versions of the Polynomial Network Training (PNETTR) algorithm (Barron *et al.*, 1984) and the Algorithm for Synthesis of Polynomial Networks (ASPN, Elder 1985). Some details of the history and methodology of these algorithms are presented in (Elder and Brown, 1995). Like ANNs, polynomial network estimation surfaces are smooth and global, but with nonlinearities entering through higher-order polynomial terms and cross-products, rather than sigmoids. The structure is adaptive rather than fixed, and the parameters are adjusted in sets, using all the data, rather than globally using one case at a time. Polynomial networks can take orders of magnitude less time to train than back-propagation ANNs (*e.g.,* Shewhart, 1992) and typically achieve better results (*e.g.,* Tenorio and Lee, 1989). However, also like ANNs, polynomial networks are rather opaque; they are difficult to dissect, unlike trees, which can be interpreted straightforwardly.

4.4.6   Decision Trees

The neural and polynomial network methods are global estimators, and hence will poorly estimate a function everywhere if it is sufficiently badly behaved anywhere (*e.g.,* deBoor, 1978). Decision trees, which recursively divide the space into different regions, instead have sharp breaks in their estimation surfaces, allowing great local responsivity. Also, the variables selected for splits may be different in each adaptively-partitioned region of the space. The flexibility of the method seems often, in practice, to make up for the crude basis function (a constant). Note that in a classification problem in which a variable (fortuitously) has a different constant value for each class, a decision tree could capture the rule perfectly, whereas classical linear discriminant analysis would actually encounter numerical instabilities, due to the negligible within-class pooled variance of the variable.

Decision trees were legitimized in the statistical community by the pioneering work on Classification and Regression Trees (CART) of Breiman *et al.* (1984). These authors neatly describe the problem and provide theory and methods to grow a tree and validate it. They depart from most previous work in that they propose expanding nodes until they reach a prescribed minimal size or are themselves pure. A cost-complexity parameter is introduced that characterizes a nested sequence of subtrees and cross-validation is used to decide how far back to prune the overly large initial tree. As with other statistical models, the usual precautions and careful pre- and post-fitting analysis are required. An advantage held by trees in this regard is that the tree metaphor can be exploited for graphical analysis.

Trees are natural for classification, but are also useful in difficult estimation problems where their simple piecewise-constant response surface and lack of smoothness constraints make them highly robust to outliers in either the predictors or the response variable. They automatically select variables, and construct models quite rapidly for an adaptive method. Importantly, trees are also probably the easiest model form to interpret (so long as they are shallow) which, in our experience, greatly improves the model's chances of actually being used. The main problem with trees is that they devour data at a rate exponential with depth; so, to uncover complex structure, extensive data is required.

4.4.7   Adaptive Splines

The extreme local responsiveness of trees can sometimes be a disadvantage. Friedman's (1991) Multiple Adaptive Regression Splines (MARS) model employs recursive partitioning to locate product spline basis functions of adjustable degree, rather than constants. This results in smooth adaptive function approximation as opposed to the crude steps or plateaus provided by regression trees. The method also considers splines involving interactions between previously selected variables, so it can orient its basis functions on other than the original data axes. To aid interpretation, model terms are collected according to their inputs and their influence is reported in an ANOVA manner, namely, the effects of individual variables and pairs of variables are collected together and graphically presented as function plots. Like CART, MARS employs cross-validation, prunes terms after over-growing, and can handle categorical variables. As a new (and somewhat complex) method, there is less accumulated experience with its use, though it has been favorably compared with ANNs (e.g., DeVeaux et al., 1993) One would expect that enforcing continuity of the response surface (and perhaps that of its slope) will be very useful for applications which have a design space densely enough populated to support (and require) the local responsivity of the spline-like basis functions.

4.5   Statistical Computing

Arguably, no matter how brilliant the model or method to describe and summarize data, software is essential if a methodology is actually to be used. KDD and machine learning communities implicitly provide software as their methods are largely described algorithmically. Statisticians on the other hand, are perfectly capable of generating scores of models and methods with well defined operating characteristics (at least asymptotically) without ever writing a line of code. But these days are largely over and it is rare that statistical methods are described or promoted without application to data.

Early general purpose statistical packages included BMDP and SPSS, from the biomedical and social sciences, respectively. Of the two most important newer systems—SAS and S, SAS is most similar in style, containing many special "procedures" for standard statistical models. S was designed as a *language* to express statistical computations, rather than as a complete package. For example, two sample t-tests were built-in to SAS, while S simply provided a high-level language to express the relevant computations (which could be assigned to a function for repeated usage). Both SAS and S are widely used for exploratory data analysis, modeling, and graphics. Each provides some degree of data management to remove that burden from users and can be extended to tailor methods for specific applications. Emerging useful packages include Lisp-Stat (Tierney, 1990), an S-inspired, object-oriented (Common Lisp) system that is being used in research circles, as well as a host of PC-based systems that demonstrate remarkable breadth and accessible interfaces.

It is still the case that specialized methods (such as discussed in the previous Section) appear first in isolation, rather than as part of a bigger system. (A useful repository for many such statistical research algorithms is the "StatLib" archive.[7]) For example, CART fits trees and trees alone.[8] Features of these stand-alone programs usually eventually make their way into more general systems, losing some efficiencies, but gaining the capabilities of an *integrated* data analysis environment essential to analysis quality and analyst productivity. Thus the CART-inspired implementation of tree-based models in the S language (Clark and Pregibon, 1990) not only allows users to manipulate their data in a variety of ways prior to fitting, but also provides an interactive graphical interface to the model and the opportunity to painlessly explore alternatives (*e.g.,* additive models).

The story is somewhat similar on the graphical front. Most stand-alone statistical graphics systems provide real-time dynamic motion that many find essential for exploring complex high-dimensional data sets. General purpose systems adequately handle most plots but lack the degree of specialization allowing friendly user interfaces or state-of-the-art graphics. (Lisp-Stat is an exception in that certain advanced features such as case-linking multiple plots are provided.) The XGobi system (Swayne, Cook, and Buja, 1992) provides a comprehensive projection and real-time motion tool set that includes "grand tours" and other "guided tours"; the graphics system can be used stand-alone or within a cooperative statistics system (*e.g.,* S).

Finally, we want to emphasize that computing is more to statistics than a vehicle for data analysis. It has revolutionized the field through the computational methodologies that statisticians now take for granted (*e.g.,* resampling methods, cross-validation, and Markov chain monte

---

[7]Send the one line message "send index" to "statlib@lib.stat.cmu.edu" for contents and retrieval instructions.

[8]Though it's recently been offered as an optional module for a popular PC package.

carlo). We expect the influence of computer science on statistics to increase in the future.

4.6 Conclusions

The tendency of the statistical community to propagate uncertainty in their models through sampling distributions, their familiarity with the need to regularize models (trade off accuracy and complexity), and their dogged perseverance in checking model assumptions and stability (through residual and graphical analyses) are strengths. Still, alternative heuristic modeling techniques have gained in popularity partly as a way to "avoid statistics" yet still address challenging induction tasks. Statisticians should learn from this the need to do a better job of communicating the value of such considerations, as well as clarifying and streamlining ways of injecting extra-data information into the modeling process.

A great deal of work goes into identifying, gathering, cleaning, and labeling the data, into specifying the question(s) to be asked of it, and into finding the right way to view it (literally and figuratively) to discover useful patterns. Despite the central importance of actually modeling the data (the focus of this chapter) that stage can take up only a small proportion of the project effort. It is hard to conceive that the entire process will ever be automated. Increased automation has not absolved researchers of the need to think in statistical terms, including matching model assumptions to the problem, seeking interpretability, quantifying variance, regulating complexity to improve generalization, and keeping a lookout for the unexpected. However, modern statistical modeling tools do make it possible for an analyst to think about the problem at a higher level (by handling some routine or massive tasks), to try numerous approaches, to estimate the uncertainty of conclusions arising out of even complex processes, and to iterate through several stages of a solution design before settling on a representation scheme (or even a blend of them). When one is comparing KDD techniques, or attempting to extract the most out of a database, it makes sense to try some of these accessible modern statistical algorithms.

References

Akaike, H. 1973. Information Theory and an Extension of the Maximum Likelihood Principle. In Proceedings of the Second International Symposium on Information Theory, eds. Petrov and Csaki, 267–281, Budapest: Kiado Academy.

Asimov, D. 1985. The Grand Tour: A Tool for Viewing Multidimensional Data. *SIAM Journal on Scientific and Statistical Computing* 6: 128–143.

Barron, A. R.; and Barron, R. L. 1988. Statistical Learning Networks: A Unifying View. In Proceedings of the Twentieth Symposium on the Interface: Computing Science and Statistics, Reston, Virginia.

Barron, R. L.; Mucciardi, A. N.; Cook, F. J.; Craig, J. N.; and Barron, A. R. 1984. Adaptive Learning Networks: Development and Application in the United States of Algorithms Related to GMDH. In *Self-Organizing Methods in Modeling: GMDH Type Algorithms,* ed. S. J. Farlow, 25–65. New York: Marcel Dekker.

Belsley, D. A.; Kuh, E.; and Welsch, R. E. 1980. *Regression Diagnostics: Identifying Influential Data and Sources of Collinearity.* New York: John Wiley & Sons.

Bishop, Y. M. M.; Fienberg, S. E.; and Holland, P. W. 1975. *Discrete Multivariate Analysis: Theory and Practice.* Cambridge, Mass.: MIT Press.

Breiman, L. 1994a. Comment on "Neural Networks" by Cheng and Titterington, *Statistical Science* 9(1): 38–42.

Breiman, L. 1994b. Stacked Regressions, Technical Report 367, Dept. Statistics, University of California, Berkeley.

Breiman, L.; Friedman, J. H.; Olshen, R. A.; and Stone, C. J. 1984. *Classification and Regression Trees.* Monterey, Calif.: Wadsworth & Brooks.

Cheng, B.; and Titterington, D. M. 1994. Neural Networks: A Review from a Statistical Perspective (With Discussion). *Statistical Science* 9(1): 2–54.

Clark, L. A.; and Pregibon, D. 1992. Tree-based Models. In *Statistical Models in S*, ed. J. M. Chambers and T. Hastie. Pacific Grove, Calif.: Wadsworth & Brooks/Cole Advanced Books and Software.

Cleveland, W. S. 1979. Robust Locally Weighted Regression and Smoothing Scatterplots. *Journal of the American Statistical. Association* 74: 829–836.

Cover, T. M.; and Hart, P. E. 1967. Nearest Neighbor Pattern Classification. *IEEE Transactions on Information Theory* 13: 21–27.

Cox, D. D., and John, S. 1993. A Statistical Method for Global Optimization. In Proceedings of the IEEE Systems, Man, and Cybernetics Society, Chicago, Oct.

deBoor, C. 1978. *A Practical Guide to Splines.* New York: Springer-Verlag.

Dempster, A. P.; Laird, N. M.; and Rubin, D. B. 1977. Maximum Likelihood from Incomplete Data Via the EM Algorithm (With Discussion). *Journal of the Royal Statistical Society B* 39: 1–38.

DeVeaux, R. D.; Psichogios, D. C.; and Ungar, L. H. 1993. A Comparison of Two Nonparametric Estimation Schemes: MARS and Neural Networks. *Computers in Chemical Engineering* 17(8): 819–837.

Diaconis, P.; and Freedman, D. 1984. Asymptotics of Graphical Projection Pursuit. *Annals of Statistics* 12: 793–815.

Efron, B.; and Gong, G. 1983. A Leisurely Look at the Bootstrap, the Jackknife, and Cross-Validation. *American Statistician* 37: 36–48.

Efron, B. 1979. Bootstrap Methods: Another Look at the Jackknife. *Annals of Statistics* 7: 1–26.

Elder, J. F. IV 1994. Comment on "Prosection Views" by Furnas and Buja. *Journal of Computational and Graphical Statistics* 3(4): 355–362.

Elder, J. F. IV 1993a. Global R^d Optimization when Probes are Expensive: the GROPE Algorithm. Ph.D. diss., Dept. of Systems Engineering, University of Virginia, May.

Elder, J. F. IV 1993b. Assisting Inductive Modeling Through Visualization. In Proceedings of the Joint Statistical Meeting, San Francisco, California, Aug. 7-11.

Elder, J. F. IV 1985. User's Manual: ASPN: Algorithm for Synthesis of Polynomial Networks, Barron Associates, Inc., Stanardsville, Virginia.

Elder, J. F. IV; and Brown, D. E. 1995. Induction and Polynomial Networks. In *Advances in Control Networks and Large Scale Parallel Distributed Processing Models (Vol. 2),* ed. M. D. Fraser. Norwood, N.J.: Ablex.

Faraway, J. J. 1991. On the Cost of Data Analysis, Technical Report 199, Dept. Statistics, Univ. Michigan, Ann Arbor.

Farlow, S. J., ed. 1984. *Self-Organizing Methods in Modeling: GMDH Type Algorithms.* New York: Marcel Dekker.

Freedman, D.; Pisani, R.; and Purves, R. 1978. *Statistics.* New York: W. W. Norton & Co.

Friedman, J. H. 1995. An Overview of Predictive Learning and Function Approximation. In *From Statistics to Neural Networks: Theory and Pattern Recognition Applications,* ed. V. Cherkassky, J. H. Friedman, and H. Wechsler. Berlin: Springer.

Friedman, J. H. 1991. Multiple Adaptive Regression Splines (With Discussion). *Annals of Statistics* 19: 1–141.

Friedman, J. H.; and Stuetzle, W. 1981. Projection Pursuit Regression. *Journal of the American Statistical Association* 76(376) 817–823.

Friedman, J. H.; and Tukey, J. W. 1974. A Projection Pursuit Algorithm for Exploratory Data Analysis. *IEEE Transactions on Computers* 23: 881–889.

Furnival, G. M.; and Wilson, R. W. 1974. Regression by Leaps and Bounds. *Technometrics* 16: 499–511.

Hampel, F. R. 1974. The Influence Curve and Its Role in Robust Estimation. *Journal of the American Statistical Association* 62: 1179–1186.

Hastie, T. and Pregibon, D. 1990. Shrinking Trees, Technical Report, AT&T Bell Laboratories.

Hastie, T.; and Tibshirani, R. 1990. *Generalized Additive Models*. London: Chapman & Hall.

Hastie, T.; Tibshirani, R.; and Buja, A. 1994. Flexible Discriminant Analysis by Optimal Scoring. *Journal of the American Statistical Association* 89(428): 1255–1270.

Huber, P. J. 1964. Robust Estimation of a Location Parameter. *Annals of Mathematical Statistics* 35: 73–101.

Ivakhnenko, A. G. 1968. The Group Method of Data Handling—A Rival of the Method of Stochastic Approximation. *Soviet Automatic Control* 3: 43–71.

Kolmogorov, A. N. 1957. On the Representation of Continuous Functions of Several Variables by Superpositions of Continuous Functions of One Variable and Addition. *Dokladi* 114: 679–681.

Lowe, D.; and Webb, A. R. 1991. Optimized Feature Extraction and the Bayes Decision in Feed-Forward Classifier Networks. *IEEE Transactions on Pattern Analysis and Machine Intelligence* 13: 355–364.

Mallows, C. L. 1973. Some Comments on Cp. *Technometrics* 15: 661–675.

McCullagh, P.; and Nelder, J. A. 1989. *Generalized Linear Models (Second Ed.)* London: Chapman & Hall.

Michie, D.; Spiegelhalter, D. J.; and Taylor, C. C. 1994. *Machine Learning, Neural and Statistical Classification*. New York: Ellis Horwood.

Miller, A. J. 1990. *Subset Selection in Regression*. New York: Chapman & Hall.

Mosteller, F.; and Tukey, J. W. 1977. *Data Analysis and Regression*. Reading Mass.: Addison-Wesley.

Nelder, J. A.; and Wedderburn, R. W. M. 1972. Generalized Linear Models. *Journal of the Royal Statistical Society A* 135: 370–384.

O'Sullivan, F.; Yandell, B. S.; and Raynor, W. J. Jr. 1986. Automatic Smoothing of Regression Functions in Generalized Linear Models. *Journal of the American Statistical Association* 81: 96–103.

Parzen, E. 1962. On Estimation of a Probability Density Function and Mode. *Annals of Mathematical Statistics* 33: 1065–1076.

Ripley, B. 1993. Statistical Aspects of Neural Networks. In *Chaos and Networks—Statistical and Probabilistic Aspects,* ed. O. Barndorff-Nielsen, D. Cox, J. Jensen, and W. Kendall, London: Chapman & Hall.

Rissanen, J. 1978. Modeling by Shortest Data Description. *Automatica* 14: 465–471.

Schreuder, H. T. 1986. Quenouille's Estimator. *Encyclopedia of Statistical Science* 7: 473–476. New York: John Wiley & Sons.

Scott, D. W. 1992. *Multivariate Density Estimation: Theory, Practice, and Visualization.* New York: Wiley.

Shewhart, M. 1992. A Neural-Network-Based Tool. *IEEE Spectrum* February: 6.

Swayne, D. F.; Cook, D.; and Buja, A. 1992. XGobi: Interactive Dynamic Graphics in the X Window System with a Link to S. In Proceedings of the 1991 American Statistical Association Meetings.

Tenorio, M. F.; and Lee, W. T. 1989. Self-Organizing Neural Networks for the Identification Problem. In *Advances in Neural Information Processing Systems,* ed. D. S. Touretzky, 57–64. San Mateo, Calif.: Morgan Kauffman.

Tierney, L. 1990. *LISP-STAT* New York: John Wiley & Sons.

Tukey, J. W. 1977. *Exploratory Data Analysis.* Reading, Mass.: Addison-Wesley.

Weiss, S. M.; and Kulikowski, C. A. 1991. *Computer Systems that Learn: Classification and Prediction Methods from Statistics, Neural Networks, Machine Learning, and Expert Systems.* San Mateo, Calif.: Morgan Kaufmann.

Werbos, P. 1974. Beyond Regression: New Tools for Prediction and Analysis in the Behavioral Sciences. Ph.D. diss., Harvard, August.

Wolpert, D. 1992. Stacked Generalization. *Neural Networks* 5: 241–259.

II CLASSIFICATION AND CLUSTERING

5 Inductive Logic Programming and Knowledge Discovery in Databases

Sašo Džeroski
Jožef Stefan Institute

Abstract

Inductive logic programming (ILP) can be viewed as machine learning in a first-order language, where relations are present in the context of deductive databases. It is relevant for knowledge discovery in relational and deductive databases, as it can describe patterns involving more than one relation. The chapter introduces ILP and gives a survey of basic ILP techniques, as well as other ILP topics relevant to KDD. KDD applications of ILP are discussed, two of which are described in some detail: biological classification of river water quality and predicting protein secondary structure.

5.1 KDD and Machine Learning

Knowledge discovery in databases (KDD) is concerned with identifying interesting patterns and describing them in a concise and meaningful manner (Frawley et al. 1991). Frawley et al. (1991) also recognize that machine learning can be applied to KDD problems. If we interpret patterns as classes or concepts, clustering (unsupervised learning) can be used to identify patterns and concept learning (supervised) to describe them.

Attribute-value learning systems, such as C4.5 (Quinlan 1993), AS-SISTANT (Cestnik et al. 1987), and CN2 (Clark and Boswell 1991), can and have been applied to KDD problems. However, these approaches have serious limits. The patterns discovered by the above learning systems are expressed in attribute-value languages which have the expressive power of propositional logic. These languages are limited and do not allow for representing complex structured objects and relations among objects or their components. The domain (background) knowledge that can be used in the learning process is also of a very restricted form and other relations from the database cannot be used in the learning process.

Recent developments in inductive learning focus on the problem of constructing a logical (intensional) definition of a relation (Quinlan 1990) from example tuples known to belong or not to belong to it, where other relations (background knowledge) may be used in the induced definition.

Table 5.1
A Relational Database with Two Relations (tables): Potential-Customer and
Married-To.

Potential-Customer

Person	Age	Sex	Income	Customer
Ann Smith	32	F	10 000	yes
Joan Gray	53	F	1 000 000	yes
Mary Blythe	27	F	20 000	no
Jane Brown	55	F	20 000	yes
Bob Smith	30	M	100 000	yes
Jack Brown	50	M	200 000	yes

Married-To

Husband	Wife
Bob Smith	Ann Smith
Jack Brown	Jane Brown

In this way, new relations can be specified by a small number of example
tuples, which are then generalized to induce a logical definition. Alternatively, existing relations can be compressed into their corresponding
logical definitions.

As the intensional definitions induced can be recursive (Quinlan 1990),
we may say that they are expressed in the formalism of *deductive databases* (Ullman 1988). The logic programming school in deductive databases (Lloyd 1987) argues that deductive databases can be effectively
represented and implemented using logic and logic programming. Within
this framework, the induction of logical definitions of relations can be
considered logic program synthesis and has been recently named *Inductive Logic Programming (ILP)* (Muggleton 1992a; De Raedt 1992;
Lavrač and Džeroski 1994).

Early ILP systems, e.g., MIS (Shapiro 1983) and CIGOL (Muggleton
and Buntine 1988), did not address the problem of handling noisy data.
On the other hand, recent ILP systems, such as FOIL (Quinlan 1990)
and LINUS (Lavrač et al. 1991), are capable of noise-handling, as well
as handling continuous-valued attributes. In this way, they come closer
towards applicability for KDD problems.

Before proceeding further, let us illustrate the use of attribute-value learning and ILP for KDD. Consider the relational database shown in Table 5.1, containing information about the potential customers of an imaginary enterprise. Suppose we are interested in distinguishing between persons who are potential customers and those who are not (field Customer in the table Potential-Customer).

We could use an attribute-value learning system on the table Potential-Customer, where the field Customer would be the class and the fields Age, Sex and Income the attributes. In this way, the following two patterns could be discovered:

IF Income(Person) $\geq$ 100 000 THEN Potential-Customer(Person)

IF Sex(Person) = F AND Age(Person) $\geq$ 32 THEN Potential-Customer(Person).

If we use an ILP system to define the relation Potential-Customer in terms of itself and the relation Married-To, we can find the following patterns:

IF Married(Person,Spouse) AND Income(Person) $\geq$ 100 000

THEN Potential-Customer(Spouse)

IF Married(Person,Spouse) AND Potential-Customer(Person)

THEN Potential-Customer(Spouse).

The latter is written as $potential\_customer(Spouse, SAge, SSex, SIncome) \leftarrow married(Person, Spouse), potential\_customer(Person, Age, Sex, Income)$ in logic programming notation.

The above example illustrates that attribute-value learning systems can be used to discover patterns in an isolated file of database records, i.e., a single relation in a relational database, where records (tuples) can be viewed as training instances. ILP, on the other hand, can be used to discover patterns involving several relations in a database. If we want to learn concepts that involve several relations in a database using propositional approaches, we have to resort to creating a single universal relation. In the above example, the universal relation would include the fields Spouse-Age, Spouse-Sex, Spouse-Income, and Spouse-Customer, in addition to the fields of the relation Potential-Customer. This may be inconvenient and impractical (the universal relation can be very large) and suggests the use of ILP approaches for KDD.

The chapter first introduces the problem of inductive logic program-

Table 5.2
A Simple ILP problem: learning the *daughter* relationship.

Training examples	Background knowledge			
⊕ daughter(sue,eve).	mother(eve,sue).	parent(X,Y) ←	female(ann).	male(pat).
⊕ daughter(ann,pat).	mother(ann,tom).	mother(X,Y).	female(sue).	male(tom).
⊖ daughter(tom,ann).	father(pat,ann).	parent(X,Y) ←	female(eve).	
⊖ daughter(eve,ann).	father(tom,sue).	father(X,Y).		

ming by giving some terminology, a definition of the problem and a simple example. It then gives a survey of basic ILP techniques, including relative least general generalization, inverse resolution, searching refinement graphs, using rule models, and transforming ILP problems to propositional form. Recent advances in ILP relevant to KDD are outlined next. Finally, KDD applications of ILP are discussed: applications of ILP to biological classification of river water quality (Džeroski et al. 1994), and prediction of the secondary structure of a protein from its amino-acid sequence (Muggleton et al. 1992).

5.2   Inductive Logic Programming

This section first gives a simple example that will be used later to illustrate how ILP techniques work. It proceeds to introduce the necessary database and logic programming terminology. It then discusses several dimensions of ILP and finally defines the problem of empirical inductive logic programming.

5.2.1   An Example ILP Problem

Let us illustrate the ILP task on a simple problem of learning family relations. The task is to define the relation $daughter(X, Y)$, which states that person X is a daughter of person Y, in terms of the background knowledge relations $female$ and $parent$. These relations are given in Table 5.2. There are two positive and two negative examples of the *target* relation *daughter*.

In the hypothesis language of logic programs, it is possible to formulate the following definition of the target relation:

$$daughter(X, Y) \leftarrow female(X), parent(Y, X).$$

This definition is a view that defines the target relation intensionally in terms of the background knowledge relations.

Table 5.3
Database and logic programming terms.

DB terminology	LP terminology
relation name p	predicate symbol p
attribute of relation p	argument of predicate p
tuple $\langle a_1, \ldots, a_n \rangle$	ground fact $p(a_1, \ldots, a_n)$
relation p -	predicate p -
a set of tuples	defined extensionally by a set of ground facts
relation q	predicate q
defined as a view	defined intensionally by a set of rules (clauses)

5.2.2 Deductive Databases and Logic Programming

Before discussing ILP further, let us first introduce some basic terminology from the areas of logic programming and deductive databases. An n-ary *relation p* is a set of tuples, i.e., a subset of the Cartesian product of n domains $D_1 \times D_2 \times \ldots \times D_n$, where a *domain* (or a *type*) is a set of values. We assume that a relation is finite unless stated otherwise. A set of relations forms a *relational database* (RDB) (Ullman 1988).

A deductive database (DDB) consists of a set of *database clauses*. A database clause is a *typed program clause* of the form:

$$p(X_1, \ldots, X_n) \leftarrow L_1, \ldots, L_m.$$

where the body of a clause is a conjunction of positive literals $q_i(Y_1, \ldots, Y_{n_i})$ and/or negative literals *not* $q_j(Y_1, \ldots, Y_{n_j})$. The basic difference between program clauses and database clauses is in the use of types. In typed clauses, a type is associated with each variable appearing in a clause. The type of a variable specifies the range of values which the variable can take. For example, in the relation *lives_in*(X, Y), we may want to specify that X is of type *person* and Y is of type *city*.

A set of program clauses with the same predicate symbol p in the head forms a *predicate definition*. A predicate can be defined *extensionally* as a set of ground facts or *intensionally* as a set of database clauses (Ullman 1988). It is assumed that each predicate is either defined extensionally or intensionally. A relation in a database is essentially the same as a predicate definition in a logic program. Table 5.3 relates the database (Ullman 1988) and logic programming (Lloyd 1987) terms that will be used throughout the chapter.

Database clauses use variables and function symbols in predicate arguments. Recursive types and recursive predicate definitions are allowed. *Deductive hierarchical databases* (DHDB) (Lloyd 1987) are deductive databases restricted to nonrecursive predicate definitions and to nonrecursive types. The latter determine finite sets of values which are constants or structured terms with constant arguments.

5.2.3   Dimensions of ILP

Inductive logic programming systems (as well as other inductive learning systems) can be divided along several dimensions. First of all, they can learn either a *single concept* or *multiple concepts* (predicates). Second, they may require all the training examples to be given before the learning process (*batch learners*) or may accept examples one by one (*incremental learners*). Third, during the learning process, a learner may rely on an oracle to verify the validity of generalizations and/or classify examples generated by the learner. The learner is called *interactive* in this case and *non-interactive* otherwise. Fourth, a learner may invent new terms (new predicates). This results in extending the learner's vocabulary which may facilitate the learning task. Finally, a learner may try to learn a concept from scratch or can accept an initial hypothesis (theory) which is then revised in the learning process. The latter systems are called *theory revisors.*

Although these dimensions are in principle independent, existing ILP systems are situated at two ends of the spectrum. At one end are batch non-interactive systems that learn single predicates from scratch, while at the other are interactive and incremental theory revisors that learn multiple predicates. Following (De Raedt 1992) we call the first type of ILP systems *empirical ILP systems* and the second type *interactive ILP systems.*

MIS (Shapiro 1983) and CLINT (De Raedt 1992) are typical interactive ILP systems: they learn definitions of multiple predicates from a small set of examples and queries to the user. On the other hand, empirical ILP systems typically learn a definition of a single predicate from a large collection of examples. This class of ILP systems includes FOIL (Quinlan 1990), GOLEM (Muggleton and Feng 1990), and LINUS (Lavrač et al. 1991). At present, it seems that empirical ILP systems are more relevant to practical applications. Thus, the applications described in this chapter involve empirical ILP systems, an empirical ILP problem will be used to illustrate the basic ILP techniques, and the discussion will

concern mainly empirical ILP. However, the basic techniques described
are used in both interactive and empirical ILP systems.

5.2.4   Empirical Inductive Logic Programming

The task of empirical single predicate learning in ILP can be formulated
as follows:

Given:

- a set of training examples $\mathcal{E}$, consisting of true $\mathcal{E}^+$ and false $\mathcal{E}^-$
  ground facts of an unknown predicate p,

- a concept description language $\mathcal{L}$, specifying syntactic restrictions
  on the definition of predicate p,

- background knowledge $\mathcal{B}$, defining predicates q_i (other than p)
  which may be used in the definition of p

Find:

- a definition $\mathcal{H}$ for p, expressed in $\mathcal{L}$, such that $\mathcal{H}$ is complete, i.e.,
  $\forall e \in \mathcal{E}^+ : \mathcal{B} \wedge \mathcal{H} \vdash e$, and consistent, i.e., $\forall e \in \mathcal{E}^- : \mathcal{B} \wedge \mathcal{H} \not\vdash e$, with
  respect to $\mathcal{E}$ and $\mathcal{B}$.

One usually refers to the true facts $\mathcal{E}^+$ as *positive* $(\oplus)$ *examples*, the
false facts $\mathcal{E}^-$ as *negative* $(\ominus)$ *examples* and the definition of p as the
definition of the *target* relation. Positive examples are tuples known to
belong to the target relation, while negative examples are tuples known
not to belong to the target relation. A definition of the target predicate
is sought that will characterize the examples precisely (i.e., will explain
all of the positive and none of the negative examples). When learning
from noisy examples, the completeness and consistency criteria need
to be relaxed, i.e., an approximate characterization of the examples is
considered sufficient.

The symbol $\vdash$ denotes the relation of derivability under the assumption of a particular deductive inference rule, such as resolution: $T \vdash e$
means that e can be deductively derived from T. In database terms,
$T \vdash e$ would mean that the query e succeeds when posed to the database
T. The task of empirical ILP is to construct an intensional definition
(view) for the target relation p in terms of other relations from a given

database. One possible use of the constructed view is to replace the facts (examples) about p, thus saving storage space.

The language of concept descriptions $\mathcal{L}$ is usually called the *hypothesis language*. It is typically some subset of the language of program clauses. The complexity of learning grows with the expressiveness of the hypothesis language $\mathcal{L}$. Therefore, to limit the complexity of learning, $\mathcal{L}$ has to be limited by imposing restrictions on hypothesized clauses. Typical restrictions on the concept description language include the restriction to DHDB clauses and the restriction to constrained clauses (clauses that do not introduce new variables in the body).

5.3   Basic ILP Techniques

ILP techniques search for clauses in the hypothesis language that are consistent with the training examples. The space of clauses is structured by the generality relation between clauses, called θ-subsumption. A clause c is more general than clause d if c can be matched with a subset of d. For example, the clause $daughter(X, Y) \leftarrow female(X)$ is more general than the clause $daughter(ann, Y) \leftarrow female(ann), parent(Y, ann)$.

The basic ILP techniques considered here have been all used in empirical ILP systems and are thus relevant to KDD. Some of the techniques have been also used or even first introduced in interactive ILP systems. The techniques summarized below are: relative least general generalization, inverse resolution, searching refinement graphs, using rule models, and transforming ILP problems to propositional form.

5.3.1   Relative Least General Generalization

Plotkin's notion of least general generalization (lgg) (Plotkin 1969) is important for ILP since it forms the basis of cautious generalization. Cautious generalization assumes that if two clauses c_1 and c_2 are true, it is very likely that their most specific generalization $lgg(c_1, c_2)$ will also be true. The lgg of two clauses is computed by computing the lgg of each pair of literals in the heads and bodies, respectively. The lgg of two literals is computed by matching them and substituting the parts that don't match by a variable. We will not give the definition of lgg here, but will rather illustrate it on an example. If $c_1 = daughter(mary, ann) \leftarrow female(mary), parent(ann, mary)$ and $c_2 =$

$daughter(eve, tom) \leftarrow female(eve), parent(tom, eve)$, then $lgg(c_1, c_2) =$ $daughter(X, Y) \leftarrow female(X), parent(Y, X)$ (X stands for $lgg(mary,$ $eve)$ and Y for $lgg(ann, tom)$).

The *relative least general generalization* (*rlgg*) of two clauses c_1 and c_2 is the least general clause which is more general than both c_1 and c_2 with respect (*relative*) to background knowledge B. Relative least general generalization is the basic technique used in the ILP system GOLEM (Muggleton and Feng 1990), where the background knowledge B is restricted to ground facts. If K denotes the conjunction of all these facts, the *rlgg* of two ground atoms A_1 and A_2 (positive examples), relative to B is defined as:

$$rlgg(A_1, A_2) = lgg((A_1 \leftarrow K), (A_2 \leftarrow K))$$

Given the positive examples $e_1 = daughter(mary, ann)$ and $e_2 = daughter(eve, tom)$ and the background knowledge B for the family example in Section 5.2.1, the least general generalization of e_1 and e_2 relative to B is computed as:

$$rlgg(e_1, e_2) = lgg((e_1 \leftarrow K), (e_2 \leftarrow K))$$

where K denotes the conjunction of the literals $parent(ann, mary)$, $parent(ann, tom)$, $parent(tom, eve)$, $parent(tom, ian)$, $female(ann)$, $female(mary)$, and $female(eve)$.

For notational convenience, the following abbreviations are used: *d-daughter, p-parent, f-female, a-ann, e-eve, m-mary, t-tom, i-ian*. The conjunction of facts from the background knowledge (comma stands for conjunction) is

$$K = p(a, m), p(a, t), p(t, e), p(t, i), f(a), f(m), f(e).$$

The computation of $rlgg(e_1, e_2)$ produces the following clause

$$d(V_{m,e}, V_{a,t}) \leftarrow p(a, m), p(a, t), p(t, e), p(t, i), f(a), f(m), f(e),$$
$$p(a, V_{m,t}), p(V_{a,t}, V_{m,e}), p(V_{a,t}, V_{m,i}), p(V_{a,t}, V_{t,e}),$$
$$p(V_{a,t}, V_{t,i}), p(t, V_{e,i}), f(V_{a,m}), f(V_{a,e}), f(V_{m,e}).$$

where $V_{x,y}$ stands for $rlgg(x, y)$, for each x and y. In general, a *rlgg* of a set of training examples can contain infinitely many literals or at least grow exponentially with the number of examples. Since such a clause can be intractably large, GOLEM uses a determinacy constraint on introducing new variables into the body of the *rlgg*. Even under this constraint, *rlggs* are usually long clauses with many irrelevant literals.

Eliminating irrelevant literals yields the clause

$$d(V_{m,e}, V_{a,t}) \leftarrow p(V_{a,t}, V_{m,e}), f(V_{m,e}),$$

which stands for $daughter(X, Y) \leftarrow female(X), parent(Y, X)$.

The ILP system GOLEM based on *rlgg* has been applied to several practical problems, including protein secondary structure prediction (predicting the shape of a protein from its sequence of amino acids) (Muggleton et al. 1992) and learning structure-activity relationships (relating the effectiveness of a drug, e.g., the degree to which it slows bacterial growth, to its chemical structure) (King et al. 1992).

5.3.2 Inverse Resolution

The basic idea of *inverse resolution* (introduced as a generalization technique to ILP by Muggleton and Buntine (1988)) is to invert the *resolution* rule of deductive inference (Robinson 1965). The basic resolution step in propositional logic derives the proposition $p \lor r$ given the premises $p \lor \overline{q}$ and $q \lor r$. In first-order logic, resolution is more complicated, involving substitutions. The conclusion reached from clauses c and d by a resolution inference step is denoted by $res(c, d)$ and is called the resolvent of c and d.

To illustrate resolution in first-order logic, we use the example from Section 5.2.1. Suppose that background knowledge $\mathcal{B}$ consists of the clauses $b_1 = female(mary)$ and $b_2 = parent(ann, mary)$ and $\mathcal{H} = \{c\} = \{daughter\ (X, Y) \leftarrow female(X), parent(Y, X)\}$. Let $\mathcal{T} = \mathcal{H} \cup \mathcal{B}$. Suppose we want to derive the fact $daughter(mary, ann)$ from $\mathcal{T}$. To this end, we proceed as follows:

- First, the resolvent $c_1 = res(c, b_1)$ is computed under substitution $\theta_1 = \{X/mary\}$. This means the substitution θ_1 is first applied to c to obtain $daughter(mary, Y) \leftarrow female(mary)$, $parent(Y, mary)$, which is then resolved with b_1 as in the propositional case. The resolvent of $daughter(X, Y) \leftarrow female(X), parent(Y, X)$ and $female(mary)$ is thus $c_1 = res(c, b_1) = daughter(mary, Y) \leftarrow parent\ (Y, mary)$.

- The next resolvent $c_2 = res(c_1, b_2)$ is computed under the substitution $\theta_2 = \{Y/ann\}$. The clauses $daughter(mary, Y) \leftarrow parent$ $(Y, mary)$ and $parent(ann, mary)$ resolve in $c_2 = res(c_1, b_2) = daughter(mary, ann)$.

Inverse resolution, as implemented in CIGOL (Muggleton and Buntine 1988), uses a generalization operator based on inverting substitution (Buntine 1988). Given a clause W, an *inverse substitution* θ^{-1} of a substitution θ is a function that maps terms in $W\theta$ to variables, such that $W\theta\theta^{-1} = W$. Let $c = daughter(X, Y) \leftarrow female(X), parent(Y, X)$ and the substitution $\theta = \{X/mary, Y/ann\}$:

$$c' = c\theta = daughter(mary, ann) \leftarrow female(mary), parent(ann, mary).$$

By applying the inverse substitution $\theta^{-1} = \{mary/X, ann/Y\}$ the original clause c is obtained:

$$c = c'\theta^{-1} = daughter(X, Y) \leftarrow female(Y), parent(Y, X).$$

In the general case, inverse substitution is substantially more complex. It involves the *places* of terms in order to ensure that the variables in the initial clause W are appropriately restored in $W\theta\theta^{-1}$.

Let the background knowledge $\mathcal{B}$ contain the two facts (clauses) $b_1 = female(mary)$ and $b_2 = parent(ann, mary)$. Let the current hypothesis $\mathcal{H} = \emptyset$. Suppose that the learner encounters the positive example $e_1 = daughter(mary, ann)$. The inverse resolution process might then proceed as follows:

- In the first step, inverse resolution attempts to find a clause c_1 which will, together with b_2, entail e_1 and can be added to the current hypothesis $\mathcal{H}$ instead of e_1. Using the inverse substitution $\theta_2^{-1} = \{ann/Y\}$, an inverse resolution step generates the clause $c_1 = ires(b_2, e_1) = daughter(mary, Y) \leftarrow parent(Y, mary)$. Clause c_1 becomes the current hypothesis $\mathcal{H}$, such that $\{b_2\} \cup \mathcal{H} \vdash e_1$.

- Inverse resolution then takes $b_1 = female(mary)$ and the current hypothesis $\mathcal{H} = \{c_1\} = \{daughter(mary, Y) \leftarrow parent(Y, mary)\}$. By computing $c' = ires(b_1, c_1)$, using the inverse substitution $\theta_1^{-1} = \{mary/X\}$, it generalizes the clause c_1 with respect to background knowledge $\mathcal{B}$, yielding $c' = daughter(X, Y) \leftarrow female(X)$,

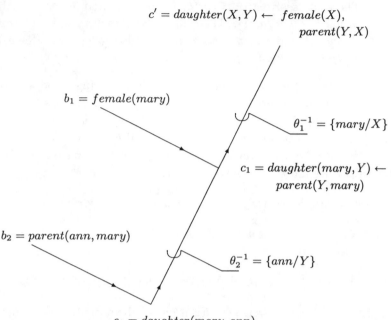

$$c' = daughter(X, Y) \leftarrow female(X),$$
$$parent(Y, X)$$

$$b_1 = female(mary)$$

$$\theta_1^{-1} = \{mary/X\}$$

$$c_1 = daughter(mary, Y) \leftarrow$$
$$parent(Y, mary)$$

$$b_2 = parent(ann, mary)$$

$$\theta_2^{-1} = \{ann/Y\}$$

$$e_1 = daughter(mary, ann)$$

Figure 5.1
An inverse linear derivation tree.

$parent(Y, X)$. In the current hypothesis $\mathcal{H}$, clause c_1 can now be re-placed by the more general clause c' which together with $\mathcal{B}$ entails the example e_1. The induced hypothesis is $\mathcal{H} = \{daughter(X, Y) \leftarrow female(X), parent(Y, X)\}$.

The corresponding inverse linear derivation tree is illustrated in Figure 5.1.

The generalization operator illustrated in the above example is called the *absorption* operator (the **V** operator), and is used in the interactive ILP systems MARVIN (Sammut and Banerji 1986) and CIGOL (Muggleton and Buntine 1988) to generate hypotheses. Several other inverse resolution operators are used in CIGOL. An important operator is *intra-construction*, also called the **W** operator, which combines two **V** operators. This operator generates clauses using predicates which are not available in the initial learner's vocabulary. The ability to introduce new predicates is referred to as *predicate invention*.

While most systems based on inverting resolution are interactive, an empirical system based on mode-directed inverse resolution (PROGOL [Muggleton 1995]) has been recently developed. It has been applied to the problem of predicting the mutagenicity of chemical compounds from their structure (Srinivasan et al. 1994).

5.3.3   Searching Refinement Graphs

The basic specialization ILP technique is *top-down search of refinement graphs*. Top-down learners start from the most general clause and repeatedly refine (specialize) it until it no longer covers negative examples. During the search they ensure that the clause considered covers at least one positive example. The ILP technique of top-down search of a refinement graph was first used in the interactive ILP system MIS (Model Inference System (Shapiro 1983)). It is also used in the empirical ILP system FOIL (Quinlan 1990) and its derivatives, e.g., mFOIL (Džeroski and Bratko 1992) and FOCL (Pazzani and Kibler 1992).

For a selected hypothesis language $\mathcal{L}$ and given background knowledge $\mathcal{B}$, the hypothesis space of program clauses is a lattice, structured by the θ-subsumption generality ordering. In this lattice, a *refinement graph* can be defined as a directed, acyclic graph in which *nodes* are program clauses and *arcs* correspond to the basic refinement operations: substituting a variable with a term and adding a literal to the body of a clause.

Part of the refinement graph for the family relations problem is depicted in Figure 5.2. The search for a clause starts with the clause $daughter(X, Y) \leftarrow$, which covers two negative examples. The refinements of this clause are then considered, of which $daughter(X, Y) \leftarrow female(X)$ and $daughter(X, Y) \leftarrow parent(Y, X)$ cover only one negative example each. These two clauses have a common refinement

$$daughter(X, Y) \leftarrow female(X), parent(Y, X)$$

which covers no negative examples. The search of the refinement lattice is usually heuristic, as for instance in FOIL (Quinlan 1990).

5.3.4   Using Rule Models

The system MOBAL (Morik et al. 1993) contains a learning module based on the use of *rule models*. Rule models are a form of declarative bias, more specifically declarative language bias. They explicitly specify the

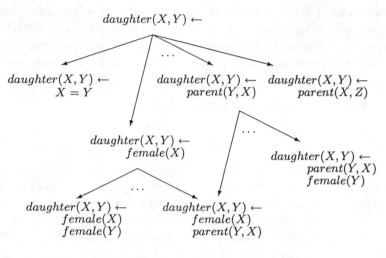

Figure 5.2
Part of the refinement graph for the family relations problem.

form of clauses that can appear in the hypothesis and are used as templates for constructing hypotheses. They are provided by the user or can be derived from previously learned rules by the model acquisition tool within MOBAL.

A *rule model* R has the form $T \leftarrow L_1, \ldots, L_m$ where T and L_i are literal schemas. Each *literal schema* L_i has the form $Q_i(Y_1, \ldots, Y_{n_i})$ or *not* $Q_j(Y_1, \ldots, Y_{n_j})$ where all non-predicate variables Y_k are implicitly universally quantified. The *predicate variable* Q_i can be instantiated only to a predicate symbol of the specified arity n_i.

The search for hypotheses in MOBAL is guided by the rule models. The hypothesis space that is actually searched is the set of all predicate ground instantiations of rule models with predicates from the background knowledge $\mathcal{B}$. An *instantiation* Θ is a second-order substitution, i.e., a finite set of pairs P/p where P is a predicate variable and p is a predicate symbol. An instantiation of a rule model R (denoted by $R\Theta$) is obtained by replacing each predicate variable in R by the corresponding predicate symbol from the set Θ. A second-order rule model R is *predicate ground* if all of its predicate variables are instantiated; in this case, R becomes a first-order rule (clause).

For learning the *daughter* relation from the family relations problem of Section 5.2.1, the user needs to define the following model:

$$P(X,Y) \leftarrow R(X), Q(Y,X).$$

In this case, the correct clause $daughter(X,Y) \leftarrow female(X), parent$ (Y,X) can be induced. The above model could also be instantiated to the clause $son(X,Y) \leftarrow male(X), parent(Y,X)$. We can thus see that one rule model can be useful for solving several learning problems.

The space of clauses specified by the rule models is still very large. For each rule model, all possible instantiations of predicate variables are tried systematically and the resulting clauses are tested against the examples and background knowledge. A hierarchical order of rule models, based on extended θ-subsumption, allows MOBAL to prune parts of the hypothesis space.

MOBAL has been applied to the practical problem of learning access rules for telecommunications equipment in a security context (Morik et al. 1993).

5.3.5 Transforming ILP Problems to Propositional Form

The ILP system LINUS (Lavrač et al. 1991; Lavrač and Džeroski 1994) is based on the following idea: background knowledge can give rise to new attributes for propositional learning. An ILP problem is transformed from relational to attribute-value form and solved by an attribute-value learner. This approach is feasible only for a restricted class of ILP problems. Thus, the hypothesis language is restricted to function-free program clauses which are *typed* (each variable is associated with a predetermined set of values), *constrained* (all variables in the body of a clause also appear in the head), and *nonrecursive* (the predicate symbol from the head does not appear in any of the literals in the body), i.e., to function-free constrained DHDB clauses.

The LINUS algorithm consists of the following three steps:

- The learning problem is transformed from relational to attribute-value form.

- The transformed learning problem is solved by an attribute-value learner.

- The induced hypothesis is transformed back into relational form.

Table 5.4
Propositional form of the *daughter* relation problem.

Class	Variables		Propositional features							
	X	Y	f(X)	f(Y)	m(X)	m(Y)	p(X,X)	p(X,Y)	p(Y,X)	p(Y,Y)
⊕	mary	ann	true	true	false	false	false	false	true	false
⊕	eve	tom	true	false	false	true	false	false	true	false
⊖	tom	ann	false	true	true	false	false	false	true	false
⊖	eve	ann	true	true	false	false	false	false	false	false

The above algorithm allows for a variety of approaches developed for propositional problems, including noise-handling techniques in attribute-value algorithms, such as ASSISTANT (Cestnik et al. 1987) or CN2 (Clark and Niblett 1989; Clark and Boswell 1991), to be used for learning relations. It is illustrated on the simple ILP problem of learning family relations from Section 5.2.1. The task is to define the relation $daughter(X, Y)$, which states that person X is a daughter of person Y, in terms of the background knowledge relations *female*, *male* and *parent*. All the variables are of type *person*, which is defined as $person = \{ann, eve, ian, mary, tom\}$. There are two positive and two negative examples of the target relation. The training examples and the relations from the background knowledge are given in Table 5.2.

The first step of the algorithm, i.e., the transformation of the ILP problem into attribute-value form, is performed as follows. The possible applications of the background predicates on the arguments of the target relation are determined, taking into account argument types. Each such application introduces a new attribute. In our example, all variables are of the same type *person*. The corresponding attribute-value learning problem is given in Table 5.4, where f stands for *female*, m for *male* and p for *parent*. The attribute-value tuples are generalizations (relative to the given background knowledge) of the individual facts about the target relation.

In Table 5.4, *variables* stand for the arguments of the target relation, and *propositional features* denote the newly constructed attributes of the propositional learning task. When learning function-free clauses, only the new attributes are considered for learning.

In the second step, an attribute-value learning program induces the following if-then rule from the tuples in Table 5.4:

$$Class = \oplus \quad \textbf{if} \quad [female(X) = true] \quad \wedge \quad [parent(Y, X) = true]$$

In the last step, the induced if-then rules are transformed into DHDB clauses. In our example, we get the clause

$$daughter(X, Y) \leftarrow female(X), parent(Y, X).$$

LINUS has been applied to the problem of learning diagnostic rules for early rheumatic diseases from a medical database (Lavrač et al. 1993). DINUS (Džeroski et al. 1992; Lavrač and Džeroski 1994) is an extension of LINUS that learns determinate clauses, the same class of clauses learned by GOLEM (Muggleton and Feng 1990). It has been applied to the problem of behavioral cloning, i.e., learning control rules for dynamic systems (Džeroski et al. 1995).

Note that several different techniques may be employed within a single ILP system. For example, rule models in MOBAL are used in combination with top-down search. Bidirectional search, combining top-down and bottom-up search for clauses, may also be used in an ILP system (Siou 1994).

5.4   Recent Developments in ILP Relevant to KDD

This section outlines three recent advances in ILP relevant to KDD: multiple predicate learning (De Raedt et al. 1993), inductive data engineering (Flach 1993), and clausal discovery (De Raedt and Bruynooghe 1993).

5.4.1   Multiple Predicate Learning

The task of empirical multiple predicate learning is to learn the logical definitions of m different predicates $p_1, \ldots, p_m$, from a set of training examples $\mathcal{E}$ of these predicates and a background theory $\mathcal{B}$, containing predicate definitions for $q_1, \ldots, q_l$ (De Raedt et al. 1993). It is similar to empirical single predicate learning, but involves additional problems that arise when learning mutually dependent predicates. These include the consideration of clauses only at a local level, determining the order of learning the predicates, overgeneralization and mutual recursion.

An example task of multiple predicate learning would be to learn the definitions of the target predicates $male\_ancestor(X, Y)$ and $female\_ancestor(X, Y)$ in terms of the background knowledge predicates $mother(X, Y)$ and $father(X, Y)$. To illustrate the problems encountered when learning multiple predicates, consider the following definitions induced by FOIL (Quinlan 1990).

$$male\_ancestor(X, Y) \leftarrow$$
$$father(X, W), mother(M, W), female\_ancestor(M, Y)$$

$$female\_ancestor(X, Y) \leftarrow$$
$$mother(X, W), father(F, W), male\_ancestor(F, Y)$$

The definitions are correct, but not operational: they would cause an endless recursion if executed. No ground facts about the target relations can be derived from these definitions.

The ILP system MPL (De Raedt et al. 1993) has been designed specifically for learning multiple predicates. It is based on a top-down search and considers clauses both locally and globally, backtracking when inconsistencies are detected. It induces the following correct definition of the predicates $male\_ancestor(X, Y)$ and $female\_ancestor(X, Y)$.

$$female\_ancestor(X, Y) \leftarrow mother(X, Y).$$
$$male\_ancestor(X, Y) \leftarrow father(X, Y).$$
$$female\_ancestor(X, Y) \leftarrow mother(X, Z), female\_ancestor(Z, Y).$$
$$male\_ancestor(X, Y) \leftarrow father(X, Z), female\_ancestor(Z, Y).$$
$$male\_ancestor(X, Y) \leftarrow father(X, Z), male\_ancestor(Z, Y).$$
$$female\_ancestor(X, Y) \leftarrow$$
$$female\_ancestor(X, Z), male\_ancestor(Z, Y).$$

5.4.2 Inductive Data Engineering

The term inductive data engineering (IDE) is used to denote the interactive restructuring of databases by means of induction (Flach 1993). The main idea is to use induction to determine integrity constraints that are valid (or almost valid) in a database and then use the constraints to decompose (restructure) the database. The integrity constraints used in the IDE system INDEX (Flach 1993) include functional and multivalued dependencies.

An unstructured database typically contains redundant information. INDEX decomposes such a relation into more primitive relations by using attribute dependencies. It defines the original relation as an intensional relation in terms of the primitive relations. In ILP terms, INDEX invents new predicates. It interacts with the user during the restructuring process, e.g., when choosing which dependency to decompose the relation upon.

If a dependency is satisfied on a given relation, it suggests a horizontal decomposition, where the original relation is reconstructed by a join operation. If a dependency is not satisfied, but is considered interesting (e.g., it is almost satisfied), it may suggest a vertical decomposition, where the original relation is reconstructed by a set union operation. The dependency is typically satisfied in the relations created by vertical decomposition, thus suggesting further horizontal decompositions.

To illustrate the IDE process, consider a train schedule represented by a single unstructured relation

$$train(Direction, Hour, Minutes, FirstStop)$$

(Flach 1993). The multivalued dependency $[] \rightarrow\rightarrow Hour$ (trains run every hour) is almost satisfied, suggesting a vertical decomposition. The relation $train$ is then split into two relations: $regular\_train$ (trains that run every hour) and $irregular\_train$: $train(A, B, C, D) \leftarrow regular\_train$ $(A, B, C, D) \lor irregular\_train(A, B, C, D)$. The dependency $[] \rightarrow\rightarrow Hour$ is satisfied for the relation $regular\_train$. Consequently, we can perform a horizontal decomposition: $regular\_train(D, H, M, FS) \leftarrow hour(H)$, $reg\_train(D, M, FS)$.

5.4.3   Clausal Discovery

The ILP setting described in Section 5.2, including single and multiple predicate learning, interactive and empirical ILP, is the normal ILP setting (Muggleton and De Raedt 1994). Classification rules are induced in the normal ILP setting; if the induced rules are sufficiently accurate, they may replace the examples; namely, the examples can be derived from the rules. A radically different approach is taken in the nonmonotonic ILP setting: given a database, a set of constraints is to be found that hold for the database. As the constraints can have the form of first-order clauses, the approach is known as clausal discovery (De Raedt and Bruynooghe 1993).

To illustrate clausal discovery in the nonmonotonic ILP setting, consider a database containing facts about family relations: $mother(X, Y)$, $father(X, Y)$, and $parent(X, Y)$. The following integrity constraints, among others, have been discovered by the ILP system CLAUDIEN (De Raedt and Bruynooghe 1993):

$$mother(X, Y) \lor father(X, Y) \leftarrow parent(X, Y)$$

$$parent(X, Y) \leftarrow father(X, Y)$$
$$\leftarrow mother(X, Y), father(X, Y)$$
$$\leftarrow parent(X, X)$$

The third and fourth constraint state that it is impossible that X is at the same time both the mother and the father of Y, and that it is impossible for a person to be his own parent. Unlike in the normal ILP setting, if we throw away the database, the learned theory may not be able to reconstruct it.

CLAUDIEN searches a refinement graph for full clauses. The language of the clauses is specified through a declarative bias specification language, thus focusing the search to relevant clauses. Potential applications of CLAUDIEN are described in (Dehaspe et al. 1994), including the discovery of attribute dependencies and integrity constraints. As the nonmonotonic setting allows for more efficient induction than the normal setting (De Raedt and Džeroski 1994), we are likely to see KDD applications of clausal discovery. Section 5.5 describes the application of CLAUDIEN to discovering rules for biological classification of river water quality.

5.5   KDD Applications of ILP

Several ILP applications have emerged recently. They vary considerably in the degree of sophistication and significance with respect to the area of application. Most of these are laboratory demonstrations (some of them using real data) rather than fielded real-world applications. Surveys of ILP applications can be found in (Bratko and King 1994; Bratko and Džeroski 1995), and (Lavrač and Džeroski 1994). Lavrač and Džeroski (1994) identify knowledge discovery in databases as one of the main application areas of ILP.

Applications of ILP to different problems of knowledge discovery in databases include learning rules for early diagnosis of rheumatic diseases from a medical database (Lavrač et al. 1993), and biological classification of river water quality from an environmental database (Džeroski et al. 1994). ILP has also been applied to several tasks of knowledge discovery in biomolecular databases, where the results achieved have come close to practical significance. These applications are: modeling the structure-activity relationships for two series of drugs (King et al. 1992;

Hirst et al. 1995a; Hirst et al. 1995b), prediction of the local secondary structure (shape) of a protein from its amino-acid sequence (Muggleton et al. 1992), and prediction of the mutagenicity of compounds using only their chemical structure (Srinivasan et al. 1994). In all three cases, ILP approaches have generated rules that perform as well or better than conventional approaches and provide insight into the relevant stereo-chemistry.

In the remainder of this section, we give a summary of the applications of ILP to biological classification of river water quality (Džeroski et al. 1994), and prediction of the secondary structure of a protein from its amino-acid sequence (Muggleton et al. 1992). While the datasets in these applications arc not tremendously large by today's standards, they nonetheless represent real-world datasets used in specific scientific studies.

5.5.1   Biological Classification of River Water Quality

Increasing importance is placed on the use of riverine ecology as a means of monitoring and classifying river quality, both in terms of water quality and its broader environmental quality (Ruck et al. 1993). The various biological flora and fauna, such as attached algae, macrophytes and benthic (or river bed) macro-invertebrates, are seen as continuous monitors of the rivers' "health," and field data on these are used to classify the river. In the case of water quality monitoring and classification, the biological methods are used to complement the more traditional chemical methods. An introduction to biological monitoring theory and techniques can be found in (De Pauw and Hawkes 1993).

At present, the most suitable single group for monitoring purposes is considered to be the benthic macro-invertebrates. These animals form part of the community associated with the river bed and are relatively immobile. They are present in all rivers, except in cases of extreme pollution, and cover a range of life modes and trophic levels. Taxonomic classification of these organisms to family or genus level is not too demanding, and qualitative identification is often carried out at the river bank. Also the different species are known to have different sensitivities to pollutants, thus the structure of the benthic macro-invertebrate community is affected by both degradable organic matter (sewage) and toxic pollutants (pesticides and heavy metals).

The task addressed here is to interpret benthic samples of macro-invertebrates in water quality terms. In other words, given are samples of the river beds at different sites and their classification into one of five quality classes. The task is to learn general rules that will be able to classify new samples (Džeroski et al. 1994). The study used 292 field samples of benthic communities collected from British Midlands rivers, classified by an acknowledged expert river ecologist (H. A. Hawkes). The samples come from the database maintained by the National River Authority of the United Kingdom, where the results of monitoring the environmental quality of British rivers are stored.

Two ILP systems were applied to the problem of classification of biological samples. GOLEM (Muggleton and Feng 1990) works in the normal ILP setting, where the task is to find classification rules that explain the training examples, while CLAUDIEN (De Raedt and Bruynooghe 1993) works in the nonmonotonic ILP setting, where the task is to find valid rules that are confirmed by the training examples. A propositional learning system, CN2 (Clark and Boswell 1991; Džeroski et al. 1993) was also applied to learn classification rules.

For the normal ILP setting, the problem was formulated as follows: for each class a separate ILP problem was created, where the positive examples are the samples classified in that class, and all the other samples are negative examples. Thus, the target predicates were $b1a(X)$, $b1b(X)$, $b2(X)$, $b3(X)$, and $b4(X)$. The background knowledge consisted of eighty predicates of the form $family(X, A)$, each denoting that $family$ is present in sample X at abundance level A. (In several cases, identification was carried to levels other than family, e.g., species or genera level. For simplicity, we will use the term family throughout, regardless of the taxonomic identification level.) Predicates of this kind include $tipulidae(X, A)$, $asellidae(X, A)$, etc. In addition, the background predicate $greater\_than(A, B)$ was available, stating that abundance level A is greater than abundance level B.

The default settings of GOLEM were used, except for the fact that rules were allowed to cover up to five negative examples. GOLEM produced three rules for class B1a, fourteen rules for B1b, sixteen for B2, two for B3, and none for B4. For example, the rule $b1a(X) \leftarrow leuctridae(X, A)$ states that a sample belongs to the best water quality class if Leuctridae are present. This rule covers forty-three positive and four negative examples, and agrees with expert knowledge; the family Leuctridae is an indicator of good water quality. Another good rule is the following: $b1b(X) \leftarrow ancylidae(X, A), gammaridae(X, B),$ $hydropsychidae(X, C),$ $rhyacophilidae(X, D),$ $greater\_than(B, A),$ $greater\_than(B, D)$. Gammaridae in abundance is a good indicator of class B1b, along with the other families present.

Out of the thirty-five rules, twenty-five are considered good or acceptable by the expert, but some of them are judged to be too specific. Note that GOLEM cannot use the absence of particular families in the rules within the representation adopted here. Together with GOLEM's strategy of looking for the most specific rules consistent with the examples, this may have influenced the generality (specificity) of the generated rules. This may also be the reason that no rules for class B4 were induced. Namely, the absence of most families is characteristic for this class.

Unlike GOLEM, CLAUDIEN (De Raedt and Bruynooghe 1993) checks all possible rules, within a specified language, for consistency with the given examples. Only tests of the presence of different families were allowed in the antecedents (no absence tests and no abundance level tests), while one or more quality classes were allowed in the consequents. Rules were required to cover at least thirty examples.

Altogether, seventy-nine rules were generated. Of these, twenty-eight involved the presence of a single family. These rules in fact specify the range of quality classes in which a certain family is present. The rule $b1a(X) \vee b1b(X) \leftarrow perlodidae(X, A)$ specifies that Perlodidae are found in good quality water (classes B1a and B1b). If Rhyacophilidae are also present, then the water is almost certainly of class B1a: $b1a(X) \leftarrow$ $perlodidae(X, A), rhyacophilidae(X, B)$. Both rules are judged by the expert to be good.

Only nine rules had a single class (B1a) in the conclusion. The others had a number of possible classes in the conclusion, which was considered natural and understandable by the expert. This indicates that class B1a is easy to characterize in terms of the families present, while for the other classes references to the abundance levels or absence of certain families is required in order to find significant rules (that cover at least thirty samples). Overall, two thirds of the rules were considered to be good. The rest were not outright wrong, but still unacceptable to the expert for a number of reasons, such as mentioning families which are irrelevant (according to the expert opinion) for a particular water quality class.

In summary, the rules induced by the ILP systems GOLEM and CLAUDIEN were found to be consistent with the expert knowledge to a great extent. Compared to other methods for automating the classification process, such as neural networks, ILP produces symbolic rules that can be used as a knowledge base for an expert system. The rules generated by CLAUDIEN were judged to be the most intuitive and promising. This is due to the coverage of more than one class by a single rule; this is important as the classification problem is based on a discretization of a continuous space. The fact that a single family is used in some rules also contributes to the overall intuitiveness of the CLAUDIEN rules.

Rules generated by GOLEM were considered too specific. The CN2 rules were quite general, but relied too heavily on the absence of certain families. According to the expert, rules should rely on the presence rather than absence of families as the latter may be due to reasons other than water quality (e.g., seasonal variations). However, the absence of some families seems to be necessary for rules classifying into poorer water quality classes.

The best direction for further work seems the selective use of absence information, which can be easily achieved using the declarative bias facilities of CLAUDIEN, together with the use of diversity information. The performance of the rules obtained in this way will be tested on an independent data set and compared to the corresponding performance of neural networks and Bayesian systems (Ruck et al. 1993; Walley et al. 1992). If their performance so merits the rules will then be used as a knowledge base of an expert system for biological classification of river water quality.

5.5.2 Predicting Protein Secondary Structure

We now briefly review the problem of learning rules for predicting the secondary structure of proteins, to which GOLEM has been applied (Muggleton et al. 1992). We first describe the problem, then the relevant background knowledge, and finally the results.

A protein is basically a string of amino acids (or *residues*). Predicting the three-dimensional shape of proteins from their amino acid sequence is widely believed to be one of the hardest unsolved problems in molecular biology. It is also of considerable interest to the pharmaceutical industry since the shape of a protein generally determines its function.

The sequence of amino acids is called the *primary structure* of the protein. Spatially, the amino acids are arranged in different patterns (spirals, turns, flat sections, etc.). The three-dimensional spatial shape

Table 5.5
Rules for predicting α-helix secondary structure.

Level 0 rule

$alpha0(A, B) \leftarrow$ $octf(D, E, F, G, B, H, I, J, K),$
$position(A, D, Q), not\_p(Q), not\_k(Q),$
$position(A, E, O), not\_aromatic(O), small\_or\_polar(O),$
$position(A, F, R),$
$position(A, G, P), not\_aromatic(P),$
$position(A, B, C), very\_hydrophobic(C), not\_aromatic(C),$
$position(A, H, M), large(M), not\_aromatic(M),$
$position(A, I, L), hydrophobic(L),$
$position(A, K, N), large(N), ltv(N, R).$

Level 1 rule

$alpha1(A, B) \leftarrow$ $octf(D, E, F, G, B, H, I, J, K),$
$alpha0(A, F), alpha0(A, G).$

Level 2 rule

$alpha2(A, B) \leftarrow$ $octf(C, D, E, F, B, G, H, I, J),$
$alpha1(A, B), alpha1(A, G), alpha1(A, H).$

of a protein is called the *secondary structure*. When trying to predict the shape (*secondary structure*) it is easier to consider only one particular shape (pattern), instead of the multitude of possibilities; the α-helix (spiral) shape was considered by Muggleton et al. (1992).

The target relation $alpha(Protein, Position)$ specifies that the residue at position *Position* in protein *Protein* belongs to an α-helix. Negative examples state all residue positions in particular proteins which are not in an α-helix secondary structure. For instance, the positive example $alpha(1HMQ, 104)$ means that the residue at position 104 in protein 1HMQ (hemerythrin met) is in an α-helix. The negative example $alpha(1HMQ, 105)$ states that the residue at position 105 in the same protein is not in an α-helix (it actually belongs to a β-coil secondary structure).

To learn rules to identify whether a position in a protein is in an α-helix, Muggleton et al. (1992) use the following information as background knowledge.

- The relation $position(A, B, C)$ states that the residue of protein

A at position B is the amino-acid C. Each residue can be any one of the 20 possible amino-acids and is denoted by a lower case character. For example, the fact $position(1HMQ, 111, g)$ says that the residue at position 111 in protein $1HMQ$ is glycine (using the standard one-character amino acid coding).

- The following arithmetic relations allow indexing of the protein sequence, relative to the residue for which secondary structure is being predicted. They have to be provided explicitly, as GOLEM has no built-in arithmetics. The relation $octf(A, B, C, D, E, F, G, H, I)$ specifies nine adjacent positions in a protein, i.e., it says that positions A to I occur in sequence. One fact in this relation may be, for instance, $octf(19, 20, 21, 22, 23, 24, 25, 26, 27)$. The $alpha\_triplet(A, B, C)$, $alpha\_pair(A, B)$ and $alpha\_pair4(A, B)$ relations allow a similar kind of indexing, which specifies residues that are likely to appear on the same face of an α-helix. They might be defined declaratively by the following three facts: $alpha\_triplet(n, n+1, n+4)$, $alpha\_pair(n, n+3)$, $alpha\_pair4(n, n+4)$.

- Physical and chemical properties of individual residues are described by unary predicates. These properties include hydrophobicity, hydrophilicity, charge, size, polarity, whether a residue is aliphatic or aromatic, whether it is a hydrogen donor or acceptor, etc. Sizes, hydrophobicities, polarities, etc., are represented by constants, such as $polar0$ and $hydro0$. The use of different constant names for polarity zero $polar0$ and hydrophobicity zero $hydro0$ is necessary to prevent unjustified generalizations in GOLEM (these could be prevented by explicit statement of types instead). Relations between the constants, such as $less\_than(polar0, polar1)$, are also provided as background knowledge.

Let us now proceed with a very short description of the experimental setup and the results (Muggleton et al. 1992). Sixteen proteins from the Brookhaven database (Bernstein et al. 1977) were used, twelve for training and four for testing. Without addressing in detail how GOLEM was run to induce rules from the training data, let us mention that each of the induced rules was allowed to misclassify up to 10 instances and some subjective statistical criteria were used to judge its significance before allowing it into the set of rules used for classification. The induced rules covered around 60% of the instances.

To improve the coverage of these preliminary rules, the learning process was iterated. The predicted secondary structure positions found using the initial rules (called level 0 rules) were added to the background information. GOLEM was then run again to produce new (level 1) rules. This was necessary as the level 0 predictions were speckled, i.e., only short α-helix sequences were predicted. The level 1 rules in effect filtered the speckled predictions and joined together short sequences of α-helix predictions. The learning process was iterated once more with level 1 predictions added to the background knowledge and level 2 rules were induced. Finally, the symmetric variants of the rules induced at level 1 and level 2 were added to the rule set (e.g., $alpha1(A,B) \leftarrow octf(D,E,F,G,B,H,I,J,K)$, $alpha0(A,F)$, $alpha0(A,G)$): this was suggested by a domain expert that inspected the rules.

Applying GOLEM to the training set produced twenty-one level 0 rules, five symmetric level 1 rules and two symmetric level 2 rules. For illustration, Table 5.5 gives one rule from each level. The induced rules achieved accuracies of 78% on the training and 81% on the testing set. For comparison, the best previously reported result is 76%, achieved by using a neural network approach (Kneller et al. 1990). The rules induced by GOLEM also have the advantage over the neural network method of being more understandable. The propositional learner PROMIS (King and Sternberg 1990) achieved 73% accuracy using the same data set as GOLEM. However, as the representation power of PROMIS is limited, it was not able to find some of the important relationships between residues that GOLEM found to be involved in α-helix formation.

5.6 Discussion

We have given a brief introduction to inductive logic programming, as well as the basic techniques currently in use in ILP: relative least general generalization, inverse resolution, top-down search of refinement graphs, the use of rule models, and the transformation of ILP problems to propositional form. We have also outlined some recent developments in ILP relevant to KDD: multiple predicate learning, inductive data engineering and clausal discovery. Finally, we have described two applications of ILP to KDD problems: biological classification of river water quality and predicting protein secondary structure. The remainder of the chapter gives a discussion on where to find out more about ILP, what ILP approaches to use for different kinds of KDD problems, and current hot topics in ILP research.

5.6.1   More Information on ILP

As the field of inductive logic programming is relatively young, most of the publications in the area appear in conference and workshop proceedings. There have been four international workshops on inductive logic programming, with proceedings published as technical reports (Muggleton 1991; Muggleton 1992b; Muggleton 1993; Wrobel 1994). The proceedings contain papers describing theoretical advances in inductive logic programming, practical implementations of ILP systems and applications of inductive logic programming.

A special section of the *SIGART Bulletin*, 5(1), January 1994, is devoted to ILP. It includes an introductory paper, as well as papers dealing with major topics within ILP, such as top-down search for logic program clauses and applications of ILP. The paper (Muggleton 1991b) introduced the term inductive logic programming. The most complete survey paper so far is (Muggleton and De Raedt 1994).

The collection of papers "Inductive Logic Programming" (Muggleton 1992a) contains many revised and extended papers from The Proceedings of the First International Workshop on Inductive Logic Programming (Muggleton 1991b), as well as many other papers relevant to the field. The book "Interactive Theory Revision: An Inductive Logic Programming Approach" (De Raedt 1992) gives a thorough account on interactive inductive logic programming, focusing on the ILP system CLINT. The book "Knowledge Acquisition and Machine Learning: Theory, Methods and Applications" (Morik et al. 1993) describes the ILP toolbox MOBAL and its applications.

An extensive overview of empirical ILP techniques, including descriptions of several empirical ILP systems is given in the book "Inductive Logic Programming: Techniques and Applications" (Lavrač and Džeroski 1994). The book gives a general introduction to the field, which we have summarized in Sections 5.2 and 5.3. It also gives a detailed account of handling imperfect (noisy) data in ILP, an important topic for practical applications. Part IV of the book concentrates on applications

Table 5.6
ILP resources on the internet.

Resource	How to reach it
ILPNET WWW	`http://www-ai.ijs.si/ilpnet.html`
ILP Newsletter	Send email to `ilpnet@ijs.si`
ILP Data sets	`ftp://ftp.gmd.de:/MachineLearning/ILP/public/data`
ML Repository	`ftp://ftp.ics.uci.edu:/pub/machine-learning-databases`
ILP Publications	`ftp://ftp.gmd.de:/MachineLearning/ILP/public/papers`
ILP References	`ftp://ftp.gmd.de:/MachineLearning/ILP/public/bib`
ILP Systems	`ftp://ftp.gmd.de:/MachineLearning/ILP/public/software`

of inductive logic programming. It describes several applications in detail and gives and overview of several other ILP applications, including protein secondary structure prediction as described in Section 5.5.2.

For the enthusiastic reader, Table 5.6 gives a list of ILP resources available on the Internet. These include ILP publications, ILP datasets, and ILP systems. The main sources are the ILPNET World-Wide-Web server in Ljubljana and the Machine Learning Archive in Bonn. The former provides general information on ILP and ILP research, as well as pointers to other sources of information on ILP.

5.6.2   When to Use What

Giving definite recommendations as to which of the variety of ILP approaches is suitable for which problem is a difficult task. This is not easy even for attribute-value systems which have been around for much longer and have reached maturity. Nevertheless, we will attempt to lay out a few guidelines.

If interested in learning classification rules for a given relation which would rely on other relations, one should use an ILP system operating within the normal ILP setting. In addition to revealing regularities in the data, such a set of classification rules can be used to replace the table it was derived from (provided it is accurate enough). If one is only interested in regularities in his database (possibly clausal integrity constraints) that need not be used for classification, the CLAUDIEN ILP system can be recommended. CLAUDIEN (De Raedt and Bruynooghe 1993) operates in the nonmonotonic ILP setting.

In the normal setting, interactive ILP systems, such as CLINT (De Raedt 1992), should be used when interaction with the user is desired or the database studied is at an early stage of construction. However, empirical ILP systems are presently more appropriate for use in KDD, especially in the context of a database that is past the initial stages of development.

MPL (De Raedt et al. 1993) can be recommended for learning classification type logical definitions for several mutually dependent predicates. Other ILP systems, e.g., MOBAL (Morik et al. 1993), can also be used for this task. The use of MOBAL is especially recommended (both for single and multiple predicate learning) if the user has knowledge of the form of patterns to be discovered: this knowledge can be provided to MOBAL in the form of rule models.

Regarding the other empirical ILP systems for single predicate learning, the following recommendations can be made. If constrained or determinate clauses suffice for the application, LINUS and DINUS (Lavrač and Džeroski 1994) are a good choice. They rely on attribute-value systems to do the learning and are thus capable of handling noisy data and real-valued attributes. Most ILP systems do not have noise-handling capabilities. However, there are several exceptions, e.g., FOSSIL (Furnkranz 1994) and MILP (Kovačič 1994). Also, FOIL (Quinlan 1990) and GOLEM (Muggleton and Feng 1990) have some rudimentary noise-handling capabilities.

Top-down systems, such as FOIL, are better for finding simpler patterns, even in the presence of noise (in this case use mFOIL (Džeroski and Bratko 1992)). Bottom-up systems, such as GOLEM, are better at finding complicated patterns from data without imperfections, because they start with the most specific hypothesis in the hypothesis language that explains the examples. To conclude this recommendation section, we recommend that the reader gain access to the ILP systems from the Machine Learning Archive in Bonn (see Table 5.6) and try them out on their favorite KDD problem.

5.6.3   Hot Topics in ILP Research

Having started from a sound theoretical basis, current ILP research is increasingly turning to topics that are relevant for practical applications. One such topic is the computational complexity of ILP algorithms. Although theoretic by nature, this topic is of immediate practical interest: provably efficient ILP algorithms are obviously desirable. Research in this area has identified several classes of patterns (logic programs) that can be efficiently induced by current ILP systems, e.g., determinate logic programs (Džeroski et al. 1992). It has also shown that the nonmonotonic ILP setting allows for more efficient clausal discovery than the normal ILP setting (De Raedt and Džeroski 1994).

The study of the computational complexity of ILP problems/algorithms has shown that current ILP algorithms would scale relatively well with the increasing number of examples or facts in the background knowledge database. However, they would not scale well with the number of arguments of the predicates (relations) involved, and in some cases with the complexity of the patterns searched. There are also indications that the use of declarative bias can help to resolve these problems.

Declarative bias is an active area of ILP research. Formalisms for specifying declarative bias include rule models (Morik et al. 1993), clause sets (Bergadano and Gunetti 1994), and antecedent description grammars (Cohen 1994). The bias specification mechanism of (Ade et al. 1995) is a generalization of these approaches and is used in the ILP system CLAUDIEN (De Raedt and Bruynooghe 1993).

Finally, handling imperfect (noisy) data and numerical constraints in ILP are also among the main topics of ILP research. This includes upgrading propositional techniques to the first-order case (Lavrač and Džeroski 1994), as well as using MDL-based heuristics (Kovačič 1994) for noise handling. Relational regression is used (Džeroski et al. 1995) to learn numerical constraints in the normal setting, and a similar regression-based approach can be used in the nonmonotonic setting.

5.7 Conclusion

ILP is concerned with the induction of first-order rules in the form of clausal theories or logic programs. The induction process happens in the context of a deductive database, i.e., a set of intensional and extensional relations. ILP can thus be used for discovering patterns that involve several relations. The expressive power of the pattern language is a strong motivation for the use of ILP in a KDD context. While efficiency and scaling problems may be expected when using ILP for KDD, recent ILP systems provide powerful tools to cope with these problems, e.g., facilities for specifying a strong declarative bias. Handling imperfect data and real-valued attributes is also increasingly present in ILP systems. In their efforts to prove the practical value of their systems,

ILP researchers are sure to address KDD applications: we hope that their work will be complemented with work by KDD practitioners, thus helping to discover new and useful knowledge.

Acknowledgments

This chapter is based on an invited talk at the AAAI'93 Workshop on Knowledge Discovery in Databases. Section 5.2, Section 5.3, and Section 5.5.2, are based on Chapter 2, Chapter 3, and Chapter 14.1 of the book "Inductive Logic Programming: Techniques and Applications" by Nada Lavrač and Sašo Džeroski, published by Ellis Horwood in 1994. The author acknowledges the support of the Slovenian Ministry of Science and Technology and the ESPRIT III Project No. 6020 "Inductive Logic Programming."

References

Adé, H.; De Raedt, L.; and Bruynooghe, M. 1995. Declarative Bias for Bottom-up ILP Systems. *Machine Learning,* 20: 119–154.

Bergadano, F.; and Gunetti, D. 1994. Learning Clauses by Tracing Derivations. In Proceedings of the Fourth International Workshop on Inductive Logic Programming, 11-30. Bonn, Germany: GMD.

Bernstein, F.; Koetzle, T.; Williams, G.; Meyer, E.; Brice, M.; Rodgers, J.; Kennard, O.; Shimanouchi, T.; and Tasumi, M. 1977. The Protein Data Bank: A Computer-based Archival File for Macromolecular Structures. *Journal of Molecular Biology,* 112: 535–542.

Bratko, I.; and Džeroski, S. 1995. Engineering Applications of Inductive Logic Programming. *New Generation Computing (Special Issue on Inductive Logic Programming),* 13: 313–333.

Bratko, I.; and King, R. 1994. Applications of Inductive Logic Programming. *SIGART Bulletin (Special Issue on Inductive Logic Programming),* 5(1): 43–49.

Buntine, W. 1988. Generalized Subsumption and Its Applications to Induction and Redundancy. *Artificial Intelligence,* 36(2): 149–176.

Cestnik, B.; Kononenko, I.; and Bratko, I. 1987. ASSISTANT 86: A Knowledge Elicitation Tool for Sophisticated Users. In *Progress in Machine Learning,* eds. I. Bratko and N. Lavrač, 31–45. Wilmslow, UK: Sigma Press.

Clark, P.; and Boswell, R. 1991. Rule Induction with CN2: Some Recent Improvements. In Proceedings of the Fifth European Working Session on Learning, 151–163. Berlin: Springer-Verlag.

Clark, P.; and Niblett, T. 1989. The CN2 Induction Algorithm. *Machine Learning,* 3(4): 261–283.

Cohen, W. 1994. Grammatically Biased Learning: Learning Logic Programs Using an Explicit Antecedent Description Language. *Artificial Intelligence,* 68: 303–366.

De Pauw, N.; and Hawkes, H. 1993. Biological Monitoring of River Water Quality. In Proceedings of the Freshwater Europe Symposium on River Water Quality Monitoring and Control, 87–111. Birmingham, UK: Aston University.

De Raedt, L. 1992. *Interactive Theory Revision: An Inductive Logic Programming Approach.* London: Academic Press.

De Raedt, L.; and Bruynooghe, M. 1993. A Theory of Clausal Discovery. In Proceedings of the Thirteenth International Joint Conference on Artificial Intelligence, 1058–1063. San Mateo, Calif.: Morgan Kaufmann.

De Raedt, L.; and Džeroski, S. 1994. First Order jk-clausal Theories Are PAC-Learnable. *Artificial Intelligence,* 70: 375–392.

De Raedt, L.; Lavrač, N.; and Džeroski, S. 1993. Multiple Predicate Learning. In Proceedings of the Thirteenth International Joint Conference on Artificial Intelligence, 1037–1042. San Mateo, Calif.: Morgan Kaufmann.

Dehaspe, L.; Van Laer, W.; and De Raedt, L. 1994. Applications of a Logical Discovery Engine. In Proceedings of the Fourth International Workshop on Inductive Logic Programming, 291–304. Bonn, Germany: GMD.

Džeroski, S.; and Bratko, I. 1992. Handling Noise in Inductive Logic Programming. In Proceedings of the Second International Workshop on Inductive Logic Programming. Tokyo: ICOT.

Džeroski, S.; Todorovski, L.; and Urbančic, T. 1995. Handling Real Numbers in ILP: A Step Towards Successful Behavioral Cloning. In Proceedings of the Eighth European Conference on Machine Learning, 283–286. Berlin: Springer-Verlag.

Džeroski, S.; Dehaspe, L.; Ruck, B.; and Walley, W. 1994. Classification of River Water Quality Using Machine Learning. In Proceedings of the Fifth International Conference on the Development and Application of Computer Techniques to Environmental Studies, volume I, 129–137. Southampton, UK: Computational Mechanics Publications.

Džeroski, S.; Cestnik, B.; and Petrovski, I. 1993. Using the m-Estimate in Rule Induction. *Journal of Computing and Information Technology,* 1(1): 37–46.

Džeroski, S.; Muggleton, S.; and Russell, S. 1992. PAC-Learnability of Determinate Logic Programs. In Proceedings of the Fifth ACM Workshop on Computational Learning Theory, 128–135. New York: ACM Press.

Flach, P. 1993. Predicate Invention in Inductive Data Engineering. In Proceedings of the Sixth European Conference on Machine Learning, 83–94. Berlin: Springer-Verlag.

Frawley, W.; Piatetsky-Shapiro, G.; and Matheus, C. 1991. Knowledge Discovery in Databases: An Overview. In *Knowledge Discovery in Databases,* eds. G. Piatetsky-Shapiro and W. Frawley, 1–27. Menlo Park, Calif.: The AAAI Press.

Furnkranz, J. 1994. FOSSIL: A Robust Relational Learner. In Proceedings of the Seventh European Conference on Machine Learning, 122–137. Berlin: Springer-Verlag.

Hirst, J.; King, R.; and Sternberg, M. 1995a. Quantitative Structure-Activity Relationships: Neural Networks and Inductive Logic Programming Compared Against Statistical Methods. I. The Inhibition of Dihydrofolate Reductase by Pyrimidines. *Journal of Medical Chemistry.* Forthcoming.

Hirst, J.; King, R.; and Sternberg, M. 1995b. Quantitative Structure-Activity Relationships: Neural Networks and Inductive Logic Programming Compared Against Statistical Methods. II. The Inhibition of Dihydrofolate Reductase by Triazines. *Journal of Medical Chemistry.* Forthcoming.

King, R.; Muggleton, S.; Lewis, R.; and Sternberg, M. 1992. Drug Design by Machine Learning: The Use of Inductive Logic Programming to Model the Structure-Activity Relationships of Trimethoprim Analogues Binding to Dihydrofolate Reductase. *Proceedings of the National Academy of Sciences,* 89: 11322–11326.

King, R.; and Sternberg, M. 1990. Machine Learning Approach for the Prediction of Protein Secondary Structure. *Journal of Molecular Biology,* 216: 441–457.

Kneller, D.; Cohen, F.; and Langridge, R. 1990. Improvements in Protein Secondary Structure Prediction by an Enhanced Neural Network. *Journal of Molecular Biology,* 214: 171–182.

Kovačič, M. 1994. MILP-a Stochastic Approach to Inductive Logic Programming. In Proceedings of the Fourth International Workshop on Inductive Logic Programming, 123–138. Bonn, Germany: GMD.

Lavrač, N.; and Džeroski, S. 1994. *Inductive Logic Programming: Techniques and Applications.* Chichester, UK: Ellis Horwood.

Lavrač, N.; Džeroski, S.; Pirnat, V.; and Križman, V. 1993. The Utility of Background Knowledge in Learning Medical Diagnostic Rules. *Applied Artificial Intelligence,* 7: 273–293.

Lavrač, N.; Džeroski, S.; and Grobelnik, M. 1991. Learning Nonrecursive Definitions of Relations with LINUS. In Proceedings of the Fifth European Working Session on Learning, 265–281. Berlin: Springer-Verlag.

Lloyd, J. 1987. *Foundations of Logic Programming,* Second Edition. Berlin: Springer-Verlag.

Morik, K.; Wrobel, S.; Kietz, J.-U.; and W. Emde 1993. *Knowledge Acquisition and Machine Learning: Theory, Methods and Applications.* London: Academic Press.

Muggleton, S., ed. 1993. Proceedings of the Third International Workshop on Inductive Logic Programming. Ljubljana, Slovenia: Jožef Stefan Institute.

Muggleton, S., ed. 1992a. *Inductive Logic Programming.* London: Academic Press.

Muggleton, S., ed. 1992b. Proceedings of the Second International Workshop on Inductive Logic Programming. Tokyo: ICOT.

Muggleton, S., ed. 1991a. Proceedings of the International Workshop on Inductive Logic Programming. Porto, Portugal: University of Porto.

Muggleton, S. 1991b. Inductive Logic Programming. *New Generation Computing,* 8(4): 295–318.

Muggleton, S.; and Buntine, W. 1988. Machine Invention of First-Order Predicates by Inverting Resolution. In Proceedings of the Fifth International Conference on Machine Learning, 339–352. San Mateo, Calif.: Morgan Kaufmann.

Muggleton, S.; and De Raedt, L. 1994. Inductive Logic Programming: Theory and Methods. *Journal of Logic Programming,* 19/20: 629–679.

Muggleton, S.; and Feng, C. 1990. Efficient Induction of Logic Programs. In Proceedings of the First Conference on Algorithmic Learning Theory, 368–381. Tokyo: Ohmsha.

Muggleton, S.; King, R.; and Sternberg, M. 1992. Protein Secondary Structure Prediction Using Logic. *Protein Engineering,* 5: 647–657.

Muggleton, S. 1995. Inverse Entailment and Progol. *New Generation Computing (Special Issue on Inductive Logic Programming),* 13: 245–286.

Pazzani, M.; and Kibler, D. 1992. The Utility of Knowledge in Inductive Learning. *Machine Learning,* 9(1): 57–94.

Plotkin, G. 1969. A Note on Inductive Generalization. In *Machine Intelligence 5,* eds. B. Meltzer and D. Michie, 153–163. Edinburgh, UK: Edinburgh University Press.

Quinlan, J. 1993. *C4.5: Programs for Machine Learning.* San Mateo, Calif.: Morgan Kaufmann.

Quinlan, J. 1990. Learning Logical Definitions from Relations. *Machine Learning,* 5(3): 239–266.

Robinson, J. 1965. A Machine-oriented Logic Based on the Resolution Principle. *Journal of the ACM,* 12(1): 23–41.

Ruck, B.; Walley, W.; and Hawkes, H. 1993. Biological Classification of River Water Quality Using Neural Networks. In Proceedings of the Eight International Conference on Artificial Intelligence in Engineering, 361–372. Amsterdam, The Netherlands: Elsevier.

Sammut, C.; and Banerji, R. 1986. Learning Concepts by Asking Questions. In *Machine Learning: An Artificial Intelligence Approach,* Volume II, 167–191. eds. R. Michalski, J. Carbonell, and T. Mitchell. San Mateo, Calif.: Morgan Kaufmann.

Shapiro, E. 1983. *Algorithmic Program Debugging.* Cambridge, Mass.: The MIT Press.

Siou, E. 1994. A Bidirectional Search for Clauses. In Proceedings of the Fourth International Workshop on Inductive Logic Programming, 365–376. Bonn, Germany: GMD.

Srinivasan, A.; Muggleton, S.: King, R.; and Sternberg, M. 1994. Mutagenesis: ILP Experiments in a Non-determinate Biological Domain. In Proceedings of the Fourth International Workshop on Inductive Logic Programming, 217–232. Bonn, Germany: GMD.

Ullman, J. 1988. *Principles of Database and Knowledge Base Systems,* Volume I. Rockville, Mass.: Computer Science Press.

Walley, W.; Boyd, M.; and Hawkes, H. 1992. An Expert System for the Biological Monitoring of River Pollution. In Proceedings of the Fourth International Conference on the Development and Application of Computer Techniques to Environmental Studies, 1030–1047. Amsterdam, The Netherlands: Elsevier.

Wrobel, S., ed. 1994. Proceedings of the Fourth International Workshop on Inductive Logic Programming. Bonn, Germany: GMD.

6 Bayesian Classification (AutoClass): Theory and Results

Peter Cheeseman
RIACS, NASA Ames Research Center

John Stutz
NASA Ames Research Center

Abstract

We describe AutoClass, an approach to unsupervised classification based upon the classical mixture model, supplemented by a Bayesian method for determining the optimal classes. We include a moderately detailed exposition of the mathematics behind the AutoClass system.

We emphasize that no current unsupervised classification system can produce maximally useful results when operated alone. It is the interaction between domain experts and the machine searching over the model space, that generates new knowledge. Both bring unique information and abilities to the database analysis task, and each enhances the others' effectiveness. We illustrate this point with several applications of AutoClass to complex real world databases, and describe the resulting successes and failures.

6.1 Introduction

This chapter is a summary of our experience in using an automatic classification program (AutoClass) to extract useful information from databases. It also gives an outline of the principles that underlie automatic classification in general, and AutoClass in particular. We are concerned with the problem of automatic discovery of classes in data (sometimes called clustering, or unsupervised learning), rather than the generation of class descriptions from labeled examples (called supervised learning). In some sense, automatic classification aims at discovering the "natural" classes in the data. These classes reflect basic causal mechanisms that makes some cases look more like each other than the rest of the cases. The causal mechanisms may be as boring as sample biases in the data, or could reflect some major new discovery in the domain. Sometimes, these classes were well known to experts in the field, but unknown to AutoClass, and other times the classes were a surprise to the experts because they revealed something important about the domain that was previously unknown. Such discovery of previously unknown structure occurs most frequently when there are many relevant attributes describing each case, because humans are poor at seeing structure in a large number of dimensions.

We wish to emphasize that the discovery of important structure in data (classes) is rarely a one-shot process of throwing some database at AutoClass (or similar program) and getting back something useful. Instead, discovery of important structure is usually a *process* of finding classes, interpreting the results, transforming and/or augmenting the data, and repeating the cycle. In other words, the process of discovery of structure in databases is an example of the well known hypothesize-and-test cycle of normal scientific discovery. We believe that a strong interaction between the discovery program and the expert will be the common pattern in Knowledge Discovery in Databases (KDD) for the foreseeable future, because each have complementary strengths. A structure searching program like AutoClass can search huge amounts of data looking for multi-dimensional structures with a speed and accuracy that no human could hope to match. An expert, on the other hand, has domain knowledge that the program lacks. This enables the expert to interpret the results of the search in a way that computers cannot. Knowledge discovery is then an interactive process that involves finding patterns, interpreting them, generating new hypothesis, getting more data and then repeating the process. We shall illustrate this process through case studies from our experience in using AutoClass.

We first give a quick outline of what AutoClass does and how it does it, followed by a more detailed description of the theory and details. We then give a number of case studies of AutoClass in action.

6.2   Bayesian Classification

The word "classification" is ambiguous. Often it means assigning a new object/case to one of an existing set of possible classes. As used in this chapter, however, it means *finding* the classes themselves from a given set of "unclassified" objects/cases (unsupervised classification). Once such a set of classes has been found, they can be the basis for classifying new cases in the first sense.

In the Bayesian approach to unsupervised classification, the goal is to find the most probable set of class descriptions (a classification) given

$X = \{X_1, \ldots, X_I\}$	the set data instances X_i
$\vec{X}_i = \{X_{i1}, \ldots, X_{iK}\}$	the vector of attribute values X_{ik}, for instance X_i
i	indexes instances, $i = 1, \ldots, I$
j	indexes classes, $j = 1, \ldots, J$
k	indexes attributes, $k = 1, \ldots, K$
l	indexes discrete attribute values, $l = 1, \ldots, L$
c	indicates inter-class probabilities & parameters
S	denotes the space of allowed p.d.f.'s $\vec{V}, T$
$T = T_c, T_1, \ldots, T_J$	denotes the abstract mathematical form of the p.d.f.
$\vec{V} = \vec{V}_c, \vec{V}_1, \ldots, \vec{V}_J$	the set of parameter values instantiating a p.d.f.
π_j	class mixture probability, $\vec{V}_c = \{\pi_1, \ldots, \pi_J\}$
$\mathcal{I}$	implicit information not specifically represented

Table 6.1
Symbols used in this chapter.

the data and prior expectations. The introduction of priors automatically enforces a tradeoff between the fit to the data and the complexity of the class descriptions, giving an automatic form of Occam's razor (section 6.3.4). Alternate approaches, such as maximum likelihood, that try to find the class descriptions that best predict the data, have trouble because the best such classification is a set of single case classes, perfectly fitting each case, with a class for each unique case. This extreme "classification" has little predictive power for new cases.

6.2.1   AutoClass Model Overview

We limit ourselves to data for which instances can be represented as ordered vectors of attribute values. In principle, each attribute represents a measurement of some instance property common to all instances. These are "simple" properties in the sense that they can be represented by single measurements: discrete values such as "true" or "false," or integer values, or real numbers. For example, medical case #8, described as (age = 23, blood-type = A, weight = 73.4kg, ...) would have $X_{8,1} = 23$, $X_{8,2} = A$, etc. We make no attempt to deal with relational data where attributes, such as "married-to," have values that are other instances. Note however, that these limitations are solely a property of our specific method of modeling classes, and could be overcome by using more expressive models.

In discussing a probabilistic model, we refer to a probability distribution or density function (p.d.f.) that gives the probability of observing an instance possessing any particular attribute value vector. Ideally, such a model would take into account everything known about the processes potentially involved in generating and observing an instance. A Bayes Net relating input and output attributes would be suitable for instances of a well-understood process. For general KDD systems like AutoClass, where little is known about underlying processes, relatively simple statistical models are used.

Probabilistic models invariably contain free parameters, such as Bernoulli probabilities or the Gaussian mean and variance, which must either be fixed or removed (by integration) before instance probabilities can be computed. Thus it is useful distinguish between the p.d.f.'s functional form and its parameter values, and we denote these by T and $\vec{V}$ respectively. S will denote the space of allowed p.d.f.'s $\vec{V}, T$, while $\mathcal{I}$ denotes implicit information not specifically represented.

For AutoClass, our fundamental model is the classical finite mixture distribution. This is a two part model. The first gives the interclass mixture probability that an instance X_i is a member of class C_j, independently of anything else we may know of the instance:

$$\mathsf{P}(X_i \in C_j \mid \vec{V_c}, T_c, S, \mathcal{I}).$$

The interclass p.d.f. T_c is a Bernoulli distribution characterized by the class number J and the probabilities of $\vec{V_c}$. Each class C_j is then modeled by a class p.d.f., $\mathsf{P}(\vec{X_i} \mid X_i \in C_j, \vec{V_j}, T_j, S, \mathcal{I})$, giving the probability of observing the instance attribute values $\vec{X_i}$ conditional on the assumption that instance X_i belongs in class C_j. The class p.d.f. T_j is a product of individual or covariant attribute p.d.f.'s T_{jk}; e.g. Bernoulli distributions for nominal attributes, Gaussian densities for real numbers, Poisson distributions for number counts, etc. It is not necessary that the various T_j be identical, only that they all model the same subset of the instance attributes.

We differ from most other classifiers in that we never *assign* any instances to the classes. Instead we use a weighted assignment, weighting on the probability of class membership: $\mathsf{P}(\vec{X_i}, X_i \in C_j \mid \vec{V_j}, T_j, S, \mathcal{I})$. We hold that no finite amount of evidence can determine an instance's class membership. We further hold that the classification p.d.f. T and parameter values $\vec{V}$ constitute a more informative class description than any set of instance assignments. As a practical matter, the weighted assignment approach eliminates the brittle behavior that boundary surface instances can induce in classification systems that decide assignments. More importantly, it allows any user to apply decision rules appropriate to that user's current goals.

6.2.2   AutoClass Search Overview

Given a set of data X we seek two things: for any classification p.d.f. T we seek the maximum posterior (MAP) parameter values $\vec{V}$, and irrespective of any $\vec{V}$ we seek the most probable T. Thus there are two levels of search. For any fixed T specifying the number of classes and their class models, we search the space of allowed parameter values for the maximally probable $\vec{V}$. This is a real valued space of generally high dimension, subject to strong constraints between the parameters. There are many local maxima and we have no simple way to determine the global maximum except by generate and test. Thus parameter level search requires an expensive numerical optimization.

The model level search involves the number of classes J and alternate class models T_j. There are several levels of complexity. The basic level involves a single p.d.f. T_j common to all classes, with search over the number of classes. A second level allows the individual T_j to vary from class to class. Model level search is subject to the usual combinatorial explosion of possibilities as attribute number increases, but the Occam factor inherent in the Bayesian approach limits the probability of complex class models for any choice of model and non-delta priors (section 6.3.4).

Note that we have described the search problem for unsupervised classification. Supervised classification is much easier: since we already *know* the class assignments, the parameter level search reduces to a single step computation of the MAP parameter values. The model level search retains some of its combinatorial complexity, but with known class memberships we can seek the most probable model for each class individually. The additional information obtained by knowing the class assignments makes it much easier to explore the space of allowed class models, and obtain maximally informative class descriptions.

6.3   AutoClass in Detail

We begin with the standard assumption that the data instances X_i are conditionally independent given the classification p.d.f. $\vec{V}, T$. Thus we claim that any similarity between two instances is accounted for by their class memberships, and that there are no further interactions between data. Under this assumption the joint data probability is just the product of the individual instance probabilities.

6.3.1   AutoClass Basic Model

Our classification level, or interclass, model $\vec{V_c}, T_c$ is the classical Finite Mixture model of Everitt & Hand (1981) and Titterington et al. (1985). This postulates that each instance belongs to one and only one, unknown, member of a set of J classes C_j, with a probability $P(X_i \in C_j \mid \vec{V_c}, T_c, S, \mathcal{I})$. Note that this probability is independent of the instance attribute vector $\vec{X_i}$. In principle the classes constitute a discrete partitioning of the data, and thus the appropriate p.d.f. is a Bernoulli distribution. Its parameters $\vec{V_c}$ are a set of probabilities $\{\pi_1, \ldots, \pi_J\}$, constrained that $0 \le \pi_j \le 1$ and $\sum_j \pi_j = 1$. Thus we have:

$$P(X_i \in C_j \mid \vec{V_c}, T_c, S, \mathcal{I}) \equiv \pi_j. \tag{6.3.1}$$

Since the Dirichlet (multiple Beta) distribution is conjugate[1] to the Bernoulli, we use a uniform minimum information version for the prior probability distribution on the π_j:

$$P(\pi_1, \ldots, \pi_J \mid T_c, S, \mathcal{I}) \equiv \frac{\Gamma(J+1)}{[\Gamma(1+1/J)]^J} \prod_j \pi_j^{\frac{1}{J}} \tag{6.3.2}$$

The MAP parameter estimates for the supervised case, where I_j is the number of instances assigned to C_j, are then $\widehat{\pi}_j = (I_j + 1/J)/(I + 1)$.

The instances X_i from each class are assumed to possess attribute vectors $\vec{X_i}$ that are independently and identically distributed w.r.t. the class as $P(\vec{X_i} \mid X_i \in C_j, \vec{V_j}, T_j, S, \mathcal{I})$. The p.d.f. $\vec{V_j}, T_j$ thus gives the conditional probability that an instance X_i would have attribute values $\vec{X_i}$ if it were *known* that the instance is a member of class C_j. This class distribution function is a product of distributions modeling conditionally independent attributes k:[2]

---

[1] A conjugate prior is one which, when multiplied with the direct probability, gives a posterior probability having the same functional form as the prior, thus allowing the posterior to be used as a prior in further applications.

[2] For exposition we show all attributes as if independent, with independent p.d.f.'s and parameter priors. The shift to partially or fully covariant attributes is only a

$$P(\vec{X}_i \mid X_i \in C_j, \vec{V}_j, T_j, S, \mathcal{I}) = \prod_k P(X_{ik} \mid X_i \in C_j, \vec{V}_{jk}, T_{jk}, S, \mathcal{I}). \quad (6.3.3)$$

Individual attribute models $P(X_{ik} \mid X_i \in C_j, \vec{V}_{jk}, T_{jk}, S, \mathcal{I})$ include the Bernoulli and Poisson distributions, and Gaussian densities. They are detailed in the next section.

Combining the interclass and intraclass probabilities, we get the direct probability that an instance X_i with attribute values $\vec{X}_i$ is a member of class C_j:

$$P(\vec{X}_i, X_i \in C_j \mid \vec{V}_j, T_j, \vec{V}_c, T_c, S, \mathcal{I})$$
$$= \pi_j \prod_k P(X_{ik} \mid X_i \in C_j, \vec{V}_{jk}, T_{jk}, S, \mathcal{I}). \quad (6.3.4)$$

The normalized class membership probability is obtained from this by normalizing over the set of classes.

The probability of observing an instance X_i with attribute values $\vec{X}_i$, regardless of its class is then:

$$P(\vec{X}_i \mid \vec{V}, T, S, \mathcal{I}) = \sum_j (\pi_j \prod_k P(X_{ik} \mid X_i \in C_j, \vec{V}_{jk}, T_{jk}, S, \mathcal{I})). \quad (6.3.5)$$

Thus the probability of observing the database X is:

$$P(X \mid \vec{V}, T, S, \mathcal{I})$$
$$= \prod_i [\sum_j (\pi_j \prod_k P(X_{ik} \mid X_i \in C_j, \vec{V}_{jk}, T_{jk}, S, \mathcal{I}))]. \quad (6.3.6)$$

So far we've only described a classical finite mixture model. We convert this to a Bayesian model by introducing priors, at this point only on the parameters, obtaining the joint probability of the data and the parameter values:

$$P(X\vec{V} \mid TS\mathcal{I}) = P(\vec{V} \mid TS\mathcal{I})P(X \mid \vec{V}TS\mathcal{I}) \quad (6.3.7)$$
$$= \; P(\vec{V}_c \mid T_cS\mathcal{I}) \prod_{jk} [P(\vec{V}_{jk} \mid T_{jk}S\mathcal{I})]$$
$$\prod_i [\sum_j (\pi_j \prod_k P(X_{ik} \mid X_i \in C_j, \vec{V}_{jk}T_{jk}S\mathcal{I}))].$$

---

matter of bookkeeping.

6.3.2   AutoClass Search and Evaluation

We seek two things: For any given classification form $T = T_c, T_1, \ldots, T_J$ and data X, we want the MAP parameter values obtained from the parameters' posterior p.d.f.:

$$P(\vec{V} \mid X, T, S, \mathcal{I}) = \frac{P(X, \vec{V} \mid T, S, \mathcal{I})}{P(X \mid T, S, \mathcal{I})} = \frac{P(X, \vec{V} \mid T, S, \mathcal{I})}{\int d\vec{V}\, P(X, \vec{V} \mid T, S, \mathcal{I})}. \qquad (6.3.8)$$

Independently of the parameters, we want the MAP model form, conditional on the data, where the posterior probability of the p.d.f. form T is:

$$
\begin{aligned}
P(T \mid X, S, \mathcal{I}) \;&=\; \frac{P(T \mid S, \mathcal{I}) P(X \mid T, S, \mathcal{I})}{P(X \mid S, \mathcal{I})} \\[2mm]
&=\; \frac{P(T \mid S, \mathcal{I}) \int d\vec{V}\, P(X, \vec{V} \mid T, S, \mathcal{I})}{P(X \mid S, \mathcal{I})} \qquad (6.3.9) \\[2mm]
&\propto\; P(T \mid S, \mathcal{I}) \int d\vec{V}\, P(X, \vec{V} \mid T, S, \mathcal{I}) \qquad (6.3.10) \\[2mm]
&\propto\; \int d\vec{V}\, P(X, \vec{V} \mid T, S, \mathcal{I}) = P(X \mid T, S, \mathcal{I}). \qquad (6.3.11)
\end{aligned}
$$

The proportionality in (6.3.10) is due to dropping the normalizing constant $P(X \mid S, \mathcal{I})$, which is not generally computable. This is not a problem, since we are only interested in relative probabilities of a limited number of alternate models T. The proportionality in (6.3.11) holds when we take the prior probability $P(T \mid S, \mathcal{I})$ to be uniform over all T of interest. This is reasonable when we have no strong reason to favor one model over another. $P(T \mid S, \mathcal{I})$ is only a single discrete probability. In any but toy problems, the product over the data probabilities and/or the parameter priors will quite dominate any non-zero $P(T \mid X, S, \mathcal{I})$. Thus we implicitly use $P(T \mid S, \mathcal{I})$ to exclude models deemed impossible, by ignoring those models, and substitute $P(X \mid T, S, \mathcal{I})$ for $P(T \mid X, S, \mathcal{I})$ when making decisions.

Frustratingly, attempts to directly optimize over or integrate out the parameter sets $\vec{V}_{jk}$, in equation (6.3.7), founder on the J^I products resulting from the product over sums. Only minuscule data sets can be processed without approximation.

The classical application of the mixture assumption suggests a useful approach. If we *knew* the true class memberships, as in supervised classification, and augmented the instance vectors X_i with this information, the probabilities $P(X_i' \mid X_i' \in C_j, \vec{V}_j, T_j, S, \mathcal{I})$ would be zero whenever $X_i' \notin C_j$. The sum over j in equation (6.3.7) would degenerate into a single non-zero term. Merging the two products over k, and shifting the attribute product within, gives

$$P(X', \vec{V} \mid T, S, \mathcal{I})$$

$$= \quad P(\vec{V} \mid T, S, \mathcal{I}) \prod_j [\prod_{X_i' \in C_j} (\pi_j \prod_k P(X_{ijk}' \mid \vec{V}_{jk}, T_{jk}, S, \mathcal{I}))] \qquad (6.3.12)$$

$$= \quad P(\vec{V} \mid T, S, \mathcal{I}) \prod_j [\pi_j^{n_j} \prod_k P(X_{jk}'' \mid \vec{V}_{jk}, T_{jk}, S, \mathcal{I})] \qquad (6.3.13)$$

where n_j is the number of cases assigned to C_j, and the X_{jk}'' are sets of statistics, corresponding to attribute p.d.f.'s T_{jk}, obtained from the $X_i' \in C_j$.

This pure product form cleanly separates the classes with their member instances. Class parameters can be optimized or integrated out, without interaction with the other class's parameters. The same holds for the independent attribute terms within each class. Clearly, for supervised classification, the optimization and rating of a model is a relatively straightforward process. Unfortunately, this does not hold for unsupervised classification.

One could use the mixture assumption directly, applying this known assignment approach to every partitioning of the data into J non-empty subsets. But the number of such partitionings is Stirling's $S_I^{(J)}$, which approaches J^I for small J. This technique is only useful for verifying our approximations with extremely small data and class sets.

We are left with approximation. Since equations (6.3.4) and (6.3.7) are easily evaluated for *known* parameters, the obvious approach is a variation of the EM algorithm of Dempster et al. (1977) and Titterington et al. (1985). Given the set of class distributions T_j, and the current MAP estimates of the values for π_j and $\vec{V}_{jk}$, the normalized class conditional probabilities of equation (6.3.4) provide us with weighted assignments w_{ij} in the form of normalized class probabilities:

$$w_{ij} \equiv \frac{P(\vec{X}_i, X_i \in C_j \mid \vec{V}, T, S, \mathcal{I})}{\sum_j P(\vec{X}_i, X_i \in C_j \mid \vec{V}, T, S, \mathcal{I})}$$

$$\propto \quad \pi_j \prod_k P(X_{ik} \mid X_i \in C_j, \vec{V}_{jk}, T_{jk}, S, \mathcal{I}). \qquad (6.3.14)$$

We can use these instance weightings to construct weighted statistics corresponding to the known class case. For a discrete attribute, these are the class weighted number of instances possessing each discrete value w_{jkl}. For a real valued attribute modeled by a Gaussian, these are the class weighted number, mean, and variance:

$$w_j = \sum_i w_{ij};$$

$$m_{jk} = w_j^{-1} \sum_i w_{ij} X_{ik};$$

$$s_{jk}^2 = w_j^{-1} \sum_i w_{ij}(X_{ik} - m_{jk})^2. \tag{6.3.15}$$

Using these statistics as if they represented known assignment statistics permits reestimation of the parameters with the partitioning of equation (6.3.13). This new parameter set then permits reestimation of the normalized probabilities. Cycling between the two reestimation steps carries the current parameter and weight estimates toward a mutually predictive and locally maximal stationary point.

Unfortunately, there are usually numerous locally maximal stationary points. And excepting generate-and-test, we know of no method to find, or even count, these maxima—so we are reduced to search. Because the parameter space is generally too large to allow regular sampling, we generate pseudo-random points in parameter (or weight) space, converge to the local maximum, record the results, and repeat for as long as time allows.

Having collected a set of local maxima for model T, and eliminated the (often many) duplicates, we use the local statistics $X'' = \{w_j, X_{jk}''\}$ to approximate $P(X \mid T, S, \mathcal{I})$ using:

$$P(X'' \mid T, S, \mathcal{I})$$
$$\equiv \int d\vec{V} \, [P(\vec{V} \mid T, S, \mathcal{I}) \prod_j (\pi_j^{w_j} \prod_k P(X_{jk}'' \mid \vec{V}_{jk}, T_{jk}, S, \mathcal{I}))]. \tag{6.3.16}$$

However $P(X'' \mid T, S, \mathcal{I})$ cannot be used as a direct approximation to $P(X \mid T, S, \mathcal{I})$, because the equivalence between $P(X, V \mid T, S, \mathcal{I})$ and $P(X,'' V \mid T, S, \mathcal{I})$ holds only when the weights w_{ij} used to compute the X_{jk}'' are indicators: $w_{ij} \in \{0,1\}$ and $\sum_j w_{ij} = 1$. As the w_{ij} diverge from indicator values, $P(X'' \mid T, S, \mathcal{I})$ becomes significantly less than $P(X \mid T, S, \mathcal{I})$. This is easily seen by computing the ratio of the likelihoods given by the two methods at the MAP parameters $\widehat{V}$:

$$
\frac{\mathsf{P}(X \mid \widehat{V}, T, S, \mathcal{I})}{\mathsf{P}(X'' \mid \widehat{V}, T, S, \mathcal{I})}
$$

$$
= \frac{\prod_i [\sum_j (\widehat{\pi}_j \prod_k \mathsf{P}(X_{ik} \mid X_i \in C_j, \widehat{V_{jk}}, T_{jk}, S, \mathcal{I}))]}{\prod_j (\widehat{\pi}_j{}^{w_j} \prod_k \mathsf{P}(X''_{jk} \mid \widehat{V_{jk}}, T_{jk}, S, \mathcal{I}))}. \qquad (6.3.17)
$$

This ratio is is observed to approach 1 when the weights w_{ij} and parameters $\vec{V_{jk}}$ are mutually predictive *and* the weights approach indicator values. As values diverge from either condition, this ratio's value increases drastically. Thus we approximate $\mathsf{P}(X \mid T, S, \mathcal{I})$ as:

$$
\mathsf{P}(X \mid T, S, \mathcal{I})^* \equiv \mathsf{P}(X'' \mid T, S, \mathcal{I}) \frac{\mathsf{P}(X \mid \widehat{V}, T, S, \mathcal{I})}{\mathsf{P}(X'' \mid \widehat{V}, T, S, \mathcal{I})}. \qquad (6.3.18)
$$

This substitution of $\mathsf{P}(X \mid T, S, \mathcal{I})^*$ for $\mathsf{P}(X \mid T, S, \mathcal{I})$ is a gross simplification, and currently the weakest point in our development. Mathematically we are claiming that $\mathsf{P}(X \mid \vec{V}, T, S, \mathcal{I})$ and $\mathsf{P}(X'' \mid \vec{V}, T, S, \mathcal{I})$, taken as functions of $\vec{V}$, are everywhere in the same proportion as at the MAP value $\widehat{V}$. We have no reason to believe this claim. However, we find that both probabilities fall off rapidly, in orders of magnitude, as $\vec{V}$ diverges from the $\widehat{V}$. Moreover, the rate of this fall off is approximately exponential in the number of data. Thus for even moderate[3] amounts of data, the only significant contributions to either $\mathsf{P}(X \mid T, S, \mathcal{I})$ or $\mathsf{P}(X'' \mid T, S, \mathcal{I})$ come from the region of $\vec{V}$ near $\widehat{V}$, where the proportion is most likely to hold.

The $\mathsf{P}(X \mid T, S, \mathcal{I})^*$ defined above is computed for fixed X'' corresponding to a particular local $\widehat{V}$. For any given p.d.f. form T, we expect repeated EM searches to find diverse distinct stationary points, with corresponding distinct MAP parameter sets $\widehat{V}$. How then, can we claim that any one $\mathsf{P}(X \mid T, S, \mathcal{I})^*$ represents $\mathsf{P}(X \mid T, S, \mathcal{I})$, when the latter is supposed to be the integral over the full parameter space $\vec{V}$ and implicitly includes all weightings compatible with the data? Our experience shows that the largest $\mathsf{P}(X \mid T, S, \mathcal{I})^*$ can dominate the other peak integrals to a remarkable degree. Ratios between the two largest integrals of

---

[3]Moderate, in this context, may be taken to be of order 100 instances per class. This varies with the degree that T and $\widehat{V}$ give distinct classes, which may be characterized by the degree to which the w_{ij} approach indicator values.

10^4 to 10^9 are routine when the number of attribute values, $I \times K$, exceeds a few hundred. With a few million attribute values, the ratio may easily reach $e^{100} \approx 10^{44}$. In such circumstances we feel justified in reporting the largest known $\mathsf{P}(X' \mid T\,\mathcal{I})^*$ as a reasonable approximation to $\mathsf{P}(X \mid TS\,\mathcal{I})$, and in using it as our approximation to $\mathsf{P}(T \mid XS\,\mathcal{I})$. But it must be admitted that we have not proven that non-peak regions never make significant contribution to $\mathsf{P}(T \mid XS\,\mathcal{I})$, nor have we satisfactorily determined the conditions under which our assumptions hold.

When one or more subsets of n_m class p.d.f.'s T_j have identical functional form, the corresponding blocks of $\widehat{V_j}$ may be interchanged without altering $\mathsf{P}(X \mid T, S, \mathcal{I})$. In effect, the probability peak at $\widehat{V}$ possesses $n_m!$ mirror images. Thus for any such n_m, $\mathsf{P}(X \mid T, S, \mathcal{I})^*$ needs to be scaled by $n_m!$. The magnitude of this scaling is usually small relative to that of $\mathsf{P}(X \mid T, S, \mathcal{I})^*$, but may be significant when comparing T with very different numbers of classes.

Thus we rate the various models T by their best $\mathsf{P}(X \mid TS\,\mathcal{I})^*$ and report on them in terms of the corresponding MAP parameterizations $\widehat{V}$. If one model's marginal dominates all others, it is our single best choice for classifying the database. Otherwise we report the several that do dominate.

6.3.3   AutoClass Attribute Models

Each class model is a product of conditionally independent probability distributions over singleton and/or covariant subsets of the attributes. For the medical example given in section 6.2.1, blood type is a discrete valued attribute which we model with a Bernoulli distribution while age and weight are both scalar real numbers that we model with a log-Gaussian density.

The only hard constraint is that all class models, used in any classifications that are to be compared, must model the same attribute set. Attributes deemed irrelevant to a particular classification cannot simply be ignored, since this would affect the marginal probabilities, as is shown below.

AutoClass provides basic models for simple discrete (nominal) and several types of numerical data. We have not yet identified a satisfactory distribution function for ordered discrete (ordinal) data. In each case we adopt a minimum or near minimum information prior, the choice being limited among those providing integrable marginals. This limitation has seriously retarded development of the more specific models, but numerical integration is considered to be too costly for EM convergence.

In the following we describe in detail the basic elements of the independent Bernoulli and Gaussian models, and note other attribute probability distributions that we use to assemble the class models.

- Discrete valued attributes (sex, blood-type, ...)—Bernoulli distributions with uniform Dirichlet conjugate prior. For the singleton case with L_k possible values, the parameters are $\vec{V}_{jk} \equiv \{q_{jk1} \cdots q_{jkL_k}\}$, such that $0 \leq q_{jkl} \leq 1$, $\sum_l^{L_k} q_{jkl} = 1$, where

$$P(X_{ik} = l \mid X_i \in C_j, \vec{V}_{jk}, T_{jk}, S, \mathcal{I}) \equiv q_{jkl} \tag{6.3.19}$$

$$P(q_{jk1}, \ldots, q_{jkL_k} \mid T_{jk}, S, \mathcal{I}) \equiv \frac{\Gamma(L_k + 1)}{[\Gamma(1 + \frac{1}{L_k})]^{L_k}} \prod_{l=1}^{L_k} q_{jkl}^{\frac{1}{L_k}} \tag{6.3.20}$$

$$\widehat{q}_{jkl} = \frac{w_{jkl} + \frac{1}{L_k}}{w_j + 1} \tag{6.3.21}$$

For the covariant case, say sex and blood type jointly, we apply the above model to the cross product of individual attribute values. Thus female and type A would form a single value in the cross product. The number of such values, and thus the number of parameters required, is the product of the individual attribute's L_k . However the prior of equation (6.3.20) severely limits the probability of large covariant p.d.f.'s, as discussed in section 6.3.4.

- Real valued location attributes (spatial locations)—Gaussian densities with either a uniform or Gaussian prior on the means. We use a Jeffreys prior (6.3.24) on a singleton attribute's standard deviation, and the inverse Wishart distribution (Box & Tiao 1973) as the variance prior of covariant attribute subsets. For a single attribute with uniform priors, using the statistics defined in equation (6.3.15):

$$P(X_{ik} \mid X_i \in C_j, \mu_{jk}, \sigma_{jk}, T_{jk}, S, \mathcal{I}) \frac{1}{\sqrt{2\pi}\sigma_{jk}} e^{-\frac{1}{2}\left(\frac{X_{ik} - \mu_{jk}}{\sigma_{jk}}\right)^2}, \tag{6.3.22}$$

$$P(\mu_{jk} \mid T_{jk}, S, \mathcal{I}) = \frac{1}{\mu_{k_{max}} - \mu_{k_{min}}}, \widehat{\mu}_{jk} = m_{jk}, \qquad (6.3.23)$$

$$P(\sigma_{jk} \mid T_{jk}, S, \mathcal{I}) = \sigma_{jk}^{-1} \left[\log \frac{\sigma_{k_{max}}}{\sigma_{k_{min}}} \right]^{-1}, \widehat{\sigma}_{jk}^2 = s_{jk}^2 \frac{w_j}{w_j + 1}. \qquad (6.3.24)$$

- Real valued scalar attributes (age, weight)—Log-Gaussian density model obtained by applying the Gaussian model to $\log(X_{ik} - min_k)$. See Aitchison & Brown (1957).

- Bounded real valued attributes (probabilities)—Gaussian Log-Odds obtained by applying the Gaussian to $\log((X_{ik} - min_k) / (max_k - X_{ik}))$ (under development).

- Circular or angular real valued attributes—von Mises-Fisher distributions on the circle and n-sphere (under development) See Mardia et al. (1979).

- Integer count valued attributes—Poisson distribution with uniform prior per Loredo (1992). No covariant form has been developed.

- Missing values—Discrete valued attribute sets are extended to include "missing" as an additional attribute value, to be modeled as any other value. Numerical attributes use a binary discrete probability q_{jk} for "missing" and $1 - q_{jk}$ for "known," with the standard numerical model conditioned on the "known" side. With the Gaussian model this gives:

$$P(X_{ik} = missing \mid X_i \in C_j, q_{jk}, \mu_{jk}, \sigma_{jk}, T_{jk}, S, \mathcal{I}) \equiv q_{jk}, \quad (6.3.25)$$

$$P(X_{ik} = r \mid X_i \in C_j, q_{jk}, \mu_{jk}, \sigma_{jk}, T_{jk}, S, \mathcal{I})$$

$$\equiv \frac{(1-q_{jk})}{\sqrt{2\pi}\sigma_{jk}} e^{-\frac{1}{2}\left(\frac{r-\mu_{jk}}{\sigma_{jk}}\right)^2}. \qquad (6.3.26)$$

- Hierarchical models—represent a reorganization of the standard mixture model, from a flat structure, where each class is fully independent, to a tree structure where multiple classes can share one or more model terms. A class is then described by the attribute model nodes along the branch between root and leaf. This makes it possible to avoid duplicating essentially identical attribute distributions common to several classes. The advantage of such hierarchical models lies in eliminating excess parameters, thereby increasing the model posterior. See Hanson et al. (1991) for a full description of our approach. Other approaches are possible: see Boulton & Wallace (1973).

- Irrelevant attributes—Irrelevant attributes pose a problem which we have only recently recognized. If an attribute is deemed irrelevant to *all* classification models under consideration, it can simply be deleted from the database. If an attribute is deemed irrelevant to only some of the models, one is tempted to simply eliminate it from consideration by those models, and to model it in the others. This is what we have done in AutoClass, but it is an error.

Consider two models $\vec{V}_j, T_j$ and $\vec{V}_j{}', T_j'$, identical in both form and parameter values except that the latter includes an additional $\vec{V}_{jk'}{}', T_{jk'}'$, modeling one additional attribute k'. Let $T_{jk'}'$ be any appropriate p.d.f. except a delta function, Then for any instance X_i:

$$\mathsf{P}(\vec{X}_i \mid X_i \in C_j, \vec{V}_j, T_j, S, \mathcal{I})$$
$$> \mathsf{P}(\vec{X}_i \mid X_i \in C_j', \vec{V}_j{}', T_j', S, \mathcal{I}). \tag{6.3.27}$$

This is a simple consequence of the fact that a non-delta p.d.f. cannot predict any value with probability 1. Taken to the limit, we find that a class model which ignores all attributes will always be more probable than one which models any attributes. Obviously, the results of modeling with different attribute sets are incommensurable.

How should we handle irrelevant attributes? For a classifier, an attribute is irrelevant when all classes possess identical p.d.f.'s for that attribute. In the hierarchical model described above, this can be achieved by pushing the attribute model $\vec{V}_{jk}, T_{jk}$ up to the root node, where it is inherited by all leaves. In an ordinary mixture model the same effect can be obtained by using a common T_{jk} with every $\vec{V}_{jk}$ fixed at the MAP values estimated from a single class classification model. This will suffice for the case when all classes within a classification ignore the attribute, and allow comparison between classifications that deem different attribute subsets irrelevant. The case where only some classes within a classification ignore an attribute is yet undecided.

In principle, our classification model should also include a prior distribution $P(T \mid S, \mathcal{I})$ on the number of classes present and the individual class model forms T_j. Currently we take this distribution to be uniform and drop it from our calculations. Thus we ignore any prior information on alternate classification model probabilities, relying solely on our parameter priors for the Occam factor preventing over fitting of the models. We find this quite sufficient.

6.3.4   The Occam Factor

We have several times mentioned an "Occam Factor," implying that Bayesian parameter priors can somehow prevent the over fitting that is a problem with maximum likelihood optimization of any kind of probabilistic model. Consider that every single parameter introduced into a Bayesian model brings its own multiplicative prior to the joint probability, which *always* lowers the marginal. If a parameter fails to raise the marginal by increasing the direct probability by a greater factor than the prior lowers the marginal, we reject the model incorporating that parameter. In the mixture models used by AutoClass, each class requires a full set of attribute model parameters, each with its own prior. Those priors always favor classifications with smaller numbers of classes, and do so overwhelmingly, once the number of classes exceeds some small fraction[4] of the database size.

Similar effects limit model complexity within the classes. Simple independent attribute models are usually favored simply because they require fewer parameters than the corresponding covariant models. Ten real valued attributes require 20 parameters for modeling with independent Gaussians, and 55 for the full covariant Gaussian. Ten binary discrete attributes also require 20 parameters for modeling with independent Bernoulli distributions, but 1024 are needed for a fully covariant Bernoulli distribution. One needs a great many very highly covariant instances to raise a fully covariant model's marginal above the independent model's.

Both of the foregoing effects are confirmed throughout our experience with AutoClass. For data sets of a few hundred to a few thousand instances, class models with large order covariant terms are generally rated far lower than those combining independent and/or small order

---

[4]Typically of order 1%, but potentially larger for very distinct classes.

covariant terms. We have yet to find a case where the most probable number of classes was not a small fraction of the number of instances classified. Nor have we found a case where the most probable number of model parameters was more than a small fraction of the total number of attribute values. Over fitting simply does not occur when Bayesian mixture models are correctly applied.

6.3.5   The AutoClass Implementation

AutoClass was written in Lisp, taking full advantage of the extraordinary programming environment provided by the Symbolics Lisp Machine. It has been adapted to operate in most Lisp environments, and a data parallel version exists for star-Lisp on the CM-3. A C translation is in preparation. Some details regarding the computational considerations encountered in implementing AutoClass will be found in Stutz & Cheeseman (1995). A NASA technical report giving fuller details of the mathematics and implementation is in preparation.

6.4   Case Studies

6.4.1   Infrared Astronomical Satellite (IRAS) Data.

The first major test of AutoClass on a large scale real-world database was the application of AutoClass to the IRAS Low Resolution Spectral Atlas. This atlas consisted of 5425 mean spectra of IRAS point sources. Each spectrum consists of 100 "blue" channels in the range 7 to 14 microns, and another 100 "red" channels in the range from 10 to 24 microns. Of these 200 channels, only 100 contain usable data. These point source spectra covered a wide range of intensities, and showed many different spectral distributions. We applied AutoClass to this spectral database by treating each of the 100 spectral channels (intensities) as an independent normally distributed single real value. The log-normal model is preferable for such scalar data, but several percent of the reported intensity values were negative. Also, adjacent spectral values are expected to be highly correlated, but it was not obvious how to incorporate neighbor correlation information. Thus we knew from the beginning that we were missing important information, but we were curious how well AutoClass would do despite this handicap.

Our very first attempts to apply AutoClass to the spectral data did not produce very good results, as was immediately apparent from visual inspection. Fortunately, inspection also exposed the cause of the problem. The spectra we were given had been "normalized"—in this case normalization meant scaling the spectra so that all had the same peak height. This normalization meant that noisy spectra were artificially scaled up (or down) depending on whether the noise at the peak was higher or lower than the average. Since all values in a single spectrum were scaled by the same constant, an incorrect scaling constant distorted all spectral values. Also, spectra with a single strong peak were scaled so that the rest of the spectrum was close to the noise level. We solved the "normalization problem" by renormalizing the data ourselves so that area under all the curves is the same. This method of normalization is much less sensitive to noise than the peak normalization method.

The experts who provided us with this data tried to make life easy for us by only giving us the brightest spectra from 1/4 of the sky (without telling us about this sampling bias). When we found this out, we requested all the spectra in the atlas to work with. Because this larger atlas included much noisier spectra, we found a new problem—some spectral intensities were negative. A negative intensity, or measurement, is physically impossible, so these values were a mystery. After much investigation, we finally found out that the processing software had subtracted a "background" value from all spectra. This pre-processing, of course, violates the basic maxim that analysis should be performed on the data actually measured, and all "corrections" should be done in the statistical modeling step.

Once these problems had been removed, we used AutoClass II to classify all 5425 spectra. The results of this classification are presented in Cheeseman et al. (1989), and it revealed many interesting new discoveries. The first observation is that the AutoClass classes (77 of them) gave a significantly different classification than that previously provided with the atlas. This earlier IRAS spectral classification was based on expected features and human generated criteria based on visual inspection. AutoClass was able to make many subtle distinctions between spectra that superficially look similar, and these distinctions were not previously known. Some of the classes, such as the blackbody emission classes, and the silicate emission classes were known from previous studies, but the fine distinctions within these broad classes were not previously known.

The IRAS spectral classification also revealed other astronomically significant results. For example, by finding which classes the few known carbon stars occurred in, we were able to triple the number of known (or suspected) carbon stars. AutoClass also revealed a large number of blackbody stars with a significant IR excess, presumably due to dust surrounding the star. Another indirect result of the classification is that the average spectral intensities of a class cancel the noise present in single spectra, making finer detail visible. For example, this noise suppression revealed a very weak spectral "bump" at 13 microns in some classes that is completely invisible in the individual spectra. Many of these discoveries are discussed in Goebel et al. (1989).

The AutoClass classification was sufficiently good, that it revealed problems with the data that had been previously missed. In particular, some of the blackbody sub-classes showed an excess of energy at the blue end of the spectrum. There is no plausible physical mechanism that could produce such a blue excess in blackbody stars, so this result was a mystery. Eventually, we discovered that this excess was the result of incorrect calibration. Originally, Vega (a 10,000 degree star) was chosen as the reference star, but later in the mission the reference star was switched to α Tau (a 4000 degree star). Unfortunately, the software was not altered to reflect this change, thus causing the calibration error. Of course, none of this change information was documented, so it took considerable search for us to find the cause.

Other calibration errors and artifacts of the data processing also gradually came to light as we discussed our results with the domain experts. In particular, we found out that the spectra were often contaminated with cosmic ray "spikes," and that a "filter" in the software removed these spikes from the data before averaging the different spectra together. Unfortunately, this filter could not tell the difference between a strong spectral line and a cosmic ray hit, so it often eliminated perfectly good spectra and yet still passed contaminated spectra. Again the lesson to be drawn from this experience is that the raw observation data should be made available, and effects such as cosmic rays and background noise should be statistically modeled—the data itself should not be modified!

6.4.2 IRAS Lessons

A major lesson of our IRAS experience is that experts tend to pass on only the minimum information that they think the data analyst needs. They are attempting to be helpful—but in practice they are not treating the analyst as a full partner. We kept finding new unexplained results, and only by confronting the experts with them would they reveal other sources of data, or processing steps they had neglected to mention. Finally, in frustration, we insisted that our experts give us *all* the data that they had, and *all* the documentation on the data processing that had been performed instead of feeding it to us piecemeal. Even then we found out about other data (e.g. star variability index), that could have aided the classification, well after we had published our classification. We believe that a data analyst using tools like AutoClass must become moderately expert in the field. This is in order to understand all the biases in the data collection; to understand the processing that occurred before the data was made available for analysis; to ensure that all the relevant data has been located; and to aid the interpretation process.

Another major lesson learned from the IRAS experience is that finding new and interesting results (classes) is not enough—unless some plausible interpretation of these results can be found, they will probably be ignored. This interpretation step often involves follow up data or analysis to test possible hypotheses. As an example, we discovered subtle distinctions in the silicate emission spectra (e.g. classes $\beta 1$ and $\beta 11$ in Cheeseman et al. (1989),) and needed to explain these differences. Since the creators of the IRAS atlas had provided visual matches for each point source, we used this data to see how stellar type related to the discovered classes. Also, the average galactic latitude of the classes was significantly different, indicating that one class is more distant, and intrinsically brighter. The most likely interpretation of these results is that there are different classes of M-giants, with different galactic distributions, and these classes can be distinguished by subtle differences in their infrared spectra. Note that we could do this follow up investigation relatively easily because the IRAS spectral atlas included considerable auxiliary data about each point-source (galactic coordinates, variability, optical identification, etc.).

Finding the classes in a database is only part of the task—the remaining task is to communicate the class descriptions to the expert. AutoClass generates reports that fully describe the classes, but these can be difficult to interpret for a novice. In the IRAS classification case, we generated spectral plots that displayed the class spectral values graphically. This graphical output is shown in Cheeseman et al. (1989), and is immediately understood by domain experts. We also classified the classes (a meta-classification) and used these meta-classes to organize the full classification. The experts found this meta-classification very helpful. We cannot over-emphasize the importance of generating easily understood outputs, but unfortunately, really good outputs tend to be domain specific.

6.4.3   DNA Intron Data

This project began when we received a database of about 3000 donor and acceptor sites (intron/exon boundaries) from human DNA. In most species, the DNA that codes for a particular protein (a gene) is broken up by the insertion of stretches of DNA (introns) that are spliced out of the corresponding messenger RNA before it is used to produce proteins. The segments of DNA that contribute to the final RNA are called exons. The beginning of exon/intron boundary is called the donor site, and the corresponding intron/exon end is called the acceptor site. The intron length (between a donor and an acceptor site) can vary from a minimum of about 80 bases, to many thousands of bases. The donor database consisted of an ordered list of the possible bases (A,G,C,T) at the 10 bases before the splice site, and 40 bases of the adjoining intron (and similarly for the acceptor site database). It has been traditionally assumed that in human DNA there is only one general type of donor and acceptor site, because they all use the same splicing machinery. We decided to test this assumption by applying AutoClass to both the donor and acceptor databases separately.

Our initial classification revealed many classes that describe essentially one unique base sequence per class. In other words, there are splice sites that are practically duplicated many times in human DNA. Further investigation showed that most of these nearly identical sites occurred in the same gene, usually in an uninterrupted sequence. When the nearly identical sites occur in different genes, these genes were found to be practically identical as a result of gene duplication. Since duplication within a gene, and duplication of genes themselves is well known in the molecular biology community, these very tight classes were of no interest.

In order to eliminate the duplication problem, we pruned the data to eliminate all sequences that had greater than 50% identity. This pruning reduced our data by roughly 30%, and allowed AutoClass to find 3 classes in the remaining data (for both the donor and acceptor sites). Inspection of these classes showed a very obvious pattern. For the largest class (about 33%) *every* position in both donors and acceptors was "C rich"—that is, every position had a significantly higher probability of having a C than the global average. The other 2 classes (donor and acceptor) were TA rich and G rich respectively. Note that this pattern was discovered even though AutoClass was treating each position independently, indicating a strong causal mechanism producing this uniform base bias. This base bias even extended into the exon region, although the signal was much weaker there. This is surprising, because the choice of bases in an exon is thought to be dictated entirely by its corresponding biological function through the protein it encodes.

Having found these clear classes, we entered the next phase of data analysis: trying to interpret the discovered pattern. One question that occurred to us was whether the class of donor site was correlated with the class of the corresponding acceptor site. Unfortunately, our original databases did not record the corresponding sites in the separate donor and acceptor databases. Also, the original databases were extracted from a very old version of GenBank, using obscure (and irreproducible) filtering techniques. We were fortunate in finding collaborators in the Stanford University Molecular Biology Lab[5], who extracted all human introns (with flanking exons) from the current version of GenBank for us. This gave us a much larger database, and all the auxiliary information we needed to do followup studies.

Our followup studies revealed the following:

- The class of a donor site was indeed highly correlated with the corresponding acceptor site. For the C-rich class, for example, not only were both the donor and acceptor sites C-rich, but the entire intron between them was C-rich. A similar pattern was observed for the other classes.

- The same classes were observed in mouse genes, and where there are corresponding genes in mice and humans, they have the same classes, indicating that whatever created the pattern we observed has persisted for at least 60 million years.

- The base-frequency pattern extends into the flanking exons, but not as strongly as that observed in the introns.

---

[5]Our collaborators were Doug Brutlag and Tod Klingler

- If one intron is, say, TA rich, then there is a high probability that any neighboring introns will also be TA rich.

From these observations, we can reasonably conclude that DNA gene relative base frequency patterns can persist for long stretches (in some cases many thousands of bases). Also, these base frequencies occur in other species and the frequency type is preserved throughout evolution. Recent sequencing of whole chromosomes (from yeast and worms) show similar long stretches of G + C rich (or poor) variation, on both coding and non-coding regions. All of these observations point toward some unknown essential mechanism that operates on DNA and creates/maintains/uses these base frequency patterns. Note that Auto-Class, combined with human interpretation and additional testing found this general pattern, even though it extends well beyond the original very restricted database. Unfortunately, these results have not been published, so these discoveries remain unknown to the molecular biology community.

6.4.4   LandSat Data

The largest database that we have applied AutoClass to is a 1024×1024 array of LandSat pixels, where each pixel records 7 spectral intensities from a 30m square ground patch. Our test image covers about a 30km square region in Kansas, taken by the LandSat/TM satellite in August 1989. Our goal was to find classes in this set of over 1 million "cases" (i.e. pixels). This large image data set put such strong computational demands on our standard LISP AutoClass (running on a Symbolics machine) that we developed a parallel version of AutoClass (in LISP) to run on a Connection machine, and later on a CM-2. Fortunately, the structure of AutoClass lends itself to parallelization, so that recent parallel versions allow large database processing in reasonable time.

Instead of treating each spectral value independently within a class (as we did in early versions of AutoClass), we allowed the values to be fully correlated with each other, with separate correlations for each class. The theory behind this correlated version of AutoClass is presented in Hanson et al. (1991). This model still assumes that the pixels are independent of their neighbors. That is, we do not take into account the spatial correlation of neighboring pixels, even though we know this is a strong source of additional information. We did this only because

AutoClass is a general purpose tool that cannot be easily modified to fit the known structure of a new domain. We are currently investigating methods for integrating spatial correlation information from multiple images.

Like other case studies described in this chapter, the results from LandSat data classification were improved significantly by transforming the data (preprocessing), so that the assumptions built into AutoClass better fit the input data. In the case of LandSat pixels, it is well known that the observed intensity of a patch on the ground is affected by the ground slope of that patch. This means that if we attempt a classification on the given observed intensities, we get different classes for the same ground cover type, depending on their particular ground slopes. For this reason, it is better to use the *ratio* of spectral intensities for each pixel instead, since the ratio is not affected by a common scaling factor, such as the ground slope effect. For all pixels, we replaced the given spectral values with the ratio of the spectral value to the sum of all spectral values (for that pixel). Note that this transformation of the data does not destroy information, since the original values can be recovered (to within numerical noise). Since the spectral ratios are strictly positive (i.e. they are scale parameters), we assume that their value distribution is log-normally distributed, so we use Log(spectral ratio) as our input data.

Readers may wonder why we rail against preprocessing of data by others, yet do the same thing ourselves. Our answer is twofold. Firstly, we encourage transformations of the data that do not destroy information (reversible transformations), if this makes the transformed data better fit the assumptions of the particular data analysis technique being used. Secondly, our major objection is to *undocumented* preprocessing, especially when the informal data description does not match the data as given.

Before we ran AutoClass on our transformed data, we histogramed the Log(spectral ratio) values to see if our log-normal distribution was reasonable. We were surprised to find that the data values were highly quantized, with large numbers of pixels having exactly the same value. Further investigation revealed that although the original spectral intensity values were recorded at 8-bit accuracy, most pixels were assigned to a much smaller range of intensity bins. That is, although there were 256 possible intensity values, in practice only a very small subset of these values were observed. This is because the camera's dynamic range was selected to record the extreme values of intensity (to avoid saturation effects), so that nearly all values occur within a much smaller range. We "dithered" these values by adding small random errors with a standard deviation of 1/2 a bin width, thus "smoothing" the data values. This dithering corrupted the data, but it avoided problems associated with the strong quantization effect.

The results of classifying all the pixel intensity data, using full correlation between the spectral values in each class description, are presented in Kanefsky et al. (1994). This classification found 93 classes in the best classification, and these classes were themselves classified to produce a meta-classification. This meta-classification makes the individual classes easier to interpret. By far the greatest aid to interpreting these pixel classes is to threshold the class membership probability so as to assign each pixel to its most probable class, then to plot the 2-D distribution of the resulting classes. For many classes, these 2-D plots immediately suggest an interpretation to the human eye, such as roads, rivers, valley bottoms, valley edges, fields of particular crops, etc. Other classes (with many fewer members) seem to contain pixels with a mixture of basic types. For example, a pixel partially falling on a highway, and partially falling on surrounding grass, results in a mixed pixel. If there are enough of these mixed pixels, with roughly the same mixing proportion, they form a class of their own. Clearly, in the mixed pixel case, the classes are not particularly meaningful, but it is surprising that the majority of classes seem to be composed of pure pixels of a single type.

We find that applying a general purpose classification tool like AutoClass can produce interesting and meaningful classes, even when the tool's basic assumptions do not fit the data very well. In particular, failing to take neighbor pixel class correlation into account, and the assumption that every pixel belongs to one and only one class, do not fit the LandSat pixel data well, yet the results are surprisingly good. A better classification of LandSat type data requires a special purpose classification tool that takes into account the known properties of the domain.

6.5   Summary of Lessons Learned

The above case studies illustrate a number of lessons learned in applying AutoClass to real databases. We summarize these lessons as follows:

- *Data analysis/Knowledge discovery is a process.* Discovery of patterns in data is only the beginning of a cycle of interpretation followed by more testing.

- *General data mining tools are only good for exploratory analysis.* Once the initial patterns have suggested new domain specific hypotheses, these hypotheses need to be further investigated using tools adapted to the hypotheses.

- *Beware undocumented or irreversible data preprocessing.* Key terms that may indicate information destroying pre-processing include calibrated, corrected, averaged, normalized, adjusted, compressed, and so forth.

- *Beware hidden biases in data collection.* Such bias may dominate the resulting classes, as in the initial Intron classes.

- **Difficulty in extracting data from experts.** Experts tend to supply only the information they think is needed. An analyst must become a mini-expert in the domain to really understand the data.

- *Data transformation to fit analysis tool.* These transformations can greatly aid pattern discovery. Try different representations. Try different pattern discovery tools.

- *Visually inspecting the data before use.* This step usually catches gross errors and obvious patterns.

- **Unsupervised classification versus supervised classification.** Discovery of (unsupervised) classes may or may not be of help in predicting a target variable.

- *Domain-specific display of resulting classes.* What your program outputs is all that the domain expert sees. To make that output useful, it is necessary to provide display and interpretation appropriate to the specific problem domain.

Acknowledgments

We thank Will Taylor, Mathew Self, Robin Hanson, Bob Kanefsky, Jim Kelley, Don Freeman, and Chris Wallace, without whose help AutoClass would not be half so useful as it is today. We are also indebted to too many to mention, for the questions and problem domains that have forced us to extend and refine our ideas and understanding.

References

Aitchison, J. and Brown, J. A. C. 1957. *The Lognormal Distribution.* Cambridge: Cambridge University Press.

Boulton, D. M.; and Wallace, C. S. 1973. An Information Measure of Hierarchic Classification. *Computer Journal,* 16(3): 57-63.

Box, G. E. P.; and Tiao, G. C. 1973. *Bayesian Inference in Statistical Analysis.* Reading, Mass.: Addison-Wesley.

Cheeseman, P.; Stutz, J.; Self, M.; Taylor, W.; Goebel, J.; Volk, K.; and Walker, H. 1989. Automatic Classification of Spectra From the Infrared Astronomical Satellite (IRAS), NASA Reference Publication #1217, National Technical Information Service, Springfield, Virginia.

Dempster, A. P.; Laird, N. M.; and Rubin, D. B. 1977. Maximum Likelihood from Incomplete Data Via the EM Algorithm. *Journal of the Royal Statistical Society, Series B,* 39(1): 1-38.

Everitt, B. S.; and Hand, D. J. 1981. *Finite Mixture Distributions.* London: Chapman and Hall.

Goebel, J.; Volk, K.; Walker, H.; Gerbault, F.; Cheeseman, P.; Self, M.; Stutz, J.; and Taylor, W. 1989. A Bayesian Classification of the IRAS LRS Atlas. *Astronomy and Astrophysics* 222, L5-L8.

Hanson, R., Stutz, J., and Cheeseman, P. 1991. Bayesian Classification with Correlation and Inheritance. In Twelfth International Joint Conference on Artificial Intelligence, 692-698. San Mateo, Calif.: Morgan Kaufmann.

Kanefsky, B., Stutz, J., and Cheeseman, P. 1994. An Improved Automatic Classification of a Landsat/TM Image From Kansas (FIFE). Technical Report, FIA-94-01, NASA Ames Research Center, Moffet Field, California.

Loredo, T. 1992. The Promise of Bayesian Inference for Astrophysics. *In Statistical Challenges in Modern Astronomy,* ed. E. Feigelson and G. Babu. New York: Springer-Verlag.

Mardia, K. V.; Kent, J. T.; and Bibby, J. M. 1979. *Multiavariant Analysis*. New York: Academic Press.

Stutz, J.; and Cheeseman, P. 1994. AutoClass—a Bayesian Approach to Classification. *In Maximum Entropy and Bayesian Methods, Cambridge, 1994,* eds. J. Skilling and S. Sibisi. Dordrecht, The Netherlands: Kluwer Academic Publishers.

Titterington, D. M.;, Smith, A. F. M.; and Makov, U. E. 1985. *Statistical Analysis of Finite Mixture Distributions*. New York: John Wiley & Sons.

7 Discovering Informative Patterns and Data Cleaning

Isabelle Guyon, Nada Matić, and Vladimir Vapnik
AT&T Bell Laboratories

Abstract

We present a method for discovering informative patterns from data. With this method, large databases can be reduced to only a few representative data entries. Our framework also encompasses methods for cleaning databases containing corrupted data. Both on-line and off-line algorithms are proposed and experimentally checked on databases of handwritten images. The generality of the framework makes it an attractive candidate for new applications in knowledge discovery.

7.1 Introduction

Databases often contain redundant data. It would be convenient if large databases could be replaced by only a subset of informative patterns. A difficult, yet important, problem is to define what informative patterns are. We use the learning theoretic definition (Rissanen 1989; Haussler, Kearns, & Schapire, 1991; MacKay, 1992) given a model trained on a sequence of patterns, a new pattern is informative if it is difficult to predict by a model trained on previously seen data. With that definition, we derive on-line and batch algorithms for discovering informative patterns. The techniques are developed for classification problems, but are also applicable to regression and density estimation problems.

Informative patterns are often intermixed with other "bad" outliers which correspond to errors introduced non-intentionally in the database. For databases containing errors, our algorithms can be used for computer-aided data cleaning, with or without supervision. We review results of several experiments in handwriting recognition (Boser, Guyon, & Vapnik 1992; Matić et al 1992; Guyon et al 1992; Matić et al 1993;) which demonstrate the usefulness of our data cleaning techniques.

7.2 Discovering Informative Patterns

In this section, we assume that the data is perfectly clean. First, we give an intuition of what informative patterns ought to be. Then, we show that this intuition coincides with the information theoretic definition. Finally, we derive algorithms to discover informative patterns.

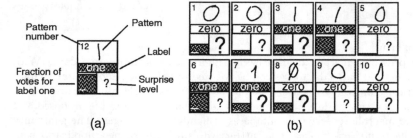

(a)   (b)

Figure 7.1
Small example database containing "zeros" and "ones." (a) A data entry. (b) A sequence of data entries during a training session showing the variation of the surprise level. The patterns which are most surprising are most informative.

7.2.1   Informative Patterns Are Most Surprising

In Figure 7.1, we constructed a small example database containing only handwritten zeros and ones. Most patterns of a given category look similar. A typical zero is a circle and a typical one is a vertical bar. However, there exist other shapes of zeros and ones. If we wanted to keep only a few data representatives, we would probably keep at least one example of each basic shape.

To choose the best data representatives, we run an imaginary experiment. Imagine that we find 100 people who do not know what the shape of a zero and that of a one are. We teach these people to recognize zeros and ones by letting them examine the patterns of our database in sequence. Every time we show them a new image, we first hide the label and let them make a guess.

We represent in Figure 7.1 the fraction of votes for label "one" for a particular sequence of data. Since we assume that our subjects have never seen a zero nor a one before the experiment, about 50% guess "zero" and 50% guess "one" when they are shown the first pattern. But, for the second example of the same shape, the majority makes the correct guess. As learning goes on, familiar shapes are guessed more and more accurately and the percentage of wrong guesses raises only occasionally when a new shape appears.

We represent with the size of a question mark the average amount of surprise generated among our subjects when the true label is uncovered. People who guess the correct label are not surprised while people who make the wrong guess are surprised. We see from Figure 7.1 that a large average surprise level coincides with the appearance of a new shape. Therefore, the level of surprise is a good indication of how informative a pattern is.

More formally, let x_k be a pattern, $y_k \in \{0, 1\}$ its associated label, $k - 1$ the number of data entries seen thus far and $\hat{y}_k$ the label predicted for pattern x_k. The level of surprise is inversely related to the probability of guessing the correct label $P_k(\hat{y}_k = y_k) = P(\hat{y}_k = y_k | x_k, (x_0, y_0), (x_1, y_1), ...(x_{k-1}, y_{k-1}))$. This probability of making the correct guess is precisely what is involved in Shannon's information gain:

$$I(k) = -\log P_k(\hat{y}_k = y_k) =$$
$$-y_k \log P_k(\hat{y}_k = 1) - (1 - y_k) \log(1 - P_k(\hat{y}_k = 1)) \qquad (7.2.1)$$

In the information theoretic sense, the data entries that are most informative are those that are most surprising.

7.2.2 Machine Learning Techniques to Estimate the Information Gain

It is somewhat unrealistic to hire 100 ignorant people to estimate the information gain. Let us now replace people with machines.

In the machine learning framework, patterns drawn from a database are presented to the learning machine which makes predictions. The prediction error is evaluated and used to improve the accuracy of further predictions by adjusting the learning machine parameters.

Assume first that we trained 100 different learning machines (substituting our 100 people), each one predicting its own value of $\hat{y}_k$. This is similar to a "Bayesian" approach (Mackay, 1992) for which predictions are made according to the vote of an ensemble of machines. Formula 7.2.1 can be readily used to determine the information gain. Although this is a perfectly valid method, we propose here a more practical one: we train a single learning machine to provide an estimate $\hat{P}_k(y_k = 1)$ of the probability that the correct label is "one" (Figure 7.2). Our prediction $\hat{y}_k$ will be the most likely category according to $\hat{P}_k(y_k = 1)$. In formula 7.2.1, we substitute $\hat{P}_k(y_k = 1)$ for $P_k(\hat{y}_k = 1)$.

Many machine learning techniques can be applied to discover informative patterns. For example, the learning machine can be a simple

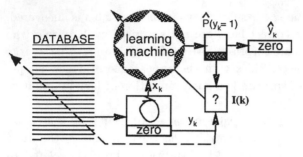

Figure 7.2
A learning machine used to predict the information gain (or surprise level). In the classical machine learning framework, the goal is to train the learning machine, either to provide a model of the data or to make predictions. In our framework the goal is to discover the informative patterns of the database (dashed line).

K-nearest-neighbor classifier (Duda & Hart, 1993). All patterns presented to the classifier are stored. $\hat{P}_k(y_k = 1)$ is given by the fraction of the K training patterns that are nearest to x_k which have label "one."

Another example is a neural network trained with a "cross-entropy" cost function which is the average over the training patterns of the Shannon information gain. The squared loss $(y_k - \hat{P}_k(y_k = 1))^2$, which also is often used, provides an *information criterion* which ranks patterns in the same order as the Shannon information gain. This is due to the fact that on the $[0, 1]$ interval, $-\log P(y_k = 1)$ and $(1 - P(y_k = 1))^2$ are both convex functions, one bounding the other one. Therefore, $-\log P(y_1 = 1) < -\log P(y_2 = 1)$ if and only if $(1 - y_1)^2 < (1 - y_2)^2$.

In the following, we use the size of the symbol "question mark," in the Figures, and the notation $I(k)$, in the text, to represent the *information criteria* used to measure the "surprise level."

7.2.3   On-line Algorithms and Batch Algorithms

In an on-line algorithm, patterns are presented in sequence and the learning machine adjusts its parameters at each presentation of a new pattern. This is a situation similar to that of our example of section 7.2.1. In that case, we could say that a pattern is informative if the information criterion exceeds a pre-defined threshold. The disadvantage of this method is that informative patterns depend on the sequence in which patterns are presented. Nonetheless, there may be practical situations where the data is only available on-line.

In a batch algorithm, conversely, all data entries are available at once and the information criterion is independent of pattern ordering. This implies that if there are p data entries in the database we need to train p machines, each one on all the data but one pattern, and then try to predict that last pattern. In practice, this is feasible only if training is inexpensive, as for the K-nearest-neighbor algorithm.

For other batch algorithms, we prefer to train the learning machine only once on all of the data. We then approximate the information criterion of each pattern with an estimate of how much the *cumulative information criterion* would decrease if we removed that pattern from the training set. For instance, on can use as cumulative information criterion the value of the cost function on the training set at the solution; the information criterion of each pattern is then its contribution to the overall cost.

For batch algorithms all the patterns of the database are uniquely ranked according to their information criterion. The m most informative patterns can be selected to represent the entire database.

7.2.4   Minimax Algorithms

Minimax algorithms are batch algorithms that are particularly well suited to discovering informative patterns. Most algorithms train the learning machine to minimize the average loss (e.g., the mean-square-error). Minimax algorithms minimize the maximum loss:

$$\min_{w} \max_{k} \ell(k) \qquad\qquad (7.2.2)$$

where w represents the parameters of the learning machine and k runs over all data entries, and $\ell(.)$ is some loss function. Minimax algorithms are extreme cases of "active learning" methods which emphasize patterns with large information gain (MacKay, 1992). The solution of a minimax algorithm is a function of only a small subset of the training patterns, precisely called "informative patterns" (Vapnik, 1982). These are the patterns that have maximum loss.

In Addendum A, we describe a minimax algorithm for classification problems: the Optimum Margin Classifier (Vapnik, 1982; Boser, Guyon & Vapnik 1992; Guyon, Boser & Vapnik 1993). The algorithm maximizes the minimum distance of the training patterns to the decision boundary. It can be shown that the solution w^* is a linear combination of basis functions of the informative patterns:

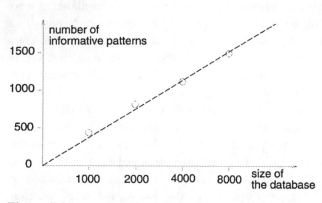

Figure 7.3
Variation of the number of informative patterns as a function of the number of
patterns in the database. Experiments are carried out on a database of handwritten
digits, encoded with 16 real-valued global features derived from the pen trajectory
information. A polynomial classifier of degree 2 is trained with a minimax
algorithm (Optimal Margin Classifier). The informative patterns are the patterns
for which $I(k) = \alpha_k^* \neq 0$.

$$w^* = \sum_{k=1}^{p}(2y_k - 1)\alpha_k^*\varphi(x_k), \quad \alpha_k^* \geq 0, \tag{7.2.3}$$

where $y_k \in \{0,1\}$ indicates the class membership, the $\varphi(.)$ are basis
functions and α_k^* are coefficients (all null except for the informative
patterns). We use the value of the cost function at the solution as the
cumulative information criterion:

$$I = \sum_{k=1}^{p}\alpha_k^*, \tag{7.2.4}$$

from which we derive an estimate of the information loss incurred by
removing the informative pattern k:

$$I(k) = \alpha_k^*. \tag{7.2.5}$$

One important question is: what is the rate of growth of the number
of informative patterns as a function of the size of the database? The
results of experiments carried out on a database of handwritten digits
using the Optimal Margin Classifier suggest a logarithmic growth, in
the regime when the number of patterns is small compared to the total
number of distinct patterns (Figure 7.3).

Other minimax algorithms have been proposed for classification, regression and density estimation (Demyanov & Malozemov 1972; Cortes & Vapnik 1993)

7.3   Data Cleaning

In this section we tackle the problem of real world databases which may contain corrupted data entries. We propose data cleaning algorithms and analyze experimental results.

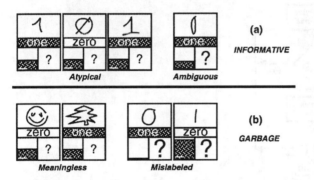

Figure 7.4
(a) Informative patterns versus (b) garbage patterns. Informative patterns are intermixed with garbage patterns which also generate a lot of surprise (i.e. have a large information gain).

7.3.1   Garbage Patterns Are Also Surprising

The information theoretic definition of an informative pattern does not always coincide with the common sense definition. In Figure 7.4, we show examples of patterns drawn from our database of "zeros" and "ones" which have a large information gain. We see two kinds of patterns:

- Patterns that are actually informative: atypical shapes or ambiguous shapes.

- Garbage patterns: meaningless or mislabeled patterns.

Truly informative patterns should be kept in the database while garbage patterns should be eliminated.

Purely automatic cleaning could be performed by eliminating systematically all patterns with suspiciously large information criterion. However, this is dangerous since valuable informative patterns may also be eliminated. Purely manual cleaning, by examining all patterns in the database, is tedious and impractical for very large databases. We propose a computer-aided cleaning method where a human operator must check only those patterns that have largest information criterion and are therefore most suspicious.

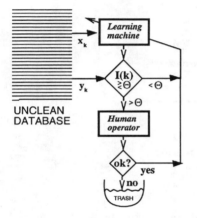

Figure 7.5
Flow diagram of on-line cleaning. In the process of learning, patterns for which the information criterion exceeds a threshold θ are examined by a human operator. Good patterns are kept in the database and sent to the recognizer for adaptation. Bad patterns are removed from the database.

7.3.2   On-line Algorithms and Batch Algorithms

In Figure 7.5 we present our on-line version of data cleaning. It combines cleaning and training in one single session. The learning machine is initially trained with a few clean examples. At step k of the cleaning process, a new pattern x_k is presented to the learning machine. The prediction of the learning machine and the desired value y_k are used to compute the information criterion $I(k)$. If $I(k)$ is below a given threshold θ, the pattern is directly sent to the learning machine for adaptation. Otherwise, the pattern is sent to the human operator for checking. Depending on the decision of the operator, the pattern is either trashed or sent to the learning machine for adaptation.

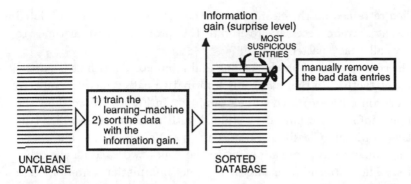

Figure 7.6
Block diagram of batch cleaning. The learning machine is trained on unclean data.
The information criterion is evaluated for each pattern by estimating how much
information would be lost if that pattern are removed. The database is sorted
according to the information criterion. Only the top ranked patterns are examined
for cleaning by the human operator. After cleaning, the learning machine needs to
be retrained to obtain a good model and/or make good predictions.

When all the data has been processed, both training and cleaning
are completed, since the learning machine is trained only on clean data.
This is an advantage if further use is made of the learning machine. But
on-line cleaning has several disadvantages:

- One has to find an appropriate threshold θ.

- Training the learning machine may be slower than checking the
  patterns which may result in wasting the time of the operator.

- The method depends on the order of presentation of the patterns;
  it is not possible to reverse a decision on whether a pattern is good
  or bad.

When possible, batch methods are preferred for cleaning (Figure 7.6).
Training is performed on all patterns, including garbage patterns, with
any training algorithm. After training, the information criterion of the
patterns is computed as explained in sections 7.2.3 and 7.2.4. Typically,
one uses the contribution of the training patterns to the value of the
cost function at the solution. The data entries are then sorted in decreasing order of information criterion. The patterns are examined by
the operator, starting from the top (most suspicious) until the number
of consecutive "good" patterns exceeds a given threshold. The classifier

is then retrained on the clean data. If the database contains correlated errors, it may be necessary to iterate this procedure several times to remove all "bad" patterns.

The combination of batch cleaning and minimax algorithms is particularly attractive. In that case, only informative patterns (with non zero information criterion) need to be examined. In Figure 7.7 we show the first few informative patterns obtained with a minimax classifier (the Optimum Margin Classifier (Boser, Guyon & Vapnik 1992). The classifier is trained to discriminate between the digit "two" and all the other digits. The patterns with largest α_k^* (our information criterion from equation 7.2.5) is a garbage pattern.

Figure 7.7
The informative patterns obtained by a minimax algorithm (the Optimum Margin Algorithm), for the separation of handwritten digit "two" against all other digit categories (Boser, Guyon & Vapnik 1992). Patterns are represented by a 16 x 16 grey-level pixel-map. The informative patterns are shown in order of decreasing information criterion.(a) Informative patterns for class 2: a garbage pattern comes first. (b) Informative patterns for all other classes: several ambiguous or atypical shapes are among the patterns with the largest information criterion.

7.3.3   Point of Optimal Cleaning

In the experiments described in this section (Matić et al 1992) we use the following experimental setup. We train a neural network to recognize handwritten lowercase letters. The representation is 630 local features of the pen trajectory. A training data set of 9513 characters and a validation data set of 2000 characters from disjoint set of writers is used for cleaning (the validation set does not get cleaned). The network is a convolutional neural network with local connections and shared weights. It is trained by minimizing a mean-square-error cost function with the backpropagation algorithm. Weights are initialized to small random values. Training is stopped after 30 iterations through the training set. No weight decay is used.

We may wonder how reliable our cleaning techniques are: did we examine all the patterns that should be candidates for cleaning? Among the patterns that were candidates for cleaning, did we remove too many or too few patterns?

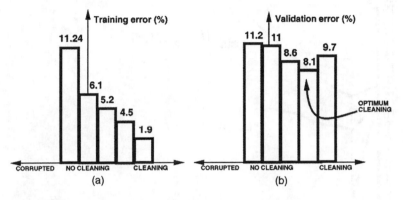

Figure 7.8
Data cleaning results (Matić et al 1992) depicting a point of optimal cleaning. These results are obtained with an on-line cleaning method on a handwriting recognition task using a neural network classifier (see text).

We can again use our learning machine to provide us with an answer. In the experiments of Figure 7.8, we vary the amount of cleaning (Matić et al 1992). Starting with the "uncleaned" database, several levels of cleaning are applied by the human operator. Each stage is more strict, i.e. he lowers the tolerance for marginal-quality characters. To test the power of the cleaning technique, we also corrupt the initial, uncleaned database, by artificially mislabeling 5% of the characters in the training set (left most column). A version of on-line cleaning called "bootstrap" cleaning is used: small batches of data are processed at a time instead of a single pattern. The classification error is used as information criterion.

We observe that, as more patterns are removed through the cleaning process, the error rate on the training set decreases. This is understandable since the learning task becomes easier and easier to the learning machine. The validation error however goes through a minimum. This is because we remove first only really bad patterns, then we start removing valuable informative patterns that we mistook for garbage patterns. As explained in the next paragraph, this behavior of the validation error is general and can be predicted theoretically. The minimum of the validation error is the point of optimal cleaning. If our validation error does not go through a minimum, more patterns should be examined and considered for cleaning.

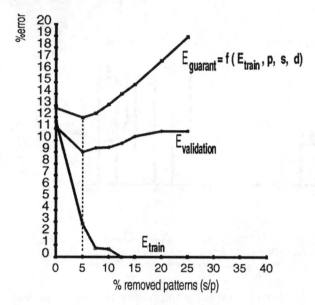

Figure 7.9
Detection of the point of optimal cleaning with the Vapnik-Chervonenkis prediction. These results are obtained with a batch cleaning method. The experimental setup is the same as in Figure 7.8. $E_{guarant}$ is rescaled to fit on the figure.

It is not always possible nor desirable to split the database into a training and a validation set. Another way of obtaining the point of optimum cleaning is to use the predictions of the Vapnik-Chervonenkis (VC) theory (Vapnik 1982). According to the VC-theory (see Addendum B), the point of optimum cleaning is the minimum of the so-called *guaranteed risk*, which is a bound on $E_{validation}$, the validation set frequency of errors:

$$E_{guarant} = E_{train}(s) + \beta \; \frac{d(\ln \frac{2(p-s)}{d} + 1) + s(\ln \frac{p}{s} + 1)}{p - s} \tag{7.3.6}$$

where β is a constant, $E_{train}(m)$ is the frequency of training errors when s suspicious patterns have been removed from the training set, p is the number of training patterns before cleaning and d is the VC-dimension. β and d are estimated as explained in Addendum B.

References	Database	Db. size	Num. of inf. pat.	Cleaning time (h)	% test error unclean train	% test error clean train
Boser-92	OCR digits	7,300	690	1	15	10.5
Matić-93	on-line lower	16,000	3,130	1	11	6.5
Guyon-92	on-line ASCII	100,000	10,983	5	30	6

Table 7.1
Results obtained on various databases of handwritten patterns. The cleaning time is the time spent by the operator browsing through the informative patterns (not including the learning machine training time). Only the training data is cleaned. The test errors are computed on separate unclean test sets of more than 2000 examples from a disjoint set of writers. Without cleaning, the last database is completely worthless.

In Figure 7.9 (Matić et al 1992) we compare the prediction of the VC-theory and that of the validation set. The experimental setup is the same as in the previous experiment, except that training is performed with an "active learning" technique (Guyon et al 1992). The information criterion is the total time each pattern spent in the active set. The number of patterns before cleaning is $p = 9513$. We use a constant $\beta = 0.5$ and our estimation of the VC-dimension of the neural network is $d = 2000$ (approximately one third of the number of free parameters).

We obtain good agreement between the prediction of the VC-theory and that of the validation set, even with a very rough estimate of the VC-dimension. In fact, for the particular network architecture that we use, the position of the point of optimum cleaning is insensitive to a change in the estimate of the VC-dimension in the range $300 < d < 5000$.

7.4   Conclusions

We presented a computer-aided method for detecting informative patterns and cleaning data. We used this method on various databases of handwritten characters. The results are summarized in table 7.1. It is important to stress that the number of informative patterns varies sub-linearly with the number of data entries and that therefore the cleaning time varies sub-linearly with the number of data entries. The point of optimum cleaning can be predicted by the VC-theory which does not require splitting the data between a training set and a validation set. Our cleaning method clearly improves the quality of the data, as measured by the improvement in classification performance on a test set independent from the training set. Our framework is general and applies to other problems than classification problems (regression or density estimation) which makes it attractive for new applications in knowledge discovery.

Acknowledgments

Discussions with colleagues AT&T Bell Labs and at UC Berkeley are gratefully acknowledged. Special thanks to B. Boser who contributed many ideas.

Addendum 7.A: Optimal Margin Classifier (OMC)

This addendum summarizes the OMC algorithm described in Vapnik (1982), Boser, Guyon, and Vapnik (1992), Guyon, Boser and Vapnik (1993).

We seek a decision function for pattern vectors $\mathbf{x}$ of dimension n belonging to one of two classes A and B. The input to the training algorithm is a set of p examples $\mathbf{x}_k$ with labels $g_k \in \{-1, 1\}$ indicating the class membership $(g_k = 2y_k - 1)$. From these training examples the algorithm finds the parameters of the decision function $D(\mathbf{x})$ during a learning phase. After training, the classification of unknown patterns is predicted according to the following rules: $\mathbf{x} \in$ A, if $D(\mathbf{x}) > 0$ and $\mathbf{x} \in$ B otherwise. The OMC algorithm applies to classifiers linear in their parameters, but not restricted to linear dependencies in their input components, such as perceptrons and kernel-based classifiers.

Duality

Perceptrons and kernel-based classifiers are often considered two very distinct approaches to classification. However, for a number of training algorithms, they constitute *dual* representations of the same decision function. Perceptrons (Duda & Hart 1973) have a decision function defined as:

$$D(\mathbf{x}) = \mathbf{w} \cdot \varphi(\mathbf{x}) + b = \sum_{i=1}^{N} w_i \varphi_i(\mathbf{x}) + b, \qquad (7.4.7)$$

where the φ_i are predefined functions of $\mathbf{x}$, and the w_i and b are the adjustable parameters of the decision function. This definition encompasses that of polynomial classifiers. In that particular case, the φ_i are products of components of vector $\mathbf{x}$. Kernel-based classifiers, have a decision function defined as:

$$D(\mathbf{x}) = \sum_{k=1}^{p} \alpha_k K(\mathbf{x}_k, \mathbf{x}) + b, \tag{7.4.8}$$

The coefficients α_k and the bias b are the parameters to be adjusted and the $\mathbf{x}_k$ are the training patterns. The function K is a predefined kernel, for example a potential function (Aizerman, Braverman & Rozonoer 1964) or any *radial basis function* (RBF).

A perceptron classifier admits a dual kernel representation if its weight vector is a linear combination of the training patterns in φ-space:

$$\mathbf{w} = \sum_{k=1}^{p} \alpha_k \varphi(\mathbf{x}_k) \ . \tag{7.4.9}$$

Reciprocally, a kernel classifier admits a dual perceptron representation if the kernel function possesses a finite (or infinite) expansion of the form:

$$K(\mathbf{x}, \mathbf{x}') = \sum_{i} \varphi_i(\mathbf{x}) \, \varphi_i(\mathbf{x}') \ . \tag{7.4.10}$$

Such is the case for instance for some symmetric kernels. Examples of kernels that we have been using include

$$
\begin{aligned}
K(\mathbf{x}, \mathbf{x}') &= (\mathbf{x} \cdot \mathbf{x}' + 1)^q && \text{(polynomial of order q)}, \\
K(\mathbf{x}, \mathbf{x}') &= \tanh(\gamma \, \mathbf{x} \cdot \mathbf{x}') && \text{(neural units)}, \\
K(\mathbf{x}, \mathbf{x}') &= \exp(\gamma \, \mathbf{x} \cdot \mathbf{x}') - 1 && \text{(exponential)}, \\
K(\mathbf{x}, \mathbf{x}') &= \exp\left(-\|\mathbf{x} - \mathbf{x}'\|^2/\gamma\right) && \text{(gaussian RBF)}, \\
K(\mathbf{x}, \mathbf{x}') &= \exp\left(-\|\mathbf{x} - \mathbf{x}'\|/\gamma\right) && \text{(exponential RBF)}, \\
K(\mathbf{x}, \mathbf{x}') &= (\mathbf{x} \cdot \mathbf{x}' + 1)^q && \\
& \quad \exp\left(-\|\mathbf{x} - \mathbf{x}'\|/\gamma\right) && \text{(mixed polynomial} \\
& && \text{\& RBF)}.
\end{aligned} \tag{7.4.11}
$$

These kernels have positive parameters (the integer q or the real number γ) which can be determined with a *structural risk minimization* or *cross-validation* procedure (see Addendum B).

The OMC algorithm computes the maximum margin solution in the kernel representation. This is crucial for making the computation tractable when training very large VC-dimension classifiers (see Addendum B). Training a classifier in the kernel representation is computationally advantageous when the dimension N of vectors $\mathbf{w}$ (or the VC-dimension $N+1$) is large compared to the number of parameters α_k, which equals the number of training patterns p. This is always true if the kernel function possesses an infinite expansion (7.4.10). Our experimental results (Boser, Guyon & Vapnik 1992; Guyon, Boser & Vapnik 1993) indicate that this argument holds in practice even for low order polynomial expansions when the dimension n of the input space is sufficiently large.

Minimizing the Maximum Loss

The margin, defined as the Euclidean distance between the decision boundary and the closest training patterns in φ-space can be computed as

$$M = \min_k \frac{g_k D(\mathbf{x}_k)}{\|\mathbf{w}\|} . \tag{7.4.12}$$

The goal of the maximum margin training algorithm is to find the decision function $D(\mathbf{x})$ which maximizes M, that is the solution of the optimization problem

$$\max_{\mathbf{w}} \min_k \frac{g_k D(\mathbf{x}_k)}{\|\mathbf{w}\|} . \tag{7.4.13}$$

In the classical framework of loss minimization, Problem 7.4.13 is equivalent to minimizing (over $\mathbf{w}$) the maximum loss. The loss function is defined as $\ell(\mathbf{x}_k) = -g_k D(\mathbf{x}_k)/\|\mathbf{w}\|$.

One of the benefits of minimax algorithms is that the solution is a function only of a restricted number of training patterns, namely the informative patterns. This results in high computational efficiency in those cases when the number m of informative patterns is small compared to both the total number of training patterns p and the dimension N of φ-space.

Formulation as a Quadratic Programming Problem

The Problem 7.4.13 is reformulated in the dual α-space as the quadratic programming problem of maximizing the cost function (Vapnik 1982):

$$J(\alpha, b) = \sum_{k=1}^p \alpha_k \left(1 - b g_k\right) - \frac{1}{2}\alpha \cdot H \cdot \alpha, \tag{7.4.14}$$

under the constrains:

$$\begin{cases} \alpha_k \geq 0 \\ \sum_k g_k \alpha_k = 0 \ . \end{cases} \tag{7.4.15}$$

The $p \times p$ square matrix H has elements $H_{kl} = g_k g_l K(\mathbf{x}_k, \mathbf{x}_l)$, where $K(\mathbf{x}, \mathbf{x}')$ is a kernel, such as the ones proposed in (7.4.11), which can be expanded as in (7.4.10). A unique solution exists if H is positive semi-definite.

The quadratic programming problem thus defined can be solved efficiently by standard numerical methods (Luenberger 1984). Numerical computation can be further reduced by processing iteratively small chunks of data (Vapnik 1982). The computational time is linear the dimension n of $\mathbf{x}$-space (not the dimension N of φ-space) and in the number p of training examples and polynomial in the number $m < \min(N + 1, p)$ of informative patterns. It can be theoretically proven that it is a polynomial in m of order lower than 10, but experimentally an order 2 is observed.

Properties of the OMC solution

This formulation of the problem in dual space is obtained with the formalism of Lagrange multipliers and using the scaling constraint that the margin is at a distance $1/\|\mathbf{w}\|$ of the decision boundary. This imposes:

$$\begin{cases} g_k D(\mathbf{x}_k) = 1 & \text{for all informative patterns,} \\ g_k D(\mathbf{x}_k) > 1 \text{ and } \alpha_k^* = 0 & \text{for the other training patterns,} \end{cases} \tag{7.4.16}$$

where α_k are the Lagrange multipliers.

Only the informative patterns appear in the solution with non-zero weight α_k^*:

$$\begin{aligned} D(\mathbf{x}) &= \sum_k g_k \alpha_k^* K(\mathbf{x}_k, \mathbf{x}) + b^*, \qquad \alpha_k^* \geq 0, \\ &= \mathbf{w}^* \cdot \varphi(\mathbf{x}) + b, \\ \mathbf{w}^* &= \sum_k g_k \alpha_k^* \varphi(x_k), \\ b^* &= -\frac{1}{2} \left(\mathbf{w}^* \cdot \varphi(\mathbf{x}_A) + \mathbf{w}^* \cdot \varphi(\mathbf{x}_B) \right), \end{aligned}$$

where $\mathbf{x}_A$ and $\mathbf{x}_B$ are two arbitrary informative patterns of class A and B. Using the kernel representation, with a factorized kernel (such as 7.4.11), the classification time is linear in n (not N) and in m (not p).

Using (7.4.16), (7.4.14) and (7.4.15), it can be shown that the value of the cost function at the solution is:

$$J(\alpha^*, b^*) = \frac{1}{2}\|\mathbf{w}\|^2 = \frac{1}{2}\sum_k \alpha_k^* \qquad (7.4.17)$$

In the text, we use as *cumulative information criterion* $I = 2\, J(\alpha^*, b^*)$.

Another property of the OMC algorithm is that its prediction error on a test set is bounded by m/p (Boser, Guyon & Vapnik 1992). Therefore, maximum margin solutions obtain good generalization even when the problem is grossly underdetermined, i.e. the number of training patterns p is much smaller than the number of adjustable parameters, $N + 1$.

Addendum 7.B: Vapnik-Chervonenkis Dimension

In this addendum, we review the notion of Vapnik-Chervonenkis Dimension or VC-dimension (Vapnik 1982).

Capacity and Guaranteed Risk

A common way of training a given classifier is to adjust the parameters $\mathbf{w}$ in the classification function $D(\mathbf{x}, \mathbf{w})$ to minimize the *training error* E_{train}, i.e., the frequency of errors on a set of p training examples. E_{train} estimates the expected risk based on the empirical data provided by the p available examples. The method is thus called *empirical risk minimization*. But the classification function $D(\mathbf{x}, \mathbf{w}^*)$ which minimizes the empirical risk does not necessarily minimize the *generalization error*, i.e., the expected value of the risk over the full distribution of possible inputs and their corresponding outputs. Such generalization error E_{gen} cannot in general be computed, but it can be estimated on a separate test set (E_{test}).

Any family of classification functions $\{D(\mathbf{x}, \mathbf{w})\}$ can be characterized by its capacity. The Vapnik-Chervonenkis dimension (or VC-dimension) (Vapnik 1982) is such a capacity, defined as the maximum number d of training examples which can be learned without error, *for all possible binary labelings*. In some simple cases, the VC-dimension is given by the number of free parameters of the classifier (e.g., for classifiers linear in their parameters, the VC-dimension is $N + 1$, where N is the dimension of φ-space, the space spanned by the $\varphi(\mathbf{x})$ vectors, see Addendum A). In most cases it is quite difficult to determine it analytically.

The VC-theory provides bounds. Let $\{D(\mathbf{x}, \mathbf{w})\}$ be a set of classification functions of capacity d. For p training examples that are independently and identically distributed, $p > d$, with probability $(1 - \eta)$, simultaneously for all classification functions $D(\mathbf{x}, \mathbf{w})$, the generalization error E_{gen} is lower than a *guaranteed risk* defined by:

$$E_{guarant} = E_{train} + \beta \; \varepsilon(p, d, E_{train}, \eta) \; , \tag{7.4.18}$$

where $\varepsilon(p, d, E_{train}, \eta)$ is equal to:

$$\varepsilon_0 = \frac{d(\ln \frac{2p}{d} + 1) - \ln\eta}{p} \tag{7.4.19}$$

for small E_{train}, and equal to $\sqrt{\varepsilon_0}$ for E_{train} close to one (Vapnik 1982; Le Cun, Levin & Vapnik 1994). The smaller ε, the closer the *guaranteed risk* is to the training error, therefore the more we can trust the method of *empirical risk minimization*. The first term in ε roughly behaves like $(d/p)^\alpha$, where $1/2 < \alpha < 1$. It says that generalization is likely to be better if $p \geq d$. The second term, $\ln\eta/p$, says that the surer we want to be of the inequality $E_{gen} \leq E_{guarant}$, the looser the bound. This second term is usually ignored in the experiments.

For a fixed number of training examples p, the training error decreases monotonically as the capacity d increases, while the ε term increases monotonically. As a result, the *guaranteed risk* goes through a minimum which usually coincides with a minimum in the generalization error. Before the minimum, the problem is *overdetermined*: the capacity is too small for the amount of training data. Beyond the minimum the problem is *underdetermined*. The key issue is therefore to match the capacity of the classifier to the amount of training data in order to get best generalization performance. The method of *structural risk minimization* (SRM) (Vapnik 1982; Le Cun, Levin & Vapnik 1994) provides a way of achieving this goal.

Let us choose a family of classifiers $\{D(\mathbf{x}, \mathbf{w})\}$, and define a structure consisting of nested subsets of elements of the family:

$$S_1 \subset S_2 \subset \ldots \subset S_r \subset \ldots .$$

By defining such a structure, we ensure that the capacity d_r of the subset of classifiers S_r is less than d_{r+1} of subset S_{r+1}. The method of SRM amounts to finding the subset S^{opt} for which the classifier $D(\mathbf{x}, \mathbf{w}^*)$ which minimizes the empirical risk within such subset yields the best overall generalization performance.

Two problems arise in implementing SRM: (i) How to find a good structure? (ii) How to select S^{opt}?

A good structure reflects the *a priori* knowledge of the designer, and only a few guidelines can be provided from the theory to solve problem (i). The designer must find the best compromise between two competing terms: E_{train} and ε. Reducing d causes ε to decrease, but E_{train} to increase. A good structure should be such that decreasing the VC-dimension happens at the expense of the smallest possible increase in training error. Examples of structures include varying the number of hidden units in a neural network and varying the order of a polynomial in a polynomial classifier.

Problem (ii) arises because we have no direct access to E_{gen}. Several methods can be used, including *guaranteed risk minimization* (GRM) which consists of using $E_{guarant}$ instead of E_{gen}, *cross-validation* which consists of using the error $E_{validation}$ calculated on a validation set, distinct from the training set and the test set and the *leave-one-out* method which consists of calculating $E_{validation}$ by averaging the results of rotating through the training set, training on all patterns but one, and testing on that pattern.

Removing patterns from the training data, as performed during data cleaning, is a special case of SRM. The number s of suspicious patterns removed establish a structure. The expression of the *guaranteed risk* is slightly different for this particular problem because the pattern selection process adds degrees of freedom:

$$E_{guarant} = E_{train}(s) + \beta \; \frac{d(\ln\frac{2(p-s)}{d} + 1) + s(\ln\frac{p}{s} + 1) - \ln\eta}{p - s} \qquad (7.4.20)$$

It is similar to equation 7.4.18 (in the small training error case), where p has been replaced by $p - s$, except for the additional term $s(\ln\frac{p}{s} + 1)/(p-s)$, which shows that number of patterns removed s behaves like an additional capacity.

For the *optimal margin classifier* the GRM method does not apply because the training error is always zero when a solution exists. The method of *cross-validation* is then used to determine the point of optimum cleaning.

Effective VC-dimension

Using SRM with *cross-validation* does not require knowing the VC-dimension and is therefore the simplest and most commonly used method.

Using SRM with GRM is presumably better because it does not rely on reserving patterns for the validation set, but it is more involved. First, the constant β predicted by the theory is always too pessimistic and it must be empirically determined. Second, except in very trivial case, the VC-dimension d is not known analytically. Moreover, the VC-dimension *per se* is not a very good measure of capacity because it does not take into account the properties of the loss function and the training algorithm. It is preferable to substitute it an empirical value, the *effective* VC-dimension, which is generally smaller than the VC-dimension predicted analytically.

The functional form of the *guaranteed risk* provides nevertheless useful theoretical insights to predict the behavior of the generalization error. Several methods have been proposed to determine empirical values of d and β (Le Cun, Levin & Vapnik 1994). We recommend the following simple protocol:

- Choose a classification task defined by a training and validation set.
- Choose a classifier $D(\mathbf{x}, \mathbf{w})$.
- Calculate the training error E_{train} and also the validation error $E_{validation}$ of the classifier for various number of training examples p.
- Determine the unknowns β and the *effective* VC-dimension d by fitting the expression of $[E_{guarant} - E_{train}]$ (ignoring the $\ln\eta$ term) to the experimental points given by $[E_{validation} - E_{train}]$.

More accurate estimates are obtained by splitting the data into a training set and test set in different ways and averaging the results.

The GRM method is advantageous compared to *cross-validation* mainly if β and d are invariant with respect to the classification task. Otherwise, the same data needs to be used to train, to determine β and d and to compute $E_{guarant}$. The only benefit is then that the functional form of $E_{guarant}$ is used to smooth $E_{validation}$.

Confidence in the invariance of β and d with respect to the classification task is built by repeating the experiment on various data sets. Our experiments indicate that for the neural networks that we use, trained with the backpropagation algorithm with small weight random initialization, but no weight decay, we have $\beta \simeq 0.5$ and $d \simeq f/3$, where f is the number of free parameters (Matić et al 1992).

References

Aizerman, M.; Braverman, E.; and Rozonoer, L. 1964. Theoretical Foundations of the Potential Function Method in Pattern Recognition Learning. *Automation and Remote Control*, 25(6): 821–837.

Boser, B.; Guyon, I.; and Vapnik, V. 1992. A Training Algorithm for Optimal Margin Classifiers. In *Proceedings of the Fifth Annual Workshop on Computational Learning Theory*. Baltimore, Md: ACM Press, 144–152.

Cortes, C.; and Vapnik, V. 1993. The Soft Margin Classifier. Technical Memorandum 11359-931209-18TM, AT&T Bell Labs, Holmdel, NJ.

Demyanov, V. F.; and Malozemov, V. N. 1972. *Introduction to Minimax*. New York: Dover Press.

Duda, R.; and Hart, P. 1973. *Pattern Classification and Scene Analysis*. New York: John Wiley and Sons.

Guyon, I.; Henderson, D.; Albrecht, P.; Le Cun, Y.; and Denker, J. 1992. Writer Independent and Writer Adaptive Neural Network for On-Line Character Recognition. In *From Pixels to Features III*, ed. S. Impedovo. Amsterdam: Elsevier, 493–506.

Guyon, I.; Boser, B.; and Vapnik, V. 1993. Automatic Capacity Tuning of Very Large VC Dimension Classifiers. In *Advances in Neural Information Processing Systems 5*, ed. S. Hanson, S. et al. San Francisco: Morgan Kaufmann, 147–155.

Haussler, D.; Kearns, M.; and Shapire, R. 1991. Bounds on the Sample Complexity of Bayesian Learning Using Information Theory and the VC Dimension. In *Proceedings of the Fourth Annual Workshop on Computational Learning Theory*, Baltimore, Md: ACM Press.

Le Cun, Y.; Levin, E.; and Vapnik, V. 1994. Measuring the VC-Dimension of a Learning Machine. *Neural Computation*, 6(5): 851–884.

Luenberger, D. 1984. *Linear and Non-linear Programming*. Reading, Mass.: Addison Wesley.

MacKay, D. 1992. Information-Based Objective Functions for Active Data Selection. *Neural Computation*, 4(4): 590–604.

Matić, N.; Guyon, I.; Bottou, L.; Denker, J.; and Vapnik, V. 1992. Computer Aided Cleaning of Large Databases for Character Decognition. In

Proceedings of the Eleventh International Conference on Pattern Recognition, Volume II. Los Alamitos, CA: IEEE Computer Society Press, 330–333.

Matić, N.; Guyon, I.; Denker, J.; and Vapnik, V. 1993. Writer Adaptation for On-line Handwritten Character Recognition. In *Proceedings of Second International Conference on Pattern Recognition and Document Analysis.* Los Alamitos, Calif.: IEEE Computer Society Press, 187–191.

Rissanen, J. 1989. *Stochastic Complexity in Statistical Inquiry.* Singapore: World Scientific.

Vapnik, V. 1982. *Estimation of Dependencies Based on Empirical Data.* New York: Springer-Verlag.

8 Transforming Rules and Trees

Brian R. Gaines
University of Calgary

Abstract

The problem of transforming the knowledge bases of expert systems using induced rules or decision trees into comprehensible knowledge structures is addressed. A knowledge structure is developed that generalizes and subsumes production rules, decision trees, and rules with exceptions. It gives rise to a natural complexity measure that allows them to be understood, analyzed and compared on a uniform basis. The structure is a directed acyclic graph with the semantics that nodes are premises, some of which have attached conclusions, and the arcs are inheritance links with disjunctive multiple inheritance. A detailed example is given of the generation of a range of such structures of equivalent performance for a simple problem, and the complexity measure of a particular structure is shown to relate to its perceived complexity. The simplest structures are generated by an algorithm that factors common subpremises from the premises of rules. A more complex example of a chess dataset is used to show the value of this technique in generating comprehensible knowledge structures.

8.1 Introduction

It is fitting to commence this chapter with a quotation from Ross Quinlan's foreword to the first volume of the *Knowledge Discovery in Databases* series:

"In one of several illuminating essays on different facets of knowledge, Donald Michie (1986) identifies *concept expressions* as those correct and effectively computable descriptions that can also be assimilated and used by a human being. As a counterexample, he cites a case in which ID3 derived a decision tree for a chess end game from a complete set of positions. The tree was absolutely correct and computationally efficient but, alas, completely incomprehensible to human chess experts. As he put it, "It was not a question of a few glimmers of sense here and there scattered through a large obscure structure, but just a total blackout." In Michie's view, which I share, such a structure does not qualify as knowledge." (Quinlan, 1991).

The inductive models produced of significant databases typically have such large trees or numbers of rules that they are not comprehensible to people as meaningful knowledge from which they can gain insights into the basis of decision making. This problem is common to both the manually and inductively derived rule sets, and seems intrinsic to the use of tree or rule structures as the basis of performance systems (Li, 1991).

It is not obvious that an excellent performance system necessarily implies the existence of a comprehensible knowledge structure to be discovered. Human practical reasoning does not require overt knowledge structures (Gaines, 1993b) and the supposition of an implicit structure, or 'mental model', is a construct of the observer (Clancey, 1993). In the knowledge acquisition community 'expertise transfer' paradigms have been replaced in recent years by 'knowledge modeling' paradigms (Schreiber, Wielinga and Breuker, 1993) that impute the resultant overt knowledge to the modeling process, not to some hypothetical knowledge base within the expert. Clancey, who has played a major role in promoting this paradigm shift (Clancey, 1989; 1993), has done so in part based on his experience in developing overt knowledge structures from MYCIN rules to support GUIDON (Clancey, 1987) as a teaching system based on MYCIN.

The development of excellent performance systems will remain a major practical objective regardless of the comprehensibility of the basis of their performance. However, the challenge of increasing human knowledge through developing understanding of that basis remains a significant research issue in its own right. Can one take a complex knowledge base that is difficult to understand and derive from it a better and more comprehensible representation? If so, to what extent can the derivation process be automated? This chapter presents techniques for restructuring production rules and decision trees to generate more comprehensible knowledge structures.

8.2   Comprehensibility of Knowledge Structures

In attempting to improve the comprehensibility of knowledge structures it would be beneficial to have an operational and psychologically well-founded measure of comprehensibility. However, there are in general no such measures. This is not to say that one has to fall back on subjective judgment alone. There are general considerations that smaller structures tend to be more comprehensible, coherent structures more meaningful, those using familiar concepts more understandable, and so on. The internal analog weights and connections of neural networks with graded relations of varying significance are at one extreme of incomprehensibility. Compact sets of production rules are better but not very much so if there are no clear relations between premises or obvious bases of interaction between the rules. Taxonomic structures with inheritance relations between concepts, and concept definitions based on meaningful properties, are probably most assimilable by people, and tend to be the basis of the systematization of knowledge in much of the scientific literature. Ultimately, human judgment determines what is knowledge, but it is not a suitable criterion as a starting point for discovery since the most interesting discoveries are the ones that are surprising. The initial human judgment of what becomes accepted as an excellent knowledge structure may be negative. The process of assimilation and acceptance takes time.

One feature of knowledge structures, that is highly significant to discovery systems, is that *unicity*, the existence of one optimal or preferred structure, is the exception rather than the rule. There will be many possible structures with equivalent performance as models, and it is inappropriate to attempt to achieve unicity by an arbitrary technical criterion such as minimal size on some measure. The relative evaluation of different knowledge structures of equivalent performance involves complex criteria which are likely to vary from case to case. For example, in some situations concepts may be preferred that are deemed more appropriate in being usual, familiar, theoretically more interpretable or coherent, and so on. A structure based on these concepts may be preferred over a smaller one that uses less acceptable concepts. Thus, a discovery system that is able to present alternatives and accept diverse criteria for discrimination between them may be preferred over one that attempts to achieve unicity through purely combinatorial or statistical criteria. On the other hand, it is a significant research objective in its own right to attempt to discover technical criteria that have a close correspondence to human judgment.

These have been the considerations underlying the research presented in this chapter: to generate knowledge structures that have a form similar to those preferred by people; to explore a variety of possible structures and accept as wide a range of possible of external criteria for assessing them automatically or manually; and to develop principled statistical criteria that correspond to such assessments to the extent that this is possible.

8.3   Exception Directed Acyclic Graphs (EDAGS)

The starting point for the research has been empirical induction tools that generate production rules or decision trees. One early conclusion was that a hybrid structure that had some of the characteristics of both rules and trees was preferable to either alone. This structure can be viewed either as a generalization of rules allowing exceptions, or as a generalization of trees such that the criteria at a node do not have to be based on a single property or be mutually exclusive, and the trees are generalized to partial orders allowing branches to come together again. These generalizations allow substantially smaller knowledge structures to be generated than either rules or trees alone, and overcome problems of trees in dealing with disjunctive concepts involving replication of subtrees.

Figure 8.1 exemplifies this knowledge structure, termed an *exception directed acyclic graph* (EDAG). It may be read as a set of rules with exceptions or as a generalized decision tree. Its operational interpretation is:

- All paths through the graph are traced from each of its root nodes.
- For each node on a path, if the premise (if any) is true then the conclusion (if any) is noted for that path, replacing any previous conclusion noted for the path.
- A path is traced until a premise fails to hold, or a leaf node is reached.
- When a path has been traced, any conclusion noted is asserted.

Several features of EDAGs may be noted:

- The graph is not rooted and may have several disconnected parts.
- Concepts at a branch do not have to be mutually exclusive, so multiple conclusions can arise. An interesting example is conclusion 9 which is concluded unconditionally once premise 2 applies.

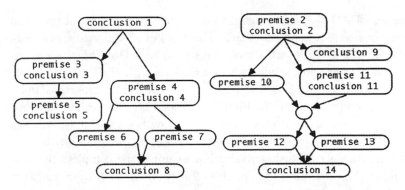

Figure 8.1
Knowledge structure—exception directed acyclic graph.

- As shown at premise 2, the structure is not binary. There may be more than two nodes at a branch.

- As shown at conclusion 8, the structure is not a tree. Branches may rejoin, corresponding to rules with a common exception or common conclusion

- As shown at premise 6, a premise does not have to have a conclusion. It may just be a common factor to all the premises of its child nodes. As in decision trees, not all premises in an EDAG are directly premises of rules.

- As shown at conclusions 1 and 8, a conclusion does not have to have a premise. It may be a default conclusion, or a common conclusion to all the premises on its parent nodes.

- As shown by the null node between premises 10 and 12, it may be appropriate to insert an empty node to avoid arrows crossing.

- The notion of "premise" used is that of any potentially decidable predicate; that is, one with truth values, true, false or unknown. The unknown case is significant because, as illustrated later, conclusions from the EDAG as a whole may be partially or wholly decidable even though some premises are undecidable in a particular case—usually because some information is missing for the case.

A set of production rules without a default and without exceptions forms a trivial EDAG with no connections. An ID3-style decision tree forms an EDAG that is restricted to be a tree, with the set of premises fanning out from a node restricted to be tests of all the values of a particular attribute. Rules with exceptions form an EDAG in which every node has a conclusion. Rules with exceptions with their premises factored for common sub-premises (Gaines, 1991d) form a general EDAG.

The direction of arrows in Figure 8.1 indicates the decision-making paths. However, if the arrows are reversed they become the 'isa' arrows of a semantic network showing inheritance among premises, with multiple inheritance read disjunctively. For example the complete premise leading to the conclusion 14 is premise 2 $\land$ (premise 10 $\lor$ premise 11) $\land$ (premise 12 $\lor$ premise 13).

The complete premise for nodes with child nodes involves the negation of the disjunction of the child nodes, but not of their children. For example, the complete premise leading to the conclusion 1 is $\neg$(premise 3 $\lor$ premise 4), with premises 5 through 7 playing no role.

This last result is important to the comprehensibility of an EDAG. The 'meaning' of a node can be determined in terms of its path(s) back to the root and its child nodes. The other parts of the tree are irrelevant to whether the conclusion at that node will be selected. They remain potentially relevant to the overall conclusion in that they may contribute additional conclusions if the structure is not such that conclusions are mutually exclusive.

From a psychological perspective, the interpretation of the EDAG may be seen as each node providing a well-defined 'context' for its conclusion, where it acts as an exception to nodes back to the root above it, and it has as exceptions the nodes immediately below it. This notion of context is that suggested by Compton and Jansen (1990) in their analysis of 'ripple-down rules', the difference being that EDAG contexts are not necessarily mutually exclusive.

8.4   Inducing EDAGS

Induct (Gaines, 1989) is used to generate EDAGs through a three-stage process. First, it is used to generate rules with exceptions. Second, the premises of the rules are factored to extract common sub-premises (which are not necessarily unique, e.g. A $\land$ B, B $\land$ C and C $\land$ A may be factored in pairs by A, B or C). Third, common exception structures

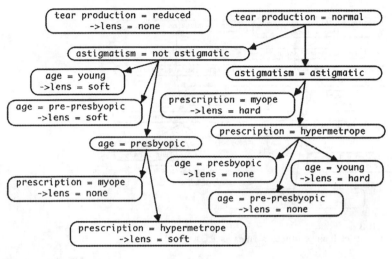

Figure 8.2
ID3 contact lens decision tree as EDAG.

are merged. Currently, a greedy algorithm is used that reports the first factorization found, and does not search over all factorizations to achieve a global minimum. The second and third stages of factoring can be applied to any set of production rules represented as an EDAG, and it is appropriate to do so to C4.5 and PRISM rules when comparing methodologies and illustrating EDAGs as knowledge structures.

The familiar contact lens prescription problem (Cendrowska, 1987) will be used to illustrate the EDAG as a knowledge structure. The problem involves three 2-valued attributes, one 3-valued attribute, and a 3-valued conclusion. Figure 8.2 shows the ID3 decision tree for the lens problem as an EDAG, and Figure 8.3 shows the PRISM production rules as an EDAG. The representation in itself adds nothing to the results, but the examples illustrate the subsumption of these two common knowledge structures. The representation of the rules can be improved by factoring the premises to produce the EDAG shown in Figure 8.4.

Figures 8.2 through 8.4 are trivial EDAGs in the sense in that no exceptions are involved. More interesting examples can be generated using C4.5's methodology of: reducing the number of production rules by specifying a default conclusion; removing the rules with that conclusion; and making the other rules exceptions to the default. This can be applied

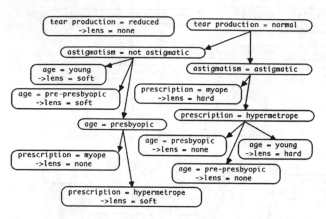

Figure 8.3
PRISM contact lens production rules as EDAG.

to the PRISM rules in Figure 8.4 by making "none" the default and removing the four rules with "none" as a conclusion on the left. Both PRISM and C4.5 then generate the same set of rules with exceptions which can be factored into the EDAG shown in Figure 8.5.

Induct generates multi-level exceptions in that an exception may itself have exceptions. Figure 8.6 shows the EDAG generated by Induct from the 24 lens cases. On the left, the "soft" conclusion is generated by a simple premise that has an exception. On the right, the "hard" conclusion is generated by the same rules as in Figure 8.5.

Varying the distribution of the data set can lead to different exception structures. Figure 8.7 shows the EDAG is generated by Induct when the data is biased to have a lower proportion of the "hard" exceptions. 46 cases have been used—2 x 24 with the 2 examples of the "hard" exception removed from the second set. The data is logically unchanged, but the statistical test that Induct uses to determine whether to generate an exception is affected. The exceptions are now statistically more "exceptional."

8.5 Complexity Measuures for EDAGS

Figures 8.2 through 8.7 show that many different EDAGs can be derived having the same performance. It is also apparent that the simpler

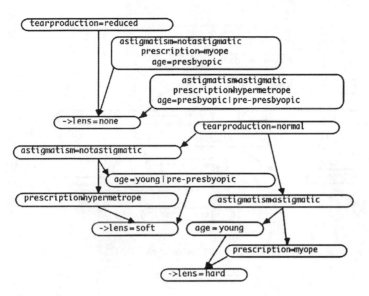

Figure 8.4
PRISM contact lens production rules, factored as EDAG.

ones present a more comprehensible knowledge structure. Figures 8.5 through 8.7 show that simple comprehensible knowledge structures are not unique. Each represents a reasonable basis for understanding and explaining contact lens decisions. Figure 8.6 may appear marginally better than the alternatives in Figures 8.5 and 8.7, but one can imagine a debate between experts as to which is best—Figure 8.5 has only one layer of exceptions—Figure 8.7 is more balanced in its treatment of astigmatism.

It is interesting to derive a complexity measure for an EDAG that corresponds as closely as possible to the psychological factors leading to judgments of the relative complexity of different EDAGs. As usual, the basis for a structural complexity measure is enumerative, in that one counts the components in the representation (Gaines, 1977). The obvious components are the nodes, the arcs, and the premise and conclusion clauses. Since the graphs are not trees, branches can rejoin with possible line crossings causing visual confusion. This correlates with the extent to which nodes are disjunctive and have several outgoing arcs. A possible measure is the number of outgoing arcs in excess of one for a node, which may be calculated as arcs + final nodes - nodes. Induct also

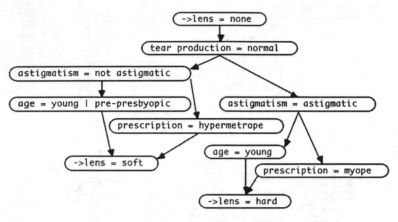

Figure 8.5
PRISM/C4.5 contact lens rules with default, factored as EDAG.

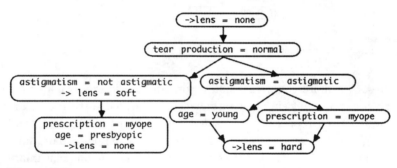

Figure 8.6
Induct rules with exceptions, factored as EDAG.

allows the option of a disjunction of values within a clause, and such a disjunction is weighted by the number of values mentioned, e.g. $x = 5$ counts 1, $x \in \{5, 8\}$ counts 2, and $x \in \{5, [8, 12]\}$ counts 3 (where [8,12] specifies the interval from 8 through 12).

The derivation of an overall complexity measure from these component counts has to take into account the required graph reductions which should lead to complexity measure reductions. The basic requirements are shown in Figure 8.8. It is apparent that clause and crossing reduction should dominate node reduction.

One suitable formula is that shown in Figure 8.8, that the: complexity of an EDAG =

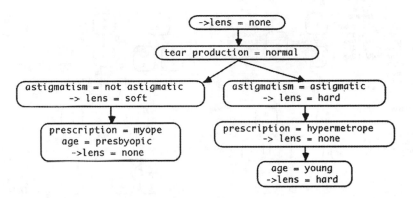

Figure 8.7
Alternative Induct rules with exceptions, factored as EDAG.

$$(\text{nodes} + \text{excess arcs} \times 2 + \text{clauses} \times 2)/5 \qquad (8.5.1)$$

where the scaling by 5 is for normalization.

For binary decision trees and production rules there are relations between the numbers in Equation (1) that allow one to give the complexity measure more specific interpretations:

$$\text{complexity of a binary decision tree} \; = \; \text{number of nodes} \qquad (8.5.2)$$

which is the usual measure of the complexity of a binary decision tree;

$$\text{complexity of production rules} \; =$$
$$0.6 \times \text{ number of rules} + 0.4 \times \text{ number of premise clauses} \qquad (8.5.3)$$

which is a weighted mean of two usual measures of the complexity of a set of production rules.

It would be appropriate to conduct empirical psychological experiments with a range of EDAGs and evaluate the correlation between the understanding of knowledge measured in various ways and the complexity measure developed here. Sufficient data would also allow other complexity measures to be evaluated. Nosek and Roth's (1990) empirical comparison of formal knowledge representation schema exemplifies what can be done. Shum and Hammond (1994) have surveyed studies of comprehensibility of data structures more generally.

Figure 8.9 shows the component counts and the computed complexity measures for the solutions to the lens problems shown in Figures

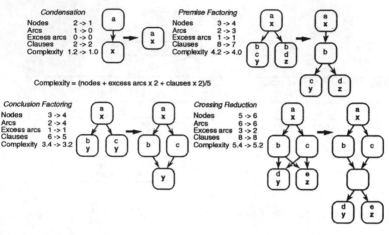

Figure 8.8
Complexity reductions required to correspond to graph reductions.

Fig.	Example	Nodes N	Final Nodes F	Arcs A	Excess E = A +F-N	Clauses C	Complexity (N+2E+2 C)/5
2	ID3	14	9	12	7	23	14.8
3	PRISM	9	9	0	0	34	15.4
4	PRISM, factored	13	3	13	3	19	11.4
5	C4.5 default, factored	10	2	11	3	11	7.6
6	Induct, factored	8	2	8	2	11	6.8
7	Induct variant, factored	7	2	6	1	13	7.0

Figure 8.9
Comparison of complexity of contact lens EDAGs.

2 through 7. The computed complexity measure does appear to have a reasonable correspondence to the variations in complexity that are subjectively apparent.

8.6   A Chess Example

The contact lens example is useful for illustration but too simple for the significance of the complexity reduction to be evaluated. This section presents a somewhat more complex example based on one of Quinlan's (1979) chess datasets that Cendrowska (1987) also analyzed with Prism.

```
line = f: game = safe (324.0)
line = t:                              (black king, rook, knight, in li)
  |  r>>k = f: game = safe (162.0)
  |  r>>k = t:                              (rook bears on black kin
  |  |  r>>n = f: game = safe (81.0)
  |  |  r>>n = t:                              (rook bears on knigh
  |  |  |  k-n = 1:
  |  |  |  |  n-wk = 2: game = safe (9.0)      (knight to white king =
  |  |  |  |  n-wk = 3: game = safe (9.0)
  |  |  |  |  n-wk = 1:
  |  |  |  |  |  k-r = 1: game = safe (2.0)      (black king to rook =
  |  |  |  |  |  k-r = 2: game = lost (3.0)
  |  |  |  |  |  k-r = 3: game = lost (3.0)
  |  |  |  k-n = 2:
  |  |  |  |  n-wk = 2: game = safe (9.0)
  |  |  |  |  n-wk = 3: game = safe (9.0)
  |  |  |  |  n-wk = 1:
  |  |  |  |  |  k-r = 2: game = lost (3.0)
  |  |  |  |  |  k-r = 3: game = lost (3.0)
  |  |  |  |  |  k-r = 1:
  |  |  |  |  |  |  r-wk = 1: game = lost (1.0)
  |  |  |  |  |  |  r-wk = 2: game = safe (1.0)
  |  |  |  |  |  |  r-wk = 3: game = safe (1.0)
  |  |  |  k-n = 3:
  |  |  |  |  k-r = 2: game = lost (9.0)
  |  |  |  |  k-r = 3: game = lost (9.0)
  |  |  |  |  k-r = 1:
  |  |  |  |  |  r-wk = 1: game = lost (3.0)
  |  |  |  |  |  r-wk = 2: game = safe (3.0)
  |  |  |  |  |  r-wk = 3: game = safe (3.0)
```

Figure 8.10
ID3 chess decision tree.

The data consists of 647 cases of a rook versus knight end game situation described in terms of four 3-valued and three 2-valued attributes leading to one of two conclusions. All the solutions described are 100% correct.

Figure 8.10 shows the 30 node decision tree produced by ID3 and Figure 8.11 shows the 15 rules produced by C4.5 for the chess data. Cendrowska (1987) reports a substantially larger tree and the same number of rules with some additional clauses. Figures 8.12 and 8.13 shows the rules produced by C4.5 factored in 2 ways. The EDAG in Figure 8.13 introduces an additional (empty) node to make it clear that the possible exceptions are the same on both branches. Figure 8.14 shows an EDAG produced by Induct. All three EDAGs are interesting in not being trees and involving different simple presentations of the same knowledge.

Figure 8.15 shows the complexities of various EDAGs solving the chess problem. The decision tree published by Cendrowska (1987) is more complex than that produced by ID3. PRISM generates the same 15 production rules as does C4.5 except that two of the rules have redundant clauses. This has a small effect on the relative complexity of the production rules, but a larger effect on that of the factored rules since those from PRISM do not factor as well because of the redundant clauses.

```
                               r>>n = f -> game = saf
                               r>>k = f -> game = saf
                               line = f -> game = saf
                    k-n = 1 & n-wk = 2 -> game = sa
                    k-n = 1 & n-wk = 3 -> game = sa
                    k-r = 1 & r-wk = 2 -> game = sa
                    k-r = 1 & r-wk = 3 -> game = sa
                    k-n = 2 & n-wk = 2 -> game = sa
                    k-n = 2 & n-wk = 3 -> game = sa
  k-r = 2 & n-wk = 1 & line = t & r>>k = t & r>>n = t -> game =
  k-r = 3 & n-wk = 1 & line = t & r>>k = t & r>>n = t -> game =
  n-wk = 1 & r-wk = 1 & line = t & r>>k = t & r>>n = t -> game =
  k-n = 3 & r-wk = 1 & line = t & r>>k = t & r>>n = t -> game =
  k-n = 3 & k-r = 2 & line = t & r>>k = t & r>>n = t -> game =
  k-n = 3 & k-r = 3 & line = t & r>>k = t & r>>n = t -> game =
```

Figure 8.11
C4.5 chess rules.

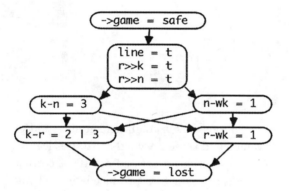

Figure 8.12
C4.5 chess rules with exception, factored as EDAG.

The three solutions shown in Figures 8.12 through 8.14 are similar in complexity as one might expect. They are different, yet equally valid, ways of representing the solution.

The reduction between the tree in Figure 8.10 or the rules in Figure 8.11 and the EDAGs in Figures 8.12 through 8.14 does seem to go some way to meeting Michie's objections to trees or rule sets as knowledge structures that Quinlan (1991) cites. It is more plausible to imagine a chess expert using the decision procedures of Figures 8.12 through 8.14 than those of Figures

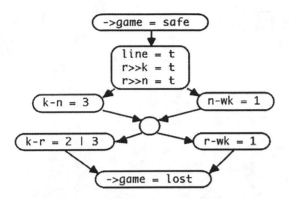

Figure 8.13
C4.5 chess rules with exception, factored with crossing reduction.

8.7   Inference with EDAGS—Unknown Values

Inference with EDAGs when all premises are decidable is simple and has already been described. However, inference when some premises are unknown as to their truth values involves some subtleties that are significant. Consider the EDAG of Figure 8.16 where Premise-1 is unknown but Premise-2 is true and the attached conclusion is the same as the default. One can then infer Conclusion = A regardless of what the truth value of Premise-1 might be.

The required reasoning is simple to implement and is incorporated in the EDAG-inference procedure of KRS (Gaines, 1991a; Gaines, 1993a) a KL-ONE-like knowledge representation server. The evaluation of a premise as true, false or unknown is common in such systems. It is simple to mark the EDAG such that a node is disregarded if: it has an unknown premise but has a child node that is definitely true; or it has the same conclusion as another node whose premise is true.

The importance of pruning the list of possible conclusions is that it is the basis of acquiring further information, for example, by asking the user of the system. It is important not to request information that may be expensive to obtain but is irrelevant to the conclusion. Cendrowska (1987) makes this point strongly in comparing modular rules with decision trees; that, for example, in contact lens prescription the measurement of tear production is time-consuming and unpleasant, and should be avoided if possible. She notes that it is not required in the 3 rules

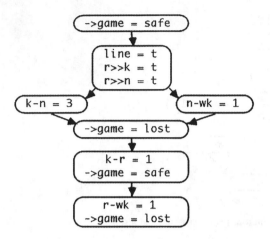

Figure 8.14
Induct chess rules with exceptions, factored as EDAG.

produced by PRISM shown at the middle left of Figure 8.3 but is the first attribute tested in the ID3 decision tree of Figure 8.2. She argues that the tree requires the testing of this attribute unnecessarily in certain cases.

However, the three decidable cases with unknown values of tear production (corresponding to the premises of the three rules at the middle left of Figure 8.3) are all correctly evaluated by the EDAG of Figure 2 using the reasoning defined above, as they are by all the other EDAGs of Figures 8.4 through 8.7. The problem Cendrowska raises is a question of properly using the tree as a basis for inference, rather than a distinction between trees and production rules.

Since the complexity figures in Figure 8.9 indicate that the PRISM rules are, on one reasonable measure, more complex than the ID3 tree, it would seem that the arguments for rules being better than trees are not justified. Certainly the highly restrictive standard decision tree can be improved in comprehensibility by the use of exceptions and factoring, but whether the resultant structure is a more general rule, or a set of rules with exceptions, is a matter of perspective.

The simple pruning procedure described above is sufficient to deal with the tear production problem raised by Cendrowska. However, it is inadequate to properly account for all the nine decidable cases with unknown values (corresponding to the premises of the rules in Figure 8.3).

Fig.	Example	Nodes N	Final Nodes F	Arcs A	Excess E = A +F-N	Clauses C	Complexity (N+2E+2C)/5
-	Cendrowska tree	78	52	76	50	130	87.6
-	PRISM production rules	15	15	0	0	73	32.2
10	ID3 decision tree	30	20	28	18	50	33.2
11	C4.5 production rules	15	15	0	0	70	31.0
-	PRISM default, factored	9	1	11	3	12	7.8
12	C4.5 default, factored	7	1	9	3	10	6.6
13	C4.5 default+, factored	8	1	9	2	10	6.4
14	Induct exceptions, factored	7	1	7	1	11	6.2

Figure 8.15
Comparison of complexity of chess EDAGs.

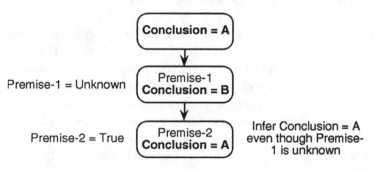

Figure 8.16
Inference with unknown values.

For example, someone whose tear production is normal, astigmatism is astigmatic and age is young but whose prescription is unknown should be inferred as lens is hard. However, this inference cannot be made with the ID3 tree of Figure 8.2 using the procedure described above alone. KRS copes with this situation by keeping track of the relation between child nodes that are such that one of them must be true. In the case just defined it infers that the conclusion is lens is hard because the two nodes with lens = hard conclusions at the lower right of Figure 8.2 are both possible, one of them must be true, and both have the same conclusion.

KRS also disregards a node if the conclusion is already true of the entity being evaluated, again to prevent an unnecessary attempt to acquire further information. The four strategies described are such as to reduce the list of possible conclusions to the logical minimum, and form a complete inference strategy for EDAGs.

It should be noted that the completeness of inference is dependent on the possibility of keeping track of relations between child nodes. This is simple for the classification of single individuals based on attribute-value data. It is far more complex for EDAG-based inference with arbitrary KL-ONE knowledge structures involving related individuals, where it is difficult to keep track of all the relations between partially open inferences. This corresponds to managing the set of possible extensions of the knowledge base generated by resolving the unknown premises, and is inherently intractable

8.8   EDAG Knowledge Discovery Tools

EDAGs are simple to support through visualization and graphic editing tools interfaced to induction and evaluation systems. Figure 8.17 shows the Induct and KMap tools in KSSn (Gaines, 1994) being used to edit and evaluate EDAGs for the chess end game discussed above.

At the top left is an Induct server window with the chess data loaded. At the top right is a partial view of a KMap window with the C4.5 rules of Figure 8.11 represented graphically, and at the bottom is a KMap window with the ID3 rules of Figure 8.10 represented graphically.

KMap is a general visual language tool for knowledge structures (Gaines, 1991c) and concept maps (Gaines and Shaw, 1994) Induct exports its derived EDAGs as graphs in KMap, and edited graphs in KMap may be pasted back into Induct for evaluation of error rates

The text in the bottom part of the Induct window at the top left of Figure 8.17 was generated by copying the EDAG in the KMap window at the bottom, pasting it into the Induct window, and then clicking the "Evaluate" button to cause Induct to evaluate the performance of the EDAG on the chess data.

The graphic interface between KMap and Induct makes it simple for an expert or knowledge engineer to experiment with the induced knowledge structures, investigate the roles of different parts, and attempt to improve the comprehensibility of what has been derived.

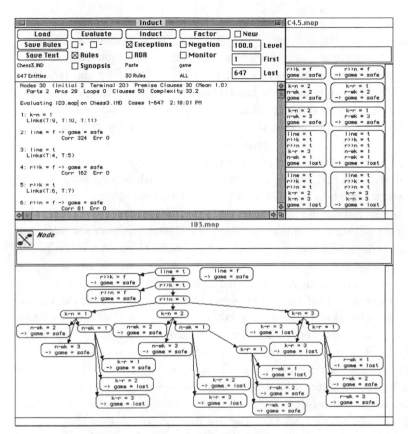

Figure 8.17
Graphic EDAG induction and editing tools.

8.9   Discussion and Conclusions

The factorization of systems of rules with exceptions is proposed as a means for simplifying induced rules to derive more comprehensible knowledge structures. The resultant structure is an example of a knowledge structure, an exception directed acyclic graph, that subsumes both trees and rules. EDAGs make apparent the conceptual structures underlying inference through inheritance and structure sharing. EDAG inference is computationally simple, even under conditions of partial information, and its simplicity should make it easily understood by people.

The EDAGs studied in this article are simple and leave open the question of the scalability of the methodology to more significant problems.

A recent study (Gaines, 1995) has used EDAGs to reconstruct Shapiro's (1987) "structured induction" of a solution to the rook version pawn end-game when the pawn is about to queen. Replacing the ID3 trees with EDAGs results in a very much smaller solution to the problem that is more comprehensible. In addition, Induct directly induces an EDAG for the complete problem with a structure similar in size and conceptual relations to the structured induction solution.

The EDAGs studied in this article have all related to noise-free data. However, C4.5 and Induct are both effective with noisy data, and can be used to generate EDAGs with probabilistic conclusions.

A number of studies have developed graph-like decision structures that relate to EDAGs. Compton and Jansen's (1990) *ripple-down rules* generalize binary decision trees by allowing a node to contain a compound premise, and interior nodes to contain conclusions which are asserted if the tree cannot be traversed further. Gaines (1991) shows that ripple-down rules are a particular case of *rules with exceptions* that can encode some knowledge structures more compactly. Oliver (1993) and Kohavi (1994) have shown how various forms of *decision graphs* may be induced and provide a more compact alternative than decision trees.

Many questions remain open. Psychological studies of the nature of comprehensibility of knowledge structures are necessary to give substance to the intuitions that lie behind the developments reported in this chapter. The current EDAG structure may be too 'flat' in that there is no means to lift the same knowledge component out of different parts of the graph.

All that can be said currently is that the approach is promising and provides a synthesis of trees and rules that goes beyond both and may indicate an interesting new avenue of research and development in knowledge discovery systems.

Acknowledgments

This work was funded in part by the Natural Sciences and Engineering Research Council of Canada. I am grateful to Paul Compton and Ross Quinlan for access to their research and for discussions that have influenced this work. I am also grateful to the anonymous referees for helpful comments. I am grateful to Padhraic Smyth for a detailed critique of the original chapter which has greatly improved it.

References

Cendrowska, J. 1987. An Algorithm for Inducing Modular Rules. *International Journal of Man-Machine Studies* 27(4): 349–370.

Clancey, W. J. 1987. From GUIDON to NEOMYCIN and HERACLES in Twenty Short Lessons. *Current Issues in Expert Systems,* 79–123. London: Academic Press.

Clancey, W. J. 1989. Viewing Knowledge Bases as Qualitative Models. *IEEE Expert* 4(2): 9–23.

Clancey, W. J. 1993. The Knowledge Level Reinterpreted: Modeling Sociotechnical Systems. *International Journal of Intelligent Systems* 8(1): 33–49.

Compton, P.; and Jansen, R. 1990. A Philosophical Basis for Knowledge Acquisition. *Knowledge Acquisition* 2(3): 241–258.

Gaines, B. R. 1977. System Identification, Approximation and Complexity. *International Journal of General Systems* 2(3): 241–258.

Gaines, B. R. 1989. An Ounce of Knowledge Is Worth a Ton of Data: Quantitative Studies of the Trade-off Between Expertise and Data Based on Statistically Well-founded Empirical Induction. In *Proceedings of the Sixth International Workshop on Machine Learning,* 156–159. San Mateo, Calif.: Morgan Kaufmann.

Gaines, B. R. 1991a. Empirical Investigations of Knowledge Representation Servers: Design Issues and Applications Experience with KRS. *ACM SIGART Bulletin* 2(3): 45–56.

Gaines, B. R. 1991b. Integrating Rules in Term Subsumption Knowledge Representation Servers. In *Proceedings of the Ninth National Conference on Artificial Intelligence,* 458–463. Menlo Park, Calif.: AAAI Press.

Gaines, B. R. 1991c. An Interactive Visual Language for Term Subsumption Visual Languages. In *Proceedings of the Twelfth International Joint Conference on Artificial Intelligence,* 817–823. San Mateo, Calif.: Morgan Kaufmann.

Gaines, B. R. 1991d. Refining Induction into Knowledge. In *Proceedings of the AAAI Workshop on Knowledge Discovery in Databases,* 1–10. Menlo Park, California: AAAI.

Gaines, B. R. 1993a. A Class Library Implementation of a Principled Ppen Architecture Knowledge Representation Server with Plug-in Data Types. In *Proceedings of the Thirteenth International Joint Conference on Artificial Intelligence,* 504–509. San Mateo, Calif.: Morgan Kaufmann.

Gaines, B. R. 1993b. Modeling Practical Reasoning. In *International Journal of Intelligent Systems* 8(1): 51–70.

Gaines, B. R. 1994. Class Library Implementation of an Open Architecture Knowledge Support System. *International Journal Human-Computer Studies.* 41(1–2): 59–107.

Gaines, B.R. 1995. Inducing Knowledge. In *Proceedings of the Ninth Knowledge Acquisition for Knowledge-Based Systems Workshop.* Alberta: University of Calgary.

Gaines, B. R.; and Shaw, M. L. G. 1994. Concept Maps Indexing Multimedia Knowledge Bases. Presented in the Working Notes of the 1994 AAAI Workshop on Indexing and Reuse in Multimedia Systems, 36–45. Menlo Park, California: AAAI.

Kohavi, R. 1994. Bottom-up Induction of Oblivious Read-once Decision Graphs: Strengths and Limitations. In *Proceedings of the Twelfth National Conference on Artificial Intelligence,* 613–618. Menlo Park, Calif.: AAAI Press.

Li, X. 1991. What's So Bad About Rule-based Programming? *IEEE Software,* 103–105.

Nosek, J. T.; and Roth, I. 1990. A Comparison of Formal Knowledge Representations as Communication Tools: Predicate Logic Versus Semantic Network. *International Journal of Man-Machine Studies* 33: 227–239.

Oliver, J. J. 1993. Decision Graphs—An Extension of Decision Trees. In *Proceedings of Fourth International Workshop on AI and Statistics,* 343–350.

Quinlan, J. R. 1979. Discovering Rules by Induction from Large Collections of Examples. *Expert Systems in the Micro Electronic Age,* 168–201. Edinburgh: Edinburgh University Press.

Quinlan, J. R. 1991. Foreword. In *Knowledge Discovery in Databases,* ix–xii. Menlo Park, Calif.: AAAI Press.

Schreiber, A. T., Wielinga, B. J. and Breuker, J. A., ed. 1993. *KADS: A Principled Approach to Knowledge-based System Development.* London: Academic Press.

Shapiro, A. D. 1987. *Structured Induction in Expert Systems.* Wokingham, UK: Addison-Wesley.

Shum, S. B.; and Hammond, N. 1994. Argumentation-based Design Rationale: What Use at What Cost? *International Journal of Human-Computer Studies* 40(4): 603–652.

III TREND AND DEVIATION ANALYSIS

9 Finding Patterns in Time Series: A Dynamic Programming Approach

Donald J. Berndt & James Clifford
New York University

Abstract

Knowledge discovery in databases presents many interesting challenges within the context of providing computer tools for exploring large data archives. Electronic data repositories are growing quickly and contain data from commercial, scientific, and other domains. Much of this data is inherently temporal, such as stock prices or NASA telemetry data. Detecting patterns in such data streams or time series is an important knowledge discovery task. This chapter describes some experiments with a dynamic programming approach to the problem. The pattern detection algorithm is based on the dynamic time warping technique used in the speech recognition field.

9.1 Introduction

Almost every business transaction, from a stock trade to a supermarket purchase, is recorded by computer. In the scientific domain, the Human Genome Project is creating a database of every human genetic sequence. NASA observation satellites can generate data at the rate of a terabyte per day. Overall, it has been estimated that the world data supply doubles every 20 months (Frawley et al. 1991). Many databases, whether formed from streams of stock prices, NASA telemetry, or patient monitors, are inherently temporal. The challenge of knowledge discovery research is to develop methods for extracting valuable information from these huge repositories of data—most of which will remain unseen by human eyes.

The last decade has witnessed a tremendous growth of interest and research in the field of temporal databases, as illustrated in Tansel et al. (1993). Among the temporal data models that have been proposed in the literature, some directly model time-series data (Clifford and Croker 1987); the advantages of these models have recently been clarified in Clifford et al. (1994). But before we can use the results of queries on time series within regularities, we must be able to detect temporal patterns, such as "rising interest rates," in the underlying time series data. Such patterns form part of the domain-specific vocabulary in many areas of expertise. For instance, the patterns in Figure 9.1 are drawn from technical analysis of the stock market (Little and Rhodes 1978). Finding these patterns, or time-series fragments, is an interesting sub-problem within the context of discovering higher-level relationships and is the focus of some of the work we are doing within the overall problem of knowledge discovery in temporal databases. The detection of patterns in time series requires an approximate or "fuzzy" matching process. Once identified, pattern instances may then be used to construct higher-level rules or regularities, such as "panic reversals are often associated with high trading volumes."

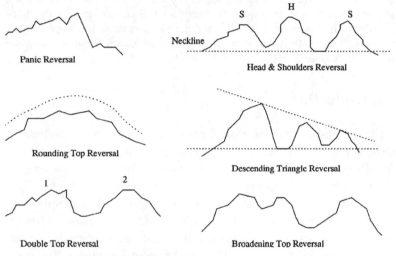

Figure 9.1
Bearish technical analysis patterns.

For example, consider the line graphs in Figure 9.2 depicting lynx and snowshoe hare populations over nearly a century (Odum 1971; Clapham 1973).[1] What type of patterns emerge from the data? One pattern seems to be that the "lynx population rises after an increase in the snowshoe hare population"—fairly natural given the predator/prey relationship. In addition, the "lynx population appears to be less volatile than the snowshoe hare population." Lastly, there are two "spikes" in the hare population that might be explained by a third data stream—perhaps they are associated with "fashion sense" as tracked by sales of rabbit

---

[1]The ratio of predator to prey seems too large, but the data are derived from commercial trapping, not from scientific observation.

fur garments! Of course, Figure 9.2 might represent data collected from any domain—just replace the labels. One could imagine the hare population to be data tracking a computer industry stock index and the lynx population to be a particular issue being "pulled" by movements of the index.

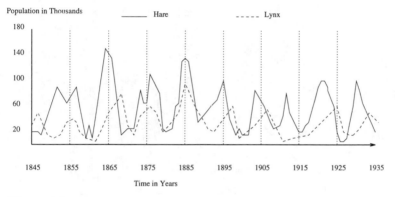

Figure 9.2
Changes in the lynx and snowshoe hare populations as determined by the number of pelts from the Hudson's Bay Company.

Humans are very good at visually detecting such patterns, but programming machines to perform the same task is a difficult problem. The difficulty arises in capturing the ability to match patterns with some notion of "fuzziness." Similar approximate pattern detection tasks are found in several fields. Related work in statistics (Jain and Dubes 1988), signal processing (Poor 1988), genetic algorithms (Goldberg 1989; Packard 1990), and speech recognition (Ainsworth 1988) offers a variety of useful techniques.

9.2   Dynamic Time Warping

The problem of recognizing words in continuous human speech seems to include many of the important aspects of pattern detection in time series. Word recognition is usually based on matching pre-stored word templates against a waveform of continuous speech, converted into a discrete time series. Successful recognition strategies are based on the ability to match words approximately in spite of wide variations in timing and pronunciation. Recently, speech recognition researchers have used dynamic programming as the basis for both isolated and connected word recognition (Ainsworth 1988; Rabiner and Levinson 1990; Sakoe and Chiba 1990).

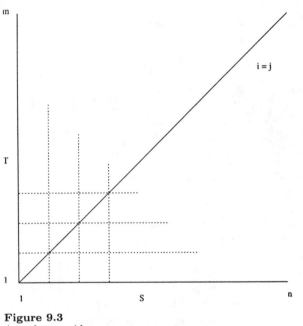

Figure 9.3
An n-by-m grid.

The technique of *dynamic time warping* (DTW) uses a dynamic programming approach to align the time series and a specific word template so that some distance measure is minimized (for an extended discussion see Rabiner and Levinson [1990]; Sakoe and Chiba [1990]). Since the time axis is stretched (or compressed) to achieve a reasonable fit, a template may match a wide variety of actual time series. Specifically, the pattern detection task involves searching a time series, S, for instances of a template, T, where:

$$S = s_1, s_2, \ldots, s_i, \ldots s_n \tag{9.2.1}$$

$$T = t_1, t_2, \ldots, t_j, \ldots t_m \tag{9.2.2}$$

The sequences S and T can be arranged to form a n-by-m plane or grid (see Figure 9.3), where each grid point, (i, j), corresponds to an alignment between elements s_i and t_j. A *warping path*, W, maps or aligns the elements of S and T, such that the "distance" between them is minimized.

$$W = w_1, w_2, \ldots, w_p \qquad\qquad (9.2.3)$$

That is, W is a sequence of grid points, where each w_k corresponds to a point $(i, j)_k$, as shown in Figure 9.4 (Sakoe and Chiba 1990). For example, point w_3 in Figure 9.4 indicates that s_2 is aligned with t_3. When there is no timing difference, the warping path coincides with the diagonal line, $i = j$.

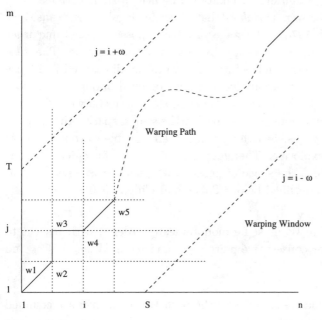

Figure 9.4
An example warping path.

In order to formulate a dynamic programming problem, we must have a distance measure between two elements. Many distance measures are possible—two obvious candidates for a distance function, δ, are the magnitude of the difference or the square of the difference[2]:

$$\delta(i,j) = \mid s_i - t_j \mid \qquad\qquad (9.2.4)$$
$$\delta(i,j) = (s_i - t_j)^2 \qquad\qquad (9.2.5)$$

Once a distance measure is defined, we can formally define the dynamic time warping problem as a minimization over potential warping paths based on the cumulative distance for each path, where δ is a distance measure between two time series elements.

$$DTW(S,T) = min_W \left[\sum_{k=1}^{p} \delta(w_k) \right] \qquad\qquad (9.2.6)$$

In dynamic programming formulations, we need a *stage variable, state variables,* and *decision variables* that describe legal state transitions (Larson and Casti 1978). The stage variable imposes a monotonic order on events and is simply represented by time in our formulation. The state variables are the individual points on the grid as illustrated in Figure 9.3. The decision variables are less easily recognized in our formulation, but correspond to the restrictions on permissible paths between two grid points. These restrictions serve to reduce the search space—the space of possible warping paths. Searching through all possible warping paths is combinatorially explosive. Therefore, out of concern for efficiency, it is important to reduce the space of possible warping paths; several types of restrictions are outlined below (Sakoe and Chiba 1990).

1. **Monotonicity**

   The points in W must be monotonically ordered with respect to time; i.e. for consecutive pairs w_{k-1} and w_k in W, $i_{k-1} \le i_k$ and $j_{k-1} \le j_k$.

2. **Continuity**

   The allowable steps taken by the path W in the grid are confined to neighboring points, i.e. $i_k - i_{k-1} \le 1$ and $j_k - j_{k-1} \le 1$.

3. **Warping Window**

   Allowable points can be constrained to fall within a given warping window, $\mid i_k - j_k \mid \le \omega$, where ω is a positive integer window width (see Figure 9.4).

---

[2]A given distance measure allows warping paths to be ranked. It may also be useful to define relative (i.e. percentage-based) distance measures to make individual distances more comparable. For example, consider comparing the distance between stock prices of $8 and $10 with that of $98 and $100.

4. **Slope Constraint**

   Allowable warping paths can be constrained by restricting the slope, thereby avoiding excessively large movements in a single direction.

5. **Boundary Conditions**

   Lastly, boundary conditions further restrict the search space. The most restrictive variant uses constrained endpoints, such as $i_1 = 1$, $j_1 = 1$ and $i_p = n$, $j_p = m$. Rather than simply anchoring the points, we can relax the endpoint constraint by introducing an "offset" in the above conditions. Lastly, a starting point may be specified, with subsequent path constraints replacing a fixed ending point (Rabiner and Levinson 1990).

The dynamic programming formulation is based on the following recurrence relation, which defines the cumulative distance, $\gamma(i,j)$, for each point.

$$\gamma(i,j) = \delta(i,j) + min[\gamma(i-1,j), \gamma(i-1,j-1), \gamma(i,j-1)] \qquad (9.2.7)$$

That is, the cumulative distance is the sum of the distance between current elements (specified by a point) and the minimum of the cumulative distances of the neighboring points. The above formulation is a *symmetric* algorithm since both predecessor points off the diagonal are used. An *asymmetric* formulation would use only one of the points, $(i-1,j)$ or $(i,j-1)$. Experimental results suggest that symmetric algorithms perform better in the speech recognition domain (Sakoe and Chiba 1990). The dynamic programming algorithm fills in a table of cumulative distances as the computation proceeds, removing the need to re-calculate partial path distances. Upon completion, the optimal warping path can be found by tracing backward in the table—choosing the previous points with the lowest cumulative distance.

9.3   A Simple Example

In order to illustrate the DTW approach, we use the simple "mountain-shaped" test patterns shown in Figure 9.5. The collection starts with a mountain that increases in increments of 20, with subsequent patterns "flattened" until we reach a horizontal line at 40.[3]

---

[3]The units in this example have no particular meaning.

Synthetic Values

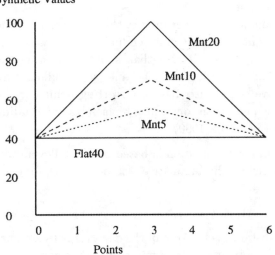

Figure 9.5
A collection of mountain-shaped patterns.

We ran a naïve DTW algorithm on all combinations of mountain patterns. That is, each pattern acted as both a series and a template during the matching process. In this naïve algorithm we used fixed endpoints and some simple constraints on warping path slope (including the monotonicity and continuity restrictions).

For example, consider the matching process with *Mnt20* acting as the underlying series and *Mnt10* the template to be matched. The matrix of cumulative distances (γ) is shown in Table 9.1, with the optimal cumulative distance of 70 in the upper right-hand corner. The warping path representing the best fit is shown below, with the appropriate Table 9.1 cells highlighted.

$$(6,6)(5,5)(5,4)(4,3)(3,3)(2,3)(1,2)(0,1)(0,0) \tag{9.3.8}$$

The warping path is a sequence of (i, j) pairs, indicating an alignment between a series element, s_i, and template element, t_j. For instance, the Table 9.1 entry $(4, 3)$ on the warping path indicates that $s_4 = 80$ is aligned with $t_3 = 70$.

Table 9.1
Cumulative distance matrix for *Mnt20* and *Mnt10*.

6	90	50	70	110	130	90	**70**
5	90	30	50	90	90	**70**	70
4	80	20	40	60	70	**60**	80
3	60	20	**20**	50	**60**	70	100
2	30	**10**	30	70	90	90	110
1	**10**	10	40	90	120	130	140
0	**0**	20	60	120	160	180	180
Mnt10/Mnt20 Distances (γ)	0	1	2	3	4	5	6

9.3.1   Measures of Fit

Once the best warping path is found, a score describing the "fit" of the template and underlying time series segment must be calculated. The score is intended to quantify the degree of fit achievable by stretching or compressing the series and template with regard to time. In addition, the score must allow comparisons so that matches can be ranked. We might be interested in comparisons of multiple matches of a single template against a long series, or against multiple series, as well as in comparisons of the fit of various templates with a series.

Normalization   The cumulative distance associated with the best warping path is a "raw" score, which cannot even be used to compare matches along a single time series. If a template is matched along a segment of time series values that are small in magnitude, the raw cumulative distance will be less than that found when matching a similarly shaped segment with larger values. This situation is illustrated by the time series in Figure 9.6, where three recurring segments with the same "shape" differ only in scale. Figure 9.6 also shows the corresponding cumulative distances or raw scores, resulting from matching a similarly shaped five-point template at each point along the length of the time series. Note that the raw scores of the matches increase along with the underlying time series. Ideally, matches differing only in scale should be comparable—requiring normalization of the raw scores. There are many ways to normalize the cumulative distances; a simple one is just to di-

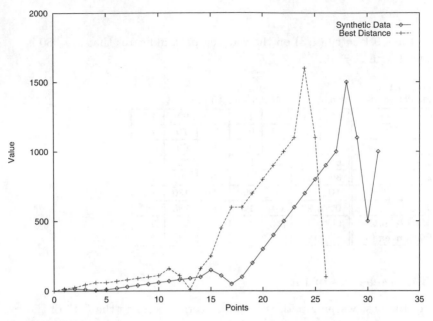

Figure 9.6
A time series containing a repetitive pattern with changes in scale and the
associated best cumulative distances.

vide by the value of the anchor point, i.e. the value of the initial point
of the match in the time series. Figure 9.7 shows the normalized scores
with three clearly comparable matches, indicated by low scores.

Baseline Score   Once we have a normalized cumulative distance, we
must still determine if the "fit" is good enough. We could use the normalized distance directly, or we could compare this distance with a baseline
score, yielding a relative score. That is, we can use the ratio of the
cumulative warping path distance to some baseline distance. We have
experimented with several baseline calculations, including a boundary
around the time series segment and simple straight-line approximations.
In Figure 9.8, the scores are relative to the fit of a straight line drawn
through the average of the time series segment. The score is set to zero
if the warping path distance exceeds the baseline, thereby keeping the
score in the [0, 1] range. An example of a boundary baseline is shown
in Figure 9.9, where the baseline is a relative band centered around the
series. For instance, a data point of 50 would be bounded by 25 and
75, assuming the band width to be 100% of the data value. Returning

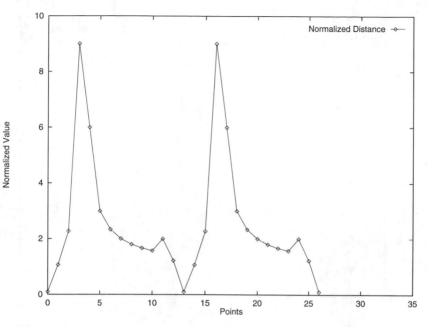

Figure 9.7
Normalized distances with comparable points.

to the example used in Section 9.3, the resulting scores with respect
to a baseline are summarized in Table 9.2. The cells on either side of
the diagonal represent the opposite series acting as a template, thereby
changing the baseline and resulting score.

Table 9.2
Score matrix for the "mountain" templates.

Scores Template/Series	Flat40	Mnt5	Mnt10	Mnt20
Flat40	1.00	0.86	0.76	0.61
Mnt5	0.84	1.00	0.91	0.73
Mnt10	0.68	0.89	1.00	0.85
Mnt20	0.36	0.62	0.81	1.00

An alternative technique for scoring could be based on statistical correlation. The DTW algorithm could be used to find the best alignment
and then the correlation between the data elements of the warping path
could be used to form an overall score. However, short templates will
lead to short warping paths and small sample sizes for correlation.

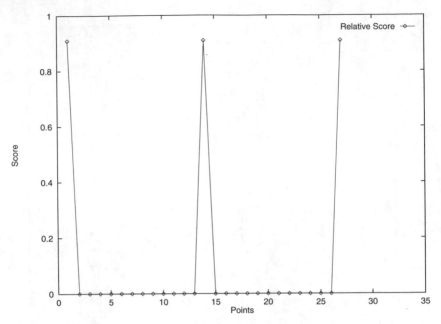

Figure 9.8
Normalized dumulative distances relative to a baseline score.

9.3.2   Algorithm Analysis

Dynamic time warping is based on dynamic programming, a well-studied technique involving the calculation of a matrix, which may later be searched to recover the solution (Baase 1988; Sedgewick 1993). In the case of dynamic time warping, the n-by-m grid of cumulative distances is calculated as depicted in Figure 9.3. Therefore, each matching process is $O(nm)$, where m is the template size and n is the size of the time series segment. The restrictions on the search space, discussed in Section 9.2, allow the running time of the algorithm to be reduced. For example, a warping window could be used to remove the corners of the grid—reducing running time by a half or more. The matching process is "slid" along the entire time series so the running time of the complete search is $O(nml)$, where l is the length of the time series. However, constants are important here as well. If the matching process is robust enough, we may not need to use every point as an anchor for a match. By skipping points, l can be reduced by half or more. In addition, the independence of each matching process should allow the entire search to be conducted in parallel.

9.4   Predator/Prey Experiments

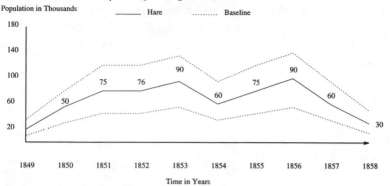

Figure 9.9
Double top peak in the hare population near 1850.

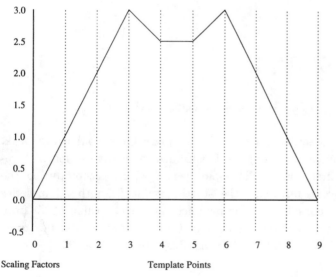

Scaling Factors   Template Points

Figure 9.10
An example double top template expressed in relative terms.

Consider again the time series in Figure 9.2. The hare population exhibits two "double-topped" peaks which will form the basis for our pattern detection. These peaks may indicate some interesting phenomena: perhaps heavy lynx hunting for pelts caused a break in the normal spike-shaped cycles. In the entirely different domain of stock market technical analysis, involving the search for many such patterns, this particular form is similar to what is called a "double top reversal" as shown in Figure 9.1. Figure 9.9 is a close-up of the peak occurring near 1850, including the boundary which would be used to calculate a baseline score as discussed in Section 9.3.1.

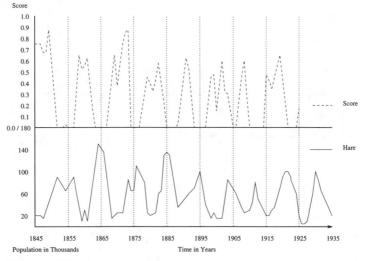

Figure 9.11
Dynamic time warping scores and hare population data.

Figure 9.10 describes an example template for a double top peak. In our experiment, the template is specified in relative terms with respect to the first point. This point serves as an anchor during the matching process, inheriting the starting value from the time series segment being considered. For instance, an anchor value of 20 from the underlying time series would result in a template instance of $< 20, 40, 60, 80, 70, 70, 80, 60, 40, 20 >$, as illustrated in Table 9.3.

Table 9.3
A template instance derived by scaling.

Pattern Scaling	Template Instance

Pattern Scaling	0	1	2	3	2.5	2.5	3	2	1	0
Template Instance	20	40	60	80	70	70	80	60	40	20

After matching the template at each point along the hare population series, again using the DTW algorithm described in Section 9.3, the two

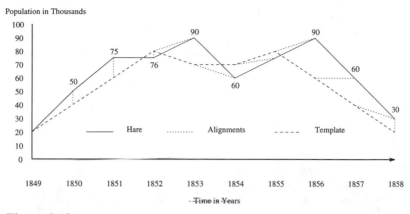

Figure 9.12
The series/template alignment anchored near 1850.

highest scores obtained were anchored at 1849 (0.87) and 1870 (0.86).
These points correspond nicely with the double-topped peaks in Figure
9.2. Most other scores were substantially lower, with only a few reaching
over 0.6. This matching problem is fairly difficult since there are several
areas which might be classified as double-peaked and the template is
quite simple. A more complex template should be harder to match
closely, and therefore be more selective. The graph of the scores over
the hare population data is shown in Figure 9.11. The particular warping
path anchored near 1850 is shown in Figure 9.12, with the warping path
alignments represented by dotted lines.

9.5   Stock Market Experiments

Figure 9.13 shows the Dow Jones Industrial Average (DJIA) from 1989
through the middle of 1993. This DJIA series was used to run experiments based on the templates depicted in Figure 9.14. These templates
vary in length from 9 to 12 trading days, and represent relative changes
of around 10%.

We ran the DTW algorithm on the these four templates using a combination of the warping path restrictions described in Section 9.2. In
particular, we varied the size of the warping window and slope constraint, while maintaining fixed endpoints. The warping window size is
expressed as the percentage of the cumulative distance matrix which is

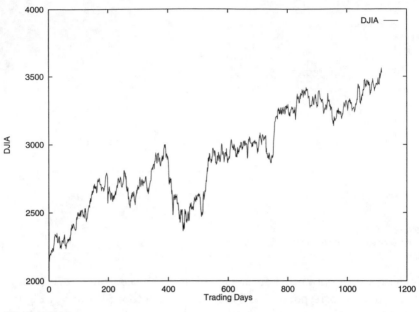

Figure 9.13
The DJIA from 1989 to 1993.

legal territory for warping paths. The slope constraint is expressed as
the number of consecutive moves allowable in the same direction. As
the restrictions are tightened, there is less freedom to skew the time
alignments. One would expect fewer matches given less freedom, and
this is the case in Figure 9.15. However, the reduction in matches is not
too dramatic, indicating that the method is fairly robust with respect to
parameter choice. As one would expect, the average length of warping
paths increases as restrictions on possible alignments are relaxed. Figure
9.16 shows the actual scores for one of the patterns.

9.6   Conclusion

The knowledge discovery sub-problem of finding patterns in time series
data is a challenging research issue. It is certainly important if we consider how much data is inherently temporal, such as stock prices, patient
information, or credit card transactions. Our preliminary experiments
with techniques based on dynamic time warping are encouraging. However, the performance on very large databases may be a limitation. In a

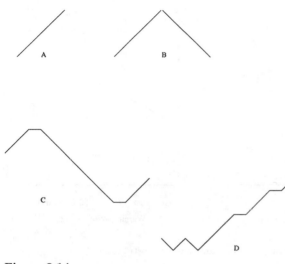

Figure 9.14
The templates used for searching the DJIA.

recent paper, Faloutos et al. (1994) discussed an approach based on discrete fourier transform (DFT) techniques. The features of a time series
are extracted and used as an index for the search. The abstraction introduced in this scheme helps to provide higher levels of performance, but
also means the search may return both the segments that match nicely
and also some that do not match well. Dynamic time warping may provide a nice technique for refining the results of this fast subsequence
search.

In the overall context of knowledge discovery, our goal is that once
we can detect patterns such as a double top peak, we can then express
higher-level relationships or "knowledge" as rules. That is, a natural
extension of this work is to search for associations between patterns.
For example, the following rule expresses one possible relationship in
the hares and lynx domain, where $t1$ and $t2$ represent a time interval.

$$double\_top(hare, t1, t2) \rightarrow heavy\_hunting(lynx, t1, t2) \qquad (9.6.9)$$

We plan to develop more refined DTW algorithms and evaluate them
in the context of a prototype knowledge discovery tool. In addition,
we plan to explore parallel versions of these techniques in order to improve performance. Since the DTW algorithm is based on independent
matches of a template against segments of a time series, we can partition

Number of Matches

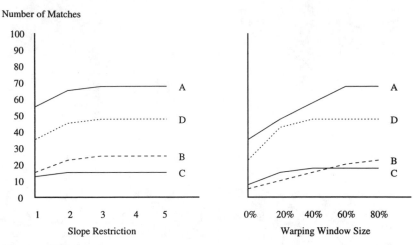

Figure 9.15
The number of matches for varying slope and window restrictions.

the time series and use parallel matching processes. The granularity of the computations can be controlled by changing the time series interval size. These independent tasks can then be distributed to multiple processors.

Acknowledgments

This research was supported by the NSF under grant IRI-9318773. The authors would like to thank Vasant Dhar, Alex Tuzhilin, and Norm White for many fruitful discussions during the course of this research.

References

Ainsworth, W. A. 1988. *Speech Recognition by Machine*. London: Peter Peregrinus Ltd.

Baase, S. 1988. *Computer Algorithms*. Reading, Massachusetts: Addison-Wesley, Second Edition.

Clifford, J., and Croker, A. 1987. The Historical Relational Data Model (HRDM) and Algebra Based on Lifespans. In Proceedings of the International Conference on Data Engineering, 528–537, Los Angeles, California: IEEE Computer Society Press.

Clifford, J., Croker, A., and Tuzhilin, A. 1994. On Completeness of Historical Relational Data Models. *ACM Transactions on Database Systems*,

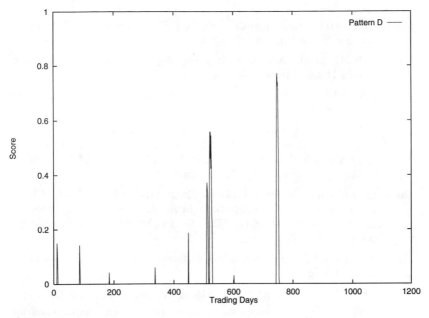

Figure 9.16
The scores for pattern D.

19(1).

Clapham Jr., W. B. 1973. *Natural Ecosystems*. New York: Macmillan Publishing Company.

Frawley, W. J., Piatetsky-Shapiro, G., and Matheus, C. J. 1991. Knowledge Discovery in Databases: An Overview. In *Knowledge Discovery in Databases*, eds. Piatetsky-Shapiro, G., and Frawley, W. J., 1–27. Menlo Park, California: The AAAI Press.

Faloutos, C., Ranganathan, M., Manolopoulos, Y. 1994. Fast Subsequence Matching in Time-series Databases. In Proceedings of the 1994 ACM SIGMOD.

Goldberg, D. E. 1989. *Genetic Algorithms in Search, Optimization, and Machine Learning*. New York: Addison-Wesley Publishing Company.

Jain, A. K., and Dubes, R. C. 1988. *Algorithms for Clustering Data*. Englewood Cliffs, New Jersey: Prentice Hall.

Larson, R. E., and Casti, J. L. 1978. *Principles of Dynamic Programming*. Basel, Switzerland: Marcel Dekker Inc.

Little, J. B., and Rhodes, L. 1978. *Understanding Wall Street*. Cockeysville, Maryland: Liberty Publishing Company.

Odum, E. P. 1971. *Fundamentals of Ecology.* Philadelphia: W. B. Saunders Company, Third Edition.

Packard, N. H. 1990. A Genetic Learning Algorithm for the Analysis of Complex Data. *Complex Systems*, 4, 543–572.

Poor, H. V. 1988. *An Introduction to Signal Detection and Estimation.* New York: Springer-Verlag.

Rabiner, L. R., and Levinson, S. E. 1990. Isolated and Connected Word Recognition—Theory and Selected Applications. In *Readings in Speech Recognition*, eds. Waibel, A. and Lee, K., 115–153. San Mateo, California: Morgan Kaufmann Publishers, Inc.

Sakoe, H., and Chiba, S. 1990. Dynamic Programming Algorithm Optimization for Spoken Word Recognition. In *Readings in Speech Recognition*, eds. Waibel, A. and Lee, K., 159–165. San Mateo, California: Morgan Kaufmann Publishers, Inc.

Sedgewick, R. 1993. *Algorithms in Modula-3.* Reading, Massachusetts: Addison-Wesley.

Tansel, A., Clifford, J., Gadia, S., Jajodia, S., Segev, A., and Snodgrass, R. 1993. *Temporal Databases: Theory, Design, and Implementation.* Redwood City, California: Benjamin/Cummings Publishing Company.

10 Explora: A Multipattern and Multistrategy Discovery Assistant

Willi Klösgen

German National Research Center for Computer Science (GMD)

Abstract

To be beneficial for diverse application domains, versatile discovery systems integrate large scale search, visualization, and navigation and offer many options, including pattern types, concept languages, evaluation and search strategies. The user must select the appropriate options when focusing a single discovery process. We introduce main problem types of discovery and sketch their option profiles to get guidelines for option selection. The problem types are illustrated by application examples indicating the versatility of Explora. Evaluation and search strategies and their implementation in Explora are studied in detail.

10.1 Versatile Discovery Systems

Knowledge discovery in databases (KDD) is the search for patterns that exist in databases, but are hidden among the volumes of data. These patterns can supply valuable knowledge, if data is sufficiently conclusive and contains problem relevant attributes for many representative cases of the domain.

Three paradigms are fundamental in support of data exploration: search, visualization, and navigation. While search in hypothesis spaces is nearly autonomous, visualization and navigation are mainly user driven approaches. In general, KDD is a semi-automatic process that should combine all three paradigms.

KDD applications use many pattern types, including rules, classification trees, and deviation detection. Concept spaces can be constructed referring to propositional or first order languages. Different strategies for hypotheses evaluation and search can be applied. The problem type of an application determines which patterns and strategies are appropriate. We introduce main problem types determined by analysis goals and problem characteristics such as data conclusiveness and amount of user knowledge.

Explora (Hoschka and Klösgen 1991) is a KDD system that assists its users and does not try to replace the analyst. To offer assistance

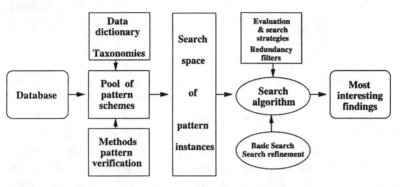

Figure 10.1
Functional model of Explora.

functionality and to take more tasks than query and statistical systems do when supporting "manual" exploration, Explora can be supplied with domain knowledge, can process imprecise instructions, and can be adapted to a user's individual needs (Klösgen 1995a).

Figure 10.1 illustrates the general approach: Explora constructs hierarchical spaces of hypotheses, organizes and controls the search for interesting instances in these spaces, verifies and evaluates the instances in data, and supports the presentation and management of the discovered findings. The discovery kernel of the system allows to incorporate many different patterns and offers various evaluation and search strategies to adapt discovery processes to the requirements of applications.

10.1.1   Versatile Discovery Needs Assisting Systems

Discovery systems support analysts in performing KDD *processes* (Brachman and Anand, this volume) with the aim of finding new knowledge about a domain. Usually, a KDD process cannot be specified in advance or automated completely, since it depends on dynamic, result dependent goals of the analyst which emerge iteratively. Typically, a process consists of steps, each attempting at the completion of a particular task, and accomplished by applying a method. The process iterates through the domain, based on search in various hypotheses spaces. KDD systems are compared by evaluating autonomy and versatility (Matheus et al. 1993). Autonomy measures to what extent a system evaluates its decisions and produces knowledge automatically. Versatility measures the variety of domains and steps of KDD processes a system supports.

There is a tradeoff between autonomy and versatility. Highly autonomous discoverers can be developed for some domains, e.g. KEFIR (Matheus et al., this volume). However, to achieve a wide range of applicability, discoverers should be assistant systems supporting human-centered KDD processes. Such versatile systems are adaptable to the requirements of the domains.

10.1.2   Versatile Discovery Needs Multipattern and Multistrategy Systems

To be adaptable to diverse domains and problems, systems must provide patterns, concept languages, search and evaluation strategies. KDD is based on searching for interesting instances of statistical patterns. A *pattern* is defined by a schema of a finding (Frawley et al. 1991; Klösgen and Zytkow, this volume) and can be seen as a generic statement with free variables. An *instance* of a pattern is a concrete statement in a high level language that describes a hypothesis. Patterns must be *comprehensible*, i.e. they should be understood directly by the analysts.

The high level pattern language is a formalism to communicate new knowledge on a domain. The kind of statements constructed in such a language depends on the pattern and varies from natural-language-like sentences like rules to more abstract statements like trees or even statements in a graphical language. The typical KDD patterns are rules, classification and regression trees, conceptual clustering, and deviation detection. Multipattern systems offer all these patterns.

The *concept language* is an important component of a pattern language. Concepts are subsets of cases which may be relevant in the domain. Typical concept languages are propositional or first order languages. Restrictions on the allowed terms of the language determine which subsets of cases are available for findings.

KDD strategies can be divided into paradigms such as search, visualization, navigation, and low level strategies for searching and evaluating patterns. Visualization gives a feeling for the contents of the data and presents findings (Klösgen 1992). Especially for spatial and time referenced data, interactive tools such as linked windows allow selected interesting areas in one data view to be examined simultaneously in the context of other views. E.g., the Natural Hazards domain (Major and Mangano 1995) needs a Geographical Information System for direct examination of findings based on a map. A loose integration of visualization with autonomous search can support KDD. However, a tighter integration is still missing.

Navigation refers to browsing in spaces of hypotheses, guided by the user. E.g., the user wonders why a finding he expected was not presented and directs the system to analyze this finding. Navigation operators relying on a set of semantic relations between objects were tentatively implemented in Explora (Hoschka and Klösgen 1991), but the overall integration of navigation, visualization, and autonomous search is not yet solved.

Findings are discovered by searching for instances of selected patterns. These instances must be interesting enough, according to some criteria. Interestingness has several facets: *Evidence* indicates the significance of a finding measured by a statistical criterion. *Redundancy* amounts to the similarity of a finding with respect to other findings and measures to what degree a finding follows from another one. *Usefulness* relates a finding to the goals of the user. *Novelty* includes the deviation from prior knowledge of the user or system. *Simplicity* refers to the syntactical complexity of the presentation of a finding, and *generality* is determined by the fraction of the population a finding refers to.

Multistrategy systems offer tools to treat all these facets of interestingness and a whole spectrum of evaluation functions. To search in hypotheses spaces, they provide diverse strategies of exhaustive and heuristic search.

10.2   Main Problem Types for KDD

This section introduces main problem types to offer guidelines for pattern and strategy selection in accordance with the requirements of a domain and to give an overview about the application fields of Explora.

10.2.1   Classification and Prediction

The general analysis goal characterizing this problem type is to discover a set of rules or similar patterns for predicting the values of a dependent variable, often to be used on new cases in the domain. A discrete

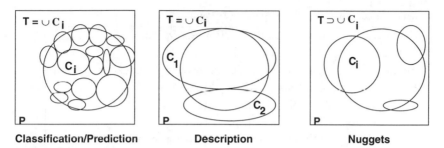

Figure 10.2
Typical concepts discovered for a target set for some problem types.

variable partitions a population of cases into k disjoint classes according to the k values of the variable. A new case is classified into one of these classes using classification trees or rules as typical patterns. In case of a continuous dependent variable, regression trees or mean patterns can be used to predict the value of the variable.

It is important for applications of this type that the concepts describe the dependency completely so that the concepts nearly partition the population or, for a binary dependent variable, partition the positive cases. Moreover, the classification accuracy must be high, and the concepts should be highly homogeneous.

Often, the classification result is further processed by another system. Then it does not matter, if the complexity of the classification result is quite high. E.g., there may be a large number of concepts, complex concept descriptions built with many selectors, and a small concept generality. Figure 10.2 illustrates this situation for a special binary case, when only the positive cases (a target set T) within a population P shall be covered by a set of concepts C_i.

Explora applications illustrate this situation. A Market Research database holds a yearly sample of 20,000 persons asked about their behavior in the financial market (banks, insurance companies). One KDD goal is to derive client profiles for companies and products (Table 10.1). These profiles are further processed by another component. To support direct marketing of a product, this component selects potential clients according to the client profile of the product. To support decisions where to open a new branch, the component compares the district where the new branch is to be opened with the client profile of the company.

Table 10.1
Client profile of bank institute "Pounds & Pennies."

Problem:	Client profile of "Pounds & Pennies"
Pattern:	Probabilistic rules
Subgoals:	High accuracy, Disjointness, Exhaustive Search
Persons:	Germany, with banking account
	9% of the persons are clients of P&P
P&P Clients:	38% of Berlin, professionals
	34% of Berlin, males, single, pensioned
	29% of Berlin, employees, high income
	25% of Berlin, students
	24% of Berlin, unskilled workmen, age > 40
	31% of Bavaria, professionals, age < 40 ...

A still planned application in the financial sector requiring a high homogeneity of concepts is the discovery of *risk and fraud profiles* for banks and insurance companies (Holsheimer et al., this volume). We will implement a new KDD system relying on parallel database and search processing to cope with huge databases (more than 1,000,000 cases) which are outside the possibilities of Explora. A third example refers to Natural Hazards. A reanalysis of the storm data (Major and Mangano 1995) in Explora classified hurricanes reaching U.S. coast.

10.2.2   Summary and Description

The next problem type is describing the dominant structure that drives a dependency. The concepts to be derived should also nearly completely partition the population or class of positive cases. However, in contrast to the type *classification and prediction,* classification accuracy and homogeneity can be reduced, but complexity must be small with a few large concepts to be easily understandable by an analyst.

Analysis of simulation results for political planning (Klösgen 1994) is an Explora application of this type. Here, the aim is not to derive an exact classification (already known by the analyst), but to generalize this very detailed classification and abstract a small number of important concepts. The database consists of a sample of 50,000 households containing socio-economic variables and data on the financial support of households according to transfer and tax laws. The typical addressee of

Table 10.2
Summary with exception sets.

Problem: Who gets no subsidies?
Pattern: Probabilistic rules; refinement of results
Households: West Germany, with children, 1994
55% of households get no subsidies. These are:
95% of TaxableIncome > 40000.
Exceptions (5%) with subsidies:
Children > 2, TaxableIncome 40000 - 80000   (96%)
in detail: Children = 3, TaxableIncome 40000 - 62000   (99%)
Children = 4, TaxableIncome 40000 - 86000   (99%)
Children > 4, TaxableIncome 40000 -116000   (100%)

results as examplified by Table 10.2 is a politician who needs a stringent overview about the consequences of a tax or transfer law. The discovery results are arranged as exception sets which are similar to exception dags used as knowledge structure by Gaines (this volume).

Another example refers again to the Market Research database and demonstrates that the same data can be searched for findings belonging to different problem types. Now, the aim is to give to a manager of a banking institute an overview on the deviations between 2 years in the client profiles of the company or product. A deviation detection pattern is used in Explora for this problem.

10.2.3   Nuggets

This problem type (Riddle et al. 1994) is dominant when data are highly inconclusive or when the distribution of cases to classes is highly asymmetric in a classification or prediction problem, e.g., if there are only a few positive and many more negative cases. The concepts to be discovered can not be expected to completely partition the population or the class of positive cases. Only a few concepts are discovered as indicated by Figure 10.2. Not a whole decision tree, but only a few branches are important. Two subtypes can be introduced, characterized by a high (resp. low) accuracy and homogeneity requirement.

The example (Table 10.3) analyses a database on political elections containing data on German election districts for federal elections after 1948. Deviations between two consecutive elections for a political party

Table 10.3
Nuggets in an election database.

Problem:	Where CDU had high losses in 1980?	
Pattern:	Means	
El. Districts:	West Germany, 1980	
	CDU lost 4.2%	
High losses in:	North, much agriculture	-7.1%
	South-West, low pop-density, few catholics	-6.9%
	Middle, low pop-density, medium industry	-6.1%

Table 10.4
Option profiles of problem types.

Options	Classif/Pred	Description	FineNuggets	CoarseNuggets
patterns	rule, tree, mean-patt.	rule, mean, deviation	rule, mean, deviation	rule, mean, deviation
granularity of concept space	fine	coarse	fine	coarse
disjoint-overlapping concepts	disjoint	both	disjoint	both
concept accuracy	high	low	high	low
concept homogeneity	high	low	high	low
concept simplicity	low	high	low	high
concept generality	low	high	low	high
evaluation-balance	balanced	balanced	unbalanced	unbalanced
exhaustive search	if possible	if possible	unnecessary	unnecessary

("CDU") are investigated to identify homogeneous sets of districts where the party has suffered high losses. Another "nuggets" application of Explora exploits hospital data on 3,000 thyroid patients.

10.2.4   Option Profiles for Problem Types

To fix steps of a discovery process, an analyst has to select various options (Table 10.4) referring to patterns, concept languages, evaluation functions, and search strategies.

10.3   Patterns

Explora offers a stock of predefined patterns which are generally useful for diverse domains and allows to incorporate new patterns which may be appropriate for special domains. A data management interface and the embedding of patterns into a general search algorithm facilitate extensions by new patterns.

Patterns of a first set compare a subset of a population (concept) with the whole population. For a second (or third) set of patterns, a concept is unusual when compared in two (or k) populations. In each set, patterns differ according to the scale of dependent variables. This arrangement resembles method-finding tables of statistics based on problem (one-, two-, k-sample comparison) and variable type. The general form of a pattern offered in Explora is:

(1) Distribution of dependent variables is unusual for a concept.

The main search dimension is given by a space of concepts which is built according to the chosen concept language. This dimension builds the "inner loop" for ordering pattern instances, i.e. concepts are varied, while other pattern arguments still remain constant. Further search dimensions refer to sets of segments, ranges, and dependent variables. See (Klösgen 1995b) for more details.

The following definition of "unusual" specializes (1) for the first pattern set:

(1.1) A concept is unusual within a population, if the distribution of dependent variable(s) in the concept differs significantly from the distribution in the population.

According to the type of the dependent variables, (1.1) is further specialized, e.g.:

(1.1.1) Share of a target group is significantly larger in a concept than in a population.

(1.1.2) In population: If case belongs to concept, then case belongs to target group.

(1.1.3) In population: If case belongs to target group, then case belongs to concept.

(1.1.4) Distribution of a dependent variable in a concept differs significantly from its distribution in a population.

(1.1.5) Mean of dependent variable is significantly larger in concept than in population.

For 2-population patterns, the term "unusual" is defined in the following way:

(1.2) A concept is unusual, if distribution of dependent variable in concept C in first population is significantly different from distribution in C in second population.

The concept is compared in two (resp. k) populations. According to the type of dependent variables, there are specializations as (1.1.i). Also other patterns, like functional dependency (Zytkow and Zembowicz 1993), are available in Explora.

The examples show patterns as a schema that is applied to candidates. For each candidate, one must check, if the pattern exists. The candidates in the examples were mainly concepts. All concepts must be tested to find the valid instances of the pattern. But a pattern has still other arguments like a target group, a population, a time point. Therefore, we regard a pattern as a statement schema with several arguments. To each argument belongs a partially ordered set of objects. We apply a verification method in the product space of these object spaces.

Pattern specification (Klösgen 1992) means defining a schema and implementing a verification method. A schema is defined descriptively by filling out a form with specifications on arguments, search characteristics, presentation and explanation. The verification method of a pattern is implemented procedurally consisting of an interface to get the data requested by a pattern instance and a statistical evaluation. The method usually is a small program calling data management and statistical subprocedures. Specialization techniques of object oriented programming simplify implementation of the method.

10.4   Concept Spaces

The search for patterns is mainly done in concept spaces. Explora constructs concepts as sets of cases with a propositional language. The number of concepts that can be constructed depends on the language type. For languages of strictly conjunctive form of order n with no internal disjunctions, this number is often limited enough to prevent severe combinatorial problems. However, these problems usually occur for disjunctive normal forms without any order limitations. A concept lattice is given by a space of concept extensions (set inclusion as partial ordering) and a space of concept descriptions (language terms partially ordered by generality). The ordering of concept descriptions is used in Explora to search in concept spaces.

Explora relies on strictly conjunctive forms of order n. Concepts are built by conjunctions of selectors, allowing at most n conjunctions. The order n can be specified by the user. A selector defines a selection condition with an attribute and one or several values of the attribute domain. In case of an ordered domain, one or several intervals may appear in a selector. An internal disjunction includes several values or intervals. The user can select the attributes and for each attribute, the subset of its domain that shall be used in the concept language.

To restrict the number of internal disjunctions (all intervals with values of an ordinal or all disjunctions of a nominal attribute), the user can define a hierarchical structure (taxonomy) and include only the disjunctions interesting in the domain. Further, several interval structures for an ordinal variable can be generated like the partially ordered sets of all or of one-sided intervals. For continuous variables, Explora can generate several discretizations, e.g. quantiles.

Disjunctions of conjunctive concepts are generated for most patterns implicitly in Explora. E.g., a rule set consisting of conjunctive rules can be considered as one rule built as disjunction of the rules of that set. However, this can be regarded as an heuristic approach, because only a subset of all disjunctions in disjunctive normal form is treated by the search process.

In case of a dataset with several relations, one can use n-ary predicates ($n = 1$ is the attributive case of propositional logic) to represent concepts in some sublanguage of predicate logic (Dzeroski, this volume). An example of a sufficient rule for a target predicate *client-of* is given by:

> *lives-in (person, region), laborer (person), small-town (region), exists-in(branch, region), belongs-to (branch, company), aggressive-advertising (company)* $\Rightarrow$ *client-of (person, company)*

Sets of object tuples (pairs of persons and companies) belong to the premises and conclusions of predicative rules, contrasted to sets of cases for attributive rules.

In Explora, an object set is associated with an argument of a pattern. The objects represent domain objects, e.g. political parties, companies, products, regions, time points. But not only these primary objects, which are introduced mainly via a data dictionary, are important. Explora derives secondary from other objects by *operations*. A concept is a secondary object, e.g. the subset "Married persons." Explora includes general operations to build concepts, combinations of concepts (e.g. all conjunctions of order n), or interval structures on ordered objects. To the main components of a structure belong:

- set of elements (usually represented as indices or vectors of indices)
- partial ordering of the set (successor and predecessor relations)
- ordering of the set (depth first, breadth first)
- natural language representations of the elements (e.g. "Married persons")
- meanings of the elements (e.g. extensions of married persons in database)

Other operations could build concept spaces based on propositional disjunctive normal forms or spaces of FOL expressions.

10.5   Evaluation Functions

Pattern instances are evaluated to measure facets of interestingness. We concentrate here on *evidence* and *generality*. *Redundancy* is discussed in 10.6. Simplicity can be treated by choosing options of the concept language like order of conjunctions or by introducing explicit complexity terms into evaluation functions. *Novelty* and *usefulness* are not yet used in Explora. Some proposals to treat novelty based on adaptive system behavior by learning from the user when selecting among presented findings are discussed in (Klösgen 1995a). Matheus et al. (this volume) treat usefulness: the utility of a finding is determined based on its estimated benefit from a possible action connected to it.

In Explora, interestingness is evaluated locally in the search process by the verification method when processing a single instance and globally treating a set of pattern instances by redundancy filters and search refinement. An application test within the method can verify some constraints for interestingness.

Statistical tests in the verification methods compute evidence. For exploration, we need no exact tests, because we perform many tests in a hypotheses space. A significance threshold too small leads to many findings, some of which are statistically not justified, because they are merely a result of random chance. Using an explorative test, we decide whether a distinct value of a random variable differs from an expected

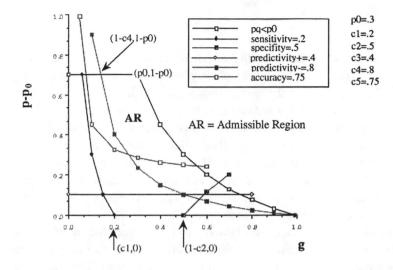

Figure 10.3
Constraints in p-g space.

value significantly. We calculate the expected value and (mostly an estimation of) the variance of the random variable. For an exact test, we need the distribution function of the variable, but for exploration, we can use approximations. In our explorative tests, we use the expected value and the variance, and as boundaries for regarding a value as significant, deviations of the value from the expected value that exceed a fixed multiple of the standard deviation. For more details, see (Klösgen 1992).

10.5.1 Evaluation Functions for Rule Patterns

The rule pattern treats the case of a binary dependent variable (1.1.1), dealing with a population P, a target group T, and a concept C. Let $p = |C \cap T|/|C|$, $p_0 = |T|/|P|$, $g = |C|/|P|$. We can assume: $C, T \subset P$.

Rules belonging to fixed P and T are evaluated in a p-g space, where p is the strength (certainty factor) and g is the generality (coverage) of the concept C.

Constraints (Figure 10.3) are conditions on true or false positives or negatives defined as sensitivity, specificity, positive predictivity, negative predictivity, and accuracy of a rule (e.g., Weiss et al. 1990). A sensitivity constraint is defined by:

sensitivity $::= |C \cap T|/|T| \geq c_1$ and is equal to $pg \geq p_0 c_1$

requiring a minimal number of true positives in C. The specificity constraint allows a maximal number of false positives in C. The user can specify constraints to localize implicitly interesting regions in the p-g space. They are used in the verification method to filter instances before evaluation. Some constraints can also be used by the search algorithm to cut subspaces of concepts. If a sensitivity constraint is satisfied for a concept, then it is also satisfied for all superconcepts. The reverse is valid for a specificity constraint. If this constraint is satisfied for a concept, then it is also satisfied for all subconcepts. These are examples of redundancy filters (true → predecessor-true, true → successor-true) which are used to prune the search space.

Axioms, equivalence relations, and balance for evaluation functions. Piatetsky-Shapiro (1991) introduced three axioms that rule evaluation functions should satisfy. Major and Mangano (1995) added a fourth axiom. These axioms mainly constitute monotony requirements with respect to p and g.

1. $E(p_0, g) = 0$
2. $E(p, g_0)$ monotonically increases in p for fixed g_0
3. $E(p, g)$ monotonically decreases in g for $p = constant/g$
4. $E(p_1, g)$ monotonically increases in g for fixed $p_1 > p_0$

Equivalence relations can be introduced for evaluation functions. We define two functions as equivalent with respect to a search strategy, if the sets of findings which are generated based on the search strategy are identical for both functions.

An exhaustive strategy to discover disjoint concepts can iteratively select the concept with the highest evaluation and eliminate all overlapping concepts. Then only the ordering of the evaluation values is relevant. All functions with the same ordering are *order-equivalent*. The search refinement algorithm of Explora provides another example (Klösgen 1995). Functions that differ only by a positive, multiplicative constant are equivalent in this case *(factor-equivalent)*.

Evaluation functions used for decision-trees are focused on producing the best overall tree. They are balanced with regard to the positive and negative examples. We can analyze two symmetry properties of evaluation function by contrasting positive versus. negative examples and by comparing a concept with its complement. Let C^* be the complement of some concept C within the population P, and E^* the evaluation function

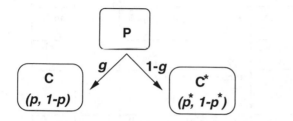

$$p = |T \cap C| / |C|$$

$$p^* = |T \cap C^*| / |C^*|$$

$$g = |C| / |P|$$

Figure 10.4
Split corresponding to a single rule (if C then T).

which is dual to E, i.e. is based on the negative examples (the complement of the target set T within the population). We define an evaluation function as type1-balanced, iff $E(C) = E(C^*)$ and as type2-balanced, iff $E(C) = E^*(C)$. Balance properties are important for diverse application types (Table 10.4).

Evaluation functions can be attributed mostly to Breiman et al. (1984). Adapting the CART approach to a single rule, the split of Figure 10.4 is evaluated. An impurity function $i(t)$ is defined on the nodes, and the goodness of a split is evaluated as the decrease in impurity:

$$\Delta i(s, t) = i(t) - gi(t_L) - (1 - g)i(t_R)$$

Evaluation functions are compiled in Table 10.5. Within the family

$$E(p, g) = g^a (p - p_0)$$

with $0 \leq a \leq \infty$, the cases $a = 0$ (resp. $a = \infty$) rely only on p (resp. on g, $E(p, g) = g$). The axioms are satisfied for $a \leq 1$, the third axiom is not satisfied for $a \geq 1$.

Comparison of evaluation functions can be studied by their isolines (points with equal evaluation values) in the p-g-space. A detailed analytical study of isolines is out of the scope of this chapter. However, Figure 10.5 illustrates the situation.

In Explora, the user typically gives a qualitative option (e.g. low, medium, high accuracy) and the system transforms this into a quantitative parameter (e.g. an exponent in a formula). By tuning a slider (e.g.

Table 10.5
Evaluation functions for rules.

No	Test/Impurity function; Reference	Evaluation function	Axiom	Sym.
1	Binomial test; Klösgen 1992	$E(p,g) = \sqrt{g}(p - p_0)$	all	no
2	$i = p(1 - p)$; Breiman et al. 1984	$E(p,g) = (g/(1 - g))(p - p_0)^2$	all	both
3	$i = p\,ln(p) + (1 - p)ln(1 - p)$; Quinlan	factor-equivalent to 2	all	both
4	Gini diversity index; Breiman	factor-equivalent to 2	all	both
5	twoing criterium; Breiman	factor-equivalent to 2	all	both
6	chi-square; Piatetsky-Shapiro 1991	factor-equivalent to 2	all	both
7	Inferrule; Uthurusamy 1991	order-equivalent to 2	all	both
8	Piatetsky-Shapiro 1991	$E(p,g) = g(p - p_0)$	all	no
9	accuracy; Weiss et al. 1990	$E(p,g) = g(2p - 1) + 1 - p_0$	2-4	both
10	$i = min(p, 1 - p)$; Breiman	factor-equivalent to 9	2-4	both

"still higher accuracy"), the user can modify implicitly the parameter, if he is not yet satisfied with the discovery results.

The functions 1 (high), 2 (medium), 8 (low) of Table 10.5 are associated in Explora to the qualitative options.

10.5.2   Evaluation Functions for the Multiclass Problem

A dependent variable with n values partitions P into n disjoint subsets T_i (1.1.4). Let $p_i = |C \cap T_i|/|C|, p_{i_0} = |T_i|/|P|, p_{i*} = |C^* \cap T_i|/|C^*|$

Evaluation functions (Table 10.6) usually consist of two components, which capture the size of the concept by some term in g and the strength by the distance of the vectors p and p_0. Equivalence and balance-properties of functions can be defined as in the 2-class problem, axioms must be generalized for vectors p and p_0. As in the binary case, Explora offers a family of evaluation functions $E(p,g) = f(g,a)d(p,p_0)$ with alternative functions f and d. The parameter a controls accuracy.

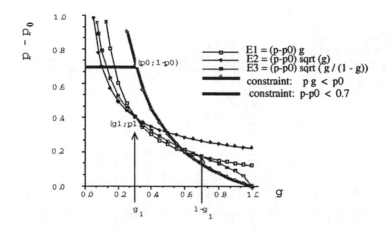

Example: $g_1 = 0.3, p_1 = 0.7, p_0 = 0.3$

Figure 10.5
Isolines for evaluation functions.

Unbalanced functions are used for nuggets.

10.5.3   Evaluation Functions for Mean Patterns

For a continuous dependent variable y, we use the mean pattern (1.1.5). Let m_0 be the mean of y in the population P, m its mean in the concept C, and m^* its mean in the complementary concept C^*. As above, we introduce a family of functions

$$E(m, g) = g^a(m - m_0)$$

where the parameter a is again used in Explora to comply with the accuracy requirements of the application.

These evaluations are extended to the k- population patterns (1.2) and (1.3) of subsection 3. Also criteria referring to the median are used for an ordinal variable (e.g. mean absolute deviation from median as impurity function).

10.6   Search

Explora uses a general search approach. Search runs in any multi-dimensional space constructed as product of partially ordered dimensions. Here, the approach is discussed in KDD context, where dimensions are determined by KDD patterns. For Scientific Discovery, other

Table 10.6
Evaluation functions for the multiclass problem.

No	Test/Impurity function; Ref.	Evaluation function	Axiom	Sym.
1	Gini index; Breiman	$E(p,g) = (g/(1-g))\Sigma(p_i - p_{i0})^2$	all	both
2	Inferrule; Uthurusamy	order-eqivalent to 1	all	both
3	twoing criterium; Breiman	$E(p,g) = (g/(1-g))(\Sigma|p_i - p_{i0}|)^2$	all	both
4	information gain; Quinlan	$i = \Sigma(p_i ln(p_i))$	all	both
5	chi-square test	$E(p,g) = (g/(1-g))\Sigma(p_i - p_{i0})^2/p_{i0}$	all	both
6	split 1 in C, C^* and use C	$E(p,g) = g\Sigma(p_i - p_{i0})^2$	all	no
7	split $i = 1 - max(p_j)$	$E(p,g) = g\ max(p_j)$	2-4	no
8	Riddle et al. 1994	$E(p,g) = max(p_j)$	2-4	no

Table 10.7
Evaluation functions for the continuous problem.

No	Test/Impurity function; Reference	Evaluation function	Sym.
1	mean test; Klösgen 1992	$E(m,g) = \sqrt{g}(m - m_o)$	no
2	Variance reduction; Breiman	$E(m,g) = (g/(1-g))(m - m_0)^2$	yes
3	Explora	$E(m,g) = g(m - m_o)$	no

kinds of patterns based on chemical reactions, genetic structures, or physical components may be integrated into the approach.

A pattern embedded in the algorithm determines the component dimensions. Patterns of Explora have 3 to 5 dimensions. Redundancy filters and search priorities are associated with dimensions. The filters— "if node is true, then its successor (predecessor) is true (false, not interesting)" —are used to prune the search space. Explora constructs a product space for a pattern, induces a partial ordering, and searches over its nodes. A pattern specific verification method checks the hypothesis which belongs to a node using related parts of the database. We consider here the main search dimension of KDD patterns and describe how Explora organizes and performs an exhaustive or heuristic search in concept spaces. Compare (Klösgen 1995b) for details of the steps of the search algorithm.

10.6.1   Exhaustive Search

If a high accuracy of discovery results is required and the size of a concept space is limited enough or time constraints are not so rigid, exhaustive search is run in Explora. Exhaustive search must be organized systematically, i.e. as efficient as possible without any redundant steps. If the exhaustive search is slow, then it is useful to present intermediate results. After a first "brute force" search phase, Explora presents intermediate results, and the user can then start a refinement phase, connected to selected intermediate results.

To eliminate redundancy, strong filters "if concept true, then successor (predecessor) true (false)" are applied to cut subspaces of concepts from search. The weak redundancy filters "if concept true, then successor (predecessor) is not interesting" are applied to cut subspaces of concepts from search for a first brute force phase. If a refinement is subsequently run for the concept, the subspace cut in the first phase is also examined. Refinement methods analyze whole sets of concepts (and not a single concept) and solve main problems of brute force search, such as hidden dependencies between independent variables, heterogeneity within groups of cases, the tradeoff between generality and strength, and the tradeoff between diversity and significance of findings (Klösgen 1995b).

10.6.2   Heuristic Search

If the number of independent attributes is large and the granularity of taxonomies and intervals is high, then the size of the concept space is so large that an exhaustive search is not possible. This is not only a problem of computer time, but also of main memory constraints. Explora manages a structure for a concept space requiring memory. By dynamic generation and processing of this structure, the constraints could be relaxed, but there will still remain applications that require heuristic approaches such as best-first, beam, or other search procedures.

Best-first search is scheduled by Explora in concept spaces by recursively applying its brute force search process. Since the search depth is restricted for each application by treating only the next specialization level of a concept, the overall search effort is decreased considerably compared to an exhaustive search. After each search, the best concept is determined relying on a balanced evaluation function and the search process is applied again, in case of binary trees, using the concept and its complement as new population. Constraints limit the recursion.

Best-first search not only limits the search effort, but also generates a disjoint and covering set of concepts. Therefore, it is also useful, if such a disjoint cover is desired, to use the results of exhaustive brute force search to generate and evaluate trees with the aim to find an "optimal" tree.

Beam search moderates some problems which may occur with best-first search due to its local optimization nature and can recursively be applied to a set of n concepts. After each search, the best n concepts are determined (using an evaluation function) and the search process is applied again using the best n concepts as new populations. As for best-first search, each search space has search depth 1. The refinement algorithm of Explora is included in evaluation to avoid overlappings.

Beam search produces a set of n concepts. But as in CN2 (Clark and Niblett 1989), beam search itself can be applied iteratively to generate a disjoint and covering set of concepts. The best concept is selected after each iteration, and in the next iterations, only concepts that do not overlap with the already generated concepts are included in search.

Stepwise search: A large number of independent variables causes heavy combinatorial problems. Often the user can select a subset of those variables which may be important, given the pattern and the dependent variable. Additionally, Explora offers a heuristic search based on a stepwise selection of independent variables. Statistical methods for model selection are adapted to identify (small) sets of relevant variables.

Using forward selection, the variable is determined in an initial step producing the best concepts in a concept space of depth 1. Conjunctions of the best variables of a step with one of the other variables at a time form the search space for the next step. When terminating the iteration after n steps, n variables are selected, which are then used to construct a full concept space, possibly with a larger granularity of taxonomies.

Disjunctions of concepts: If concepts are in disjunctive normal form, the concept space can cause severe combinatorial problems. An exhaustive or heuristic search can in a first step identify conjunctive concepts.

Then disjunctions of these concepts are evaluated to find the best ones, e.g. by a beam search.

10.6.3   Concept Driven and Parallel Search

Explora relies on a concept driven search approach in the sense that a concept space is constructed statically before search or dynamically during search. Each concept is a node in that space which stores associated information such as the result of the verification method and links to the successor and predecessor nodes in the space. Search is based on the partial ordering in the concept space.

When a concept is evaluated, many accesses to the data base are necessary which can make it very time consuming. Explora uses its own data management level oriented to discovery requirements ensuring that these accesses are efficient (Klösgen 1995). In principle, search in concept spaces must be possible along all paths and not be limited by data access optimization.

Search approaches based on parallel processing can cope with much larger problems (Holsheimer et al., this volume). Parallelization can be applied to data management and search. In some cases, the database can also be partitioned to several subsets which are searched in parallel.

Searching with genetic algorithms (De Jong et al. 1993) is not oriented at the partial ordering of the concept space, but on genetic operations like mutation and crossover. Genetic algorithms could be combined with concept driven search, by generating the initial set of concepts for genetic algorithms with some rough concept driven approach, and then using genetic algorithms to refine these initial concepts. The same strategy could also be applied for incremental discovery.

10.7   Conclusion

To efficiently support an analyst in KDD, a system must act as an assistant, because discovery is an interactive process which depends on the goals of the analyst and emerges iteratively. Since this process cannot always be specified in advance, a system cannot replace an analyst by automating KDD completely. On the other hand, "manual" exploration of large datasets, i.e. testing single hypotheses specified individually by the user, does not meet the requirements of "data mining." KDD systems must assist the analyst in generating, searching, and evaluating spaces of hypotheses.

Explora operates on data and domain knowledge to discover new knowledge about a domain. Data dictionary knowledge, taxonomies, global statistical characteristics, and interestingness specifications constitute the domain knowledge within Explora. Some of this knowledge can be generated also by discovery. Future generations of systems will include discovered knowledge in their domain knowledge to a still higher extent and use these findings for further discovery processes. Explora processes imprecise instructions by transforming qualitative goals specified by the user into numerical parameters of algorithms. Such goal specifications are necessary to adapt discovery processes to the needs of the user and the domain. Future, more advanced discovery systems will incorporate more learning and adaptive behavior. Discovery methods should also be used to learn from the user by monitoring and analyzing his reactions on the discovered and presented findings to assess the novelty facet of interestingness.

Acknowledgments

I wish to thank G. Piatetsky-Shapiro for his useful comments on this chapter.

References

Breiman, L.; Friedman, J.; Olshen, R.; and Stone, C. 1984. *Classification and Regression Trees.* Belmont, Calif.: Wadsworth.

Clark, P.; and Niblett, T. 1989. The CN2 Induction Algorithm. *Machine Learning* 3: 261–283.

De Jong, K.; Spears, W.; and Gordon, D. 1993. Using Genetic Algorithms for Concept Learning. *Machine Learning* 13: 161–188.

Frawley, W., Piatetsky-Shapiro, G., and Matheus, C. 1991. Knowledge Discovery in Databases: An Overview. In *Knowledge Discovery in Databases,* 1–27, eds. G. Piatetsky-Shapiro and W. Frawley. Menlo Park, Calif.: AAAI Press.

Hoschka, P.; and Klösgen, W. 1991. A Support System for Interpreting Statistical Data. In *Knowledge Discovery in Databases,* 325–346, eds. G. Piatetsky- Shapiro and W. Frawley. Menlo Park, Calif.: AAAI Press.

Klösgen, W. 1995a. Assistant for Knowledge Discovery in Data. In *Assisting Computer: A New Generation of Support Systems,* ed. P. Hoschka. Forthcoming.

Klösgen, W. 1995b. Efficient Discovery of Interesting Statements in Databases. *The Journal of Intelligent Information Systems* 4(1): 53–69.

Klösgen, W. 1994. Exploration of Simulation Experiments by Discovery. In Proceedings of the AAAI-94 Workshop on Knowledge Discovery in Databases, 251–262, eds. U. Fayyad and R. Uthurusamy. Menlo Park: AAAI Press.

Klösgen, W. 1992. Problems for Knowledge Discovery in Databases and their Treatment in the Statistics Interpreter EXPLORA. *International Journal for Intelligent Systems* 7(7): 649–673.

Major, J.; and Mangano, J. 1995. Selecting Among Rules Induced from a Hurricane Database. *The Journal of Intelligent Information Systems* 4(1).

Matheus, C.; Chan, P.; and Piatetsky-Shapiro, G. 1993. Systems for Knowledge Discovery in Databases. *IEEE Transactions on Knowledge and Data Engineering* 5(6): 903–913.

Piatetsky-Shapiro, G. 1991. Discovery, Analysis, and Presentation of Strong Rules. In *Knowledge Discovery in Databases,* 229–248, eds. G. Piatetsky-Shapiro and W. Frawley. Menlo Park, Calif.: AAAI Press.

Quinlan, J. 1986. Induction of Decision Trees. *Machine Learning* 1: 81–106.

Riddle, P.; Segal, R.; and Etzioni, O. 1994. Representation Design and Brute-Force Induction in a Boeing Manufacturing Domain. *Applied Artificial Intelligence* 8: 125–147.

Uthurusamy, R.; Fayyad, U.; and Spangler, S. 1991. Learning Useful Rules from Inconclusive Data. In *Knowledge Discovery in Databases,* 141–158, eds. G. Piatetsky- Shapiro and W. Frawley. Menlo Park, Calif.: AAAI Press.

Weiss, S.; Galen, R.; and Tadepalli, P. 1990. Maximizing the Predictive Value of Production Rules. *Artificial Intelligence* 45: 47–71.

Zytkow, J.; and Zembowicz, R. 1993. Database Exploration in Search of Regularities. *Journal of Intelligent Information Systems* 2: 39–81.

IV DEPENDENCY DERIVATION

11 Bayesian Networks for Knowledge Discovery

David Heckerman
Microsoft Research

Abstract

We examine a graphical representation of uncertain knowledge called a Bayesian network. The representation is easy to construct and interpret, yet has formal probabilistic semantics making it suitable for statistical manipulation. We show how we can use the representation to discover new knowledge by combining domain knowledge and statistical data.

11.1 Introduction

Many techniques for knowledge discovery rely solely on data. In contrast, the knowledge encoded in expert systems usually comes solely from an expert. In this chapter, we examine a knowledge representation, called a *Bayesian network,* that lets us have the best of both worlds. Namely, the representation allows us to discover new knowledge by combining expert domain knowledge with statistical data.

A Bayesian network is a graphical representation of uncertain knowledge that most people find easy to construct and interpret. In addition, the representation has formal probabilistic semantics, making it suitable for statistical manipulation (Howard, 1981; Pearl, 1988). Over the last decade, the Bayesian network has become a popular representation for encoding uncertain expert knowledge in expert systems (Heckerman et al., 1995a). More recently, researchers have developed methods for learning Bayesian networks from a combination of expert knowledge and data. The techniques that have been developed are new and still evolving, but they have been shown to be remarkably effective in some domains (Cooper and Herskovits 1992; Aliferis and Cooper 1994; Heckerman et al. 1995b).

Using Bayesian networks, the knowledge discovery process goes as follows. First, we encode the existing knowledge of an expert or set of experts in a Bayesian network, as is done when building a probabilistic expert system. Then, we use a database to update this knowledge, creating one or more new Bayesian networks. The result includes a refinement of the original expert knowledge and sometimes the identification of new distinctions and relationships. The approach is robust to errors in the knowledge of the expert. Even when expert knowledge is unreliable and incomplete, we can often use it to improve the discovery process.

Knowledge discovery using Bayesian networks is similar to that using neural networks. The process employing Bayesian networks, however, has two important advantages. One, we can easily encode expert knowledge in a Bayesian network and use this knowledge to increase the efficiency and accuracy of knowledge discovery. Two, the nodes and arcs in learned Bayesian networks often correspond to recognizable distinctions and causal relationships. Consequently, we can more easily interpret and understand the knowledge encoded in the representation.

This chapter is a brief tutorial on Bayesian networks and methods for learning them from data. In Section 11.2, we discuss the representation itself. In Sections 11.3 through 11.6, we describe methods for learning the probabilities and structure of a Bayesian network. In Sections 11.7 and 11.8, we discuss methods for identifying new distinctions about the world and integrating these distinctions into a Bayesian network. We restrict our discussion to Bayesian and quasi-Bayesian methods for learning. An interesting and often effective non-Bayesian approach is given by Pearl and Verma (1991) and Spirtes et al. (1993). Also, we limit our discussion to problem domains where variables take on discrete states. More general techniques are given in Buntine (1994) and Heckerman and Geiger (1994). Finally, the interested reader may wish to read the companion article in this volume by Buntine, which provides additional examples of the Bayesian-network representation as well as an introduction to some of the more complex issues associated with learning Bayesian networks.

11.2   Bayesian Networks

Before we discuss methods for learning Bayesian networks, let us examine the Bayesian philosophy and the representation itself. A primary element of the language of probability (Bayesian or otherwise) is the event. By *event*, we mean a state of some part of our world in some time interval in the past, present, or future. A classic example of an event is that a particular flip of a coin will come up heads. A perhaps more interesting event is that gold will close at more than $400 per ounce on January 1, 2001.

Given an event e, the prevalent conception of its probability is that it is a measure of the frequency with which e occurs, when we repeat many times an experiment with possible outcomes e and $\bar{e}$ (not e). A different notion is that the probability of e represents the *degree of belief* held by a person that the event e will occur in a single experiment. The interpretation of a probability as a frequency in a series of repeat experiments is traditionally referred to as the *objective* or *frequentist* interpretation. In contrast, the interpretation of a probability as a degree of belief is called the *subjective* or *Bayesian* interpretation.

In the Bayesian interpretation, a probability or belief will always depend on the state of knowledge of the person who provides that probability. Thus, we write the probability of e as $p(e|\xi)$, which is read as the probability of e *given* ξ. The symbol ξ represents the state of knowledge of the person who provides the probability. Also, in this interpretation, a person can assess a probability based on information that he *assumes* to be true. We write $p(e_2|e_1, \xi)$ to denote the probability of event e_2 *given* that event e_1 is true and given background knowledge ξ.

A *variable* represents a distinction about the world. It takes on values from a collection of mutually exclusive and collectively exhaustive states, where each state corresponds to some event. A variable may be *discrete*, having a finite or countable number of states, or it may be *continuous*. For example, a two-state or *binary* variable can be used to represent the possible outcomes of a coin flip; whereas a continuous variable can be used to represent the weight of the coin. In this chapter, we use lower-case letters (usually near the end of the alphabet) to represent single variables and upper-case letters to represent sets of variables. We write $x = k$ to denote that variable x is in state k. When we observe the state for every variable in set X, we call this set of observations a state of X, and write $X = k$. Sometimes, we leave the state of a variable or set of variables implicit. The *probability distribution over a set of variables X*, denoted $p(X|\xi)$, is the set of probabilities $p(X = k|\xi)$ for all states of X. Given sets of variables X and Y, we write $p(X|Y, \xi)$ to denote the set probability distributions $p(X|Y = k, \xi)$ for all states of Y.

A Bayesian network is a person's model for some *problem domain* or *universe*, which consists of a set of variables. A Bayesian network for the domain $U = \{x_1, \ldots, x_n\}$ represents the joint probability distribution $p(U|\xi)$. The representation consists of a set of *local* conditional probability distributions, combined with a set of assertions of conditional independence that allow us to construct the global joint distribution from the local distributions.

To illustrate the representation, let us consider the domain of troubleshooting a car that won't start. The first step in constructing a Bayesian network is to decide what variables and states to model. One possible choice of variables for this domain is *Battery* (*b*) with states good and bad, *Fuel* (*f*) with states not empty and empty, *Gauge* (*g*) with states not empty and empty, *Turn Over* (*t*) with states yes and no, and *Start* (*s*) with states yes and no. Of course, we could include many more variables (as we would in a real-world example). Also, we could model the states of one or more of these variables at a finer level of detail. For example, we could let *Gauge* be a continuous variable with states ranging from 0% to 100%.

The second step in constructing a Bayesian network is to construct a directed acyclic graph that encodes assertions of conditional independence. We call this graph the *Bayesian-network structure*. Given a domain $U = \{x_1, \ldots, x_n\}$ and an ordering on the variables $(x_1 \ldots, x_n)$, we can write the joint probability distribution of U using the chain rule of probability as follows:

$$p(x_1, \ldots, x_n | \xi) = \prod_{i=1}^{n} p(x_i | x_1, \ldots, x_{i-1}, \xi). \tag{11.2.1}$$

Now, for every x_i, there will be some subset $\Pi_i \subseteq \{x_1, \ldots, x_n\}$ such that x_i and $\{x_1, \ldots, x_n\}$ are conditionally independent given Π_i. That is,

$$p(x_i | x_1, \ldots, x_{i-1}, \xi) = p(x_i | \Pi_i, \xi) \tag{11.2.2}$$

These conditional independencies define the Bayesian-network structure. The nodes in the structure correspond to variables in the domain. The parents of x_i correspond to the set Π_i. In our example, using the ordering (b, f, g, t, s), we have the conditional independencies

$$
\begin{aligned}
p(f|b, \xi) &= p(f|\xi) \\
p(t|b, f, g, \xi) &= p(t|b, \xi) \\
p(s|b, f, g, t, \xi) &= p(s|f, t, \xi)
\end{aligned}
\tag{11.2.3}
$$

Consequently, we obtain the structure shown in Figure 11.1.

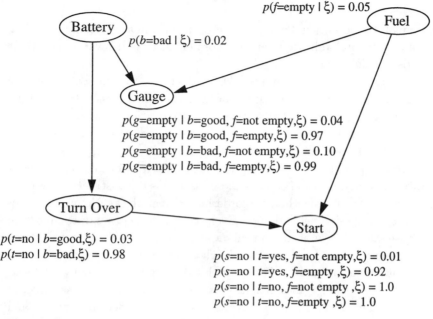

Figure 11.1
A Bayesian-network for troubleshooting a car that won't start. Arcs are drawn from cause to effect. The local probability distribution(s) associated with a node are shown adjacent to the node.

The final step in constructing a Bayesian network is to assess the local distributions $p(x_i|\Pi_i, \xi)$—one distribution for every state of Π_i. These distributions for our automobile example are shown in Figure 11.1. Combining Equations 11.2.1 and 11.2.2, we see that a Bayesian network for U always encodes the joint probability distribution for U.

The problem of computing probabilities of interest from a (possibly implicit) joint probability distribution is called *probabilistic inference*. Given any Bayesian network, we can use the joint probability distribution determined by that network to do probabilistic inference. For example, suppose we want to compute the probability distribution of *Fuel* given that the car doesn't start. From the rules of probability we have

$$p(f|s = no, \xi) = \frac{p(f, s = no|\xi)}{p(s = no|\xi)} = \frac{\sum_{b,g,t} p(b, f, g, t, s = no|\xi)}{\sum_{b,f,g,t} p(b, f, g, t, s = no|\xi)} \quad (11.2.4)$$

In a real-world problem with n variables, this approach is not feasible, because it entails summing over 2^n or more terms. Fortunately, we can exploit the conditional independencies encoded in a Bayesian network to make this probabilistic inference more efficient; and several algorithms exist for doing so.

A drawback of Bayesian networks as defined is that network structure depends on variable order. If the order is chosen carelessly, the resulting network structure may fail to reveal many conditional independencies in the domain. As an exercise, the reader should construct a Bayesian network for the automobile domain using the ordering (s, t, g, f, b). Fortunately, in practice, we can usually assert causal relationships among variables in a domain, and can use these assertions to construct a Bayesian-network structure without preordering the variables. Namely, to construct a Bayesian network for a given set of variables, we draw arcs from cause variables to their immediate effects. In almost all cases, doing so results in a Bayesian network whose conditional-independence implications are accurate. For example, the network in Figure 11.1 was constructed using the assertions that *Gauge* is the direct causal effect of *Battery* and *Fuel*, *Turn Over* is the direct causal effect of *Battery*, and *Start* is the direct causal effect of *Turn Over* and *Fuel*.

In large part, it is this connection between causal relationships and conditional independence that has made the representation attractive as a modeling tool to expert-system engineers. Nonetheless, there are times when expert knowledge is unreliable, incomplete, or is difficult to obtain. It this case, we can use data to update or learn the probabilities and structure of a Bayesian network. In the remainder of this tutorial, we consider this task.

11.3   Learning Probabilities: The One-Variable Case

Because Bayesian networks have a probabilistic interpretation, we can use traditional techniques from Bayesian statistics to learn these models from data. Several of the techniques that we need can be discussed in the context of learning the probability distribution of a single variable. In this section, we examine this case.

Consider a common thumbtack—one with a round, flat head that can be found in most supermarkets. If we throw the thumbtack up in the air and let in land on a hard, flat surface, it will come to rest either on its point (*heads*) or on its head (*tails*), as shown in Figure 11.2a.[1] Suppose we give the thumbtack to someone, who then flips the thumbtack many times and measures the fraction of flips that it comes up heads. A frequentist would say this long-run fraction is a probability, and would observe flips of the thumbtack to estimate this probability. In contrast, from the Bayesian perspective, we recognize the possible values of this fraction as a variable—call it θ—whose true value is uncertain. We express our uncertainty about θ with a probability distribution $p(\theta|\xi)$, and update this distribution as we observe flips of the thumbtack.

We note that, although θ is not a degree of belief, collections of long-run fractions like θ satisfy the rules of probability. In this chapter, we shall refer to θ as a *physical probability* (after Good, 1959) to distinguish it from a degree of belief.[2] Figure 11.2 shows one possible probability distribution for θ.

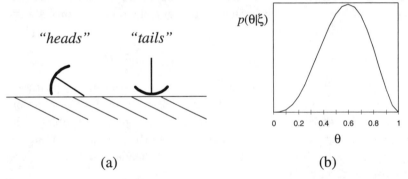

Figure 11.2
(a) The outcomes of a thumbtack flip. (b) A probability distribution for θ, the long-run fraction of heads associated with a thumbtack.

Now suppose we have a database $D = \{x_1, \ldots, x_m\}$ of outcomes of flipping the thumbtack. If we knew the value of θ, then our probability for heads on any flip would be equal to θ, no matter how many outcomes we observe. That is,

$$p(x_l = heads|\theta, x_1, \ldots, x_{l-1}, D, \xi) = \theta \tag{11.3.5}$$

---

[1]This example is taken from Howard (1970).
[2]The variable θ is also referred to as a frequency, objective probability, and true probability.

where x_l is the outcome of the lth flip of the thumbtack. Similarly, we have

$$p(x_l = tails|\theta, x_1, \ldots, x_{l-1}, D, \xi) = 1 - \theta \qquad (11.3.6)$$

In particular, the outcomes are mutually independent given θ.

In reality, we are uncertain about the value of θ. In this case, we can use the expansion rule of probability to determine our probability that the next toss of the thumbtack will come up heads:

$$p(x = heads|\xi) = \int p(x = heads|\theta, \xi)\, p(\theta|\xi)\, d\theta = \int \theta\, p(\theta|\xi)\, d\theta \equiv E(\theta|\xi)$$

where $E(\theta|\xi)$ denotes the expectation of θ with respect to the distribution $p(\theta|\xi)$. That is, our probability for heads on the next toss is just the expectation of θ. Furthermore, suppose we flip the thumbtack once and observe heads. Using Bayes' theorem, the posterior probability distribution for θ becomes

$$p(\theta|x = heads, \xi) = c\, p(x = heads|\theta, \xi)\, p(\theta|\xi) = c\, \theta\, p(\theta|\xi)$$

where c is some normalization constant. That is, we obtain the posterior distribution for θ by multiplying its prior distribution by the function $f(\theta) = \theta$ and renormalizing. This procedure is depicted graphically in Figure 11.3. As expected, the posterior is shifted to the right and is slightly narrower. In general, if we observe h heads and t tails in the database D, then we have

$$p(\theta|t\ heads, h\ tails, \xi) = c\, \theta^h (1 - \theta)^t\, p(\theta|\xi)$$

That is, once we have assessed a prior distribution for θ, we can determine its posterior distribution given any possible database. Note that the order in which we observe the outcomes is irrelevant to the posterior—all that is relevant is the number of heads and the number of tails in the database. We say that h and t are a *sufficient statistic* for the database.

In this simple example, our outcome variable has only two states (*heads* and *tails*). Now, imagine we have a discrete outcome variable x with $r \geq 2$ states. For example, this variable could represent the outcome of a roll of a loaded die ($r = 6$). We denote the physical probabilities of the outcomes $\Theta_x = \{\theta_{x=1}, \ldots, \theta_{x=r}\}$, and assume that each state

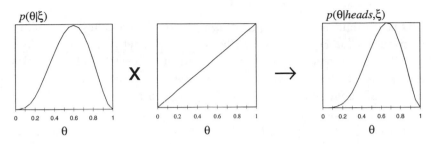

Figure 11.3
A graphical depiction of the use of Bayes' theorem to compute the posterior
probability distribution of the physical probability θ.

is possible so that each $\theta_{x=k} > 0$. In addition, we have $\sum_{k=1}^{r} \theta_{x=k} = 1$.
Also, if we know these physical probabilities, then the outcome of each
"toss" of x will be conditionally independent of the other tosses, and

$$p(x_l = k | x_1, \ldots, x_{l-1}, \Theta_x, \xi) = \theta_{x=k} \tag{11.3.7}$$

Any database of outcomes $\{x_1, \ldots, x_m\}$ that satisfies these conditions is
called an $(r-1)$-*dimensional multinomial sample with physical probabil-*
ities Θ_x (Good, 1965). When $r = 2$, as in the thumbtack example, the
sequence is said to be a *binomial sample*. The concept of a multinomial
sample (and its generalization, the random sample) will be central to
the remaining discussions in this chapter.

Analogous to the thumbtack example, we have

$$p(x = k | \xi) = \int \theta_{x=k} \, p(\Theta_x | \xi) \, d\Theta_x \equiv E(\theta_{x=k} | \xi) \tag{11.3.8}$$

where $p(x = k | \xi)$ is our probability that $x = k$ in the next case. Note
that, because $\sum_{k=1}^{r} \theta_{x=k} = 1$, the distribution for Θ_x is technically a
distribution over the variables $\Theta_x \setminus \{\theta_{x=k}\}$ for some k (the symbol $\setminus$
denotes set difference). Also, given any database D of outcomes, we
have

$$p(\Theta_x | D, \xi) = c \cdot \prod_{k=1}^{r} \theta_{x=k}^{N_k} \, p(\Theta_x | \xi) \tag{11.3.9}$$

where N_k is the number of times $x = k$ in D, and c is a normalization
constant. Note that the counts $N_1, \ldots, N_r$ are a sufficient statistic for
the multinomial sample.

Given a multinomial sample, a user is free to assess any probability distribution for Θ_x. In practice, however, one often uses the Dirichlet distribution because it has several convenient properties. The variables Θ_x are said to have a *Dirichlet distribution with exponents* $N'_1, \ldots, N'_r$ when the probability distribution of Θ_x is given by

$$p(\Theta_x|\xi) = \frac{\Gamma(\sum_{k=1}^{r} N'_k)}{\prod_{k=1}^{r} \Gamma(N'_k)} \prod_{k=1}^{r} \theta_{x=k}^{N'_k-1}, \quad N'_k > 0 \qquad (11.3.10)$$

where $\Gamma(\cdot)$ is the *Gamma* function, which satisfies $\Gamma(x+1) = x\Gamma(x)$ and $\Gamma(1) = 1$. When the variables Θ_x have a Dirichlet distribution, we also say that $p(\Theta_x|\xi)$ *is Dirichlet*. The exponents N'_k must be greater than 0 to guarantee that the distribution can be normalized. Note that the exponents N'_k are a function of the user's state of information ξ. When $r = 2$, the Dirichlet distribution is also known as a *beta distribution*. The probability distribution on the left-hand-side of Figure 11.3 is a beta distribution with exponents $N'_{heads} = 3$ and $N'_{tails} = 2$. The probability distribution on the right-hand-side of the figure is a beta distribution with exponents $N'_{heads} = 4$ and $N'_{tails} = 2$.

From Equation 11.3.9, we see that if the prior distribution of Θ_x is Dirichlet, then the posterior distribution of Θ_x given database $D = \{x_1, \ldots, x_m\}$ is also Dirichlet:

$$p(\Theta_x|D, \xi) = c \prod_{k=1}^{r} \theta_{x=k}^{N'_k+N_k-1} \qquad (11.3.11)$$

We say that the Dirichlet distribution is closed under multinomial sampling, or that the Dirichlet distribution is a *conjugate family of distributions* for multinomial sampling. Also, when Θ_x has a Dirichlet distribution, the expectation of $\theta_{x=k}$ with respect to this distribution—equal to the probability that $x = k$ in the first observation—has a simple expression:

$$E(\theta_{x=k}|\xi) = p(x = k|\xi) = \frac{N'_k}{N'} \qquad (11.3.12)$$

where $N' = \sum_{k=1}^{r} N'_k$. As we shall see, these properties make the Dirichlet a useful prior for learning.

According to Equation 11.3.12, we can assess a Dirichlet distribution for Θ_x by assessing the probability distribution $p(x|\xi)$ for the next observation and N'. The number N' is sometimes called an *equivalent sample size* for a Dirichlet distribution, because it is equal to the number of observations we would have to make starting from complete ignorance (each N'_k very close to zero) in order to arrive at that distribution. Note that N' is a measure of a user's confidence in the values of Θ_x: the larger the value of N', the more certain the user is about the values.

So far, we have only considered a variable with discrete outcomes. In general, we can imagine a physical probability distribution over a variable (discrete or continuous) from which database cases are drawn at random. This physical probability distribution typically can be characterized by a finite set of *parameters*. If the outcome variable is discrete, then the physical probability distribution has a parameter corresponding to each physical probability in the distribution (and, herein, we sometimes refer to these physical probabilities as parameters). If the outcome variable is continuous, the physical probability distribution may be (e.g.) a normal distribution. In this case, the parameters would be the mean and variance of the distribution. A database of cases drawn from a physical probability distribution is often called a *random sample.*

Given such a physical probability distribution with unknown parameters, we can update our beliefs about these parameters given a random sample from this distribution using techniques similar to those we have discussed. For random samples from many named distributions—including normal, Gamma, and uniform distributions—there exist corresponding conjugate priors that offer convenient properties for learning probabilities similar to those properties of the Dirichlet. These priors are in the *exponential family.* The reader interested in learning about these distributions should read DeGroot (1970, Chapter 9).

11.4   Learning Probabilities: Known Structure

The notion of a random sample generalizes to domains containing more than one variable as well. Given a domain $U = \{x_1, \ldots, x_n\}$, we can imagine a multivariate physical probability distribution for U. If U contains only discrete variables, this distribution is just a finite collection of discrete physical probabilities. If U contains only continuous variables, this distribution could be (e.g.) a multivariate-normal distribution characterized by a mean vector and covariance matrix. Using conjugate priors for the parameters of such distributions, such as those discussed in

DeGroot (1970), we can update our priors about the parameters of these distributions given a database.

Now, however, let us consider the following wrinkle. Suppose we know that this multivariate physical probability distribution can be encoded in some particular Bayesian-network structure B_S. We may have gotten this information—for example—from our causal knowledge about the domain. In this section, we consider the task of learning the parameters of B_S. We discuss only the special case where all the variables in U are discrete and where the random sample (i.e., database) $D = \{C_1, \ldots, C_m\}$ contains no missing data—that is, each case C_l consists of the observation of *all* the variables in U (we say that D is *complete*). In Section 11.7, we consider the more difficult problem where D contains missing data. Buntine (1994) and Heckerman and Geiger (1994) discuss the case where U may contain continuous variables.

When a database D is a random sample from a multivariate physical probability distribution that can be encoded in B_S, we simply say that D is a random sample from B_S. As an example, consider the domain U consisting of two binary variables x and y. Let $\theta_{xy}, \theta_{x\bar{y}}, \theta_{\bar{x}y}$, and $\theta_{\bar{x}\bar{y}}$ denote the parameters (i.e., physical probabilities) for the joint space of U, where $\theta_{x\bar{y}}$ is the physical probability of the event where x is true and y is false, and so on. (Note that, in using the overbar, we are departing from our standard notation.) Then, saying that D is a random sample from the network structure containing no arc between x and y, is the assertion that the parameters of the joint space satisfy the independence constraints $\theta_{xy} = \theta_x \theta_y, \theta_{x\bar{y}} = \theta_x \theta_{\bar{y}}$, and so on, where—for example— $\theta_x = \theta_{xy} + \theta_{x\bar{y}}$ is the physical probability associated with the event where x is true. It is not difficult to show that this assertion is equivalent to the assertion that the database D can be decomposed into two multinomial samples: the observations of x are a multinomial sample with parameter θ_x, and the observations of y are a multinomial sample with parameter θ_y.

As another example, suppose we assert that a database for our two variable domain is a random sample from the network structure $x \rightarrow y$. Here, there are no constraints on the parameters of the joint space. Furthermore, this assertion implies that the database is made up of at most three binomial samples: (1) the observations of x are a binomial sample with parameter θ_x, (2) the observations of y in those cases (if any) where x is true are a binomial sample with parameter $\theta_{y|x}$, and (3) the observations of y in those cases (if any) where x is false are a binomial sample with parameter $\theta_{y|\bar{x}}$. Consequently, the occurrences of x in D are conditionally independent given θ_x, and y in case C is conditionally independent of the other cases in D given $\theta_{y|x}$, $\theta_{y|\bar{x}}$, and x in case C. We can graphically represent the conditional-independence assertions associated with these random samples using a Bayesian-network structure as shown in Figure 11.4a.

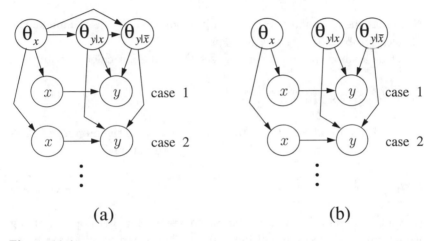

(a)   (b)

Figure 11.4
(a) A Bayesian-network structure for a two-binary-variable domain $\{x, y\}$ showing conditional independencies associated with the assertion that the database is a random sample from the structure $x \rightarrow y$. (b) Another Bayesian-network structure showing the added assumption of parameter independence.

Given the collection of random samples shown in Figure 11.4a, it is tempting to apply our one-variable techniques to learn each parameter separately. Unfortunately, this approach is not correct when the parameters are dependent as shown in the figure. For example, as we see occurrences of x and update our beliefs about θ_x, our beliefs about $\theta_{y|x}$ and $\theta_{y|\bar{x}}$ will also change. Suppose, however, that all of the parameters are independent, as shown in Figure 11.4b. Then, provided the database is complete, we can update each parameter separately.

In the remainder of this section, we shall assume that all parameters are independent. We call this assumption—introduced by Spiegelhalter and Lauritzen (1990)—*parameter independence*. In Section 11.7, we discuss methods for handling dependent parameters.

To complete the discussion, we need some notation. Let B_S^h denote the assertion (or hypothesis) that a database D is a random sample from a Bayesian network structure B_S. Given B_S, let r_i be the number of states of variable x_i; and let $q_i = \prod_{x_l \in \Pi_i} r_l$ be the number of states of Π_i. Let θ_{ijk} denote the physical probability of $x_i = k$ given $\Pi_i = j$ for $i = 1, \ldots, n$, $j = 1, \ldots, q_i$, $k = 1, \ldots, r_i$. In addition, let

$$\Theta_{ij} \equiv \cup_{k=1}^{r_i} \{\theta_{ijk}\} \qquad \Theta_{B_S} \equiv \cup_{i=1}^{n} \cup_{j=1}^{q_i} \Theta_{ij}$$

Note that the parameters Θ_{B_S} in conjunction with B_S determine all the physical probabilities of the joint space.

Let us assume that each variable set Θ_{ij} has a Dirichlet distribution:

$$p(\Theta_{ij}|B_S^h, \xi) = c \cdot \prod_{k=1}^{r_i} \theta_{ijk}^{N'_{ijk}-1} \tag{11.4.13}$$

where c is a normalization constant. Then, if N_{ijk} is the number of cases in database D in which $x_i = k$ and $\Pi_i = j$, we obtain

$$p(\Theta_{ij}|D, B_S^h, \xi) = c \cdot \prod_{k=1}^{r_i} \theta_{ijk}^{N'_{ijk}+N_{ijk}-1} \tag{11.4.14}$$

where c is some other normalization constant. Furthermore, applying Equation 11.3.12 to each multinomial sample, we can compute the probability that $x_i = k$ and $\Pi_i = j$ in C_{m+1}, the next case to be seen after the database:

$$p(C_{m+1}|D, B_S^h, \xi) = \prod_{i=1}^{n} \prod_{j=1}^{q_i} \frac{N'_{ijk} + N_{ijk}}{N'_{ij} + N_{ij}} \tag{11.4.15}$$

where $N'_{ij} = \sum_{k=1}^{r_i} N'_{ijk}$ and $N_{ij} = \sum_{k=1}^{r_i} N_{ijk}$.

11.5   Learning Structure

In the previous section, we considered the situation where we are uncertain about the physical probabilities, but certain about the network structure that encodes these probabilities. Now, suppose we are not only uncertain about the probabilities, but also uncertain about the structure that encodes them. As with any set of events, we can express this uncertainty by assigning a prior probability $p(B_S^h|\xi)$ to each possible hypothesis B_S^h. Furthermore, we can update these probabilities as we see cases. In so doing, we learn about the structure of the domain.

As in the previous section, let B_S^h denote the (now uncertain) hypothesis that the database D is a random sample from the Bayesian network structure B_S. From Bayes' theorem, we have

$$p(B_S^h|D, \xi) = c\, p(B_S^h|\xi)\, p(D|B_S^h, \xi) \tag{11.5.16}$$

where c is a normalization constant. Also, from the product rule, we have

$$p(D|B_S^h, \xi) = \prod_{l=1}^{m} p(C_l|C_1, \ldots, C_{l-1}, B_S^h, \xi) \tag{11.5.17}$$

We can evaluate each term on the right-hand-side of this equation using Equation 11.4.15, under the assumption that the database D is complete. For the posterior probability of B_S^h given D, we obtain

$$p(B_S^h|D, \xi) =$$

$$c \cdot p(B_S^h|\xi) \cdot \prod_{i=1}^{n} \prod_{j=1}^{q_i} \left\{ \left[\frac{N'_{ij1}}{N'_{ij}} \cdot \frac{N'_{ij1}+1}{N'_{ij}+1} \cdots \frac{N'_{ij1}+N_{ij1}-1}{N'_{ij}+N_{ij1}-1} \right] \cdot \right.$$

$$\left[\frac{N'_{ij2}}{N'_{ij}+N_{ij1}} \cdot \frac{N'_{ij2}+1}{N'_{ij}+N_{ij1}+1} \cdots \frac{N'_{ij2}+N_{ij2}-1}{N'_{ij}+N_{ij1}+N_{ij2}-1} \right] \cdots$$

$$\left. \left[\frac{N'_{ijr_i}}{N'_{ij}+\sum_{k=1}^{r_i-1}N_{ijk}} \cdot \frac{N'_{ijr_i}+1}{N'_{ij}+\sum_{k=1}^{r_i-1}N_{ijk}+1} \cdots \frac{N'_{ijr_i}+N_{ijr_i}-1}{N_{ij}+N'_{ij}-1} \right] \right\} =$$

$$c \cdot p(B_S^h|\xi) \cdot \prod_{i=1}^{n} \prod_{j=1}^{q_i} \frac{\Gamma(N'_{ij})}{\Gamma(N'_{ij}+N_{ij})} \cdot \prod_{k=1}^{r_i} \frac{\Gamma(N'_{ijk}+N_{ijk})}{\Gamma(N'_{ijk})}$$

$$\tag{11.5.18}$$

Using these posterior probabilities and Equation 11.4.15, we may compute the probability distribution for the next case to be observed after we have seen a database. From the expansion rule, we obtain

$$p(C_{m+1}|D, \xi) = \sum_{B_S^h} p(C_{m+1}|D, B_S^h, \xi)\, p(B_S^h|D, \xi) \tag{11.5.19}$$

There are two important points to be made about this approach. One, it can happen that two Bayesian-network structures represent exactly

the same sets of probability distributions. We say that the two structures are *equivalent* (Verma and Pearl, 1990). For example, for the three
variable domain $\{x, y, z\}$, each of the network structures $x \to y \to z$,
$x \leftarrow y \to z$, and $x \leftarrow y \leftarrow z$ represents the distributions where x and z
are conditionally independent of y. Consequently, these network struc-
tures are equivalent. As another example, a *complete network structure*
is one that has no missing edges—that is, it encodes no assertions of
conditional independence. A domain containing n variables has $n!$ complete network structures: one network structure for each possible ordering of the variables. All complete network structures for a given domain
represent the same joint probability distributions—namely, all possible
distributions—and are therefore equivalent.

In general, two network structures are equivalent if and only if they
have the same structure ignoring arc directions and the same v-structures
(Verma and Pearl, 1990). A *v-structure* is an ordered tuple (x, y, z) such
that there is an arc from x to y and from z to y, but no arc between
x and y. Using this characterization of network-structure equivalence,
Chickering (1995) has created an efficient algorithm for characterizing
all Bayesian-network structures that are equivalent to a given network
structure.

Given that B_S^h is the assertion that the physical probabilities for the
joint space of U can be encoded in the network structure B_S, it follows
that the hypotheses associated with two equivalent network structures
must be identical. Consequently, two equivalent network structures must
have the same (prior and posterior) probability. For example, in the two
variable domain $\{x, y\}$, the network structures $x \to y$ and $y \to x$ are
equivalent, and will have the same probability. In general, this property is called *hypothesis equivalence.* In light of this property, we should
associate each hypothesis with an equivalence class of structures rather
than a single network structure, and our methods for learning network
structure should actually be interpreted as methods for learning equivalence classes of network structures (although, for the sake of brevity, we
often blur this distinction).[3]

---

[3]Hypothesis equivalence holds provided we interpret Bayesian-network structures
simply as representations of conditional independence. Nonetheless, stronger definitions of Bayesian networks exist where arcs have a causal interpretation (e.g., Pearl
and Verma, 1991). Heckerman et al. (1995b) argue that, although it is unreasonable
to assume hypothesis equivalence when working with causal Bayesian networks, it
is often reasonable to adopt a weaker assumption of *likelihood equivalence,* which

The second important point about this approach is that, in writing Equation 11.5.19, we have assumed that the hypothesis equivalence classes are mutually exclusive. In reality, these hypotheses are not mutually exclusive. For example, in our two-variable domain, both network structures $x \rightarrow y$ and the empty network structure can encode parameters satisfying the equality $\theta_y = \theta_{y|x}$. Therefore, the hypotheses associated with these non-equivalent network structures overlap. Nonetheless, in this approach, we assume that the priors on parameters for any given network structure have bounded distributions, and hence the overlap of hypotheses will be of measure zero.

In principle, the approach we have discussed in this section is essentially all there is to learning network structure. In practice, when the user believes that only a few alternative network structures are possible, he can directly assess the priors for the possible network structures and their parameters, and subsequently use Equations 11.5.18 and 11.5.19 or their generalizations for continuous variables and missing data. For example, Buntine (1994) has designed a software system whereby a user specifies his priors for a set of possible models using Bayesian networks in a manner similar to that shown in Figure 11.4. The system then compiles this specification into a computer program that learns from a database.

Nonetheless, the number of network structures for a domain containing n variables is more than exponential in n. Consequently, when the user cannot exclude almost all of these network structures, there are several issues that must be considered. In particular, computational constraints can prevent us from summing over all the hypotheses in Equation 11.5.19. Can we approximate $p(C_{m+1}|D,\xi)$ accurately by retaining only a small fraction of these hypotheses in the sum? If so, which hypotheses should we include? In addition, how can we efficiently assign prior probabilities to the many network structures and their parameters? In the subsections that follow, we consider each of these issues.

11.5.1   Scoring Metrics

The most important issue is whether we can approximate $p(C_{m+1}|D,\xi)$ well using just a small number of network-structure hypotheses. This

---

says that the observations in a database can not help to discriminate two equivalent network structures.

question is difficult to answer in theory. Nonetheless, several researchers have shown experimentally that even a single "good" network structure often provides an excellent approximation (Cooper and Herskovits 1992; Aliferis and Cooper 1994; Heckerman et al., 1995b). We give an example in Section 11.6. These results are somewhat surprising, and are largely responsible for the great deal of recent interest in learning Bayesian networks.

Given this observation, another important consideration is how to identify "good" network structures. The approach that has been adopted by many researchers is to use a *scoring metric* in combination with a search algorithm. The scoring metric takes prior knowledge, a database, and a set of network structures, and computes the goodness of fit of those structures to the prior knowledge and data. The search algorithm identifies network structures to be scored. In this section, we discuss scoring metrics. In Section 11.5.4, we discuss search algorithms.

An obvious scoring metric for a single network-structure (equivalence class) is the relative posterior probability of that structure given the database. For example, we can compute $p(D, B_S^h|\xi) = p(B_S^h|\xi)\, p(D|B_S^h, \xi)$ or compute a *Bayes factor*: $p(B_S^h|D, \xi)/p(B_{S0}^h|D, \xi)$ where B_{S0}^h is some reference network structure such as the empty network structure. When we use Equation 11.5.18 to compute this relative posterior probability, the scoring metric is sometimes called the *Bayesian Dirichlet* (BD) metric. A network structure with the highest posterior probability is often called a *maximum a posteriori* (MAP) structure. To score a set of distinct network structures S we can use $\sum_{B_S \in S} p(D, B_S^h|\xi)$. Note that practitioners typically compute logarithms of the probabilities to avoid numerical underflow.

Madigan and Raferty (1994) suggest an alternative scoring metric that uses relative posterior probability in conjunction with heuristics based on the principle of Occam's Razor.

Other scoring metrics approximate the posterior-probability metric. In Section 11.7, we discuss algorithms that can find a local maximum in the probability $p(D|B_S^h, \Theta_{B_S}, \xi)$ as a function of Θ_{B_S} (the physical probabilities associated with network structure B_S). We cannot use such a local maximum as a score for B_S, because it will always favor the most complex network structures, which place no constraints on the parameters Θ_{B_S}. Nonetheless, we can use a local maximum of $p(D|B_S^h, \Theta_{B_S}, \xi)$ as a score for B_S if we also penalize structures based on their complexity.

Akaike (1974) suggests the scoring metric

$$\log p(D|M, \widehat{\Theta}_{B_S}, \xi) + \mathrm{Dim}(M)$$

where M is a model, $\widehat{\Theta}_{B_S}$ denotes the values of Θ_{B_S} that maximize the probability, and $\mathrm{Dim}(M)$ is the number of logically independent parameters in M. This scoring metric is sometimes called the A information criterion (AIC). For a Bayesian network, the penalty is given by

$$\mathrm{Dim}(B_S) = \prod_{i=1}^{n} \prod_{j=1}^{q_i} q_i(r_i - 1)$$

Schwarz (1978) suggests a similar scoring metric with a penalty term given by $(1/2)\mathrm{Dim}(M)\log(m)$, where m is the number of cases in the database. This metric is sometimes called the Bayesian information criterion (BIC).

Another metric that approximates the posterior-probability metric is minimum description length (MDL) (Rissanen 1987). The MDL of a network structure is the sum of the number of bits required to encode the model (which increases with increasing model complexity) and the number of bits required to encode the database given the model (which decreases with increasing model complexity) relative to a particular coding scheme. We note that, in the limit, as the number of cases in the database approach infinity, the BD metric with uniform priors on structures, BIC, and MDL give the same relative scores (Kass and Raferty, 1993). Unfortunately, in practice, this asymptotic equivalence is rarely achieved.

11.5.2   Priors on Structures

The posterior-probability metrics require that we assign a prior probability to every possible network structure. In this section, we present an efficient method for doing so described by Heckerman et al. (1995b).

The approach requires that the user constructs a *prior network structure* for the domain. The method assumes that this structure is a user's "best guess" of the network structure that encodes the physical probabilities.

Given a prior network structure P, we compute the prior probability of B_S as follows. For every variable x_i in U, let δ_i denote the number of nodes in the symmetric difference of $\Pi_i(B_S)$ and $\Pi_i(P)$: ($\Pi_i(B_S) \cup$

$\Pi_i(P)) \setminus (\Pi_i(B_S) \cap \Pi_i(P))$. Then, B_S and the prior network differ by $\delta = \sum_{i=1}^{n} \delta_i$ arcs. We compute the prior probability by penalizing B_S by a constant factor $0 < \kappa \leq 1$ for each such arc. That is, we set

$$p(B_S^h|\xi) = c\,\kappa^\delta \qquad (11.5.20)$$

where c is a normalization constant, which we can ignore. Note that this approach assigns equal priors to equivalent network structures only when the prior network structure is empty (see Heckerman et al. [1995b] for a discussion of this point).

This formula is simple, as it requires only the assessment of a prior network structure and a single constant κ. Nonetheless, if the user is willing, he can provide more detailed knowledge by assessing different penalties for different nodes x_i and for different parent configurations of each node (Buntine, 1991). Another variant of this approach is to allow the user to categorically assert that some arcs in the prior network must be present. We can again use Equation 11.5.20, except that we set to zero the priors of network structures that do not conform to these constraints.

11.5.3   Priors on Network Parameters

The posterior-probability metrics also require that we assign priors to network parameters for all possible network structures. Several authors have discussed similar practical approaches for assigning these priors when many structures are possible (Cooper and Herskovits, 1991, 1992; Buntine, 1991; Spiegelhalter et al., 1993; Heckerman et al., 1995b). In this section, we describe the approach of Heckerman et al.

Their approach is based on a result from Geiger and Heckerman (1995). Namely, if all allowed values of the physical probabilities are possible, then parameter independence and hypothesis equivalence[4] imply that the physical probabilities for complete network structures must have Dirichlet distributions as specified in Equation 11.4.13 with the constraint

$$N'_{ijk} = N'\,p(x_i = k, \Pi_i = j|B_{S_C}^h, \xi) \qquad (11.5.21)$$

where N' is the user's equivalent sample size for the domain, $B_{S_C}^h$ is the hypothesis corresponding to any complete network structure, and

---

[4]Actually, Geiger and Heckerman (1995) proved this result using only likelihood equivalence.

$p(x_i = k, \Pi_i = j | B^h_{S_C}, \xi)$ is the user's probability that $x_i = k$ and $\Pi_i = j$ in the first case to be seen in the database.

Under these conditions, the priors on parameters for all complete network structures may be determined by (1) constructing a *prior network* for the first case to be seen (from which the probabilities in Equation 11.5.21 may be computed) and (2) assessing the equivalent sample size (i.e., confidence) in that prior network. In Section 11.6, we give an example of a prior network.

To determine priors for parameters of incomplete network structures, Heckerman et al. (1995b) use the assumption of *parameter modularity*, which says that given two network structures B_{S1} and B_{S2}, if x_i has the same parents in B_{S1} and B_{S2}, then

$$p(\Theta_{ij} | B^h_{S1}, \xi) = p(\Theta_{ij} | B^h_{S2}, \xi)$$

for $j = 1, \ldots, q_i$. They call this property parameter modularity, because it says that the distributions for parameters Θ_{ij} depend only on the structure of the network that is local to variable x_i—namely, Θ_{ij} only depends on x_i and its parents. For example, consider the network structure $x \to y$ and the empty structure for our two-variable domain with corresponding hypotheses $B^h_{x \to y}$ and B^h_{xy}. In both structures, x has the same set of parents (the empty set). Consequently, by parameter modularity, $p(\theta_x | B^h_{x \to y}, \xi) = p(\theta_x | B^h_{xy}, \xi)$.

Given the assumptions of parameter modularity and independence, it is a simple matter to construct priors for the parameters of an arbitrary network structure given the priors on complete network structures. In particular, given parameter independence, we construct the priors for the parameters of each node separately. Furthermore, if node x_i has parents Π_i in the given network structure, we identify a complete network structure where x_i has these parents, and use parameter modularity to determine the priors for this node. The result is a special case of the BD metric, called the BDe metric, that assigns equal scores to equivalent network structures. In Section 11.6, we illustrate the use of this metric.

11.5.4   Search Methods

In this section, we examine search methods for identifying network structures with high scores. Essentially all such search methods make use of a property of the scoring metrics that we call decomposability. Given a network structure for domain U, we say that a measure on that structure is *decomposable* if it can be written as a product of measures, each of which is a function only of one node and its parents. For example, from Equation 11.5.18, we see that the probability $p(D|B_S^h, \xi)$ given by the BD metric is decomposable. Consequently, if the prior probabilities of network structures are decomposable (as they are in Equation 11.5.20), then so is the BD metric. Thus, we can write

$$p(D, B_S^h|\xi) = \prod_{i=1}^{n} s(x_i|\Pi_i) \qquad (11.5.22)$$

where $s(x_i|\Pi_i)$ is only a function of x_i and its parents. Most Bayesian and non-Bayesian metrics for complete databases are decomposable. Given a decomposable metric, we can compare the score for two network structures that differ by the addition or deletion of arcs pointing to x_i, by computing only the term $s(x_i|\Pi_i)$ for both structures.

First, let us consider the special case of finding the network structure with the highest score among all structures in which every node has at most one parent. For each arc $x_j \to x_i$ (including cases where x_j is null), we associate a weight $w(x_i, x_j) \equiv \log s(x_i|x_j) - \log s(x_i|\emptyset)$. From Equation 11.5.22, we have

$$\log p(D, B_S^h) = \sum_{i=1}^{n} \log s(x_i|\pi_i) = \sum_{i=1}^{n} w(x_i, \pi_i) + \sum_{i=1}^{n} \log s(x_i|\emptyset) \quad (11.5.23)$$

where π_i is the (possibly) null parent of x_i. The last term in Equation 11.5.23 is the same for all network structures. Thus, among the network structures in which each node has at most one parent, ranking network structures by sum of weights $\sum_{i=1}^{n} w(x_i, \pi_i)$ or by score has the same result. Finding the network structure with the highest weight is a special case of a well-known problem of finding *maximum branchings* (Edmonds, 1967). Algorithms for finding maximum branchings can be used regardless of the metric we use, as long as one can associate a weight with every edge. Therefore, this algorithm is appropriate for any decomposable metric. When using metrics that assign equal scores to equivalent network structures, however, we have

$$s(x_i|x_j) \, s(x_j|\emptyset) = s(x_j|x_i) \, s(x_i|\emptyset)$$

Thus, for any two edges $x_i \to x_j$ and $x_i \leftarrow x_j$, the weights $w(x_i, x_j)$ and $w(x_j, x_i)$ are equal. Consequently, the directionality of the arcs plays no role for such metrics, and the problem reduces to finding the undirected forest for which $\sum w(x_i, x_j)$ is a maximum. This search can be done using a maximum spanning tree algorithm.

Now, let us consider the case where we find the best network from the set of all networks in which each node has no more than k parents. Unfortunately, the problem for $k > 1$ is NP-hard (Chickering et al. 1995). Therefore, heuristic search algorithms are used.

Most of the commonly discussed search methods for learning Bayesian networks make successive arc changes to the network, and employ the property of decomposability to evaluate the merit of each change. The possible changes that can be made are easy to identify. For any pair of variables, if there is an arc connecting them, then this arc can either be reversed or removed. If there is no arc connecting them, then an arc can be added in either direction. All changes are subject to the constraint that the resulting network contains no directed cycles. We use E to denote the set of eligible changes to a graph, and $\Delta(e)$ to denote the change in log score of the network resulting from the modification $e \in E$. Given a decomposable metric, if an arc to x_i is added or deleted, only $s(x_i | \Pi_i)$ need be evaluated to determine $\Delta(e)$. If an arc between x_i and x_j is reversed, then only $s(x_i | \Pi_i)$ and $s(x_j | \Pi_j)$ need be evaluated.

One simple heuristic search algorithm is *local search*. First, we choose a graph. Then, we evaluate $\Delta(e)$ for all $e \in E$, and make the change e for which $\Delta(e)$ is a maximum, provided it is positive. We terminate search when there is no e with a positive value for $\Delta(e)$. Using decomposable metrics, we can avoid recomputing all terms $\Delta(e)$ after every change. In particular, if neither x_i, x_j, nor their parents are changed, then $\Delta(e)$ remains unchanged for all changes e involving these nodes as long as the resulting network is acyclic. Candidates for the initial graph include the empty graph, a random graph, a graph determined by one of the polynomial algorithms described previously in this section, and the prior network.

A potential problem with any local-search method is getting stuck at a local maximum. In one method for escaping local maxima, called *iterated hill-climbing*, we apply local search until we hit a local maximum. We then randomly perturb the current network structure, and repeat the process for some manageable number of iterations. Other methods for escaping local maxima include best-first search (Korf, 1993), simulated annealing (Metropolis et al., 1953), and Gibbs' sampling (see

Section 11.7.2).

11.6   A Real-World Example

Figure 11.5 illustrates an application of these techniques to the real-world domain of ICU ventilator management, taken from Heckerman et al. (1995b). Figure 11.5a is a hand-constructed Bayesian network for this domain, called the Alarm network (Beinlich et al., 1989) (the probabilities are not shown). Figure 11.5c is a database of 10,000 cases that is sampled from the Alarm network. Figure 11.5b is a hypothetical prior network for the domain. Heckerman et al. (1995b) constructed this network by adding, deleting, and reversing arcs in the Alarm network and by adding noise to the probabilities of the Alarm network.

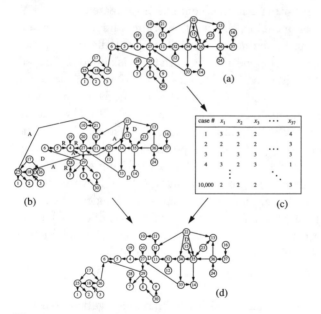

Figure 11.5
(a) The Alarm network structure. (b) A prior network encoding a user's beliefs about the Alarm domain. (c) A 10,000-case database generated from the Alarm network. (d) The network learned from the prior network and a 10,000 case database generated from the Alarm network. Arcs that are added, deleted, or reversed with respect to those in the Alarm network are indicated with A, D, and R, respectively. (Taken from Heckerman et al., 1995b.)

Figure 11.5d shows the most likely network structure found by local search initialized with the prior network structure using the BDe metric, an equivalent sample size $N' = 64$, and priors on network structures determined by Equation 11.5.20 with $\kappa = 1/(N' + 1)$. Comparing the three network structures, we see that the learned network structure is much closer to that of the Alarm network than that of the prior network. Furthermore, the joint distribution encoded by the learned network is much closer to that of the Alarm network than that of the prior network. In particular, whereas the cross entropy of the joint distributions of the prior network with respect to that of the Alarm network is 5.6, the cross entropy of the joint distribution of the learned network with respect to that of the Alarm network is 0.03.[5] The learning algorithm has effectively used the database to "correct" the prior knowledge of the user.

11.7 Missing Data

In real databases, observations of one or more variables in one or more cases are typically missing. In this section, we consider extensions to previous methods that can handle missing data. We caution the reader that the methods we discuss assume that whether or not an observation is missing is independent of the actual states of the variables. For example, these methods are not appropriate for a medical database where data about drug response is missing in those patients who became too sick to take the drug.

11.7.1 Fill-In Methods

First, let us consider the simple situation where we observe a single incomplete case C in domain U. Let C' denote the variables not observed in the case. We can compute the posterior distribution of Θ_{ij} as follows:

$$p(\Theta_{ij}|C,\xi) \;=\; \sum_{U} p(U|C,\xi)\, p(\Theta_{ij}|C,C',\xi) \tag{11.7.24}$$

$$=\; (1 - p(\Pi_i = j|C,\xi))\, \{p(\Theta_{ij}|\xi)\} +$$

---

[5]By way of comparison, the cross entropy of an empty network whose probabilities are determined from the marginals of the Alarm network with respect to that of the Alarm network is 13.6.

$$\sum_{k=1}^{r_i} p(x_i = k, \Pi_i = j | C, \xi) \left\{ p(\Theta_{ij} | x_i = k, \Pi_i = j, \xi) \right\}$$

where x_i and Π_i refer to these variables in case C. Each term in curly brackets in Equation 11.7.24 is a Dirichlet distribution. Thus, unless both x_i and all the variables in Π_i are observed in case C, the posterior distribution of Θ_{ij} will be a linear combination of Dirichlet distributions. Such distributions are sometimes called *Dirichlet mixtures*; and the probabilities $(1 - p(\Pi_i = j | C, \xi))$ and $p(x_i = k, \Pi_i = j | C, \xi), k = 1, \ldots, r_i$ are called *mixing coefficients*.

If we observe two cases, then the situation becomes more complex, because the computation of the mixing coefficients involves finding the means of Dirichlet mixtures. In general, as shown (e.g.) in Cooper and Herskovits (1992), the computational complexity of the exact computation of $p(D, B_S^h | \xi)$ can be exponential in the number of missing variable entries in the database.

Thus, in practice, we require an approximation. One approach is to approximate each correct posterior distribution Θ_{ij} with a single Dirichlet distribution, and continue to use Equation 11.5.17 along with the formula for the mean of a Dirichlet distribution. Several such approximations have been described in the literature. For example, Titterington (1976) describes a method called *fractional updating*, wherein for each unobserved variable, we pretend that we have observed a fractional number of instances of each state of that variable. In particular, he suggests the approximation:

$$p(\Theta_{ij} | C, \xi) \approx c \prod_{k=1}^{r_i} \theta_{ijk}^{p(x_i = k, \Pi_i = j | C, \xi)} p(\Theta_{ij} | \xi) \tag{11.7.25}$$

One drawback of this method is that it falsely increases the equivalent sample sizes of the Dirichlet distributions associated with each Θ_{ij}, because it replaces each missing datum with a fractional sample. Cowell et al. (1995) suggest an approach that does not have this problem. Namely, they approximate Θ_{ij} by a single Dirichlet whose means and average variance $\sum_{k=1}^{r_i} Var(\theta_{ijk})/r_i$ are the same as those for the correct Dirichlet mixture.

These approximations process the data in the database sequentially, and make use of the assumption of parameter independence and properties of the Dirichlet distribution. Other methods—including Gibbs sampling, the EM algorithm, and gradient descent—process all the data at once, and can handle continuous domain variables and dependent parameters.

11.7.2   Gibbs Sampling

Gibbs sampling, described—for example—by Geman and Geman (1984), is a special case of Markov chain Monte-Carlo methods for approximate inference (Hastings, 1970). Given variables $X = \{x_1, \ldots, x_n\}$ with some joint distribution $p(X|\xi)$, we can use a Gibbs sampler to approximate the expectation of any function $f(X)$ with respect to $p(X|\xi)$ $(E(f(X)|\xi))$ as follows. First, we choose an initial state of each of the variables in X somehow. Next, we pick some variable x_i, unassign its current state, and compute its probability distribution given the assignments to the other $n-1$ variables. Then, we sample a state for x_i based on this probability distribution, and compute $f(X)$. Finally, we iterate the previous two steps, keeping track of the average value of $f(X)$. In the limit as the number of samples approach infinity, this average is equal to $E(f(X)|\xi)$ provided two conditions are met. First, the Gibbs sampler must be *irreducible*: The probability distribution $p(X)$ must be such that we can eventually sample any possible state of X given any possible initial state of X. For example, if $p(X)$ contains no zero probabilities, then the Gibbs sampler will be irreducible. Second, each x_i must be chosen infinitely often. In practice, an algorithm for deterministically rotating through the variables is typically used. For a good introductory discussion on Gibbs sampling—including methods for initialization and a discussion of convergence—see York (1992).

Now, suppose we have a database $D = \{C_1, \ldots, C_m\}$ with missing data and a new case C_{m+1}, and we want to approximate $p(C_{m+1}|D, B_S^h, \xi)$ for a given network structure B_S. One reasonable variant of Gibbs sampling for performing this estimation goes as follows. First, we initialize the parameters Θ_{B_S} somehow. Second, for each case C_l in D containing missing data and for every variable x_i that is unobserved in C_l, we assign the state of x_i using the assigned values of Θ_{B_S}, creating a complete database D'. This step can be done using any standard Bayesian network inference algorithm. Third, we reassign the parameters Θ_{B_S} according to the posterior distribution $p(\Theta_{B_S}|D', B_S^h, \xi)$. Finally, we iterate the previous two steps, and use the average of $p(C_{m+1}|\Theta_{B_S}, B_S^h, \xi)$ computed after each iteration to approximate $p(C_{m+1}|D, B_S^h, \xi)$. Note that, in principle, this approach can be used when domain variables are continuous and parameters are dependent.

11.7.3   EM Algorithm

The expectation–maximization (EM) algorithm is an approximation algorithm that can find a local maximum of a probability $p(\cdot|\Theta,\xi)$ as a function of parameters Θ (Dempster et al., 1977). For example, given a database $D = \{C_1, \ldots, C_m\}$ with missing data, we can use the EM algorithm to find a local maximum for $p(D|B_S^h, \Theta_{B_S}, \xi)$. We can then use this maximum (e.g.) to compute a BIC score for B_s. Like the Gibbs sampler, the EM algorithm can handle models with missing data and continuous variables.

The EM algorithm can be viewed as a deterministic version of the Gibbs sampler. To illustrate the method, suppose we wish to find a local maximum for $p(D|B_S^h, \Theta_{B_S}, \xi)$. We begin by assigning values to Θ_{B_S} somehow. Next, rather than sample a complete database D', we compute the *expected sufficient statistics* for the missing entries in the database. In particular, we compute

$$E(N_{ijk}|\Theta_{B_S},\xi) = \sum_{l=1}^{m} p(x_i = k, \Pi_i = j|C_l, \Theta_{B_S}, \xi) \qquad (11.7.26)$$

When x_i and all the variables in Π_i are observed in case C_l, the term for this case requires no computation: it is either zero or one. Otherwise, we can use any Bayesian network inference algorithm to evaluate the term. This computation is called the *expectation step* of the EM algorithm.

Next, rather than sample new values for Θ_{B_S}, we use the expected sufficient statistics as if they were actual sufficient statistics from a database D', and set the new values of Θ_{B_S} to be those that maximize $p(D'|B_S^h\Theta_{B_S}, \xi)$. Namely, we set

$$\theta_{ijk} = \frac{E(N_{ijk}|\Theta_{B_S},\xi)}{E(N_{ij}|\Theta_{B_S},\xi)}$$

This assignment is called the *maximization step* of the EM algorithm.

Dempster (1977) showed that, under certain regularity conditions, iteration of the expectation and maximization steps will converge to a local maximum of the probability $p(D|B_S^h, \Theta_{B_S}, \xi)$.

To use the EM algorithm in practicé, we need a closed-form expression for the maximization step. Such expressions exist when the likelihood

$p(D|B_S^h, \Theta_{B_S}, \xi)$ is in the exponential family, as is the case for discrete variables. When the likelihood does not have this form, we can use general optimization methods to maximize $p(D|B_S^h, \Theta_{B_S}, \xi)$ (Press et al. 1992). These approaches—for example, gradient descent, conjugate gradient, and quasi-Newton methods—require derivatives of the function to be maximized. Buntine (1994) discusses how we can use the structure of B_s to simplify the computation of these derivatives.

11.8   Learning New Variables

In a database with missing data, a particular variable may be observed in some cases, or it may never be observed. In the latter situation, we say that the variable is *hidden*.

Any of the methods described in the previous section can be used to learn Bayesian networks containing hidden variables. The network structure may be fixed and only the physical probabilities uncertain, or both the network structure and parameters may be uncertain. One example of learning the probabilities of a fixed structure with hidden variables is the AutoClass algorithm of Cheeseman and Stutz (in this volume), which performs *unsupervised classification*. The model underlying the algorithm is a Bayesian network with a single hidden variable whose states correspond to unknown classes. The number of states of the hidden variable is uncertain and has a prior distribution. Also, this hidden variable renders sets of observable variables conditionally independent. The algorithm searches over variations of this model (including the number of states of the hidden variable), using a version of the EM algorithm in conjunction with an approximate Bayesian scoring metric to select the model variation with the highest posterior probability.

In addition, we can use methods for learning with missing data to identify (under uncertainty) the existence of new variables. Namely, we hypothesize a mutually exclusive and exhaustive set of Bayesian-network structures, some containing hidden variables and some not. We assign priors to each structure and its parameters, and then update these priors with data using one of the described algorithms for handling missing data.

11.9   Pointers to the Literature

Like all tutorials, this tutorial is incomplete. For those readers interested in learning more about graphical models and methods for learning them, we offer the following additional references. A more detailed guide to the literature can be found in Buntine (1995).

Charniak (1991) provides an easy-to-read introduction to the Bayesian-network representation. Spiegelhalter et al. (1993) and Heckerman et al. (1995) give simple discussions of methods for learning Bayesian networks for domains containing only discrete variables. Buntine (1994) and Heckerman and Geiger (1994) provide more detailed discussions. Experimental comparisons of different learning approaches can be found in Cooper and Herskovits (1992), Aliferis and Cooper (1994), Lauritzen et al. (1994), Cowell et al. (1995), and Heckerman et al. (1995b).

In addition to directed models, researchers have also explored graphs containing undirected edges as a knowledge representation. These representations are discussed (e.g.) in Lauritzen (1982), Verma and Pearl (1990), and Frydenberg (1990). Bayesian methods for learning such models from data are described by Dawid and Lauritzen (1993) and Buntine (1994).

Finally, several software systems for learning graphical models have been implemented. Thomas, Spiegelhalter, and Gilks (1992) have created a system that takes a learning problem specified as a Bayesian network and compiles this problem into a Gibbs-sampler computer program. Badsberg (1992) and Højsgaard et al. (1994) have built systems that can learn directed, undirected, and mixed graphical models using a variety of scoring metrics.

Acknowledgments

I thank David Chickering, Eric Horvitz, Koos Rommelse, and Padhraic Smyth for their comments on earlier versions of this manuscript.

References

Akaike, H. 1974. A New Look at the Statistical Model Identification. *IEEE Transactions on Automatic Control,* 19: 716–723.

Aliferis, C.; and Cooper, G. 1994. An Evaluation of an Algorithm for Inductive Learning of Bayesian Belief Networks Using Simulated Data Sets. In *Proceedings of Tenth Conference on Uncertainty in Artificial Intelligence*, 8–14. San Francisco: Morgan Kaufmann.

Badsberg, J. 1992. Model Search in Contingency Tables by Coco. In *Computational Statistics*, 251–256, ed. Y. Dodge and J. Wittaker. Heidelberg: Physica Verlag.

Beinlich, I.; Suermondt, H.; Chavez, R.; and Cooper, G. 1989. The ALARM Monitoring System: A Case Study with Two Probabilistic Inference Techniques for Belief Networks. In *Proceedings of the Second European Conference on Artificial Intelligence in Medicine*, 247–256. Berlin: Springer Verlag.

Buntine, W. 1991. Theory Refinement on Bayesian Networks. In *Proceedings of Seventh Conference on Uncertainty in Artificial Intelligence*, 52–60. San Francisco: Morgan Kaufmann.

Buntine, W. 1994. Operations for Learning with Graphical Models. *Journal of Artificial Intelligence Research*, 2: 159–225.

Buntine, W. 1995. A Guide to the Literature on Learning Graphical Models. Technical Report IC-95-05, NASA Ames Research Center.

Charniak, E. 1991. Bayesian Networks Without Tears. *AI Magazine*, 12: 50–63.

Chickering, D. 1995. A Transformational Characterization of Equivalent Bayesian Network Structures. In Proceedings of the Eleventh International Joint Conference on Artificial Intelligence, Montreal, 87–98. San Francisco: Morgan Kaufmann.

Chickering, D.; Geiger, D.; and Heckerman, D. 1995. Learning Bayesian Networks: Search Methods and Experimental Results. In *Proceedings of Fifth Conference on Artificial Intelligence and Statistics*, 112–128. Society for Artificial Intelligence in Statistics.

Cooper, G.; and Herskovits, E. 1992. A Bayesian Method for the Induction of Probabilistic Networks from Data. *Machine Learning*, 9: 309–347.

Cooper, G.; and Herskovits, E. 1991. A Bayesian Method for the Induction of Probabilistic Networks from Data. Technical Report SMI-91-1, Section on Medical Informatics, Stanford University.

Cowell, R.; Dawid, A.; and Sebastiani, P. 1995. A Comparison of Sequential Learning Methods for Incomplete Data. Technical Report 135, Department of Statistical Science, University College London.

DeGroot, M. 1970. *Optimal Statistical Decisions.* New York: McGraw-Hill.

Dempster, A.; Laird, N.; and Rubin, D. 1977. Maximum Likelihood from Incomplete Data Via the EM Algorithm. *Journal of the Royal Statistical Society*, B 39:1–38.

Edmonds, J. 1967. Optimum Branching. *J. Res. NBS,* 71B: 233–240.

Frydenberg, M. 1990. The Chain Graph Markov Property. *Scandinavian Journal of Statistics,* 17: 333–353.

Geiger, D.; and Heckerman, D. 1995. A Characterization of the Dirichlet Distribution Applicable to Learning Bayesian Networks. Technical Report MSR-TR-94-16, Microsoft, Redmond, Wash.

Geman, S.; and Geman, D. 1984. Stochastic Relaxation, Gibbs Distributions and the Bayesian Restoration of Images. *IEEE Transactions on Pattern Analysis and Machine Intelligence,* 6: 721–742.

Good, I. 1959. Kinds of Probability. *Science,* 129: 443–447.

Good, I. 1965. *The Estimation of Probabilities.* Cambridge, Mass.: The MIT Press.

Hastings, W. 1970. Monte Carlo Sampling Methods Using Markov Chains and Their Applications. *Biometrika,* 57: 97–109.

Heckerman, D. and Geiger, D. 1994. Learning Bayesian Networks. Technical Report MSR-TR-95-02, Microsoft, Redmond, Wash.

Heckerman, D.; Mamdani, A.; and Wellman, M. 1995a. Special Issue on Real-World Applications of Bayesian Networks. *Communications of the ACM,* March.

Heckerman, D.; Geiger, D.; and Chickering, D. 1995b. Learning Bayesian Networks: The Combination of Knowledge and Statistical Data. *Machine Learning.*

Højsgaard, S.; Skjøth, F.; and Thiesson, B. 1994. User's Guide to BIFROST. Technical Report, Department of Mathematics and Computer Science, Aalborg, Denmark.

Howard, R. 1970. Decision Analysis: Perspectives on Inference, Decision, and Experimentation. *Proceedings of the IEEE,* 58: 632–643.

Howard, R.; and Matheson, J. 1981. Influence Diagrams. In *Readings on the Principles and Applications of Decision Analysis,* volume II, 721–762. ed. R. Howard and J. Matheson. Menlo Park, Calif.: Strategic Decisions Group.

Kass, R.; and Rafferty, A. 1993. Bayes Factors and Model Uncertainty. Technical Report 571, Department of Statistics, Carnegie Mellon University.

Korf, R. 1993. Linear-Space Best-First Search. *Artificial Intelligence,* 62: 41–78.

Lauritzen, S. 1982. *Lectures on Contingency Tables.* University of Aalborg Press, Aalborg, Denmark.

Lauritzen, S.; Thiesson, B.; and Spiegelhalter, D. 1994. Diagnostic Systems Created by Model Selection Methods: A Case Study. In *AI and Statistics IV,* 143–152, ed. P. Cheeseman and R. Oldford. New York: Springer-Verlag.

Madigan, D.; and Rafferty, A. 1994. Model Selection and Accounting for Model Uncertainty in Graphical Models Using Occam's Window. *Journal of the American Statistical Association,* 89: 1535–1546.

Metropolis, N.; Rosenbluth, A.; Rosenbluth, M.; Teller, A.; and Teller, E. 1953. *Journal of Chemical Physics,* 21: 1087–1092.

Pearl, J. 1988. *Probabilistic Reasoning in Intelligent Systems: Networks of Plausible Inference.* San Francisco: Morgan Kaufmann.

Pearl, J.; and Verma, T. 1991. A Theory of Inferred Causation. In *Knowledge Representation and Reasoning: Proceedings of the Second International Conference,* 441–452, ed. J. Allen, R. Fikes, and E. Sandewal. San Francisco: Morgan Kaufmann.

Press, W.; Teukolsky, S.; Vetterling, W.; and Flannery, B. 1992. *Numerical Recipes in C.* New York: Cambridge University Press.

Rissanen, J. 1987. Stochastic Complexity (with Discussion). *Journal of the Royal Statistical Society, Series B,* 49: 223–239, 253–265.

Schwarz, G. 1978. Estimating the Dimension of a Model. *Annals of Statistics,* 6: 461–464.

Spiegelhalter, D.; Dawid, A.; Lauritzen, S.; and Cowell, R. 1993. Bayesian Analysis in Expert Systems. *Statistical Science,* 8: 219–282.

Spiegelhalter, D. and Lauritzen, S. 1990. Sequential Updating of Conditional Probabilities on Directed Graphical Structures. *Networks,* 20: 579–605.

Spirtes, P.; Glymour, C.; and Scheines, R. 1993. *Causation, Prediction, and Search.* New York: Springer-Verlag.

Thomas, A.; Spiegelhalter, D.; and Gilks, W. 1992. Bugs: A Program to Perform Bayesian Inference Using Gibbs Sampling. In *Bayesian Statistics,* 837–842, ed. J. Bernardo, J. Berger, A. Dawid, and A. Smith. New York: Oxford University Press.

Titterington, D. 1976. Updating a Diagnostic System Using Unconfirmed Cases. *Applied Statistics,* 25: 238–247.

Verma, T.; and Pearl, J. 1990. Equivalence and Synthesis of Causal Models. In *Proceedings of Sixth Conference on Uncertainty in Artificial Intelligence,* 220–227. San Francisco: Morgan Kaufmann.

York, J. 1992. *Bayesian Methods for the Analysis of Misclassified or Incomplete Multivariate Discrete Data.* PhD diss., Department of Statistics, University of Washington, Seattle.

12 Fast Discovery of Association Rules

Rakesh Agrawal
IBM Almaden Research Center

Heikki Mannila
University of Helsinki

Ramakrishnan Srikant
IBM Almaden Research Center

Hannu Toivonen
University of Helsinki

A. Inkeri Verkamo
University of Helsinki

Abstract

Association rules are statements of the form "98% of customers that purchase tires and automobile accessories also get automotive services." We consider the problem of discovering association rules between items in large databases. We present two new algorithms for solving this problem. Experiments with synthetic data show that these algorithms outperform previous algorithms by factors ranging from three for small problems to more than an order of magnitude for large problems. We show how the best features of the two proposed algorithms can be combined into a hybrid algorithm. Scale-up experiments show that the hybrid algorithm scales linearly with the number of transactions and that it has excellent scale-up properties with respect to the transaction size and the number of items in the database. We also give simple information-theoretic lower bounds for the problem of finding association rules, and show that sampling can be in some cases an efficient way of finding such rules.

12.1   Association Rules

Recently, Agrawal, Imielinski, and Swami (1993) introduced a class of regularities, *association rules*, and gave an algorithm for finding such rules. An association rule is an expression $X \Rightarrow Y$, where X and Y are sets of items. The intuitive meaning of such a rule is that transactions of the database which contain X tend to contain Y. An example of such a rule might be that 98% of customers that purchase tires and automobile accessories also have automotive services carried out.

Application domains for association rules range from decision support to telecommunications alarm diagnosis and prediction. The prototypical application is in analysis of sales data. Bar-code technology has made it possible for retail organizations to collect and store massive amounts of sales data, referred to as *basket* data. A record in such data typically consists of the transaction date and the items bought in the transaction. Finding association rules from such basket data is valuable for cross-marketing and attached mailing applications. Other applications include catalog design, add-on sales, store layout, and customer segmentation based on buying patterns.

The following is a formal statement of the problem (Agrawal *et al.* 1993): Let $\mathcal{I} = \{i_1, i_2, \ldots, i_m\}$ be a set of literals, called items. Let $\mathcal{D}$ be a set of transactions, where each transaction T is an itemset such that $T \subseteq \mathcal{I}$. (In other words, $\mathcal{I} = \{i_1, i_2, \ldots, i_m\}$ is a set of attributes over the binary domain $\{0, 1\}$. A tuple T of the database $\mathcal{D}$ is represented by identifying the attributes with value 1.) Associated with each transaction is a unique identifier, called its *TID*. A set of items $X \subset \mathcal{I}$ is called an *itemset*. We say that a transaction T *contains* an itemset X, if $X \subseteq T$. An *association rule* is an implication of the form $X \Rightarrow Y$, where $X \subset \mathcal{I}, Y \subset \mathcal{I}$, and $X \cap Y = \emptyset$. The rule $X \Rightarrow Y$ holds in the transaction set $\mathcal{D}$ with *confidence c* if $c\%$ of transactions in $\mathcal{D}$ that contain X also contain Y. The rule $X \Rightarrow Y$ has *support s* in the transaction set $\mathcal{D}$ if $s\%$ of transactions in $\mathcal{D}$ contain $X \cup Y$. Negatives, or missing items, are not considered of interest in this approach. Our rules are somewhat more general than in (Agrawal *et al.* 1993) in that we allow a consequent to have more than one item.

Given a set of transactions $\mathcal{D}$, the problem of mining association rules is to generate *all* association rules that have certain user-specified minimum support (called *minsup*) and confidence (called *minconf*). Note that we are interested in *discovering* all rules rather than *verifying* whether a particular rule holds. Verification has the limitation that we may miss surprising rules and changing trends. Our discussion is neutral with respect to the representation of $\mathcal{D}$. For example, $\mathcal{D}$ could be a data file, a relational table, or the result of a relational expression.

This article is the result of research undertaken independently as part of the Quest project at IBM Almaden Research Center (Agrawal and

Srikant 1994) and research at the University of Helsinki (Mannila *et al.* 1994).

12.1.1   Related Work

Related, but not directly applicable, work includes the induction of classification rules (Breiman *et al.* 1984; Quinlan 1993), discovery of causal rules (Spiegelhalter *et al.*1993), learning of logical definitions (Muggleton and Feng 1992), fitting of functions to data (Langley *et al.* 1987), and clustering (Cheeseman *et al.* 1988; Fisher 1987). The closest work in the machine learning literature is the KID3 algorithm presented in (Piatetsky-Shapiro 1991). If used for finding all association rules, this algorithm will make as many passes over the data as the number of combinations of items in the antecedent, which is exponentially large. Related work in the database literature is the work on inferring functional dependencies from data (Mannila and Räihä 1992; Mannila and Räihä 1994).

There has been work on quantifying the "usefulness" or "interestingness" of a rule (Piatetsky-Shapiro 1991; Piatetsky-Shapiro and Matheus 1994). What is useful or interesting is often application-dependent. The need for a human in the loop and providing tools to allow human guidance of the rule discovery process has been articulated, for example, in (Brachman *et al.* 1993) and (Klemettinen *et al.* 1994). We do not discuss these issues in this chapter, except to point out that these are necessary features of a rule discovery system that may use our algorithms as the engine of the discovery process.

12.1.2   Chapter Organization

The rest of this chapter is organized in the following manner. In Section 12.2, we describe new algorithms, Apriori and AprioriTid, for discovering all itemsets that have at least *minsup* support. We give an algorithm for using the itemsets to generate association rules in Section 12.3.

In Section 12.4, we provide empirical results of the performance and compare the Apriori and AprioriTid algorithms against the AIS (Agrawal *et al.* 1993) and SETM (Houtsma and Swami 1993) algorithms, the two other algorithms available in the literature. We describe how the Apriori and AprioriTid algorithms can be combined into a hybrid algorithm,

AprioriHybrid, and demonstrate the scale-up properties of this algorithm.

We study the theoretical properties of the problem of finding association rules in Section 12.5. Section 12.6 is a short conclusion.

12.2   Discovering Large Itemsets

The problem of discovering all association rules of sufficient support and confidence can be decomposed into two subproblems (Agrawal *et al.* 1993):

1. Find all combinations of items that have transaction support above minimum support. Call those combinations *large* itemsets and all other combinations *small* itemsets. We describe new algorithms, Apriori and AprioriTid, for solving this problem.

2. Use the large itemsets to generate the desired rules. We provide an algorithm for this problem in Section 12.3. The general idea is that if, say, $ABCD$ and AB are large itemsets, then we can determine if the rule $AB \Rightarrow CD$ holds by computing the ratio r = support($ABCD$)/support(AB). Only if $r \geq$ *minconf*, then the rule holds. Note that the rule will have minimum support because $ABCD$ is large.

It is easy to see that this two-step approach is in a sense optimal: the problem of finding large itemsets can be reduced to the problem of finding all association rules that hold with a given confidence. Namely, if we are given a set of transactions $\mathcal{D}$, we can find the large itemsets by adding an extra item j to each transaction in $\mathcal{D}$ and then finding the association rules that have j on the right-hand side and hold with confidence 100%.

The algorithms for discovering all large itemsets make multiple passes over the data. In each pass, we start with a *seed* set of large itemsets and use the seed set for generating new potentially large itemsets, called *candidate* itemsets. We find the support count for these candidate itemsets during the pass over the data. At the end of the pass, we determine which of the candidate itemsets are actually large, and they become the seed for the next pass. This process continues until no new large itemsets are found. In the first pass, we count the support of individual items and determine which of them are large. This could be considered breadth-first search in the space of potentially large itemsets.

In both the AIS (Agrawal *et al.* 1993) and SETM (Houtsma and Swami 1993) algorithms candidate itemsets are generated on-the-fly during the database pass. Specifically, after reading a transaction, it is determined which of the itemsets found large in the previous pass are present in the transaction. New candidate itemsets are generated by extending these large itemsets with other items in the transaction. However, as we will see, this approach results in unnecessarily generating and counting too many candidate itemsets that turn out to be small.

On the other hand, the Apriori and AprioriTid algorithms generate the candidate itemsets to be counted in a pass by using only the itemsets found large in the previous pass—without considering the transactions in the database. The basic combinatorial property used is that any subset of a large itemset must be large. Therefore, the candidate itemsets having k items can be generated by joining large itemsets having $k-1$ items, and deleting those that contain any subset that is not large. This procedure results in generation of a much smaller number of candidate itemsets, i.e., in effect pruning the search space.

The AprioriTid algorithm has the additional property that the database is not used at all for counting the support of candidate itemsets after the first pass. Rather, an encoding of the candidate itemsets used in the previous pass is employed for this purpose. (This encoding tells us what candidates were present in which transactions.) In later passes, the size of this encoding can become much smaller than the database, thus saving much reading effort.

Notation   Assume for simplicity that items in transactions and itemsets are kept sorted in their lexicographic order. We call the number of items in an itemset its *size*, and call an itemset of size k a k-itemset. We use the notation $c[1] \cdot c[2] \cdot \ldots \cdot c[k]$ to represent a k-itemset c consisting of items $c[1], c[2], \ldots c[k]$, where $c[1] < c[2] < \ldots < c[k]$. Associated with each itemset is a count field to store the support for this itemset.

We summarize in Table 12.1 the notation used in the algorithms. The set $\widehat{C}_k$ is used by AprioriTid and will be further discussed when we describe this algorithm.

Table 12.1
Notation.

k-itemset	An itemset having k items.
L_k	Set of large k-itemsets (those with minimum support). Each member of this set has two fields: i) itemset and ii) support count.
C_k	Set of candidate k-itemsets (potentially large itemsets). Each member of this set has two fields: i) itemset and ii) support count.
$\widehat{C}_k$	Set of candidate k-itemsets when the TIDs of the generating transactions are kept associated with the candidates.

```
1)    L₁ = {large 1-itemsets};
2)    for ( k = 2; L_{k-1} ≠ ∅; k++ ) do begin
3)        C_k = apriori-gen(L_{k-1});  // New candidates
4)        forall transactions t ∈ D do begin
5)            C_t = subset(C_k, t);  // Candidates contained in t
6)            forall candidates c ∈ C_t do
7)                c.count++;
8)        end
9)        L_k = {c ∈ C_k | c.count ≥ minsup}
10)   end
11)   Answer = ∪_k L_k;
```

Figure 12.1
Algorithm apriori.

12.2.1   Algorithm Apriori

Figure 12.1 gives the Apriori algorithm. The first pass of the algorithm simply counts the number of occurrences of each item to determine the large 1-itemsets. A subsequent pass, say pass k, consists of two phases. First, the large itemsets L_{k-1} found in the $(k-1)$th pass are used to generate the candidate itemsets C_k, using the apriori-gen function described in Section 12.2.1. Next, the database is scanned and the support of candidates in C_k is counted. The candidates in C_k that are contained in a given transaction t can be determined efficiently by using the *hash-tree*, described when we talk about the subset function momentarily.

Apriori Candidate Generation   The apriori-gen function takes as an argument L_{k-1}, the set of all large $(k-1)$-itemsets. It returns a superset of the set of all large k-itemsets. First, in the *join* step, we join

L_{k-1} with L_{k-1} to obtain a superset of the final set of candidates C_k. The union $p \cup q$ of itemsets $p, q \in L_{k-1}$ is inserted in C_k if they share their $k - 2$ first items:

1) **insert into** C_k
2) **select** $p[1], p[2], \ldots, p[k-1], q[k-1]$
3) **from** L_{k-1} p, L_{k-1} q
4) **where** $p[1] = q[1], \ldots, p[k-2] = q[k-2], p[k-1] < q[k-1]$;

Next, in the *prune* step, we delete all itemsets $c \in C_k$ such that some $(k-1)$-subset of c is not in L_{k-1}. To see why this generation procedure maintains completeness, note that for any itemset in L_k with minimum support, any subset of size k–1 must also have minimum support. Hence, if we extended each itemset in L_{k-1} with all possible items and then deleted all those whose $(k-1)$-subsets were not in L_{k-1}, we would be left with a superset of the itemsets in L_k.

The join is equivalent to extending L_{k-1} with each item in the database and then deleting those itemsets for which the $(k$–1$)$-itemset obtained by deleting the $(k$–1$)$th item is not in L_{k-1}. Thus at this stage, $C_k \supseteq L_k$. For the same reason, the pruning stage where we delete from C_k all itemsets whose $(k-1)$-subsets are not in L_{k-1} also does not delete any itemset that could be in L_k.

As an example, let L_3 be $\{\{1\ 2\ 3\}, \{1\ 2\ 4\}, \{1\ 3\ 4\}, \{1\ 3\ 5\}, \{2\ 3\ 4\}\}$. After the join step, C_4 will be $\{\{1\ 2\ 3\ 4\}, \{1\ 3\ 4\ 5\}\ \}$. The prune step will delete the itemset $\{1\ 3\ 4\ 5\}$ because the itemset $\{1\ 4\ 5\}$ is not in L_3. We will then be left with only $\{1\ 2\ 3\ 4\}$ in C_4.

The prune step requires testing that all $(k$–1$)$-subsets of a newly generated k-candidate-itemset are present in L_{k-1}. To make this membership test fast, large itemsets are stored in a hash table.

Subset Function   Candidate itemsets C_k are stored in a *hash-tree*. A node of the hash-tree either contains a list of itemsets (a *leaf* node) or a hash table (an *interior* node). In an interior node, each bucket of the hash table points to another node. The root of the hash-tree is defined to be at depth 1. An interior node at depth d points to nodes at depth $d + 1$. Itemsets are stored in the leaves. When we add an itemset c, we start from the root and go down the tree until we reach a leaf. At an interior node at depth d, we decide which branch to follow by applying a hash function to the dth item of the itemset, and following the pointer in the corresponding bucket. All nodes are initially created

1) $L_1 = \{$large 1-itemsets$\}$;
2) $\widehat{C}_1 =$ database $\mathcal{D}$;
3)   **for** ($k = 2$; $L_{k-1} \neq \emptyset$; $k{+}{+}$) **do begin**
4) $C_k =$ apriori-gen(L_{k-1}); // New candidates
5) $\widehat{C}_k = \emptyset$;
6)   **forall** entries $t \in \widehat{C}_{k-1}$ **do begin**
7)   // determine candidates contained in the transaction t.TID
            $C_t = \{c \in C_k \mid (c[1] \cdot c[2] \cdot \ldots \cdot c[k{-}1]) \in t$.set-of-itemsets $\wedge$
                $(c[1] \cdot c[2] \ldots \cdot c[k{-}2] \cdot c[k]) \in t$.set-of-itemsets$\}$;
8)   **forall** candidates $c \in C_t$ **do**
9) c.count$++$;
10)   **if** $(C_t \neq \emptyset)$ **then** $\widehat{C}_k \mathrel{+}= \; < t$.TID$, C_t >$;
11)   **end**
12) $L_k = \{c \in C_k \mid c$.count $\geq$ minsup$\}$
13)   **end**
14)   Answer $= \bigcup_k L_k$;

Figure 12.2
Algorithm aprioriTid.

as leaf nodes. When the number of itemsets in a leaf node exceeds a specified threshold, the leaf node is converted to an interior node.

Starting from the root node, the subset function finds all the candidates contained in a transaction t as follows. If we are at a leaf, we find which of the itemsets in the leaf are contained in t and add references to them to the answer set. If we are at an interior node and we have reached it by hashing the item i, we hash on each item that comes after i in t and recursively apply this procedure to the node in the corresponding bucket. For the root node, we hash on every item in t.

To see why the subset function returns the desired set of references, consider what happens at the root node. For any itemset c contained in transaction t, the first item of c must be in t. At the root, by hashing on every item in t, we ensure that we only ignore itemsets that start with an item not in t. Similar arguments apply at lower depths. The only additional factor is that, since the items in any itemset are ordered, if we reach the current node by hashing the item i, we only need to consider the items in t that occur after i.

12.2.2   Algorithm AprioriTid

The AprioriTid algorithm, shown in Figure 12.2, also uses the apriori-gen function (given in Section 12.2.1) to determine the candidate item-sets before the pass begins. The new feature of this algorithm is that the database $\mathcal{D}$ is not used for counting support after the first pass. Rather, the set $\widehat{C}_k$ is used for this purpose. Each member of the set $\widehat{C}_k$ is of the form $< TID, \{X_k\} >$, where each X_k is a potentially large k-itemset present in the transaction with identifier TID. For $k = 1$, $\widehat{C}_1$ corresponds to the database $\mathcal{D}$, although conceptually each item i is re-placed by the itemset $\{i\}$. For $k > 1$, $\widehat{C}_k$ is generated by the algorithm (step 10). The member of $\widehat{C}_k$ corresponding to transaction t is $<t.TID$, $\{c \in C_k | c$ contained in $t\}>$. If a transaction does not contain any can-didate k-itemset, then $\widehat{C}_k$ will not have an entry for this transaction. Thus, the number of entries in $\widehat{C}_k$ may be smaller than the number of transactions in the database, especially for large values of k. In addition, for large values of k, each entry may be smaller than the correspond-ing transaction because very few candidates may be contained in the transaction. However, for small values for k, each entry may be larger than the corresponding transaction because an entry in C_k includes all candidate k-itemsets contained in the transaction. We further explore this trade-off in Section 12.4.

Example   Consider the database in Figure 12.3 and assume that the minimum support is 2 transactions. Calling apriori-gen with L_1 at step 4 gives the candidate itemsets C_2. In steps 6 through 10, we count the support of candidates in C_2 by iterating over the entries in $\widehat{C}_1$ and generate $\widehat{C}_2$. The first entry in $\widehat{C}_1$ is $\{ \{1\} \{3\} \{4\} \}$, corresponding to transaction 100. The C_t at step 7 corresponding to this entry t is $\{ \{1\ 3\} \}$, because $\{1\ 3\}$ is a member of C_2 and both $(\{1\ 3\}-\{1\})$ and $(\{1\ 3\}-\{3\})$ are members of t.

Calling apriori-gen with L_2 gives C_3. Making a pass over the data with $\widehat{C}_2$ and C_3 generates $\widehat{C}_3$. Note that there is no entry in $\widehat{C}_3$ for the transactions with TIDs 100 and 400, since they do not contain any of the itemsets in C_3. The candidate $\{2\ 3\ 5\}$ in C_3 turns out to be large and is the only member of L_3. When we generate C_4 using L_3, it turns out to be empty, and we terminate.

Database	
TID	Items
100	1 3 4
200	2 3 5
300	1 2 3 5
400	2 5

$\widehat{C}_1$

TID	Set-of-Itemsets
100	{ {1}, {3}, {4} }
200	{ {2}, {3}, {5} }
300	{ {1}, {2}, {3}, {5} }
400	{ {2}, {5} }

L_1

Itemset	Support
{1}	2
{2}	3
{3}	3
{5}	3

C_2

Itemset	Support
{1 2}	1
{1 3}	2
{1 5}	1
{2 3}	2
{2 5}	3
{3 5}	2

$\widehat{C}_2$

TID	Set-of-Itemsets
100	{ {1 3} }
200	{ {2 3}, {2 5}, {3 5} }
300	{ {1 2}, {1 3}, {1 5}, {2 3}, {2 5}, {3 5} }
400	{ {2 5} }

L_2

Itemset	Support
{1 3}	2
{2 3}	2
{2 5}	3
{3 5}	2

C_3

Itemset	Support
{2 3 5}	2

$\widehat{C}_3$

TID	Set-of-Itemsets
200	{ {2 3 5} }
300	{ {2 3 5} }

L_3

Itemset	Support
{2 3 5}	2

Figure 12.3
Example.

12.3   Generating Rules

The association rules that we consider are somewhat more general than in (Agrawal *et al.* 1993) in that we allow a consequent to have more than one item. In this chapter we give an efficient generalization of the algorithm in (Agrawal *et al.* 1993).

For every large itemset l, we output all rules $a \Rightarrow (l - a)$, where a is a subset of l, such that the ratio support(l)/support(a) is at least *minconf.* The support of any subset $\tilde{a}$ of a must be as great as the support of a. Therefore, the confidence of the rule $\tilde{a} \Rightarrow (l - \tilde{a})$ cannot be more than the confidence of $a \Rightarrow (l - a)$. Hence, if a did not yield a rule involving all the items in l with a as the antecedent, neither will $\tilde{a}$. It follows that for a rule $(l - a) \Rightarrow a$ to hold, all rules of the form $(l - \tilde{a}) \Rightarrow \tilde{a}$ must also hold, where $\tilde{a}$ is a non-empty subset of a. For example, if the rule $AB \Rightarrow CD$ holds, then the rules $ABC \Rightarrow D$ and $ABD \Rightarrow C$ must also hold.

This characteristic is similar to the property that if an itemset is large

```
1)   forall large k-itemsets l_k, k ≥ 2 do begin
2)       H_1 = { consequents of rules from l_k with one item in the consequent };
3)       call ap-genrules(l_k, H_1);
4)   end

5)   procedure ap-genrules(l_k: large k-itemset, H_m: set of m-item consequents)
6)       if (k > m + 1) then begin
7)           H_{m+1} = apriori-gen(H_m);
8)           forall h_{m+1} ∈ H_{m+1} do begin
9)               conf = support(l_k)/support(l_k − h_{m+1});
10)              if (conf ≥ minconf) then
11)                  output the rule (l_k − h_{m+1}) ⇒ h_{m+1}
                         with confidence = conf and support = support(l_k);
12)              else
13)                  delete h_{m+1} from H_{m+1};
14)          end
15)          call ap-genrules(l_k, H_{m+1});
16)      end
```

Figure 12.4
Rule generation algorithm.

then so are all its subsets. From a large itemset l, therefore, we first generate all rules with one item in the consequent. We then use the consequents of these rules and the function apriori-gen in Section 12.2.1 to generate all possible consequents with two items that can appear in a rule generated from l, etc. An algorithm using this idea is given in Figure 12.4.

12.4   Empirical Results

To assess the relative performance of the algorithms for discovering large itemsets, we performed several experiments. We first describe the synthetic datasets used in the performance evaluation. Then we show the performance results on synthetic data and discuss the trends in performance. We obtained similar results on real-life datasets (Agrawal and Srikant 1994; Mannila *et al.* 1994). Finally, we describe how the best performance features of Apriori and AprioriTid can be combined into an AprioriHybrid algorithm and demonstrate its scale-up properties.

The experiments were performed on an IBM RS/6000 530H workstation. To keep the comparison fair, we implemented all the algorithms
using the same basic data structures.

12.4.1   Synthetic Data

To evaluate the performance of the algorithms over a large operating
region, we developed synthetic transactions data. These transactions
attempt to mimic the transactions in the retailing environment. Our
model of the "real" world is that people tend to buy sets of items together. Each such set is potentially a maximal large itemset. An example of such a set might be sheets, pillow case, comforter, and ruffles.
However, some people may buy only some of the items from such a set.
A transaction may contain more than one large itemset. For example,
a customer might place an order for a dress and jacket when ordering
sheets and pillow cases, where the dress and jacket together form another
large itemset. In our model, transaction sizes are small with respect to
the total number of items, i.e. the data is sparse. The transaction sizes
are typically clustered around a mean and a few transactions have many
items. Typical sizes of large itemsets are also clustered around a mean,
with a few large itemsets having a large number of items.

To create synthetic datasets, we used the following method. First we
generated 2000 potentially large itemsets from 1000 items. We picked
the size of a set from a Poisson distribution with mean equal to $|I|$
= 2, 4, or 6, and we randomly assigned items to the set. To model
that large itemsets often have common items, some fraction of items in
subsequent itemsets were chosen from the previous itemset generated.
Each itemset has a weight associated with it, which corresponds to the
probability that this itemset will be picked. This weight is picked from
an exponential distribution with unit mean, and is then normalized so
that the sum of the weights for all the itemsets is 1.

Then we generated $|\mathcal{D}|$ = 100,000 transactions. The average size $|T|$
of a transaction was 5, 10 or 20, and the size was picked from a Poisson distribution. Each transaction was assigned a series of fractions of
potentially large itemsets, to model that all the items in a large itemset
are not always bought together.

The number of transactions was to set to 100,000 because, as we will
see in Section 12.4.2, SETM could not be run for larger values. However,
for our scale-up experiments, we generated datasets with up to 10 million

Table 12.2
Parameters and sizes of datasets.

Name	$|T|$	$|I|$	$|\mathcal{D}|$	MB
T5.I2.D100K	5	2	100K	2.4
T10.I4.D100K	10	4	100K	4.4
T20.I4.D100K	20	4	100K	8.4
T20.I6.D100K	20	6	100K	8.4

Table 12.3
Execution times for T10.I4.D100K (sec).

Algorithm	Minimum Support (%)				
	2.0	1.5	1.0	0.75	0.5
SETM	41	91	659	929	1639
Apriori	3.8	4.8	11.2	17.4	19.3

transactions (838MB for $|T| = 20$). Table 12.2 summarizes the dataset parameter settings. A more detailed description of the synthetic data generation can be found in (Agrawal and Srikant 1994).

12.4.2   Experiments with Synthetic Data

Figure 12.5 shows the execution times for the four synthetic datasets given in Table 12.2 for decreasing values of minimum support. As the minimum support decreases, the execution times of all the algorithms increase because of increases in the total number of candidate and large itemsets.

Apriori outperforms AIS for all problem sizes, by factors ranging from 2 for high minimum support to more than an order of magnitude for low levels of support. For small problems, AprioriTid did about as well as Apriori, but its performance degraded to be about twice as slow for large problems.

For SETM, we have only plotted the execution times for the dataset T5.I2.D100K in Figure 12.5. The execution times for SETM for T10.I4. D100K are given in Table 12.3. We did not plot the execution times in Table 12.3 on the corresponding graphs because they are too large compared to the execution times of the other algorithms. For the two datasets with transaction sizes of 20, SETM took too long to execute and we aborted those runs as the trends were clear. Clearly, Apriori outperforms SETM by more than an order of magnitude for large datasets.

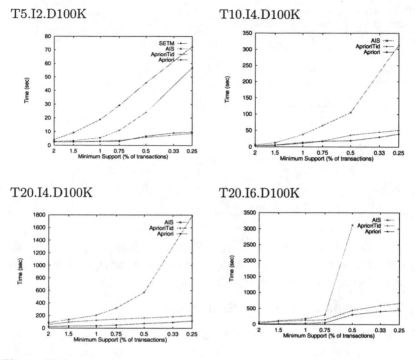

Figure 12.5
Execution times: synthetic data.

12.4.3   Explanation of the Relative Performance

To explain these performance trends, we show in Figure 12.6 the sizes of the large and candidate sets in different passes for the T10.I4.D100K dataset for the minimum support of 0.75%. L_k is the lower bound for all the curves. Note that the Y-axis in this graph has a log scale.

The problem with the SETM algorithm is the size of its $\widehat{C}_k$ sets. Recall that the size of the set $\widehat{C}_k$ is given by $\sum_{c \in C_k}$ support-count(c). Thus, the sets $\widehat{C}_k$ are roughly S times bigger than the corresponding C_k sets, where S is the average support count of the candidate itemsets. Unless the problem size is very small, the $\widehat{C}_k$ sets have to be written to disk, and externally sorted twice, causing the SETM algorithm to perform poorly. For datasets with more transactions, the performance gap between SETM and the other algorithms will become even larger.

The problem with AIS is that it generates too many candidates that

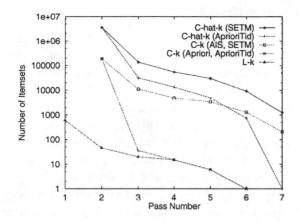

Figure 12.6
Sizes of the large and candidate sets (T10.I4.D100K, minsup = 0.75%).

later turn out to be small, causing it to waste too much effort. Apriori also counts too many small sets in the second pass (recall that C_2 is really a cross-product of L_1 with L_1). However, this wastage decreases dramatically from the third pass onward.

AprioriTid also has the problem of SETM that $\widehat{C}_k$ tends to be large. However, the apriori candidate generation used by AprioriTid generates significantly fewer candidates than the transaction-based candidate generation used by SETM. As a result, the $\widehat{C}_k$ of AprioriTid has fewer entries than that of SETM. In addition, unlike SETM, AprioriTid does not have to sort $\widehat{C}_k$. Thus, AprioriTid does not suffer as much as SETM from maintaining $\widehat{C}_k$.

AprioriTid has the nice feature that it replaces a pass over the original dataset by a pass over the set $\widehat{C}_k$. Hence, AprioriTid is very effective in later passes when the size of $\widehat{C}_k$ becomes small compared to the size of the database. Thus, we find that AprioriTid beats Apriori when its $\widehat{C}_k$ sets can fit in memory and the distribution of the large itemsets has a long tail. When $\widehat{C}_k$ doesn't fit in memory, there is a jump in the execution time for AprioriTid, such as when going from 0.75% to 0.5% for datasets with transaction size 10 in Figure 12.5. In this region, Apriori starts beating AprioriTid.

12.4.4   Algorithm AprioriHybrid

Based on the observations above, we can design a hybrid algorithm, which we call AprioriHybrid, that uses Apriori in the initial passes and switches to AprioriTid when it expects that the set $\widehat{C}_k$ at the end of the pass will fit in memory.

We use the following heuristic to estimate if $\widehat{C}_k$ would fit in memory in the next pass. At the end of the current pass, we have the counts of the candidates in C_k. From this, we estimate what the size of $\widehat{C}_k$ would have been if it had been generated. This size, in words, is ($\sum_{\text{candidates } c \in C_k}$ support(c) + number of transactions). If $\widehat{C}_k$ in this pass was small enough to fit in memory, and there were fewer large candidates in the current pass than the previous pass, we switch to AprioriTid.

We have run performance tests with the datasets described earlier, and AprioriHybrid performs better than Apriori and AprioriTid in almost all cases. AprioriHybrid does a little worse than Apriori when the pass in which the switch occurs is the last pass; AprioriHybrid thus incurs the cost of switching without realizing the benefits. AprioriHybrid did up to 30% better than Apriori, and up to 60% better than AprioriTid.

12.4.5   Scale-up Experiment

Figure 12.7 shows how AprioriHybrid scales up as the number of transactions is increased from 100,000 to 10 million transactions. We used the combinations (T5.I2), (T10.I4), and (T20.I6) for the average sizes of transactions and itemsets respectively. All other parameters were the same as for the data in Table 12.2. The sizes of these datasets for 10 million transactions were 239MB, 439MB and 838MB respectively. The minimum support level was set to 0.75%. The execution times are normalized with respect to the times for the 100,000 transaction datasets in the first graph and with respect to the 1 million transaction dataset in the second. As shown, the execution times scale quite linearly. Although we do not give the graphs, similar experiments showed that the Apriori algorithm also scales linearly.

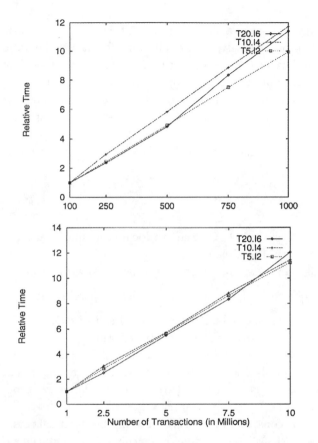

Figure 12.7
Number of transactions scale-up.

12.5   Theoretical Analyses

The algorithms presented in the previous sections perform quite well in practice. Their running time is bounded by $O(\|C\| \cdot |\mathcal{D}|)$, where $\|C\|$ denotes the sum of the sizes of candidates considered and $|\mathcal{D}|$ denotes the size of the database.

12.5.1   A Lower Bound

The quantity $\|C\|$ can be exponential in the number of items, as all itemsets can be large. If there are only a few large sets, the above algorithms still investigate several candidates. Next we show that this is to some degree inevitable. Namely, we now give an information-theoretic lower bound for finding one association rule in a restricted model of computation where the only way of getting information from a database $\mathcal{D}$ is by asking questions of the form "is the set X large." This model is realistic in the case the database $\mathcal{D}$ is large and stored using a database system.

Assume the database $\mathcal{D}$ has m items. In the worst case one needs at least

$$\log \binom{m}{k} \approx k \log(m/k)$$

questions of the form "is the set X large" to locate one maximal large set, where k is the size of the large set.

The proof of this claim is simple. Consider a database with exactly 1 maximal large set of size k. There are $\binom{m}{k}$ different possible answers to the problem of finding the maximal large set. Each question of the form "is the set X large" provides at most 1 bit of information.

This lower bound is not optimal for small values of k. For example, assume that there is exactly one large set of size 1. Then any algorithm for finding this set has to use at least $\Theta(m)$ queries of the above type. However, the bound is fairly tight for larger values of k.

Loveland (1987) has considered the problem of finding "critical sets." Given a function $f : \mathcal{P}(R) \to \{0,1\}$ that is *upwards monotone* (i.e., if $f(Y) = 1$ and $Y \subseteq X$, then $f(X) = 1$), a set X is *critical* if $f(X) = 1$, but $f(Z) = 0$ for all subsets Z of X. Thus maximal large itemsets are complements of critical sets of the upwards monotone function $f(X) = 0$, if X is large, and $f(X) = 1$, otherwise. For example for $k = m/2$, the lower bound above matches exactly the upper bound provided by one of Loveland's algorithms.

12.5.2   Probabilistic Analysis of Random Databases

The number of large sets is an important factor influencing the running times of the algorithms. We now show that in one model of random databases all large itemsets have small size.

Consider a random database $\mathcal{D} = \{T_1, \ldots, T_n\}$ over items $\mathcal{I} = \{i_1, i_2, \ldots, i_m\}$; assume that each transaction T_k of the database contains any item i_j with probability q, and assume that the entries are independent. Then the probability that T_k contains i_j for all i_j in a given itemset X is q^h, where $h = |X|$. The number x of such transactions has a binomial distribution with parameters n and q^h.

The Chernoff bounds (Alon and Spencer 1992; Hagerup and Rüb 1989/90) state that for all $a > 0$ we have

$$Pr[x > nq^h + a] < e^{-2a^2/n}.$$

We thus obtain

$$Pr[x > sn] = Pr[x > nq^h + n(s - q^h)] < e^{-2n(s-q^h)^2}$$

where n is the number of transactions $|\mathcal{D}|$ and s is the minimum support *minsup*. Thus the expected number of large itemsets of size h is bounded by $m^h e^{-2n(s-q^h)^2}$, where m is the number of items. This is less than 1 provided $s > \sqrt{(h \ln m)/n} + q^h$. For large databases and thus for large n the first term is very small. Hence if $s > q^h$, the expected number of large sets of size is small. (For $s = minsup = 0.01$ and $q = 0.1$, this means $h \geq 2$; for $s = 0.0001$ and $q = 0.1$, this means $h \geq 4$.) Thus a random database typically has only very few large itemsets. Of course, databases occurring in practice are not random.

12.5.3   Analysis of Sampling

The running times of the algorithms depended linearly on the size of the database. One possibility of lowering this factor is to use only a sample of transactions. We show that small samples are sometimes quite good for finding large itemsets.

Let s be the support of a given set X of items. Consider a random sample with replacement of size h from the database. Then the number of transactions in the sample that contain X is a random variable x with binomial distribution of h trials, each having success probability s. We can again use the Chernoff bounds. The probability that the estimated support is off by at least α is

$$Pr[x > h(s + \alpha)] < e^{-2\alpha^2 h^2/h} = e^{-2\alpha^2 h},$$

i.e., bounded by a quantity exponential in h.

Table 12.4 presents sufficient sample sizes, given values for α and probabilities of error more than α. For accuracy to be within support

Table 12.4
Sufficient sample sizes, given values for α and probabilities of error more than α.

$\alpha =$	1%	0.1%	0.01%	0.001%
$Pr[error > \alpha] \approx 1\%$	23000	$2.3 \cdot 10^6$	$2.3 \cdot 10^8$	$2.3 \cdot 10^{10}$
$Pr[error > \alpha] \approx 5\%$	15000	$1.5 \cdot 10^6$	$1.5 \cdot 10^8$	$1.5 \cdot 10^{10}$
$Pr[error > \alpha] \approx 10\%$	11500	$1.15 \cdot 10^6$	$1.15 \cdot 10^8$	$1.15 \cdot 10^{10}$

of an itemset $\pm$ 1%, samples of some dozens of thousands of examples can be sufficient. For association rules with support in fractions of a percent (where we would like accuracy to be within 0.01% or 0.001%), these bounds indicate that sampling is not effective. Note that the completeness guarantee of finding *all* the rules satisfying the minimum support and confidence constraints is lost when we use sampling.

12.6   Conclusions and Open Problems

Association rules are a simple and natural class of database regularities, useful in various analysis and prediction tasks. We have considered the problem of finding all the association rules satisfying user-specified support and confidence constraints that hold in a given database.

We presented two new algorithms, Apriori and AprioriTid, for discovering all significant association rules between items in a large database of transactions. We compared these algorithms to algorithms introduced in earlier work, the AIS (Agrawal *et al.* 1993) and SETM (Houtsma and Swami 1993) algorithms. We presented experimental results, using synthetic data, showing that the proposed algorithms always outperform AIS and SETM. We obtained similar results with real data (Agrawal and Srikant 1994; Mannila *et al.* 1994). The performance gap increased with the problem size, and ranged from a factor of three for small problems to more than an order of magnitude for large problems.

We showed how the best features of the two proposed algorithms can be combined into a hybrid algorithm, called AprioriHybrid, which then becomes the algorithm of choice for this problem. The scale-up properties of AprioriHybrid and Apriori demonstrate the feasibility of using these algorithms in real applications involving very large databases. However, the implementation of AprioriHybrid is more complex than Apriori. Hence the somewhat worse performance of Apriori may be an acceptable tradeoff in some situations. We have also analyzed the theoretical properties of the problem of finding association rules.

Several problems remain open and are subject to further research.

- Multiple taxonomies (*is-a* hierarchies) over items are often available. An example of such a hierarchy is that a dish washer *is a* kitchen appliance *is a* heavy electric appliance, etc. We would like to be able to find association rules that use such hierarchies.

- We did not consider the quantities or values of the items bought in a transaction, which are important for some applications. Finding such rules needs further work.

- We may be interested in only those rules in which certain items appear in the consequent and/or antecedent. Pushing constraints on antecedents into the computation is quite straightforward, but the exploitation of constraints on the consequent is an interesting problem. More generally, the question is about using the user input or domain knowledge to improve the execution efficiency of the mining process.

References

Agrawal, R., Imielinski, T., and Swami, A. 1993. Mining Association Rules between Sets of Items in Large Databases. In *Proceedings, ACM SIG-MOD Conference on Management of Data*, 207–216. Washington, D.C.

Agrawal, R., and Srikant, R. 1994. Fast Algorithms for Mining Association Rules. IBM Research Report RJ9839, June 1994, IBM Almaden Research Center, San Jose, Calif..

Alon, N.; and Spencer, J. H. 1992. *The Probabilistic Method.* New York: John Wiley Inc.

Brachman, R., et al. 1993. Integrated Support for Data Archeology. Presented at the AAAI Workshop on Knowledge Discovery in Databases, Washington, D.C.

Breiman, L.; Friedman, J. H.; Olshen, R. A.; and Stone, C. J. 1984. *Classification and Regression Trees.* Belmont, Calif.: Wadsworth.

Cheeseman, P.; Kelly, J.; Self, M.; Stutz, J.; Taylor, W.; and Freeman, D. 1988. AutoClass: A Bayesian Classification System. In *Proceedings, Fifth International Conference on Machine Learning*, 54–64. San Mateo, Calif.: Morgan Kaufmann.

Fisher, D. H. 1987. Knowledge Acquisition Via Incremental Conceptual Clustering. *Machine Learning* 2(2): 139–172.

Hagerup, T., and Rüb, C. 1989/90. A Guided Tour of Chernoff Bounds. *Information Processing Letters* 33: 305–308.

Houtsma, M.; and Swami, A. 1993. Set-Oriented Mining of Association Rules. Research Report RJ 9567, Oct. 1993, IBM Almaden Research Center, San Jose, Calif.

Klemettinen, M., Mannila, H., Ronkainen, P., Toivonen, H., and Verkamo, A. I. 1994. Finding Interesting Rules from Large Sets of Discovered Association Rules. In *CIKM'94: Conference on Information and Knowledge Management*, 401–407. Gaithersburg, Md.

Langley, P.; Simon, H.; Bradshaw, G.; and Zytkow, J. 1987. *Scientific Discovery: Computational Explorations of the Creative Process*. Cambridge, Mass.: The MIT Press.

Loveland, D. W. 1987. Finding Critical Sets. *Journal of Algorithms* 8: 362–371.

Mannila, H., and Räihä, K.-J. 1992. On the Complexity of Inferring Functional Dependencies. *Discrete Applied Mathematics* 40: 237–243.

Mannila, H., and Räihä, K.-J. 1994. Algorithms for Inferring Functional Dependencies from Relations. *Data & Knowledge Engineering* 12(1): 83–99.

Mannila, H., Toivonen, H., and Verkamo, A. I. 1994. Efficient Algorithms for Discovering Association Rules. In Knowledge Discovery in Databases, Tech. Report WS-94-03, American Association for Artificial Intelligence, Menlo Park, Calif.

Muggleton, S., and Feng, C. 1992. Efficient Induction of Logic Programs. In *Inductive Logic Programming*, 281–298, ed. S. Muggleton. London: Academic Press.

Piatetsky-Shapiro, G. 1991. Discovery, Analysis, and Presentation of Strong Rules. In *Knowledge Discovery in Databases*, 229–248, ed. G. Piatetsky-Shapiro and W. Frawley. Menlo Park, Calif.: AAAI Press.

Piatetsky-Shapiro, G., and Frawley, W., eds, 1991. *Knowledge Discovery in Databases*. Menlo Park, Calif.: AAAI Press.

Piatetsky-Shapiro, G., and Matheus, C. J. 1994. The Interestingness of Deviations. Presented at the AAAI Workshop on Knowledge Discovery in Databases, Seattle, Wash.

Quinlan, J. R. 1993. *C4.5: Programs for Machine Learning*. San Mateo, Calif.: Morgan Kaufmann.

Spiegelhalter, D.; Dawid, A.; Lauritzen, S.; and Cowell, R. 1993. Bayesian Analysis in Expert Systems. *Statistical Science* 8(3): 219–283.

13 From Contingency Tables to Various Forms of Knowledge in Databases

Robert Zembowicz
Wichita State University

Jan M. Żytkow
Wichita State University
Polish Academy of Sciences

Abstract

Knowledge comes in different species, such as equations, contingency tables, taxonomies, rules, and concepts. Experience proves that knowledge in various forms can be automatically mined from databases, but the existing automated discovery systems require many improvements. We argue that contingency tables are the basic form of 2-D regularities while other forms of knowledge can be treated as their special cases. We show how simple tests, applied to knowledge in the form of contingency tables, distinguish various special forms of 2-D knowledge, leading to automated solutions of problems in two categories. First, different forms of knowledge may require search in different hypotheses spaces, but if data do not fit any hypothesis in a given space much time could be saved if that space was not searched at all. We solve this problem by testing non-existence of solutions in particular spaces. The search in a particular space is conducted only if the possibility of a solution is not excluded. The second problem comes from the recurring observation of users who show serious confusion when faced with thousands of regularities discovered in a database. This problem is important because the exploration of even a modestly sized database frequently leads to large numbers of regularities. As a response, we describe tests which classify regularities into different categories and are followed by automated methods which combine large numbers of regularities in each category into concise, useful forms of taxonomies, inclusion graphs and other multi-dimensional theories.

13.1 Towards Autonomous Exploration of Databases

Integration of many discovery capabilities into one system is the goal of some KDD researchers. Although various systems can run a large scale "homogeneous" search in simple problem spaces, the integration that would combine many discovery goals, switching automatically from one goal to another, is difficult to achieve. Such integration is not only of practical importance, but is also critical for the complete understanding of the discovery process. As long as the parameters of each individual search, such as the depth of search, the acceptance threshold, and the operators to be applied, can be adjusted by the user, subtle forms of user intervention are difficult to capture and to eliminate. In order to eliminate various forms of user intervention, our systems must know how to instantiate each search automatically in response to particular situations. The more steps performed automatically by a successful search, without consulting a user, the better the understanding of the discovery process.

13.1.1   49er: Search for 2-D Regularities

Although full automation of data mining is our ultimate goal, we recognize that concrete progress is possible only by gradual automation of individual steps. Before we discuss several solutions that enhance automation of our 49er (Forty-Niner) data mining system (Żytkow & Zembowicz, 1993), let us present the initial search mechanism of 49er. During that search, which applies on any relational table (data matrix), 49er discovers knowledge in the form of regularities represented by statements of the form "Pattern P holds for all data in range R". Examples of patterns include contingency tables, equations, and logical equivalence. Every range considered by 49er is a data subset distinguished by a conjunction of simple conditions, each partitioning the values of a single attribute into two approximately equal subsets. 49er systematically searches for regularities in the set of all data, then partitions the data into subsets and searches for regularities in the subsets. Within each range of data, 49er tries to detect 2-D regularities for all combinations of attribute pairs admissible by the user. Initially, 49er examines the contingency table for each pair of attributes, but as we describe in this chapter, if the system finds that the contingency table follows a specific pattern, a more subtle discovery mechanism can be invoked, such as a search in the space of equations.

49er applies statistical tests of significance and strength to all hypotheses, qualifying them as regularities if test results exceed acceptance thresholds. Significance is the probability Q that a given pattern has been generated randomly for variables which are really independent. Values close to 0 mean that such a situation is very unlikely, while values close to 1 make it very likely. 49er measures the predictive strength for contingency tables by Cramer's V coefficient, which we discuss later. Both Q and V are derived from the χ^2 statistic which measures the distance between actual and expected events.

13.1.2   Significance Thresholds

In searching for regularities, 49er examines huge numbers of hypotheses. As a result, the system typically finds many regularities, but can we be sure that all the regularities are genuine? There is always a chance that a randomly created pattern looks like an authentic relationship. The statistical measures of significance estimate the probability with which a given pattern could be created randomly. About ten randomly created patterns in a million should have the significance measure on the order of 10^{-5}. Researchers typically accept regularities with $Q < 0.05$, but when examining 10^5 random patterns and applying that threshold, 49er would admit some 5,000 spurious regularities. Tests on randomly generated data confirm this estimate (Żytkow & Zembowicz, 1993). Our analysis of significance is different from Jensen's (1991), who considers many hypotheses for a single data set, while we consider one contingency table per dataset.

To minimize the number of pseudo-regularities generated by random fluctuation, we should set a demanding threshold of acceptance. But then we risk ignoring regularities which are real but weak. To avoid spurious regularities, but not to overlook weak but genuine relations, 49er uses thresholds which depend on the estimated number of independent hypotheses in the form of contingency tables, to be considered within a given search: for N independent hypotheses, the threshold is on the order of $1/N$. This practically guarantees a negligible number of spurious regularities. We suggest that the user increase that threshold by the order of 10 or more, if weak regularities are considered important. This approach is deemed successful when the threshold of K/N leads to significantly more than K regularities.

When 49er partitions the data, the smaller the data subsets, the less chance there is to detect a regularity which is more significant than a fixed threshold. At the same time, when smaller partitions are allowed, the threshold must become more demanding, because the number of hypotheses increases. The search terminates "naturally" when even the strongest pattern that occurs for a given data subset is not significant.

Threshold selection reflects also user expectations for domain knowledge and other research objectives. For instance, in the preliminary exploration we may wish to concentrate on the few really outstanding regularities, ignoring all the rest.

13.1.3   49er: Automated Knowledge Refinement

Theoretical reasons for automation go hand in hand with the practical advantages of automated exploration. Several years ago we believed (Żytkow & Baker, 1991) that after a substantial initial search for 2-D regularities, the user will examine the results and decide on further refinements, gradually helping the system to refine the knowledge and to combine regularities into multi-dimensional theories. Manual inspection of 49er's intermediate findings turned out to be not that useful. Even in small databases, the initial search reveals hundreds or thousands of regularities. This turns out to be too many for users to inspect and comprehend in order to prescribe methods of analysis for the next step. Another reason for automation is that a typical user makes wrong choices when deciding on which discovery tool to use next, and how to instantiate the search. A combined working knowledge of search, statistics, data management, and knowledge management is too much even for a well-educated user. In response, we expanded 49er's automated search, using the methods described in this chapter.

A general purpose data miner is very convenient because with little preparation it can work on any database, liberating the user from manual data analysis in order to focus the initial search on one or another form of knowledge. It is difficult to tell apriori which forms of knowledge will occur and which will not occur in a given database. The search should be open to all possibilities, but at the same time limited to a size manageable within the resources. In the absence of concrete user expectations, 49er applies the following strategy. It searches the space of all attribute pairs in many data subsets, looking for contingency tables which are statistically significant. Then it applies various tests to those tables to reveal special forms of knowledge. Two mechanisms follow.

First, the functional and multifunctional relationships are refined respectively to specific equations or to systems of equations, where each equation is confined to a specific scope. Second, regularities that indicate equivalence or subset are summarized into taxonomies and subset graphs. They capture knowledge of many dimensions, yet take little storage. They are convenient to visualize, easy to understand, and preserve empirical contents of the discovered knowledge. These methods continue to make theory improvements as far as the discovered knowledge permits, before the user is asked for new directions. Other systems that build contingency tables, for instance, EXPLORA (Hoschka & Klösgen, 1991) can use our approach.

13.2   The Basic Forms of 2-D Knowledge

To minimize the complexity of search for knowledge, 49er starts from 1-D patterns (histogram analysis) and then moves on to search for 2-D regularities. A huge variety of 2-D patterns, however, calls for decomposition of the search space. This, in turn, requires understanding of relations between patterns. Some 2-D classes of patterns are more universal, while others are special cases. The foundations of mathematics tell us that relations are the basic conceptual structures. One such 2-D relation, set membership $(x \in y)$, is sufficient to reconstruct the core of mathematics. Other relations are special cases, such as functional relations and equivalence relations.

Contingency tables are even more basic. While a relation can be viewed as a subset of the Cartesian product of the values of several attributes, a contingency table provides, for each cell in a Cartesian product, the count of all events in the data with the combination of attribute values characteristic for that cell. Relations are special cases, with the count of zero in some cells and without information about the relative frequency of events. Regularities in the form of contingency tables play a role analogous to relational and functional regularities. They summarize data, provide predictions, and are a convenient tool for knowledge visualization. The following partial order with contingency tables on the left shows other patterns as special cases:

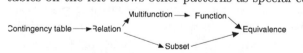

Contingency tables have been used as a general tool for expressing knowledge (Gokhale & Kullback, 1978; Fienberg, 1980; Whittaker, 1990) which cannot be summarized into specialized patterns such as equations. For us, contingency tables are an excellent starting point for automated recognition of other types of knowledge.

Table 13.1
Searches for various forms of knowledge triggered by dedicated tests.

Form of knowledge	Search triggered by:
Concept hierarchies	equivalence relationship test
Subset networks	subset test
Functions	functionality test based on function definition
Multifunctions	test based on definitions of functionality & continuity
Decision trees	predictive power of contingency tables
Causal networks	dependencies between attributes for all records & in slices

Different types of relations can be recognized by tests applied to contingency tables. We discuss those tests in the subsequent sections. In Table 13.1 we summarize the discovery method triggered by each test. Some of these methods refine 2-D tables into other 2-D forms, while other combine many 2-D regularities of the same type into n-D theories.

13.3   Various Forms of 2-D Knowledge in Databases

49er has been applied to databases in many areas, often returning hundreds or thousands 2-D regularities. The majority of databases yield regularities of many types, but the numbers of regularities in each type show significant and characteristic differences across many domains.

For instance, the majority of contingency tables discovered in personnel records are imprecise and do not belong to the special types discussed in this chapter. Occasional equations link variables such as length of employment and salary. Scientific databases are very different. The results reached by 49er show that scientists prepare their data very carefully, trying to make them conclusive for the discovery process. Significant and strongly predictive regularities in the categories of functions, equivalencies and subsets crop up in large numbers. Table 13.2 summarizes the characteristic 2-D patterns found by 49er in databases from many domains.

Table 13.2
Summary of 49er's findings for databases from different domains. Contingency
tables are mentioned if their substantial numbers do not reduce to other forms.
Regularities in other forms have been discovered through contingency tables.

Database	The Main Forms of 2-D Knowledge
navy/training	contingency tables, few equations
navy/recruitment	contingency tables, few equations
juvenile crime	contingency tables, equations, subsets
university enrollment	contingency tables
questionnaire	contingency tables, equations
soybean diseases	equivalences, subsets
bio-species	equivalences, some subsets
geobotany	subsets, equivalences, contingency tables
geographic information systems	multifunctions

13.4   From Equivalence Tables to Concept Hierarchies

Equivalence relations are common in biological databases, especially
when records characterize properties of different, but related species.
It is not uncommon in such databases to find hundreds of contingency
tables in the category of equivalence.

The equivalence of two attributes means that A and B lead to equal
partitions of all records by the values of both attributes. In 49er, the
simplest equivalences are discovered as 2×2 or 2×3 contingency tables
that lead to 2 classes per attribute, for instance:

(a)	A	38	0
	$\neg A$	0	53
		B	$\neg B$

(b)	a_1	81	1
	a_2	2	63
	A	b_1	b_2	B

(c)	a_1	2	34	46
	a_2	64	1	0
	A	c_1	c_2	c_3	C

The equivalence in example (a) can be written as $A \equiv B$ (or $A \Leftrightarrow B$).
The approximate equivalence (b) can be written as $(A = a_1 \ \& \ B = b_1) \vee$
$(A = a_2 \ \& \ B = b_2)$, and similarly (c) as $(A = a_1 \ \& \ C = c_2$ or $c_3) \vee (A =$
$a_2 \ \& \ C = c_1)$. Statements like "$A = a_1$" or "$C = c_2$ or c_3" (in short,
$C = c_2, c_3$) are called *descriptors*.

Noticing equivalences can lead to run-time speed-up in search for
knowledge. If B turns out to be equivalent to A, all regularities for
B are the same as those for A. We can therefore disregard B, reducing the number of attributes, reducing the search, and simplifying the
interpretation and presentation of findings.

13.4.1   Testing for Equivalence

To test whether a contingency table approximates an equivalence, we use Cramer's V coefficient. V is based on the value of the chi-square statistic (χ^2), which measures the distance between tables of actual and expected counts. For a given $M_{row} \times M_{col}$ contingency table and for a given number N of records,

$$V = \sqrt{\chi^2/(N\min(M_{row} - 1, M_{col} - 1))}.$$

V measures the predictive power of a regularity. The regularity between x and y has a larger predictive power if for a given value of x or y the value of the other variable can be predicted more precisely. The strongest, unique predictions are possible when for each value of one attribute there is exactly one corresponding value of the other attribute. In those cases $V = 1$. On the other extreme, when the actual distribution is equal to expected, then $\chi^2 = 0$ and $V = 0$. V is not dependent on the size of the contingency table nor on the number of records. Thus it can be used as a homogeneous measure on regularities found in different subsets and for different combinations of attributes. A table is qualified as equivalence when it exceeds a threshold for V set typically at 0.9.

13.4.2   Taxonomy Formation

For each identified equivalence relation which also exceeds the earlier discussed threshold of significance, 49er forms a simple *hierarchy unit*, such as the two hierarchy units below, linked by the "+" sign. They have been formed for examples (b) and (c) above. "All" at the root means that the regularity holds for all data.

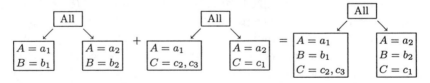

In the next step of taxonomy formation 49er merges all hierarchy units if they share a common descriptor in each subclass. The example above shows how two units are merged into the unit following the "=" sign. Each class in the merged hierarchy unit can be characterized by one of the three alternative descriptors. Hierarchy units can be treated as simple one-layer taxonomies. A multilevel taxonomy is formed from the merged units. In preparation, all hierarchy units are sorted according to the number of alternative descriptors, in descending order. The hierarchy unit with the largest number of descriptors is placed at the root of the hierarchy tree, then the next largest is attached to all bottom level nodes, etc., as illustrated in Figure 13.1. The descriptors in each new node are compared against descriptors of all the ancestor nodes to detect contradictions. For instance, the descriptor "Stem-Cankers = 1 or 2" that characterizes Class 4 contradicts "Stem-Cankers = 0" characteristic to Class 6. Contradiction with an ancestor node indicates empty descendent node which must be removed. For that reason Class 4 under Class 6 and other classes shown in *italics* in Figure 13.1 have been removed from the taxonomy. The algorithm is summarized below. For details see Troxel et. al (1994).

Main Algorithm: Build concept hierarchy
> Create hierarchy units from equivalence relations
> Merge similar hierarchy units
> Sort merged hierarchy units by the decreasing number of descriptors
> hierarchy ← single node labeled "ALL"
> **for** each hierarchy unit, add hierarchy unit to hierarchy

Procedure: Merge similar hierarchy units
> **for** each pair of hierarchy units
>> **if** both units share a common descriptor in each subclass
>>> Merge two hierarchy units into one

Procedure: Add hierarchy unit to hierarchy
> **for** each leaf in the hierarchy
>> Attach children in the hierarchy unit to the leaf
>> Remove children incompatible with the path to the root
>> **if** there is only one child left, merge this child with its parent

Figure 13.1 illustrates both the process of hierarchy formation and the final concept hierarchy discovered by 49er in the soybean database. All nodes shown in *italic* have been removed after proven empty. Four leaves remained, labeled D1, D2, D3, and D4. Each covers exactly one soybean disease. Neither the knowledge that the data describe four classes, however, nor the identity of each class were given to the program. It has been inferred through other knowledge discovered by 49er.

Alternative class definitions can be formed by different choices of descriptors available at each node, leading to very flexible class definitions. Each node n in the hierarchy can be uniquely described by a conjunction of single descriptors, picked up from each node (concept) on the path from the root to n. Note that at least two different but (approximately) equivalent descriptors are available at each node. For instance, class D2, that is, Class6/Class3/Class1/Class7 in the right part of Figure 13.1 can be described by "InternalDiscolor=2." All other descriptors can be inferred. Class D4 can be described by "Sclerotia=0 & StemCankers=1,2 & FruitingBodies=0 & Roots=0."

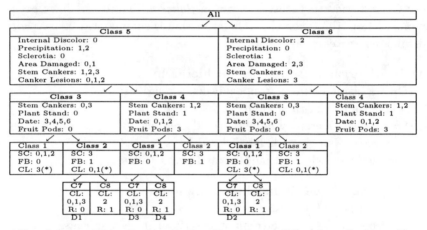

Abbreviations: FB = Fruiting-Bodies; R = Roots; SC = Stem-Cankers; CL = Canker-Lesions

Figure 13.1
The taxonomy generation process, depicted from the top (Classes 5 and 6) till the bottom (Classes 7 and 8). Empty classes are shown in *italic*. They have been removed from the taxonomy.

13.4.3   Comparison with COBWEB on Soybean Data

Applied to soybean data, COBWEB (Fisher, 1987) discovered the same four disease classes. Detailed results, published by Fisher for class D2 (a disease called Charcoal Rot), indicate that COBWEB found eight descriptors for D2, compared to 13 descriptors discovered by 49er. This shows a substantial increase in empirical content (predictive power) reached by accumulating 2-D relations. For details see Troxel et. al

(1994).

13.4.4   Taxonomy as a Limited Form of Knowledge

Knowledge contained in a taxonomy can be expressed by statements of several types. Our examples below refer to the situation depicted in Figure 13.2.

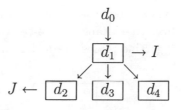

Figure 13.2
Fragment of taxonomy: d_0 represents the conjunction of tests-descriptors on the path prior to d_1; d_1 is the test leading to d_1; all children of d_1 are distinguished by descriptors d_2, d_3, d_4. I is the conjunction of descriptors inferred at node d_1, while J is a similar conjunction inferred at node d_2.

- Child class d_2 is a non-empty subset of parent class d_1:
  $\exists x[d_0(x) \ \& \ d_1(x) \ \& \ d_2(x)]$.

- Taxonomy is exhaustive and disjoint (xor below is exclusive or):
  $[d_0(x) \ \& \ d_1(x)] \rightarrow [d_2(x) \ \text{xor} \ d_3(x) \ \text{xor} \ d_4(x)]$.

  When d_1 has two children: $[d_0(x) \ \& \ d_1(x)] \rightarrow [d_2(x) \equiv \neg d_3(x)]$.

- Empirical content of a taxonomy is represented by statements:
  $d_0(x) \ \& \ d_1(x) \rightarrow I(x)$, $d_0(x) \ \& \ d_1(x) \ \& \ d_2(x) \rightarrow J(x)$,
  where $I(x) = i_1(x) \ \& \ \dots \ \& \ i_k(x)$, $J(x) = j_1(x) \ \& \ \dots \ \& \ j_l(x)$,
  $i_m(x)$, and $j_n(x)$ are the descriptors that can be inferred in the classes labeled respectively by d_1 and d_2.

Notice that knowledge included in a taxonomy falls into the category of monadic logic; membership criterion for each class is represented by a unary predicate, while empirical content of each class and relations between classes are represented by logical relations between such predicates. Knowledge represented by monadic predicates is very limited compared to the expressive power of equations and contingency tables, and to the full expressive power of the first order logic.

13.5   From Subset Tables to Subset Networks

Theories based on the subset relations are even more limited in expressive power than taxonomies, but they can combine large numbers of subset relations.

13.5.1   Testing for Subset

The inclusion relation between the scopes of two Boolean attributes may be determined from the "triangular," 4-cell contingency tables. For example, the following table represents inclusion of attribute A in B, $A \subset B$,

$$
\begin{array}{c|c|c|}
A & \text{a} & 0 \\
\hline
\neg A & \text{b} & \text{d} \\
\hline
 & B & \neg B
\end{array}
$$

a, b, d indicate non-zero counts of records, $c = 0$. This table could be also interpreted as implication of property B from property A, that is by $A \Rightarrow B$.

Four inclusion cases are possible for 2×2 contingency tables, depending on which cell has zero counts. To allow some small level of noise and error, we admit some exceptions. For example, instead of $c = 0$ we require $max(c/(a+c), c/(d+c)) < \delta$, where δ is the tolerance (typically 10%).

Similarly to equivalence, subset relation is not limited to Boolean attributes and can be inferred from large contingency tables. For instance, if a table includes 0 counts for the combination of values d_3 and e_7 of attributes D and E, then $D = d_3 \subset \neg E = e_7$. If D and E have many values, there is little practical value in such subset relations because they cover only very limited cases and possess little empirical content.

13.5.2   Inclusion Network

In many databases a significant number of 2-D regularities represent inclusions (Moraczewski et. al, 1995). A large number of inclusions can be conveniently combined into an inclusion graph, in which vertices represent attributes while directed edges stand for inclusion between extensions of attributes.

Constructing the inclusion graph 49er stores equivalent attributes on the same node to reduce the subset edges. For example, if $A \subset B$ and

$B \equiv C$, then $A \subset C$ is removed. Transitivity of the inclusion also permits reduction of the graph: if $A \subset B$ and $B \subset C$, then the inclusion $A \subset C$ is removed. These steps reduce the number of nodes and edges in the inclusion graph while preserving its predictive content.

To divide the typically large inclusion graphs into meaningful pieces, 49er uses the maximum subsets, which are not subsets of any other node in the inclusion graph. For each maximum node M, it extracts the subgraph G_M of all subsets of M. Such subgraphs typically have a strong domain-specific interpretation, representing, for instance, all species which inhabit various selective parts of the environment settled by the species M. After removing all edges shared with any other subgraph $G_{M'}$, the remaining subgraph G_M^* has the interpretation of all species which are more selective than M but are not part of the environment of any other species, except those under M. Each G_M^* graph can be interpreted in domain-specific terms. The following algorithm describes inclusion graph formation and analysis.

Algorithm: Build Inclusion Graph and extract subgraphs G_M^*

given the list of significant contingency tables
Select inclusions from contingency tables
Build inclusion graph
Remove redundant edges
for each maximum node M
$G_M \leftarrow$ graph of all subsets of M
$G_M^* \leftarrow G_M$ after removing edges shared with any other graph $G_{M'}$

13.5.3   Geobotanical Database Exploration

Consider application of 49er on a geobotanical database that resulted from 20-year studies of Warsaw flora (Sudnik-Wójcikowska 1987) and consists of 1181 Boolean attributes (presence of plant taxa in a given area) and 225 records (areas in the grid covering the whole city). The search in the space of 2-D attribute combinations without slices evaluated $0.5 \times 1181 * 1180 \approx 7 \times 10^5$ hypotheses. Although many interesting regularities are usually found in data subsets, the number of attributes in this database prohibits data slicing. Allowing only a partition into two slices per attribute leads to $0.5 \times 1180 \times 1179 \times 2 \times 1181 \approx 1.6 \times 10^9$ hypotheses to be tested. 49er would take some 2 years to complete this task. In 10 hour search without slices 49er discovered 16577 statistically significant contingency tables. 49er determined that 594 tables capture equivalences of attributes, and applied the taxonomy formation method described in the previous section. The merging of hierarchy units resulted in interesting discoveries. One grid element included 29 species which turned out to be not established permanently in the flora; it showed that they occur in the vicinity of a mill. Another 9-attribute class, occupying just two grid elements, contained species fugitive from gardens. Since these and all other merged hierarchy units were extremely unbalanced, and hierarchy formation did not lead to any node reduction, the resultant multi-level hierarchy has not been interesting.

6364 contingency tables passed the test for approximate subset. After merging equivalent nodes and removing redundant edges, this number was reduced to 2475. 2358 contingency tables express "positive" inclusions (that is, $A \subset B$) while the remaining 117 represent exclusions of ranges of the corresponding plant taxa A and B ($A \subset \neg B$ or $\neg A \subset B$). These are not used in the inclusion graph. The algorithm described earlier in this chapter formed 302 subgraphs G_M^*, each corresponding to one maximum element M. The species in each G_M^* are characteristic to a specific environment. The further away from M, the narrower is the ecological amplitude of the species. For instance, in a subgraph of species preferring moist areas, the root corresponds to a common meadow plant *Ranunculus acris*, growing on wet soils, that is missing only in the downtown and several dryer areas, while one of the lowest descendents is *Calla palustris*, growing only in peat-bogs, very wet, natural habitats (Moraczewski et. al, 1995).

13.6   From Contingency Tables to Equations

Equations are typically discovered in data coming from high precision experiments. 49er also discovered approximate equations in databases of Navy training and recruitment, juvenile crime, questionnaires, and biological data. Whenever they apply, equations are a preferred form of knowledge because they can be used to make unique predictions and strong explanations. Equations are very compact: little space is required to store an equation compared to the original data (cf. Table 13.3). Equations can be also easily generalized and expanded to more dimensions, so that their advantages are magnified.

Table 13.3
Example of contingency table for which a linear equation $(y = -0.12 + 1.10x)$ was found.

y	7	0	0	6	29	56	15	
	6	0	1	28	131	100	8	
	5	0	5	92	214	85	3	
	4	1	37	242	258	28	0	
	3	3	97	352	203	10	0	
	2	20	241	298	54	4	0	
	1	19	128	71	7	0	0	
		1	2	3	4	5	6	x

The search for equations applies whenever the types of attributes permit, but it is relatively time consuming. Even at the rate of few seconds per search, when repeated for thousands of attribute combinations and data subsets, equation finding search is prohibitive. 49er applies the functionality test to contingency tables (Zembowicz & Żytkow, 1993) to determine whether there is a chance to find an equation for a given table. The search for equations is performed only if the test succeeds.

13.6.1   Functionality Test

The test is based on the mathematical definition of functional relationship:

Definition: Given a set D of value pairs (x_i, y_i), $i = 1, \ldots, N$ of two variables x and y, and the range X of x; **y is a function of x in X** iff for each x_0 in X, there is exactly one value y_0 of y, such that (x_0, y_0) is in D.

The following algorithm approximates the above definition:

Algorithm: Test approximate functional relationship between x and y

given the contingency table of actual record counts and set X of values of x

AV ← average number of records per cell

for each value in X

find all groups of cells with adjacent values of y and counts > AV

if # of groups > α **then return** NO–FUNCTION

if average # of groups $> \beta$ **then return** NO–FUNCTION
else return FUNCTION

This algorithm is controlled by two modifiable parameters, α and β, which measure local (α) and global (β) uniqueness in y; that is, the number of values of y for the same value of $\dot{x}$. The default values used by 49er are: $\alpha = 2$ (data from experiments) or 3 (databases), $\beta \approx 1.5$. For $\alpha = 3$ the functionality test fails when for a value in X there are more than 3 adjacent groups of cells with above average density of points. This higher value 3 of α solves the problem of rare outliers, allowing up to 2 outliers if they happen rarely. However, many outliers or frequent discontinuities in y should fail the test, therefore the value of β is much smaller and close to 1. Note that the test with both parameters set to 1 corresponds to the strict mathematical definition of functionality given above. Presence of error, noise, and other data imperfections force values of α and β to be larger than 1. The noise handling by varying the number of cells in the table is treated in detail by Zembowicz & Żytkow (1993).

13.6.2   Equation Finder's Search

The task of equation finding can be formally defined by the input of n datapoints (x_i, y_i), $i = 1, ..., n$. The output is the list of acceptable equations.

Equation Finder's search can be decomposed into (1) generation of new terms, (2) selection of pairs of terms, (3) generation and evaluation of equations for each pair of terms. The combination of these three searches can be summarized by the following algorithm:

Algorithm: Find Equation

```
T ← (x y)              ; the initial list of terms for search #1
old-T ← NIL            ; the list of terms already used
E ← a set of polynomial equation models
                       ; list of models for search #3
loop until new terms in T exceed threshold of complexity
    2T ← list of new pairs of terms created from T and old-T
                       ; the list generated by search #2,
                       ; initially ((x y))
    for each pair in 2T and for each model in E
```

find and evaluate the best equation
if at least one equation accepted, **then**
        return all accepted equations and HALT the search
old-T ← old-T augmented with T
T ← list of new terms created from old-T

13.7   From Contingency Tables to Multifunctions

Multifunctions are two or more superimposed functions; see Figure 13.3 for an example of multifunctions in a geographic information system. If a functional dependence is defined by *one value of y for each value of x*, N-functional dependence can be defined as systematic occurrence of *up to N values of y for each value of x*. The functionality test, after minor enhancements, can be used to test for multifunctions.

13.7.1   Another Use of the Functionality Test

We will now discuss an extension of the functionality test that selects the tables which can lead to discovery of multifunctions. The data pass our functionality test when, for most values of x, there is one group of cells adjacent in y, with counts above the average. However, if the test consistently shows two groups of cells, it could mean that there are *two* functional dependencies in data: $y = f_1(x)$ and $y = f_2(x)$.

The existence of two or more functional dependencies in data is practically useful (Piatetsky-Shapiro & Matheus, 1991). For example, in data on the weight of African elephants of different age, one can find two distinct dependencies between weight and age. That indicates two kinds of African elephants: large bush elephants (*Loxodonta africana*) and smaller forest elephants (*Loxodonta cyclotis*). Such a discovery of two or more functional dependencies in data could lead to the discovery of new concepts. Piatetsky-Shapiro and Matheus (1991) present another method for detection of multifunctions, limited to linear functions.

13.7.2   Multiple Equation Finder's Search

Multiple Equation Finder (MEF) uses an extended version of the functionality test to discover multiple functional relationships. If the test returns a high value of β, MEF checks continuity of cell groups in the x direction, then partitions the data and runs Equation Finder for every group of adjacent cells. If successful, it finally tries to extend the range of discovered equations and merge different groups if they can be described simultaneously by the same equation. The following algorithm depicts the MEF search.

Algorithm: Multiple Equation Finder
    run Test for Functionality
    if average # of groups $< \beta$ **then** run Equation Finder
    else
        for each group of high-density cells adjacent in y
            merge the group with other groups adjacent in x
        for every group spanning many subranges of x,
            run Equation Finder
        for each pair of groups described by similar equations
            run Equation Finder and merge groups if covered
                by one equation

13.7.3 Industrial Application: Vectorizing Maps

Multiple Equation Finder has found a Geographic Information System (GIS) application. Consider a GIS user, who has a number of paper maps with his own geographic features (pipelines, cables, land boundaries, etc) overlaid on the top of basic geographic features (streets, railroads, rivers, etc). The GIS system comes with all basic features in its geographic database, but user features are not included. The user has to vectorize all his features to add them to the database. The following algorithm uses Multiple Equation Finder in order to aid this process.

Algorithm: Vectorize New Map Features
    given bit image from scanner
        synchronize bit image with geographic map
        remove points corresponding to the map features present
          in the database
        run Multiple Equation Finder; consider only linear equations
        create new features from the discovered equations
        remove points corresponding to new features

The remaining features, typically represented by about 1% of points from the scanner, are vectorized manually. Since the database consists

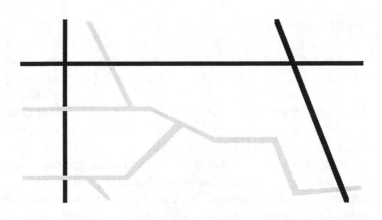

Figure 13.3
Example of map containing user features (shaded points) overlayed on the top of streets (dark lines).

of vectors, the search for equations inside the MEF is very fast, because it considers only linear equations.

13.8   From Contingency Tables to Other Forms of Knowledge

Other forms of knowledge can be also reached through contingency tables. Lacking space, we will only mention how to use contingency tables to build causal graphs.

Spirtes, Glymour & Scheines (1993) demonstrated in their TETRAD system how correlations between attributes and vanishing conditional correlations can be used to build causal dependency graphs. 49er's initial search for 2-D contingency tables for all data and in data slices provides sufficient raw material for TETRAD's algorithm: measures of dependence between attributes and non-existence of dependence between the same attributes in the data slices made for other attributes. The greatest computational effort lies in obtaining the conditional dependencies (in slices). Little extra work is needed to build a causal dependency graph.

13.9   Limitations of Contingency Tables

The main limitations of our approach to discovery (based on contingency tables) are the large sizes of some contingency tables and small volumes of data available in data slices. While the majority of attributes in databases have a very limited number of values, there are exceptions. In those special cases, contingency tables may be very large or there may not be enough memory to build them. In addition, large tables are often sparse, creating problems for some of our tests. Binning of the values can help, but different binning methods may hide some patterns.

Small sizes of data slices combined with their large numbers may lead 49er to spurious regularities, which are just statistical fluctuations of random relationships. 49er's significance threshold is varied to avoid spurious regularities, but especially in small databases the search follows a thin line between a large percentage of spurious results and loss of some results because of a too demanding significance threshold.

Acknowledgments

Special thanks to Kim Swarm and Molly Troxel for their contributions to research on taxonomy formation, to Ireneusz Moraczewski for his work on subset graphs, to Gregory Piatetsky-Shapiro, Mary Edgington and two anonymous reviewers for their valuable comments and suggestions.

References

Fienberg, S. E. 1980. *The Analysis of Cross-Classified Categorical Data.* Cambridge, Mass.: The MIT Press.

Fisher, D.H. 1987. Knowledge Acquisition Via Incremental Conceptual Clustering, *Machine Learning* 2: 139-172.

Gokhale, D.V. and Kullback, S. 1978. *The Information in Contingency Tables,* New York: M. Dekker.

Hoschka, P., and Klösgen, W. 1991. A Support System for Interpreting Statistical Data. In *Knowledge Discovery in Databases,* ed. G. Piatetsky-Shapiro and W. Frawley. Menlo Park, Calif.: The AAAI Press.

Jensen, D. 1991. Knowledge Discovery Through Induction with Randomization Testing. Presented at the 1991 AAAI Workshop on Knowledge Discovery in Databases, Anaheim, Calif.

Moraczewski, I.; Zembowicz, R.; and Żytkow, J. M. 1995. Geobotanical Database Exploration. Presented at the 1995 AAAI Spring Symposium, Stanford Calif.

Piatetsky-Shapiro, G.; and Matheus, C. J. 1991. Knowledge Discovery Workbench: An Exploratory Environment for Discovery in Business Databases. Presented at the 1991 AAAI Workshop on Knowledge Discovery in Databases, Anaheim, Calif.

Spirtes, P.; Glymour, C.; and Scheines R. 1993. *Causality, Prediction and Search*. Berlin: Springer-Verlag.

Sudnik-Wojcikowska, B. 1987. *The Flora of Warsaw and Its Changes in Nineteenth and Twentieth Centuries* (in Polish), Warsaw: Warsaw University Publications.

Troxel, M.; Swarm, K.; Zembowicz, R.; and Żytkow, J. M. 1994. Concept Hierarchies: a Restricted Form of Knowledge Derived from Regularities. In: Proceedings of Methodologies for Intelligent Systems, ed. M. Zemankova and Z. Ras. Berlin: Springer-Verlag.

Whittaker, J. 1990. *Graphical Models in Applied Multivariate Statistics*. New York: John Wiley and Sons.

Zembowicz, R.; and Żytkow, J. M. 1993. Testing the existence of Functional Relationships in Data. Presented at the 1993 AAAI Workshop on Knowledge Discovery in Databases, Washington, D.C.

Żytkow, J.; and Baker, J. 1991. Interactive Mining of Regularities in Databases. In *Knowledge Discovery in Databases,* ed. G. Piatetsky-Shapiro and W. Frawley, Menlo Park, Calif.: The AAAI Press

Żytkow, J.; and Zembowicz, R., 1993. Database Exploration in Search of Regularities. *Journal of Intelligent Information Systems* 2: 39–81.

V INTEGRATED DISCOVERY SYSTEMS

14 Integrating Inductive and Deductive Reasoning for Data Mining

Evangelos Simoudis
IBM

Brian Livezey
Lockheed Missiles and Space Company, Inc.

Randy Kerber
AT&T Global Information Solutions

Abstract

Data mining is the process of finding previously unknown and potentially interesting patterns and relations in large databases. The extracted information can (1) be organized by a data analyst into a prediction or classification model, (2) be used to refine an existing model, or (3) provide a summary of the database(s) being mined. A wide variety of techniques are available to perform data mining. However, frequently, a single data mining technique is insufficient for extracting knowledge from a data set. Instead, several techniques must be employed cooperatively to solve a data mining problem. In this chapter we discuss how rule induction, deductive databases, and data visualization can be used cooperatively to create high quality, rule-based models by mining data stored in relational databases. We also present the *Recon* data mining framework which integrates these three techniques.

14.1 Data Mining

Data mining is the process of extracting and refining useful knowledge from large databases. The extracted information can be used to form a prediction or classification model, identify trends and associations, refine an existing model, or provide a summary of the database(s) being mined. A number of data mining techniques, e.g., rule induction, neural networks, and conceptual clustering, have been developed and used individually in domains ranging from space data analysis (Fayyad and Smyth 1993) to financial analysis (Ziarko, Golan, and Edwards 1993). Frequently, a single data mining technique is insufficient for extracting knowledge from a data set. Instead, several techniques must be employed cooperatively to support a single data mining application. In this chapter we discuss how rule induction, deductive databases, and data visualization can be used cooperatively to create high quality, rule-based models by mining data stored in relational databases. We also present the *Recon* data mining framework which integrates these three techniques.

The operations performed during data mining are discussed in Section 14.2. *Recon*'s architecture is described in Section 14.3. Issues relating to the distribution of data among *Recon*'s data mining modules are discussed in Section 14.4. The interaction among the three data mining techniques used in *Recon* are described in Section 14.5. A model-creation example from the domain of stock portfolio creation is presented in Section 14.6. Related work is discussed in Section 14.7, and conclusions are presented in Section 14.8.

14.2   Model Development and Data Mining

Making effective and accurate decisions directly from data stored in databases is difficult for two reasons. First, these databases are frequently very large. For example, typical marketing databases contain several gigabytes of demographic and purchasing data. Identifying good prospective customers for a particular product using the contents of such databases requires sifting and reasoning through this data. Second, the database is usually described in terms of low-level concepts and relations that are cognitively distant from the concepts used by the decision-maker. For example, a marketing database may be described in terms of every purchase made by the individual members of each household, rather than in terms of concepts such as "repeat customer," "good customer," "high-risk credit customer," etc., that are most useful to a marketing professional. Models developed by mining such large databases are used to alleviate these problems and enable effective and accurate decision-making. Models can be statistical, neural, or symbolic, depending on the data mining technique used.

A symbolic model consists of *concepts*, e.g., "good customer," and *rules* that relate concepts. The quality of each rule is measured by its discriminating power, its generality, and its interestingness. For example, consider the following rule, called *rule1*, which states: "if the revenues of a publicly-traded corporation are five times its profits for three consecutive quarters, then the return on investment of its stock during the next quarter will be greater than 20%." This rule will be classified as (1) very discriminating if, for example, it correctly predicts the return on investment for eight out of the ten stocks, (2) very general if it is very predictive during several time periods and is relevant for a large number of stocks, and (3) very interesting if it provides a useful insight to the financial analyst. The rule "the return on investment of stocks issued by pharmaceutical companies is greater than 20%" may have been very discriminating during the summer of 1992 but not at present. The rule is not very general because it only applies during a single time period and it only characterizes stocks of pharmaceutical companies, a small percentage of the stocks traded in the various exchanges. It may, however, be very interesting if the stocks of pharmaceutical companies do not usually provide high returns on investment.

Mining databases to develop a model can be performed in either a top-down or a bottom-up fashion. During *top-down data mining* the analyst defines concepts and rules in terms of the entities and relations included in the database, and proceeds by progressively extending these concepts to higher-level ones. During *bottom-up data mining* the system automatically creates concepts and rules that either specialize or generalize those defined by the analyst. Therefore, the data mining process is performed by interweaving three operations: (1) *generation*, and *testing* of concepts and rules hypothesized by the analyst, (2) automatic, or semi-automatic, generation and *refinement* of concepts and rules by the data mining system, and (3) *integration* of the best of the manually generated and automatically discovered concepts and rules into a cohesive model.

Analysts often hypothesize value-prediction and classification rules as well as trends and associations. For example, an investment analyst may have hypothesized *rule1*. Since the quality of this rule is not known *a priori*, the rule must be tested against historical data. The test results allow the user to establish the quality of each rule and of each concept it includes. The testing could lead the analyst to accept the rule and incorporate it into the model being developed, refine the rule, or reject it altogether. In some cases, such analysis may lead the analyst to discover erroneous data.

Analysts cannot generate all the concepts and rules that might be included in a model. The data mining system explores the contents of the database to automatically identify concepts and rules supported by the data. For example, by exploring the target database, a rule induction component may form a rule stating that "if a company's earnings per share growth is greater than 50% during six consecutive quarters, then the return on investment of its stock during the quarter following this period will be greater than 20%." The concepts and rules resulting from automatic discovery can be ranked according to their discriminating power. The discovered rules can also be tested on a different database so that their predictive ability and generality can be established. Using all of the provided information, the user selects a subset of the discovered concepts and rules, possibly edits them, and incorporates them into the model being developed.

14.3   Recon's Architecture

Recon consists of: a command module, a server, one or more data mining modules, a knowledge repository, and interfaces to relational database management systems. In *Recon*, top-down data mining is performed using a deductive database (Kellogg and Livezey 1992), (Livezey and Simoudis 1994). Bottom-up data mining is performed using a rule induction system (Kerber 1991), and a data visualization system (Simoudis, Klumpar, and Anderson 1994). *Recon*'s architecture is shown in Figure 14.1.

The analyst uses the command module to connect to a particular database. The server interacts with the database management system of the connected database by issuing Structured Query Language (SQL) commands through the database Application Programming Interface (API). The *Recon* server distributes data and knowledge among the connected database and the data mining modules.

14.4   The Recon Server

Recon's data and knowledge distribution operations are performed by the *Recon* server. The server maintains the target database, allows the user to direct data from the deductive database to the other data mining modules, maintains the knowledge repository, and distributes stored knowledge and data to other *Recon* modules.

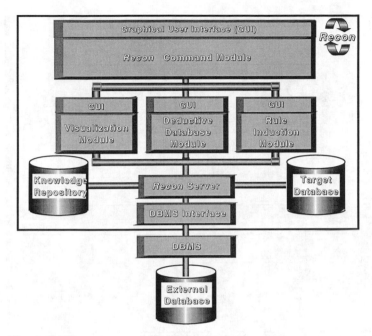

Figure 14.1
The architecture of the *Recon* data mining framework.

The target database is created and refined through interaction between the user and the *Recon* server. In particular, after the user connects to a database, the *Recon* server automatically extracts the database's schema and displays it in the Query Matrix. A portion of the extracted information from a database of corporate stocks is shown in Figure 14.2.

The Query Matrix presents the database's entities and relations along the vertical axis and attributes along the horizontal axis. The squares in the matrix indicate which attributes appear in which entities. More detailed information about a particular table can be seen by selecting a relation in the Query Matrix.

Using the base relations from the Query Matrix, the analyst can employ the deductive database to define new domain-specific concepts; this process is described in Section 14.5.2. *Recon*'s server automatically incorporates each concept into the target database's schema, displaying it in the Query Matrix, so that it can be used seamlessly with the base relations in forming subsequent queries or concept definitions. These definitions can be sent to the rule induction module to be incorporated

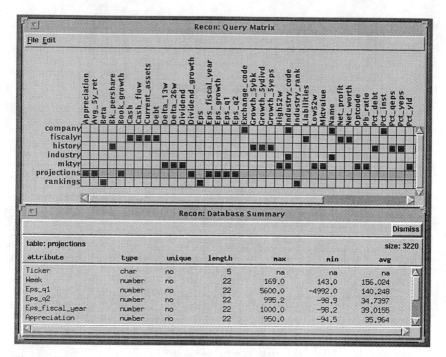

Figure 14.2
Schema information of a database with corporate stocks.

as antecedents in the discovered rules.

Often, analysts use *Recon*'s data mining modules on only a subset of the database. These subsets, called *data sources*, are defined by querying the target database. Data sources are maintained by the *Recon* Server and are stored either explicitly by saving the results of the appropriate query, or implicitly by saving the query itself. In addition, the *Recon* server can randomly sample a database or a data source if a smaller subset of the database is desired.

14.5   Deduction, Induction, and Visualization

In this section we describe how *Recon*'s three data mining modules can be used cooperatively to create a rule-based classification model. In a typical scenario, the analyst first gets a "feel" for the contents of the target database by using the visualization module. In particular, the analyst uses histograms and bar charts to view the distribution of values for each attribute in the database, as well as 2-dimensional and 3-dimensional scatter plots to discover interrelations between attributes. If in the process, the analyst identifies relations between various attributes, he can encode them as new concepts using the deductive database. Furthermore, the analyst generates, tests, and refines concepts and rules using the deductive database. As part of the testing process, data generated by the deductive database may be sent to the visualization module for more detailed exploration. In addition, the analyst invokes the rule induction module and initiates the automatic concept and rule discovery task. At any point, the analyst may (1) interrupt the rule discovery operation, (2) use the *Recon* server to import induced rules into the deductive database where they are integrated with other previously stored knowledge, or alternatively to import previously-defined concepts and rules into the rule induction module thereby "seeding" this module's knowledge base, and (3) restart the induction process. The knowledge maintained by the deductive database, which includes both knowledge defined by the analyst, as well as induced knowledge, can be sent to *Recon*'s knowledge repository for long term storage.

14.5.1 Data Visualization

Data visualizationis particularly appropriate for (1) obtaining a global view of a data set and (2) noticing important phenomena that hold for a relatively small subset of a data set. *Recon*'s visualization module is based on the RAVE system (Simoudis, Klumpar, and Anderson 1994) with one exception. While RAVE includes a knowledge base that allows it to automatically decide and suggest to the user how to visualize a particular data set, *Recon*'s visualization module does not include this feature. Instead, it allows the user to simultaneously plot and view multiple visualizations. In this way the user can request, for example, that the histograms of all the attributes in a particular data source be plotted so that he can examine their value distributions. Each visualization is presented in a separate interactive window.

Based on conclusions reached by examining the global view of the contents of a data set, the analyst may decide to concentrate on particular components and/or subsets of the data. For example, after the analyst designates the dependent variable—in this case the 26-week return on investment, i.e., (roi_26w)—in a data source, the visualization module generates 2-dimensional scatter plots between each independent variable

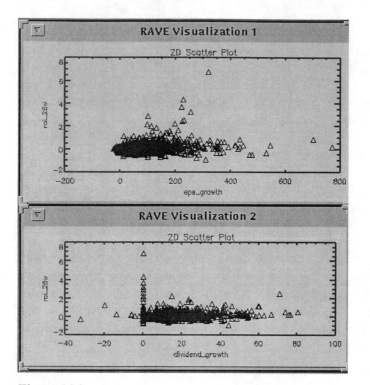

Figure 14.3
Plots relating earnings per share growth and dividend growth of stocks to the
return on investment.

and the dependent variable, two of which are shown in Figure 14.3. By
examining these two visualizations the analyst notices that when the
earnings per share growth is greater than 50%, the return on investment
is greater than 20%, and when the dividend growth is also greater than
50%, the return on investment is also greater than 20%. Based on this
observation, the analyst uses the deductive database to encode the concept of "strong stock" as one that has earnings per share greater than
50% and dividend growth greater than 50%.

Visualization methods are valuable because phenomena that are easy
to spot using visualization often tend to be "drowned out" by the rest
of the data when statistical methods are used. Furthermore, the analyst
does not need to know specifically the type of phenomena he is looking
for in order to notice something interesting. In addition, when used on
data with distributions that are not well-behaved, visualizations tend
to be more effective than many statistical methods, because the latter

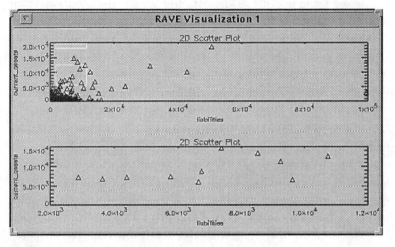

Figure 14.4
Visualization of data about publicly traded companies.

often make limiting assumptions about the data distributions.

The visualization process begins with the user selecting a data source from the *Recon* server and importing it into the visualization module. *Recon*'s visualization module permits the analyst to:

- Mark subsets of the data set that are of particular interest. Each such subset is plotted using a different color. For example, in the example provided above, the analyst may mark the stocks whose earnings per share growth is greater than 50%.

- Focus on a portion of the displayed data. For example, Figure 14.4 shows a simple visualization that includes two scatter plots produced by *Recon*'s visualization module created in order to determine the relationship between current-assets and liabilities of solvent companies. The top scatter plot includes the entire contents of the data source. The bottom scatter plot provides more detail of the area indicated by the rectangle on the top scatter plot. In this case, it was selected to include companies that show an almost linear relationship between current-assets and liabilities.

- Select a portion of the data displayed in one visualization, e.g., a two-dimensional scatter plot, and visualize the values of attributes of interest using another visualization, e.g., a two-dimensional line plot. For example, after establishing, through the use of a two-dimensional scatter plot, that there exists an almost-linear relationship between the values of the current assets and current liabilities attributes, the analyst can select the data points that obey this relationship and display the values of their quarterly earnings over a period of a year using a two-dimensional line plot.

- Select a subset of the data to export to another *Recon* module for further analysis. For example, after noticing that within certain value ranges earning per share growth, divident growth, and other attributes are predictive of high twenty-six-week return on investment, the analyst can export part of the data source to the rule induction module and use it to obtain precise symbolic expressions of such interrelations, along with all of the value ranges over which they hold, and discover additional interrelations that may not have been initially visible.

14.5.2   Deductive Database

Recon's deductive database is used for formulating queries, defining *concepts*, representing concept interrelations to be validated, and refining existing concepts and concept interrelations.

A concept is defined in terms of its name, a set of attributes, and one or more relations among the attributes. An attribute may either belong to one of the database's base relations or be part of another previously defined concept. The user selects the appropriate relations and/or concepts from the Query Matrix and relates the attributes by specifying equalities and inequalities among the attributes. The new concept is incorporated into the Query Matrix and can be used in future queries, concept definitions, and rules.

For example, the user might define the concept *high-growth* to characterize stocks whose *earnings-per-share-growth* and *dividend-growth* are both greater than 50%, thus expressing symbolically the knowledge he discovered through the use of visualization techniques. This concept is defined in terms of another concept (projections) and some constraints as shown in Figure 14.5.

A database that contains such user-defined knowledge is called a *deductive database*. The values of concepts are not stored in the database;

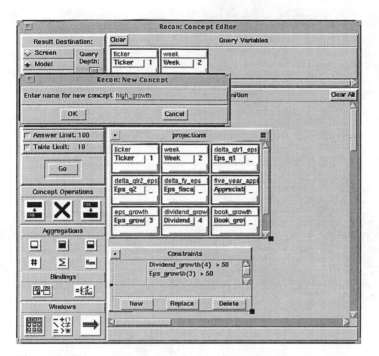

Figure 14.5
Concepts are defined graphically in terms of other existing concepts.

they are computed dynamically via deductive inferences in response to a user's query. In particular, after the user has graphically expressed a query, in terms of base and user-defined concepts, the query is automatically expanded by the deductive database until it consists solely of base relations and computable functions. The deductive database transforms each expanded query into a set of optimized SQL expressions (McGuire 1991). The expanded query is then posed to the target database.

The deductive database provides justifications for query responses. The justifications detail the exact chain of reasoning that led to the result in question. In this way, the user can better understand the results and determine whether the definitions of particular concepts need to be refined, or whether the data in the target database is anomalous.

For example, Figure 14.6 illustrates why the stock with ticker symbol "APS" was considered to be *high-growth*. We can see that its *earnings-per-share-growth* and *dividend-growth* both exceed the specified thresholds. For sophisticated queries, e.g., queries involving recursion and disjunction over large collections of inter-related concepts, explanations

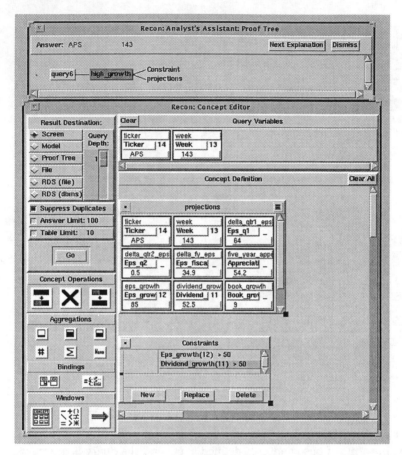

Figure 14.6
Answers are explained in terms of the concepts from which they were derived.

permit the analyst to determine which of potentially numerous derivation paths contributed to the result in question.

The analyst also uses the deductive database to form "if... then ..." rules. The antecedents and consequents of these rules may contain a mixture of user-defined concepts and database entities. The deductive database expands the rule into two queries which, after optimization, are posed to the target database. The first query returns the set of records that support the rule. The second query returns the set of records that match the rule's left-hand side but do not match its right-hand side. From the returned information the analyst can assess the rule's quality.

14.5.3   Rule Induction

While the deductive database allows the analyst to express knowledge and test it against the target database, rule induction is used to automatically explore the target database to discover rules that characterize its contents. The user must divide the data presented to the rule induction module into a small number of classes between which he wishes to distinguish. This operation can be done either outside *Recon*, or by using the deductive database. For example, assume that the target database contains historical data about the quarterly performance of stocks, including the quarterly return on investment of each stock. Further assume that the analyst defines two classes: "high return on investment" for stocks with quarterly return on investment greater than 20%, and "low return on investment" for the rest of the stocks. The induced rules express generalizations over the input data that are useful for distinguishing between these two classes.

Recon's rule induction module searches for rules via continual modification of existing rules. Since it is rarely possible to find a single, perfect discriminating rule that matches all examples in one class and no examples in any other class, *Recon*'s rule induction module produces a collection of rules. The rule induction module uses an agenda to schedule modification tasks. It performs three types of modification tasks: specialization, generalization, and constructive induction. Each task on the agenda is assigned a score by the agenda evaluation function, which considers factors such as discriminating power, conciseness, generality, and statistical significance of the rule. On each agenda cycle, the task with the highest score is removed from the agenda and executed. Each new rule produced via a modification task is analyzed using a set of heuristics that decide whether to add it to the list of best rules, discard it, or add it to the agenda for further modification. This process repeats until the agenda is empty, a preset termination condition is satisfied, or the user decides to terminate the search.

Recon's rule induction module has three distinct advantages and characteristics. First, it is able to produce high quality rules even when the input data is noisy and incomplete (for performance results see [Kerber 1991]). Second, it generates human-understandable "if ... then ..." rules, the same representation used by *Recon*'s deductive database. Finally, it is able to accept knowledge defined using the deductive database. Such domain knowledge expedites the rule discovery task while simultaneously improving the quality of the induced rules.

The user can establish the predictive ability and generality of the induced rules by testing them against the contents of other data sources imported from the *Recon* server. The user can request an explanation of why a particular prediction was made. In response to such a request, the rule induction module displays the rules that contributed to that prediction. Examination of rules that contributed to incorrect predictions may lead the analyst to ignore certain attributes or refine concept definitions before subsequent induction sessions. The analyst might repeat this process several times in order to produce a set of high-quality rules that can be stored in the knowledge repository.

14.6   Using Recon for Stock Portfolio Creation

We now provide a simple example of how an investment analyst can use *Recon* to create a rule-based model for selecting stocks that yield a high return on investment. Creating rule-based stock selection models is a very appropriate domain for data mining because of the large number of stocks from which the money manager can select to create a portfolio and the vast amount of historical data available. The use of data mining techniques allows the analyst to consider many more factors and much more data, thus leading to the development of more accurate value-prediction models.

We assume that the investment analyst has access to a database with monthly data about a universe of stocks. The process begins by creating the target database through *Recon*'s server. Assume that the target database contains data on 1500 stocks over a period of seven years. The user's goal is to create a portfolio of approximately 100 stocks.

First, the user sends the target database to the visualization module. By comparing several scatter plots, as discussed in Section 14.5.1, the user discovers that *earnings-per-share-growth* and *dividend-growth* are good indicators for high return on investment.

Next, the analyst uses the deductive database to interactively test his knowledge about indicators that can discriminate stocks which have the potential of providing high return on investment. He defines the *high-growth* concept described in Section 14.5.2.

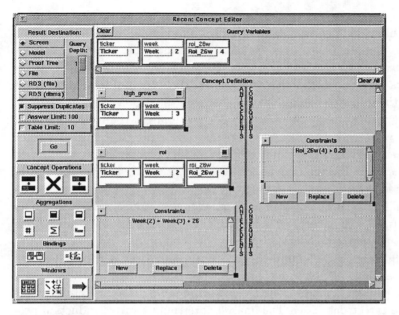

Figure 14.7
A rule expressed using *Recon*'s deductive database.

The analyst then uses the deductive database to formulate concept interrelations and test them against the target database. An example rule states that "If a stock is *high-growth* at time t, then its *return on investment* two quarters, i.e., twenty six weeks, later will be greater than 20%." The definition of this rule is shown in Figure 14.7. The two concepts used in this rule are shown on the left hand side of the Concept Definition region of the Concept Editor. In the Constraints box, which is also placed on the left hand side of the rule, the user indicates the "week" in which the stock was considered *high-growth* preceeds the week in which it's *return-on-investment* was measured by 26. Finally, the rule's right hand side consists of the constraint that the value of the attribute return on investment (roi_26w) must be greater than 20% (0.20 in the figure).

Once the user instructs *Recon* to test the stated rule, the system retrieves from the database two sets of answers: the records (stocks) that support the rule and those which refute it. The user inspects these two sets in the following way. First, he determines whether the rule accurately discriminates by seeing how many records support the rule compared to how many records refute it. Second, he establishes how general the rule is by determining how many records were retrieved compared to the number of records in the database. Finally, he uses the deductive database's explanation facility to determine precisely why some of the stocks were classified as they were. These three types of evaluation might lead the user to refine his rule by changing the definition of *high-growth* to encompass more (or fewer) stocks or he might change his expectations with respect to return on investment. In our case, the stated rule has returned 15 supporting records and eight refuting records. Based on these results, the user decides that he has discovered a useful indicator for high return on investment, i.e., the *high-growth* concept, and a useful interrelation between *high-growth* and twenty-six-week return on investment. He incorporates both of the new concept and the new rule into the evolving model.

While the analyst interactively creates indicators and tests concept interrelations, *Recon*'s rule induction module automatically discovers other concept interrelations by exploring a randomly selected sample of the target database. The analyst interrupts the rule induction process and requests the rules discovered thus far. Before presenting them to the user, the rule induction module sorts the discovered rules based upon their discrimination power, determined by the percentage of the instances from each class in the target database the rule matches. Figure 14.8 shows a subset of the induced rules. The columns labeled "High" and "Low" indicate what percentage of each of the two sets the rule matched.

The user tests the discovered concept interrelations by applying them to another randomly selected data set. For each stock in this set, the rule induction module displays its return on investment prediction, along with the confidence level associated with the prediction, as well as the stock's actual return on investment.

The user can select individual stocks from this list and request the rationale for the associated prediction. Of particular interest are those cases where the wrong prediction was made with a high degree of confidence. The explanation consists of the set of rules that were used to make the particular prediction. For example, the explanation for the stock with ticker symbol STL is shown in Figure 14.9. Associated with each rule is the weight that the rule contributed to the prediction. The sum of the individual rule weights determines the overall confidence in the prediction.

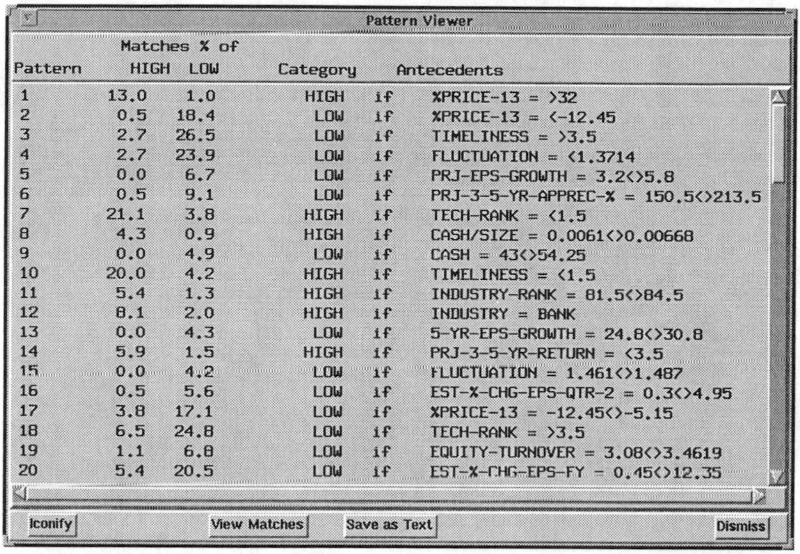

Pattern	Matches % of HIGH	LOW	Category	Antecedents
1	13.0	1.0	HIGH	if XPRICE-13 = >32
2	0.5	18.4	LOW	if XPRICE-13 = <-12.45
3	2.7	26.5	LOW	if TIMELINESS = >3.5
4	2.7	23.9	LOW	if FLUCTUATION = <1.3714
5	0.0	6.7	LOW	if PRJ-EPS-GROWTH = 3.2<>5.8
6	0.5	9.1	LOW	if PRJ-3-5-YR-APPREC-X = 150.5<>213.5
7	21.1	3.8	HIGH	if TECH-RANK = <1.5
8	4.3	0.9	HIGH	if CASH/SIZE = 0.0061<>0.00668
9	0.0	4.9	LOW	if CASH = 43<>54.25
10	20.0	4.2	HIGH	if TIMELINESS = <1.5
11	5.4	1.3	HIGH	if INDUSTRY-RANK = 81.5<>84.5
12	8.1	2.0	HIGH	if INDUSTRY = BANK
13	0.0	4.3	LOW	if 5-YR-EPS-GROWTH = 24.8<>30.8
14	5.9	1.5	HIGH	if PRJ-3-5-YR-RETURN = <3.5
15	0.0	4.2	LOW	if FLUCTUATION = 1.461<>1.487
16	0.5	5.6	LOW	if EST-X-CHG-EPS-QTR-2 = 0.3<>4.95
17	3.8	17.1	LOW	if XPRICE-13 = -12.45<>-5.15
18	6.5	24.8	LOW	if TECH-RANK = >3.5
19	1.1	6.8	LOW	if EQUITY-TURNOVER = 3.08<>3.4619
20	5.4	20.5	LOW	if EST-X-CHG-EPS-FY = 0.45<>12.35

Iconify   View Matches   Save as Text   Dismiss

Figure 14.8
Rules discovered by *Recon*'s rule induction module.

By examining the evidence for *incorrect* predictions, the user can identify low-quality rules. It is assumed that a high quality value-prediction model will have low error rate, thus few incorrect predictions. Therefore, analyzing the rules that were used in making these predictions is not expected to be a cognitively difficult task. However, we are also currently investigating the application of visualization and clustering techniques to automatically organize induced rules and thus better facilitate the user's inspection task.

In this case, the user decides to delete the attributeINDUSTRY from the target database because he feels it was only relevant during the time period covered in the data used to generate the rules and is not a generally useful indicator. The user restarts the rule induction process with the revised target database. Finally, the user selects the desired set of discovered rules and sends them to the *Recon* server where they are incorporated into the knowledge repository.

The model developed through the interoperation of these three components—visualization, deductive database, and rule induction—is then applied on a universe of current stocks. The top 100 of the stocks for which the model predicts a high return on investment are included in the portfolio.

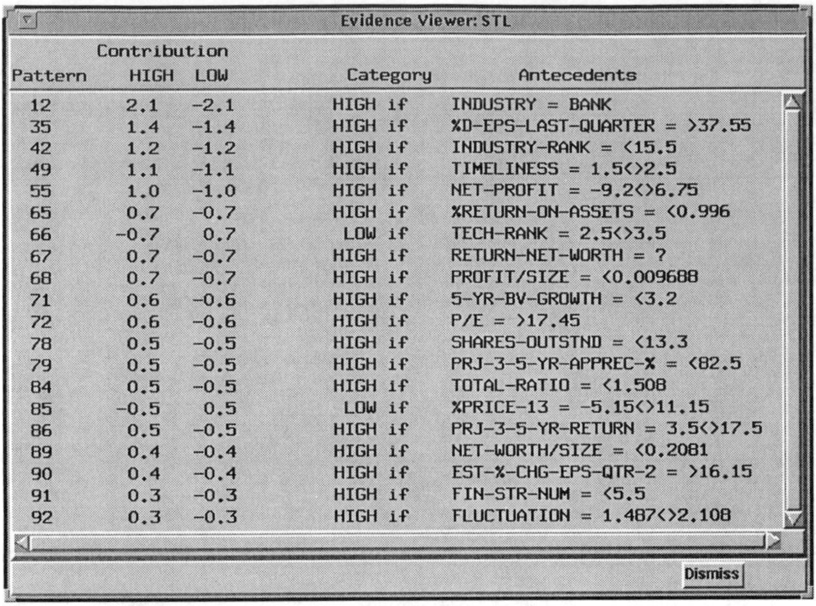

	Contribution			
Pattern	HIGH	LOW	Category	Antecedents
12	2.1	-2.1	HIGH if	INDUSTRY = BANK
35	1.4	-1.4	HIGH if	%D-EPS-LAST-QUARTER = >37.55
42	1.2	-1.2	HIGH if	INDUSTRY-RANK = <15.5
49	1.1	-1.1	HIGH if	TIMELINESS = 1.5<>2.5
55	1.0	-1.0	HIGH if	NET-PROFIT = -9.2<>6.75
65	0.7	-0.7	HIGH if	%RETURN-ON-ASSETS = <0.996
66	-0.7	0.7	LOW if	TECH-RANK = 2.5<>3.5
67	0.7	-0.7	HIGH if	RETURN-NET-WORTH = ?
68	0.7	-0.7	HIGH if	PROFIT/SIZE = <0.009688
71	0.6	-0.6	HIGH if	5-YR-BV-GROWTH = <3.2
72	0.6	-0.6	HIGH if	P/E = >17.45
78	0.5	-0.5	HIGH if	SHARES-OUTSTND = <13.3
79	0.5	-0.5	HIGH if	PRJ-3-5-YR-APPREC-X = <82.5
84	0.5	-0.5	HIGH if	TOTAL-RATIO = <1.508
85	-0.5	0.5	LOW if	%PRICE-13 = -5.15<>11.15
86	0.5	-0.5	HIGH if	PRJ-3-5-YR-RETURN = 3.5<>17.5
89	0.4	-0.4	HIGH if	NET-WORTH/SIZE = <0.2081
90	0.4	-0.4	HIGH if	EST-X-CHG-EPS-QTR-2 = >16.15
91	0.3	-0.3	HIGH if	FIN-STR-NUM = <5.5
92	0.3	-0.3	HIGH if	FLUCTUATION = 1.487<>2.108

Evidence Viewer: STL

Dismiss

Figure 14.9
Evidence for the return on investment prediction for STL.

14.7 Related Work

A growing number of data mining systems using artificial intelligence
techniques have been developed in recent years. We compare *Recon*
to those that have been most widely reported in literature. Since we
have strongly argued for the cooperative use of multiple data mining
techniques, and moreover for the use of both hypothesis testing and
pattern discovery (top-down and bottom-up data mining) techniques,
the comparison is done along two dimensions; the type of data mining operations supported by each system, and the degree of integration
among each system's components. We compare *Recon* to five systems:
IMACS (Brachman, *et al* 1993), KNOWLEDGE MINER (Shen 1994), KDW
(Piatetsky-Shapiro and Matheus 1992), INLEN (Kaufman, Michalski, and
Kerschberg 1991), and MLT (Uszynski 1992). A more complete list of
data mining systems, along with a more elaborate comparison methodology, is provided in (Piatetsky-Shapiro 1993).

Of these systems IMACS, and KNOWLEDGE MINER support hypothesis testing using deductive databases. IMACS includes a visualization
component that is tightly integrated with the deductive database. Vi-

sualization in IMACS is used primarily to graphically display the records retrieved by the deductive database in the process of testing a hypothesis. *Recon* has four basic differences with IMACS. First, *Recon*'s deductive database interacts with commercial relational databases through SQL; IMACS requires that data from such databases be loaded in memory before hypotheses can be tested. This requirement limits the use of IMACS to databases that fit in the main memory of the computer on which it is running. Second, *Recon*'s visualization component can be used to display the results of testing a hypothesis *and* to perform interactive visual exploration of a data set. Third, *Recon* includes a rule induction module to perform pattern discovery. Fourth, because *Recon* interacts with existing databases through SQL, its deductive database cannot be used to express concepts and rules as complex as IMACS can.

With the exception of *Recon*, the KNOWLEDGE MINER is the only other system reported in literature that supports both hypothesis testing and pattern discovery. Similar to IMACS, the deductive database also plays the central data mining role in the KNOWLEDGE MINER. This system includes a Bayesian clustering component to perform pattern discovery. This component is tightly integrated with the deductive database. The KNOWLEDGE MINER differs from *Recon* in two ways. First, the KNOWLEDGE MINER does not include a visualization component. Our experience with developing real-world data mining applications has shown that visualization is important both for the effective presentation of data mining results, in addition to the "logical visualization of knowledge" that can be performed through the use of rule induction, but also for the interactive exploration of the data. Second, in the KNOWLEDGE MINER each data mining operation is always driven by the system's deductive database. Rule induction is only used to refine rules that have been hypothesized by the analyst. In *Recon*, all three of the integrated techniques are "first class citizens"—the user may start a data mining task using whichever of the techniques is most appropriate for the problem at hand.

The KDW, INLEN, and MLT systems only support pattern discovery operations. While none of these three systems includes an interactive visualization component similar to Recon's, within the pattern discovery regime these systems are similar to *Recon* in two ways. First, each system includes a variety of techniques to perform this operation.[1] INLEN, and MLT integrate several techniques to support each type of pattern discovery, e.g., the MLT system includes at least three rule and tree induction components, thus providing the capability for broad experimentation during the pattern discovery operation. Such experimentation is necessary in research but not as much in application development. Second, all systems allow knowledge sharing between the pattern discovery modules they integrate. However, the four systems differ in the degree of component integration they support. In particular, *Recon* and KDW are loosely integrated systems. The components of INLEN and MLT are more tightly integrated. The advantage of the loose integration style is that additional components can easily be incorporated into the system adhering to this style, and existing components can be replaced with new ones that exhibit superior performance.

14.8   Conclusions

We have successfully applied *Recon* in: (1) financial domains to develop prediction models from data about stocks, bonds, and commodities, (2) manufacturing domains to extract information that allowed for the correction of manufacturing process failures, and (3) household purchasing data to identify loyal customers for specific product classes. Our work to date has allowed us to reach the following conclusions:

1. Effective data mining is performed through the interweaving of: generation, testing, refinement, and integration of concepts and concept interrelations from data stored in large databases

2. The cooperative use of deductive databases, rule induction, and data visualization results in high quality, rule-based models.

3. *Recon* supports the identified operations and integrates the three data mining techniques in a way that allows their cooperative use.

Current work on *Recon* includes the improvement of the search techniques used by its artificial intelligence modules, improvement of the server's functionality, and the application of the system in additional domains.

---

[1]While in this chapter we have only discussed its rule induction module, *Recon* also includes a conceptual clustering and a neural network module.

References

Brachman, R.; Selfridge, P.; Terveen, L.; Altman, B.; Halper, F.; Kirk, T.; Lazar, A.; McGuiness, D.; Resnick, L.; and Borgida, A. 1993. Integrated Support for Data Archaeology. Presented at the 1993 AAAI Workshop on Knowledge Discovery in Databases, Washington, D.C.

Fayyad, U.; and Smyth, P. 1993. Automated Analysis of a Large-Scale Sky Survey: the SKICAT System. Presented at the 1993 AAAI Workshop on Knowledge Discovery in Databases, Washington, D.C.

Kaufman, K.; Michalski, R.; and Kerschberg, L. 1991. Mining for Knowledge in Databases: Goals and General Description of the INLEN System. Presented at the 1991 AAAI Workshop on Knowledge Discovery in Databases, Anaheim, Calif.

Kerber, R. 1991. Learning Classification Rules from Examples. Presented at the 1991 AAAI Workshop on Knowledge Discovery in Databases, Anaheim, Calif.

Kellogg, C.; and Livezey, B. 1992. Intelligent Data Exploration and Analysis. In *Proceedings of the Conference on Information and Knowledge Management (CIKM-92)*.

Livezey, B.; and Simoudis, E. 1994. A Deductive Front-End for Relational Databases In *Applications of Deductive Databases,* ed. R. Ramakrishna. Kluwer Academic Publishers.

McGuire, J. 1991. Query Optimization to Support a Deductive Analysis Tool. Technical Report AIC 91-109, Lockheed Artificial Intelligence Center.

Piatetsky-Shapiro, G., and Matheus, C. 1992. Knowledge Discovery Workbench for Exploring Business Databases. *International Journal of Intelligent Systems* 7.

Shen, W.; Mitbander, B.; Ong, K.; and Zaniolo, C. 1994. Using Metaqueries to Integrate Inductive Learning and Deductive Database Technology. In Knowledge Discovery in Databases: Papers from the 1994 AAAI Workshop. AAAI Tech. Rep. WS-94-03, Menlo Park, Calif.

Simoudis, E., Klumpar, D., and Anderson, K. 1994. Rapid Visualization Environment: RAVE. In *Proceedings of the Ninth Goddard Conference on Space Applications of Artificial Intelligence*.

Uszynski, M. 1992. Machine Learning Toolbox. *European Economic Community*. Esprit II.

Ziarko, W.; Golan, R.; and Edwards, D. 1993. An Application of Datalogic/R Knowledge Discovery Tool to Identify Strong Predictive Rules in Stock Market Data. Presented at the 1993 AAAI Workshop on Knowledge Discovery in Databases, Washington, D.C.

15 Metaqueries for Data Mining

Wei-Min Shen
USC Information Sciences Institute

KayLiang Ong
MCC

Bharat Mitbander
Tandem Computers

Carlo Zaniolo
University of California, Los Angeles

Abstract

This chapter presents a framework that uses metaqueries to integrate inductive learning methods with deductive database technologies in the context of knowledge discovery from databases. Metaqueries are second-order predicates or templates, and are used for (1) Guiding deductive data collection, (2) Focusing attention for inductive learning, and (3) Assisting human analysts in the discovery loop. We describe in detail a system that uses this idea to unify a Bayesian Data Cluster with the Logical Data Language ($LDL++$), and show the results of three case studies, namely, discovering regularities from a knowledge base, discovering patterns and errors from a large telecommunication database, and discovering patterns and errors from a large chemical database. The patterns discovered using metaqueries are implication rules with probabilities. These rules can link information from many tables in databases, and they can be stored persistently for multiple purposes, including error detection, integrity constraints, or generation of more complex metaqueries.

14.1 Introduction

Recent progress in knowledge discovery from databases (Cercone and Tsuchiya 1993; Piatetsky-Shapiro 1993) has shown that inductive hypothesis generation, deductive hypothesis verification, and human intituation, are all crucial components for an effective discovery system.

Inductive learning is essential for generating hypotheses from data automatically, deductive database technology is a natural tool for gathering evidence in support of existing hypotheses, while human intuition (which may be inspired by the results of machine discovery) is necessary for generating and selecting the most promising hypotheses in a practical manner. However, the integration of these three components are still poorly supported by today's discovery systems. Most systems simply provide a set of tools (deductive or inductive alike) for humans to choose at arbitration, and once a tool is selected, no attempt is made to exploit the synergy between these three intrinsically related discovery "engines."

In this chapter, we propose an approach to the integration via second-order predicates called *metaqueries*. A metaquery is in essence a second-order template that specifies the type of patterns to be discovered. For example, let P, Q and R be variables for predicates, then a metaquery

$$P(X, Y) \land Q(Y, Z) \Rightarrow R(X, Z)$$

specifies that the patterns to be discovered are transitivity relations $p(X, Y) \land q(Y, Z) \Rightarrow r(X, Z)$, where p, q, and r are specific predicates. One possible result of this metaquery is the pattern

$$citizen(X, Y) \land officialLanguage(Y, Z) \Rightarrow speaks(X, Z)$$
with a probability (say 0.93),

where *citizen*, *officialLanguage*, and *speaks* are relations that bind to P, Q, and R, respectively, in the current database.

In general, a metaquery can be viewed as a two-part specification: the left-hand side specifies a constraint on how data should be prepared, and the right-hand side specifies an action to be applied on the prepared data. For example, the left-hand of the above example, when P and Q are bound to specific predicates p and q respectively, is a constraint on how to fetch those data pairs (X, Z) that satisfy $p(X, Y) \land q(Y, Z)$. The right-hand of that example, when R is bound to a specific predicate r, is interpreted as an action that computes the ratio of (X, Z) pairs, among those returned by the left-hand side, that satisfy $r(X, Z)$. (In fact, the precise syntax for the right-hand side of the above metaquery is $RuleStrengthComputer\ (R(X, Z))$, where $RuleStrengthComputer$ is an action that performs the described procedure.)

At the present, the framework supports the following four basic metaquery actions:

- *RuleStrengthComputer*(r, $[X, Z, ...]$), where r is a predicate and $[X, Z, ...]$ is a tuple of variables for a given set of data. This action returns an expression r(X,Z,...) along with a number (such as the probability 0.93 in the above example) indicating the ratio of the given data tuples that satisfy the predicate r(X,Z,...).

- *Plotter*($[X, Z, ...]$). This action simply plots the given set of data.

- *Classifier*($[X, Z, ...]$). This action uses the CDL incremental learning algorithm (Shen 1994) to return a set of class descriptions that best classify the given data.

- *Cluster*($[X, Z, ...]$). This action uses a Bayesian-based Cobweb clustering algorithm (Fisher 1987; Shen 1994) to return a set of cluster descriptions that best cluster the given data.

As shown in Figure 14.1, metaqueries serve as the link between the inductive and deductive aspects of knowledge discovery, effectively facilitating a deductive-inductive-human discovery loop. Metaqueries outline the data collecting strategy for the deductive part of the loop; they serve as the basis for the generation of specific queries, which are obtained by instantiating the variables in the metaqueries with values representing tables and columns in the database of interest. These instantiated queries are then run against the database to collect relevant data. Users can either type their metaqueries directly, or have the system generates some initial metaqueries automatically. Furthermore, metaqueries also serve as a generic description of the class of patterns to be discovered and help guide the process of data analysis and pattern generation in the inductive part of the loop. The patterns discovered from the database adhere to the format of the current metaquery. Notice that, unlike many other discovery systems, patterns discovered using metaqueries can link information from many tables in databases. Furthermore, these patterns are all relational, while most machine learning systems can only learn propositional patterns.

Metaqueries can be specified by human experts or alternatively, they can be automatically generated from the database schema. Either way, they serve as a very important interface between human "discoverers" and the discovery system. Using metaqueries, human experts can focus

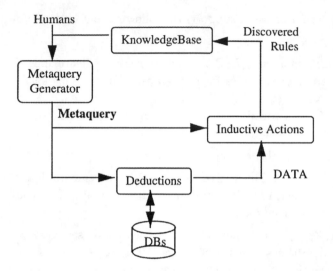

Figure 14.1
The metaquery framework and the discovery loop.

the discovery process onto more profitable areas of the database; the system generated metaqueries provide valuable clues to the human expert regarding good start points for the database searches and also serve as the evolutionary basis for the development of user specified metaqueries more attuned to the discovery goals as envisaged by the human expert.

The above ideas are implemented in a system called the *Knowledge Miner* (KM). Up to date, the induction component of KM is an unsupervised Bayesian Data Cluster (Shen 1994), and the deduction component of KM is a state of the art deductive database technology called *LDL++* (Naqvi and Tsur 1989, Arni, Ong, Tsur, and Zaniolo 1993), which is well suited for both knowledge representation and data querying. Under this implementation, the patterns discovered under metaqueries are actual *LDL++* rules, and their usage is very flexible. Used as queries, they can retrieve the actual data that satisfy or violate a particular rule; Used as integrity constraints, they can alert or filter future "illegal" transactions; Used as logical rules, they can help to generate new metaqueries.

In the rest of this chapter, Section 14.2 gives an overview of the KM framework and its various components. Sections 14.3 and 14.4 describe in detail the *LDL++* language and the unsupervised Bayesian Data

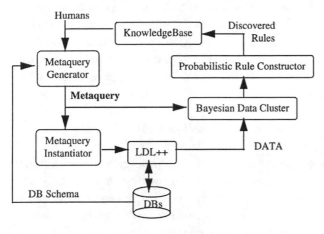

Figure 14.2
Knowledge Miner: A metaquery-driven framework.

Cluster, respectively. Sections 5 to 7 present three case studies in the application of the metaquery approach to knowledge discovery in a knowledge base, a telecommunication database, and a chemical database respectively. Finally, the chapter is concluded with a set of open problems associated with this approach and our plan for future work.

14.2   Knowledge Miner:
A MetaQuery-Driven Framework

In this section, we give an overview of the metaquery driven framework, and a specific system called "Knowledge Miner" that implements the ideas described above.

Figure 14.2 illustrates the configuration of Knowledge Miner. Given a database and its schema, the metaquery generator (to be described later) suggests a series of valid metaqueries. Users can either pick some of the suggested metaqueries or they can specify their own metaqueries to be run.

On being provided with a metaquery as input, the instantiator generates a set of corresponding $LDL++$ queries by instantiating the predicate variables in the metaquery with relevant table names and column names as appropriate. These $LDL++$ queries are then run against the database to gather the data in the desired fashion. The resulting data is fed to the Bayesian Data Cluster, which classifies the data into classes and then passes the classification information to the Probabilistic Rule Constructor. The constructor then builds relations and patterns in the format specified in the current metaquery. The classification information produced by the Bayesian Data Cluster can also be stored persistently in a database.

Consider, for example, a database that has 4 tables, each with an arity of 2. Suppose that table1 and table2 specify ingredients of chemical compounds, and table3 and table4 specify two properties of compounds, P_1 and P_2, respectively. (These information can be presented to KM by experts or be extracted automatically from the schema by the metaquery generator.) If we are interested in finding the relation between ingredients and properties, then a proper metaquery is as follows:

$$Ingredients(X, c_1, c_2) \wedge Property(X, Y) \Rightarrow Cluster(Y)$$

where X and Y are variables, c_1 and c_2 are constants, and $Cluster$ is the inductive action to be performed on Y. Given this metaquery, the instantiator instantiates it into a series of $LDL++$ queries with variables bound to appropriate table and column names. In the current example, such $LDL++$ queries are:

$$Q1(Y) \quad \leftarrow \quad table1(X, c1),\ table2(X, c2),\ table3(X, Y)$$
$$Q2(Y) \quad \leftarrow \quad table1(X, c1),\ table2(X, c2),\ table4(X, Y)$$

Each rule is run against the database, and a set of values that satisfy the constraints on the right-hand side of the rule is fed into the Bayesian Data Cluster. The cluster classifies these values into a set of classes, each with a mean value, a variance, and a likelihood. For example, when $c_1=$'BX89' and $c_2=$'GF102', the Y values that satisfy the first rule may be classified into two classes: (m_1, v_1, l_1) and (m_2, v_2, l_2), where m_i are mean values, v_i are variances, and l_i are the likelilhood of the class.

These clustering results are then fed into the Rule Constructor, which uses the current metaquery as a template to generate a final rule. For example, suppose the two classes above are: $(m_1=2.4, v_1=3.5, l_1=0.97)$ and $(m_2=202.0, v_2=0.5, l_2=0.03)$, then the final rule constructed using the metaquery may look like this:

ingredients='BX89'&'GF102' ∧ property=P_1 ⇒ Clusters(P_1)={(2.4,3.5, 0.97), (202.3, 0.5, 0.03)}

This rule says for all compounds that contains ingredients 'BX89' and 'GF102', the majority values of their property P_1 are near 2.4, but there are few values scattered around 202.3.

We now discuss each of the components of KM in detail. In particular, the following two sections cover the $LDL++$ language and the Bayesian Data Cluster. The Metaquery Generator will be discussed after the presentation of experimental results obtained using KM.

14.3   The $LDL++$ Deductive Database System

The $LDL++$ system is a deductive database system based on the integration of a logic programming system with relational database technology. It provides a logic-based language that is suitable for both database queries and knowledge representation. More details on the $LDL++$ system and language can be found in (Naqvi and Tsur 1989; Arni, Ong, Tsur, and Zaniolo 1993; Zaniolo 1994). In this section, we will briefly describe some of the salient aspects of the $LDL++$ system as relevant to KM and also highlight the benefits of using $LDL++$ in the Knowledge Miner framework.

The $LDL++$ query language is based on Horn clause logic (Lloyd 1984; Apt 1990) and a $LDL++$ program is essentially a set of declarative rules. For example, the following rules

$$ancestor(X, Y) \quad \leftarrow \quad parent(X, Y).$$
$$ancestor(X, Y) \quad \leftarrow \quad ancestor(X, Z), parent(Z, Y).$$

specify that a new relation **ancestor** can be defined based on the relation **parent**. X, Y and Z are variables and **ancestor** and **parent** are predicate symbols, both with arity of 2. By declarativeness, we mean that the ordering between the rules is unimportant and will not affect the results returned. Deduction of all values of the ancestor relation is achieved through an iterative bottom-up execution model.

The language supports a rich set of complex data types such as complex objects, lists and sets in addition to other basic types such as integer, real and string. Examples of each of these complex types are **rectangle(1,2)**, **[1,2]** and **{1,2}** respectively.

With such a rich set of data types, the *LDL++* language is well suited for representing knowledge discovered from databases. Furthermore, complex constraints in the metaqueries can be easily specified in the language. Through the metalevel query facility in *LDL++*, constraints represented in the form of data can be used to generate rules at run-time.

From the database query perspective, in comparison to SQL, the *LDL++* language extends the ability of KM to impose more complex constraints on the data it retrieves beyond what is possible in SQL. This is illustrated by the recursive rules that define `ancestor`—such constraints cannot be specified in SQL directly. Moreover, cascading or nested queries can be easily represented in LDL++ in the form of rules.

Systemwise, the *LDL++* system was designed with an open architecture. Even though it was designed independently of KM needs, it meets many of the KM demands. It is "opened" to procedural languages such as C/C++ in two ways: It provides an Application Programming Interface (API) that allows applications to drive the system and, an External Function Interface (EFI) that allows C/C++ routines to be imported into the inference engine. It is also "opened" to external databases such as Sybase, Oracle, Ingres and DB2 through its External Database Interface (EDI).

Referring to Figure 14.2, we can observe that the *LDL++* system has to interface with the Instantiator, the Database and the Bayesian Data Cluster. It interfaces with the Instantiator through its API, the Bayesian Data Cluster with its EFI and the Database with its EDI.

Both tables in the external databases and C/C++ interface routines are modeled as predicates through its EDI and EFI respectively. As a result, these external resources are transparent to the inference engine and the KM can plug in a different database or another learning algorithm with ease, without making any changes to the overall implementation. The EDI facilitates the retrieval of data as well as the archiving of statistical metadata into persistent storage.

The EDI are designed to provide access data from multiple, heterogeneous databases simultaneously in one single query. Furthermore, it also provides the capability to fuse the data from the various and combine into one single view for knowledge discovery. This empowers KM to discover relationships between data from different sources. Again, the data access is transparent to KM and no changes are required to take advantage of this capability.

The following example shows the *LDL++* schema declaration to access an external Sybase relation `employee` in the database `payroll` running on the server `server1`.

Example 1 Schema Declaration to external Sybase server.

```
database({
        sybase::employee(NAME:char(30),SALARY:int,
                    MANAGER:char(30))
                from server1
                use payroll
                user_name 'john'
                application_name 'downsizing'
                interface_filename
                        '/tmp/ldl++/demo/interfaces'
                password nhoj
        } ).
```

Predicates on external relations in rules are translated to standard SQL queries that are applicable to all relational databases with an SQL interface. The *LDL++* system generates SQL queries that off-load join, select, and project operations (and negation and aggregate operations as well) to the external database server. This is done using the rewriting optimizations that collapse one or more rules using external relations and comparison predicates into one single SQL statement. To illustrate, consider the following example

Example 2 SQL Generation

```
    expensive_employee(Name) <-
                employee(Name, Salary1, Manager),
                Salary1 > 75000,
                employee(Manager, Salary2, _),
                Salary1 > Salary2.
```

The rule in the example defines expensive employees as those who make over 75,000 and more than their managers. The *LDL++* compiler will collapse the body literals and transform them into one SQL node as shown below:

```
        expensive_employee(Name) <- sql_node(Name).
```

Where the SQL query corresponding to sql_node, that is sent to the server is:

```
SELECT    employee_0.NAME
FROM      employee employee_0, employee employee_1
WHERE     employee_0.SALARY > 75000 AND
          employee_1.NAME = employee_0.MANAGER AND
          employee_0.SALARY > employee_1.SALARY
```

Consequently, access to the external database via $LDL++$ is as efficient as any queries written directly in SQL. Rules with negated goals are also supported and implemented via the NOT EXIST construct of SQL.

Last but not least, once the statistical data is derived and high-probability rules are created, they are represented directly in $LDL++$ for enforcing the integrity of the database.

14.4   Bayesian Data Clustering

Since most our applications involve unsupervised data classification, we have chosen to integrate a cluster as our first inductive action. To classify the retrieved data, we use a *conceptual clustering* approach based on the Cobweb algorithm (Fisher 1987) but adapted to use discriminant functions derived from Bayesian probability theory (Jaynes 1993; Shen 1994). We feel that the latter lends a stronger mathematical basis to the evaluation process.

The Cobweb algorithm facilitates incremental, unsupervised learning of concept hierarchies from attribute-based instances. The concepts formed represent nodes in a concept tree, with each non-leaf node further partitioned into its more specific children nodes. Thus, more general concepts are located near the root of the tree and more specific concepts are located towards the leaves. Each node in the concept tree describes a class of instances and hence each cut of the concept tree represents a partition of all the known instances.

Given a new instance, the task of the Cobweb algorithm is to create a new concept hierarchy that incorporates the knowledge embodied in the instance. The classification of the new instance proceeds recursively through each level of the concept hierarchy, following a path composed of increasingly specific concept nodes. At each level in the concept hierarchy, the classification process is focussed on the immediate subtree (i.e. the children) of the current node and essentially reduces to the best choice among the following four alternatives, namely:

- *Incorporate* the instance into an existing concept. Select the child concept which best fits the new instance to host it.

- *Create* a new child concept to host the new instance.

- *Merge* two children concepts and use the resulting combined concept to host the new instance.

- *Split* a child concept i.e. replace it with its children and then choose the best child to host the instance.

According the Bayesian theory, the best choice among these alternatives is the one that gives the maximal value of the *Bayesian Evaluation Function*, described in the addendums of this chapter. The algorithm recursively applies the above classification process at each level of the concept hierarchy, incorporating the instance into concepts of increasing specificity. The algorithm halts when it classifies the instance into either:

- A singleton node at the leaf, or

- A new concept at any level in the hierarchy.

In the Knowledge Miner framework, the Bayesian Data Cluster interfaces with the *LDL++* module through the latter's EFI. It receives the data extracted by *LDL++* as input, classifies it and returns the concept tree as output. The module interface provides all the requisite functionality to the external process/user for fine-tuning the classification process.

14.5   Discoveries from a Large Knowledge Base

In this and the following two sections, we present the results of three applications of Knowledge Miner to a large common-sense knowledge base called Cyc, a telecommunication database containing a large number of real telephone circuits and a chemical research database representing over 30 years of chemical research results respectively.

Cyc is a large common-sense knowledge base developed at MCC, containing over one million logical assertions (think of them as relations if you like). We applied an earlier version of the Knowledge Miner system

(Shen 1992) to two large collections of objects in Cyc: *Person* and *Organization*. At the time, the *Person* collection contained 633 objects and 77 relevant relations, while the *Organization* collection contained 1550 objects and 150 relevant relations.

The metaquery we used in these experiments is as follows:

$$P(X\ Y) \wedge Q(Y\ Z) \Rightarrow R(X\ Z)$$

where P, Q, and R are variables for binary relations, and X, Y, and Z are variables for objects.

This metaquery is instantiated on combinations of the 77 relations in the *Person* collection and the 150 relations in the *Organization* collection respectively. From the data in Cyc, 146 patterns were discovered (i.e., were found to have enough supporting data) from the *Person* collection, and 250 from the *Organization* collection. Example patterns discovered from the *Person* collection are as follows:

> acquaintedWith(x y)∧languageSpoken(y z)⇒
>   languageSpoken(x z)
> studentAtInstitution(x y)∧hasProfessor(y z)⇒likedBy(x z)
> primeMinisterOfCountry(x y) ∧ eq(y z) ⇒headOfGovernmentOf(x z)
> computersFamiliarWith(x y)
>   ∧languagesThisFamilyOfMachinesCanRun(y z)⇒programsIn(x z)
> presidentOfCountry(x y)∧officialLanguage(y z)⇒
>   languageSpoken(x z)
> likedBy(x y)∧wearsClothing(y z)⇒wearsClothing(x z)
> birthDate(y z)∧allSuperAbstrac(x y)⇒birthDate(x z)
> laterSubAbstractions(x y) ∧ eq(y z) ⇒
>   startsBeforeStartingOf(x z)
> children(x y) ∧ eq(y z) ⇒relative(x z)
> duringActorIn(x y) ∧ eq(y z) ⇒canPerform(x z)
> isAwareOf(x y) ∧ allSubAbstrac(y z) ⇒isAwareOf(x z)
> residences(x y)∧officialLanguage(y EnglishLanguage)⇒
>   speaks(x EnglishLanguage)
> memberOfPoliticalParty(x y)∧allInstances(y CommunistParty)⇒
>   ideology(x Communist)
> staffMembers(x y)∧eq(y MCC)⇒
>   probableExpertiseInComputers(x UserLevel)

All of these assertions were new to Cyc (i.e, cannot be inferred by Cyc itself at the time). Most of these assertions are interesting because they specify things that are true with high, but less than one, probabilities.

These rules can be used by Cyc as default rules for reasoning. For example, the pattern studentAtInstitution(x y)∧hasProfessor(y z)⇒ likedBy (x z) says that if x is a student in an institution, then x must be liked by all the professors in that institution. This is not always true but is a good default rule. Given the fact that more and more knowledge bases are capable of reasoning nonmonotonically, this kind of default knowledge is important if you don't know whether a particular student x is liked by a particular professor z.

14.6   Discoveries from a Telecommunication Database

We also applied KM to a large telecommunication database. This database contains approximately 300MB of information about existing telephone circuits in a regional Bell company. There are two types of circuits in the database: point to point circuits, and multiple-leg circuits. Each circuit (or leg) is a sequence of connected components such as *channel, cable, station, equipment, test point*, etc.. Each component is associated with a set of features. For example, an *equipment* has location, function, channelID, and others. A *channel* has starting and ending locations, conductivity, and others.

We were interested in finding the feature correlation between components that are directly connected in some circuit. So the metaquery used was as follows:

$$Linked(X, Y) \wedge Feature1(X) \wedge Feature2(Y) \Rightarrow equal(X, Y)$$

where X and Y are variables for components. From this metaquery, the instantiator generated a series of *LDL++* queries, with *Linked* bound to a circuit connection table, and *Feature1* and *Feature2* bound to various columns in each component table. Running these *LDL++* queries against the database, the KM system generated 281 patterns in about 7 hours. Two examples of patterns that have high probabilities are:

    (P=1.0) linked(EQPT,EQPT)⇒
        equal(chanID(EQPT),chanID(EQPT))
    (P=0.98) linked(CHANNEL,EQPT)⇒
        equal(endLocation(CHANNEL),location(EQPT))

Two examples of patterns that have low probabilities are:

(P=0.015) linked(LOOP,CABLE)⇒
    equal(startLocation(LOOP),endLocation(CABLE))
(P=0.004) linked(EQPT,CHANNEL)⇒
    equal(calcSigVoice(EQPT),ovrdSigVoice(CHANNEL))

Two examples of patterns that have middle probabilities are:

(P=0.59) linked(TPoint,TPoint)⇒
    equal(accsys(TPoint),accsys(TPoint))
(P=0.40) linked(EQPT,TPoint)⇒
    equal(hierchyIND(EQPT),analRingSigDir(TPoint))

We presented these rules to experts in this field and most of the rules were deemed to make perfect sense. There are a number of ways that these rules can be used: Those with high probabilities can run directly (they are in fact *LDL++* queries) against the database to find the set of data that violate the rules. Such data is very likely to be erroneous. Similarly, one can run the low probability rules to find the data that obeys the rules—this data is also very likely to be erroneous. These rules can also be used as data validation filters for future data entry. Any input data that violates the high-probability rules (or obeys the low-probability rules) should be flagged and checked before actually being entered into the database. The rules with middle probabilities are also interesting and useful in that they identify subsets of the database that need further investigation. One can then introduce new metaqueries that are constrained to focus on these subsets and subsequently generate new rules with high and low probabilities.

14.7   Discoveries from a Chemical Research Database

We are currently applying the KM system to a real chemical research database. This database contains results representing over 30 years of chemical research and experiments. Conceptually speaking, it has information about the ingredients and the properties of various compounds. The ingredients are specified in a single table, while the properties are distributed over more than 50 tables. All these tables are linked via the compound identification.

We are interested in discovering the relationship between ingredients and properties, so the following metaquery is employed:

$Ingredient(C\ X\ Y) \wedge Property(C\ Z) \Rightarrow Cluster(Z)$

where C is a variable for compound identification, X and Y are variables for ingredients, and Z is a variable for property. As one may expect given the large number of properties in the database, this metaquery is too time consuming to run. So we restrict it by constraining the variables X and Y to be bound only to those ingredients that are commonly used.

Using the restricted metaquery, KM returns a set of patterns describing the relationships between specific ingredients and properties. One example of these patterns is the relationship between an ingredient *3060* and the *densityBM* property of the compound:

$$\text{ingredient}(C,3060,X) \wedge \text{densityBM}(C,Y) \Rightarrow$$
$$\text{Clusters}(Y) = \{(1.243,0.46,0.99), (\text{-}999.9,0.2,0.01)\}$$

The rule indicates that for this type of compounds, the majority (99%) of values of property densityBM are near 1.243 (with a variance 0.46). Thus, the ingredient 3060 has a very specific effect on the compound's densityBM property, irrespective of the other ingredient X. This information is extremely valuable to the chemists. This rule also indicates (with a very low probability cluster) that there may be some noisy data in the densityBM table.

We are currently experimenting with various metaqueries, and the results will be reported in the near future.

14.8   Generating Initial Metaqueries

As we have seen so far, metaqueries play an important role in the KM discovery system. However, good metaqueries do not come easy. They must balance the computational expense on one hand with the potential profit of discovery on the other. One may have an extremely general metaquery for a database, but it's demands on computational resources may be untenable. On the other hand, one may have an extremely specific metaquery with fast response characteristics, but it may not discover anything interesting. The ideal case would be to have a metaquery general enough to support the discovery of interesting patterns, but constrained enough to do so without making unreasonable demands on computational and time resources.

Obviously, designing the right metaquery is a difficult problem—in addition to knowledge about the database schema, one also needs good judgment and a healthy dose of intuition. We do not claim to have reduced this process to an exact science—indeed, we have not solved this problem. Instead, our philosophy, as reflected in the KM methodology, is to play the role of an informed assistant and afford a human expert the fullest flexibility and help in defining the best metaqueries he or she can. For example, one thing we find useful is to have the system automatically generate a set of initial metaqueries, which can then be analyzed and refined by the human expert. As more rules are discovered from the database, the system should be able to generate more metaqueries in an interactive fashion. This is the task of the Metaquery Generator in KM.

The Metaquery Generator accepts two inputs: the database schema and the rules discovered from the database. Initially, the generator examines the database schema and generates simple metaqueries that address the relationships across tables. Certain types of information from the schema can provide useful guidance in narrowing down the set of possible metaqueries. These include:

1. Keys

2. Column Types

3. Column Names

Some example heuristics based on these information types include:

- Since the key column of a table is always unique, we can pretty much eliminate it from consideration as a possible candidate for instantiation in metaquery.

- When joining any two tables, we need to determine the join columns i.e. a column from each table which could be deemed equal. In this case, the basic criterion is that both columns must have the same types to even have a reasonable chance at success.

- If the column names are the same, the likelihood is greater that the two tables should be joined based on those two columns.

Discovered rules can also be used to guide the generation of metaqueries. For example, knowing the probabilistic distribution of the candidate columns for joining two tables, we can determine whether a metaquery based on the same will generate useful results or not. Thus, less useful metaqueries will not be suggested to the users. Another way to generate metaqueries is to generalize the existing rules. For example, the system BLIP (Theime 1989) uses the heuristic of "turning constants to variables" to acquire metalevel rules from domain-level rules entered by users.

The Metaquery Generator is by no means complete. We have yet to generate complex queries automatically. There is also potentially a lot more useful information that can be gleaned from the database schema and the discovered rules that could be gainfully applied to the generation process. This is ongoing work and we are engaged in a little discovery activity ourselves—we will have more to report as more experiments are carried out.

14.9   Related Work

The number of knowledge mining systems that uses artificial intelligence techniques are growing but few combines deductive techniques with inductive techniques. (Matheus, Chan and Piatetsky-Shapiro 1992) compares in detail the methodologies between the various systems.

A comparison framework was suggested by (Simoudis, Livezey and Kerber 1994) based on two aspects. The first is based on the operations supported and the second is based the degree of integration. The list of operations are:

- testing and refinement of rules hypothesized
- automatic discovery of rules by the system
- integration of the best of the hypothesized and discovered rules into a cohesive model

which are all supported by the Recon (Simoudis, Livezey and Kerber 1994) and the IMACS (Brachman, Selfridge, Terveen, Altman, Halper, Kirk, Lazar, McGuiness, Resnick. and Borgida 1993) system. All these three operations are also supported by our *metaqueries* approach. Other systems such as KDW (Piatetsky-Shapiro and Matheus 1992), INLEN (Kaufman, Michalski and Kerschberg 1991), MLT (Usznski 1992) support only a subset of these operations.

One significant difference between IMACS and the Recon or our *metaqueries* approach is that the former loads all data into memory from databases for processing while the latter two systems interface database directly and retrieve data as needed at processing time. All three systems

are supported by some form of deductive engine. However, since `Recon`
can only support non-recursive queries and thus, limited by the SQL
it generates, `IMACS` can express and process more complex structures.
Our metaqueries approach, which uses the *LDL++* deductive database
engine that can support a full range of both recursive and non-recursive
queries, has similar expressive and processing power as `IMACS`.

In terms of integration, `Recon`, `KDW` and our *metaqueries* uses a loose
architecture where the various components are separated into distinct
modules and they interface through well-defined interfaces. In the *metaqueries* approach, second-order predicates or templates are used to interface with the users or the visualization module, first-order predicates
are used to interface with the deductive database engine, SQL statements are used to interface with the underlying databases, first-order
predicates are used to interface with the clustering routines and rules
are generated as input to the knowledge base. `IMACS`, `INLEN` and `MLT`
are in comparison more tightly integrated systems.

14.10   Conclusions and Future Work

We have presented a framework for using metaqueries to integrate induction and deduction for knowledge discovery from databases. The
framework has been implemented in the Knowledge Miner system to
integrate two very advanced deductive and inductive technologies: the
LDL++ system and the Bayesian Data Cluster. Applications of Knowledge Miner to several real-world databases and a knowledge base have
demonstrated that the metaquery approach is indeed viable and shows
much promise.

Our experiments with the system thus far have been fruitful, but a
lot more work needs to be done before the KM system can be truly
useful in a variety of discovery environments. On the theoretical side,
we are exploring more advanced learning algorithms with a better, more
intelligent clustering capability as well as a higher efficiency in terms of
computational time and space used.

On the practical side too, there are a number of issues on the agenda.
One is to have the ability to connect with legacy databases provided by
various vendors. The *LDL++* system can currently access data from
Sybase, Ingres, Rdb and Oracle. We plan to extend it to also access

other database products such as IBM/DB2 and IBM/IMS. A second issue is the design and implementation of an appropriate visualization tool for the graphical presentation of the results of the discovery process.

Lastly, we will also explore new uses for the discovered rules and statistical data. In addition to using them to enforce integrity constraints for future updates and for generating new metaqueries, we believe that they can also be effectively used for estimating the cost of queries and also for supporting some forms of fuzzy querying. These beliefs remain to be verified.

Addendum 15.A: The Bayesian Evaluation Function

An instance is described by its attributes. Thus, if K is the number of attributes, an instance D can be defined as a vector of K values for these attributes:

$$D \equiv (x_1 = v_1, ..., x_k = v_k, ..., x_K = v_K)$$

A concept is a collection of related or similar instances. The size of a concept C, denoted as $|C|$, is the number of its instances. The concept C can be defined as a vector of K probability distribution functions on the K attributes of its instances:

$$C \equiv (f_1, ..., f_k, ..., f_K).$$

where f_k is determined by the kth values of all its instances. For instance, if $v_{k1}, v_{k2}, \ldots, v_{kN}$ are the kth values of N instances $D_1, D_2, \ldots, D_N$, respectively, then, assuming a normal distribution, the probability distribution function f_k can be estimated as:

$$f_k(x_k|D_1 \cdots D_N I) = M_k \exp\left\{-\frac{(x_k - a_k)^2}{2\sigma_k^2}\right\} \qquad (14.10.1)$$

where I is the background information

$$M_k = \frac{1}{\sigma_k\sqrt{2\pi}},$$

is a normalization constant to satisfy the constraint:

$$\int_{-\infty}^{+\infty} f_k(x_k|D_1 \cdots D_N I)dx_k = 1,$$

a_k, the mean of f_k, can be estimated as:

$$a_k = \frac{1}{N} \sum_{j=1}^{N} v_{kj} \qquad (14.10.2)$$

and σ_k^2, the variance of f_k, can be estimated as:

$$\sigma_k^2 = \frac{1}{N} \sum_{j=1}^{N} (v_{kj} - a_k)^2. \qquad (14.10.3)$$

The values of a_k and σ_k^2 can also be estimated incrementally for the nth instance based on the values of the same for the $n - 1$th instance (see Addendum 15.B). The incremental values are estimated as:

$$a_{kn} = a_{k(n-1)} + \frac{v_{kn} - a_{k(n-1)}}{n} \qquad (14.10.4)$$

and

$$\sigma_{kn}^2 = \frac{n-1}{n} \left[\sigma_{k(n-1)}^2 + (a_{k(n-1)} - a_{kn})^2 \right] + \frac{(v_{kn} - a_{kn})^2}{n} \qquad (14.10.5)$$

Let $H = (C_1, \ldots, C_J)$ represent the children of concept C. Let child C_j $(1 \le j \le J)$ be the one selected to host new instance D, and let H_j represent the new set of children nodes obtained after the definition of C_j changes to incorporate D. Then how good the assignment of D to C_j can be estimated by the probability:

$$P(H_j|DH) = P(H_j|H)\frac{P(D|H_jH)}{P(D|H)} \qquad (14.10.6)$$

Clearly, the best child concept to host D is C_i such that

$$P(H_i|DH) = \max_{j=1,\ldots,J} \{P(H_j|DH)\} \qquad (14.10.7)$$

Assume that $P(H_j|H)$ are equal for all j, then to compare $P(H_j|DH)$ we need only compute $P(D|H_jH)$. Notice that

$$P(D|H_jH) = \sum_{j=1}^{J} P(DC_j|H_jH) = \sum_{j=1}^{J} P(C_j|H_jH)P(D|C_jH_jH) \quad (14.10.8)$$

and

$$P(C_j|H_jH) = \frac{|C_j|}{|C|} \qquad (14.10.9)$$

and

$$P(D|C_jH_jH) = P(D|C_j) \qquad (14.10.10)$$

$P(D|C)$ represents the degree to which instance D belongs to concept C and is computed as:

$$P(D|C) = \prod_{k=1}^{K} P(v_k|f_k) \qquad (14.10.11)$$

The term $P(v_k|f_k)$ can be computed easily. If the kth attribute is continuous-value numeric attribute, then

$$P(v_k|f_k) \approx f_k(v_k)\Delta x_k \qquad (14.10.12)$$

where Δx_k is a small constant range around v_k. If the kth attribute is discrete (ordered or not), then

$$P(v_k|f_k) = \frac{\text{num. of insts whose } k\text{th value is } v_k}{\text{num. of insts in } C} \qquad (14.10.13)$$

Addendum 15.B: Incremental Update of a_k and σ_k^2

The parameters of f_k (a_k and σ_k^2) can be computed incrementally. Let $a_{k(N-1)}$ and $\sigma_{k(N-1)}^2$ be the parameters of f_k after $N-1$ instances. When the Nth instance is seen, we can use $a_{k(N-1)}$, $\sigma_{k(N-1)}^2$, and v_{kN} (the kth value of the Nth instance) to compute the new parameters a_{kN} and σ_{kN}^2.

To compute the new mean value a_{kN}, notice that

$$
\begin{aligned}
a_{kN} &= \frac{1}{N}\sum_{j=1}^{N} v_{kj} \\
&= \frac{1}{N}\sum_{j=1}^{N-1} v_{kj} + \frac{v_{kN}}{N} \\
&= \frac{N-1}{N}a_{k(N-1)} + \frac{v_{kN}}{N} \\
&= a_{k(N-1)} + \frac{v_{kN} - a_{k(N-1)}}{N} \qquad (14.10.14)
\end{aligned}
$$

To compute the new variance σ^2_{kN}, we first observe that

$$\sum_{j=1}^{N-1}(v_{kj} - a_{kN})^2 =$$

$$\sum_{j=1}^{N-1}(v_{kj} - a_{k(N-1)})^2 + (N-1)(a_{k(N-1)} - a_{kN})^2 \qquad (14.10.15)$$

(see Addendum for the proof of Equation 14.10.15), therefore,

$$
\begin{aligned}
\sigma^2_{kN} &= \frac{1}{N}\sum_{j=1}^{N}(v_{kj} - a_{kN})^2 \\
&= \frac{1}{N}\sum_{j=1}^{N-1}(v_{kj} - a_{kN})^2 \\
&\quad + \frac{(v_{kN} - a_{kN})^2}{N} \\
&= \frac{1}{N}\left[\sum_{j=1}^{N-1}(v_{kj} - a_{k(N-1)})^2 + (N-1)(a_{k(N-1)} - a_{kN})^2\right] \\
&\quad + \frac{(v_{kN} - a_{kN})^2}{N} \\
&= \frac{1}{N}\left[(N-1)\sigma^2_{k(N-1)} + (N-1)(a_{k(N-1)} - a_{kN})^2\right] \\
&\quad + \frac{(v_{kN} - a_{kN})^2}{N} \\
&= \frac{N-1}{N}\left[\sigma^2_{k(N-1)} + (a_{k(N-1)} - a_{kN})^2\right] \\
&\quad + \frac{(v_{kN} - a_{kN})^2}{N} \qquad (14.10.16)
\end{aligned}
$$

These calculations are incremental in the sense that there is no need to refer to any earlier values of instances: $v_{k1}, v_{k2}, \ldots, v_{k(N-1)}$.

Finally, we give the proof of Equation 14.10.15 as follows:

Proposition:

$$\sum_{j=1}^{M}(v_j - c)^2 = \sum_{j=1}^{M}(v_j - b)^2 + M(b - c)^2$$

where

$$b = \frac{1}{M} \sum_{j=1}^{M} v_j$$

Proof: First, notice that

$$(x - c)^2 = [(x - b) + (b - c)]^2 = (x - b)^2 + 2(x - b)(b - c) + (b - c)^2$$

thus,

$$
\begin{aligned}
\sum_{j=1}^{M} (v_j - c)^2 &= (v_1 - b)^2 + 2(v_1 - b)(b - c) + (b - c)^2 + \\
&\quad (v_2 - b)^2 + 2(v_2 - b)(b - c) + (b - c)^2 + \\
&\quad \vdots \\
&\quad (v_M - b)^2 + 2(v_M - b)(b - c) + (b - c)^2 \\
&= \sum_{j=1}^{M} (v_j - b)^2 + 2(b - c) \sum_{j=1}^{M} (v_j - b) + M(b - c)^2 \\
&= \sum_{j=1}^{M} (v_j - b)^2 + 2(b - c) \left[\sum_{j=1}^{M} v_j - Mb \right] + M(b - c)^2 \\
&= \sum_{j=1}^{M} (v_j - b)^2 + 0 + M(b - c)^2 \\
&= \sum_{j=1}^{M} (v_j - b)^2 + M(b - c)^2
\end{aligned}
$$

QED.

References

Apt, Krzysztof R. 1990. Logic Programming. Ch. 10 in *Handbook of Theoretical Computer Science,*, 493–574, ed. J. van Leeuwen.

Arni, Ong, Tsur, and Zaniolo. 1994. *LDL++: A Second Generation Deductive Database System*, Working Paper.

Brachman, R.; Selfridge, P.; Terveen, L.; Altman, B.; Halper, F.; Kirk, T.; Lazar, T.; McGuiness, D.; Resnick, L.; and Borgida, A. 1993. Integrated Support for Data Archaeology. Pesented at the 1993 AAAI Workshop on Knowledge Discovery in Databases, Washington D.C.

Cercone, N.; and Tsuchiya, M. ed. 1993. Special issue on Learning and Discovery in Databases. *IEEE Transactions on Knowledge and Data Engineering,* 5 (6).

Fisher, D., 1987. Knowledge Acquisition Via Incremental Conceptual Clustering, *Machine Learning,* 2:139-172.

Jaynes, E. 1995. *Probability Theory—The Logic of Science,* Cambridge: Cambridge University Press.

Kaufman, K.; Michalski, R.; and Kerschberg, L., 1991. Mining for Knowledge in Databases: Goals and General Description of the INLEN System, Presented at the 1991 IJCAI Workshop on Knowledge Discovery in Databases.

Kerber, R.; and Livezey, B.; and Simoudis, E. 1994. Recon: A Framework for Database Mining. *International Journal of Intelligent Information Systems.*

Lloyd, J., 1984.*Foundations of Logic Programming,* ch. 1. New York: Springer-Verlag.

Matheus, C.; Chan, P. K.; and Piatetsky-Shapiro, G., 1993. Systems for Knowledge Discovery in Databases, *IEEE Transactions on Knowledge and Data Engineering,* 5 (6).

Naqvi and Tsur. 1989. *A Logical Language for Data and Knowledge Bases.* San Francisco: W. H. Freeman Company.

Piatetsky-Shapiro G.; and Matheus C., 1992. Knowledge Discovery Workbench for Exploring Business Databases, *International Journal of Intelligent Systems,* 7.

Shen, W.-M. 1992. Discovering Regularities from Knowledge Bases. *International Journal of Intelligent Systems,* 7(7), 623-636.

Shen, W.-M. 1994. *Autonomous Learning from the Environment.* New York: Computer Science Press

Simoudis, E.; Livezey, B.; and Kerber, R. 1994. Integrating Inductive and Deductive Reasoning for Database Mining. In Knowledge Discovery in Databases: Papers from the 1994 AAAI Workshop, 37–48. AAAI Tech. Rep. WS-94-03, Menlo Park, Calif.

Theime, S. 1989. The Acquisition of Model-Knowledge for a Model-Driven Machine Learning Approach. In *Knowledge Representation and Organization in Machine Learning,* ed. K. Morik. Berlin: Springer-Verlag.

Usznski, M. 1992.Machine Learning Toolbox, Technical Report, European Economic Community, Espirit II.

Zaniolo, C. 1992. Intelligent Databases: Old Challenges and New Opportunities. *Journal of Intelligent Information Systems,* 1: 271-292.

16 Attribute-Oriented Induction in Data Mining

Jiawei Han and Yongjian Fu
Simon Fraser University

Abstract

Attribute-oriented induction is a set-oriented database mining method which generalizes the task-relevant subset of data attribute-by-attribute, compresses it into a generalized relation, and extracts from it the general features of data. In this chapter, the power of attribute-oriented induction is explored for the extraction from relational databases of different kinds of patterns, including characteristic rules, discriminant rules, cluster description rules, and multiple-level association rules. Furthermore, it is shown that the method is efficient, robust, with wide applications, and extensible to knowledge discovery in advanced database systems, including object-oriented, deductive, and spatial database systems. The implementation status of DBMiner, a system prototype which applies the method, is also reported here.

16.1 Introduction

With an upsurge of the application demands and research activities on knowledge discovery in databases (Matheus, Chan and Piatetsky-Shapiro 1993; Piatetsky-Shapiro and Frawley 1991), an *attribute-oriented induction method* (Cai, Cercone and Han 1991; Han, Cai and Cercone 1993) has been developed as an interesting technique for mining knowledge from data. The method integrates a machine learning paradigm (Michalski 1983), especially learning-from-examples techniques, with database operations, extracts generalized rules from an interesting set of data, and discovers high-level data regularities.

The development of the attribute-oriented induction method is motivated by the following observations. First, although certain regularities, such as association rules, can be discovered and expressed at the primitive concept level by interesting data mining techniques (Piatetsky-Shapiro 1991; Agrawal, Imielinski and Swami 1993), stronger and often more interesting regularities can be discovered at high concept levels and expressed in concise terms. Thus it is often necessary to generalize low level primitive data in databases to relatively high level concepts for effective data mining. Second, since autonomous discovery often generates too many rules without focus, it is recommended to initiate a knowledge discovery process by a user's request which represents relatively constrained search on a specified subset of data for desired knowledge. Third, the availability of certain background knowledge, such as conceptual hierarchies, not only improves the efficiency of a discovery process but also expresses user's preference for guided generalization, which may lead to an efficient and desirable generalization process.

Based on these observations, a set-oriented, generalization-based induction method, called *attribute-oriented induction*, has been developed, which collects an interesting set of data as an initial data relation, performs on it the induction process including attribute removal, concept hierarchy ascension, generalization operator application, etc. attribute-by-attribute, eliminates duplications among generalized tuples (but with *counts* accumulated), and derives generalized relations and rules. The method has been implemented in a data mining system prototype, DBMINER (previously called DBLEARN, and been tested successfully against large relational databases.

In this chapter, the power of attribute-oriented induction in data mining is examined in two aspects: (1) attribute-oriented induction for mining different kinds of rules, including characteristic rules, discriminant rules, association rules, and cluster description rules, and (2) extension of the method for data mining in advanced database systems, including object-oriented, deductive, and spatial database systems. The study outlines the high potential of the method for efficient and effective knowledge discovery in large databases.

The remainder of the chapter is organized as follows. In Section 16.2, a brief summary of the methodologies of attribute-oriented induction is presented. In Section 16.3, the extraction of different kinds of rules by the induction method is examined. In Section 16.4, the extension of the method towards knowledge discovery in advanced database systems are discussed. The implementation of DBMINER is discussed in Section 16.5, and the study is summarized in Section 16.6. Because of the broad scope of the discussion, the chapter is descriptive in nature. More rigorous treatment can be found in the references.

16.2   A Brief Summary of Attribute-Oriented Induction Methodology

A data mining request should include the specification of the interesting subset of data and the kind of rules to be discovered, as shown in a DBMINER query below.

Example 16.1 The following query, presented in an SQL-like syntax, requests to use the database "NSERC94" (containing the information about 1994-1995 NSERC[1] research grants), and find a characteristic rule from two relations, award and organization, which satisfies the condition specified in the where-clause and in relevance to four attributes:

> province, amount, percentage(count), percentage(amount),

where $percentage(x) = x/total\_x\%$ (the ratio of x versus *total* x). A *characteristic rule* is an assertion that characterizes all or most of the data undergoing examination (called the *target class*).

```
use NSERC94
find characteristic rule for 'CS_Grants'
from award A, organization O
where A.org_code = O.org_code and A.disc_code = 'Computer Science'
      in relevance to province, amount, percentage(count),
      percentage(amount)
```

The process first collects the interesting set of data (target class) by executing an SQL query based on the condition specified in the where-clause which contains a high-level concept "Computer Science." Since the database stores only the detailed discipline code such as 25502 for "database management," the concept hierarchy for discipline code should be consulted in the data retrieval. Similarly, concept hierarchies should be consulted in the generalization of data in the attributes province and amount.

A *concept hierarchy* defines a sequence of mappings from a set of concepts to their higher-level correspondences. It is usually partially ordered according to a general-to-specific ordering, with the most general concept usually defined by a reserved word "*any*" and the most specific concepts corresponding to the specific data in the database.

---

[1]the Natural Sciences and Engineering Research Council of Canada

Concept hierarchies represent necessary background knowledge which directs the generalization process. Using a concept hierarchy, the discovered rules can be represented in terms of generalized concepts and stated in a simple and explicit form, which is desirable to most users.

Many concept hierarchies, such as `geo_location(city, province, country)`, are stored in the database implicitly, which can be made explicit by specifying certain attribute mapping rules. Some hierarchies can be provided by knowledge engineers or domain experts, which is reasonable even for large databases since a concept hierarchy registers only the *distinct* discrete attribute values or ranges of numerical values for an attribute, which is, in general, not very large. To certain extent, concept hierarchies can also be generated automatically (Fisher 1987; Chu and Chiang 1994) based on data semantics and/or data distribution statistics. Moreover, a given concept hierarchy may not be best suited for a particular learning task, which therefore often needs to be dynamically refined for desired learning results (Han and Fu 1994).

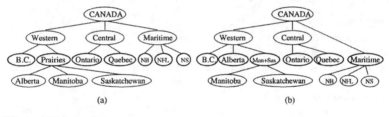

(a)   (b)

Figure 16.1
The given and refined concept hierarchies for the attribute "province."

Example 16.2 The given concept hierarchy for *province*, based on the geographic and administrative regions of Canada (Figure 16.1a), may not reflect the characteristics of research grant distribution of Computer Science in Canada. Such a hierarchy needs to be dynamically refined based on the query, attribute threshold (the desired number of higher level attribute values), and data distribution. The refinement is performed by identifying and promoting "big" nodes and grouping the small ones while maximally preserving the original shape of the hierarchy (thus the semantic meaning) (Han and Fu 1994). The refined hierarchy for the query of Example 16.1 is described in Figure 16.1b.

Different concept hierarchies can be constructed on the same attribute based on different viewpoints or preferences. For example, the birthplace can be organized according to administrative regions, geographic locations, size of cities, etc. Usually, a popularly referenced hierarchy is associated with an attribute as the default one. Other hierarchies can be chosen explicitly by users in a data mining process. A concept hierarchy can also be in the shape of lattice or DAG (directed acyclic graph). Moreover, it is sometimes preferable to perform induction in parallel along with more than one hierarchy and select a promising one based on some intermediate generalization results.

16.2.1   Attribute-Oriented Induction for Mining Characteristic Rules

The attribute-oriented induction method is examined here using the DBMINER query presented in Example 16.1.

In a generalized relation, some or all of its attribute values are generalized data, that is, nonleaf nodes in the concept hierarchies. It is usually desired that an attribute in a (generalized) relation contains only a small number of distinct values. A system may set a small integer as a default, desired *attribute threshold* for each attribute, which should be adjustable by users, because a user may know better which particular attribute should have more distinct values (thus a larger threshold) than others. An attribute is at the desirable level if it contains no more distinct values than its attribute threshold. Moreover, the attribute is at the *minimum desirable level* if it would contain more distinct values than the threshold when it were specialized to a level lower than the current one. A particular generalized relation R' of an initial relation R is the *prime relation* of R if every attribute in R' is at the minimum desirable level. Besides threshold control, one may also allow a user to specify explicitly a level in the hierarchy as the level to be generalized.

For mining characteristic rules, the attribute-oriented induction is performed in the following steps (Han and Fu 1994).

1. *Initial data collection:* The learning request is transformed into an SQL query and executed to collect the set of data relevant to the learning task (as an initial relation).

2. *Derivation of the generalization plan for each attribute:* If there is a large set of distinct values in an attribute of the initial relation, the attribute should be generalized by either attribute removal or attribute generalization. The former is performed when there is

no generalization operator on the attribute, or its higher-level concepts are expressed in another attribute. The latter is performed otherwise by (1) determining the *prime level* (generalized) concepts for each attribute, which is the level (possibly determined after the refinement of concept hierarchy) that makes the number of distinct generalized values just within its attribute threshold, and (2) linking them with the data in the initial relation to form generalization pairs.

3. *Prime relation derivation:* Perform attribute-oriented generalization, by substituting lower level concepts with its corresponding prime level concepts, which leads to a prime relation, by eliminating duplicated tuples and accumulating the counts in the retained generalized tuples.

The method described above integrates relational database operations with attribute-oriented generalization and leads to an efficient induction process. Step 1 is a typical relational query whose optimization relies on the well-developed relational technology. Let the initial relation and the derived prime relation contain n and p tuples respectively. Step 2 involves one scan (or less if a sampling technique is adopted) of the initial relation, with the worst-case time complexity of $O(n)$. Step 3 scans the initial relation, generalizes the relation attribute by attribute, and inserts generalized tuples into the result relation, which takes $O(n)$ time if p is small, or $O(n \log p)$ time if the tuples in the result relation are ordered and a binary or tree-based search is applied.

Conceptually, the induction process described above can be viewed as a data generalization and compression process, which compresses an initial relation into a usually much smaller prime relation expressed at high concept levels.

Knowledge rules or general data distributions can be extracted from the prime relation by statistics and/or machine learning tools. There are many techniques for extraction of interesting generalized information from a prime relation:

1. *Direct presentation of the prime relation.* This is effective if the prime relation is small. Otherwise, further reduction of the prime relation is often desirable.

2. *Reduction of the number of attributes in the prime relation.* A simple method is to project on different sets of attributes to extract different

generalized feature tables. Example 16.3 shows a prime relation and a feature table for `count%` in relevance to `amount` and `province`. Moreover, many techniques developed in previous studies on machine learning (Michalski, Carbonell and Mitchell 1986), statistics, fuzzy set and rough set theories (Ziarko 1994), etc. can be applied to the evaluation of the importance of different sets of attributes and projection on the appropriate ones.

3. *Further generalization of the prime relation.* A *relation threshold* can be specified (or set by default) to indicate the maximum number of tuples that the *final generalized relation* should contain. There are usually alternative choices to select a candidate attribute for further generalization. The interestingness of the final generalized relation relies on the selection of the attributes to be generalized and the selection of generalization operators, based on data semantics, user preference, generalization efficiency, etc. Criteria, such as the preference of a larger reduction ratio on the number of tuples or the number of distinct attribute values, the simplicity of the final discovered rules, etc., can also be used for selection.

The above discussion shows that knowledge rules can be represented in the form of generalized relations, generalized feature tables, or generalized rule(s), in which a tuple in the generalized relation is transformed into conjunctive normal form, and multiple tuples are transformed into disjunctive normal form. Interesting rules can often be discovered by following different paths leading to several generalized relations for comparison. Following different paths corresponds to the way in which different people may learn differently from the same set of examples. The generalized relations can be examined by users or experts interactively to filter out trivial rules and preserve interesting ones (Zytkow and Baker 1991). Therefore, a user-friendly graphical interface is implemented in DBMINER for users to try different alternatives for interactive mining of desired rules.

Example 16.3 Following Example 16.1, part of an original relation, `award`, is shown in Table 16.1. Part of the prime relation is in Table 16.2. A feature table of `count%` extracted from Table 16.2 is in Table 16.3. Each entry in Table 16.3 represents the percentage of the `count` of the corresponding "feature" (pattern) with respect to the `total count`.

16.2.2   Feasibility of Attribute-Oriented Induction

A major strength of attribute-oriented induction over tuple-oriented induction is its efficiency in the induction process. The former performs generalization on each attribute *uniformly* for all the tuples in the initial relation in the formation of the prime relation, which contrasts with the latter that explores different possible combinations for a large number of tuples in the same generalization phase. An exploration of different possible generalization paths for different tuples at the early generalization stage will not be productive since these combinations will be merged in further generalization. Different possible combinations should be explored only when the relation has been generalized to a relatively small prime relation.

Table 16.1
A portion of the original table *award*.

grantee_id	name	department	org_code	year	amount	⋯
156274	BAERLOCHER FJ	Biology	1620	1994	16000	⋯
⋯	⋯	⋯	⋯	⋯	⋯	⋯

Table 16.2
A portion of the *prime relation*.

amount	province	count%	amount%
0-20Ks	Alberta	4.53%	3.26%
0-20Ks	British Columbia	7.41%	4.64%
⋯	⋯	⋯	⋯

Table 16.3
A feature table of *count%* extracted from Table 16.2.

amount	province						total %
	Al.	B.C.	Mar.	Ontario	Queb.	Sas+Man	
0-20Ks	4.53	7.41	6.79	24.49	13.79	3.70	60.70
20Ks-40Ks	3.70	5.35	1.03	12.76	5.14	1.65	29.63
40Ks-60Ks	0.21	1.23	0.00	5.14	1.03	0.00	7.61
60Ks-	0.21	0.21	0.00	1.23	0.21	0.21	2.06
Total	8.64	14.20	7.82	43.62	20.16	5.56	100.00

Attribute-oriented induction is robust and handles noise and/or exceptional cases elegantly because it incorporates statistical information (using count) and generates disjunctive rules. The association of count with each disjunct leads naturally to learning *approximate rules*, for which the conditions with negligible weight can be dropped in generalization and rule formation since a negligible weight implies a minimal influence to the conclusion.

Count association facilitates incremental learning (Fisher 1987) in large databases as well: when a new tuple is inserted into a database, its concepts (attribute values) are first generalized to the same concept level as those in the generalized relation and then merged naturally into the generalized relation.

Furthermore, with the association of count information, data sampling (Kivinen and Mannila 1994) and parallelism can be explored in knowledge discovery. Attribute-oriented induction can be performed by sampling a subset of data from a huge set of relevant data or by first performing induction in parallel on several partitions of the relevant data set and then merging the generalized results.

As a generalization-based method, attribute-oriented induction confines its power to the discovery of knowledge rules at general concept levels. There are applications which require the discovery of knowledge at primitive concept levels, such as finding (primitive) association or dependency rules, or finding functional relationships (e.g., "$y = f(x)$") between two numerical attributes (e.g., height and weight). Attribute-oriented induction does not suit such applications. Moreover, attribute-oriented induction needs reasonably informative concept hierarchies for generalization of nonnumerical attributes, and over-generalization should be guarded against by setting thresholds flexibly and/or interactively. Nevertheless, the method is useful in most database-oriented applications which need to generalize some or all of the relevant attributes.

16.3 Discovery of Different Kinds of Rules

Besides mining characteristic rules, attribute-oriented induction can be used to discover discriminant rules, cluster description rules, and multilevel association rules, as illustrated in this subsection. Moreover, other kinds of rules, including data evolution regularities and deviation rules, can also be discovered based on the similar philosophy.

16.3.1 Mining Discriminant Rules

A *discriminant rule* is an assertion which discriminates concepts of the class being examined (the *target class*) from other classes (called *con-*

trasting classes). For example, to distinguish one disease from others, a discriminant rule should summarize the symptoms that discriminate this disease from others.

A discriminant rule can be discovered by generalizing the data in both target class and contrasting class(es) *synchronously* in an attribute-oriented fashion and excluding the properties that overlap in both classes in the generalized rule. Usually, a property, which is quite good at discriminating a class, may still have minor overlaps with other classes in a large data set. Thus it is often preferable to associate quantitative information with a rule or with the tuples in a generalized relation to indicate how precisely a property can be used to distinguish a target class from others. Such a quantitative measurement, called *discriminating weight* (Han, Cai and Cercone 1993), can be defined as the ratio of the frequency that a property occurring in the target class versus that occurring in both (target and contrasting) classes. Obviously, a property with a discriminating weight close to 1 is a good discriminator; whereas that close to 0 is a negative discriminator (the properties unlikely occurring in the target class).

Based on these considerations, the method for discovery of discriminant rules is outlined as follows.

1. Collect the relevant set of data respectively into the target class and the contrasting classes.

2. Extract the *prime target relation* (the prime relation corresponding to the initial relation in the target class) in a similar way as the attribute-oriented induction at learning characteristic rules. Then generalize the concepts of the initial relation(s) in the contrasting class(es) to the same level as those in the prime target relation, which results in the *prime contrasting relation(s)*.

3. To generate qualitative discriminant rules, compare the tuples in the prime target relation against those in the prime contrasting relation(s), and mark those tuples which overlap in both relations. The discriminating properties are represented by the unmarked tuples.

4. To generate quantitative discriminant rules, compute the discriminating weight for each property and output the properties whose discriminating weight is close to 1 (together with the discriminating weight).

This method summarizes the major differences of a target class from a contrasting class at a high concept level. Notice that machine learning techniques, such as a decision-tree method like ID3 (Quinlan 1986) and C4.5 (Quinlan 1992), have been used to classify objects and find discriminating behaviors. To these algorithms, the attribute-oriented induction can be viewed as a preprocessing stage which performs a preliminary generalization using domain knowledge (such as concept hierarchies) to make rules expressible at a relatively high concept level to achieve both processing efficiency and representation clarity. Examples in ID3 or C4.5 algorithms assume that concepts to be classified are already at a relatively high level, such as "mild" (temperature) and "high" (humidity) (Quinlan 1986), which may not be the cases for the actual data stored in large databases but can be easily achieved by attribute-oriented generalization. After such generalization, one may choose either presenting directly the characteristic and/or discriminant rules as described above (which are in the relational form, desirable for some applications, and allowing the same tuples appearing in different classes but with weights associated), or integrating with an ID3-like algorithm for further concept classification and compact rule generation.

16.3.2   Mining Cluster Description Rules

In a large database, it is often desirable to cluster data according to data semantics (called *conceptual clustering* (Michalski and Stepp 1983)) and associate (description) rules with such clusters. For example, students in a university can be clustered (i.e., classified) based on different attribute(s), including major, age, height, academic performance, etc., however, clustering on one attribute may generate more meaningful and concise descriptions than that on another. It is important to determine desired classifying attribute(s) and desired concept level(s) for conceptual clustering in a particular set of data.

Attribute-oriented induction can be applied to conceptual clustering as follows (Han, Cai and Cercone 1991). First, the interested set of data is collected by a database query, and the attribute-oriented induction generalizes the set of data to an appropriate high concept level, which results in a generalized relation. Second, this generalized relation is mapped into a table with the generalized attribute values as rows and columns, and the occurrence frequency (i.e., *count*) as the table entry value. After filtering out the entries with very low frequency (treated as noise), the nonempty entries can be merged into bigger slots and mapped into a set of candidate schemes with each corresponding to a set of rules to be generated. Based on a combined measurement of *sparseness* (the problem space covered by the generated rules but not covered by the evidence data) and *complexity* of the generated rules, the candidate scheme which minimizes the combined measurement can be selected as the *classifying scheme*, and the set of rules which distinguish one class from others can be associated with the class, as *cluster description rules*. Such a process iterates until no further classification effort is necessary.

This iterative process leads to the generation of a preferred hierarchy for the interested set of data, with a set of description rules associated with each node of the hierarchy.

An alternative (but of the same spirit) conceptual clustering method is to first perform attribute-oriented induction as described above, and then construct a decision tree from the generalized relation using a method similar to ID3 (Quinlan 1986) and associate the corresponding rules with each node in the tree.

16.3.3   Mining Multiple-Level Association Rules

An *association rule* represents an association relationship among a set of patterns (values) in a database (Agrawal, Imielinski and Swami 1993). For example, an association rule discovered from a shopping transaction database may disclose that a customer who buys milk will have 90% possibility to buy bread as well.

The association relationship can be characterized by *support* σ and *confidence* φ. The support of pattern A occurring in set S is denoted as $\sigma(A/S)$. The confidence that "if A occurs in S, then B occurs in S" can be derived by the formula, $\varphi((A \rightarrow B)/S) = \sigma((A \wedge B)/S)/\sigma(A/S)$.

In a database with a large number of concrete patterns, there may not exist many *strong* associations (i.e., with *large* support and *high* confidence) between concrete patterns. However, there may exist many interesting association relationships for the patterns at high concept levels. For example, although there may not exist noticeable associations between particular brands, categories, and sizes of milk and bread, there may exist strong evidence to associate milk and bread together. Therefore, it is interesting to generalize patterns to different concept levels and discover multiple-level association rules.

The following algorithm demonstrates a top-down technique (from a high level to lower ones) for deriving multiple-level association rules: find all the large patterns $A_1, \ldots, A_m$ in set S (i.e., $\sigma(A_1 \wedge \ldots \wedge A_m/S) \geq \sigma_l$, where σ_l is the minimum support at level l). Notice that a user may set different σ_l's at different levels based on data characteristics or search interests and adjust them interactively based on the patterns returned.

1. Collect the task-relevant set S from the database by a query, and generalize the data in S to a high concept level by attribute-oriented induction.

2. At this concept level, search S to find large single-item sets. Combine them to form candidate large two-item sets and check against the database to find large two-item sets, and so on, until all the large k-item sets are found.

3. Go down one level l, find all the large item sets at level l based on the same method of Step 2 for all the children of the large items at level $l - 1$, i.e., one level higher.

4. Progressively walk down the hierarchy to find large item sets at each level until no large one-item set is found or it reaches the leaf level of the hierarchy.

The method first finds large patterns at a high concept level and progressively deepens the search to find such patterns among their descendants at lower concept levels until it reaches the primitive-level concepts in the database. Notice that the search at a lower concept level is confined to only those patterns whose ancestors have passed the testing at their corresponding higher concept levels. Also, the corresponding rules in the form of "$A_1 \wedge A_k \rightarrow A_m$" (and their confidence ratios) can be derived straightforwardly. A detailed algorithm is presented in Han and Fu (1995).

16.4   Towards Knowledge Discovery in Advanced Database Systems

In this section, we briefly examine the extension of attribute-oriented induction to knowledge discovery in advanced and/or special purpose databases, including object-oriented, deductive, and spatial databases.

16.4.1   Attribute-Oriented Induction in Object-Oriented Databases

An object-oriented database organizes a large set of complex objects into classes which are in turn organized into class/subclass hierarchies with rich data semantics. Each object in a class is associated with (1) an object-identifier, (2) a set of attributes which may contain sophisticated data structures, set- or list- valued data, class composition hierarchies, multimedia data, etc., and (3) a set of methods which specify the computational routines or rules associated with the object class.

Knowledge discovery in object-oriented databases can be performed by first generalizing a set of complex data components into relatively simple generalized concepts and then applying the attribute-oriented induction method to generalize them into a generalized prime relation (Han, Nishio and Kawano 1994).

To facilitate generalization of complex data objects, it is important to implement efficiently a set of generalization operators on the components of object-oriented databases, including object identifiers, unstructured and structure values, class composition hierarchies, inherited and derived data, methods, etc., illustrated as follows.

1. **Generalization of object identifiers**: Since objects belong to certain classes which in turn are organized into certain class/subclass hierarchies, an object identifier can be first generalized to its corresponding lowest subclass name which can in turn be generalized to a higher level class/subclass name by climbing up the class/subclass hierarchy.

2. **Generalization of structured data**: The generalization of complex structure-valued data, such as set-valued or list-valued data and data with nested structures, can be explored in several ways in order to extract interesting patterns. Take set-valued attributes as an example. A set-valued attribute can be typically generalized in two ways: (1) generalization of each value in a set into its corresponding higher level concepts, or (2) derivation of the general behavior of a set, such as the number of elements in the set, the types or value ranges in the set, the weighted average for numerical data, etc. For example, the *hobby* of a person, such as {*tennis, hockey, chess, violin, nintendo*}, can be generalized into a set of high level concepts, such as {*sports, music, computer_games*}, or into 5 (the number of hobbies in the set), etc.

3. Generalization on inherited and derived properties: In an OODB, an attribute or a method in an object class may not be explicitly specified in the class itself but is inherited from its higher level classes or derivable (computable) by applying some deduction rules or methods. From the knowledge discovery point of view, it is unnecessary to distinguish the data stored within the class from those inherited from its superclass(es) or derived using rules or methods. As long as the set of relevant data are collected by query processing, the knowledge discovery process will treat them in the same way as those stored in the object class and perform generalization accordingly.

4. Generalization on class composition hierarchies: An attribute value in an object may itself be an object, whose attributes may in turn be composed by other objects, thus forming a class composition hierarchy. Generalization on a class composition hierarchy can be viewed as generalization on a set of (possibly infinite, if the nesting is recursive) nested structured data. Although the reference to a composite object may traverse via a long sequence of references along the corresponding class composition hierarchy, the longer sequence it traverses, the weaker semantic linkage between the original object and its referenced ones in most cases. Therefore, in order to discover relatively interesting knowledge, generalization should be performed only on the composite objects closely related to the currently focused class(es) but not on those which have only remote and rather weak semantic linkages.

Besides object-oriented data generalization, attribute-oriented induction can also be applied to schema formation and schema evolution in object-oriented databases. This can be done by first generalizing object-oriented data and then performing conceptual clustering on the generalized data, a process similar to mining cluster description rules discussed in Section 16.3.2.

16.4.2   Integration of Knowledge Discovery and Deductive Database Techniques

A *deductive database* is a database which consists of data, rules, and integrity constraints and performs deductive reasoning on large sets of data. Integration of deduction and induction mechanisms not only leads to discovery of new knowledge in deductive databases but also enhances the power of knowledge discovery mechanisms.

There are at least four cases that a knowledge discovery mechanism may interact with the deductive database technology.

1. *Data derived by applying deduction rules:* With the availability of deduction rules, new data can be derived by deductive query processing. Knowledge discovery can be performed on the data so derived, which is the case that deduction rules are used for the collection of the task-relevant set of data; whereas the knowledge discovery mechanism itself remains intact.

2. *Rules representing (partially) generalized data:* With the availability of conceptual hierarchy and knowledge discovery mechanisms, it is possible that a deduction rule plays the role of a generalized rule which defines a portion of generalized data. If a knowledge discovery query is to discover the regularity of a set of data which is a superset of the data covered by the rule, the rule can be merged with the corresponding (intermediate) generalized relation of the other portion of the data for further generalization.

3. *Deduction rule-specified concept hierarchy:* A rule may also be used to specify concept hierarchies (Dhar and Tuzhilin 1993). For example, a rule which claims that "*a student is excellent if (s)he is an undergraduate student with GPA $\geq$ 3.5 or if (s)he is a graduate student with GPA $\geq$ 3.75*" defines a portion of the concept hierarchy for the attribute GPA. Such a rule can be stored as a part of the concept hierarchy and be used in generalization (Cheung, Fu and Han 1994).

4. *Rule-directed knowledge discovery:* Certain rules can be used for directing a knowledge discovery process. For example, "$A \wedge B \rightarrow C$" can be used as a meta-rule to inform the system to find rules in such a logical form from a large set of data (Shen et al. 1994). A rule "*buy milk $\rightarrow$ buy bread*" can be used as a guide for finding similar kinds of rules, which may result in the association of credibility with the rule, such as "*if one buys milk, there is a 90% possibility that (s)he will buy bread*" or deepening the rule by associating it with lower level concepts, such as "*if one buys 2% Dairyland milk, there is a 45% possibility that (s)he will buy Wonder whole wheat bread.*"

16.4.3   Attribute-Oriented Induction in Spatial Databases

A *spatial database* system stores, manages and manipulates spatial (i.e., space-related) data and, in most cases, nonspatial data as well for geographic information systems and many other applications (Elmasri and Navathe 1994).

Spatial data mining refers to the discovery of interesting relationships between spatial and nonspatial data and/or among spatial data in spatial databases. An example for the former (spatial-nonspatial) is the finding of weather patterns related to different geographic regions; whereas that for the latter is the finding of general spatial relationships (e.g., nearby, far-away, etc.) between service stations and highways.

The discovery of general relationships between spatial and nonspatial data can be performed by attribute-oriented induction in two ways: (1) spatial-dominant generalization, and (2) nonspatial-dominant generalization.

The *spatial-dominant generalization* first performs generalization on task-relevant spatial data using user/expert-provided spatial data hierarchies (such as geographic regions, etc.), hierarchical spatial data structures (such as R-trees, quad-trees, etc.), or spatial clustering algorithms (Ng and Han 1994) to generalize or cluster spatial data, and then generalize the nonspatial data associated with each spatial cluster or partition.

On the other hand, the *nonspatial-dominant generalization* first performs attribute-oriented induction on task-relevant, nonspatial data—which generalizes nonspatial primitives to high level concepts and merges database tuples and their associated spatial data pointers into a small number of generalized entries. Then spatial merging operations can be performed on the spatial data in each generalized entry to form a small number of merged spatial entities (e.g., regions) for each entry.

Example 16.4 Weather patterns related to geographic regions in British Columbia can be discovered by either spatial-dominant or nonspatial-dominant generalization.

The former merges scattered small regions into several major regions in the province (based on the administrative or geographic hierarchies), which partitions accordingly the associated nonspatial data, such as temperature and precipitation. Attribute-oriented induction can then be performed on each partition to extract general weather patterns associated with each generalized region.

The latter generalizes the climate data, such as temperature and precipitation, into a small number of generalized entries (such as wet and cold), or concrete range values, which collects the associated spatial data pointers when merging nonspatial components. Then spatial merging (or region growing) can be performed on the spatial entities in the same generalized entry.

The selection of the two methods can be based on the availability of background knowledge, generalization efficiency, and the preference of generalization results.

Besides concept tree ascension and spatial data handling techniques, aggregation and approximation play an important role in spatial data mining. When generalizing scattered regions into clustered regions, it is necessary not only to merge or cluster the regions of similar types within the same general class but also to ignore some scattered regions with different types if they are unimportant to the study. For example, different pieces of land for different agricultural usages can be merged into one large piece of land by spatial merge. However, such an agricultural land may contain highways, houses, small stores, etc. If the majority land is used for agriculture, the scattered spots for other purposes can be ignored, and the whole region can be claimed as an agricultural area by approximation.

16.5   Integration of Attribute-Oriented Induction with DBMS

Based on the methodology of attribute-oriented induction, a data mining system prototype, DBMINER, has been developed in our research and integrated with commercial relational database systems.

Figure 16.2 shows the configuration of the DBMINER system, which consists of several major modules, including graphical user interface, knowledge discovery, concept hierarchy manipulation, and SQL server modules. These modules are tightly coupled together for efficient, set-oriented processing.

The system has the following main features. First, it integrates data mining with relational database systems and provides an SQL-like knowl-

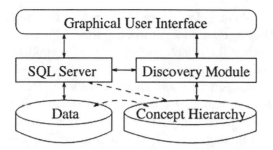

Figure 16.2
The configuration of the DBMINER system.

edge discovery interface for relational system-based data retrieval and relational operation-based data generalization, and thus facilitates its integration with the existing commercial relational database systems. Second, a graphical user interface has been constructed for the specification of parameters and for flexible and interactive data mining. Moreover, the system can perform automatic generation of concept hierarchies for numeric data and dynamic adjustment of hierarchies based on data statistics.

The prototype is implemented in C on the UNIX system, using a client-server architecture, accessing relational databases via a Sybase server. A PC database system-based version is also under construction and experimentation. Experiments have been conducted on relational databases, including NSERC research grant databases and several very large ones provided by industry firms, with good performance and satisfactory results. The system has also been used for experiments on spatial data mining. The system discovers successfully the characteristic rules and discriminant rules. The extraction of other kinds of rules in relational database systems is currently under implementation and experimentation.

16.6   Conclusions

We have explored in this chapter the power of an interesting induction method, the attribute-oriented induction, in data mining. As a set-oriented, generalization-based data mining method, attribute-oriented induction extracts effectively different kinds of knowledge rules, including characteristic rules, discriminant rules, cluster description rules, and multiple-level association rules in relational database systems. Furthermore, it is shown that the method is efficient, robust, with wide applications, and extensible to knowledge discovery in advanced database systems, including object-oriented, deductive, and spatial databases. However, the method is a generalization-based technique and requires the availability of some background knowledge (such as concept hierarchies). Thus it may not be suitable for mining knowledge without generalization or without background knowledge.

Knowledge discovered by attribute-oriented induction has interesting applications at querying database knowledge, cooperative query answering, multiple layered database construction, and semantic query optimization, as reported in our previous studies (Han, Fu and Ng 1994). In general, data mining provides a powerful tool for automatic generation and verification of knowledge in the construction of large knowledgebases.

Knowledge discovery represents an important and promising direction in the development of data and knowledge-base systems. Our preliminary study of the attribute-oriented induction mechanism leads to an efficient implementation of a data mining system. Besides further advance of our study on the attribute-oriented induction methodology, we are also investigating other data mining methods (Agrawal, Imielinski and Swami 1993; Chu and Chiang 1994; Kivinen and Mannila 1994; Matheus, Chan and Piatetsky-Shapiro 1993; Michalski et al. 1992; Piatetsky-Shapiro and Frawley 1991; Shen et al. 1994; Uthurusamy, Fayyad and Spangler 1991; Ziarko 1994) and working on the integrated method for discovery of various kinds of knowledge in different kinds of database and information systems.

Acknowledgments

Research is partially supported by the Natural Sciences and Engineering Research Council of Canada under the grant OGP0037230 and by the Networks of Centres of Excellence Program (with the participation of PRECARN association) under the grant IRIS-HMI-5. The authors would like to express their thanks to Yandong Cai and Yue Huang for their implementations of the early versions of the DBLEARN system and their experiments of the attribute-oriented induction method for knowledge discovery in relational databases. Also, the authors would like to express their thanks to them and to Colin Carter, Nick Cercone, David Cheung, Son Dao, Ada Fu, Randy Goebel, Howard Hamilton, Xiaohua Hu, Hiroyuki Kawano, Rizwan Kheraj, Kris Koperski, Peter Leung, Ling Liu, Wei Lu, Gabor Melli, Wendy Moore, Raymond T. Ng, Shojiro Nishio, Beng-Chin Ooi, Simon Tang, Wei Wang, and Osmar R. Zaïane for their discussions on the research issues related to knowledge discovery in databases, and finally, to Gregory Piatetsky-Shapiro whose comments have substantially improved the quality of this chapter.

References

Agrawal, R.; Imielinski, T.; and Swami, A. 1993. Mining Association Rules Between Sets of Items in Large Databases. In Proceedings of the ACM-SIGMOD International Conference on Management of Data, 207–216, Washington, D.C.: ACM Press.

Cai, Y.; Cercone, N.; and Han, J. 1991. Attribute-Oriented Induction in Relational Databases. In *Knowledge Discovery in Databases,* ed. G. Piatetsky-Shapiro and W. J. Frawley, 213–228. Menlo Park, Calif.: AAAI Press.

Cheung, D. W.; Fu, A. W.-C.; and Han., J. 1994. Knowledge Discovery in Databases: A Rule-Based Attribute-Oriented Approach. In Proceedings of the International Symposium on Methodologies for Intelligent Systems, 164-173, Charlotte, North Carolina.

Chu, W. W.; and Chiang, K. 1994. Abstraction of High Level Concepts from Numerical Values in Databases. In Knowledge Discovery in Databases: Papers from the 1994 AAAI Workshop, 37–48. AAAI Tech. Rep. WS-94-03, Menlo Park, Calif.

Dhar, V.; and Tuzhilin, A. 1993. Abstract-Driving Pattern Discovery in Databases. *IEEE Transactions on Knowledge and Data Engineering,* 5 (6): 926–938.

Elmasri, R.; and Navathe, S. B. 1994. *Fundamentals of Database Systems, Second Edition.* Menlo Park, Calif. Benjamin/Cummings.

Fisher, D. H. 1987. Knowledge Acquisition Via Incremental Conceptual Clustering. *Machine Learning,* 2:139–172.

Han, J.,; Cai, Y.; and Cercone, N. 1991. Concept-Based Data Classification in Relational Databases. Presented at the 1991 AAAI Workshop on Knowledge Discovery in Databases, Anaheim, Calif.

Han, J.; Cai, Y.; and Cercone, N. 1993. Data-Driven Discovery of Quantitative Rules in Relational Databases. *IEEE Transactions on Knowledge and Data Engineering*, 5: 29–40.

Han, J.; and Fu, Y. 1995. Discovery of Multiple-Level Association Rules from Large Databases. In Proceedings of the International Conference on Very Large Data Bases, 420–431. Zurich, Switzerland.

Han, J.; and Fu, Y. 1994. Dynamic Generation and Refinement of Concept Hierarchies for Knowledge Discovery in Databases. In Knowledge Discovery in Databases: Papers from the 1994 AAAI Workshop, 157–168. AAAI Tech. Rep. WS-94-03, Menlo Park, Calif.

Han, J.; Fu, Y.; and Ng, R. 1994. Cooperative Query Answering Using Multiple-Layered Databases. In Proceedings of the Second International Conference on Cooperative Information Systems, 47–58. Toronto, Canada.

Han, J.; Nishio, S.; and Kawano, H. 1994. Knowledge Discovery in Object-Oriented and Active Databases. In *Knowledge Building and Knowledge Sharing*, ed. F. Fuchi and T. Yokoi, 221–230. Ohmsha, Ltd. and IOS Press.

Kivinen, J.; and Mannila, H. 1994. The Power of Sampling in Knowledge Discovery. In Proceedings of the Thirteenth ACM Symposium on Principles of Database Systems, 77–85. Minneapolis, Minn.: ACM Press.

Matheus, C.; Chan, P. K.; and Piatetsky-Shapiro, G. 1993. Systems for Knowledge Discovery in Databases. *IEEE Transactions on Knowledge and Data Engineering*, 5 (6): 903–913.

Michalski, R. S. 1983. A Theory and Methodology of Inductive Learning. In *Machine Learning: An Artificial Intelligence Approach, Vol. 1*, ed. Michalski et al., 83–134. San Francisco: Morgan Kaufmann.

Michalski, R. S.; Carbonell, J. G.; and Mitchell, T. M. 1986. *Machine Learning, An Artificial Intelligence Approach, Vol. 2*. San Francisco: Morgan Kaufmann.

Michalski, R. S.; Kerschberg, L.; Kaufman, K. A.; and Ribeiro, J. S. 1992. Mining for Knowledge in Databases: The INLEN Architecture, Initial Implementation and First Results. *Journal, Intelligent Information Systems*, 1: 85–114.

Michalski, R. S.; and Stepp, R. 1983. Automated Construction of Classifications: Conceptual Clustering Versus Numerical Taxonomy. *IEEE Transactions Pattern Analysis and Machine Intelligence*, 5:396–410.

Ng, R.; and Han, J. 1994. Efficient and Effective Clustering Method for Spatial Data Mining. In Proceedings of the International Conference on Very Large Data Bases, 144–155, Santiago, Chile.

Piatetsky-Shapiro, G.; and Frawley, W. J. 1991. *Knowledge Discovery in Databases.* Menlo Park, Calif.: AAAI Press.

Piatetsky-Shapiro, G. 1991. Discovery, Analysis, and Presentation of Strong Rules. In *Knowledge Discovery in Databases,* ed. G. Piatetsky-Shapiro and W. J. Frawley, 229–238. Menlo Park, Calif.: AAAI Press.

Quinlan, J. R. 1992. *C4.5: Programs for Machine Learning.* San Francisco: Morgan Kaufmann.

Quinlan, J. R. 1986. Induction of Decision Trees. *Machine Learning,* 1: 81–106.

Shen, W.; Mitbander, B.; Ong, K.; and Zaniolo, C. 1994. Using Metaqueries to Integrate Inductive Learning and Deductive Database Technology. In Knowledge Discovery in Databases: Papers from the 1994 AAAI Workshop, 335–346. AAAI Tech. Rep. WS-94-03, Menlo Park, Calif.

Uthurusamy, R.; Fayyad, U. M.; and Spangler, S. 1991. Learning Useful Rules from Inconclusive Data. In *Knowledge Discovery in Databases,* ed. G. Piatetsky-Shapiro and W. J. Frawley, 141–158. Menlo Park, Calif.: AAAI Press.

Ziarko, W. 1994. *Rough Sets, Fuzzy Sets and Knowledge Discovery.* Berlin: Springer-Verlag.

Zytkow J.; and Baker, J. 1991. Interactive Mining of Regularities in Databases. In *Knowledge Discovery in Databases,* ed. G. Piatetsky-Shapiro and W. J. Frawley, 31–54. Menlo Park, Calif.: AAAI Press.

VI NEXT GENERATION DATABASE SYSTEMS

17 Using Inductive Learning To Generate Rules for Semantic Query Optimization

Chun-Nan Hsu and Craig A. Knoblock
University of Southern California

Abstract

Semantic query optimization can dramatically speed up database query answering by knowledge intensive reformulation. But the problem of how to learn the required semantic rules has not been previously solved. This chapter presents a learning approach to solving this problem. In our approach, the learning is triggered by user queries. Then the system uses an inductive learning algorithm to generate semantic rules. This inductive learning algorithm can automatically select useful join paths and attributes to construct rules from a database with many relations. The learned semantic rules are effective for optimization because they will match query patterns and reflect data regularities. Experimental results show that this approach learns sufficient rules for optimization that produces a substantial cost reduction.

17.1   Introduction

This chapter presents an approach to learning semantic knowledge for semantic query optimization (SQO). SQO optimizes a query by using semantic rules, such as *all Maltese seaports have railroad access*, to reformulate a query into a less expensive but equivalent query. For example, suppose we have a query to *find all Maltese seaports with railroad access and 2,000,000 ft³ of storage space*. From the rule given above, we can reformulate the query so that there is no need to check the railroad access of seaports, which may save some execution time. Many SQO algorithms have been developed (Hammer and Zdonik 1980; King 1981; Shekhar et al. 1988; Shenoy and Ozsoyoglu 1989). Average savings from 20 to 40 percent using hand-coded knowledge are reported in the literature.

A learning approach to automatic acquisition of semantic knowledge is crucial to SQO. Most of the previous work in SQO assumes that semantic knowledge is given. King (1981) proposed using *semantic integrity constraints* given by database programmers to address the knowledge acquisition problem. An example of semantic integrity constraints is that *Only female patients can be pregnant*. However, integrity constraints do not reflect properties of data that affect the query execution cost, such as, relation sizes and distributions of attribute values. Moreover, integrity constraints rarely match query patterns. It is difficult to encode semantic knowledge that both reflects database properties and matches query patterns. The approach presented in this chapter uses example queries to trigger the learning so as to match query patterns, and induces effective semantic rules that reflect regularities of data.

Unlike most rule mining systems (Agrawal et al. 1993; Mannila et el. 1994), which are designed to derive rules from a single database table, our inductive learning algorithm can learn semantic rules from a database with many relations. Consider a database with three relations: person, car, and company. An interesting rule about persons might involve the companies they work for, or the cars they drive, or even the manufacturers of their cars. Our inductive learning algorithm can select relevant join paths and attributes automatically instead of requiring users to do this difficult and tedious task. With semantic rules describing regularities of joined relations, the SQO optimizer will be more effective because it is able to delete a redundant join or introduce new joins in a query.

The remainder of this chapter is organized as follows. The next section illustrates the problem of semantic query optimization for databases. Section 17.3 presents an overview of the learning approach. Section 17.4 describes our inductive learning algorithm for databases with many relations. Section 17.5 shows the experimental results of using learned knowledge in optimization. Section 17.6 surveys related work. Section 17.7 reviews the contributions and describes some future work.

17.2   Semantic Query Optimization

Semantic query optimization is applicable to different types of databases. Nevertheless, we chose the relational model to describe our approach because it is widely used in practice. The approach can be easily extended to other data models. In this chapter, a *database* consists of a set of relations. A *relation* is then a set of instances. Each *instance* is a vector of attribute values. The number of attributes is fixed for all instances in a relation. The values of attributes can be either a number or a string, but with a fixed type. Figure 17.1 shows the schema of an example database with two relations and their attributes. In this database, the relation geoloc stores data about geographic locations, and the attribute glc_cd is a geographic location code.

Although the basic SQO approach (King 1981) applies only to conjunctive queries, it can be extended to optimize complex queries with disjunctions, *group-by* or aggregate operators. The idea is that a complex query can be decomposed into conjunctive subqueries. The system can then apply SQO to optimize each subquery and propagate constraints among them for global optimization. We have developed such an SQO algorithm to optimize heterogeneous multidatabase query plans (Hsu and Knoblock 1993a). Rules learned for optimizing conjunctive queries can be used for optimizing complex queries. In this chapter, we will focus on the problem of learning and SQO for conjunctive queries.

The queries considered here are conjunctive Datalog queries, which corresponds to the select-from-where subset of SQL. A query begins with a predicate answer. There can be one or more arguments to answer. For example,

```
Q1: answer(?name):-
        geoloc(?name,?glc_cd,"Malta,"_,_),
        seaport(_,?glc_cd,?storage,_,_,_),
        ?storage > 1500000.
```

retrieves all geographical location names in Malta. There are two types of literals. The first type corresponds to a relation stored in a database. The second type consists of built-in predicates, such as > and member.

Semantic rules for query optimization are expressed in terms of Horn clauses. Semantic rules must be consistent with the data. To clearly distinguish a rule from a query, we show queries using the Prolog syntax and semantic rules in a standard logic notation. A set of example rules is also shown in Figure 17.1.

Rule R1 states that the latitude of a Maltese geographic location is greater than or equal to 35.89. R2 states that all Maltese geographic locations *in the database* are seaports. R3 states that all Maltese seaports have storage capacity greater than 2,000,000 ft^3. Based on these rules, we can infer five equivalent queries of Q1. Three of them are shown in Figure 17.2. Q21 is deduced from Q1 and R3. This is an example of *constraint deletion* reformulation. From R2, we can delete one more literal on seaport and infer that Q22 is also equivalent to Q1. In addition to deleting constraints, we can also add constraints to a query based on the semantic rules. For example, we can add a constraint on ?latitude

Schema:
```
geoloc(name,glc_cd,country,latitude,longitude),
seaport(name,glc_cd,storage,silo,crane,rail).
```

Semantic Rules:
```
R1: geoloc(_,_,"Malta,"?latitude,_) ⇒ ?latitude ≥ 35.89.
R2: geoloc(_,?glc_cd,"Malta,"_,_) ⇒ seaport(_,?glc_cd,_,_,_,_).
R3: seaport(_,?glc_cd,?storage,_,_,_) ∧
    geoloc(_,?glc_cd,"Malta,"_,_)
    ⇒ ?storage > 2000000.
```

Figure 17.1
Schema of a geographic database and semantic rules.

to Q22 from R1, and the resulting query Q23 is still equivalent to Q1. Adding a new constraint could be useful when the new constraint is on an indexed attribute. Sometimes the system can infer that a query is unsatisfiable because it contradicts a rule (or a chain of rules). It is also possible for the system to infer the answer directly from the rules. In both cases, there is no need to access the database to answer the query, and we can achieve nearly 100 percent savings.

Now that the system can reformulate a query into equivalent queries based on the semantic rules, the next problem is how to select the equivalent query with the lowest cost. The exact execution cost of a query depends on the physical implementation and the contents of the databases. However, we can usually estimate an approximate cost from the database schema and relation sizes. In our example, assume that the relation geoloc is very large and is sorted only on glc_cd, and assume that the relation seaport is small. Executing the shortest query Q22 requires scanning the entire set of geoloc relations and is thus even more expensive than executing the query Q1. The cost of evaluating Q21 will be less than that of Q1 and other equivalent queries because a redundant constraint on ?storage is deleted, and the system can still use the sorted attribute glc_cd to locate the answers efficiently. Therefore, the system will select Q21.

The difference between conventional query optimization (Jarke and Koch 1984; Ullman 1988) and SQO is that the latter uses semantic knowledge to extend the search space. Conventional syntactic query optimization searches for low-cost queries logically equivalent to input queries. Optimization by reordering literals/constraints in a query be-

```
Q21: answer(?name):-
       geoloc(?name,?glc_cd,"Malta,"_,_),
       seaport(_,?glc_cd,_,_,_,_).
Q22: answer(?name):-
       geoloc(?name,_,"Malta,"_,_).
Q23: answer(?name):-
       geoloc(?name,_,"Malta,"?latitude,_),
       ?latitude ≤ 35.89.
```

Figure 17.2
Equivalent queries.

longs in this category. SQO, in addition, searches for low-cost queries equivalent to an input queries given some semantic knowledge. Therefore, its search space is much larger and the potential savings that can be achieved are also much larger than those from syntactic optimization alone.

17.3   General Learning Framework

This section presents a general learning framework for the learning problem of SQO. Figure 17.3 illustrates the organization of a database system with an SQO optimizer and a learning system. The optimizer uses semantic rules in a rule bank to optimize input queries, and then sends optimized queries to the DBMS to retrieve data. When the DBMS encounters an expensive input query, it triggers the learning system to learn a set of rules from the data, and then saves them in the rule bank. These rules will be used to optimize future queries. The system will gradually learn a set of effective rules for optimization.

Figure 17.4 illustrates a simplified scenario of our learning framework. This learning framework consists of two components, an inductive learning component, and an operationalization component. A query is given to trigger the learning. The system applies an inductive learning algorithm to induce an *alternative query* equivalent to the input query with a lower cost. The operationalization component then takes the input query and the learned alternative query to derive a set of semantic rules. Previously, Yu and Sun (1989) have shown that semantic rules for SQO can be derived from two equivalent queries. However, they did not show how to automatically generate equivalent queries. Our approach can automatically induce a low-cost alternative query of an expensive

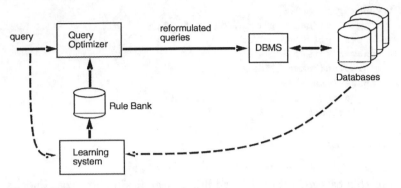

Figure 17.3
Structure of the database system with SQO optimizer and learner.

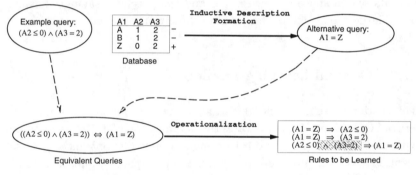

Figure 17.4
A simplified learning scenario.

input query. The derived rules will thus match query patterns and be effective for SQO in reformulating expensive queries into low-cost equivalent queries.

In Figure 17.4, instances (or tuples) in the database are labeled as positive (+) if they satisfy the input query and negative (–) otherwise. The learned alternative query must cover all positive instances but no negative instances so that it retrieves the same data as the input query and is equivalent to the input query. Given a set of data instances classified as positive or negative, the problem of inducing a description that covers all positive data instances but no negatives is known as *supervised inductive learning* in machine learning (Shavlik and Dietterich 1990). Since a query is a description of the data to be retrieved, inductive learning algorithms that learn descriptions expressed in the query language can be used in our framework.

Most supervised inductive learning algorithms are designed for accurate classification of unseen data instances. In our framework, however, the algorithm is also required to induce a low-cost description, that is, a low-cost alternative query that can be evaluated by the DBMS efficiently. Previously, we have developed an inductive learning algorithm that learns low-cost queries from single-table databases (Hsu and Knoblock 1993a). Section 17.4 describes in detail a more advanced algorithm that learns conjunctive Datalog queries from relational databases. This algorithm can be extended to databases with more advanced data models, such as object-oriented and deductive databases.

The operationalization component derives semantic rules from two equivalent queries. It consists of two stages. In the first stage, the system transforms the equivalence of two equivalent queries into the required syntax (Horn clauses) so that the optimizer can use semantic rules efficiently. For the example in Figure 17.4, the equivalence of the two queries is transformed into two implication rules:

$(1)\ (A2 \leq 0) \wedge (A3 = 2) \implies (A1 = \text{`Z'})$

$(2)\ (A1 = \text{`Z'}) \implies (A2 \leq 0) \wedge (A3 = 2)$

Rule (2) can be further expanded to satisfy the Horn-clause syntax requirement:

$(3)\ (A1 = \text{`Z'}) \implies (A2 \leq 0)$

$(4)\ (A1 = \text{`Z'}) \implies (A3 = 2)$

After the transformation, we have proposed rules (1), (3), and (4) that satisfy our syntax requirement. In the second stage, the system tries to compress the antecedents of rules to reduce their match costs. In our example, rules (3) and (4) contain only one literal as antecedent, so no further compression is necessary. If the proposed rule has many antecedent literals, then the system can use the *greedy minimum set cover* algorithm (Coremen et al. 1989) to eliminate unnecessary constraints. The problem of minimum set cover is to find a subset from a given collection of sets such that the union of the sets in the subset is equal to the union of all sets. Negating both sides of (1) yields:

$(5)\ \neg(A1 = \text{`Z'}) \implies \neg(A2 \leq 0) \vee \neg(A3 = 2)$

The problem of compressing rule (1) is thus reduced to the following: given a collection of sets of data that satisfy $\neg(A2 \leq 0) \vee \neg(A3 = 2)$, find the minimum number of sets that cover the set of data satisfying $\neg(A1 = \text{`Z'})$. Suppose the resulting minimum set that covers $\neg(A1$

```
C0:seaport(?name,_,?storage,_,_,_),
   ?storage <= 150000.
C1:geoloc(?name1,_,?cty,_,_),
   member(?cty,["Tunisia,""Italy,""Libya"]).
C2:geoloc(?name1,?glc_cd,_,_,_),
   seaport(?name2,?glc_cd,_,_,_,_).
```

Figure 17.5
Two forms of constraints used in queries.

= 'Z') is ¬(A2 ≤ 0), we can eliminate ¬(A3 = 2) from rule (5) and negate both sides again to form the rule:

(A2 ≤ 0) ⟹ (A1 = 'Z')

17.4   Learning Alternative Queries

The previous section has described a general learning framework and how the operationalization component derives rules from the equivalence of input and alternative queries. This section describes an inductive learning approach to learning low-cost alternative queries. The scenario shown in Figure 17.4 is a simplified example where the database consists of only one table. However, real-world databases usually have many relations, and users can specify joins to associate different relations in a query. The inductive learning approach described below can learn low-cost conjunctive Datalog queries from real-world databases with many relations.

Before we discuss the approach, we need to clarify two forms of constraints implicitly specified in a Datalog query. Consider the geographic database schema in Figure 17.1. Some example constraints for this database are shown in Figure 17.5. Among these constraints, C0 and C1 are *internal disjunctions*, which are constraints on the values of a single attribute. An instance of seaport satisfies C0 if its ?storage value is less than 150,000. An instance of geoloc satisfies C1 if its ?cty value is "Tunisia" or "Italy" or "Libya". The other form of constraint is a *join constraint*, which specifies a constraint on values of two or more attributes from different relations. A pair of instances of geoloc and seaport satisfy a join constraint C2 if they share common values on the attribute glc_cd (geographic location code).

Our inductive learning algorithm is extended from the greedy algorithm that learns internal disjunctions from a single-table database proposed by Haussler (1988). Of the many inductive learning algorithms, Haussler's was chosen because its hypothesis description language is the most similar to database query languages. His algorithm starts from an empty hypothesis of the concept description to be learned. The algorithm proceeds by constructing a set of *candidate constraints* that are consistent with all positive instances, and then using a *gain/cost* ratio as the heuristic function to select and add candidates to the hypothesis. This process of candidate construction and selection is repeated until no negative instance satisfies the hypothesis.

The top level algorithm of our inductive learning is shown in Figure 17.6. We extended Haussler's algorithm to allow join constraints in the description of hypotheses, i.e., alternative queries to be learned. To achieve this, we extended the candidate construction step to allow join constraints to be considered, and we extended the heuristic function to evaluate both internal disjunctions and join constraints.

The algorithm takes a user query Q and the database relations as its inputs. We use Q22 in Figure 17.2 and the database fragment shown in Figure 17.7 as an example to explain the algorithm. The primary relation of a query is the relation that must be accessed to answer the input query. For example, the primary relation of Q22 is geoloc because the output variable, ?name, of the query is bound to an attribute of geoloc. If output variables are bound to attributes from different relations, then the primary relation is a relation derived by joining those relations.

Initially, the system determines the primary relation of an input query and labels the instances in the relation as positive or negative. An instance is positive if it satisfies the input query; otherwise, it is negative. In our example, the primary relation is geoloc and its instances are labeled according to Q22 as shown in Figure 17.7. The next subsection will describe how to construct and evaluate candidate constraints, which can be either an internal disjunction or a join constraint. Then subsection 17.4.2 will describe a preference heuristic to restrict the number of candidate constraints in each iteration.

17.4.1 Constructing and Evaluating Candidate Constraints

For each attribute of the primary relation, the system can construct an internal disjunction as a candidate constraint by generalizing attribute values of positive instances. The constructed constraint is consistent

```
INPUT Q = input query; DB = database relations;
BEGIN
   LET r = primary relation of Q;
   LET AQ= alternative query (initially empty);
   LET C = set of candidate constraints (initially empty);
   Construct candidate constraints on r and add them to C;
   REPEAT
      Evaluate gain/cost of candidate constraints in C;
      LET c = candidate constraint with the highest gain/cost in C;
      IF gain(c) > 0 THEN
         Merge c to AQ, and C = C - c;
         IF AQ ⇔ Q THEN RETURN AQ;
         IF c is a join constraint on a new relation r' THEN
            Construct candidate constraints on r' and add them to C;
         ENDIF;
      ENDIF;
   UNTIL gain(c) = 0;
   RETURN fail, because no AQ is found to be equivalent to Q;
END.
```

Figure 17.6
Inductive algorithm for learning alternative queries.

```
geoloc("Safaqis,"     8001, Tunisia, ...)  seaport("Marsaxlokk"   8003 ...)
geoloc("Valletta,"    8002, Malta,   ...)+ seaport("Grand Harbor" 8002 ...)
geoloc("Marsaxlokk,"  8003, Malta,   ...)+ seaport("Marsa"        8005 ...)
geoloc("San Pawl,"    8004, Malta,   ...)+ seaport("St Pauls Bay" 8004 ...)
geoloc("Marsalforn,"  8005, Malta,   ...)+ seaport("Catania"      8016 ...)
geoloc("Abano,"       8006, Italy,   ...)  seaport("Palermo"      8012 ...)
geoloc("Torino,"      8007, Italy,   ...)  seaport("Traparri"     8015 ...)
geoloc("Venezia,"     8008, Italy,   ...)  seaport("AbuKamash"    8017 ...)
```

Figure 17.7
A database fragment.

with positive instances because it is satisfied by all positive instances. In our example database, for attribute country, the system can generalize from the positive instances a candidate constraint:

geoloc(?name,_,?cty,_,_), ?cty = "Malta,"

because the country value of all positive instances is Malta.

Similarly, the system considers a join constraint as a candidate constraint if it is consistent with all positive instances. This can be verified by checking whether all positive instances satisfy the join constraint. Suppose the system is verifying whether join constraint C2 in Figure 17.5 is consistent with the positive instances. Since for all positive instances, there is a corresponding instance in seaport with a common glc_cd value, the join constraint C2 is consistent and is considered as a candidate constraint.

Table 17.1
Cost estimates of constraints in a query.

Internal disjunctions, on NON-indexed attribute	$\lvert \mathcal{D}_1 \rvert$
Internal disjunctions, on indexed attribute	$\mathcal{I}$
Join, over two NON-indexed attributes	$\lvert \mathcal{D}_1 \rvert \cdot \lvert \mathcal{D}_2 \rvert$
Join, over two indexed attributes	$\frac{\lvert \mathcal{D}_1 \rvert \cdot \lvert \mathcal{D}_2 \rvert}{max(\mathcal{I}_1, \mathcal{I}_2)}$

Once we have constructed a set of candidate internal disjunctive constraints and join constraints, we need to measure which one is the most promising and add it to the hypothesis. In Haussler's algorithm, the evaluation function is a *gain/cost* ratio, where *gain* is defined as the number of negative instances excluded and *cost* is defined as the syntactic length of a constraint. Note that the negative instances excluded in previous iterations will not be counted as gain for the constraints being evaluated. The gain/cost heuristic is based on the generalized problem of minimum set cover where each set is assigned a constant cost. Haussler used this heuristic to bias the learning for short hypotheses. In our problem, we want the system to learn a query expression with the lowest evaluation cost. We define the *gain* part of the heuristic as the number of excluded negative instances in the primary relation, and define the *cost* of the function as the estimated evaluation cost of the candidate constraint.

The motivation of this formula is also from the generalized minimum set covering problem. The gain/cost heuristic has been proved to generate a set cover within a small ratio bound $(\ln \lvert n \rvert + 1)$ of the optimal set covering cost (Coremen et al. 1989), where n is the number of input sets. However, in this problem, the cost of a set is a constant and the total cost of the entire set cover is the sum of the cost of each set. This is not always the case for database query execution, where the cost of each constraint is dependent on the execution ordering. To estimate the actual cost of a constraint is very expensive. We therefore use an approximation here.

The evaluation cost of individual constraints can be estimated using standard query size estimation techniques (Ullman 1988). A set of simple estimates is shown in Table 17.1. For an internal disjunction on a non-indexed attribute of a relation $\mathcal{D}$, a query evaluator has to scan the entire relation to find all satisfying instances. Thus, its evaluation cost is proportional to $|\mathcal{D}|$, the size of $\mathcal{D}$. If the internal disjunction is on an indexed attribute, then its cost is proportional to the number of instances satisfying the constraint, denoted as $\mathcal{I}$.

For join constraints, let $\mathcal{D}_1$ and $\mathcal{D}_2$ denote the relations that are joined, and $\mathcal{I}_1$, $\mathcal{I}_2$ denote the number of the distinct attribute values used for join. Then the evaluation cost for the join over $\mathcal{D}_1$ and $\mathcal{D}_2$ is proportional to $|\mathcal{D}_1| \cdot |\mathcal{D}_2|$ when the join is over attributes that are not indexed, because the query evaluator must compute a cross product to locate pairs of satisfying instances. If the join is over indexed attributes, the evaluation cost is proportional to the number of instance pairs returned from the join, $\frac{|\mathcal{D}_1| \cdot |\mathcal{D}_2|}{max(\mathcal{I}_1, \mathcal{I}_2)}$. This estimate assumes that distinct attribute values distribute uniformly in instances of joined relations. If possible, the system may sample the database for more accurate estimation.

For the example at hand, two candidate constraints are the most promising:

```
C3:geoloc(?name,_,"Malta,"_,_).
C4:geoloc(?name,?glc_cd,_,_,_),
    seaport(_,?glc_cd,_,_,_,_).
```

Suppose |geoloc| is 30,000, and |seaport| is 800. The cardinality of glc_cd for geoloc is 30,000 again, and for seaport is 800. Suppose both relations have indices on glc_cd. Then the evaluation cost of C3 is 30,000, and C4 is $30,000 * 800/30,000 = 800$. The gain of C3 is $30,000 - 4 = 29,996$, and the gain of C4 is $30,000 - 800 = 29,200$, because only 4 instances satisfy C3 (See Figure 17.7) while 800 instances satisfy C4. (There are 800 seaports, and all have a corresponding geoloc instance.) So the gain/cost ratio of C3 is $29,996/30,000 = 0.99$, and the gain/cost ratio of C4 is $29,200/800 = 36.50$. The system will select C4 and add it to the hypothesis.

17.4.2 Searching the Space of Candidate Constraints

When a join constraint is selected, a new relation and its attributes are introduced into the search space of candidate constraints. The system can consider adding constraints on attributes of the newly introduced relation to the partially constructed hypothesis. In our example, a new relation seaport is introduced to describe the positive instances in geoloc. The search space is now expanded into two levels, as illustrated in Figure 17.8. The expanded constraints include a set of internal disjunctions on attributes of seaport, as well as join constraints from seaport to

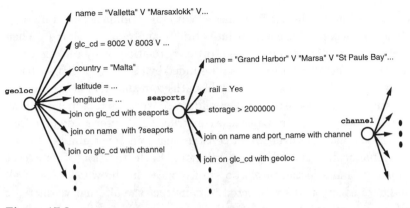

Figure 17.8
Candidate constraints to be selected.

another relation. If a new join constraint has the maximum gain/cost ratio and is selected later, the search space will be expanded further. Figure 17.8 shows the situation when a new relation, say **channel**, is selected, the search space will be expanded one level deeper. At this moment, candidate constraints will include all unselected internal disjunctions on attributes of **geoloc**, **seaport**, and **channel**, as well as all possible joins with new relations from **geoloc**, **seaport** and **channel**. Exhaustively evaluating the gain/cost of all candidate constraints is impractical when learning from a large and complex database.

We adopt a search method that favors candidate constraints on attributes of newly introduced relations. That is, when a join constraint is selected, the system will estimate only those candidate constraints in the newly expanded level, until the system constructs a hypothesis that excludes all negative instances (i.e., reaches the goal) or no more consistent constraints in the level with a positive gain are found. In the later case, the system will backtrack to search the remaining constraints on previous levels. This search control bias takes advantage of underlying domain knowledge in the schema design of databases. A join constraint is unlikely to be selected on average, because an internal disjunction is usually much less expensive than a join. Once a join constraint (and thus a new relation) is selected, this is strong evidence that all useful internal disjunctions in the current level have been selected, and it is more likely that useful candidate constraints are on attributes of newly joined relations. This bias works well in our experiments. But certainly there are cases when the heuristic prunes out useful candidate constraints.

The complexity of the algorithm is briefly analyzed as follows. When a new relation r is introduced as a primary relation or by selection of a join, the number of relation scans is bounded by $(1+J(r))+(A(r)+J(r))$, where $J(r)$ is the number of legal join paths to r and $A(r)$ is the number of attributes of r. Constructing candidate constraints requires scanning the relations $1+J(r)$ times, because constructing all internal disjunctions on r needs one scan over r and constructing join constraints needs an additional scan over each joined relation. Each iteration of gain/cost evaluation and selection needs to scan r once. In the worst case, if all candidate constraints are selected to construct the alternative query, it will require scanning the relations $A(r) + J(r)$ times. Since usually a query involves a small number of relations and expansions in learning are rare, the number of relation scans is linear with respect to the number of attributes in most cases.

Returning to the example, since C4 was selected, the system will expand the search space by constructing consistent internal disjunctions and join constraints on seaport. Assuming that the system cannot find any candidate on seaport with positive gain. It will backtrack to consider candidates on geoloc again and select the constraint on country (see Figure 17.8). Now, all negative instances are excluded. The system thus learns the query:

```
Q3: answer(?name):-
        geoloc(?name,?glc_cd,"Malta,"_,_),
        seaport(_,?glc_cd,_,_,_,_).
```

The operationalization component will then take the equivalence of the input query Q22 and the learned query Q3 as input:

```
    geoloc(?name,_,"Malta,"_,_)
⇔ geoloc(?name,?glc_cd,"Malta,"_,_) ∧
    seaport(_,?glc_cd,_,_,_,_).
```

and will deduce a new rule that can be used to reformulate Q22 to Q3:

```
    geoloc(_,?glc_cd,"Malta",_,_)
⇒ seaport(_,?glc_cd,_,_,_,_).
```

This is the rule R2 we have seen in Section 17.2. Since the size of geoloc is considerably larger than that of seaport, next time when a query asks about geographic locations in Malta, the system can reformulate the query to access the seaport relation instead and speed up the query answering process.

Table 17.2
Database features.

Databases	Contents	Relations	Instances	Size(MB)
Geo	Geographical locations	16	56708	10.48
Assets	Air and sea assets	14	5728	0.51
Fmlib	Force module library	8	3528	1.05

17.5   Experimental Results

Our experiments are performed in the SIMS information mediator (Arens et al. 1993; Knoblock et al. 1994). SIMS allows users to access different kinds of remote databases and knowledge bases as if they were using a single system. For the purpose of our experiments, SIMS is connected with three remotely distributed Oracle databases via the Internet. Figure 17.2 shows the domain of the contents and the sizes of these databases. Together with the databases are 28 sample queries written by the users of the databases. However, among these queries, only 7 are multidatabase queries, and 4 of them return NIL because the data in `Assets` and `Fmlib` databases are incomplete. To test the effect of data transmission cost reduction, we wrote 6 additional multidatabase queries. Therefore, we have a total of 34 sample queries for the experiments.

We classified 28 sample queries into 8 categories according to the relations and constraints used in the queries. We then chose 8 queries randomly from each category as input to the learning system and generated 32 semantic rules. To reduce the learning cost, a multidatabase query will be decomposed into single-database subqueries by the SIMS query planner (Arens et al. 1993; Knoblock et al. 1994) before being fed into the learning system. The learned rules were used to optimize the remaining 26 queries. In addition to rules, the system also used 163 attribute range facts (e.g., the range of the `age` attribute of `employee` is from 17 to 70) compiled from the databases.

Table 17.3 shows the performance statistics. In the first column, we show the average performance of all tested queries. We divide the queries into 3 groups. The number of queries in each group is shown in the first row. The first group contains those unsatisfiable queries refuted by the learned knowledge. In these cases, the reformulation takes full advantage of the learned knowledge and the system does not need to

Table 17.3
Performance statistics.

	All	NIL Queries	≤ 60s.	> 60s.
# of queries	26	4	17	5
Time(sec), w/out reformulation	51.79	41.51	7.97	209.03
Time(sec), with reformulation	20.80	2.37	6.66	83.57
Overall % time saved	59.84%	94.28%	16.38%	60.00%
Average % time saved	29.36%	79.62%	12.56%	46.28%
Average overhead(sec)	0.08	0.07	0.07	0.11
Times range facts applied	3.84	5.25	2.82	6.2
Times rules applied	1.15	0.75	1.35	0.80

access the databases at all, so we separate them from the other cases. The second group contains those low-cost queries that take less than one minute to evaluate without reformulation. The last group contains the high-cost multidatabase queries that we wrote to test the reduction of data transmission cost by reformulation.

In Table 17.3, the second row lists the average elapsed time of query execution without reformulation. The third row shows the average elapsed time of reformulation and execution. The overall percentage time saved is the ratio of the total time saved due to the reformulation over the total execution time without reformulation. The next row shows the average percentage saving of designated sets of queries. That is, the sum of percentage time saved of each query divided by the number of queries. The savings is 59.84 percent overall and 29.36 percent on average. The reformulation yields significant cost reduction for high-cost queries, but not so high for the low-cost queries. This is not unexpected, because the queries in this group are already very cheap and the cost cannot be reduced much further. The average overhead listed in the table shows the time in seconds spent on reformulation. The overhead is very small compared to the total query processing time.

On average, the system applies range facts 3.84 times and semantic rules 1.15 times for reformulation. Note that the same range fact or rule may be applied more than once during the reformulation procedure. In fact, the system reformulates many of the queries using the range facts only. To distinguish the effect of learned rules in reformulation, we separate the queries for which the system applies at least one rule in reformulation. Range facts are still necessary for reformulating these

Table 17.4
Performance statistics for queries optimized using learned semantic rules.

	All	NIL Queries	≤ 60s.	> 60s.
# of queries	11	1	9	1
Time(sec), w/out reformulation	21.25	67.90	8.86	86.09
Time(sec), with reformulation	12.01	4.15	6.99	65.01
Overall % time saved	43.48%	93.88%	21.09%	24.49%
Average % time saved	23.67%	93.88%	15.78%	24.49%
Average overhead(sec)	0.09	0.03	0.09	0.21
Times range facts applied	4.00	2.00	3.44	11.0
Times rules applied	2.72	3.00	2.55	4.00

queries because the system uses them in the rule matching for numerically typed attributes. (Hsu and Knoblock 1993b) describes in detail the usage and acquisition of range facts. The performance statistics on those queries are shown in Table 17.4. There are 11 out of 26 testing queries in this set. The overall saving of this class is 43.48 percent, comparable to the SQO systems using hand-coded rules (King 1981; Shekhar et al. 1988; Shenoy and Ozsoyoglu 1989).

17.6   Related Work

Previously, systems for learning background knowledge for semantic query optimization were proposed by Siegel (1988) and by Shekhar et al. (1993). Siegel's system uses predefined heuristics and an example query to drive the learning. This approach is limited because the heuristics are unlikely to be comprehensive enough to detect missing rules for various queries and databases. Shekhar et al.'s system uses a data-driven approach which assumes that a set of relevant attributes is given. Focusing on these relevant attributes, their system explores the contents of the database and generates a set of rules in the hope that all useful rules are learned. Siegel's system goes to one extreme by neglecting the importance of guiding the learning according to the contents of databases, while Shekhar's system goes to another extreme by neglecting dynamic query patterns. Our approach is more flexible because it addresses both aspects by using example queries to trigger the learning and using inductive learning over the contents of databases.

The problem of Inductive Logic Programming (ILP) (Muggleton and Feng 1990; Quinlan 1990; Lavrač and Džeroski 1994) is closely related to our problem of learning alternative queries in that both problems learn definitions from databases with multiple relations. Our inductive learning approach uses a top-down algorithm similar to FOIL (Quinlan 1990) to build an alternative query. One difference between our approach and FOIL is that they learn descriptions in a different language. FOIL learns Horn-clause definitions where each clause covers a subset of positive instances but no negative instances. Our approach learns conjunctive queries which must cover all positive instances but no negative instances. Another difference is their search heuristics. FOIL uses an information-theoretic heuristic while our approach uses a set-covering heuristic for learning a low-cost description.

Approaches to mining association rules (propositional conjunctive rules) from a single table database are described by Agrawal et al. (1993) and Mannila et al. (1994). Their approach generates a set of data patterns from a table, and then converts those patterns into association rules. The data patterns are generated after the system scans the database a few times. In each pass, the system revises a set of candidate patterns, by proposing new patterns and eliminating existing patterns, as it reads in a data tuple. A "support" counter for each pattern that counts the number of tuples showing a given pattern is used to measure the interestingness of patterns. A tuple scanning approach is not appropriate when joins are allowed to express a rule because the system must consider data patterns in many relations at the same time. Also, in their approaches, the "support" counters for measuring interestingness of rules can be efficiently updated and estimated during the tuple scanning process, while the effectiveness of semantic rules for SQO is difficult to measure and estimate in that manner.

17.7   Conclusions and Future Work

This chapter demonstrates that the knowledge required for semantic query optimization can be learned inductively under the guidance of input queries. We have described a general learning framework in which inductive learning is triggered by queries, and an inductive learning algorithm for learning from many relations. Experimental results show that query optimization using learned semantic knowledge produces substantial cost reductions for a real-world multidatabase system.

A limitation to our approach is that there is no mechanism to deal with changes to databases. After a database is changed, some learned semantic rules may become inconsistent with a new database state and not useful for optimization. Our planned approach to this issue is to estimate the robustness of candidate rules and learn those rules with high robustness confidence. When the database is changed, a maintenance system will be used to update the confidence and delete those rules with low confidence. Meanwhile, as new queries arrive, the system keeps triggering learning for new rules for new database states. This way, the system can autonomously maintain a set of effective and consistent rules for optimization. We are currently developing an estimation approach to implement this idea.

Acknowledgments

This chapter is extended from (Hsu and Knoblock 1994). We wish to thank the SIMS project members: Yigal Arens, Wei-Min Shen, Chin Y. Chee and José-Luis Ambite for their help on this work. Thanks also to Yolanda Gil, Dennis McLeod, Dan O'Leary, Gregory Piatetsky-Shapiro, Paul Rosenbloom, Milind Tambe and the anonymous reviewers for their valuable comments. The research reported here was supported in part by the National Science Foundation under grant No. IRI-9313993 and in part by Rome Laboratory of the Air Force Systems Command and the Advanced Research Projects Agency under Contract No. F30602-91-C-0081.

References

Agrawal, R.; Imielinski, T.; and Swami, A. 1993. Mining Association Rules between Sets of Items in Large Databases. In Proceedings of ACM SIGMOD, 207–216. Washington, D.C.

Arens, Y.; Chee, C. Y.; Hsu, C.-N.; and Knoblock, C. A. 1993. Retrieving and Integrating Data from Multiple Information Sources. *International*

Journal on Intelligent and Cooperative Information Systems 2 (2):127–159.

Cormen, T. H.; Leiserson, C. E.; and Rivest, R. L. 1989. *Introduction To Algorithms.* Cambridge, Mass.: The MIT Press.

Hammer, M.; and Zdonik, S. B. 1980. Knowledge-based Query Processing. In Proceedings of the Sixth VLDB Conference, Washington, D.C., 137–146.

Haussler, D. 1988. Quantifying Inductive Bias: AI Learning Algorithms and Valiant's Learning Framework. *Artificial Intelligence* 36:177–221.

Hsu, C.-N.; and Knoblock, C. A. 1994. Rule Induction for Semantic Query Optimizer. In *Machine Learning: Proceedings of the Eleventh International Conference,* 112–120. San Mateo, Calif.: Morgan Kaufmann.

Hsu, C.-N.; and Knoblock, C. A. 1993a. Learning Database Abstractions for Query Reformulation. Presented at the AAAI-93 Workshop on Knowledge Discovery in Databases, Washington, D.C.

Hsu, C.-N.; and Knoblock, C. A. 1993b. Reformulating Query Plans for Multidatabase Systems. In Proceedings of the Second International Conference on Information and Knowledge Management, Washington, D.C., 423–432.

Jarke, M.; and Koch, J. 1984. Query Optimization in Database Systems. *ACM Computer Surveys,* 16:111–152.

King, J. J. 1981. Query Optimization by Semantic Reasoning. Ph.D. diss., Department of Computer Science, Stanford University.

Knoblock, C. A.; Arens, Y.; and Hsu, C.-N. 1994. Cooperating Agents for Information Retrieval. In Proceedings of the Second International Conference on Intelligent and Cooperative Information Systems, Toronto, Ontario, Canada.

Lavrač, N.; and Džeroski, S. 1994. *Inductive Logic Programming: Techniques and Applications.* Chichester, U.K.: Ellis Horwood.

Mannila, H.; Toivonen, H.; and Verkamo, A. I. 1994. Efficient Algorithms for Discovering Association Rules. In Knowledge Discovery in Databases: Papers from the 1994 AAAI Workshop, 181–192. AAAI Tech. Rep. WS-94-03, Menlo Park, Calif.

Muggleton, S.; and Feng, C. 1990. Efficient Induction of Logic Programs. In Proceedings of the First Conference on Algorithmic Learning Theory. Tokyo, Japan.

Quinlan, J. R. 1990. Learning Logical Definitions from Relations. *Machine Learning* 5: 239–266.

Shavlik, J.; and Dietterich, T. A., eds. 1990. *Readings in Machine Learning.* San Mateo, Calif.: Morgan Kaufmann.

Shekhar, S.; Hamidzadeh, B.; Kohli, A.; and Coyle, M. 1993. Learning Transformation Rules for Semantic Query Optimization: A Data-Driven Approach. *IEEE Transactions on Knowledge and Data Engineering* 5(6): 950–964.

Shekhar, S.; Srivastava, J.; and Dutta, S. 1988. A Formal Model of Trade-off Between Optimization and Execution Costs in Semantic Query Optimization. In Proceedings of the Fourteenth VLDB Conference. Los Angeles, Calif.

Shenoy, S. T.; and Ozsoyoglu, Z. M. 1989. Design and Implementation of a Semantic Query Optimizer. *IEEE Transactions on Knowledge and Data Engineering* I(3): 344–361.

Siegel, M. D. 1988. Automatic Rule Derivation for Semantic Query Optimizer. In Proceedings of the Second International Conference on Expert Database Systems, 371–385, ed. L. Kerschberg. Fairfax, Va.: George Mason Foundation.

Ullman, J. D. 1988. *Principles of Database and Knowledge-base Systems,* Vol. I–II. Palo Alto, Calif.: Computer Science Press.

Yu, C. T.; and Sun, W. 1989. Automatic Knowledge Acquisition and Maintenance for Semantic Query Optimizer. *IEEE Transactions on Knowledge and Data Engineering* I(3): 362–375.

18 Data Surveyor: Searching the Nuggets in Parallel

Marcel Holsheimer
Data Distilleries

Martin L. Kersten and Arno P. J. M. Siebes
Database Research Group, CWI

Abstract

One of the main obstacles in applying data mining techniques to large, real-world databases is the lack of efficient data management. In this chapter, we present the design and implementation of an effective two-level architecture for a data mining environment. It consists of a mining tool and a parallel DBMS server. The mining tool organizes and controls the search process, while the DBMS provides optimal response times for the few query types being used by the tool. Key elements of our architecture are its use of fast and simple database operations, its re-use of results obtained by previous queries, its maximal use of main-memory to keep the database hot-set resident, and its parallel computation of queries. Apart from a clear separation of responsibilities, we show that this architecture leads to competitive performance on large data sets. Moreover, this architecture provides a flexible experimentation platform for further studies in optimization of repetitive database queries and quality driven rule discovery schemes.

18.1 Mining on Large Databases

Recent years have shown an increased interest in data mining techniques, especially in their application to real-world databases. These databases tend to be very large (> 100K objects) and contain objects with many attributes. These vast amounts of data hide many interesting relationships, but their discovery is obstructed by two problems.

First of all, the number of potential relationships in a database is very large. Efficient search algorithms, e.g., Quinlan's ID3 algorithm (Quinlan 1986; Quinlan 1992), are needed to find the patterns quickly, and domain knowledge is needed to select the most interesting ones.

However, simply applying these algorithms to large databases causes another optimization problem, because candidate relationships have to be validated against the database. For many techniques, this results in a repetitive, expensive scan of the entire database.

A straight forward solution would be to reduce the amount of data by taking a sample from the database. In such a sample, small differences among sets of objects in the database will become less clear, and interesting relationships can easily be overlooked. So one would prefer to mine on the entire database, or at least on a very large sample.

In this chapter, we outline a two-level architecture that enables mining on large databases. Section 18.2 describes this architecture, consisting of the Surveyor mining tool and the Monet data server. Section 18.3 gives an introduction to the classification problem. Section 18.4 illustrates a general search strategy for this problem. Section 18.5 contains a brief introduction to the Monet DBMS. Section 18.6 describes the interaction. In Section 18.7, we outline how our architecture can be used to support other learning algorithms, such as ID3. Section 18.8 gives the performance figures and their analysis for this architecture. We conclude with a short indication of future and related research issues addressed within our group.

18.2   Two Level Architecture

To achieve a competitive performance on large datasets, we choose to store all data in a separate data server, that is optimized towards the efficient handling of large sets. This separation of tasks results in a two level architecture, as depicted in Figure 18.1. The front-end consists of the Surveyor mining tool that provides a graphical user interface to formulate and direct the mining activities. All data handling is performed by the back-end, the Monet database server, a parallel DBMS developed within our group, to support a variety of advanced applications (van den Berg and Kersten 1994). The front-end queries the data server for statistical information. Only this information is returned to the mining tool, the actual data remains in the data server at any time. The focal point of this chapter is on the mining algorithm, the interaction and the database performance. Details on the internals of the data mining tool and the DBMS are given elsewhere.

Although the idea of using a DBMS is not new, e.g., systems such as SKICAT use a relational DBMS (Fayyad, Weir and Djorgovski 1993),

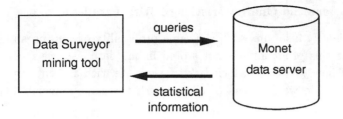

Figure 18.1
The two level architecture.

our system offers some novel optimization features like the parallel computation of column oriented operations, the reuse of results of previous queries and fast data access by keeping only a limited *hot-set* of data in main memory. This hot-set is changed dynamically during the search process to reflect the information requirements of the data mining tool.

These optimizations are equally applicable to a range of data mining systems. Moreover, other modern extendible DBMSs, e.g., Postgres (Stonebraker, Rowe and Hirohama 1990), Starburst (Lehman, Shekita and Cabrera 1992), EXODUS (Carey, Richardson and Shekita 1986) support the inclusion of specialized routines, and can thus be used as a back-end.

18.3   Inferring Risk-Profiles

One of the Dutch insurance companies has asked us to derive *risk-profiles* from their car-insurance databases. A set of risk-profiles is a classification of insurants such that the insurance company can expect all clients in the same class to cause the same claim-amount per year. The relevance of this knowledge for the insurance business is obvious.

The performance results reported later on in this chapter have been measured on a synthetic database based on this real world example. As a first approximation, we derive risk-profiles for the probability that someone will cause a claim, rather than for the expected claim-amount. In this section, we briefly explain how these risk-profiles were found; more information can be found in (Siebes 1994).

18.3.1   What are the Characteristics of Risk-Profiles?

Risk-profiles identify insurants with the same probability of causing an accident. Since this probability is not stored in the database, we face the problem of how we decide which risk to associate with a client. In other words, how do we find sets of clients with the same associated probability?

To do this, we (and insurance companies) make some assumptions. The first is that this probability depends on some properties of the client and his car and which are among the attributes in the database.

For the second assumption, note that if we have a set C of insurants that share the same associated probability p, we can estimate p. Let C' be the set of tuples in the database that correspond to the insurants in C. All tuples in C' can be seen as records of trials of the same Bernoulli experiment. The outcome of this experiment is 1 if there was an accident and 0 otherwise. So, using standard probability theory (Feller 1950), we can compute the, say 99%, confidence interval[1] $CI_{C'}$ for p.

The larger C is, the narrower $CI_{C'}$ is. Since we want to identify groups with distinct associated probabilities, narrower intervals $CI_{C'}$ are better, because we can only conclude that C and D are distinct groups if $CI_{C'} \cap CI_{D'} = \emptyset$.

The consequence of this observation is that we assume that all risk-groups (a group in which all the clients have the same associated probability) are large. A direct consequence of this assumption is that there are only a few distinct risk-groups.

The problem still is, of course, that the database can be partitioned in large subsets in many different ways. Each way would associate a different risk with a given client. In facts, these risks can vary from 0 to 1. Which partitionings are good?

The answer to this question comes in two stages. The first step is that we are not interested in arbitrary subsets of the database, but only in relatively few of them. For example, if *age* turns out to be a relevant attribute, a risk-profile that states that if the age of an insurant is in $\{19, 31, 57, 70\}$ then the probability of an accident is in $[0.25, 0.29]$ is not very plausible, whereas on that states that if the age is in $[18, 25]$ then the probability is in $[0.25, 0.29]$ is far more believable.

---

[1]The actual confidence value chosen is immaterial for this discussion, but not for insurance companies.

Similarly, if one's geographic location is important, a random selection of towns is not very plausible, whereas a region is plausible.

To make this observation a bit more precise, we introduce *descriptions*. Assume that our database is over the attribute set $\mathcal{A} = \{A_1, \ldots, A_n\}$ with domains $D_1, \ldots, D_n$, where $dom(A_i) = D_i$. A *pre-description* is then a conjunction of terms of the form: $A_i \in V_i$, where A_i is an attribute name and V_i is a range or a list of values in D_i. In our example database, $age \in [19, 24] \wedge gender = male$ would be such a pre-description. The cover of a pre-description ϕ, denoted by $\langle \phi \rangle$, is the set of all database tuples that satisfy ϕ.

From this set of pre-descriptions we choose a subset Φ as description language; its elements are called descriptions. The precise details of Φ, of course, depend on the application. However, it should always satisfy the following three constraints:

1. The number of elements of Φ should be small compared to the number of possible subsets of the database.

2. Each description should have a large cover.

3. If for two descriptions ϕ and ψ the intersection of their covers, $\langle \phi \rangle \cap \langle \psi \rangle$, is large then $\phi \wedge \psi$ is also a description.

The first two constraints are to ensure that we do not look at too many subsets of the database. The last one is to ensure that we do not consider too few; we want to find the answer, we don't want to define it. Our third assumption is then that our risk-groups can be identified by Φ.

The second step is weeding out the good subsets from the bad ones is done through the notion of homogeneity. The risk-groups consist of clients that share the same probability of causing an accident, i.e., a *homogeneous* group. Analogously, a description is called homogeneous if the set of all clients that satisfy it is homogeneous.

Intuitively, a set is homogeneous, if all its subsets yield the same associated probability. The fact that the number of elements of Φ is small compared to the number of possible sets of the database allows us to formalize this intuition as follows. A description $\phi \in \Phi$ is homogeneous[2] if:

$$\forall \psi \in \Phi : \phi \wedge \psi \in \Phi \rightarrow CI_\phi \cap CI_{\phi \wedge \psi} \neq \emptyset$$

---

[2] A related notion of homogeneity has been introduced independently by Segal and Etzioni (1994).

In other words, if we call $\phi \wedge \psi$ an extension of ϕ, a description is homogeneous if its associated probability cannot be distinguished, with 99% certainty, from those of its extensions.

So, given our three assumptions, risk-groups can be equated with homogeneous descriptions. The insurance company didn't want an arbitrary set of risk-groups, it wanted a classification of all its present and future clients. That is, they wanted to find a *cover* of the database. To formalize this problem in the terminology of descriptions, define a set $\{\phi_1, \ldots, \phi_k\}$ of descriptions to be a *disjunctive cover,* abbreviated to *discovery*, if (1) the $\langle \phi_i \rangle$ are mutually disjoint and (2) the union of all $\langle \phi_i \rangle$ is the entire set.

Classifying the insurants reduces now to finding a discovery $\{\phi_1, \ldots, \phi_l\}$ such that:

1. all ϕ_i are homogeneous;

2. ϕ_i have non-overlapping confidence intervals.

Such a discovery is said to *split* the database. A discovery that satisfies only the first requirement is called *homogeneous.*

18.3.2   Existence and Uniqueness

If Φ is carefully defined, many homogeneous discoveries will exist. For example, from a sequence $\phi_1, \ldots, \phi_n \in \Phi$ of descriptions we can generate the decision list (Rivest 1987), $\Psi = \{\phi_1, \neg\phi_1 \wedge \phi_2, \neg\phi_1 \wedge \neg\phi_2 \wedge \phi_3, \ldots, (\neg\phi_1 \wedge \cdots \wedge \neg\phi_n)\}$. This decision list is potentially a homogeneous discovery.

Whether there exist homogeneous discoveries that split the database depends more on the actual database state than on the design of Φ. In other words, there might be 0, 1 or many.

If there are 0, we are out of luck. The database simply does not contain enough information to partition the clients through risk-profiles. If there are many, we seem to be in similar straits because we can assign many different risks to the same client. However, the *quality* of the different discoveries may differ considerably. In other words, one might be naturally the best.

A detailed discussion of quality measures on discoveries is outside the scope of this chapter. One aspect, however, is interesting to note. One reason for having many homogeneous discoveries is that many descriptions are homogeneous by definition, i.e., all those descriptions which have no extensions in Φ.

These trivially homogeneous descriptions are in a sense too small to take into account. In other words, a homogeneous description with a large cover is better than one with a small cover. Extending this to discoveries, a discovery that partitions the database in large subsets is better than one that partitions it into smaller subsets.

Similarly, the better a set of descriptions distinguishes between its components, the better it is. To formalize this, define that a homogeneous set of descriptions $\{\phi_1, \ldots, \phi_l\}$ *strongly splits* the database if its descriptions differ in all aspects:

$$\forall \psi \in \Phi \; \forall i, j \in \{1, \ldots, l\} : \left[\begin{array}{ll} i \neq j & \wedge \\ \phi_i \wedge \psi \in \Phi & \wedge \\ \phi_j \wedge \psi \in \Phi & \end{array} \right] \rightarrow CI_{\phi_i \wedge \psi} \cap CI_{\phi_j \wedge \psi} = \emptyset$$

Let $\{\phi_1, \ldots, \phi_k\}$ and $\{\psi_1, \ldots, \psi_l\}$ be two homogeneous discoveries that strongly split the database and such that all $\langle \phi_i \rangle$ and $\langle \psi_j \rangle$ are large. Then for each ϕ_i there is at least one ψ_j such that $\langle \phi_i \rangle \cap \langle \psi_j \rangle \gg \emptyset$ and thus $\langle \phi_i \wedge \psi_j \rangle \in \Phi$. But since both discoveries strongly split the database, there can be at most one. So, $\langle \phi_i \rangle \approx \langle \psi_j \rangle$ and $CI_{\phi_i} \approx CI_{\psi_j}$. In other words, in this case there is essentially only one way to partition the database

The fact that the discoveries are not unique is simply caused by the fact that a set of tuples can have more than one description. For example, it could happen that almost all young clients are male and vice versa. In that case the descriptions *age = young* and *gender = male* are equally good from a theoretical point of view, but not necessarily from a practical point of view. For, it is very well possible that the description *age = young* makes sense to a domain expert, while *gender = male* does not. Hence, both options should be presented to the domain expert.

18.4   Search Strategy

If a homogeneous discovery exists that splits the database, it must contain a homogeneous description with the highest associated probability. This suggests a simple algorithm to find such a discovery:

Make a list of homogeneous descriptions as follows:

find a ϕ that has the maximal associated probability.
remove $\langle \phi \rangle$ from db and add ϕ to the list.
continue with this process until $\top$ is homogeneous on the remainder of db;
Check whether the decision list splits the database.

In the remainder of this chapter, we concentrate on finding descriptions with maximal associated probability. The associated probability of a description is taken as a measure of its quality.

To discover descriptions of high quality, the system uses an iterative search strategy, organized in a number of *phases*. The initial description R_0 is simply

$R_0 : \top$

In the first phase, this description is extended with an attribute-value condition to obtain a new description, e.g.

$R_1 : \text{age} \in [19, 24]$

and this new description is further extended with conjunctions in following phases. The heuristic to obtain a satisfactory classification is to choose description extensions with a perceived high quality. This algorithm is generally applicable and basically underlies many machine learning systems (Holsheimer and Siebes 1994). Hence, we expect that a wide variety of data mine systems may benefit from the optimizations that we discuss in the following section.

To select the extensions with the highest quality, we compute the quality of *all* possible description extensions. The combinatorial explosion of candidate descriptions is controlled using a beam search algorithm, where the best w (the beam width) extensions are selected for further exploration. Of these new descriptions, all possible extensions are computed, and again, the best w are selected. This process continues until no further improvement is possible. To compute the quality of all extensions of a description R_i, we only need to look at the cover of R_i and not at the entire database. This is caused by the 'zooming' behavior of our algorithm: the cover of an extension of R_i is always a subset of the cover of R_i. Hence, at every stage we compute the cover, and use it for the computation of the quality of the newly generated descriptions. This algorithm is described in pseudo-code as

Beamset := {initial description R_0},
while improvement and phase < d
    All_extensions := ∅,
    For each R_i in Beamset do
        C_i := cover(R_i),
        Extensions := extend(R_i),
        compute_quality(Extensions, C_i),
        All_extensions := All_extensions ∪ Extensions,
    Beamset := best(All_extensions, w)

Example 18.1 Our synthetic database contains 100K objects, half of which have had an accident. We want to find the description with the highest quality for this database:

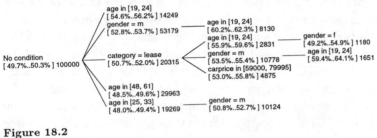

Figure 18.2
A 5 × 3 search tree.

A search tree, constructed using a 5 × 3 beam search is shown in Figure 18.2. In each node, the condition is stated together with the size of the cover and the description quality. The initial condition covers 100K objects, half of which belongs to the class. For example, the description with condition (age ∈ [19, 24]) ∧ (gender = m) covers 8130 objects. The confidence interval CI for this description is [60.2%, 62.3%].

18.5   The Monet Database Server

The DBMS used for our data mining tool is the *Monet* database server developed at CWI as a vehicle to support advanced applications and as an experimentation platform for novel database techniques (Kersten 1991; Kersten, van den Berg and Plomp 1992). Besides Data Surveyor it supports an SQL and ODMG compiler. Its salient features include:

Binary Relation Model   Monet employs a fully decomposed storage scheme and adaptive indexing to speed-up query processing (van den Berg and Kersten 1994). That is, complex objects are decomposed into a set of binary relationships using an OID to relate their components. Hence only a vertical subset of the database, consisting of the currently relevant attributes, can be loaded into main memory. A similar vertical partitioning of the database is used by the Explora system (Klösgen 1993). Such a storage scheme is very effective in situations where the database *hot-set* can be kept memory resident. This design feature has proved crucial in the efficient support of our data mining tool.

Search accelerators are introduced as soon as an operator would benefit from their existence. They exists as long as the table is kept in memory and are not stored on disk.

Inter-Operator Parallelism   The system exploits shared-store and all-cache architectures. A distributed shared-nothing approach, as described in (van den Berg and Kersten 1992), is under development. Unlike the implementations of PRISMA (Apers *et al.* 1992) and GAMMA (DeWitt *et al.* 1990), Monet does not use tuple or segment pipelining. Instead, the algebraic operators are the units for scheduling and parallel execution. Their result is completely materialized before being used in the next phase. This approach improves throughput at a slight reduction of response time.

The Monet development platform has been the Silicon Graphics R3000 and R4000 workstations with the IRIX operating system. Furthermore, a shared-memory multi-processor of 6 150Mhz CPUs and 256 Mbyte of main memory is used to exploit parallelism.

The mode of interaction is that of client/server, where a single Monet server takes care of all interactions with a specific physical database. The clients are either application programs linked with the Monet application programming interface library or to use a textual interface. The latter is used to interface with Data Surveyor. Although this implies some parsing overhead, it also provides a clean and traceable interface for debugging and to cross hardware implementation schemes.

18.5.1   Data Storage and Manipulation

A relational table is broken down into multiple Binary Association Tables (or BAT), where each database attribute is stored in a separate table. The first column, *head,* of each BAT contains a unique object identifier (oid), the second column, *tail,* contains the attribute values.

Example 18.2 To illustrate, the table 'test100k(age, carprice, category, gender, town)' introduced in Example 18.1 is stored in 5 BATs: 'test100k_age', 'test100k_carprice', etc. It contains both string values and integers. The age and category domains are dense; all values within min(age) and max(age) are represented in the database. The carprice domain is sparse. This artificial database enables us to predict the statistical properties of queries. The binary target variable accident is not stored as a single BAT, but as two BATs, 'pos_accident' and 'neg_accident', whose heads contain the oid's of objects with accident = yes and accident = no respectively.

The database of 100K objects consumes about 2.6 Mbyte of disk space. It is stored in compressed form. The BATs are automatically decompressed and loaded upon need. The tables are not sorted, nor do they carry an index to speed-up selection on the tail of the association.

The Monet kernel provides a rich set of algebraic operations on BATs, the subset relevant to the Data Mine system is summarized in Table 18.1. The result of an operation is a new BAT.

Table 18.1
A subset of the Monet operators.

BAT operator	result
AB.select(Tl,Th)	oid-value pairs where the value is larger or equal to Tl and smaller or equal to Th
AB.select(T)	oid-value pairs where the value is equal to T
semijoin(AB,CD)	oid-value pairs in AB for which there exists an oid in CD
AB.histogram	the value-frequency pairs for all values in AB

18.6   Bridging the Gap

As we outlined in Section 18.4, processing takes place in different *phases.* During each phase, the Data Surveyor system computes the quality of all extensions of the rules in the current beamset, i.e., all possible conditions on each of the attributes. For example, on the attribute 'gender', conditions would be 'gender = m' and 'gender = f', conditions on age would be 'age ∈ [19,20]', 'age ∈ [19,21]', etc.

Note that only the attributes that are not yet present in the rule have to be taken into account. Extending the rule 'gender = m' with a condition on gender is useless. This is the *vertical zooming* property: the set of interesting attributes decreases in size during the search process.

The main problem to be tackled is to efficiently compute the quality of all possible extensions. A straight forward technique is to compute the quality of each extension separately. This involves issuing two database queries, one to compute the number of objects for which the extension predict the target variable correctly, and another to compute the incorrect predictions. Although intuitively appealing, this technique is far too expensive. In Example 2, the quality of 1000 extensions have been computed, which would have resulted in 2000 database server interactions.

A more sophisticated technique, proposed by Agrawal *et al.* (1993), is to incrementally compute the quality of a set of descriptions in a single pass over the database by updating counters for each extension. To avoid excessive memory consumption, the description-set under consideration is pruned along the way. This approach works under the assumption that the database scan sequence does not influence the pruning of the classification descriptions.

18.6.1   Retrieving Statistics

We propose an alternative architecture, where the quality of all possible extensions of a rule is computed using only a few simple database operations. Data Surveyor queries the DBMS for information on the frequency of *combinations* of an attribute and the target variable in the database.

Example 18.3 The combinations of the (binary) attributes 'gender' and 'accident' are: male drivers that had an accident, males with no accident, females with an accident and females without an accident.

Knowing the number of database-objects in these four classes, Data Surveyor can compute the quality of any extensions on gender, e.g., the quality of the rule 'gender = m' is the number of male drivers that had an accident, divided by the total number of males (with or without an accident).

To compute the quality of extensions on an n-ary variable, such as hometown, Monet computes the sizes of each of the $2n$ classes. For numerical variables, e.g., age, it uses an algorithm to split the domain in ranges. The ranges are created such that objects in the same range have the same quality, and the differences between ranges are maximized.

The Data Surveyor system generates a Monet script to compute sizes of classes. First the semijoin of test100k_gender and pos_accident is computed, resulting in a BAT containing the ⟨oid, gender⟩ pairs of accidental drivers. From this BAT, the histogram is computed, i.e., a BAT containing the frequency of each value (f or m). A similar BAT is computed for the non-accident drivers, and for the other attributes:

```
t0_pos = semijoin(test100k_gender, pos_accident).histogram;
t0_neg = semijoin(test100k_gender, neg_accident).histogram;
t1_pos = semijoin(test100k_carprice, pos_accident).histogram;
t1_neg = semijoin(test100k_carprice, neg_accident).histogram;
t2_pos = semijoin(test100k_category, pos_accident).histogram;
...
t0_pos.print;
[19, 1359]
[20, 1330]
[21, 1263]

...
```

The (temporary) BATs tX_pos and tX_neg store the histograms and are printed after the above code is executed (the *delivery* phase). These results are shipped back to Data Surveyor.

18.6.2 Selection

The above computations are used to compute the extensions of the initial rule, i.e., the rule that covers the entire database. However, in the second phase of the beam search, the quality of extensions of rules such as 'age ∈ [19,24]' have to be computed (see Figure 18.2). So we have to compute the sizes of the classes *within* the cover of this rule. First we compute the database selection, corresponding to the cover, i.e., a BAT containing the oid's of young people. Next, we compute the BATs pos_accident0 and neg_accident0 containing respectively the oid's of the accident and non-accident drivers in the cover. The code is repeated for the other rules in the beamset, i.e., 'gender = m', etc.

```
{tmp0 = test100k_age.select(19,24);
          pos_accident0 = semijoin(tmp0, pos_accident);
          neg_accident0 = semijoin(tmp0, neg_accident);
}
{tmp1 = test100k_gender.select("m");
          pos_accident1 = semijoin(tmp1, pos_accident);
          neg_accident1 = semijoin(tmp1, neg_accident);
```

```
}
{tmp2 = test100k_category.select("lease");
                pos_accident2 = semijoin(tmp2, pos_accident);
        . . .
```

Since 'pos_accidentX' contains the oid's of the accidental drivers in the cover of Xth rule in the beamset, it simply replaces 'pos_accident' in computing the quality of possible extensions. The code, executed by Monet to compute the quality of the extensions of the rules in the beamset is

```
t0_pos = semijoin(test100k_gender, pos_accident0).histogram;
t0_neg = semijoin(test100k_gender, neg_accident0).histogram;
t1_pos = semijoin(test100k_gender, pos_accident3).histogram;
t1_neg = semijoin(test100k_gender, neg_accident3).histogram;
t2_pos = semijoin(test100k_gender, pos_accident4).histogram;
t2_neg = semijoin(test100k_gender, neg_accident4).histogram;
t3_pos = semijoin(test100k_carprice, pos_accident0).histogram;
t3_neg = semijoin(test100k_carprice, neg_accident0).histogram;
t4_pos = semijoin(test100k_carprice, pos_accident1).histogram;
        . . . . . . .
```

18.6.3   Session Optimization

In the third phase, we first have to compute the cover of the rules in the new beamset, e.g., the cover of 'category = lease, carprice ∈ [59000, 79995]', by taking selections on both category and carprice. At this point, we can re-use results of a previous computation, because the selection 'category = lease' is already made, and stored in 'pos_accident2' and 'neg_accident2'. The code to compute the new cover is:

```
{tmp0 = test100k_price.select(59000,79995);
                pos_accident5 = semijoin(tmp0, pos_accident2);
                neg_accident5 = semijoin(tmp0, neg_accident2);

}
```

This code contains no references to the category BAT. The BATS 'pos_accident2' and 'neg_accident2' are no longer needed and destroyed.

We already mentioned the vertical zooming behavior of this algorithm, the number of columns that are of interest decreases during the search process. Something similar happens for the number of objects, covered by a rule (horizontal zooming). Due to this zooming behavior, a smaller and smaller portion of the database is relevant for exploration. This means that the main-memory buffer requirements for retaining intermediate results stabilizes after a few iterations.

The database operations sketched above lead to an abundance of intermediate results. Although the Monet server automatically flushes the least recently used temporaries to disk, our data mining algorithm can determine precisely the subset of interest for the remainder of the session. Therefore, after each phase it releases temporaries by re-use of their name or using explicit destroy operations. Attributes that are no longer used are automatically flushed to disk.

18.6.4   Parallelism

The above program fragments illustrate the potential use of parallelism. Each cycle in the beam search can be decomposed into a *selection-*, *statistics-*, and *delivery-* phase. The computation of covers in the first phase, and the computation of statistics in the second can be ran in parallel. The last phase forces sequential processing, because the frontend itself has not been parallelized.

The Monet kernel largely relies on the scheduling of processes over the available processors. This is the default mode of operation on the SGI multi-processors, and assures that resources are divided over multiple users. The experiments were ran on a lightly-loaded system and we have assured ourself that work was evenly divided over the processors.

18.7   Construction of Decision Trees

As we stated in our introduction, our architecture can be used for other learning strategies as well. In this Section, we will shortly outline how Monet can support Quinlan's ID3 algorithm (Quinlan 1986).

ID3 induces a decision tree from a set of positive and negative examples. In a decision tree, nodes are labeled with attribute names, branches are labeled with all possible values for this attribute, and leaves are labeled with class names. To classify an object, we start at the root of the tree, and at each node, we take the branch corresponding to the value of the objects' attribute.

The tree is constructed by selecting an attribute as the root of the tree, and making branches for all different values this attribute can have. If all examples at a particular leaf belong to the same class, the leaf is labeled with this class. Otherwise, we label the node with an attribute that does not occur on the path to the root, and create branches for all possible values.

In ID3, smaller trees are preferred, on the grounds that these are more likely to classify previously unseen objects correctly. We create a small tree by a suitable selection of attributes. ID3 uses an *information-based* heuristic to select these attributes. The amount of information, needed to decide if an arbitrary object is a positive or negative example, is defined as (Quinlan, 1986):

$$I(p, n) = -\frac{p}{p+n} \log_2 \frac{p}{p+n} - \frac{n}{p+n} \log_2 \frac{n}{p+n}$$

The expected information $I(p, n)$ depends solely on p and n, the number of positive and negative examples in the database. Assume that attribute A with values $\{A_1, A_2, \ldots, A_v\}$ is used to branch, this will split the database in subsets $\{S_1, S_2, \ldots, S_v\}$. If S_i contains p_i positive examples and n_i negative examples, the information, needed to decide if an element in S_i belongs is a positive or negative example is $I(p_i, n_i)$. So the information needed to classify an element of S using a tree with A as root, is the weighted average of the information, needed to classify objects in all subtrees S_i:

$$E(A) = \sum_{i=1}^{v} \frac{p_i + n_i}{p+n} I(p_i, n_i)$$

The attribute A is selected such that the *information gain* is maximal, that is, $E(A)$ is minimal. The information, needed to compute $E(A)$, is the frequency of each of the values $A_1, A_2, \ldots, A_v$ in the set of positive and negative examples. This is *exactly* the information, that Monet returns using the histogram operation. So by using a graph search, rather than a beam search, and using the information gain criterion to select attributes, Data Surveyor can implement the ID3 algorithm. Selection results can be reused, as described in Section 18.6.3, and operations can be ran in parallel.

18.8   Performance Results

The current implementation has been subject to extensive performance assessment to isolate the bottlenecks and to direct research in both development of mining algorithms and the database kernel. The results presented here are focussed on the database activity.

In Section 18.8.1 we summarize the interaction of Data Surveyor and Monet in terms of database instructions, data exchanged and overall performance. Section 18.8.2 illustrates the effect of parallel execution.

18.8.1   Sequential Database Mining

The first experiment illustrates the global division of labor between Data Surveyor and Monet. Figure 18.3 shows the performance results for 5×5 and 7×7 beam searches. The database size ranges from 5K to 100K records, which covered a spectrum hardly reported in the literature. In these experiments, the code produced by the mining tool was executed in sequential mode by Monet. The experimentation platform was a 6-node SGI machine of 150Mhz processors and 256 Mbytes of main memory.

The graphs are read as follows. The line marked *miner* represents the time involved in the mining algorithm and management of the graphical user interface. The lines marked *cpu* and *sys* describe the processing times as measured by the database back-end. All times are in seconds. The results indicate the constant processing cost within the user interface of about 12 and 24 seconds, respectively.

These experiments indicate that the performance of the front-end is largely independent of the database size. It is primarily determined by the properties of the search algorithm. Moreover, the front-end is relatively expensive compared to the back-end processing. This is a result of our implementation strategy for Surveyor, which is programmed in Prolog and XPCE, a windowing system for Prolog applications. It has been designed with emphasis on simplicity and extensibility, so we expect that reasonable speed up can be achieved by partly switching from Prolog to C, and optimization of its algorithms.

18.8.2   Parallel Database Mining

As indicated in Section 18.6.4, our search strategy includes two processing phases that can be easily parallelized. The next experiments were set up to 1) test the implementation of the parallelization features in the database back-end and 2) assess the speed-up factor. The algorithms were modified to generate parallel code upon request by the user.

For this experiment, we repeated the 5×5 case for a 25K database by turning on the parallelization switch. We varied the number of threads from 1 to 4 to determine their global contribution. The processing time in the user interface remained the same, because it is independent of the parallelization within Monet. The results of these experiments are shown in Figure 18.4.

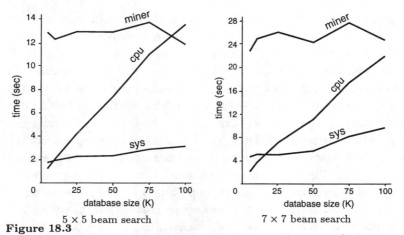

Figure 18.3
Performance results (in sec.) for different databases and beam search sizes.

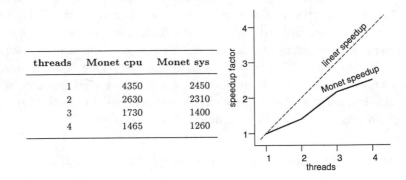

threads	Monet cpu	Monet sys
1	4350	2450
2	2630	2310
3	1730	1400
4	1465	1260

Figure 18.4
Results for parallel processing.

We may conclude that considerable speed up is obtained when multiple threads are used, although this speed up is not linear. This is caused by the locking and synchronization mechanisms in Monet, and by the fact that not all code can be run in parallel. In particular, the communication with the data mining tool is still serial. Figure 18.4 depicts the number of extensions per seconds as a function of the number of threads.

18.9   Conclusions

The two-level architecture of our data mining environment provides a performance-effective solution to data mining against real-life databases based on an iterative technique.

The Monet DBMS facilities lead to a solution, where classification of large databases can be handled within seconds on state-of-the-art multiprocessors. The repetitive nature and overlap of successive queries calls for automated support for browsing session optimization in the database server (Kersten and de Boer 1994). Thereby further off loading parts of the mining activity to the DBMS kernel. Moreover, the policy to retain most information in main memory during a transaction leads to a high demand on the available store. A more prudent memory management scheme may be required to avoid clashes with other users and to scale beyond 10M objects easily.

We are currently investigating refinements of the quality control primitives to explore rule enhancements. Other points of interest are: the use of domain knowledge to speed up the search process and distinguish interesting rules from trivial or already known knowledge; and alternative search strategies, such as simulated annealing and genetic algorithms.

Acknowledgments

We wish to thank Frank van Dijk and Fred Kwakkel for continual support in the realization of the Data Surveyor.

References

Agrawal, R.; Imielinski, T.; and Swami, A. 1993. Database Mining: A Performance Perspective. *IEEE Transactions on Knowledge and Data Engineering,* 5(6): 914–925.

Apers, P. M. G.; van den Berg, C. A.; Flokstra, J.; Grefen, P. W. P. J.; Kersten, M. L.; and Wilschut, A. 1992. PRISMA/DB: A Parallel, Main-Memory Relational DBMS. *IEEE Transactions on Knowledge and Data Engineering, Special Issue on Main-Memory DBMS.*

Carey, M.; DeWitt, D. J.; Richardson, J. E.; and Shekita, E. J. 1986. Object and File Management in the EXODUS Extensible Database System.

In Proceedings of the Twelfth International Conference on Data Bases, 91–100. Kyoto.

DeWitt, D. J.; Ghadeharizadeh, S.; Schneider, D. A.; Bricker, A.; Hsiao, H.; and Rasmussen, R. 1990. The GAMMA Database Machine Project. *IEEE Journal on Data and Knowledge Engineering,* 2 (1): 44–51.

Fayyad, U. M., and Uthurusamy, R., eds. 1994. Knowledge Discovery in Databases: Papers from the 1994 AAAI Workshop, AAAI Tech. Rep. WS-94-03, Menlo Park, Calif.

Fayyad, U. M.; Weir, N.; and Djorgovski, S. 1993. Automated Cataloging and Analysis of Ski Survey Image Databases: The SKICAT System. In Proceedings of the Second International Conference on Information and Knowledge Management, 527–536, Washington D.C.

Feller, W. 1950. *An Introduction to Probability Theory and Its Applications,* Vol 1. New York: John Wiley.

Holsheimer, M.; and Kersten, M. L. 1994. Architectural Support for Data Mining. In Knowledge Discovery in Databases: Papers from the 1994 AAAI Workshop, 217–228. AAAI Tech. Rep. WS-94-03, Menlo Park, Calif.

Holsheimer, M. and Siebes, A. P. J. M. 1994. Data Mining: The Search for Knowledge in Databases. Technical Report, CS-R9406, CWI.

Kersten, M. L.; and de Boer, M. 1994. Query Optimization Strategies for Browsing Sessions. In Proceedings IEEE International Conference on Data Engineering. Houston.

Kersten, M. L. 1991. Goblin: A DBPL Designed for Advanced Database Applications. In Second International Conference on Database and Expert Systems Applications, DEXA'91. Berlin, Germany.

Klösgen, W. 1993. Efficient Discovery of Interesting Statements in Databases. Technical Report, GMD.

Kersten, M. L.; van den Berg, C. A.; and Plomp, S. 1992. Object Storage Management in Goblin. In *In Distributed Object Management.* San Francisco: Morgan Kaufman.

Lehman, T. J.; Shekita, E. J.; and Cabrera, L. F. 1992. An Evaluation of Starburst's Memory Resident Storage Component. *Journal of Data and Knowledge Engineering,* 4(6): 555–567.

Piatetsky-Shapiro, G., and Frawley, W. J., eds. 1991. *Knowledge Discovery in Databases.* Menlo Park, Calif.: AAAI Press.

Quinlan, J. R. 1986. Induction of Decision Trees. *Machine Learning,* 1: 81–106.

Quinlan, J. R. 1992. *C4.5: Programs for Machine Learning.* San Francisco: Morgan Kaufmann.

Rivest, R. L. 1987. Learning Decision Lists. *Machine Learning,* 2:229–246.

Siebes, A. P. J. M. 1994. Homogeneous Discoveries Contain No Surprises: Inferring Risk-Profiles from Large Databases. In Knowledge Discovery in Databases: Papers from the 1994 AAAI Workshop, 97–108. AAAI Tech. Rep. WS-94-03, Menlo Park, Calif.

Stonebraker, M., Rowe, L., and Hirohama, M. 1990. The Implementation of POSTGRES. *Journal of Data and Knowledge Engineering,* 2(1): 125–142.

Segal, R., and Etzioni, O. 1994. Learning Decision Lists Using Homogeneous Rules, In Proceedings of the Twelfth National Conference on Artificial Intelligence. Menlo Park, Calif.: AAAI Press.

van den Berg, C. A., and Kersten, M. L. 1992. A Dynamic Parallel Query Processing Architecture. In *COMAD'92,* Bangalore, India.

van den Berg, C. A.; and Kersten, M. L. 1994. An Analysis of a Dynamic Query Optimization Scheme for Different Data Distributions. In *Advances in Query Processing,* 449–470, eds. J. Freytag, D, Maier, and G. Vossen. San Francisco: Morgan-Kaufmann.

VII KDD APPLICATIONS

19 Automating the Analysis and Cataloging of Sky Surveys

Usama M. Fayyad
Jet Propulsion Laboratory,
California Institute of Technology

S. George Djorgovski, & Nicholas Weir
California Institute of Technology

Abstract

This chapter presents an application of classification learning techniques to automating the reduction and analysis of a large astronomical data set: The Digital Palomar Observatory Sky Survey (POSS-II). The 3 terabytes worth of images are expected to contain on the order of 2 billion sky objects. For the primary scientific analysis of these data, it is necessary to detect, measure, and classify every sky object. The size of the complete data set precludes manual reduction, requiring an automated approach. The SKICAT system integrates techniques for image processing, data classification, and database management. The learning algorithms are trained to classify the detected objects and can classify objects too faint for visual classification with high accuracy. This increases the number of classified objects in the final catalog three-fold relative to the best results from digitized photographic sky surveys to date. The tasks of managing and matching the resulting thousands of plate catalogs is accomplished using custom software and the Sybase relational DBMS. A full array of scientific analysis tools are provided for filtering, manipulating, plotting, and listing the data in the sky object database. SKICAT represents a system in which machine learning played a powerful and enabling role, and solved a difficult, scientifically significant problem. The primary benefits of our overall approach are increased data reduction throughput; consistency of classification; and the ability to easily access, analyze, and create new information from an otherwise unfathomable data set.

19.1   Introduction

In astronomy and space sciences, we currently face a data glut crisis. The problem of dealing with the huge volume of data accumulated from a variety of sources, of correlating the data and extracting and visualizing the important trends, is now fully recognized. This problem will rapidly become more acute, with the advent of new telescopes, detectors, and space missions, with the data flux measured in terabytes. We face a critical need for information processing technology and methodology with which to manage this data avalanche in order to produce interesting scientific results quickly and efficiently. Developments in the fields of Knowledge Discovery in Databases (KDD), machine learning, and related areas can provide at least some solutions. Much of the future of scientific information processing lies in the creative and efficient implementation and integration of of these methods.

In this chapter we present an application of supervised classification learning techniques to the automation of the tasks of cataloging and analyzing objects in digitized sky images. The Sky Image Cataloging and Analysis Tool (SKICAT) (Fayyad, Weir, & Djorgovski 1993,1994; Djorgovski, Weir, & Fayyad 1994) was developed for use on the images resulting from the Second Palomar Observatory Sky Survey (POSS-II) conducted by the California Institute of Technology (Caltech). See Reid et al (1991) for a detailed description of the POSS-II effort. The photographic plates collected from the survey are being digitized at the Space Telescope Science Institute. This process will result in about 3,000 digital images of $23,040 \times 23,040$ 16-bit pixels each, totalling over 3 terabytes of data. When complete, the survey will cover the entire northern sky in three colors, detecting virtually every sky object down to an equivalent B magnitude[1] object intensity of 22.0. This is at least one magnitude fainter than previous comparable photographic surveys. We estimate that there are at least 5×10^7 galaxies and 2×10^9 stellar objects (including over 10^5 quasars) detectable in this survey. This data set will be the most comprehensive large-scale imaging survey produced to date and will not be surpassed in scope until the completion of a fully digital all-sky survey in the next decade.

The purpose of SKICAT is to enable and maximize the extraction of meaningful information from such a large database in an efficient and timely manner. The system is built in a modular way, integrating several existing algorithms and packages. There are three basic functional components to SKICAT, serving the purposes of sky object catalog con-

---

[1]This is a standard Astronomical magnitude scale for measuring relative brightness of astronomical sources. It is logarithmic, with 1 mag = -4 db; the brightest stars visible with a naked eye are first magnitude. Magnitudes are usually defined in a particular bandpass, given by a combination of a filter and a detector, e.g., the "blue" (B) band.

struction, catalog management, and high-level statistical and scientific analysis. In this chapter we place particular emphasis on the first. It is there where we have already realized the significant advantages of KDD for a data reduction problem of this magnitude. However, the subsequent tasks of managing and updating the sky object database in the face of new and better data, not to mention the large-scale statistical analysis of the full data set, similarly cry out for the application of automated information processing and exploration technology. These aspects of SKICAT comprise a significant portion of our ongoing research.

The first step in analyzing the results of a sky survey is to identify, measure, and catalog the detected objects in the image into their respective classes (e.g. stars versus galaxies). Once the objects have been classified, further scientific analysis can proceed. For example, the resulting catalog may be used to test models of the formation of large-scale structure in the universe, probe Galactic structure from star counts as in Weir, Djorgovski, & Fayyad (1995), perform automatic identifications of radio or infrared sources, and so forth (Weir, Djorgovski, & Fayyad 1993; Djorgovski, Weir, & Fayyad 1994; Weir 1994). Reducing the images to catalog entries is an overwhelming task which inherently requires an automated approach. The goal of our project is to automate this process, providing a consistent and uniform methodology for reducing the data sets. This will provide the means for objectively performing tasks that formerly required subjective and visually intensive manual analysis. Another goal of this work is to classify objects whose brightness (isophotal magnitude) is too faint for recognition by inspection, hence requiring an automated classification procedure. We do this by utilizing a limited set of high resolution CCD images in which it is possible for astronomers to assign classes to faint objects. The learning algorithm's job is to find a classifier that can predict classes of faint objects based only on measurements from the lower-resolution images (see section 19.5).

Faint objects constitute the majority of objects on any given plate. We target the classification of objects that are at least one magnitude fainter than objects classified in previous surveys using comparable photographic material. SKICAT is an example where learning algorithms proved to a be useful and powerful tool in the automation of a significant scientific data analysis task, producing tangible new scientific results (Weir, Djorgovski, & Fayyad 1995, Weir, Fayyad, & Djorgovski 1995).

The chapter begins with a brief introduction of the machine learning techniques we used, then we discuss the problem of cataloging objects in a sky survey. We then focus on the important problem of feature extraction which makes accurate classification possible. After we cover the successful results which exceeded our initial goals, we conclude by discussing our future work targeting the utilization of unsupervised learning to aid in scientific discovery in the large SKICAT-generated catalog.

19.2   Decision Trees and Rules

19.2.1   Induction of Decision Trees

A classification learning algorithm is given as input a set of *examples* that consist of vectors of attribute values (also called *feature vectors*) and a class. The goal is to output a classification scheme, known as a *classifier*, that will predict the class variable based on the values of the attributes. A particularly efficient method for producing classifiers from data is to generate a decision tree (Breiman et al, 1984; Quinlan, 1986). A decision tree consists of nodes that are tests on the attributes. The outgoing branches of a node correspond to all the possible outcomes of the test at the node. The examples at a node in the tree are thus partitioned along the branches and each child node gets its corresponding subset of examples.

A well-known greedy tree growing algorithm for generating decision trees is Quinlan's ID3 (Quinlan 1986) with extended versions called C4 (Quinlan 1990). ID3 starts with all the training examples at the root node of the tree. An attribute is selected to partition these examples. For each value of the attribute, a branch is created and the corresponding subset of examples that have the attribute value specified by the branch are moved to the newly created child node. The algorithm is applied recursively to each child node until either all examples at a node are of one class, or all the examples at that node have the same values for all the attributes. Every leaf in the decision tree represents a classification rule. Note that the critical decision in such a top-down decision tree generation algorithm is the choice of attribute at a node. Attribute selection in ID3 and C4 is based on minimizing an information entropy measure applied to the examples at a node. The measure favors attributes that result in partitioning the data into subsets that have low class entropy. A subset of data has low class entropy when the majority of examples in it belong to a single class. The algorithm basically chooses the attribute that provides the locally maximum degree of discrimination between classes. For a detailed discussion of the information entropy selection criterion see Quinlan (1986), Fayyad (1991), and Fayyad and Irani (1992a)

19.2.2   The GID3* and O-BTREE Algorithms

The criterion for choosing the attribute clearly determines whether a "good" or "bad" tree is generated by the algorithm. ID3 utilizes a heuristic criterion which favors the attribute that results in the partition having the least mutual information entropy with the class variable. However, there are weaknesses inherent in the ID3 algorithm that are due mainly to the fact that it creates a branch for each value of the attribute chosen for branching. The overbranching problem in ID3 leads to several problems, since in general it may be the case that only a subset of values of an attribute are of relevance to the classification task while the rest of the values may not have any special predictive value for the classes. These extra branches are harmful in three ways (Fayyad, 1991):

1. They result in rules that are overspecialized (conditioned on particular irrelevant attribute values).

2. They unnecessarily partition the data, thus reducing the number of examples at each node. Subsequent attribute choices will be based on an unjustifiably reduced subset of data.

3. They increase the likelihood of occurrence of the missing branches problem (see Fayyad 1991,1994 for more details).

The GID3* algorithm (Fayyad 1994) was designed mainly to overcome this problem. We generalized the ID3 algorithm so that it does not necessarily branch on each value of the chosen attribute. GID3* can branch on arbitrary individual values of an attribute and "lump" the rest of the values in a single default branch. Unlike the other branches of the tree which represent a single value, the default branch represents a subset of values of an attribute. Unnecessary subdivision of the data may thus be reduced. See Fayyad (1991,1994) for more details and for empirical evidence of improvement.

The O-Btree algorithm (Fayyad and Irani 1992a) was designed to overcome problems with the information entropy attribute selection measure itself. O-Btree creates strictly binary trees and utilizes a measure from a family of measures (called C-SEP) that detects class separation rather than class impurity. Information entropy is a member of the class of impurity measures. O-Btree employs an orthogonality rather than an impurity measure. For details on problems with entropy measures and empirical evaluation of O-Btree, the reader is referred to (Fayyad 1991; Fayyad and Irani 1992b). Both O-Btree and GID3* differ from ID3 and C4 along one additional aspect: the discretization algorithm used at each node to discretize continuous-valued attributes (Fayyad and Irani, 1992b). Whereas ID3 and C4 utilize a binary interval discretization algorithm, we use a generalized version of that algorithm which derives multiple intervals rather than strictly two. For details and empirical tests showing that this algorithm does indeed produce better trees see Fayyad (1991) and Fayyad and Irani (1993). We have found that multiple interval extraction improves performance considerably in several domains.

19.2.3   Optimized Rules from Multiple Trees: The RULER System

There are limitations to decision tree generation algorithms that derive from the inherent fact that the classification rules they produce originate from a single tree. This fact was recognized by practitioners early on by Breiman et. al (1984) and others. Tree pruning is used to overcome the fact that in any good tree there are always leaves that are overspecialized or predict the wrong class. The very reason which makes decision tree generation efficient (the fact that data is quickly partitioned into ever smaller subsets), is also the reason why overspecialization or incorrect classification occurs. It is our philosophy that once we have good, efficient, decision tree generators, they could be used to generate multiple trees, and only the best rules in each tree are kept. Figure 19.1 gives an overview of the RULER system.

RULER repeatedly divides a set of examples randomly into training and test subsets. A decision tree is generated from each training set and its rules are tested on the corresponding test set. Using Fisher's exact test—the exact hyper geometric distribution (Finney et al 1963), RULER evaluates each condition in a given rule's preconditions for relevance to the class predicted by the rule. It computes the probability that

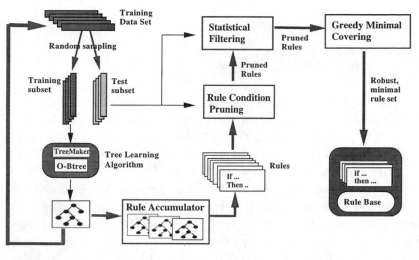

Figure 19.1
Overview of the RULER learning system

the condition is correlated with the class by chance[2]. If this probability is higher than a small threshold (say 0.01), the condition is deemed irrelevant and is pruned. After condition pruning, RULER also measures the merit of the entire rule by applying the test to the entire precondition as a unit. This process serves as a filter which passes only robust, general, and correct rules.

By gathering a large number of rules through iterating on randomly subsampled training sets, RULER builds a large rulebase of robust rules that collectively cover the entire original data set of examples. A greedy covering algorithm is then employed to select a minimal subset of rules that covers the examples. The set is minimal in the sense that no rule could be removed without losing complete coverage of the original training set. Using RULER, we can typically produce a robust set of rules that has fewer rules than any of the original decision trees used to create it. Furthermore, any learning algorithm that produces rules can be used as the rule generating component. We use decision tree algorithms since they constitute a fast and efficient method for generating a set of rules. This allows us to iterate many times without requiring extensive

---

[2]The Chi-square test is actually an approximation to Fisher's exact test when the number of test examples is large. We use Fisher's exact test because it is robust for small and large data sets.

amounts of time and computation.

19.3   The Cataloging Process

SKICAT provides an integrated environment for the construction, classification, management, and analysis of catalogs from large-scale imaging
surveys, in particular the digitized POSS-II. Due to the large amounts
of data being collected, a manual approach to detecting and classifying
sky objects in the images is infeasible: it would require on the order of
tens of man years. Existing computational methods for classifying the
images would preclude the identification of the majority of objects in
each image since they are at levels too faint for traditional recognition
algorithms or even manual inspection/analysis approaches. A principal
goal of SKICAT is to provide an effective, objective, and examinable
basis for classifying sky objects at levels beyond the limits of existing
technology. Each of the 3,000 digitized plates, consisting of $23,040^2$
pixels, is subdivided into a set of partially overlapping frames. Each
frame represents a small part of the plate that is small enough to be
manipulated and processed conveniently. Figure 19.2 depicts the overall architecture of the SKICAT catalog construction and classification
process.

Low-level image processing and object separation is performed by a
modified version of the FOCAS image processing public domain software
(Jarvis & Tyson 1981, Valdes 1984). The FOCAS image processing
steps detect contiguous pixels in the image that are to be grouped as
one object. Attributes are then measured based on this segmentation.
Based on the pixel group constituting a single detected object, FOCAS
produces basic attributes describing the object. In Section 19.4.2 we
explain the arrow going from the learning algorithm to the attribute
definition box in Figure 19.2 representing the fact that we used learning
in the attribute measurement process.

Our current goal is to classify objects into four major categories, following the original scheme in FOCAS: star (s), star with fuzz (sf), galaxy
(g), and artifact (long). However, the goal is to both achieve a higher
accuracy and classify fainter objects than has been previously achieved
using traditional computational techniques in Astronomy.

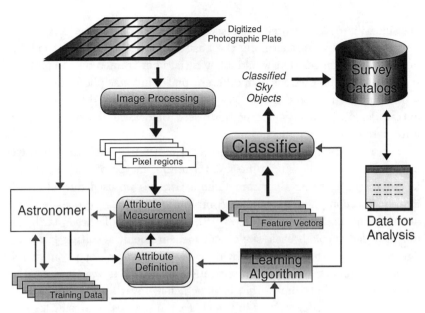

Figure 19.2
An overview of the SKICAT plate cataloging process.

19.4   Feature Extraction and Definition

A total of 40 attributes for each detected object are measured automatically.. These base-level attributes are generic quantities typically used in astronomical analyses including the following FOCAS-defined attributes:

- isophotal, aperture, core, and asymptotic "total" magnitudes
- isophotal and "total" areas
- sky brightness and sigma (variance)
- peak, intensity weighted, and unweighted positions: xc, yc, icx, icy, cx, cy
- intensity weighted and unweighted image moments: ir1, ir2, ir3, ir4, r1, r2, ixx, iyy, ixy, xx, yy, xy
- ellipticity and position angle (orientation)

Once all attributes are measured, the next problem to address is classification. However, the base-level attributes are not sufficient for accurate

classification of the fainter objects which constitute the majority of all
detected objects. Furthermore, the base-level attributes do not exhibit
desirable invariances that would allow a classifier trained on one plate to
make accurate predictions on a different plate that was photographed on
a different night with different sky conditions. Hence a difficult feature
extraction problem needs to be addressed before we can proceed with
automated classification.

In classification learning, the choice of attributes used to define examples is by far the single most determining factor of the success or
failure of the learning algorithm. The attributes we used during classification are computed through a combination of image processing and
attribute normalization processes. While a number of these attributes
are provided through basic sky object measurements resulting from image processing, they do not provide a suitable feature space in which
to perform object classification with high accuracy. It was necessary to
derive additional attributes that have sufficient invariance within a plate
(i.e. along the borders versus in the center) and across plates. This section describes how the attributes which are used in classification were
derived.

19.4.1   Normalized Attributes

We quickly determined that these base-level attributes do not exhibit
the required invariance between different regions of a single plate, and
across plates. This was exhibited both by low accuracy classifiers, and
by simple analysis of the value distributions across plates. For example,
we determined that the base-level measurements such as background
sky level, area, and average intensity are image-dependent, and thus
inherently sensitive to plate-to-plate and even frame-to-frame variation.
For the learning algorithms to be able to produce robust classifiers, new
attributes had to be derived from the base-level attributes.

Using the following approach, we compute four new normalized attributes based on the following four base-level attributes: core magnitude, log of the isophotal area, intensity weighted first moment radius,
and S, which is a function of area, core luminosity, and isophotal intensity:

$$\mathbf{S} = \frac{\mathbf{Area}}{\log[\mathbf{L_{core}}/(9 \times \mathbf{Ispht})]}.$$

First we derive a non-linear curve (the stellar locus) in the two dimensions defined by magnitude versus the original base-level attribute, for each frame within a plate. We define the new attribute to be the distance of each object from the stellar locus for that plate. We essentially subtract out the stellar locus, in order to normalize the attributes. The quantities described are used by astronomers, and many of them have physical interpretations.

The result of this process is a set of features that exhibit a good degree of invariances across plates, and within different regions on a plate. For example, a constant shift in background sky brightness, resulting in differences in intensity observations would be removed by such processing.

19.4.2   Resolution Scale and Fraction

In addition to the four normalized attributes described above, we compute two additional attributes which are particularly stable across images. However, the computation of these additional attributes requires an empirical measurement based on a selection of stars from each frame. This process was achieved through a second application of the learning algorithms during the attribute measurement process; this is shown in the loop in the bottom left corner of Figure 19.2. We refer to this as the star selection subproblem.

Due to turbulence in the Earth's atmosphere, point sources in the sky (stars) appear as blurred, quasi-Gaussian intensity distributions. By selecting some of the objects on a frame that are obviously resolved (*sure-thing stars*), one can hope to model this effect and compensate for it when classifying. To this end, we fit the pixel values of these "sure-thing stars" to define a point spread function (PSF) template. Using the PSF template, the FOCAS 'resolution' routine determines the best-fitting 'scale' (α) and 'fraction' (β) values, which parameterize the fit of a blurred (or sharpened) version of the PSF to each object (Valdes, 1982). The template used to model each object is of the form:

$$t(r_i) = \beta s(r_i/\alpha) + (1 - \beta)s(r_i)$$

where r_i is the position of pixel i, α is the broadening (sharpening) parameter, β is the fraction of broadened PSF, and $s(r_i)$ represents the pixel value at position r_i.

To form the PSF template, the sure-thing stars would normally be hand-selected from an image by the astronomer. To automate the measurement of these additional attributes, we trained a classifier to detect the "sure-thing" stars in each frame using the four normalized attributes described in the previous section. We have achieved 98% accuracy in detecting the sure-thing stars used to determine the PSF template. Once a template is formed, the resolution attributes are measured for each object on that frame automatically. See Section 19.6 for the discussion of the impact of adding these derived attributes.

19.5   Classifying Faint Objects

How can a learning algorithm learn to classify objects too faint for humans to classify? In addition to the scanned photographic plates, we have access to CCD images that span several small regions in some of the frames. CCD images are obtained from a separate telescope. The main advantage of a CCD image is higher resolution and higher signal-to-noise ratio at fainter levels. Hence, many of the objects that are too faint to be classified by inspection on a photographic plate are easily classifiable in a CCD image. In addition to using these images for photometric calibration of the photographic plates, we make use of CCD images in two very important ways for the machine learning aspect, since they provide us with:

1. class labels for faint objects in the photographic plates, and

2. the means to reliably evaluate the accuracy of the classifiers obtained from the decision tree learning algorithms.

In order to produce a classifier that classifies faint objects correctly, the learning algorithm needs training data consisting of faint objects labeled with the appropriate class. The class label is therefore obtained by examining the CCD frames. This process is illustrated in Figure 19.3. Once trained on properly labeled objects, the learning algorithm produces a classifier that is capable of properly classifying objects based on the values of the attributes measured from the lower resolution plate image. Hence, in principle, the classifier will be able to classify objects in the photographic image that are simply too faint for an astronomer to classify by inspection. Using the class labels, the learning algorithms are basically being used to solve the more difficult problem of separating the classes in the multi-dimensional space defined by the set of attributes

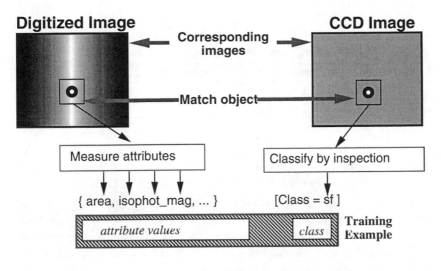

Figure 19.3
Constructing training examples for faint objects.

derived via image processing. This method is expected to allow us to classify objects that are at least one magnitude fainter than objects classified in photographic all-sky surveys to date.

19.6   Classification Results

In order to assess the accuracy of the automatically generated classifier, we used data consisting of objects collected from four different plates from regions for which we had CCD image coverage. recall that CCD plates provides us with the "ground truth" since this is the only data for which true accurate classifications are available. We performed initial tests to evaluate the accuracy of the classifiers produced by the machine learning algorithms ID3, GID3*, and O-BTree. The learning algorithms are trained on a data set from 3 plates and tested on data from the remaining plate for cross validation. This estimates our accuracy in classifying objects across plates. Note that the plates cover different regions of the sky and that CCD frames cover multiple small portions of each plate. The training data consisted of 1,688 objects that were classified manually by one of the authors (NW) by examining the corresponding CCD frames. It is noteworthy that for the majority of these objects, the astronomer would not be able to reliably determine the classes by ex-

Table 19.1
Percent of objects correctly classified by learning algorithms.

Decision Tree Algorithms			Classification Rules
ID3	GID3*	O-Btree	RULER
75.6%	90.1%	91.2%	94.2%

amining the corresponding survey (digitized photographic) images. All attributes used by the learning algorithms are derived from the survey images and not, of course, from the higher resolution CCD frames.

Using all the attributes, including the two resolution attributes derived after star selection, the classification results are shown in Table 19.1. The results for RULER above are shown with O-Btree as the decision tree generation component and were obtained by cycling through tree generation and rule merging (Figure 19.1) 10 times.

When the same experiments were conducted without using the resolution scale and resolution fraction attributes the results were significantly worse. The error rates jumped above 20% for O-BTree, above 25% for GID3*, and above 30% for ID3. The respective sizes of the trees grew significantly as well. We took this as evidence that the resolution attributes are very important for the classification task. Furthermore, the results point out that the GID3* and O-BTree learning algorithms are more appropriate than ID3 for the final classification task. We suspect that this is due mainly to the multi-interval discretization algorithm employed by them (Fayyad and Irani 1993) which differs from ID3's binary algorithm. As expected, the use of RULER resulted in improvement in performance.

19.6.1   Comparison with Neural Nets

In order to compare against other learning algorithms, and to preclude the possibility that a decision tree based approach is imposing a priori limitations on the achievable classification levels, we tested several neural network algorithms for comparison. The results indicate that neural network algorithms achieve similar, and sometimes worse, performance than the decision trees. The neural net learning algorithms tested were:

1. traditional backpropagation,
2. conjugate gradient optimization, and
3. variable metric optimization.

Unlike backpropagation, the latter two training algorithms work in batch mode and use standard numerical optimization techniques in changing the network weights (Hertz et al 1991). They compute the weight adjustments simultaneously using matrix operations based on the total error of the network on the entire training set. Their main advantage over traditional backpropagation is the significant speed-up in training time.

The results can be summarized as follows: The performance of the neural networks was fairly unstable and produced accuracy levels varying between 30% (no convergence) and 95%[3]. The most common range of accuracy on average was between 76% and 84%. Note that we had to perform multiple trials, each time varying:

1. the number of internal nodes in the hidden layer,

2. the initial network weight settings, and

3. the learning rate constant for backpropagation.

Upon examining the results of the empirical evaluation, we concluded that the neural net approach did not offer any clear advantages over the decision tree based learning algorithm. Although neural networks, with extensive training and several training restarts with different initial weights to avoid local minima, could match the performance of the decision tree classifier, the decision tree approach still holds several major advantages. The most important is that the trees, especially when turned into compact rules by RULER, were easy for domain experts to understand. In addition, unlike neural network learning algorithms, the decision tree learning algorithms GID3* and O-BTree do not require the specification of parameters such as the size of the neural net, the number of hidden layers, and random trials with different initial weight settings. Also, the required training time is orders of magnitude faster than the training time required for a neural network approach. Other groups have experimented with the neural network approach, e.g. Odewahn et al (1992), for astronomy applications.

The stability of the performance of the decision tree algorithms, and the fact that a decision tree (or classification rule) is a lot easier to interpret and understand than a neural network, provided strong reasons

---

[3]Note that these are single maxima and minima for performance, what we care about is average performance: this is what we reported in Table 19.1 for trees and rules.

for favoring the decision tree approach. We, therefore, decided to adopt the decision tree approach for our problem.

19.6.2   Verification and Reliability Estimates

As mentioned earlier, in addition to using the CCD frames to derive training data for the machine learning algorithms, we also use them to verify and estimate the performance of our classification technique. This is done by testing on data sets that are drawn independently from the training data. An additional source of internal consistency checks comes from the fact that the plates, and the frames within each plate are partially overlapping. Hence, objects inside the overlapping regions will be classified in more than one context. By measuring the rate of conflicting classifications, we can obtain further estimates of the statistical confidence in the accuracy of our classifier. For the purposes of the final catalog production, a method is being designed for resolving conflicts on objects within regions of overlap. We have not yet collected reportable results on this aspect of the problem.

In order to demonstrate the difficulty and significance of the classification results presented so far, consider the example shown in Figure 19.4. This figure shows four image patches each centered about a faint sky object that was classified by SKICAT. These images were obtained from a plate that was not provided to SKICAT in the training cycle and the objects are part of a region in the sky containing the Abell 1551 cluster of galaxies near the North Galactic Pole. SKICAT classified the top two objects as stars and the bottom two as galaxies. According to astronomers (at least two of the authors), the objects shown in Figure 19.4 are too faint for reliable classification. As a matter of fact, an astronomer visually inspecting these images would be hard pressed to decide whether the object in the lower right hand corner is a star or a galaxy. The object in the upper right hand corner appears as a galaxy based on visual inspection. Upon retrieving the corresponding higher resolution CCD images of these objects, it was clear that the SKICAT classification was indeed correct. Note that SKICAT produced the prediction based on the lower resolution survey images (shown in the figure). This example illustrates how the SKICAT classifier can correctly classify the majority of faint objects which even the astronomers cannot classify. Indeed, the results indicate that SKICAT has a better than 90% accuracy identifying objects that are one full magnitude below

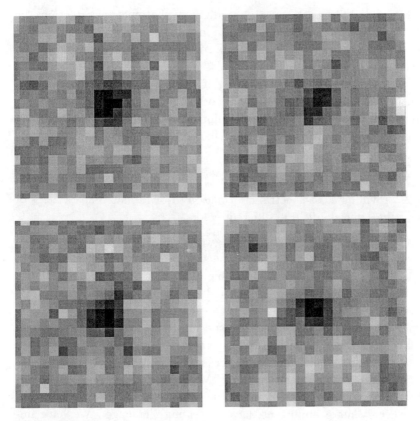

Figure 19.4
An illustrative example: four faint sky objects.

the comparable magnitude limit in previous automated Schmidt plate surveys.

19.7   Catalog Management

The current version of SKICAT uses the Sybase commercial database package for catalog storage, modification, and management. Each of the plate and CCD catalogs, must be registered in the SKICAT system tables, where a complete description and history of every catalog loaded to date is maintained. Catalog revisions, e.g., from deriving new and improved plate astrometric coordinates, photometric corrections, or even improved classifications, are also logged. The system is designed to manage a database of image catalogs constantly growing and improving with time. One of the most difficult, yet critical, aspects of the data management process is the matching of identical sky objects detected in multiple, independent images. The most important science to be derived from the POSS-II depends upon uniformly integrating object measurements from a large number of overlapping plates. The advantages are:

1. permitting the objective analysis of a much larger portion of the sky than covered by a single 6.5° × 6.5° photographic plate, and

2. providing cross-spectral information through matching catalogs of the same sky field in different colors.

It is the large solid angular coverage of all-sky surveys which set them most apart in observational phase space; this property facilitates certain types of science which are not feasible with other forms of data. In addition, cross-correlation of sources detected at different wavelengths is particularly fruitful in maximizing the scientific return from virtually any type of astronomical observation, especially from major surveys. A direct comparison of emission from astronomical objects in different parts of the electromagnetic spectrum can lead to astrophysical insights and better understanding of their nature. Matching and cross-identifications of large numbers of sources, in an objective and uniform way, is thus an increasingly more important data processing challenge. We have implemented a SKICAT utility for matching any number of catalogs, object by object, in a consistent, though user-definable, fashion. With a modest amount of programming effort, the system can even be made to accommodate astronomical catalogs from sources other than plate scans or CCDs, i.e., from vastly different spectral regimes. The resulting matched catalog contains independent entries for every measurement of every object present in the constituent catalogs. The matched catalog may be queried using a sophisticated filtering and output mechanism to generate a so-called object catalog, containing just a single entry per matched object. Such queries may generate either additional Sybase objects tables or ASCII files, suitable for input to any number of plotting and analysis packages (Weir et al 1994).

A particularly promising aspect of SKICAT is the facility, as new data are added in, to query plate and CCD overlap regions in the matched catalog and dynamically update the constituent catalogs (their photometry, astrometry, classifications, etc.) in light of these results. While this process is accomplished by applying the appropriate SKICAT tools manually at this point, it is clear that an automated approach to maintaining and improving database uniformity in this way would be rewarding. This goal, of creating a "living," growing data set, instead of a data archive fixed for all time, has been an overriding one from the very start of the development of SKICAT.

19.8   Some Experiments with Unsupervised Classification

We have also begun exploring the application and implementation of unsupervised classification techniques like AutoClass (described elsewhere in this book by Cheeseman and Stutz [1996]) for the purpose of automated machine discovery. Unlike the so-called supervised methods of classification that we have described so far, where the algorithm learns how to distinguish user-specified classes within the data, unsupervised classification consists of identifying the statistically significant classes within the data itself. For example, one could employ this type of method to try to systematically detect new classes of objects within astronomical catalogs.

Our own initial experiments in applying AutoClass to POSS-II appear to confirm the validity and usefulness of this approach. After supplying AutoClass with eight-dimensional feature vectors from a sample of several hundred objects from four fields, it analyzed the distribution of the objects in this parameter space and suggested four distinct classes within the data. Visually, the classes seem to divide into stellar objects, stellar-like objects with a low surface brightness halo, and diffuse or irregular objects with and without a central core (De Carvalho et al 1995).

However, in order to achieve these results, we had to bin the values one of the parameters (isophotal magnitude) before presenting AutoClass with the data. We thus partitioned the data by meaningful magnitude ranges before running AutoClass on each subset. We also selected the eight-dimensional subspace by hand. Nevertheless, AutoClass's success at distinguishing these apparently physically relevant classes based just upon eight image parameters suggests that far richer and innovative results may be in store when one matches multiple catalogs together, increasing the informational dimensionality of the data set many fold. Problems of extending clustering algorithms to high-dimensional spaces and large data sets still need to be addressed.

19.9   Conclusions

In this chapter, we described a KDD application to automate the processing and analysis of a large scientifically important data set. The SKICAT system integrates multiple components including image processing, feature extraction, classification learning, and high-performance DBMS. SKICAT can catalog and classify objects that are at least one magnitude fainter than objects cataloged in previous surveys. This project represents a step towards the development of an objective, reliable automated sky object classification method.

The initial results of our effort to automate sky object classification in order to automatically reduce the images produced by POSS-II to sky catalogs are indeed very encouraging. We have exceeded our initial accuracy target of 90%. This level of accuracy is required for the data to be useful in testing or refuting theories on the formation of large structure in the universe and on other phenomena of interest to astronomers. The SKICAT tool is now being employed to both process and analyze the survey images as they arrive from the digitization instrument. We are also beginning to explore the application of SKICAT to the analysis of other surveys already performed or being planned by NASA and other institutions.

By effectively defining robust features, we were able to derive classifiers with an accuracy exceeding that of humans for faint objects. Since faint objects constitute the majority of objects on any plate, the number of classified objects available for further scientific analysis is dramatically increased. In effect, this shows that the pixels contained important information that was difficult for the human visual system to extract. Projection of the high-dimensional pixel space onto a suitable lower-dimensional feature space allowed us to transform the problem into one solvable by a supervised learning algorithm. By defining additional "normalized" image-independent attributes, we were able to obtain high accuracy classifiers within and across photographic plates.

The implications of a tool like SKICAT for Astronomy may indeed be profound. One could reclassify any portion of the survey using alternative criteria better suited to a particular scientific goal (e.g. star catalogs versus galaxy catalogs). This changes the notion of a sky catalog from the classical static entity "in print," to a dynamic, ever growing, ever improving, on-line database. The catalogs will also accommodate additional attribute entries, in the event other pixel-based measurements are deemed necessary. An important feature of the survey analysis system will be to facilitate such detailed interactions with the catalogs. The catalog generated by SKICAT will eventually contain about two billion entries representing hundreds of millions of sky objects. Unlike the traditional notion of a static printed catalog, we view our effort as targeting the development of a new generation of scientific analysis tools that render it possible to have a constantly evolving, improving, and growing catalog. Without the availability of these tools for the first survey (POSS-I) conducted over four decades ago, no objective and comprehensive analysis of the data was possible. In contrast, we are targeting a comprehensive sky catalog that will be available on-line for use by the scientific community.

Acknowledgments

The majority of the funding for SKICAT was provided by NASA's Office of Space Access and Technology (Code XS): we thank Dr. M. Montemerlo for his support and program management. We thank the Sky Survey team for their expertise and effort in acquiring the plate material. The POSS-II is funded by grants from Eastman Kodak Co., The National Geographic Society, The Samuel Oschin Foundation, NSF Grants AST 84-08225 and AST 87-19465, and NASA Grants NGL 05002140 and NAGW 1710. The JPL SKICAT team included Joe Roden, John Loch, Scott Burleigh, Maureen Burl, and Jennifer Yu. This work was supported by a NSF graduate fellowship (NW), Caltech President's Fund, NASA contract NAS5-31348 (SD & NW), and the NSF PYI Award AST-9157412 (SD).

The work described in this chapter was carried out in part by the Jet Propulsion Laboratory, California Institute of Technology, under a contract with the National Aeronautics and Space Administration.

References

Breiman, L.; Friedman, J. H.; Olshen, R. A.; and Stone, C. J. 1984. *Classification and Regression Trees*. Monterey, Calif.: Wadsworth & Brooks.

Cheeseman, P.; and Stutz, J. 1996. Bayesian Classification (AutoClass): Theory and Results. In *Advances in Knowledge Discovery and Data Mining,* ed. U. Fayyad et al. Menlo Park, Calif.: AAAI Press.

DeCarvalho, R.; Djorgovski, S. G.; Weir, N.; Fayyad, U.; Cherkauer, K.; Roden, J.; and Gray, A. 1995. Clustering Analysis Algorithms and Their Applications to Digital POSS-II Catalogs. In Astronomical Data Analysis Software and Systems IV, ed. R. Hanisch. *A.S.P. Conf. Ser.*

Djorgovski, S. G.; Weir, N.; and Fayyad, U. M. 1994. Processing and Analysis of the Palomar—STScI Digital Sky Survey Using a Novel Software Technology. In Astronomical Data Analysis Software and Systems III, ed. D. Crabtree, R. Hanisch, and J. Barnes. *A.S.P. Conf. Ser.* 61 (195).

Fayyad, U. M. 1991. On the Induction of Decision Trees for Multiple Concept Learning. PhD diss., Department of Electrical Engineering & Computer Science, The University of Michigan, Ann Arbor, 1991.

Fayyad, U. M.; and Irani, K. B. 1992a. The Attribute Selection Problem in Decision Tree Generation. In Proceedings of the Tenth National Conference on Artificial Intelligence AAAI-92, 104–110. Menlo Park, Calif.: AAAI Press.

Fayyad, U. M.; and Irani, K. B. 1992b. On the Handling of Continuous-Valued Attributes in Decision Tree Generation. *Machine Learning,* 8(2).

Fayyad, U. M.; and Irani, K. B. 1993. Multi-Interval Discretization of Continuous-Valued Attributes for Classification Learning. In Proceedings of the Thirteenth International Joint Conference on Artificial Intelligence. San Francisco: Morgan Kaufmann.

Fayyad, U. M.; Weir, N.; and Djorgovski, S. G. 1993. SKICAT: A Machine Learning System for the Automated Cataloging of Large-Scale Sky Surveys. In Proceedings of the Tenth International Conference on Machine Learning.

Fayyad, U. M. 1994. Branching on Attribute Values in Decision Tree Generation. In Proceedings of the Twelfth National Conference on Artificial Intelligence AAAI-94, 601–606. Menlo Park, Calif.: AAAI Press.

Finney, D. J.; Latscha, R.; Bennett, B. M.; and Hsu, P. 1963. *Tables for Testing Significance in a 2 × 2 Contingency Table*. Cambridge: Cambridge University Press.

Hertz, J.; Krogh, A.; and Palmer, R. G. 1991. *Introduction to the Theory of Neural Computation*. Reading, Mass.: Addison-Wesley.

Jarvis, J.; and Tyson, A. 1981. FOCAS: Faint Object Classification and Analysis System. *Astronomical Journal* 86 (476).

Odewahn, S.; Stockwell, E.; Pennington, R.; Humphreys, R.; and Zumach, W. 1992. Automated Star/Galaxy Discrimination with Neural Networks. *Astronomical Journal* 103: 318.

Quinlan, J. R. 1986. The Induction of Decision Trees. *Machine Learning*, 1 (1).

Quinlan, J. R. 1990. Probabilistic Decision Trees. In *Machine Learning: An Artificial Intelligence Approach Vol. III*, ed. Y. Kodratoff & R. Michalski. San Mateo, Calif.: Morgan Kaufmann.

Reid, I. N.; Brewer, C.; Brucato, R.; McKinley, W.; Maury, A.; Mendenthall, D.; Mould, J.; Mueller, J.; Neugebauer, G.; Phinney, J.; Sargent, W.; Schombert, J.; and Thicksten, R. 1991. The Second Palomar Sky Survey. *Publications of the Astronomical Society of the Pacific*, 103 (665).

Valdes, F. 1982. The Resolution Classifier. In *Instrumentation in Astronomy IV*, 331: 465. Bellingham, Wash.:, SPIE.

Weir, N. 1994. *Automated Analysis of the Digitized Second Palomar Sky Survey: System Design, Implementation, and Initial Results*. Ph.D. diss., California Institute of Technology, Pasadena, Calif.

Weir, N.; Djorgovski, S. G.; Fayyad, U. M.; Smith, J. D.; and Roden, J. 1994. Cataloging the Northern Sky Using a New Generation of Software Technology. In *Astronomy From Wide-Field Imaging*, #161, 205, ed. H. MacGillivray. Dordrecht: Kluwer.

Weir, N.; Fayyad, U. M.; and Djorgovski, S. G. 1995. Automated Star/Galaxy Classification for Digitized POSS-II. *The Astronomical Journal*.

Weir, N., Djorgovski, S. G., and Fayyad, U. M. 1995. Initial Galaxy Counts From Digitized POSS-II. *The Astronomical Journal*.

20 Selecting and Reporting What Is Interesting

Christopher J. Matheus & Gregory Piatetsky-Shapiro
GTE Laboratories Incorporated

Dwight McNeill
GTE Service Corporation

Information by itself is a pretty thin meal,
if not mixed with other ingredients.
– *Internet quote*

Abstract

One of the most promising areas in knowledge discovery in databases is the automatic analysis of deviations. Success in this task hinges on the ability to identify a few important and relevant events among the multitude of potentially interesting deviations. In this chapter we present our approach to determining the interestingness of a deviation via the potential benefit from a relevant action. This approach has been implemented in the Key Findings Reporter (KEFIR), a system for discovering and explaining "key findings" in large, changing databases, currently being applied to the analysis of healthcare data. The system performs an automatic drill-down through data along multiple dimensions to determine the most interesting deviations of specific quantitative measures relative to their previous and expected values. It explains "key" deviations through their relationship to other deviations in the data, and, where appropriate, generates recommendations for actions in response to these deviations. KEFIR uses Netscape, a WWW browser, to present its findings in a hypertext report, using natural language and business graphics.

20.1   Introduction

Increasingly, databases are being used to record all kinds of business transactions. The timely analysis of these databases is highly desirable and may often provide a competitive advantage. As these databases grow larger—with gigabyte sizes quite common—they are overwhelming the traditional query and report based methods of data analysis.

This has led to the development of systems for automated discovery in databases (Piatetsky-Shapiro & Frawley 1991, Piatetsky-Shapiro 1993, Fayyad & Uthurusamy 1994).

While many different discovery methods (Matheus et al. 1993) have been tried, some of the most successful business applications – such as the Spotlight (Anand and Kahn 1992) and CoverStory (Schmitz, Armstrong, and Little 1990) systems for supermarket sales analysis—have been based on the detection of deviations, i.e. significant differences between measured values and corresponding references such as previous values or normative values.

Deviations are powerful because they provide a simple way of identifying interesting patterns in the data. We have studied many knowledge discovery algorithms with potential for identifying vast numbers of significant patterns from data, but most of these are unable to determine when a pattern is truly interesting to the user (Matheus et al. 1993). With deviations we have a simple way to identify things that differ from our expectations—since they differ from what we expect, they are by definition interesting at least to some degree.

KEFIR is a system for discovering, explaining, and reporting on key deviations in large databases. It performs an automatic drill-down through data along multiple dimensions to determine the most interesting deviations of specific quantitative measures relative to norms and previous values. It then explains "key" deviations through their relationships to other deviations in the data, and, where appropriate, generates simple recommendations for actions in response to deviations. The results are compiled into a written report in the form of a hypertext document, delivered using the World Wide Web (WWW) (Berners-Lee et al. 1992).

In this chapter we describe Health-KEFIR which is an application of KEFIR to the healthcare domain. In particular, we will concentrate on the problem of how to decide which deviations are the most interesting. We will argue that to properly judge the interestingness of a deviation, one should examine deviations between an observed value and *all* relevant reference values, that is all previous values, and all relevant normative values. Such a set of related (current, previous, and normative) values of a given measure is called a *finding*.

Central to KEFIR's methodology is its ability to rank deviations according to some measure of "interestingness" to the user of the system. In earlier work (Piatetsky-Shapiro 1991, Frawley, Piatetsky-Shapiro, and Matheus 1992) we examined various factors of interestingness such as novelty, utility, relevance, and statistical significance. Here, we will argue that, at least in business applications, domain-independent statistical measures of interestingness are insufficient and that the interestingness of a finding should be based on the estimated utility that could be realized by taking a specific responsive action.

In the following section we describe the process of data analysis of healthcare information, which sets the stage for our analysis of interestingness. We then describe the complete KEFIR system, and offer ideas for future work in this area.

20.2   Healthcare Data Analysis

With the steady rise in healthcare costs and the growing urgency to control these costs, timely analysis of healthcare information has become an issue of great importance. Large corporations, hospitals, health-maintenance organizations, and insurance companies all require expert analysis of their healthcare data—an endeavor that is both time consuming and very expensive. A single report may take weeks or months to prepare and can cost tens of thousands of dollars. For large corporations, which typically order many reports for different business units, healthcare consulting costs may run into millions of dollars per year. The great time and expense of preparing a report acts as a disincentive to ordering them in many cases, thus eliminating potential savings opportunities. Even when a report is ordered, it may be incomplete, because an exhaustive search of possible findings and their explanations is simply infeasible by manual means. In our own experience, we have seen examples where human experts overlooked important findings later detected by Health-KEFIR.

This situation presents a real opportunity for automating data analysis and reporting systems, especially because the methods currently employed by healthcare analysts lend themselves well to automation. These methods rely on a set of relatively standard *measures* which assess various aspects of healthcare, such as cost, price, usage, and quality (e.g. `average_hospital_payments_per_capita`, `admission_rate_per_-1000_people`, `cesarean_section_rate`). These measures are usually aggregate values taken over subsets of data. These subsets are created along two independent dimensions. One dimension defines the *population group* of interest, e.g. a business unit, a region, union employees, etc. The other dimension defines the *study area* (the type of medical problem to be analyzed for the selected population group): e.g. inpatient admissions, premature pregnancies, elective surgeries, etc.

A fundamental question in healthcare analysis is: For a given population group and study area, how do the current measure values compare to previous values and to normative values? If a measure for the population has changed dramatically or deviates significantly from the norm, then this is a potentially interesting finding. The actual interestingness depends on whether there are actions that can be taken in response, and on the benefits that might result. For example, a $1,000,000 jump in payments due to an increase in the number of regular pregnancies is probably less important than a $200,000 increase in payments due to premature deliveries, since there are no relevant actions for the first finding, while there are well-established intervention strategies for the second finding that can save a significant part of the cost *and* improve the quality of care. Thus, the *interestingness of a deviation is related to the estimated benefit achievable through available actions*—a notion which is quite generic and not limited to healthcare.

20.3   Analysis of Interestingness

In this section we present a principled approach to the analysis of interestingness.

The interestingness of a deviation, in brief, is determined by the payoff from a relevant action that can be taken in response to that deviation[1]. We note that in healthcare analysis, the interesting deviations are generally those which indicate a problem that can be corrected. In other applications deviations could lead to opportunities of other types.

In our discussion, we use D to denote a database instance and S to denote a subset of data (called a sector). A *measure*, denoted $M(S, D)$ (or simply M) is a function that returns a value when applied to a particular sector S and a database instance D. Not all measures are applicable to all sectors. We also assume, unless noted otherwise, that

---

[1] This fits into a statistician's view of an optimal utility function, as defined, e.g. by (DeGroot 1970)

the "interesting" direction for each measure is up, i.e. the increase in a measure such as payments_per_case (while bad for GTE) is interesting for health-care analysts, since it represents an opportunity for savings.

First, we will examine the interestingness of a single deviation and then show why it is important to combine temporal and normative deviations.

20.3.1   Impact of a Deviation

The basic measure of importance for business events is their financial impact. Other measures, such as quality or customer satisfaction, can also be translated to financial terms (although difficult, it is done, for example, by lawyers). The financial impact of a deviation serves as the objective component in KEFIR's measure of interestingness.

Let us begin with a concrete example. If payments_per_case for surgical admissions in the west region increased from \$14,818 to \$23,187 between 1992 and 1993, what is the financial impact of this change on the bottom line? To answer this question, we first need to select a measure M_0 that represents the bottom line. This measure should be such that any other measure M_i can be related to M_0 via some function f_i such that $M_0 = f_i(M_i, D)$. Note that f_i would generally be a function of other measures and also of the database instance. For Health-KEFIR M_0 is the total healthcare payments, denoted total_payments.

The impact should be measured with respect to the selected population group P_0 and the top-level study area (which contains all episodes of care) A_0. The intersection of P_0 and A_0 is called the top-level sector, denoted S_0.

Formally, the *impact* of the deviation of measure M_i in sector S_j from its value $M_i(S_j, D_R)$ in the reference database D_R to its value $M_i(S_j, D_C)$ in the current (observation) database D_C, denoted

$$impact(M_i, S_j, D_C, D_R \| M_0, S_0),$$

is the difference between

- the value that the bottom-line measure M_0 would have if the value of M_i for sector S_j was changed to its current value $M_i(S_j, D_C)$, while all other values would be as in D_R, and
- $M_0(S_0, D_R)$, the reference value of M_0 in sector S_0.

The equation for computing impact is:

$$impact(M_i, S_j, D_C, D_R \| M_0, S_0) = f_i(M_i(S_j, D_C), D_R) - M_0(S_0, D_R)$$

When the values of M_0 and S_0 are obvious they will be omitted.

For example, if `payments_per_case` in sector S_{surg} increased from $14,818 in 1992 ($D_R$) to $23,187 in 1993 ($D_C$), and `cases`$(S_{surg}, D_{92})$ = 149, then the impact of just that change on the bottom line measure can be computed to be (23,187 - 14,818) × 149 = $1,246,981. The formulas for computing the impact are described in more detail in the addendum.

In this example the impact represents the potential savings that would be realized if the current value of the measure was brought back to its previous value, i.e. GTE could save $1,246,981 if the `payments_per_case` measure for surgical admissions was brought back to its 1992 level. This approach has two major problems: (1) the old value may be an unrealistic target, and (2) the impact does not indicate the degree of control or *discretion* we might have in changing the measure. These two problems are discussed in the following sections.

20.3.2   Combining Trend and Normative Deviations

CoverStory, an earlier system for finding deviations in supermarket sales data (Schmitz, Armstrong, and Little 1990) looked at changes over time in a small number of predefined measures such as sales volume and share, and five additional causal measures (called factors in CoverStory) – distribution in store, price, store displays, feature ads, and price cuts— pre-determined by earlier market research to have effect on changes in sales volume. The interestingness of a change in a factor value was determined heuristically as: $Interestingness = \%Change \times FactorWeight \times MarketWeight$

Here the *FactorWeight* is a weight on one of the five causal factors, and *MarketWeight* is the square root of the market size.

In healthcare management it is not sufficient to look only at changes over time, since the past is not always the best reference for comparison— bringing a measure to its old value may in fact be quite difficult if not impossible. Instead, we are concerned with what can be done now to reduce future costs. A more realistic target in this case is the measure's expected value. In healthcare, as in other fields, there are tables of national, regional and other norms for many key measures. These tables

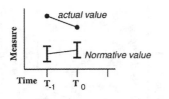

a) Finding is still significant, despite
the downward trend in the actual value

b) Finding is not important, despite
the upward trend in the actual value

Figure 20.1
Focusing only on changes can be misleading.

can be used to derive expected values for a given population (Piatetsky-Shapiro and Matheus 1994).

Figure 20.1 shows two examples of how focusing only on changes can be misleading. In Figure 20.1a, despite the downward trend in the measure, the finding is potentially interesting because the measure's value remains significantly above the norm. In Figure 20.1b, despite the upward trend in the measure, the finding is probably not as interesting because the measure's value continues to be below the norm. It is also insufficient to look only at present deviation from the norm, since this ignores the trends of the measure and of the norm.

In any case, the deviation at present reflects the potential savings which were already missed, and is only an approximation for the real measure of benefit, which is the "potential savings" achievable in the future. To determine that we need to 1) forecast the measure's future deviation from the norm, 2) translate that deviation into impact on the bottom line, and 3) determine how much of that amount we can expect to save by intervening with an appropriate action (see figure 20.2). Let us look at each of these steps in turn.

1) The Projected Deviation From the Norm: In KEFIR we forecast measure values at the end of the year by making a simple linear projection based on values from previous years. More complex forecasting strategies will be considered as additional historical data becomes available. A further refinement we are considering is knowledge-based forecasting (Lee, Oh, and Shin 1990), which could take into account domain knowledge of trends in medical inflation, normative measures, and so forth.

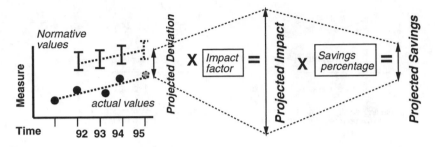

Figure 20.2
Determining future potential savings.

2) Translating the Projected Deviation Into Bottom Line Impact: After forecasting the future actual and normative values of the measure M in sector S at time T_1, we can compute the projected impact of this difference on the bottom line (see Addendum). When the formula relating M to the bottom-line measure uses only additions or multiplications, the impact can be simply computed by multiplying the projected deviation by the impact factor.

3) Actions to Reduce the Deviation: The projected impact on the bottom line is the amount that can be saved if we could bring the measure's value to the projected norm. Changing the trend of a measure, however, is possible only when relevant intervention strategies are available. For example, GTE healthcare managers have several accepted actions for containing the cost of chronic care or for reducing admissions for premature pregnancies, while they have no actions for affecting admissions for normal pregnancies.

Our healthcare domain expert has provided a number of recommended actions for various measures in different study areas. These are encoded in the system as production rules. For each rule, the expert estimated the savings percentage, i.e. the percentage of the deviation from the norm that can be saved by taking the action.

For a given finding, the system identifies matching rules and selects the rule with the highest savings percentage. It then computes the projected savings as: $ProjectedSavings(finding) = ProjectedImpact(finding) \times SavingsPercentage$

Because the healthcare field is rapidly progressing, the set of available actions will be constantly changing. To adjust to that, and to explicitly account for incompleteness in the system's knowledge, a default action of simply reporting the deviation matches any finding; this can be viewed as an encoding for the likelihood that bringing the deviation to the user's attention will lead to some (unknown to the system) corrective action. The savings percentage of the default action, however, is generally low.

20.3.3   Statistical Significance

Let us further consider the example of deviations in Surgical `payments_per_case`. The significance of this deviation would be less if the million-dollar-plus increase were attributable to a single extreme case than if it were due to several dozen high-cost cases. The rationale for this reasoning is that a single extreme case is unlikely to re-occur next year, and so there is nothing to be done; several dozen high-cost cases, however, indicate a potentially correctable pattern. Formally capturing this intuition requires analysis of statistical significance.

Estimating the potential benefit of an action as a single number (e.g. estimated benefit = $567,432) has the added problem of giving a false sense of precision. Forecasting is intrinsically an imprecise science and it would be much better to give a range and a confidence level (e.g. estimated benefit is between $400,000 and $700,000 with confidence 0.9), or even a central estimate and a standard deviation.

Computing the confidence or a standard deviation requires either knowing the a priori data distribution (impossible in our application and in most real cases), or having a large set of historical data points. In our application, we have huge amounts of data, but at this writing they only go back two years, and thus we cannot make a reliable annual forecast based only on this data. The lack of historical data and the resulting lack of standard statistical measures is, unfortunately, typical for many areas of medical cost analysis today. In the meantime, we are solving the problem by using simple approaches such as discounting findings based on less than a minimum number of cases, and using heuristic rules for dealing with extreme deviations based on a small number of cases. Methods for producing better estimates, given very incomplete data, are the topic of further research.

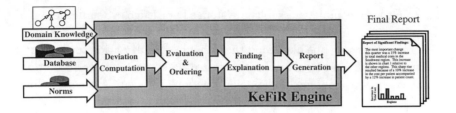

Figure 20.3
Overall design and process flow within KEFIR.

20.4   The KEFIR System

KEFIR implements the described approach to determining interestingness. However, a complete discovery system requires much more than
just detection and ordering of deviations. The deviations are intri-
cately interconnected and frequently a high-level deviation needs to be
explained via other deviations. In the area of healthcare at least, an
analysis is incomplete without some recommendations for how to rem-
edy the problems represented by the discovered deviations. Finally, the
results need to be presented in a user-friendly manner.

The overall design and process flow of the system is depicted in Figure 20.3. The healthcare data, the normative data, and domain knowledge (e.g. the measures, the population groups, the study areas, and the
recommendations) are the sources of input. The system calculates all
deviations, uses relevant recommendations to order deviations according
to their interestingness, generates explanations for the most important
deviations, and compiles the results into a written report with text,
tables, and charts.

20.4.1   The Search Space

The deviation search space that KEFIR explores has three separate components (see figure 20.4). The first component is the population group
of interest. The entire population is broken down into different populations subgroups, using criteria such as organizational unit, geographical
region, employee status, etc.

The second component is the medical study area (corresponding to
types of medical problems and treatments). The top-level study area
breakdowns, such as inpatient versus outpatient, are the same for all

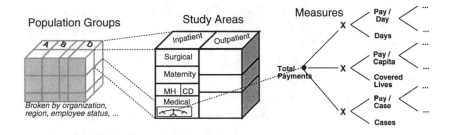

Figure 20.4
KEFIR search space of population groups, study areas, and measures

population groups. On lower levels we have fields like DRG (Diagnostic Related Group), which is a 3-digit code for the medical problem type. Since there are almost 500 distinct DRGs and lower-level study areas for different populations will generally have only a few (but different) DRGs, it does not make sense to create sub-study areas for all 500 DRGs. Instead, KEFIR dynamically computes the top N (typically 3 to 5) DRGs with the highest payments, and limits the further analysis only to those DRGs.

The third component is the set of relevant measures. These measures are independent of the population group, but do depend on the study area. While some very generic measures, such as total payments, are defined for all study areas, most measures are meaningful only for a subset of study areas (e.g. average length of stay is only meaningful for inpatient admissions).

20.4.2   Deviation Detection

The deviation search space that KEFIR explores is specified by the selected population group, the study area hierarchy, and a set of measures relevant for each study area. We refer to the *intersection* of the population group and a study area as a *sector*. The "top sector" refers to the top-level ("All episodes") study area for the selected population group. KEFIR begins its analysis by evaluating the trend and normative deviations of all the measures relevant to the top sector. New sectors are then created for each of the partitions defined by all relevant categories, and deviations are calculated for each measure in each of these new sectors. This drill down into smaller and smaller sectors continues recursively until the search space is exhausted or the number of episodes in the sector becomes too small. The result of this detection process is several hundred to several thousand deviations.

Deviations are encoded in KEFIR within structures we call *findings*. Each finding stores information for a single measure within a single sector. Both the trend and normative deviations are stored within the finding structure. Additional information is also maintained regarding the the impact of the finding, its relation to other findings (for use in explanation), matching recommendations, references to relevant measure and sector information, and miscellaneous book-keeping data.

20.4.3   Ordering Deviations

After the deviations are calculated, they are ordered in preparation for selecting the *key findings* to include in the final report. This ranking uses the interestingness measure defined earlier in this chapter. The top N findings are marked as "key findings," with N being a user definable parameter that defaults to ten.

20.4.4   Explanation

KEFIR generates explanations for all its key findings. An explanation for a given finding can come from the decomposition of a formula that defines the finding's measure, or from the breakdown of the measure into its values from the sub-sectors derived from the finding's sector. The decomposition of a measure by formulas is shown in Figure 20.4. In this example, the measure total_payments can be decomposed by three different formulas. The factors in these formulas are drivers of the total_payments measure since a change in any one directly affects a change in the value of total_payments. Using this knowledge, we can begin to explain an observed deviation in total_payments by relating it to the factor most responsible.

The breakdown of a sector into sub-sectors is illustrated in Figure 20.5. The high level inpatient sector can be broken down into sub-sectors by several different categories. The highlighted category in this example, admission_type, breaks the inpatient sector into four disjoint sub-sectors. If a deviation is observed in a measure, such as total_payments, we can determine which if any of these sub-sectors is most responsible by comparing their own deviations for that measure. Although this example

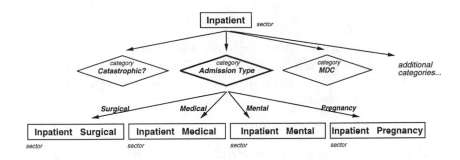

Figure 20.5
Examples of how a sector is broken down into sub-sectors using predefined categories. The resulting tree of dependent sectors is used to explain deviations by tracing the value of a measure down into the sub-sectors contributing the most to the observed deviation at the high level.

shows but a single breakdown, in practice there may be many levels, resulting in increasingly smaller and more homogeneous sub-sectors.

KEFIR explains a key finding by first evaluating all other findings affecting it through formulas or breakdowns. It then selects the one finding with the greatest influence and attempts to explain it in the same manner. This recursive process continues until there are no more interesting findings to explain, or a predefined depth (typically of three) is reached. The final result is a sequence of explanations that chain together a set of interesting findings.

20.4.5   Recommendation

The main purpose for reporting the key findings is to indicate areas where delivery of healthcare could be improved.

In many cases, the information provided by a finding is sufficient for the system to automatically suggest a specific course of action for handling the problem. Health-KEFIR uses a set of rules to identify these situations and to generate recommended actions. The following is the content of a simple recommendation rule:

```
IF measure = admissions_per_1000  &
   sector = Premature_Pregnancies &
   percent_change > 0.10
RECOMMEND "Initiate an early prenatal care program."
WITH savings percentage = 0.6
```

The recommendations were defined by our healthcare expert. Approximately 35 recommendations currently cover the most general healthcare areas. Refinements and additions to this knowledge base are on-going. With the recent addition of a WWW-based editor, expert users are now able to add and modify recommendations remotely.

20.4.6   Report Generation

The final output from KEFIR is a written report of the key findings, their explanations, and recommendations. Sentences and paragraphs are generated using simple template matching, with the option for randomized variations to produce more natural sounding text. Descriptive information relevant to the findings also appears in the report in the form of tables, bar charts, and pie charts. The report is generated in hypertext format using HTML (hyper-text markup language) to allow viewing with a WWW browser (Berners-Lee et al. 1992). When hardcopy output is desired, the HTML files are converted by a program to LaTeX, and then into postscript for printing. Figures 20.6 and 20.7 depict pages from an actual Health-KEFIR report.

20.5   The Implementation of KEFIR

KEFIR was written entirely in tcl (Ousterhout 1994) and C, making it widely portable across platforms. The system's access to data is implemented through an SQL interface which ensures portability to a wide range of database servers. We are currently running the system on a Sun SPARCstation 20 with an Informix DBMS. The design and development of KEFIR required approximately two full-time-employee (FTE) years. Another six FTE-months went into the knowledge engineering required to construct the knowledge base for Health-KEFIR. The bulk of this knowledge is represented in a collection of study areas, categories, and measures. Figure 20.8 shows parts of the structure definitions for typical instances of these objects. Health-KEFIR performs its analysis on a central workstation, but it makes its results available remotely by creating a collection of HTML (hypertext markup language) and GIF (graphic interchange file) files, and serving these over the network using NCSA's httpd (hyper-text transfer protocol) server. The information manager for GTE's Managed Healthcare Program accesses the reports using a WWW client (such as NCSA's Mosaic). From there the reports can be printed for wider distribution or copied into local files for editing into specialized reports. The user may also request the generation of new reports or edit the knowledge base of recommendations through the same WWW client.

20.6   Deployment and Testing

The initial version of Health-KEFIR was deployed in January of 1995. Deployment to GTE's regional managers across the country is scheduled for later in 1995. Initial feedback from users has been extremely positive. In comparison to healthcare consultant reports, Health-KEFIR tends to identify the same general problem areas and often uncovers new, unexpected findings deemed interesting by the users. More rigorous tests will follow as new quarters of data arrive and are turned into reports.

20.7   Limitations and Extensions

The performance of Health-KEFIR is only as good as its domain knowledge. We are adding to its rule base to broaden and improve its recommendation capabilities. New categories and measures are being added to reflect changes in the way healthcare managers desire to aggregate and decompose information.

Currently the system only handles simple trend and normative analysis. We would like to extend its capabilities to include trend analysis over multiple periods, and add model-based comparisons. While norms are useful references for average performance, it is often desirable to set other targets for comparison. For example, rather than comparisons to the average it has been argued that comparisons should be made to a "best practice" model, i.e. comparison to a target representing an achievable level of above average performance. In some situations unusual circumstances may make even the average unachievable, in which case we might wish to set sights on some target below the norm.

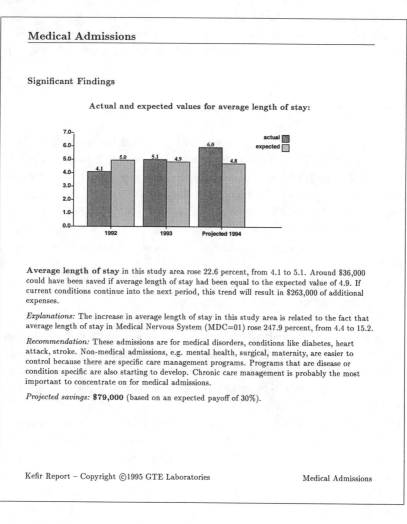

Medical Admissions

Significant Findings

Actual and expected values for average length of stay:

Average length of stay in this study area rose 22.6 percent, from 4.1 to 5.1. Around $36,000 could have been saved if average length of stay had been equal to the expected value of 4.9. If current conditions continue into the next period, this trend will result in $263,000 of additional expenses.

Explanations: The increase in average length of stay in this study area is related to the fact that average length of stay in Medical Nervous System (MDC=01) rose 247.9 percent, from 4.4 to 15.2.

Recommendation: These admissions are for medical disorders, conditions like diabetes, heart attack, stroke. Non-medical admissions, e.g. mental health, surgical, maternity, are easier to control because there are specific care management programs. Programs that are disease or condition specific are also starting to develop. Chronic care management is probably the most important to concentrate on for medical admissions.

Projected savings: **$79,000** (based on an expected payoff of 30%).

Kefir Report – Copyright ©1995 GTE Laboratories   Medical Admissions

Figure 20.6
Sample output from a KEFIR report.

Total Payments Summary

Total inpatient payments in this study area fell 22.5 percent, from $1.4 million to $1.1 million. The fact that total inpatient payments was better than the expected value of $1.2 million accounted for a savings of $147,000. If current conditions continue into the next period, this trend will result in $388,000 of savings.

The decrease in total inpatient payments in this study area is related to the fact that total inpatient payments in Medical Circulatory System (MDC=05) fell 58.7 percent, from $370,910 to $153,287. The observed deviation from the expected value is related to the fact that payments per day was 8.1% below the expected value ($910.68 versus $1,479.59).

Percent of Total Inpatient Payments by Top 5 MDC by payments

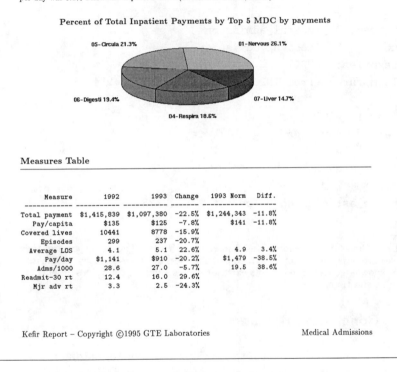

05-Circula 21.3%   01-Nervous 26.1%

06-Digesti 19.4%   07-Liver 14.7%

04-Respira 18.6%

Measures Table

Measure	1992	1993	Change	1993 Norm	Diff.
Total payment	$1,415,839	$1,097,380	-22.5%	$1,244,343	-11.8%
Pay/capita	$135	$125	-7.8%	$141	-11.8%
Covered lives	10441	8778	-15.9%		
Episodes	299	237	-20.7%		
Average LOS	4.1	5.1	22.6%	4.9	3.4%
Pay/day	$1,141	$910	-20.2%	$1,479	-38.5%
Adms/1000	28.6	27.0	-5.7%	19.5	38.6%
Readmit-30 rt	12.4	16.0	29.6%		
Mjr adv rt	3.3	2.5	-24.3%		

Kefir Report – Copyright ©1995 GTE Laboratories   Medical Admissions

Figure 20.7
Sample output from a KEFIR report (continued).

```
Category: Admission_type
   name:       {admission type}
   split_by: ADMTYP
   values:     {value: 1 sector: In_surgical}
               {value: 2 sector: In_medical}
               {value: 3 sector: In_pregnancy}
               {value: 4 sector: In_mental}

Study_area: In_medical_admission
   name:          {medical admissions}
   categories:    {MDC}
   sqltemplate: {from INPCASE where "ADMTYP = 2"}

Measure: In_ALOS
   name:       "average length of stay"
   type:       use
   units:      days
   format:     %.2f
   compute_as: {sql_code {select "AVG(DAYS)"}}
```

Figure 20.8
Samples of three of the structures used in Health-KEFIR. The slots shown in these
examples are only those that have predefined values, i.e. they represent elements of
domain knowledge. Additional slots exist for each structure, the values of which are
filled in at run time.

20.8   Concluding Remarks

KEFIR represents an approach to developing complete, automated systems for identifying, explaining, and reporting on key deviations in large,
changing databases. The successful implementation of Health-KEFIR
demonstrates the merits of the system and the potential power of the
proposed methodology. This technology has matured to a point where
wider application to other domains is now feasible and desirable. We are
currently considering an application of KEFIR to databases in the areas
of marketing and customer analysis.

Acknowledgments

We are very grateful to Shri Goyal and Bill Griffin for their encouragement of our work on discovery in databases. Zhuma Feng made significant contributions to many parts of KEFIR. We thank Bernard Silver
and Roland Zito-Wolf for their comments on drafts of this chapter.

20.9   Addendum: Calculating Impact of a Deviation

The bottom line measure M_0 is chosen so that all other measures can be
related to it via formulas. Thus, for any measure M_i there is a function
f_i such that $M_0 = f_i(M_i, D)$ and the impact of change in M_i is computed
as

$$impact(M_i, S_j, D_C, D_R \| M_0, S_0) =$$
$$f_i(M_i(S_j, D_C), D_R) - M_0(S_0, D_R) \quad (20.9.1)$$

First, let's examine the computation of impact of change in the bottom
line measure M_0 for different sectors. If $S_0 = S_1 \cup S_2 \cup \ldots \cup S_k$, (where
all S_j are disjoint) then we can write the old value of M_0 for top sector
as

$$M_0(S_0, D_R) = M_0(S_1, D_R) + \ldots +$$
$$M_0(S_j, D_R) + \ldots + M_0(S_k, D_R) \quad (20.9.2)$$

and the value $M_0^{(j)}$ that M_0 would have if M_0 would change only in S_j
but not in other sectors, is

$$M_0^{(j)}(S_0, D_R) = M_0(S_1, D_R) + \ldots +$$
$$M_0(S_j, D_C) + \ldots + M_0(S_k, D_R) \quad (20.9.3)$$

Subtracting these equations we get

$$impact(M_0, S_j, D_C, D_R) = M_0(S_j, D_C) - M_0(S_j, D_R) \quad (20.9.4)$$

i.e. the bottom-line impact of M_0 change in S_j is simply the difference
between the new and the old values of M_0 in S_j. For example, if the total
payments for surgical admissions changed from \$2.2 million in 1992 to
\$3.2 million in 1993, the impact on the bottom line would be \$1 million.

Next, we focus on a specific sector S and examine how to compute the impact of change of a specific measure M_i (other than M_0) in just that sector.

Measures are related to M_0 by different formulas. In general, we can use equation 20.9.1 to determine the impact. However, there is a much simpler method in the important special case when these formulas have only additions and multiplications (which is the case for almost all Health-KEFIR measures). Then the function f_i that expresses measure M_0 via M_i can be written as

$$M_0(S_0, D) = A(S, D) \times M_i(S, D) + B(S, D) \qquad (20.9.5)$$

where $A(S, D)$ and $B(S, D)$ depend on the sector, the database instance, and other measures, but *not* on M_i. Now, the reference value of M_0 is

$$M_0(S_0, D_R) = A(S, D_R) \times M_i(S, D_R) + B(S, D_R) \qquad (20.9.6)$$

Let $D_R^{(i)}$ denote the version of D_R where measure M_i in S has the value $M_i(S, D_C)$ (its value in D_C), and the rest of the measures are unchanged. The value of M_0 would be

$$M_0(S, D_R^{(i)}) = A(S, D_R) \times M_i(S, D_C) + B(S, D_R) \qquad (20.9.7)$$

Subtracting, we get

$$impact(M_i, S, D_C, D_R) =$$
$$A(S, D_R) \times (M_i(S, D_C) - M_i(S, D_R)) \qquad (20.9.8)$$

which is the change in measure M_i in sector S, multiplied by the impact factor $A(S, D_R)$. Note that $B(S, D)$—the contribution resulting from additive terms—drops away completely. This equation allows one to compute impact for measures related to M_0 by additions and multiplications simply by keeping track of the multiplicative factor $A(S, D_R)$.

References

Anand, T., and Kahn, G.1992. SPOTLIGHT: A Data Explanation System. In Proceedings, Eighth IEEE Conference on Applied Artificial Intelligence.

Berners-Lee, T., J.; Cailliau, R.; Groff, J. F.; and Pollermann, B. 1992. World-Wide Web: The Information Universe, *Electronic Networking: Research, Applications and Policy,* 2(1) (Spring): 52–58. Westport, Conn.: Meckler Publishing.

DeGroot, M. H. 1970. *Optimal Statistical Decisions.* New York:McGraw-Hill.

Fayyad, U. and Uthurusamy, R., eds.1994. Proceedings of the 1994 Knowledge Discovery in Databases Workshop, Tech. Report WS-94-03. Menlo Park, Calif.: AAAI Press.

Lee, J. K.; Oh, S. B.; and Shin, J. C. 1990. UNIK-FCST: Knowledge-assisted Adjustment of Statistical Forecasts. *Expert Systems with Applications,* 1(1):39–49.

Matheus, C. J.; Piatetsky-Shapiro, G.; and McNeill, D. 1994. An Application of KEFIR to the Analysis of Healthcare Information, In Proceedings of the 1994 Knowledge Discovery in Databases Workshop, ed. U. Fayyad and R. Uthurusamy. Tech. Report WS-94-03. Menlo Park, Calif.: AAAI Press.

Matheus, C. J.; Chan, P. K.; and Piatetsky-Shapiro, G. 1993. Systems for Knowledge Discovery in Databases. *IEEE Transactions on Knowledge and Data Engineering,* 5(6) (December):903–913.

McNeill, D. 1993. A Comprehensive Set of Performance Measures to Evaluate Managed Healthcare Organizations: GTE's Perspective. In *National Quality Management Conference.*

Ousterhout, J. 1994. *Tcl and TK toolkit.* Reading, Mass.: Addison-Wesley.

Piatetsky-Shapiro, G. 1991. Discovery, Analysis, and Presentation of Strong Rules, In *Knowledge Discovery in Databases,* ed G. Piatetsky-Shapiro and W. J. Frawley. Menlo Park, Calif.: AAAI Press.

Piatetsky-Shapiro, G. & Frawley, W. J. 1991. *Knowledge Discovery in Databases.* Menlo Park, Calif.: AAAI Press.

Piatetsky-Shapiro, G.; and Matheus, C. J. 1994. The Interestingness of Deviations. In Proceedings of the 1994 Knowledge Discovery in Databases Workshop, ed. U. Fayyad and R. Uthurusamy. Tech. Report WS-94-03. Menlo Park, Calif.: AAAI Press.

Piatetsky-Shapiro, G., ed. 1993. Proceedings of 1993 Knowledge Discovery in Databases Workshop, Tech. Report WS-93-02 Menlo Park, Calif.: AAAI Press.

Schmitz, J.; Armstrong, G.; and Little, J. D. C.1990. CoverStory–Automated News Finding in Marketing. In *DSS Transactions,* 46–54. Providence, R.I.: Institute of Management Sciences.

21 Modeling Subjective Uncertainty in Image Annotation

Padhraic Smyth & Usama M. Fayyad
Jet Propulsion Laboratory,
California Institute of Technology

Michael C. Burl & Pietro Perona
California Institute of Technology

Abstract

This chapter examines the problem of dealing with subjective "ground truth" in the context of knowledge discovery from image databases. In particular, the problem of evaluating the relative detection performance of human experts and algorithms is discussed. In practice, for remote-sensing applications, acquiring ground truth is often prohibitively expensive or physically impossible. Instead one must often rely on the subjective opinions of experts. These experts visually examine the images and provide a *subjective* labeling, in essence, noisy estimates of ground truth. In this chapter a probabilistic model to account for labeling reliability and bias is proposed, and a maximum likelihood scheme for parameter estimation from a labeled database is presented. The estimated model combines multiple opinions to arrive at a single consensus estimate. These estimates form the basis for comparing both human and detection algorithm performance in the form of modified receiver operation characteristics (ROCs). Experimental results are discussed in the context of a particular image analysis problem: identifying small volcanos in radar images of Venus.

21.1 Introduction

Knowledge discovery systems are often built on the principle of *supervised learning*. The system is trained using training data where the signal or category of interest is known. The trained model is subsequently used on data where the target variable is unknown and must be predicted. It is standard practice to assume that the target values in the training data have been provided by some sort of infallible supervisor or Oracle, i.e., there is no ambiguity in the target signal or category. This type of target is known as "ground truth." As an example consider loan-approval applications where the target category is "default/no-default after one year of originating the loan." If the training data consists of loans over one year old then the target variable is known with certainty. Another example occurs in the classification of remotely-sensed images into vegetation types: in this case, ground truth is interpreted in the literal sense of someone having made an independent ground-based verification by visiting the site and classifying the vegetation.

In some supervised learning applications, however, instead of "ground truth" one may have to rely on the subjective opinion(s) of one or more experts. The assumption that the training data has been labeled in a reasonably objective and reliable manner may not be appropriate. For example, medical or image data is collected and some time later a set of experts individually analyze the data and produce a set of class labels. Their decision is based only on the measured data and thus their labeling may not be perfect.

The problem dealt with in this chapter is that of inferring "ground truth" from such noisy subjective estimates of experts. Specifically, consider that the database consists of N d-dimensional feature vectors, $\underline{x}^i$, $1 \leq i \leq N$. Let Ω be the discrete-valued prediction variable or *class*, taking values in $\{\omega_1, \ldots, \omega_m\}$. Under the standard supervised classification scenario one would have for each $\underline{x}^i$ a corresponding class label $\omega^i \in \{\omega_1, \ldots, \omega_m\}$. However, under the case considered here, instead of a specific class label ω^i there is an L-ary vector $\underline{z}^i$ of *estimates* of the true class label ω^i, where L is the number of labelers (or experts). The lth component of the vector $\underline{z}^i$ corresponds to the estimate by labeler l of the class to which feature vector $\underline{x}^i$ belongs. For example, the $\underline{x}^i$ could be medical records of patients in a hospital and the $\underline{z}^i$ would then correspond to the recorded diagnoses of a set of physicians.

The "estimates" $\underline{z}^i$ can consist of guesses of the class labels directly, estimates of $p_l(\omega^i|\underline{x}^i)$ (the subjective probability from labeler l of the probability of a particular class given a particular feature vector), or some function of $p_l(\omega^i|\underline{x}^i)$. This chapter deals with combining the l estimates for each feature vector to arrive at an overall posterior probability estimate of a particular class, $\hat{p}(\omega^i|\underline{x}^i)$, given the opinions of *all* L of the labelers.

21.2   Motivation

Generating a "consensus" estimate $\hat{p}(\omega^i|\underline{x}^i)$ impacts the development of knowledge discovery algorithms in two distinct ways: (i) evaluating the relative performance of experts and algorithms, and (ii) training a knowledge discovery system in the absence of absolute ground truth.

The emphasis of this chapter is on problem (i), the performance evaluation issue. In particular, the application of a particular modeling technique to the problem of counting volcanos on the surface of Venus is discussed. The problem of how to utilize probabilistic labels in learning, problem (ii), has been dealt with in previous work: when the inferred labels have a probabilistic interpretation, a simple mixture model argument leads to straightforward modifications of various learning algorithms (Smyth 1995).

It should be noted that the issue of inferring ground truth from subjective labels has appeared in the literature under various guises. French (1985) and Lindley (1985) provide a Bayesian perspective on the problem of combining multiple opinions. In the field of medical diagnosis there is a significant body of work on latent variable models for inferring hidden "truth" from subjective diagnoses (see Agresti (1992) and Uebersax (1993) for reviews). Elsewhere more abstract theoretical models have been developed under specific assumptions on the noise present in subjective labeling patterns (Silverman 1980; Lugosi 1992). The novel contribution of this chapter is twofold: (i) this is the first application of subjective labeling models to a large-scale *image* analysis problem (to the best of the authors' knowledge), and (ii) the work discussed here compares human and algorithmic performance as opposed to simply comparing humans to each other (which is the focus of almost all related work in the literature).

The chapter begins with a background discussion on the volcano detection problem and briefly discusses the algorithmic techniques we have developed to automate the task of detecting volcanos. The practical issues involved in collecting label estimates from the scientists are described. The paper then focuses on the performance evaluation issue: given conflicting labelings from multiple experts, how should one evaluate both algorithm and human performance ? A probabilistic model is introduced and the use of the Expectation-Maximization (EM) procedure (Redner and Walker 1984) for parameter-fitting is described. Experimental results clearly demonstrate the importance of taking subjective ambiguity into account.

21.3   Volcanos on Venus

Although modern remote-sensing technology has made rapid advances in terms of data collection capabilities, scientific analysis of remotely sensed images is often a manual process. Much investigative work is still carried out using hardcopy photographs. In the area of geologic studies of remotely-sensed data there are several pre-processing steps which precede any large scale quantitative geologic analysis of the data. These steps involve locating, identifying, and characterizing local geologic features such as volcanos and craters. The output of this process is typically a published catalog of geologic features which forms the basis for more global scientific studies (for examples of such catalogs and studies see the special issue of *Journal of Geophysical Research* on Magellan data, 1992). Due to the enormity of the image databases currently being acquired by agencies such as NASA (the National Aeronautics and Space Administration), *manual* cataloging is often no longer a practical proposition. Thus, automated cataloging is a topic of considerable importance if even a fraction of the collected data is to be utilized. For details on a successful large-scale application of automated cataloging of *sky-survey data* see Fayyad, Djorgovski and Weir (this volume).

The Magellan spacecraft orbited the planet Venus from 1992 to 1994, globally mapping the surface of the planet (*Science* special issue, 1991). The mapping was performed using synthetic aperture radar (SAR) because of its ability to penetrate the dense cloud cover surrounding Venus. Magellan transmitted from Venus a data set consisting of over 30,000 high resolution (75m per pixel) radar images of the Venusian surface. The data are publicly distributed as a set of approximately 100 CD-ROMS. This data set is greater than that gathered by all previous planetary missions combined—planetary scientists are literally swamped by data (Guest et al. 1992).

The study of volcanic processes is essential to an understanding of the geologic evolution of the planet Venus (Aubele and Slyuta 1990). From a scientific viewpoint the ability to accurately locate and characterize the many volcanos is a necessary requirement before more detailed studies

Volcanoes on Venus

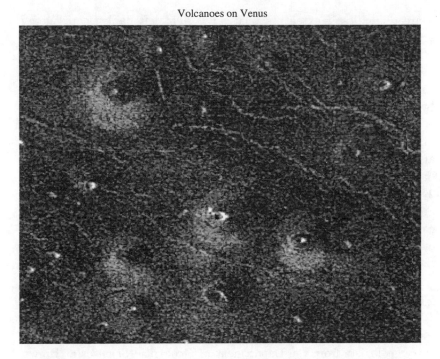

Figure 21.1
A 30km × 30km region from the Magellan SAR data containing several volcanos.

can be carried out such as analysis of spatial clustering patterns, correlation with other geologic features, and so forth. There are estimated to
be on the order of 10^6 small (less than 15km in diameter) visible volcanos
scattered throughout the 30,000 images (Aubele and Slyuta 1990). It
has been estimated that manually locating all of these volcanos would
require on the order of 10 man-years of a planetary geologist's time to
carry out. Experience has shown that even a few hours of image analysis
severely taxes the concentration abilities of human labelers.

From an engineering viewpoint, automation of the volcano detection
task presents a significant challenge to current capabilities in computer
vision and pattern recognition due to the variability among the volcanos
and the significant background "clutter" present in most of the images.
Figure 21.1 shows a Magellan subimage of size 30km square containing
at least 10 small volcanos. The radar illumination is from the lower-
left side of the image. The volcanos display a common signature to

a greater or lesser extent: a relatively bright left flank (more energy scattered back than the surrounding flatter background), a summit-pit at the center (not always visible due to the resolution of the radar), and a darker right flank (darker because the direction of the slope scatters energy away from the sensor). These are the primary visual cues used by planetary geologists for detecting small volcanos in radar images.

A standard Magellan image consists of 1000 × 1000 pixels, where the pixels are 75m in resolution for the images analyzed in this study (images at the lower resolution of 225m per pixel are also available as part of the basic Magellan data set). Small volcano diameters are typically in the 2–3km range, i.e., 30 to 50 pixels wide, and very rarely overlap. Volcanos are often spatially clustered in volcano fields. Within an image which contains all or part of a volcano field, there may be as many as 100 or more volcanos, although more typically the number is in the 10–50 range.

21.4   Volcano Labeling

Participating in the development of the detection algorithm are planetary geologists from the Department of Geological Sciences at Brown University. Their collective subjective opinion is about as expert as one can find given the available data and our current state of knowledge about the planet Venus.

In the absence of absolute ground truth, the goal of a detection system is to be as comparable in performance as possible to the scientists in terms of labeling accuracy. Absolute accuracy is not measurable for this problem. Hence, the best an automated detection system can do is to emulate the scientist's performance—this point will become clearer when performance metrics are discussed later in the chapter.

The standard manner in which labels are obtained is to have a labeler interact with an X-windows software tool whereby he or she uses mouse-clicks to locate candidate volcanos. Starting with an initially blank image, the labeler proceeds to sequentially click on the estimated centers of the volcanos. The labeler is then prompted to provide a subjective label estimate from a choice of categories 1–4 as described below—by default, locations which are not labeled are considered to have label "5" (non-volcano). In addition, the labeler also provides a diameter estimate

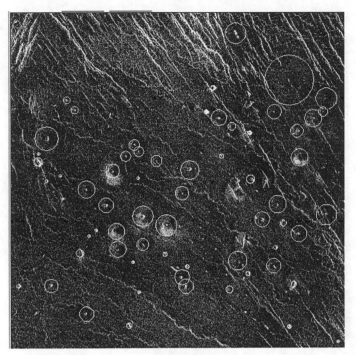

Figure 21.2
Magellan SAR image of Venus with consensus ground truth showing size and
locations of small volcanos.

by fitting a circle to the volcano (using the mouse). Figure 21.2 shows
a typical image labeled in this manner. Typically it can take from 10
minutes to 1 hour to label an image and fit diameters (depending on
how many volcanos are present)

  After completing the labeling, the result is an annotation of that image
which can be stored in standard database format. Each label event
corresponds to a unique record in the database and in turn corresponds
to a particular latitude/longitude (to the resolution of the pixels) for a
particular labeler at a particular time (since the same labeler may relabel
an image multiple times). It is this database which provides the basic
reference framework for (i) estimates of geologic parameters, (ii) training
data for the learning algorithms, and (iii) reference data for performance
evaluation. A simple form of spatial clustering is used to determine
which label events (from different labelers) actually correspond to the

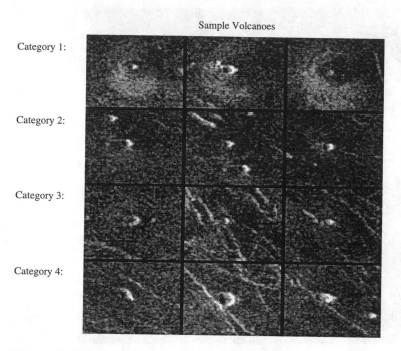

Figure 21.3
A selection of volcanos from four categories as labeled by the geologists.

same geologic feature (volcano). Mean differences of about 2.5 pixels (Euclidean distance) have been found in cross comparisons of label data from different scientists, which is reasonable considering the precision one can expect from mouse location on a screen. Hence, identifying the centers of volcanos labeled by the scientists is not in itself a significant source of uncertainty.

21.5   Volcano Sub-Categories

There is considerable subjective variability in volcano labeling: for the same image, different scientists produce different label lists, and even the same scientist produces different lists over time. To help quantify this uncertainty, the scientists label training examples into quantized probability bins or "categories," where the probability bins correspond to visually distinguishable sub-categories of volcanos. In particular, 5 categories are used:

1. where a summit pit, a bright-dark radar pattern, and apparent topographic slope are all clearly visible, probability 0.98,
2. where only 2 of the 3 criteria in category 1 are visible, probability 0.80,
3. where no summit pit is visible but there is evidence of flanks or a circular outline, probability 0.60,
4. where only a summit pit is visible, probability 0.50, and
5. where no volcano-like features are visible, probability 0.0.

The probability for category i corresponds to the mean probability that a volcano exists at a particular location *given* that it belongs to category i. These are *subjective* probability estimates and were elicited based on lengthy discussions with the planetary geologists.

Figure 21.3 shows some typical volcanos from each category. The use of quantized probability bins to attach levels of certainty to subjective image labels is not new: the same approach is routinely used in the evaluation of radiographic image displays to generate subjective ROC (receiver operating characteristic) curves (Bunch et al. 1978; Chesters, 1992). An ROC is useful for diagnostic applications since it displays the full range of possible operating thresholds for a detector (human or algorithmic). In contrast, the more oft-quoted probability of classification error criterion only represents a single point on the curve (typically the point at which the threshold on the posterior probability for deciding in favor of class 1 is set to 0.5). Thus, the ROC provides significantly more information on a detector's characteristics than a single error number.

Table 21.1 shows the confusion matrix between two geologists for a set of 4 images. The (i, j)th element of the confusion matrix counts the number of label events which correspond to labeler B generating label i and labeler A generating label j, where both labels were considered to belong to the same visual feature, i.e., were within a few pixels of each other. The $(i, 5)$ (or $(5, j)$) entries count the instances where labeler B (or A) provided label i (or j), but labeler A (or B) did not provide any label—entry (5,5) is defined to be zero. Ideally, the confusion matrix would have all of its entries on the diagonal if both labelers agreed completely on all events. Clearly, however, there is substantial disagreement, as judged by the number of off-diagonal counts in the matrix. For example, label 3's are particularly noisy, in both "directions." Label 3's are noisier than label 4's because there is less variability in the appearance of 4's compared to 3's (4's are simple pits, 3's are less well-defined). About 50% of the label 3's detected by either labeler are not detected at all by the other labeler. On the other hand, only about 10% of the label 1's of either labeler are missed by the other. *This matrix underlines the importance of modeling probabilistic labels for this particular problem.*

21.6   A Simple Model for Subjective Image Labeling

After a set of images have been labeled and the label events (mouse clicks by the scientists) spatially clustered, the result is a set of N local image windows, denoted as $\underline{x}^i$, $1 \leq i \leq N$. Each local pixel window $\underline{x}^i$ has an associated L-ary vector of labels $\underline{z}^i$, where the lth component of the vector corresponds to the label provided by lth labeler for that particular image patch. Each label is either from the set $\{1, 2, 3, 4\}$ if the labeler identified that patch as a volcano, or else is label 5 if they did not identify it at all. Thus, each local image patch in the database, $\underline{x}^i$, has been positively identified as a volcano by at least 1 of the L labelers.

Table 21.1
Confusion Matrix of Scientist A Versus Scientist B.

	Scientist A				
	Label 1	Label 2	Label 3	Label 4	Not Detected
Scientist B					
Label 1	19	8	4	1	3
Label 2	9	8	6	5	5
Label 3	13	12	18	1	37
Label 4	1	4	5	24	15
Not Detected	4	8	29	16	0

Let v and $\bar{v}$ to denote the events "volcano present" and "volcano not present" for a particular image patch. The *observed data* (in terms of label classification) for this image patch is the vector of labels, $\underline{z}$. The problem is to estimate $p(v|\underline{z})$. We propose a simple causal model relating the *observed* label data and the *hidden* data, v. The binary variable volcano/non-volcano gives rise to a set of pixel intensities $\underline{x}$. Rather than dealing with the full space of pixels, we replace $\underline{x}$ with

a quantized variable, namely the 5 categories described in the previous section. These categories are themselves *hidden* variables, like
v. Let $c \in \{1, \dots, 5\}$ denote the categories. The relationship between categories and volcanos is non-deterministic: the probabilities
$p(v|c_j)$ are those provided by the scientists as described earlier, i.e.,
$p(v|c_j) \in \{0.98, 0.8, 0.6, 0.5, 0.0\}, 1 \leq j \leq 5$.

How do the observed labels, z, enter into the picture? The observed
labels, z, are "noisy" estimates of the true category c to which a particular volcano belongs. Thus, the full causal model can be expressed in
probabilistic form as:

$$p(v|z) = \sum_j p(v|c_j)p(c_j|z) \qquad (21.6.1)$$

Hence, there are two sources of noise in inferring whether a particular
local region is a volcano or not from observed labels: (i) the probabilistic
relationship between volcanos and categories as captured by $p(v|c_j)$, and
(ii) the "estimation noise" of inferring the probability of each category
c_j given a set of noisy subjective labels z. The first set of probabilities,
$p(v|c_j)$, are provided based on the prior knowledge of the scientists as
discussed earlier and are *not* estimated from the training data.

The second set of probabilities, $p(c_j|z)$, must be estimated from the
data. This estimation process is complicated by the fact that the true
value of c is never known: it is a hidden (or latent) variable. The Addendum describes a particular maximum likelihood approach for estimating
these probabilities from data for just a single labeler: this labeler is
allowed to label each region of interest an arbitrary number of times.
To extend the model to multiple labelers we make the assumption that,
for a particular image patch, the labelers act independently given the
true category c_j. Since the estimation method is based on the number of
times labeler l labels region of interest i into category c_j, the model does
not require that each labeler labels each region of interest the same number of times: thus, one can handle the common situation in the volcano
application where some labelers only label a subset of all the available
images, other labelers only label each image once, and one or two labelers label some of the images multiple times. However, the model can
not handle the case when the labelers are correlated: for example, if an
image is labeled by labelers A and B separately and then jointly by both
working in consensus, the model can use either the individual data or

the consensus data, but not both.

Note that the overall effect of the above model will be to reduce our confidence that a typical local region is a volcano, given some labeling information. For example, this has direct implications for estimating the overall numbers of volcanos in a particular region. Local regions which produce label disagreements between experts will be downweighted compared to volcanos which receive unanimous labelings.

Table 21.2
Category-Label Probabilities for Individual Labelers as estimated via the EM Procedure.

Marginal Label Probabilities, Labeler A

Label 1	Label 2	Label 3	Label 4	Label 5
0.171	0.149	0.234	0.175	0.271

Probability(category|label), Labeler A

	Category 1	Category 2	Category 3	Category 4	Category 5
Label 1	0.137	0.635	0.058	0.150	0.021
Label 2	0.025	0.378	0.169	0.382	0.046
Label 3	0.000	0.034	0.462	0.287	0.217
Label 4	0.000	0.000	0.000	0.883	0.117
Label 5	0.000	0.040	0.103	0.039	0.817

Marginal Label Probabilities, Labeler C

Label 1	Label 2	Label 3	Label 4	Label 5
0.026	0.056	0.193	0.416	0.309

Probability(category|label), Labeler C

	Category 1	Category 2	Category 3	Category 4	Category 5
Label 1	1.000	0.000	0.000	0.000	0.000
Label 2	0.019	0.977	0.004	0.000	0.000
Label 3	0.000	0.667	0.175	0.065	0.094
Label 4	0.000	0.000	0.042	0.725	0.233
Label 5	0.000	0.000	0.389	0.000	0.611

21.7   Experimental Results

For the purposes of the experiments described here, labelings from 4 planetary geologists on the same set of 4 images were obtained. In total, the geologists found 269 distinct regions, i.e., at least 1 of the 4 labeled each such region as belonging to one of the volcano categories.

Table 21.3
First 20 regions of interest in the database: original scientist labels shown with
posterior category probability estimates as estimated via the EM procedure.

Region	Scientist Labels (z)				Posterior Probabilities (EM), $p(c_j\|z)$					$p(v\|z)$
	A	B	C	D	Cat. 1	Cat. 2	Cat. 3	Cat. 4	Cat. 5	
1	4	4	4	5	0.000	0.000	0.000	0.816	0.184	0.408
2	1	4	4	2	0.000	0.000	0.000	0.991	0.009	0.496
3	1	1	2	2	0.023	0.977	0.000	0.000	0.000	0.804
4	3	1	5	3	0.000	0.000	1.000	0.000	0.000	0.600
5	3	1	3	3	0.000	0.536	0.452	0.012	0.000	0.706
6	2	2	2	4	0.000	1.000	0.000	0.000	0.000	0.800
7	3	1	5	5	0.000	0.000	1.000	0.000	0.000	0.600
8	2	1	4	4	0.000	0.000	0.000	0.999	0.000	0.500
9	2	1	4	4	0.000	0.000	0.000	0.999	0.000	0.500
10	4	4	4	4	0.000	0.000	0.000	0.996	0.004	0.498
11	2	2	3	1	0.000	1.000	0.000	0.000	0.000	0.800
12	1	1	3	2	0.000	1.000	0.000	0.000	0.000	0.800
13	2	1	3	2	0.000	1.000	0.000	0.000	0.000	0.800
14	1	1	1	1	1.000	0.000	0.000	0.000	0.000	0.980
15	1	2	2	2	0.000	1.000	0.000	0.000	0.000	0.800
16	1	1	2	3	0.000	1.000	0.000	0.000	0.000	0.800
17	1	1	1	1	1.000	0.000	0.000	0.000	0.000	0.980
18	1	1	2	3	0.000	1.000	0.000	0.000	0.000	0.800
19	3	2	5	3	0.000	0.000	0.992	0.000	0.008	0.595
20	4	4	4	4	0.000	0.000	0.000	0.996	0.004	0.498

The Addendum describes how the problem is set up within a maximum
likelihood framework. Estimating the label-category probabilities from
the data is complicated by the fact that the category values are not
known, i.e., they are *hidden*. An efficient and general statistical algorithm for estimating model parameters involving hidden variables is the
EM procedure (Redner and Walker 1984) which iteratively re-estimates
the hidden parameters until the likelihood function reaches a local maximum (see Cheeseman and Stutz, this volume, for an application of the
EM procedure to clustering).

Applying the EM procedure (Addendum) to this data resulted in the
transition matrices for $p(l\|t)$ shown in Table 21.2 (scientists A and C)—
scientists B and D are not shown here but are qualitatively similar. From
the marginal label probabilities it is clear that scientists A and C have
quite different labeling patterns: A finds roughly equal numbers (17%)
of category 1's and 4's, while C only labels 2.6% as category 1's but
41.6% as category 4's. In terms of accuracy, if C provides a label 1 then
it is certain to be of category 1, but a label 3 has a 66.7% chance of
being category 2. Label 1 from scientist A has an 86.3% chance of not
being of category 1, including a 2% chance of not being a volcano at
all (category 5). The derived transition matrices provide a quantitative
basis for comparing the accuracy and biases of different labelers.

Table 21.3 shows the original labels for each of the first 20 regions
of interest in the database, the estimated probabilities of each category,

and the posterior probability of a volcano being present given the labels. Note that the posterior category probabilities can often not be guessed based on simple averaging or voting as a function of the labels. For example, region 5 is most likely to be a category 2 according to the posterior probabilities even though none of the labelers classified it as label 2—this is due (in part at least) to the fact that on average, a label "3" from labeler C is actually most likely to be a category "2" (see Table 21.2). In Dawid and Skene (1979) the method was applied to the problem of rating anesthesiologists—the resulting posterior probabilities were almost entirely 0 or 1 reflecting the fact that there was a relatively high level of agreement between the experts. In the volcano problem there is a relatively high level of *disagreement*, and consequently less certainty in the posterior probabilities due to the underlying difficulty of the detection problem (significant variability of volcano shape and relatively low signal-to-noise ratio).

The determination of posterior probabilities for each of the regions of interest is a fundamental step in any quantitative analysis of the volcano data. Given the category probabilities we can then estimate the probability of a volcano in a given region of interest as $p(v|\underline{z}) = \sum_j p(v|c_j)p(c_j|\underline{z})$ where the $p(c_j|\underline{z})$ terms are the posterior category probabilities provided by the EM procedure given the observed labels $\underline{z}$, and the $p(v|c_j)$ terms are the subjective volcano-category probabilities discussed earlier. In the next section we will discuss the use of receiver operating characteristic (ROC) plots for performance comparison.

21.8   Comparing Human and Algorithmic Detection Performance using ROC Curves

21.8.1   A Brief Description of the Volcano Detection Algorithm

We first briefly summarize the basic algorithm for volcano detection used in the comparative experiments. For more precise details the reader is referred to Burl et al. (1994a). Other techniques for locating volcanos in Magellan radar imagery have been described by Wiles and Forshaw (1992).

The first step in the volcano detection process uses a simple matched filter. The matched filter can be the mean of all the positive training examples or one of the volcanos themselves, chosen by cross-validation. The matched filtering results in a response image which can be thresholded to determine a set of local regions of interest or "candidate" volcanos: typically this set of regions of interest contains a large fraction of non-volcanos, including portions of linear features and so forth.

The detected regions are projected into a subspace consisting of significant principal directions of the positive examples (volcanos) in the training data. The subspace itself is determined by selecting the most significant components produced by a singular value decomposition (SVD) of the training data (Burl et al. 1994a). Supervised learning is used to produce a model which can discriminate between volcano and non-volcano local regions in the projected subspace. A simple maximum-likelihood Gaussian classifier with full covariance matrices (Duda and Hart 1973) was found to perform as well as alternative non-parametric methods such as neural networks and decision trees.

For the results described in this chapter the algorithm was trained using the labelings generated from two scientists working together—this was the default ground truth set. However, as is implicit in the discussion elsewhere in this chapter, more elaborate possibilities for training exist, e.g, using inferred probabilistic labels (Smyth 1995).

21.8.2   Comparative Results for Human Experts and Algorithm

In its simplest form the ROC plots detections (the system/human detects an object at a location where a volcano exists) versus false alarms (the system/human detects an object where no volcano exists). For a detection system which produces posterior probabilities (such as the SVD-Gaussian classifier above), a sequence of detection/false-alarm points can be plotted from the test data by varying the posterior probability threshold at which a test region of interest is classified as a volcano. Similarly, if a human categorizes his/her detections into C distinct ordered labels, then by ranking the detections according to the labels one can generate C points on the ROC plot (Bunch et al. 1987; Chesters 1992).

A complication in our application of course is that there is no "true" detection list with which to compare a particular system or human. We proceed as follows; for each human or system, we estimate based on the EM procedure a probabilistic detection list using the labels from all of the *other* labelers. For the performance results described in this chapter, each of the 4 labelers is compared with the EM-derived consensus of the other 3 and the algorithm is compared with the EM-derived consensus of all 4. The performance of the algorithmic detection method (as summarized in the Addendum) is determined as the cumulative ROC performance over each of the 4 images, where for each test image the algorithm was trained on the other 3 images.

Since the EM-derived detection list is probabilistic, each detection or false alarm is weighted. For example, if the EM posterior probability estimate of a particular region of interest is $p(v|\underline{z}) = 0.8$, then a human or algorithm which detects this region of interest has probability 0.8 of being correct (a true detection) and probability 0.2 of being incorrect (a false alarm). This is how detections and false alarms are scored when constructing the ROC plot. These "probabilistic ROCs" are the appropriate way to generate ROCs in the absence of ground truth (Burl et al. 1994b).

Figure 21.4(a) does not take into account either label-category or category-volcano probabilities, i.e., the reference list (for algorithm training and overall evaluation) is a consensus list (2 scientists working together) where labels 1,2,3,4 are ignored and all labeled items are counted equally as volcanos. The individual labelers and algorithm are then scored in the standard "non-weighted" ROC fashion. This curve is optimistic in terms of depicting the accuracy of the detectors since it ignores the underlying probabilistic nature of the labels. Even with this optimistic curve, volcano labeling is relatively inaccurate by either man or machine.

Figure 21.4(b) shows the full model where both category and estimation noise are handled. Clearly there is a substantial difference between the two plots: scientists and algorithms are all much less accurate in general when all of the uncertainty is fully modeled (Figure 21.4(b)). In Figure 21.4(a), the SVD algorithm appears to be competitive with one of the scientists. However in Figure 21.4(b), the SVD algorithm curve has shifted further away from the scientists. It turns out from closer analysis of the data that the SVD algorithm is doing particularly poorly in terms of approximating posterior probabilities and the more accurate model (Figure 21.4(b)) is more sensitive to this fact.

The poor probability approximation properties of the SVD method appear to be a function of the fact that the subspace projection destroys

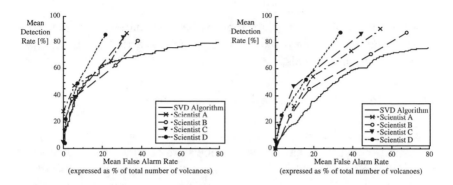

Figure 21.4
Probabilistic ROCs for both scientists and algorithms: (a) no uncertainty in the model, (b) estimation and category uncertainty included.

the implicit probabilistic information present in the labels, i.e., label 1's, 2's, etc. are jumbled up in the projected space without any particular structure. This begs the question of why one might not use other non-SVD methods ? We have conducted a significant number of experiments with a variety of other feature extraction/classification methods, including convolutional neural networks, Markov random field segmentation methods, and multiple filters, but all performed *worse* on this data than the SVD method. This gives an indication of the difficulty of this recognition problem.

We also note from the plots that there is a definite ordering in terms of accuracy among the scientists, namely, D, C, A, B. For example, B (the worst) typically generates twice as many false alarms as D (the best) for a given detection rate. None of the scientists are particularly accurate, the best being at about 88% detection for 36% false alarms. This reinforces the notion that the best one can hope for on this problem in terms of algorithmic performance, is to emulate the fallible human performance. It is worth noting that the probabilistic ROC curves are of direct interest to the scientists (independent of the algorithm's performance) in that it is the first time that human detection capabilities have been quantitatively evaluated in the context of volcano counting. The results have highlighted the subjective and ambiguous nature of the volcano-counting process and has led to the participating geologists reviewing the manner in which catalogs are generated. For example, it has been found (results not shown here) that there is greater self-consistency between groups of labelers than there is between individuals, suggesting that manual labeling is more consistent when carried out by groups rather than by individuals.

21.9   Limitations of the Labeling Model

The model described in this chapter is limited by the fact that the parameters between different labeler's models are assumed to be independent (see Heckerman, this volume, for a related discussion on parameter independence). Thus for example, the model clearly can not be used to estimate parameters both from the joint labelings of A and B and the individual labelings of A and B. It is possible to postulate more complex models which overcome parameter independence, but the maximum likelihood equations for estimation may no longer be tractable. In addition, the maximum-likelihood basis of EM raises the possibility of of over-fitting, especially on these relatively small datasets. It may be profitable in general to cast the problem in a Bayesian estimation framework rather than a maximum-likelihood one. For example, the model could easily be interpreted as a graphical model and the estimation problem solved using the Bayesian methods described in Buntine (this volume) and Heckerman (this volume).

21.10   Conclusion

This chapter focused on the treatment of uncertainty in training data in the context of evaluating human and algorithmic detection performance in image analysis, in particular, the problem of volcano detection in radar imagery of the planet Venus. A simple model for subjective ambiguity was proposed and an iterative maximum likelihood scheme was described for parameter estimation. By modeling the subjective nature of the labeling process one gets a realistic estimate of both the performance of human experts and the volcano detection algorithm. In particular, the difference between the two ROC curves in Figure 21.4 clearly shows that ignoring the subjective uncertainty aspect of the labeling can lead to significant over-confidence in terms of performance estimation.

In practical KDD problems involving the comparison of human and automated data analysis capabilities, if one suspects that the reference data was actually obtained in a subjective manner, then it is important that this source of uncertainty is taken into account. The techniques proposed in this chapter provide a framework for estimation and performance evaluation for such applications where absolute ground truth is not available. These applications are increasingly common as very large databases of image data and other data types are routinely collected and well-calibrated ground truth constitutes a tiny (and perhaps even zero) fraction of the overall data set.

Acknowledgments

The authors would like to thank Jayne Aubele and Larry Crumpler of the Department of Geological Sciences, Brown University, for their assistance in labeling images, and Maureen Burl (JPL) for assistance in obtaining the experimental results described in this paper. The research described in this paper was carried out by the Jet Propulsion Laboratory, California Institute of Technology, under a contract with the National Aeronautics and Space Administration and was supported in part by ARPA under grant number N00014-92-J-1860.

Addendum: Estimating the Label-Category Probabilities via the EM Procedure

Let N be the number of local regions of interest in the database (these are 15 pixel square image patches for the volcano application). The binary variable V takes values v and $\bar{v}$, "volcano" and "non-volcano." Let $c \subset \{1, \ldots, C\}$ denote a category. The relationship between categories and regions is non-deterministic: the probabilities $p(v|c_j)$ are those provided by the scientists as described earlier. An observed label l is a "noisy" estimate of the true category c to which a particular regions belongs. C is both the number of categories and the number of labels.

For simplicity we consider the case of just a single labeler who labels a given set of regions a number of times. The extension to multiple labelers is straightforward if one assumes that the regions are labeled independently by the labelers given the categories and that the parameters describing each labeler's model are independent of the model parameters for all of the other labelers.

Let n_{il} be the number of times that region of interest i is labeled with label l. Let c^* be the true category for a given region. Let Y_{ic}, $1 \le c \le C$, denote a binary variable which takes value 1 if $c = c^*$, and is 0 otherwise. We assume that each region is labeled independently of the others, i.e., if the labeler goes through the regions sequentially, there is no "memory" from one labeling to the next.

If one were to assume that the true category c^* is known, then one can calculate the probability of any set of labels for a given region: in particular, one can write the probability of obtaining the *observed* labels *given* a particular model for region i:

$$p(\text{observed labels}|c^*, i) \propto \prod_{l=1}^{C} p(l|c)^{n_{il}}. \tag{21.10.2}$$

Thus, unconditionally, where one does not assume knowledge of the true category c^*, and making use of the "dummy" variable Y_{ic}, one has:

$$p(\text{observed labels}, c^*|i) \propto \prod_{c=1}^{C} \left(p(c) \prod_{l=1}^{C} p(l|c)^{n_{il}} \right)^{Y_{ic}}, \tag{21.10.3}$$

where $Y_{ic} = 1$ if $c = c^*$ and 0 otherwise, and $p(c)$ is the prior probability of category c. Assuming that each region of interest is labeled independently of the others, the probability for all of the regions can be written as:

$$p(\text{observed labels}, c_i^*) \propto \prod_{i}^{N} \prod_{c=1}^{C} \left(p(c) \prod_{l=1}^{C} p(l|c)^{n_{il}} \right)^{Y_{ic}}. \tag{21.10.4}$$

Still assuming that the categories c for each region of interest are known (the Y_{ic}), the above equations can be solved to obtain maximum likelihood estimators of $p(l|c)$ and $p(c)$:

$$\hat{p}(l|c) = \frac{\sum_i Y_{ic} n_{il}}{\sum_l^C \sum_i Y_{ic} n_{il}} \tag{21.10.5}$$

and

$$\hat{p}(c) = \frac{1}{N} \sum_i Y_{ic}. \tag{21.10.6}$$

From Bayes' rule one can then show that

$$p(Y_{ic} = 1|\text{observed data}) = \frac{1}{K} \prod_l^C p(l|c)^{n_{il}} p(c) \tag{21.10.7}$$

where K is a normalization constant. Thus, given the parameters $p(l|c)$ and $p(c)$ one can infer the posterior probabilities for the category variable via Equation 21.10.7. In turn, one can infer the posterior probability that a particular region of interest is a volcano given that the "category-volcano" probabilities are known.

However, without knowing the Y_{ic} values we can not infer the parameters. Dawid and Skene (1979) noticed that one could treat the Y_{ic} as *hidden* and thus apply the well-known "Expectation-Maximization" (EM) procedure to find a local maximum of the likelihood function. The EM procedure is an iterative technique which proceeds as follows:

1. Obtain some initial estimates of the expected values of Y_{ic}, e.g.,

$$E[Y_{ic}] = \frac{n_{il}}{\sum_l n_{il}} \qquad (21.10.8)$$

2. M-step: choose the values of $p(l|c)$ and $p(c)$ which **maximize** the likelihood function (according to Equations 21.10.5 and 21.10.6), using $E[Y_{ic}]$ in place of Y_{ic}.

3. E-step: calculate the conditional **expectation** of Y_{ic}, $E[Y_{ic}|\text{data}] = p(Y_{ic} = 1|\text{data})$ (Equation 21.10.7).

4. Return to Step 2 until convergence is achieved.

In practice we have found that the procedure converges (the likelihood function does not increase with further iterations) within 5 to 10 steps for the data described in the chapter.

References

Agresti, A. 1992. Modeling Patterns of Agreement and Disagreement. *Statistical Methods in Medical Research,* 1: 201–218.

Aubele, J. C. and Slyuta, E. N. 1990. Small Domes on Venus: Characteristics and Origins. *Earth, Moon and Planets,* 50/51, 493–532.

Bunch, P. C.; Hamilton, J. F.; Sanderson G. K.; and Simmons, A. H. 1978. A Free-Response Approach to the Measurement and Characterization of Radiographic-Observer Performance. *Journal of Applied Photo. Engineering,* 4(4): 166–171.

Burl, M. C.; Fayyad, U. M.; Perona, P.; and Smyth, P. 1994a. Automating the Hunt for Volcanos on Venus. In Proceedings of the 1994 Computer Vision and Pattern Recognition Conference (CVPR-94), 302–309. Los Alamitos, Calif.: IEEE Computer Society Press.

Burl, M. C.; Fayyad, U. M.; Perona, P.; and Smyth, P. 1994b. Automated Analysis of Radar Imagery of Venus: Handling Lack of Ground Truth. In Proceedings of the IEEE Conference on Image Processing, vol.III, 236–240. Piscataway, NJ: IEEE Press.

Chesters, M. S. 1992. Human Visual Perception and ROC Methodology in Medical Imaging. *Phys. Med. Biol.,* 37(7): 1433–1476.

Dawid, A. P.; and Skene, A. M. 1979. Maximum Likelihood Estimation of Observer Error-Rates Using the EM Algorithm. *Applied Statistics,* 28(1): 20–28.

Duda, R. O. and Hart, P. E. 1973. *Pattern Classification and Scene Analysis* New York: John Wiley and Sons.

Fayyad, U. M.; Smyth, P.; Weir, N.; and Djorgovski, S. 1995. Automated Analysis and Exploration of Large Image Databases: Results, Progress, and Challenges. *Journal of Intelligent Information Systems,* 4: 7–25.

Fayyad, U. M., Smyth, P., Burl, M. C. and Perona, P. 1995. Learning to Catalog Science Images. In *Early Visual Learning,* ed. S. Nayar and T. Poggio (eds.) New York: Oxford University Press.

French, S. 1985. Group Consensus Probability Distributions: a Critical Survey. In *Bayesian Statistics 2,,* 183–202, ed. J. M. Bernardo, M. H. DeGroot, D. V. Lindley, and A. F. M. Smith. Amsterdam: Elsevier Science Publishers.

Guest, J. E.; Bulmer, M. H.; Aubele, J.; Beratan, K.; Greeley, R.; Head, J. W.; Michaels, G.; Weitz, C.; and Wiles, C. 1992. Small Volcanic Edifices and Volcanism in the Plains of Venus. *Journal of Geophysical Research,* 97(E10): 15949–15966.

Lindley, D. V. 1985. Reconciliation of Discrete Probability Distributions. In *Bayesian Statistics 2,* 375–390, ed. J. M. Bernardo, M. H. DeGroot, D. V. Lindley, and A. F. M. Smith. Amsterdam: Elsevier Science Publishers, North-Holland.

Lugosi, G. 1992. Learning with an Unreliable Teacher. *Pattern Recognition,* 25 (1): 79–87.

Magellan at Venus: Special Issue of the Journal of Geophysical Research, American Geophysical Union, 1992.

Redner, R. A.; and Walker, H. F. 1984. Mixture Densities, Maximum Likelihood, and the EM Algorithm. *SIAM Review,* 26(2): 195–239.

Science, Special Issue on Magellan Data, April 12, 1991.

Silverman, B. 1980. Some Asymptotic Properties of the Probabilistic Teacher. *IEEE Transactions on Information Theory,* IT-26 2: 246–249.

Smyth, P. 1995. Learning with Probabilistic Supervision. In *Computational Learning Theory and Natural Learning Systems 3,* ed. T. Petcshe, M. Kearns, S. Hanson, and R. Rivest. Cambridge, Mass.: The MIT Press.

Uebersax, J. S. 1993. Statistical Modeling of Expert Ratings on Medical Treatment Appropriateness. *Journal of the American Statistical Association* 88(422): 421–427.

Wiles C. R., and Forshaw, M. R. B. 1993. Recognition of Volcanos using Correlation Methods. *Image and Vision Computing,* 11(4): 188–196.

22 Predicting Equity Returns from Securities Data

Chidanand Apte & Se June Hong
T. J. Watson Research Center, IBM Research Division

Abstract

Our experiments with capital markets data suggest that the domain can be effectively modeled by classification rules induced from available historical data for the purpose of making gainful predictions for equity investments. New classification techniques developed at IBM Research, including minimal rule generation (R-MINI) and contextual feature analysis, seem robust enough for consistently extracting useful information from noisy domains such as financial markets. We will briefly introduce the rationale for our minimal rule generation technique, and the motivation for the use of contextual information in analyzing features. We will then describe our experience from several experiments with the S&P 500 data, illustrating the general methodology, and the results of correlations and simulated managed investment based on classification rules generated by R-MINI. We will sketch how the rules for classifications can be effectively used for numerical prediction, and eventually to an investment policy. Both the development of robust "minimal" classification rule generation, as well as its application to the financial markets, are part of an on-going study.

22.1   Introduction

There is currently a surge of interest in financial markets data mining. Large amounts of historical data is available for this domain in machine readable form. Analyses of this data for the purpose of abstracting and understanding market behavior, and using the abstractions for making predictions about future market movements, is being seriously explored (AI on Wall Street 91; AI on Wall Street 93). Some firms have also deployed analytical data mining methods for actual investment portfolio management (Barr and Mani 1993). We report here on our recent experiments with applying classification rule generation to S&P 500 data.

The R-MINI rule generation system (Hong 1994a) can be used for generating "minimal" classification rules from tabular data sets where one of the columns is a "class" variable and the remaining columns are "independent" features. The data set is completely discretized (i.e., continuous valued features are discretized into a finite set of discrete values, categorical features are left untouched) by a feature discretization subsystem prior to rule generation. The feature discretization performs feature ranking (of both continuous valued as well as categorical features) as well as the conversion of continuous valued features into discretized features using an optimal cutting algorithm (Hong 1994b). Once rule generation is completed, the R-MINI system can be used for classifying unseen data sets and measuring the performance using various error metrics.

The R-MINI rules are in Disjunctive Normal Form (DNF) (Indurkhya and Weiss 1991). There have been many approaches to generating DNF rules from data. These include (Michalski et al. 1986; Clark and Niblett 1989; Weiss and Indurkhya 1993b) which work in principle by iteratively forming one rule at a time to cover some examples from the training data which are removed from consideration before repeating the iteration. The other primary approach (Pagallo 1989; Quinlan 1993) is decision tree based, i.e., a decision tree is generated from a given set of training examples, using some combination of covering and pruning strategies, where each leaf of the tree represents a classification rule.

While the R-MINI approach to generating classification rules is similar to the former, it differs from both approaches in its primary goal, which is to strive for a "minimal" rule set that is complete and consistent with the training data. Completeness implies that the rules cover all of the examples in the training data while consistency implies that the rules cover no counter-examples for their respective intended classes. Others too have argued for generating complete and consistent classification models before applying error minimizing pruning processes (Breiman et al. 1984; Weiss and Kulikowski 1991). The R-MINI system utilizes a logic minimization methodology to generate "minimal" complete and consistent rules. This technique was first developed for programmable logic array circuit minimization (Hong et al. 1974) and is considered to be one of the best known logic circuit minimization techniques. The merits of striving for minimality have been well discussed (Blumer et al. 1989; Rissanen 1989). The principal hypothesis here is that a model that describes data is inversely proportional in its complexity to its accuracy. Thus, if two different models (in the same representation) both describe a particular data set, the less complex of the the two will be more accurate in its description. Complexity is measured differently for different modeling techniques. For DNF rules, it would be total number of rules and total number of tests in all the rules. A smaller description will tend to be better in its predictive accuracy, and this has been borne out in our extensive evaluations.

In the rest of this chapter, we will first describe highlights of the minimal rule generation and contextual feature analysis methodologies, followed by a detailed description of how these techniques were utilized in a specific application study, that of extracting DNF rules from capital markets data, and using these rules in a simulated investment portfolio management scheme.

22.2   Minimal Rule Generation

A data set with N features may be thought as a collection of discrete points (one per example) in an N-dimensional space. A classification rule is a hypercube in this space that contains one or more of these points. When there is more than one cube for a given class, all the cubes are Or-ed to provide a complete classification for the class. Within a cube the conditions for each part are And-ed, thereby giving the DNF representation for the overall classification model. The size of a cube indicates its generality, i.e., the larger the cube, the more vertices it contains, and potentially cover more example-points. R-MINI's minimality objective is first driven by the minimal number of cubes, and then the most general cubes. The most general cubes are prime cubes that cannot be further generalized without violating the consistency of that cube.

The minimality objective translates to finding a minimal number of prime cubes that cover all the example-points of a class and not cover any example-points of any counter-class. This objective is similar to many switching function minimization algorithms.

The R-MINI rule generation technique works with training data in which all features are completely pre-discretized. All numeric features are therefore discretized by a feature analysis and discretization subsystem prior to rule generation. Categoric features remain as they are. The rule generation technique is based upon a highly successful heuristic minimization technique that was used for minimizing large switching functions (MINI [Hong et al. 1974]). Similar heuristic minimization techniques have been developed for a publicly available switching function minimization package, ESPRESSO (Brayton et al. 1984).

We now summarize the salient steps of the R-MINI process, starting from a given set of data points. Let F be the set of initial cubes (initially, each cube corresponds to an example in the data set) for which the rules are being generated, FB be the set of initial cubes representing examples of all counter-classes, and DC is the (implicit) set of cubes representing space not covered by either F or FB.

The core heuristics used in the R-MINI system for achieving minimality consists of iterating (for a reasonable number of rounds) over two key sub-steps:

1. Generalization step, EXPAND, which takes each rule in the current set (initially each example is a rule) and opportunistically generalizes it to remove other rules that are subsumed. The sequence of operations in EXPAND are:

    2.1 Cube ordering: orders the cubes by a heuristic merit so that the cubes that are "hard" to combine with other cubes are to be processed first.

    2.2 Current cube expansion:

        2.2.1 Part ordering: decides the order of parts in which the single part expansion will proceed. Single part expansion takes a part of the given cube and turns 0s to 1s in the part, if doing so does not make the new cube contain any FB vertices. The purpose of this heuristic ordering is to effect a maximal coverage of other cubes when the cube is fully expanded.

        2.2.2 Expand each part of the cube in order. Here the cube is generalized recursively one part at a time until no more generalization is possible without violating the consistency.

    2.3 Shrinking other cubes: With the newly expanded cube, all other cubes are individually shrunk to the smallest size needed considering some of the vertices of the cube may be covered by the newly expanded cube. If a cube shrinks to a null size, it is removed from the list, thereby decreasing the number of cubes in the current F.

2.4 Shrinking the current expanded cube: The new cube is shrunk to the smallest necessary size in view of the fact that some of the vertices it covers may also be covered by other cubes.

2.5 Repeat steps 2.2)-2.4) for all surviving unexpanded cubes of F in the list in the order given by step 2.1).

2. Specialization/Reformulation, REDUCE, which takes each rule in the current set and specializes it to the most specific rule necessary to continue covering only the unique examples it covers. Cube specialization takes each cube in the order of another cube ordering heuristic designed to maximize the cube reductions, and shrinks it to the smallest size to contain the unique vertices it must cover outside the already covered vertices (by previous cubes) and the DC cover. The cube shrinking within the EXPAND shrinks cubes against the cube just expanded, whereas here the cube is shrunk against all the other cubes taken together. Redundant cubes disappear during this step.

The heuristics used for selecting what precise generalization or specialization to execute are chosen on a randomized basis. Therefore, each successive iteration may generalize and specialize in different directions. A iteration step may result either in an unchanged rule set (since completeness and consistency are enforced) or a smaller rule set. An indefinite iteration through this loop will result in monotonically decreasing classification rules that are consistent and complete at every stage in their minimization.

R-MINI's strength is in its heuristics that control the generalization and specialization. These heuristics essentially enable the generation of minimal number of rules that completely and consistently partition these example-points into unique regions. The minimization process may be viewed as a generalization process, in which regions that are adjacent to example-points but not themselves populated are available for expanding (generalizing) the rules. R-MINI's heuristics, based upon MINI's proven logic minimization heuristics, have also been empirically seen to be highly effective in generating accurate classification rule models.

This annealing style approach to rule generation (via iterative improvements) may be potentially indefinite. A limit is used that controls how long the system should keep iterating without observing a reduction.

If no reduction takes place within this limit, we can stop the minimization process. In practice, we have observed that R-MINI satisfactorily converges the rule set as long as it is allowed to go through at least 5 iterations without a reduction, on most well known test data sets as well as on some of the specific real applications in which we have been using the system.

R-MINI has been applied to several real data sets, up to those with a few hundred features and tens of thousands of examples. Preliminary evaluations suggest that complete and consistent full cover rule sets that result from applying R-MINI are much smaller than similar rule sets generated by other known techniques. Initial benchmarking studies also suggest that the predictive accuracy of R-MINI's rule sets is competitive with the DNF rule sets generated by other well known methods. An in-depth detailed discussion of the rule generation component of R-MINI appears in (Hong 1994a).

22.3   Contextual Feature Analysis

As mentioned in the previous section, R-MINI rule generation requires all features to be in categorical form, and hence the reason for discretizing all numerical features employing a feature analysis and discretization sub-system. There is also another important reason for applying this step prior to rule generation. Classification model generators will typically work only as well as the quality of the features from which they are trying to generate a model. Poor features will almost always result in weakly performing classification models.

Various approaches have been used to alleviate this problem. The decision tree based methods have relied on information theoretic measures (such as the "entropy" and "gini" functions) to determine the best feature to use at each node while expanding the decision tree (Breiman 1984). This basic principle may be thought of as a 1-level lookahead algorithm that determines the best feature to use at a node based on how well the feature partitions the training examples into their respective classes. Variants of this method include 2-level and more lookahead methods as well as employing simple conjuncts of features (instead of single features) as decision tests for nodes.

One well known method used in a DNF rule generator is backtracking based local optimization (Weiss and Indurkhya 1993b). This method works in principle by attempting to constantly improve the performance of a rule while being constructed by swapping member tests (features) with new tests. Although this method appears more powerful than the decision tree methods, it may not perform well in the presence of extremely large number of features.

In most dynamic feature selection methods the discretization of numerical features is done in-process during model generation. This has an inherent weakness due to the serial nature of selecting the landmark values, or the cut points. Consider a problem where a numeric feature inherently has two or more optimum cut points, i.e. the intervals partitioned by them are meaningful in the problem domain. It is not likely that one of these points will be chosen in a serial process where the one "best" point is sought one at a time based on its ability alone to distinguish the classes. Our approach seeks multiple "optimal" cut points based on contextual demands for the separation of values. Even when it is not done serially, if the discretization considers only the given variable's correlation to the class, the result becomes a weaker approximation to the context based consideration we employ in our approach.

The R-MINI system therefore employs a contextual feature analyzer that simultaneously ranks the features in terms of their classificatory power as well as determining the "optimal" number of cuts for each numerical feature for discretization so as to maximize that feature's ability to discriminate. Features are ranked based upon merits that are computed for each of them. Merits are computed by taking for each example in a class a set of "best" counter examples, and accumulating a figure for each feature that is a function of the example-pair feature values. Dynamic programming is then used for producing optimum cuts (Aggarwal et al. 1993) for the numeric variables by simultaneously looking at all numerical features and their value spans. The contextual merit computation algorithm works in principle as follows:

Contextual Merit and Span Generation Algorithm, CMSG

CM0)   Initialize M, and let SPAN be an empty list of triplets.
CM1)   Compute the numeric threshold vector T for numeric features.
CM2)   For each e_i of class C_1, do
        CM2.0)Initialize M_i
        CM2.1)Compute distances to all examples of C_2 and let $log_2 N_2$
               (at least 1) of the nearest distance counter examples

```
        be the BESTSET.
    CM2.2)For each counter example, e_j, in the BESTSET, do
        CMSG2.2.0)Append the triplet, (i,j,1/D²_ij) to SPAN
        CM2.2.1)   Compute M_ij:   m_k_ij = d_k_ij/D²_ij ∀k
        CM2.2.2)   Update M_i : M_i = M_i + M_ij
    CM2.3)Update M : M = M + M_i
CM3)   Return M
CMSG4)Return (generic) SPAN
```

M is the contextual merit list for the entire feature set. The SPAN list obtained as a by product, is used to discretize all the numeric features. It contains $N_1 \times log_2 N_2$ entries (order N log N). For a numeric feature, X_k, we develop a specialization, $SPAN_k$, by substituting the actual values of X_k of the pair of examples given by the i and j indices, and removing those entries if the two values are same. Each entry in the $SPAN_k$ represents two points of a span in the X_k value line, along with a "merit" value to be scored when a cut point separates the end points of the span. It is now a simple matter of invoking an optimal interval covering algorithm to find the optimum c cut points for a given c. One has a choice of dynamic programming algorithms to achieve this with varying complexity.

This process is iteratively repeated until a reasonable level of convergence emerges in the merits and the cut values. In comparison to the tree based methods, the R-MINI contextual feature analyzer may be thought of as a full-level lookahead feature analyzer. It will not suffer from falling into false local minima because of its ability to analyze merits of features in a global context. An in-depth discussion of contextual feature analysis appears in (Hong 1994b).

22.4   Experiments with S&P 500 Data

We undertook a study to determine the feasibility of applying DNF rule generation technology to managing equity investment portfolios. Initial results appear promising.

All our experiments have been conducted with S&P 500 data, for a contiguous period of 78 months. The data spans 774 securities (S&P deletes and adds new securities to its 500 index over time, so that the index continues to reflect the true market capitalization of large cap.

firms). The data comprises of 40 variables for each month for each security. The type of information conveyed through these variables is both fundamental (company performance data) as well as technical (stock performance data). Some of the variables provide trend information (ranging from month-to-month trends to 5-yearly trends). With the exception of one variable, the industry sector identifier, which is categorical, all the rest are numerical.

Also available for each monthly stream of data for a security is the monthly total return for that security, where the variables' values are all at the beginning of a month while the monthly total return (stock change + dividends) is at the end of the month. From this 1-month return variable, one can compute 3-month, 6-month, as well as 12-month returns, for each security for each month. One can also compute the difference between these returns and the capitalization weighted mean as well as simple mean for each of the returns. Thus, if one can envision the basic 40 variable set as the "features," then we have available several ways to assign classes to each of the examples (a monthly stream of feature values for a security) by picking from one of the computed returns.

We have conducted a series of compute-intensive classification experiments with this data, using different ways to assign class labels as well as different ways to partition the data. We will focus in the rest of this chapter on one particular study, which attempts to generate rules for classifying examples based upon the differential between monthly return and simple mean of monthly returns for a given stream of data. The idea here is to use these rules to predict the differential for unseen data for the following year(s) and utilize the predictions in a portfolio management scheme for maximizing the investment returns. The portfolio management strategy strives to remain constantly above the average market return, and therefore the use of the differential as a class label. A positive differential merely implies a return that is higher than the market average. The actual return could be positive or negative.

22.4.1   Generating Classification Rules for Equity Returns

There are several issues at hand for determining how much data to choose for generating DNF classification rules for this domain. A routinely used approach would be to hide a portion of the data, ranging from 10-30%, and generate rules from the remaining "training" data,

Table 22.1
Number of S&P 500 data examples per class for years 1-4.

Class	Returns	Year 1	Year 2	Year 3	Year 4
C0	< -6	880	857	559	674
C1	$\geq -6\ \&\ < -2$	1101	997	1188	936
C2	$\geq -2\ \&\ < 2$	1347	1180	1533	1295
C3	$\geq 2\ \&\ < 6$	874	883	977	1015
C4	≥ 6	699	808	560	847

and evaluate their performance on the hidden "test" data. However, that approach is not adequate for the financial markets domain. There is a strong time-dependent behavior in the securities market which needs to be accounted for. An accepted practice is to use the "sliding window" approach, in which the data is laid out in temporal sequence, and the classification generation and performance evaluation experiments are repeatedly performed on successive sets of training and test data. This method can be used for determining whether the performance of a particular approach withstands the time-dependent variations that are encountered as one moves from set to set.

Adopting this latter methodology in one of our experiments, we chose to generate classification rules from a consecutive 12 months of data, and tested the performance of those rules on the following sets of 12 month streams. The idea here was to evaluate the rate of decline in the predictive power of classification rules as one moved forward in time. Once this rate is known, one can establish a policy of re-generating the rules once every "n" years from the immediate past data so as to continue holding up the predictive performance. Our data provided us with over 6 consecutive streams of 12 month data. We are conducting our experiments from the earliest point onwards, i.e., generate classification rules from the earliest available 12 month data (year 1), apply those rules to year 2, year 3, etc. until the performance becomes unacceptable, say at year "n." Then re-generate classification rules from the 12-month data for year "n-1," and repeat the process.

For the class label, we chose the differential between the next month's 1-month total return and the S&P 500 average 1-month return. This label is essentially a numerical valued assignment. We further discretized this assignment by attempting to emulate typical security analysts' categorization method for stocks, which would include the range "strongly performing," "moderately performing," "neutral," "moderately under-performing," and "strongly under-performing." Based upon preliminary analysis of the data distribution, we chose to assign the cut-point -6, -2, +2, and +6. That is, all examples who had a class label value of 6% or more were put in one class (the "strongly performing" class), all examples with class label values of 2% or more and less than 6% were put in another class (the "moderately performing" class) and so on. Using this class partitioning scheme, Table 22.1 illustrates how the first 4 years of data break up by class. Note that although 12 months worth of data for 500 securities should translate to about 6000 examples, the actuals vary for each time period because we chose to discard examples which had one or more missing values for the 40 features. The actual examples that we worked with are 4901 for year 1, 4725 for year 2, 4817 for year 3, and 4767 for year 4.

Before proceeding to apply R-MINI's feature analysis and discretization step, we tried to carefully adjust the features based upon discussions with the domain experts. As we pointed out in the previous section, the quality of features is of extreme importance in ensuring the quality of the generated classification model. Some of our adjustments to the raw data included the normalization of some features and the inclusion of additional trend indicating features. This preprocessing usually results in the transformation of input raw features into a new set of features, and cannot be done in the absence of domain experts. However, if this expertise is available, then utilizing it to refine the features is always very desirable. Once these transformations were made, we applied R-MINI's feature discretization step to the data for Year 1, which corresponds to 4901 examples. The result of this step is the assignment of merits to all the features and the assignment of cut points to the numerical features. Table 22.2 illustrates the merit and cut assignment for this experiment. Note that features with a 0 value for cut-points indicates that the feature is categorical. Also, we chose the merit values to discard certain features from the rule generation step. These features appear the lower end of the table. Their cut points are not important, since they do not play a subsequent role in the classification experiments, and are therefore not indicated.

Using the selected features and fully discretized data values, we then apply R-MINI's rule generation step to the training data, which is now essentially a 5-class problem with 4901 examples and 30 features. Since

R-MINI uses a randomization process in its minimization phase, we run R-MINI several times (typically 5-6) on the same data set, and go with the combination of the smallest rule sets that was generated from the multiple runs. As an example, the smallest rule set size from one particular run is 569. That is, 569 rules completely and consistently classified the 4901 training examples. Figures 22.2 and 22.4.1 illustrate just 2 of these rules, where the first rule, Rule 1, is for Class 0, which corresponds to "strongly under-performing" and the second rule, Rule 481, is for Class 4, which corresponds to "strongly performing." Since R-MINI employs a randomized process in its generalization and minimization phases, different runs may potentially generate different minimal rule sets. Combining different minimal solutions allows us to simultaneously exploit the unique generalization nuances of each solution.

Table 22.2
Feature Merits and Cut Points for Year 1 Data.

Feature	Merit	Cut Points	Feature	Merit	Cut Points
ret1by1m	322	5	das	58	xx
pr2	230	4	derat	52	xx
ret1mret1	229	4	gprat	48	xx
ret1	228	4	qualty	42	xx
pr1	223	4	ccr	40	xx
pr3	216	4	ass	40	xx
pr6	201	4	growth	29	xx
valueprice	197	3	cne	21	xx
veer	152	1			
cflowprice	131	1			
earntr	122	2			
epsprice	121	2			
bookprice	115	1			
eps5	112	2			
aprice	111	1			
hsg	110	2			
per	105	1			
cap	105	1			
beta	105	1			
eps12price	100	2			
roe	94	1			
rinveq	91	2			
sects	90	0			
fund	78	2			
peg	77	1			
odl	67	2			
yld	66	1			
salshr	61	4			
epsvar	61	1			

Rule 1:
   monthr12: NOT ($5.50 \leq X < 9.50$;)
   aprice: ($X < 43.19$;)
   beta: ($X < 1.10$;)
   epsprice: NOT ($0.05 \leq X < 0.06$;)
   eps5: ($3.98 \leq X$)
   peg: ($1.54 \leq X$)
   pr3: NOT ($0.93 \leq X < 1.01$; $1.07 \leq X < 1.17$;)
   valueprice: ($0.86 \leq X$)
   veer: ($-2.37 \leq X$)
   ret1mret1: ($-10.85 \leq X$)
   ret1by1m: ($1.03 \leq X$)
Then $\Longrightarrow$ C0

Figure 22.1
Examples of R-MINI Classification Rules Generated from Year 1 Data.

22.4.2 Rule-based Regression

To be able to precisely quantify the predictive performance, especially from an investment management point of view, it is necessary that the classification rules predict the actual return, and not the discretized class segments. We have developed metrics for assigning numeric predictions for the R-MINI classification rules. While primarily motivated by the current set of experiments, it is conceivable that this approach could be used in any domain where it is required to predict numerical values. In a sense, this metric extends our R-MINI classification system for applications in non-linear multi-variate regression.

To extend the classification model to a rule-based regression model, we compute additional metrics for the rules. Based upon the training examples and the rules generated from this training data, we compute for each rule three parameters; μ, the mean of all actual class values (in this case, the differential between 1-month total return and mean S&P 500 1-month total return) of training examples covered by that rule; σ, the standard deviation of these values; and N, the total number of training examples covered by that rule.

When a rule set of this nature is applied to hidden "test" or unseen data, each example in that set will potentially have zero or more rules that apply to that example. In the case that no rules apply to an un-

Rule 481:
   beta: ($1.10 \leq X$)
   cap: ($X < 2743.50;$)
   epsvar: ($6.25 \leq X$)
   hsg: NOT ($4.89 \leq X < 9.45;$)
   peg: ($X < 1.54;$)
   pr1: ($X < 1.10;$)
   pr2: NOT ($1.06 \leq X < 1.14;$)
   pr3: NOT ($0.93 \leq X < 1.01;$)
   pr6: NOT ($0.91 \leq X < 1.02;$)
   rinveq: NOT ($5.63 \leq X < 10.64;$)
   valueprice: NOT ($0.70 \leq X < 0.86;$)
   veer: NOT ($-2.37 \leq X < 0.84;$)
   ret1mret1: NOT ($-10.85 \leq X < -4.05;$)
   ret1by1m: ($X < 1.03; 1.06 \leq X < 1.06;$)
Then $\Longrightarrow$ C4

Figure 22.2
Examples of R-MINI Classification Rules Generated from Year 1 Data.

seen example, we can assign or predict a numerical value that suggests a default for the domain, based upon priors such as the normal expected mean for the class. In the case that one or more rules apply to an unseen example, we compute an average from the rule coverage metrics, and assign that value as the class label for that example. Two straightforward averaging approaches are the simple and weighted approach. In the simple averaging approach, we compute for each example the simple average of μ of all rules that cover it as its predicted value (assigning a prediction value that is the mean of the class feature values in the training set if no rules cover it). A similar rule-based regression technique was employed in (Weiss and Indurkhya 1993). In the weighted average approach, we compute and assign a prediction of the weighted average of $\frac{\sqrt{N}}{\sigma}\mu$ of all rules that cover it. In general, weighted averaging usually leads to smoother correlations between predicted and actual values.

More sophisticated statistical averaging methods are also available within our system in addition to these. Typically, we try and determine the best averaging method to use based upon which does the best on the training example, and utilize that for making the predictions from the corresponding set of rules on unseen data.

22.4.3   Investment Portfolio Management with R-MINI Rules

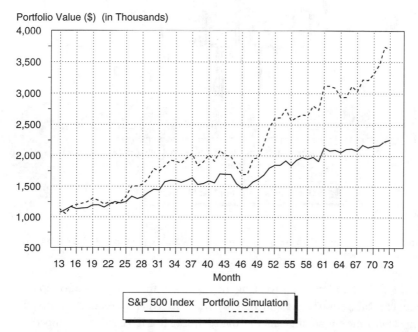

Figure 22.3
Comparing total returns of simulated S&P 500 index portfolio and a simulated
rule-managed portfolio.

To evaluate the performance of the generated rules, we applied them
to subsequent year data. For example, rules generated from data for
months 1-12, after some minimal pruning, are applied to the the following two years of data. We pruned out rules that cover 3 or less examples,
since they are assumed to be covering the noise component in the data.
For the remaining set of rules, we computed the μ, σ, and N for each
rule, and then applied them to data for months 13-48.

For effective comparison of how these rules would perform if realisti-
cally used, we constructed a portfolio management scheme based upon
these rules, and compared it to a simulated S&P 500 index fund performance. An index fund is passive in nature, and all that a S&P
500 index fund does is to constantly try and reflect the make up of

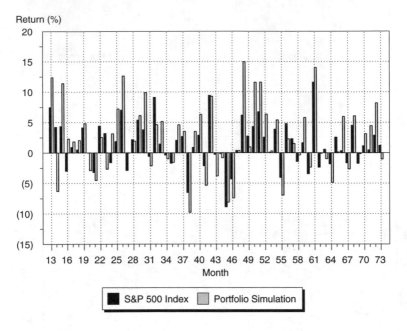

Figure 22.4
Comparing monthly returns of simulated S&P 500 index portfolio and a simulated
rule-managed portfolio.

the S&P 500 index, by investing in those companies in proportion of
their capitalization[1]. In contrast to this passively managed approach,
a portfolio management scheme based upon R-MINI rules will need to
be highly active, since every month the rules will be making predictions
which will need to be acted upon. What this active management policy
does in principle is to start out with a investment which reflects the
S&P 500 index fund, but then make trades every month based upon the
rule predictions. One strategy that we have shown to be successful is as
follows:

1. Generate rules (and use only those that cover > 3 examples).

2. Start with $1 million S&P 500 index portfolio.

3. Execute monthly action at the end of month as follows:

    (a) Update portfolio value for each equity position based upon
    the month's actual total return for that equity.

---

[1]The simulation of the passive index fund was performed on only that subset of
the available S&P 500 that did not have missing information, i.e., the data in Table
22.1. This simulation may not correspond exactly to the real S&P 500 performance,
although it is very close.

(b) Apply rules to month-end data for making predictions.

(c) Sort predictions in descending order.

(d) Sell all securities from sorted list whose predicted excess return is less than -6%, applying 0.5% transaction fee to every trade.

(e) Buy all securities from sorted list whose predicted excess return is greater than 6%, applying 0.5% transaction fee to every trade, in equal amounts.

The buy and sell cutoff points and thresholds are parameters that can be adjusted for controlling the behavior of the portfolio. For example, they can be adjusted to make the portfolio "aggressive" or "conservative." Aggressive portfolios are characterized by high turnover and large positions in limited equities. Conservative portfolios hold relatively larger number of equities and trade less. The buy/sell cutoff points and thresholds for our investment portfolio simulator can be varied to achieve different behaviors on this spectrum.

For the above settings, Figures 22.3 and 22.4 illustrate how our active portfolio performs against a passive portfolio, on a monthly basis as well as a cumulative basis. Over a six year period, three sets of rules were generated from data for years 1, 3 and 5. The year 1 rules were used for predicting returns for years 2 and 3. The year 3 rules were used for predicting returns for years 4 and 5. The year 5 rules were used for predicting returns for the remaining period, year 6. Thus there is a 5 year period over which the combined rule predictions can be evaluated against a benchmark, such as the S&P 500 index.

It can be observed that the simulated predictions-based portfolio returns a total of 270% over this period, compared to the S&P 500 index return of 110%. Compared to the 500 securities comprising the S&P 500 index, our simulated portfolio held an average of 30 securities over the 5 year period, and traded on average 5 securities per month. These characteristics can be adjusted by adjusting the buy/sell cutoff and threshold parameters. Many experiments with these parameters suggest that the simulated portfolio can be made more aggressive by carrying out much more trading and holding a lot fewer securities and consequently generating higher returns.

The monthly return plot provides insight at a more detailed level, highlighting the months when the rules actually generated predictions that were accurate enough to beat the S&P 500 index, and the months when the predictions were either weak or completely wrong. In addition to the confirmation that cumulatively the rule managed portfolio beats the S&P 500 index return, one can utilize the monthly returns to evaluate metrics such as the volatility and risk-versus-reward characteristics of the simulated rule-based portfolio. These evaluations suggest that the predictions do a reasonable job of beating the S&P 500 index without too much additional volatility or risk.

We make a few simplifying assumptions when constructing the portfolio management simulations. Issues such as the real-time granularity of the data availability, and the ability to transact stable trades, could potentially make our simulation strategy not practical. To be realistic and take all such factors into consideration, we hope to develop a more powerful portfolio management strategy that will compensate for additional real-market constraining factors such as these.

22.5   Discussion

We can draw a few key conclusions based upon our experiments. First, the S&P 500 data, as characterized by the features illustrated in Table 22.2, seem to provide adequate information for useful classification rule generation. Second, our techniques and methodology have the ability to extract this information from what is well known to be noise prone data.

The application of DNF classification rules in non-linear multi-variate regression applications is in itself another interesting direction to explore. The advantages of using DNF rules for these applications is clear; they provide a superior level of representation and interpretability in contrast to black-box style mathematical functions. Expert analysts can examine and understand these rules, and potentially even hand-edit them for improved performance.

We have demonstrated the predictive power of R-MINI's minimal rule generation philosophy in conjunction with its contextual feature analysis. We have observed that the R-MINI generated rules, when embedded in an appropriate portfolio management scheme, can outstrip passive index funds in performance.

Although automatic classification methods such as ours provide an additional level of sophistication for culling out useful information from vast amounts of data, they are certainly not to be viewed as black box entities that can be applied in isolation. Every domain and its data has its own peculiarities, and careful introspective analysis of the data is an important conjunct to leveraging these methods maximally. We have attempted to do that in these experiments, trying to understand the data entities, determining whether new and derived features need to play a role, determining which features to discard, and finally, carefully evaluating the performance of the generated rules in conjunct with experts. The nature and longevity of the predictive power of the rules suggest the style in which we need to re-generate the rules, and the specific applications that can be built around the rule models. Our approach so far has been quite promising in the results it has delivered. We have begun to explore options for embedding our methodology into an actual deployment.

References

Aggarwal, A.; Schieber, B.; and Tokuyama, T. 1993. Finding a Minimum Weight K-link Path in Graphs with Monge Property and Applications. Technical report, IBM Research Division, Yorktown Heights, New York.

Artificial Intelligence Applications on Wall Street Proceedings, 1991. Los Alamitos, Calif.: IEEE Computer Society.

Artificial Intelligence Applications on Wall Street Proceedings. Software Engineering Press, 1993.

Barr, D. and Mani, G. 1993. Neural Nets in Investment Management: Multiple Uses. In Artificial Intelligence Applications on Wall Street Proceedings, 81–87. Los Alamitos, Calif.: IEEE Computer Society.

Blumer, A.; Ehrenfeucht, A.; Haussler, D.; and Warmuth, M. 1989. Learnability and the Vapnik-Chervonenkis Dimension. *JACM*, 36:929–965.

Brayton, R.; Hachtel, G.; McMullen, C.; and Sangiovanni-Vincentelli, A. 1984. *Logic Minimization Algorithms for VLSI Synthesis*. Dortrecht, Holland: Kluwer Academic Publishers.

Breiman, L.; Friedman, J.; Olshen, R.; and Stone, C. 1984. *Classification and Regression Trees*. Monterey, Calif.: Wadsworth.

Clark, P. and Niblett, T. The CN2 Induction Algorithm. *Machine Learning*, 3:261–283.

Hong, S. J.; Cain, R.; and Ostapko, D. 1974. MINI: A Heuristic Algorithm for Two-Level Logic Minimization. *IBM Journal of Research and Development*, 18(5):443–458.

Hong, S. J. 1994a. R-MINI: A Heuristic Algorithm for Generating Minimal Rules from Examples. In Proceedings of the Third Pacific Rim International Conference on Artificial Intelligence— PRICAI' 94, 331–337.

Hong, S. J. 1994b. Use of Contextual Information for Feature Ranking and Discretization. Technical Report RC 19664, IBM Research Division, 1994.

Indurkhya, N. and Weiss, S. 1991. Iterative Rule Induction Methods. *Journal of Applied Intelligence,* 1:43–54.

Michalski, J.; Mozetic, I.; Hong, J., and Lavrac, N. 1986.   The Multi-Purpose Incremental Learning System AQ15 and its Testing Application to Three Medical Domains. In Proceedings of the American Association for Artificial Intelligence, 1041–1045. Menlo Park, Calif.: AAAI Press.

Pagallo, G. 1989. Learning DNF by Decision Trees. In Proceedings of the Eleventh International Joint Conference on Artificial Intelligence, 639–644. San Francisco: Morgan Kaufmann.

Quinlan, J. R. 1993. *C4.5: Programs for Machine Learning.* San Francisco: Morgan Kaufmann.

Rissanan, J. 1989. Stochastic Complexity in Statistical Inquiry. In *World Scientific Series in Computer Science,* 15.

Weiss, S. and Indurkhya, N. 1993a. Optimized Rule Induction. *IEEE EXPERT,* 8(6):61–69.

Weiss, S. and Indurkhya, N. 1993b. Rule-Based Regression. In Proceedings of the International Joint Conference on Artificial Intelligence.   San Francisco: Morgan Kaufmann.

Weiss, S. and Kulikowski, C. A. 1991. *Computer Systems that Learn.* San Francisco: Morgan Kaufmann.

23   From Data Mining to Knowledge Discovery: Current Challenges and Future Directions

Ramasamy Uthurusamy
General Motors R & D Center

The Purpose of Computing
is *insight*, not numbers
– *Richard Hamming*

A major contribution of this book is *its* systematic definition and discussion of the entire KDD process. This process-centered view of KDD is the unifying theme of the chapters of the book. Enabling users to gain insight from data is the common overall objective shared by the chapters. They described the relevant state-of-the-art techniques, methodologies, tools, results, and applications. In this epilogue we briefly revisit some of these to provide the basis for discussing some potentially rewarding areas of future directions in KDD research and practice.

23.1   A Synopsis of Contributions to this Book

The KDD process as defined in this book is a multi-step process that is human-centered, as it should be, if it is to be a non-trivial process of identifying valid, novel, potentially useful, and ultimately understandable patterns in data. The KDD process is enabled by an integrated, interactive, and iterative system of tools, techniques, and computational means. Such a system allows for: the selection, cleaning, transformation, and projection of data; mining the data to extract patterns and appropriate models; evaluating and interpreting the extracted patterns to decide what constitutes *knowledge*; consolidating the knowledge, resolving conflicts with previously extracted knowledge; and making the knowledge available for use by a performance element.

This process definition and discussion clarified the editors' view of the relation between knowledge discovery and data mining. Accordingly, KDD refers to the overall *process* of discovering useful knowledge from data while *data mining* refers to the application of algorithms for extracting patterns from data. The chapters of the book addressed many fundamental issues in KDD starting with an exposition of the state-of-the-practice of the human-centered KDD process that is highly interactive with many decisions made by the user.

Other basic topics covered by the chapters include: unifying view of various data mining techniques under the area of graphical models; a perspective on statistical techniques applicable to KDD; discussion and illustration of a few specific data mining techniques; methods to deal with trends and deviation analysis and finding patterns in time series data; techniques for deriving dependencies and association rules from transaction data; development of integrated discovery systems that incorporate multiple techniques to solve practical problems; development of next generation database systems to enable KDD; and finally some successful real-world applications.

In addition to the theoretical issues, we have covered application issues in KDD including guidelines for selecting an application and current challenges facing researchers and practitioners. A list of KDD terms is provided with the goal that it might serve as the seed for a common terminology for use by this multi-disciplinary field. A book is not complete in this day of networked hypermedia environments without pointers to available world-wide resources for further probing and to get a quick head start. Such a resource list follows this epilogue.

23.2   KDD: Present Challenges

> Data is an extremely valuable asset,
> but like a cash crop,
> unless harvested, it is wasted.
> – *Sid Adelman*

This book provided a definition of the KDD process to enable a common understanding and a means to compare various KDD systems. It serves as an introduction to the state-of-the-art KDD research and practice. For obvious reasons it is just that, a glimpse at some of the current activities that are noteworthy. After going through the book the reader is well aware that a lot remains to be done. Here, we will take another look at a few of the research and application issues outlined in various chapters and also a few others that demand our attention.

Representation issues, search complexity, use of prior and domain knowledge, and statistical inference are some of the core problems in KDD that are still open and require major attention. In addition to these fundamental and theoretical issues are the following primary research and application challenges for KDD: dimensionality; overfitting; statistical significance; non-stationarity due to changing data and knowledge; missing, noisy, and incomplete data; complex relations among data variables; pre-processing of data; understandability of discovered patterns; measures of interestingness of discovered patterns; human-computer interaction issues; privacy issues; integration with other systems; etc. In our opinion, the following issues also require much attention from KDD researchers and practitioners.

23.2.1   KDD Process: A Systemic View

The entire KDD process is a continuum of activities ranging from the collection and entry of large amounts of data to the sharing and use of the discovered knowledge in a decision making environment. There are literally thousands of researchers and practitioners who are involved in the various parts of this KDD process. However, each of us can identify where our work fits in this continuum and at the same time have a systemic view of the whole process. This view allows us to understand as well as explain to others the impact of our work and the remaining issues to be resolved. It also allows one to identify and assess the contribution of others as well as the claims of the commercial products that will flood this market. Hence, this process and systemic view is important and necessary to keep in mind in all of our KDD endeavors.

This systemic view requires more research to address the issues of: how to integrate results from many diverse disciplines including database, artificial intelligence, machine learning, statistics, information retrieval, etc.; development of high performance computer systems that integrate all the steps of the KDD process; training and education issues; etc. The aim is to grow the infrastructure for a knowledge processing environment where the user only needs to focus on the application issue at hand rather than having to develop everything from scratch.

23.2.2   KDD Process: A Human-Centered View

The human-centered nature of the KDD process poses many research issues. The first is the performance issue. Users interacting with an iterative KDD system expect and deserve a rapid response environment. This important issue is particularly challenging for KDD where the system has to deal with large databases and numerous algorithmic techniques designed for the various steps of the overall process. The second issue focuses on how to assist the user in the proper selection and matching of appropriate tools and techniques to achieve the goals and objectives of the user. It is a real challenge to get the system to know what it knows and impart the knowledge to decide what tools are appropriate for what problems and when. Particularly in KDD this is an important problem to address even if the user is the researcher who developed specific techniques since the whole system is needed to solve a problem. While there are developments of *knowledge discovery workbenches* and integrated systems that include more than one KDD process step they do not go far enough to address the issue of a user friendly system for use by an analyst. An analyst is usually not a KDD expert but one who has the responsibility to make sense out of the data using available KDD techniques. For any KDD system to be successful it needs to integrate well into an existing environment to provide a complete solution to an analyst. Hence, a challenge to KDD researchers and practitioners is to place more emphasis on the overall KDD process and on the tools to support its various steps. There should be more emphasis on human-computer interaction and less emphasis on total automation with the aim to support both expert and novice users.

Highly interactive human-computer environments as outlined by the KDD process enable both human-assisted computer discovery and computer-assisted human discovery. The development of appropriate tools for visualization, interpretation and analysis of discovered patterns is of paramount importance. Such interactive environments, by reducing the time to understand complex data, would enable practical solutions to many real world problems far more rapidly than either human or computer operating independently.

23.2.3   While Mining, Beware of Mines

An important aspect of KDD work is to allow users to make sense of data they *already* have. However, when we go data mining we must beware of *minefields* in the data. Contaminated data and in some cases good data might be potentially problematic *mines* if one does not do pre-processing that is appropriate to the goals at hand. Issues of privacy and spurious discoveries while mining have to be considered. Hence, techniques to handle legacy databases and means to *clean* them before attempting KDD are important and potentially useful areas for further research. Research in statistical techniques to provide safeguards and methodologies for preventing spurious discoveries are necessary.

23.2.4   Data Warehousing, Database Marketing, and OLAP

A 1994 MetaGroup survey revealed that by 1997 about 90% of Fortune 1000 Companies will be pursuing data warehousing projects. This and other factors have generated considerable interest and activity on the part of hardware and software vendors to capitalize on this trend. Hence, the recent popularity of the seemingly new trend of data warehousing is mainly due to the vendors' push and not due to the advent of any new and significant advances in database technology. Briefly, the term *Data Warehouse* refers to a database that contains subject-oriented, integrated, and historical data that is primarily utilized in analysis and decision support environments. Data warehousing is the process of creating a data warehouse by collecting and cleaning transactional data and making it available for on-line retrieval to assist in analysis and decision making. In the KDD process terms we note that the data warehouse could be equated to the output of the transformation step which just precedes the data mining step of the process.

The database community has developed a set of tools for the analysis of data warehouses that is popularly known as OLAP (On-Line Analytical Processing). OLAP tools focus on providing multi-dimensional data analysis, that is superior to SQL in computing summaries and breakdowns along many dimensions. OLAP tools require greater interaction from the users to identify interesting patterns in data. Data Mining step of the KDD process enables a potentially automated process to discover interesting and hidden patterns in data. Hence, data mining and OLAP are related facets of a new generation of intelligent information extraction and management tools. There is a potential opportunity and a challenge to develop techniques to integrate the OLAP tools of the database community and the data mining tools of the machine learning and statistical communities.

The most successful and widespread commercial application of KDD is *Database Marketing*. It is a method for analyzing customer databases, looking for patterns among existing customer preferences and using those patterns for more targeted selection of future customers. Research to develop appropriate KDD tools to aid in this analysis and application should also take into account the important issue of privacy.

23.2.5   Avoid the Hype

> The history of technology shows us that we
> overestimate what a technology can do for us in a few years
> and underestimate what it can do in a decade or two.
> – *Edward Feigenbaum, Pamela McCorduck, and Penny Nii*

At this moment the data mining and knowledge discovery field has attracted the attention of the business and commercial communities and thus is at a stage where it is necessary to separate the hype from reality. It is the responsibility of researchers and practitioners in this field to make certain the potential of this area is not overstated and that the users and businesses understand the true nature of the contributions along with its limitations. The very nature of success in this area makes it difficult to judge objectively. Truly successful KDD applications are rarely made public, particularly if the discovered knowledge is utilized for competitive advantage. It is important we make clear the value and contributions of what is being promoted in the popular press and the computer industry announcements.

23.3   KDD: Future Directions

In addition to the above challenges currently facing KDD researchers and practitioners, the following are some of the potentially rewarding areas of future directions. It is appropriate at this point to recall the excellent observations and comments on the barriers and future of knowledge discovery by Gio Wiederhold in his Foreword to this book.

23.3.1   It Is Better to Prevent than Process the Data Glut

> The idea is not to save every bit of information, but to relate
> what is known and not known to what needs to be known.
> *Vincent P. Barabba*

Data deluge is the nagging and fundamental issue of KDD. While this book adequately addressed the issue of making sense out of all that data glut, what really cries out for investigation by the KDD community is the prevention versus the cure issue. Data will continue to be collected in large quantities for valid purposes as well as for safety measures. Storage cost is no longer a factor. The philosophy of *collect now extract later*, steeped in the fear of not wanting to miss out anything that might become useful, would only add more data. Our research should focus on developing tools and techniques to address the following two questions among others. Are we collecting the right data in right amounts before focusing on extracting useful information from it? How to identify what data to collect and keep and what not to keep? The potential answers to these questions depend on the objectives and goals of the users as well as the proper application of the KDD process. Research results from the *Design of Experiments* area in statistics and input from potential users from the very beginning would help as the first step in the resolution of this issue. Learning from data and its use as well as the discovered knowledge's usage should form the basis to develop tools and techniques to determine relevant data for collection, archival, and purging. Determining what data to purge is a particularly challenging task that requires judgment, knowledge, and interaction of the user.

23.3.2   Strategic Use of Data and Discovered Knowledge

The final step of the KDD process emphasizes that the value of the discovered knowledge lies in its appropriate use. It must be consolidated and resolved with previous knowledge, shared, reported, disseminated, and acted upon. A worthwhile area of research is to develop methodologies that will assist the user in the strategic use of data and discovered knowledge, especially for competitive advantage. This involves allowing for an entirely different view and use of the discovered patterns. An important special case is where changing government policies affect the interpretation, analysis, and use of information extracted from various public and private databases. The following are some examples of strategic use of discovered knowledge. Application of KDD to healthcare data for the strategic management of service and to control cost is illustrated in the chapter on the KEFIR system. American Airlines *viewed* their reservation database *inside out* to determine near optimal fare structure for gainful yield management. MCI *viewed* the long distance call patterns to increase its collect-call market share through strategic advertisement of 1-800-collect. Canon Copier division analyzed the data to learn various facts about the operations of Xerox including the fact that Xerox is the world's best in copier service. Canon used this knowledge and strategically changed the rules of the game by developing disposable cartridges which eliminated most of the need for copier service. The analysis of the data allowed Canon to discover and commit to the opportunity for small, personal copiers. This enabled Canon to rapidly increase its market share and eventually displace Xerox as the world's most prolific copier manufacturer. Each of the above required the proper integration of discovered knowledge, domain knowledge and strategic intent to arrive at solutions that were not evident in the data per se.

23.3.3   KDD from Non-Standard and Multimedia Data

An ever increasing trend is that the databases will contain not just numeric data as in the past but large quantities of non-standard and multimedia data. Non-standard data types include non-numeric, non-textual, geometric, and graphical data as well as non-stationary, temporal, relational, and a mixture of categorical and continuous-valued data. Multimedia data include free-form multi-lingual text as well as digitized images, video, and speech/audio data. It is indeed a challenge to work towards a unifying framework for representation and problem solving and to learn and discover from large quantities of these types of data.

23.3.4   KDD in a Networked and Distributed Environment

The rapid growth of resources that are available on Internet demand the need for research to develop tools, techniques, and systems that enable discovery from such networked and distributed environments. In addition, the trend is towards a collaborative discovery by a widely distributed team of experts and analysts dynamically utilizing databases that might be separate from their own networked environment. Current research in intelligent agents is a start towards meeting these challenges posed to KDD by the world-wide web of hyper-linked multimedia data.

23.3.5   KDD Issues

While this book presented an introduction to the KDD process, further research is needed to refine the basic concepts of KDD and to resolve what is KDD and what is not KDD. Basic research to provide a better understanding of what is knowledge is necessary. There is a clear need for developing methodologies that will allow one to comparatively evaluate KDD tools and techniques that includes performance and efficiency issues. Research to address the issue of proper integration of KDD tools and techniques with well established database methods and products would enable successful practical applications. The issues discussed in this epilogue illustrate the fact that the KDD field is truly multi-disciplinary and interdependent for its success.

Acknowledgments

I would like to thank Usama Fayyad, Gregory Piatetsky-Shapiro, and Padhraic Smyth for their comments and suggestions on earlier drafts of this epilogue. The support and encouragement of my immediate management at General Motors R&D Center is gratefully acknowledged.

VIII APPENDICES

A Knowledge Discovery in Databases Terminology

Willi Klösgen
German National Research Center for Computer Science (GMD)

Jan M. Żytkow
*Wichita State University
& Polish Academy of Sciences*

Main Concerns for KDD Terminology

Knowledge discovery in databases (KDD) uses concepts and techniques developed in many areas. Artificial intelligence subfields of machine discovery, machine learning, heuristic search, and knowledge representation are among the major contributors. Resources have also been acquired from fields such as databases, statistics, various sciences, philosophy of science, logic and rough sets. High performance computing methods such as parallel techniques for data management and search are used for discovery in very large databases.

To develop mutual understanding between disciplines and attract interest in KDD from other research communities, we frequently reference technical terms that can be recognized by researchers in related disciplines. This may also give KDD researchers pointers to relevant work in other domains.

KDD is closely related to machine discovery, a domain about 10 years older. While the main emphasis of Machine Discovery has been on expanding the *autonomy* of artificial discoverers by automating new skills, KDD has been oriented towards practical results, combining *human intervention* with automated techniques. Since both fields share many discovery techniques, evaluation methods, and knowledge representation problems, we will include elements of machine discovery terminology.

Ancient Greek philosophers realized that chains of definitions cannot go on indefinitely and they recognized the need for primitive, undefined terms. We hesitate to use the term "definition" to characterize our work on terminology, but we must leave some terms undefined, hence:

> We do not define terms which are technically defined in other disciplines; those definitions can be easily found elsewhere;

We do not define common sense terms; defining them is asking for trouble;

We rely on common understanding of key terms, such as "knowledge," "theory" and "model," so that we can treat them briefly. These terms have indefinitely many shades of meanings, and they also have been technically defined in disciplines such as logic and philosophy of science.

Our explanations rely on increasingly less abstract concepts. We frequently resort to enumeration of examples.

Complex structures are explained by elements and their interrelations.

Our current term explanations are not intended to be complete. The sequencing and grouping of terms may be subject to open discussion. We invite you to join the elaboration and refinement process. All comments and revisions are most welcome. Please use email or WWW (http://orgwis.gmd.de/explora/terms.html). This terminology chapter can also be accessed via the Knowledge Discovery Mine (see the Epilogue, this volume).

Each terms that occurs in *italics* has its own entry in this chapter.

Discovery Systems

Machine discovery: develops *discovery methods* and *discovery systems* to support *knowledge discovery processes*. Although discovery methods and processes share basic commonalities, sufficient differences exist to distinguish *Knowledge Discovery in Databases*, *Automated Scientific Discovery*, automated discovery in mathematics, and discovery by autonomous intelligent robots.

Knowledge discovery process: seeks *new knowledge* about an *application domain*. Consists of many *discovery steps*, each attempting at the completion of a particular *discovery task*, and accomplished by the application of a *discovery method*. The discovery process interacts repeatedly with a given domain, using *search* in various *search spaces*. *New knowledge* is inferred from data and/or from old knowledge. *New knowledge* is recognized by a discovery system via the autonomous use of *evaluation criteria*.

Discovery step: a part of *discovery process*. The main discovery steps include *domain exploration*, data collection, *pattern extraction from data*, *inductive generalizations*, *knowledge verification*, *knowledge transformation*. A knowledge discovery process may use steps which enable further discoveries, but do not directly lead to new knowledge, such as *knowledge presentation*, management of *data*, management of *domain knowledge*, and selection of new goals. A concrete discovery step is an application of a concrete discovery method.

Discovery method: an algorithm designed to accomplish a *discovery task*. A discovery method can be a reconstruction of human activity used to acquire *new knowledge*, can combine human methods in a novel way, but can also be a new method. *Machine Discovery* adapts methods from Machine Learning (defining new concepts, taxonomy formation, conceptual clustering, learning from examples), Statistics (pattern fitting, pattern evaluation, classification and regression, cross-validation), Intelligent Database Management (parallel data base servers, query optimization), Visualization and Geographical Information Systems (interactive graphics, knowledge presentation). Low-level methods of data analysis, used under human control are collectively called *data mining*.

Discovery task: a request for a specific component of new knowledge. "Find regularity," "generalize a regularity," "combine regularities into theory" are examples of tasks. Each discovery task can be best characterized by the *search space* explored to accomplish that task, because we do not know in advance the concrete form of new knowledge or even whether any knowledge will be discovered in a given input.

Discovery system: a software (and possibly also hardware system) that autonomously performs or supports a user in performing *knowledge discovery processes*. Typically, a discovery system integrates various *discovery methods*, the majority of which are based on *search*. Discovery systems can be used in interactive or automated mode and can be compared by evaluating their *accuracy*, *autonomy*, *efficiency*, and *versatility*.

Accuracy: the degree of fit between discovered theories and data. Accuracy applies to existing data and to predictions about new data.

Autonomy: extent to which a discovery system evaluates its decisions and produces *new knowledge* automatically, without external intervention. The degree of autonomy ranges from "apprentice systems" with low autonomy to "assistant systems" to "associate" and "master systems" which are almost automatic discoverers.

Efficiency: computational effort to accomplish a given task. Expressed as a function of the complexity of inputs and size of the search space.

Versatility: the variety of *application domains* to which a *discovery system* can be applied, and the variety of alternative *discovery methods* which it can use.

Knowledge discovery in databases (KDD): concerns *knowledge discovery processes* applied to databases. KDD deals with ready data, available in all domains of science and in applied domains of marketing, planning, control, etc. Typically, KDD has to deal with *inconclusive data*, *noisy data*, and *sparse data*.

Automated scientific discovery (ASD): deals with *knowledge discovery processes* analogous to those used by scientists. In distinction to KDD, a discovery process in ASD may seek additional data to improve the quality and to expand the scope of generated knowledge, make experiments, and improve experiment design. ASD applies mainly in Natural Sciences (Astronomy, Biology, Chemistry, Physics, etc.).

Data mining: folklore term which indicates application, under human control, of low-level *data mining methods*. Large scale automated search and interpretation of discovered regularities belong to KDD, but are typically not considered part of data mining

Data mining method: an algorithm designed to analyze data, or to extract from data *patterns* in specific categories, for instance a *tree extraction method* and model fitting. Data mining methods are low level algorithms.

World

Application domain (population): a real or abstract system that exists independently from the *discovery system*. An application domain consists of *objects*, which can belong to one or several classes and jointly form the set called *universe*, and of specific *attributes* of objects and *relations* between objects. Application domains are typically limited to subsets of the set of all existing objects, as well as subsets of attributes and relations. *Discovery systems* either interact directly with application domains or (in particular in KDD) they interact with data about application domains, which can be organized as *domain models*. Discovery systems attempt to discover *domain models* and *domain theories*. Probabilistic domains can be characterized by *joint distribution* of the *attribute* values.

Joint distribution: describes for each combination of *attribute* values the probability of objects in the *application domain (population)* with this value combination. For *discrete* attributes, this is a discrete distribution.

Object (entity, event, unit): distinct member or a separate part of an *application domain*. Objects belong to classes of similar objects, such as persons, transactions, locations, events, and processes. Objects are characterized by *attributes* and *relations* to other objects.

Universe: set of all *objects* in the application domain or in the model.

Attribute (Field, variable, feature, property, magnitude): a single characteristic of *objects* in an object class. Can be viewed as mapping of objects to values of a given type combined with the mapping of meaningful operations and relations on objects into operations and relations on values.

Attribute domain: the set of possible values of an *attribute*.

Relation: set of object tuples (pairs, etc.) which have specific meaning, for instance "a is married with b" (for person objects a, b), "a has ordered b at time t" (for client object a, purchase object b, and time object t). In experimental domains the relations such as "a is heavier than b" can be empirically determined, for instance by placing objects on the scales. Relations can also be theoretically defined by relations on object values.

Attribute type: characterizes the type of values in the *attribute domain*, the operations and relations on the values which are meaningful for the objects. An *attribute* can be *nominal, ordinal, interval, continuous*, and so forth. The value types can be simple (names or numbers, one per object), but the value may be also a complex structure like a time series or an image that represents a person or a location in a multi-media application.

Nominal (categorical): *attribute* for which no relation holds between different values. The values are just labels (class names or categories) of objects.

Ordinal: *attribute* with an ordered *attribute domain*, and the ordering is empirically meaningful.

Interval: *attribute* for which the ratios of distances between pairs of values have empirical meaning. The zero and the unit are conventional. Examples of such attributes are time and temperature. Equations make sense for interval attributes.

Proportional (ratio): *attribute* for with the ratios of values have empirical meaning. The unit is conventional. Arithmetic operations of addition and multiplication by number and the ordering of values have empirical meaning. Examples of such attributes are mass and price.

Continuous: *attribute* with an *attribute domain* which is a coherent subset of real numbers.

Discrete: *attribute* which has a finite set of values or the values can be mapped on the set of integers.

Metric: distance that satisfies axioms of metric spaces. Distance can be defined on values of single attribute of interval or ratio type, on pairs of records (for instance Euclidean, Manhattan, or Mahalanobis distance on vectors of values) or pairs of Boolean attributes (for instance, the number of records on which two attributes differ).

Knowledge

Domain model: representation of an *application domain*. It may be limited to subsets of *objects*, *attributes* and *relations* in the *application domain*. Domain model represents the perspective of a *discovery process* on the application domain. The set of all the objects considered by the domain model forms the *universe* of the model. A domain model can include *data* and *domain knowledge*. The formalisms used to express domain models range from simple data files with added *data dictionary* to *knowledge representation* paradigms of Artificial Intelligence. The initial domain model is gradually elaborated in the course of knowledge discovery processes to achieve a *domain theory*.

Probabilistic domain model: assumes that *data* are considered as a sample drawn from the *joint distribution* in the *universe*. A typical probabilistic domain model is expressed in terms of marginal distributions of the joint distribution, e.g. Bayesian network, (generalized) linear model.

Domain theory: comprehensive, organized, and consistent system of claims about the *application domain*. Often we also require that, in distinction to hypotheses, theories are empirically verified. The same theory can be formally represented using different *knowledge representations*.

Domain knowledge: empirically verified or proven information specific to the *application domain*, not belonging to *data*. Typical forms are *data dictionary* knowledge, sets of contingent formulae in first order logic, systems of equations, *taxonomies*, marginal distributions and the *joint distribution*.

New knowledge: augments or refines the contents of the current *domain model* and/or *domain theory*. New knowledge can be new to the user and extend the user's mental model of the *application domain*. For an autonomous system, new knowledge may be just knowledge new to the discovery system.

Knowledge representation: formalism for expressing knowledge and reasoning with knowledge about many *application domains*. Knowledge representation paradigms include frames, production rules, semantic networks, first order logic, systems of equations. Typical knowledge representation structures used in *discovery systems* are *patterns* like *trees*, *rules*, equations, and contingency tables.

Taxonomy: hierarchical system of selected subsets of a domain, typically arranged as a tree, which is exhaustive, and disjoint.

Data

Data: consist of the collected (measured, sensed, polled, observed, etc.) *attribute* values and *relations* for *objects* in the *application domain*. Data coming from experiments include the results of manipulations (*independent* or *control* variables) and the subsequent readings of sensors (*dependent* variables). Data can be arranged in various *data formats*, for instance in one or more *data matrices*. For the sake of completeness, special values *"missing data"* or *"non-applicable data"* can be used. *Data semantics* is important to guide the discovery process, to interpret the results, and to combine data coming from various sources.

Sample set: subset of objects of an application domain (population) for which *data* are available or sought. Probabilistic properties of the sample set should be given or assumed, that relate the sample set to the whole domain universe, or weights for objects that indicate their representativity. Especially for *probabilistic domain models*, the sample set should be a representative sample of the *joint distribution*.

Data semantics: meaning of data in a database, represented by *data dictionary*. In *Automated Scientific Discovery*, the meaning of data (objects, attributes and relations) is represented by operational procedures through which (1) objects are recognized, (2) manipulators introduce the desired values, and (3) sensors acquire data.

Data format: particular data structure to collect *data*. For instance, data about a particular object can be arranged into a *record*, and many records can be arranged into a *data matrix*. *Discovery methods* may be limited to special *data types*.

Data dictionary: includes information about the *attribute types* and other aspects of attribute semantics, for instance the scope of all values, and the meaning of special values.

Inconclusive data: do not contain some *attributes* which may be essential to knowledge about the domain represented by the data. Their absence may make it impossible to discover significant knowledge about a given domain. This happens especially in database applications because databases are installed for special purposes which may differ from the purpose of *KDD*.

Noisy data: contain errors due to the nature of data collection, measurement, or sensing procedures. Imprecise values are characteristic of all data collection and typically fit a regular statistical distribution such as Gaussian, while wrong values can be data entry errors, can be caused by gross errors in instruments functions, or caused by external disturbance. Statistical methods can treat problems of noisy data, and separate different types of noise.

Missing data: happen when values for some *objects* and *attributes* are missing, because they were not measured, not answered, or simply lost. *Discovery methods* vary in the way they treat missing values. For example, they simply disregard missing values, omit the corresponding *records*, infer missing values from known values, treat missing data as a special value to be included additionally in the *attribute domain*, or average over the missing values using Bayesian techniques.

Non-applicable data: missing values, which would be either logically impossible or obvious for some *objects*, like the values "non-pregnant" and "pregnant" for "male" objects. Information about this special kind of *missing data* can be included in the *domain knowledge* and can be treated in a special way by *discovery methods*.

Sparse data: occur when the events actually represented in given data or *sample set* make only a very small (sparse) subset of the *event space*. The size of the event space, which is the product set of the *attribute domains*, is typically higher by many orders of magnitude from data sets, but by limiting the number of attributes we can reduce the size of the event space so that the data are no longer sparse.

Reliable data: data which do not contain distortions or major errors. Reliable data are repeatable when the same attributes are measured by different methods or when different *sample sets* are used. For those relations and behaviors of *objects* in the *application domain* which do not depend on time, reliable data are also repeatable when measured at different times.

Record (tuple, exemplar, case): is the collection of attribute values that represents one *object*. Record is a row in a *data matrix*.

Virtual attribute (derived, defined attribute): has its values computed from the values of other *attributes*, by a user-defined or autonomously generated transformation. The transformation of date of birth into age, or the average of several numerical attributes are examples.

Data matrix: (relational table, example set) set of *data* for a particular set of objects and attributes, systematically organized into a matrix in which each row represents the values of *attributes* for one *object* and each column represents the values of one attribute for each object.

Event space: the product set of the *attribute domains*. It represents all data which are logically possible for given *attributes*. The majority of logically possible value combinations may be physically impossible, i.e., cannot occur in the corresponding *application domain*. Various probability measures can be defined on the event space, such as expected probabilities of all events based on attribute independence or joint probabilities estimated from a sample (*contingency tables*).

Data type: (or complexity type of data): data can be characterized by their complexity type. Dimensions that determine the complexity type include the number of *object* classes and the *attribute types* of the *attributes*. Typical data types are *relational table* and *multi relational*.

Relational table (rectangular, data matrix): *data type* for one class of *objects* and a class of simple attributes for those objects attribute). In the relational database model, a single table or array can be viewed as the *data format* for data of this type.

Multi relational: *data type* characterizing *data* for several classes of *objects* with simple attributes. *Relations* are available connecting the object classes.

Time-series: *data type* where one *attribute* represents different moments of time; the records are ordered by the values of this attribute. For one value of time, other attributes store information about co-occurring properties of *objects*. Relational, object oriented, or special time series databases can be used to store time series.

Complex-structure: *data* that do not belong to the *relational*, *multi relational*, or *time-series* type. Complex-structured data are frequent in chemical, genetical, image data, text and multimedia domains.

External data: data in permanent storage. External data are often stored in a database management system. A *discovery system* can transform data available in a database system into its own special external data organization to speed up the access and processing of data.

Internal data: data that reside in the main memory. These data are typically organized in *data matrices*. *Discovery methods* may process the external data incrementally, in a loop, where at each cycle only a small part of the input data is used by the method.

Concepts & Concept Descriptions

Concept: a symbol that has a meaning (interpretation). The meaning includes extension and intension.

Extension of a concept: set of *objects* which are referred to by the concept. Extension can be limited to a given *application domain*. Extension of an attribute is a partitioning of all objects into equivalence classes, one class per each attribute value.

Intension of a concept: set of properties satisfied by all objects in the extension. In operational approach, intension is the set of methods by which objects which belong to the extension can be recognized or attribute values can be measured.

Cluster: set of objects grouped together because of their similarity or proximity. Objects are often decomposed into an exhaustive and/or mutually exclusive set of clusters.

Concept language: language used to construct *concepts*. Typical languages are *first order languages* and *propositional languages*. *Concept language* determines the concepts that can be defined, by primitive concepts, with the use of operators and connectives.

Concept space: set of all *concepts* which may be built within a *concept language*. The number of concepts in concept space can be finite, but is often unbounded (infinite).

Concept lattice: partially ordered space of concepts. Partial ordering can be determined by subset relations between concept extensions or by greater generality of concept intensions (concept descriptions).

Descriptor (selector:) statement which is satisfied for a given object when an *attribute* has one of several values for that object, for instance "Color(white or blue)." In case of an *ordinal* attribute type, one or several intervals may appear in a descriptor.

Conjunctive form: conjunction of *selectors*. Conjunctive form of order n contains at most n conjunctions. Subtypes of conjunctive forms are defined by restrictions on the construction of *selectors*. Languages of conjunctive forms of order n with no *internal disjunctions*, are used to prevent severe combinatorial problems.

Internal disjunction: use of "or" directly on attribute values, for instance "white or blue." In the case of an *ordinal* attribute, internal disjunction on intervals is possible, for instance "smaller than 2 or greater than 5." Often it is useful to limit internal disjunctions to specific values, for instance, regions that make sense on a map. Given a *taxonomy* on values of an attribute, the set of sensible disjunctions can be limited to disjunctions of taxonomy elements at the same level.

Disjunctive normal form: disjunction of conjunctive forms. For a disjunctive normal form of order n, the number of disjunctions is limited to n. Limitations on the order are necessary to avoid severe combinatorial explosion of search for the best normal form.

Languages; Hypotheses Spaces

Language: consists of terms (name-like formulae to name objects) and formulae (sentential formulae to describe situations). Formal languages are typically unbound sets of terms and formulae that can be generated from the primitive terms with the use of logical symbols (connectives, operators, and quantifiers) according to formal rules of composition (rules of syntax). Language can be interpreted when basic terms are assigned meaning in an application domain (model of a language). In extensional languages, complex terms and formulae are interpreted by compositional rules that parallel the rules of syntax. An interpreted sentential formula is a candidate for a factual statement, hypothesis, regularity, or a law.

First order languages: use subsets of predicate logic, typically function-free Horn clauses, to represent *concepts*, *rules*, and other forms of knowledge.

Propositional languages: use a set of primitive statements and logical connectives. Primitive statements can be conditions on attribute values, called *selectors* or *descriptors*. Particularly useful and common languages consist of *conjunctive forms* or *disjunctive normal forms*.

Semantics of a language (interpretation:) meaning of concepts and statements of a language. Typically the interpretation is assigned to each primitive term and then propagated to all complex terms and all statements.

Hypothesis: claim that certain statement (interpreted pattern instance) is satisfied by a particular *range* of objects in an *application domain*. During *evaluation* a hypothesis is tested against *data* and/or *domain knowledge*.

Hypotheses language: formalism and semantics to represent statements that are candidates for *knowledge* about an *application domain*. The kinds of statements constructed in such a language depend on the *pattern type* and vary from natural-language-like sentences such as *rules* to more abstract statements like *trees* or graphical statements of a graphical language. An important component of a hypotheses language is a *concept language* used to build *concepts* within patterns.

Patterns and Regularities

Pattern: generic statement that includes free variables (variables unbound by quantifiers). By quantifying the free variables or by replacing them with concrete values, pattern can be instantiated to concrete statements. Interpreted in an *application domain*, a *pattern instance* can be a *hypothesis* about that domain. *Discovery systems* use methods for *pattern detection* and *evaluation* that are limited to specific *pattern types*.

Pattern instance: produced from a *pattern* by replacing free variables with constants and/or by binding free variables with quantifiers. When interpreted in an application domain, and when the range of applications is determined, it can capture an elemental part of *new knowledge* like a single *rule* or a composite part like a system of rules or a *tree*. A pattern instance is produced by an instantiation of free variables in the generic pattern.

Regularity: a statement of the form "P holds in R," which is interpreted in the *application domain*. P is a *pattern instance*, R describes the *range* of the pattern, and the statement is true in the application domain. A *hypothesis* reaches the status of regularity after it has been tested against relevant *data* and reaches *utility* values such as *predictive accuracy* and *significance* above acceptance thresholds.

Range: set of *objects*. Typically it is defined by a logical condition on some *attributes* and their values (*concept language*), to restrict the scope of a *pattern* to a subset of *objects*, but range can also cover the whole universe (population).

Pattern parameters: free variables in the generic statement of the *pattern*.

Pattern detection (extraction:) process of instantiating and evaluating patterns, to fit particular set of data. For various *patterns* and *hypotheses spaces* special pattern extraction methods (for instance, *tree extraction methods, rule extraction methods, functional dependency extraction methods*, or *statistical pattern extraction methods*) discover *new knowledge*. Pattern detection methods rely on *search* and *evaluation*. They can be selectively invoked based on *application tests*.

Application test: filter which determines whether a given type of pattern can be detected from given data. The filter is used to avoid possibly extensive search, when the existence or interestingness of an instance can be excluded by a test.

Detection goals: general directives for *pattern extraction* specified by the user of a *discovery system* during *discovery focusing*. They relate to the purpose of *new knowledge* (for instance accurate classification or structure uncovering), to the desired *hypothesis language*, and *evaluation*, and to the admissible search effort (granularity and extent of *search*).

Pattern type: characterizes pattern dimensionality, the type of relation between dimensions and the way in which the pattern is expressed. Large categories of *logic-numerical patterns, elementary patterns*, and *statistical patterns* include many narrower types.

Logic-numerical patterns: hold the subclasses *tree, rule, functional relation*, logical patterns, and the like.

Elementary patterns: univariate patterns that do not involve a complex *search* and can be detected in rows or columns of multi-dimensional tabulations by simple methods for monotonicity, convexity, concavity, maximum, minimum, discontinuity, outliers and the like. Also simple relations between univariate patterns (for instance, all cells in one row are larger than the corresponding cells in another row). Often the columns or rows are data aggregates, produced by operations including count, sum, max, min, average, etc. For instance if columns correspond to age groups and one row to the labor force participation of women, a possible pattern could be: labor force participation of women shows an U-form.

Tree: partition of a *universe* or *sample set* into a hierarchically ordered set of *concepts*. Each concept on a hierarchical level is recursively divided into subconcepts on the next lower hierarchical level. Typically, concepts on each hierarchical level are disjoint and collectively exhaustive, and the description of the subconcepts on the next level (*concept language*) includes a further conjunctive term built with one further *attribute*. The main subtypes of this *pattern type* are *classification trees* and regression trees.

Tree extraction method: mechanism to select the next *attribute* for each *concept* on a hierarchical level, to divide the *attribute domain* of this attribute into (disjoint) subsets which correspond to the subconcepts on the next level, to terminate further partitioning of a concept, and to *prune* the tree.

Classification tree: *tree* representing a set of *classification rules* for *concept classes*. Each leave of a classification tree is associated to a concept class, where the description of the leave constitutes a sufficient condition for the concept class. Classification trees can be used to classify objects following the concept descriptions from root to leaves.

Rule: can be presented as: If LHS then RHS. In all situation in which the left hand side LHS is true, the right hand side RHS is also true or very probable. Many rules correlate two *concepts*: the LHS concept is a sufficient condition for the RHS concept. Categories of rules include *exact*, *strong*, and *probabilistic rules*.

Exact rule: allows no exceptions. Each object of the LHS *concept* of a *rule* must also be an element of the RHS concept.

Strong rule: allows some exceptions. The number of exceptions may not exceed a given limit expressed as a percentage or absolutely.

Classification rule: LHS is a sufficient condition to classify objects as belonging to the concept named in the RHS.

Characteristic rule: objects that belong to the concept named in the LHS, contain properties named in the RHS.

Functional relation: *pattern* relating a dependent *attribute* to one or several independent attributes. *Functional dependency* and equation are subtypes.

Functional dependency: exists between a dependent *attribute* and some independent attributes, if for all objects with equal values of the independent attributes the values of the dependent attribute are equal too. An approximate functional dependency allows some exceptions (e.g., due to noise).

Statistical patterns: assign probabilities to different events and form the foundation of *probabilistic domain models*.

Statistical dependency: regularity between two or more attributes in the form of *statistical pattern*, which differs from random combinations of attribute values. *Statistical dependency* captures all forms of patterns which differ from random combinations.

Probabilistic rule: relates the conditional probability P(RHS | LHS) to the probability P(RHS).

Hypotheses Evaluation

Evaluation: application of various *evaluation criteria* to measure different qualities of a *hypothesis* or piece of knowledge. In case of a composite instance like a *tree*, a system of *rules*, or an *equation*, the components of the instance (node, single rule, term of an equation) can also be evaluated. An *application test* estimates whether search in a particular hypotheses class can be successful.

Evaluation criteria: tests that we apply to patterns, hypotheses, statements, theories in order to accept them as pieces of knowledge, or to measure various qualities expected of knowledge, or to select between competing pieces of knowledge. Many mutually non-reducible measures can be used including the *validity* of a hypothesis or theory, *degree of fit* and *significance* measured against the *sample set*, the *generality* and *predictive strength*, the *reliability* on the *universe*, the degree of *redundancy* with respect to other already known pattern instances, the *simplicity* of a pattern instance, *interestingness* and the *utility*.

Validity (confirmation): the outcome of verification or confirmation process for a hypothesis. A decision based on considering the data (*evidence*) whether we can treat the hypothesis as true. Validity can be quantified by *degree of fit*, and *significance*.

Verification: the process of confronting a hypothesis against evidence in order to decide its truth value.

Validation of a method: the process of testing whether the outcomes of the method satisfy the *evaluation criteria* desired for that method.

Degree of fit (predictive accuracy:) measures how close are the relevant data in the *sample set* to the hypothesis. Can be used to anticipate the accuracy with which a regularity (hypothesis) predicts new data.

Predictive strength (empirical contents): The set of all observational predictions derived from the hypothesis.

Evidence: *reliable data*, relevant to a hypothesis or theory.

Significance: of a pattern instance measures the probability that this instance could be generated randomly according to the null hypothesis or a given set of data could be generated according to this pattern instance.

Cross-validation: a mechanism that uses a given *sample set* to generate hypotheses and estimate their validity and accuracy in the population. The *sample set* is repeatedly and randomly divided into disjoint training and test data sets. The hypotheses obtained in the training subset are verified against data in test subsets. Typical methods are n-fold cross validation, leave-one-out method, and bootstrap method.

Redundancy: relates to several *pattern instances* or to several knowledge components (e.g. nodes in a *tree*, equations in a theory). Redundancy occurs when one component follows (logically) from another. Redundancy can be quantified to measure the conditional probability of one component given another.

Generality of a statement: measure of the size of the subset of objects which are described by the statement.

Simplicity: measure of syntactic complexity of a statement or *pattern instance*.

Interestingness: measure of human interest in a given object, pattern, hypothesis, or a piece of knowledge.

Utility: quantifies the possible uses of a piece of knowledge or *pattern instance*. The utility can be related to any task of the user or to any task that a computer system can perform on the basis of this piece of knowledge.

Search

Search: process of seeking for a solution by examining alternatives. As distinct from direct methods or algorithms, search can generate tentative solutions which are evaluated and discarded when they turn out to be wrong. Search is performed in a *search space* by exploiting the structure in this space. Different *search mechanisms* can be applied to examine the search space. Search is necessary in the discovery process. For instance, search is the central approach to *pattern detection*, when many patterns must be examined before a satisfactory one is found. *Search refinement* can improve the results of a preliminary search.

Search space: set of states, and for each state, the set of moves to the neighboring states. Search spaces may consist of pre-existing data structures that represent states which can be visited during the search, and moves which guide the traversal of the space. Many search spaces, especially large ones, are constructed dynamically during search. States are created by operators. In pattern detection, the states (nodes) of a search space can correspond to *pattern instances* (e.g. *rules* or equations) or to components of pattern instances (e.g. conjunct within a *rule*, single rule within a system of rules, node of a *tree*, or term in an *equation*).

Search strategy: general approach to construct and process *search spaces.* For instance *data driven search* (forward chaining) and *hypotheses driven search* (backward chaining) impose different approaches to hypotheses generation and verification. *Heuristic search* differs from *exhaustive search* by leaving part of the space unsearched.

Search mechanism (method:) determines the order in which states are examined, and the scope of the states that are retained during search. Strategies include depth-first search, breadth-first search, best-first search, *hill climbing*, *beam search*, and many others.

Heuristic search: generates and/or processes only a part of a total *search space* which includes all possible *pattern instances* or components of pattern instances. Heuristic criteria determine which parts are included in the search. Typically heuristic search generates a satisfactory solution, but not an optimal solution. Often search spaces are so large, that only heuristic search can produce a solution in reasonable time. One step optimal search and *beam search* belong to the main heuristic search approaches.

Exhaustive search: can reach each node of a *search space*, ensuring the optimal solution, if the solutions exist, but often is not realistic because of computational complexity. It is desired but often difficult or impossible to design a non-redundant search which does not re-visit nodes and/or does not repeat moves which have been made earlier.

Hill climbing: *heuristic search* which retains one node after each step of search. At each step it selects the best neighbor of the current state, according to the optimizing criterion. If each neighbor is worse than the current state, the search halts.

Beam search: *heuristic search* strategy similar to *hill climbing*. At each step, the best n partial solutions are retained for further search according to the optimizing criterion.

Data driven search: constructs the search states and controls the search according to information derived from data. For instance, records can be accessed sequentially and nodes in the *search space* can be updated according to the information in the records. After each pass through the data, the best nodes in the search space can be selected and elaborated in the next pass. Data driven search can result in time efficient discovery because it minimizes *data* access and searches only the part of the hypotheses space constructed from the data.

Hypotheses driven search: traverses a *hypotheses space* according to a predetermined strategy and evaluates each generated (visited) hypothesis against *data*. The selection of nodes in the hypotheses space can be driven by theories of the domain.

Search refinement: refines the results of a previous *search* phase. For example, search granularity can be changed to search in the neighborhood of a previously identified node. *Pruning* is another refinement technique.

Pruning: cuts search by preventing expansion of some nodes.

Solution pruning (postpruning:) eliminates parts of a solution, for instance, branches of a *tree*, to improve overspecialized (overfitting) solutions.

Discovery focusing: the process of defining the discovery problem from the user supplied interests and expectations into the specification of a concrete search problem. Includes selection of a subset of *data* to be analyzed and the *discovery tasks*. Discovery focusing is primarily done by the user of a *discovery system*. However, a discovery system can analyze the user-supplied specifications to select appropriate *hypotheses space, concept language, evaluation* method and *search strategy*.

Visualization

Presentation specifications: determine how the *pattern instance* is presented to the user, e.g., in natural language, tabular, graphical, or audio-visual form. *Presentation templates* are typical simple presentation specifications.

Presentation template: schema for a textual or graphical presentation of a statement (*pattern instance*). Typically such a schema has some parameters. The values of the parameters are fixed by the pattern instance.

Text-based template: simple format statement containing fixed text and variable parts. The variable parts are substituted by names, numerical results, and other text. Advanced techniques include linguistic features to ensure correct natural language (for instance, English) texts.

Graphical template: uses basic graphical presentations (e.g. bar charts, histograms, pie charts, curves). Advanced techniques apply rules to select the appropriate basic graphical presentation and the design options such as number of bars, colors, and legend.

Discovery report: produced by techniques of Natural Language Generation. The report is compiled by combining primitive constructs such as *text-based* and *graphical templates* into the structure that may include sentences, paragraphs, and chapters.

Interaction graphics: visualization techniques used to explore the contents of the data. Especially for spatial and time referenced data, interactive tools such as linked windows allow the user to examine interesting areas in one data view simultaneously with other views. For instance, a Geographical Information System can be applied to examine the findings based on a map.

B Data Mining and Knowledge Discovery Internet Resources

Gregory Piatetsky-Shapiro
GTE Laboratories Incorporated

Many resources for knowledge discovery and data mining, including software, datasets, and publications are available via the Internet. Below I provide a list of the major KDD resources, including

- KDD-related world wide web sites
- Siftware: Tools for data mining and knowledge discovery
- Electronic newsletters

There are also numerous newsgroups that contain relevant discussion—the major ones are comp.ai (and its subgroups) and comp.databases (and its subgroups).

Major KDD-related WWW Sites

Knowledge Discovery Mine

URL `http://info.gte.com/~kdd/`
The knowledge discovery mine contains S*i*ftware: a catalog of KDD tools, KDD Nuggets archive, a list of relevant publications, and pointers to other resources.

The Data Mine

URL `http://www.cs.bham.ac.uk/~anp/TheDataMine.html`
The data mine contains pointers to papers, conferences, software, and other resources.

The Machine Learning Database Repository

URL `http://www.ics.uci.edu/AI/ML/Machine-Learning.html`
The Machine Learning Database Repository at University of California Irvine is the site for many data sets and domain theories that have been commonly used for testing machine learning algorithms. It also contains the archives of the ML list and several machine learning programs.

ML Net Site

URL `http://www.gmd.de/ml-archive`
This site contains machine learning publications, data, and software, related to the machine learning toolbox (MLT), inductive logic programming (ILP), the European network of excellence in machine learning (MLnet), and other projects.

Siftware: Tools for Data Mining and Knowledge Discovery

Knowledge Discovery Mine S*i*ftware Catalog

URL `http://info.gte.com/~kdd/siftware.html`
A major repository is the Knowledge Discovery Mine S*i*ftware catalog, which contains information for over 50 (public domain and commercial) tools, for the tasks of classification, clustering, dependency derivation, summarization, deviation detection, visualization, dimensional analysis, and others.

COSMIC's Program Catalog (Cybernetics Section)

URL `http://www.cosmic.uga.edu/maincat.html#45`
COSMIC's Program Catalog (cybernetics section) contains information on programs developed by NASA, including AUTOCLASS III (automatic class discovery from data), COBWEB/3 (an algorithm for data clustering and incremental concept formation), and IND (a decision tree package).

Neuronet

URL `http://www.neuronet.ph.kcl.ac.uk/`
The Neuronet site has information on many free neural network software tools.

Neural Networks FAQ

URL `http://wwwipd.ira.uka.de/~prechelt/FAQ/neural-net-faq.html`
Neural networks FAQ contains information on many free and commercial software lists.

Electronic Newsletters

KDD Nuggets

Moderator: G. Piatetsky-Shapiro
Purpose: Exchange of information relevant to knowledge discovery and data mining.
Frequency: About every week.
Contributions to: kdd@gte.com
(Un)subscription requests to: kdd-request@gte.com

Machine Learning List

Moderator: M. Pazzani
Purpose: The scientific study of machine learning.
Frequency: About every 1–2 weeks.
Contributions to: ml@ics.uci.edu.
(Un)subscription requests to: ml-request@ics.uci.edu

AI and Statistics

Moderator: D. Fisher
Purpose: Exchange of information on AI and statistics.
Frequency: About every 3 weeks or as traffic dictates;
Contributions to: ai-stats@watstat.uwaterloo.ca
(Un)subscription requests: ai-stats-request@watstat.uwaterloo.ca

DBworld

Moderator: R. Ramakrishnan
Purpose: messages of general interest to the database community
Type: Digest—weekly
Contributions to: dbworld@cs.wisc.edu
(Un)subscription requests: e-mail to listproc@cs.wisc.edu
subscribe dbworld <Your Full Name>

About the Authors

Usama M. Fayyad

Usama Fayyad is Technical Group Supervisor of the Machine Learning Systems Group at the Jet Propulsion Laboratory, California Institute of Technology. He is also an adjunct assistant professor in the Computer Science Department at the University of Souputhern California. At JPL, he is Principal Investigator of the Science Data Analysis and Visualization Task targeting applications of data mining techniques for the analysis of large science databases, as well as other tasks involving industrial applications of machine learning. He received the Ph.D. degree in Computer Science and Engineering in 1991 from the EECS Department of The University of Michigan, Ann Arbor. He holds the following degrees: B.S.E. in E.E., B.S.E. and M.S.E. in Computer Engin., and M.Sc. in Mathematics. He is a recepient of the 1993 Lew Allen Award for Excellence, the highest honor JPL awards to researchers in the early years of their professional careers. He has also received the NASA Exceptional Achievement Medal (1994). His research interests include machine learning theory and applications, knowledge discovery in large databases, data mining, statistical pattern recognition, clustering, and non-linear regression. He served on the program committees of several major conferences in AI. He has cochaired the Eleventh SPIE Applications of AI Conference (1993), the 1994 Knowledge Discovery in Databases Workshop at AAAI-94, and the First International Conference on Knowedge Discovery and Data Mining (KDD-95). He serves as general conference chair for KDD-96.

Gregory Piatetsky-Shapiro

Gregory Piatetsky-Shapiro is the Principal Member of Technical Staff at GTE Laboratories and the principal investigator of the Knowledge Discovery in Databases project. At GTE he worked on applying intelligent front-ends to heterogeneous databases, and later on developing new techniques for knowledge discovery in databases and deploying them in business applications. Piatetsky-Shapiro received four GTE Laboratories software awards and in 1995 the Leslie H. Warner Award—GTE's highest technical achievement award for KEFIR system for healthcare data analysis. His research interests also include intelligent database systems, dependency networks, and internet resource discovery. Prior to GTE, Piatetsky-Shapiro worked at Strategic Information on developing financial database systems. He earned his M.S. and Ph.D. (1984) from New York University. His Ph.D. dissertation on Self-Organizing Database Systems received NYU awards as the best dissertation in computer science and all natural sciences. Piatetsky-Shapiro initiated, organized, and chaired the first three KDD workshops (1989, 1991, and 1993). He also served on program committees of KDD–94 and KDD–95, and over a dozen other conferences and workshops in AI and Databases. Before this collection he coedited *Knowledge Discovery in Databases*, (AAAI/MIT Press, 1991) and two special journal issues on KDD. He has close to forty publications in the areas of AI and databases. Piatetsky-Shapiro founded and moderates the KDD Nuggets electronic newsletter (e-mail to kdd-request@gte.com) and maintains the Knowledge Discovery Mine site at http://info.gte.com/~kdd

Padhraic Smyth

Padhraic Smyth is a Technical Group Leader at the Jet Propulsion Laboratory. He received a Bachelor of Engineering degree from the National University of Ireland (University College Galway) in 1984, and a Masters and PhD in Electrical Engineering from the California Institute of Technology in 1985 and 1988 respectively. Since 1988 he has worked at the Jet Propulsion Laboratory as the principal investigator on a variety of problems of interest to NASA in statistical pattern recognition and machine learning, including theory and algorithms for automated and interactive analysis of large scientific datasets. Smyth has received twelve NASA certificates of recognition for technical innovation since 1990 and was a recipient of the Lew Allen Award for Excellence in Research at JPL in 1993. He is also a lecturer at the California Institute of Technology, has given tutorials on probabilistic learning at AAAI, CAIA, and IJCAI, and was appointed general chair of the Sixth International Workshop on AI and Statistics (1997).

Ramasamy Uthurusamy

Ramasamy Uthurusamy is Machine Learning Project Leader at General Motors R&D Center. His research interests include theoretical and computational issues in the application of AI to real-world problems. Currently, his research is focused in the area of knowledge discovery in databases (KDD) and its applications. Uthurusamy received the Charles McCuen Special Achievement Award from General Motors R&D Center for part of his work in GM-specific applications in these areas. He was instrumental in getting the Eleventh International Joint Conference on Artificial Intelligence (IJCAI-89) to Detroit and served as its Local Chair. He also served as the Video Program Chair for IJCAI–95. He is one of the organizers of the first three KDD workshops (1989, 1991 and 1993) and served on their program committees. He is the Coorganizer and Program Cochair of the fourth KDD workshop (KDD-94) held at AAAI-94. He is also the Coorganizer and Program Cochair of the First International Conference on Knowledge Discovery and Data Mining (KDD-95) held at IJCAI-95. He was the Program Cochair of the Eleventh SPIE Applications of AI Conference (1993). Uthurusamy has served on the program committees of several other AI conferences and workshops. Prior to joining GM Research he was with Exxon Production Research Company. He has taught at Purdue University and at the University of Idaho. He obtained his Ph.D. from Purdue University, M.S. in Computer Science from Washington State University and B.E. in Electrical Engineering from the University of Madras, India.

About the Contributors

Contact information for the editors and contributors to this book can be found in the AAAI Press section of AAAI's web site. The url is: http://www.aaai.org.

Index

Rome Antically
Challenged

RomeAntically Challenged

MARINA ADAIR

KENSINGTON BOOKS
WWW.KENSINGTONBOOKS.COM

KENSINGTON BOOKS are published by
Kensington Publishing Corp.
119 West 40th Street
New York, NY 10018

All Kensington titles, imprints, and distributed lines are available at special quantity discounts for bulk purchases for sales promotion, premiums, fund-raising, educational, or institutional use.

Special book excerpts or customized printings can also be created to fit specific needs. For details, write or phone the office of the Kensington Sales Manager: Kensington Publishing Corp., 119 West 40th Street, New York, NY 10018. Attn. Sales Department. Phone: 1-800-221-2647.

Kensington and the K logo Reg. U.S. Pat. & TM Off.

ISBN-13: 978-1-4967-2769-5 (ebook)
ISBN-10: 1-4967-2769-X (ebook)

ISBN-13: 978-1-4967-2766-4
ISBN-10: 1-4967-2766-5
First Kensington Trade Paperback Printing: August 2020

10 9 8 7 6 5 4 3 2 1

Printed in the United States of America

To my daughter, Thuy.
Your adoption story will forever
be my favorite.

Chapter 1

The moment Anh Nhi Walsh stepped into her wedding dress and shimmied the eighty-year-old silk over her hips, she knew there had been a mistake.

A mistake so terrible, all the chocolate in the world couldn't fix it.

Annie had pulled a thirty-six-hour shift, so her brain was a little slow on the uptake, but the longer she stood in her silver Jimmy Choos and yesterday's makeup, the more certain she became that even the world's best push-up bra couldn't compensate for the obvious.

This was not her dress.

"Oh my God," she whispered through her fingers.

Sure, the gown had arrived on her doorstep in the trademarked cream and blush-colored–striped box, special delivery from Bliss, Hartford's premiere bridal design boutique. And, yes, that was the silk gown Grandma Hannah had hand-carried from Ireland, now billowing around Annie's waist. But *this* was *not* Annie's dress.

Annie's dress was elegant and sophisticated, a heartfelt tribute to her grandmother, the one person Annie had wanted by her side when she finally walked down the aisle. Grandma Hannah wouldn't let something as insignificant as death keep her from her only granddaughter's wedding. But Annie had wanted to feel her in more than just spirit.

Which was why she'd commissioned a modern-day restoration of the 1941 Grecian gown with cap sleeves and embellished mermaid train, cut from the same cloth that the most important woman in Annie's life had worn on her special day.

Annie pulled the bodice of the gown to her chest and wanted to cry. The too-big, too-long, and most definitely D-cup rendition was that extra-special kick in the gut she needed to find closure.

Six years as an ER physician's assistant had instilled in her a rational calm that allowed for quick and efficient assessment of any situation. Taught her how to differentiate between the life-threatening and painfully uncomfortable. With that in mind, she pulled up the planner app on her phone.

"Add *Murder fiancé* to my to-do list," she instructed.

"*Murder fiancé* added," the digitized female voice said. "Is there anything else I can help you with?"

"Yes." Because Annie understood murder wasn't a rational response, and besides, Dr. Clark Atwood was no longer her fiancé. Or her problem.

According to the elegant handwriting on the linen thank-you card that Bliss had included with the gown, that responsibility now fell to Molly-Leigh—with a hyphen—May of the pinup curves and double-D's.

Anh Nhi—always mispronounced—Walsh of the boyish build and perky but barely-a-handful B's had moved on to bigger and better things. And that didn't include cleaning up her ex's messes.

Not anymore.

"Call Dr. Dickless," she said.

"Calling Dr. Dickless," the female voice chimed. Annie had deprogrammed her sexy 007 British narrator the day she'd heard of Clark's upcoming nuptials. She was taking her new man-free existence seriously.

Clark picked up on the first ring. "Jesus, Annie. I've been calling you for weeks," he said, as if she were the one inconveniencing his life.

"I've been busy with my new job, decorating my new place, apologizing to my relatives because it seems that 'The groom's marrying another woman' isn't an acceptable reason for airlines to grant a refund."

Three months ago, Annie had awoken to an empty bed, an emptier closet, and an awaiting text on her cell:

> **Sorry, Anh-Bon, I can't do this. U R the best thing in my life, and if I could have made it work w/ anyone, pls know that it would have been you. IDK if I'm cut out to be husband material. Forgive me.**

It had taken an entire week for her to realize that the wedding, the romantic Roman honeymoon with walks along the River Tiber, the future they'd spent years building toward was gone.

It had taken only a single Instagram post of her—*so recent I still have the ring*—ex and a perky blonde with the caption "I finally found my one *true love*" for Annie to give her two weeks' notice—which was more courtesy than Clark had spared her—and apply for a temporary ER position in Rome.

Once the offer came in, she packed her suitcase, sent in a change of address, left the ring and the rest of the gifts behind for Clark to return, and promised herself a future full of exciting opportunities and exotic destinations. She had become a traveling PA because she'd wanted to see the world, and her six-year layover in Hartford was over.

Now, it was her time.

"You do have a lot going on—how did you find the time to add 'Murder fiancé' to the top of your to-do list?" he asked, and Annie flipped her phone over to check for a listening device. She was about ready to rip out the battery when Clark added, "You still have me as a recipient on your calendar."

"Just because I forgot to delete you doesn't give you the right to read my personal stuff," she accused.

"Hard to ignore a death threat or my personal favorite, "Alone time with B.O.B." Clark let out a low whistle. "Five times a week. How many batteries are you burning through?"

"Not as many as when I was with you." Humiliation vibrated through her as she thought back to the numerous reminders she'd put on her to-do list over the past few months. "And if you saw that, then you had to have seen that I contacted Bliss to cancel the alterations and return my grandmother's dress. Untouched." She looked at her reflection in the mirror. "The dress has been touched, Clark. A lot."

"Yeah, about that." She could hear the familiar squeak of leather as Clark reclined in his office chair. "I guess there was a mix-up between orders, and your grandmother's dress was used to make, uh, Molly-Leigh's gown."

Annie eased onto the couch and rested her head on her knees.

"How did Molly-Leigh end up at Bliss?" she asked. The question exposed an ache so deep, it was as if she were reliving the breakup all over again. Because Bliss wasn't the kind of off-the-rack-shop most brides visited. It was a custom gown boutique that specialized in vintage restoration and had a yearlong wait-list.

Bliss didn't work with just any bride, and Annie hadn't wanted any old dressmaker to handle her most precious family heirloom. Which was now retrofitted to support Dolly Parton, the New Year's Eve ball in Times Square, and the scales of justice—that never seemed to tip in her favor.

"She saw a sketch of your dress in the wedding journal and fell in love with it."

Annie jerked her head up and glanced out the window to the back deck, breathing out a sigh of relief when she spotted her wedding journal. The evening's marine layer had come in fast, leaving a light dusting of dew, but it was right where she'd tossed it, beside the pool, under the patio table, in a box labeled DIRTY LAUNDRY, DRY OATMEAL, AND BROKEN DREAMS. "How did she see my wedding journal?"

"*Our* wedding journal," he corrected, and a bad feeling be-

gan to swirl in her belly. "I had one of the nurses make a copy of it for me."

"That's an inappropriate use of hospital staff and supplies. And why? You barely went to any of the appointments."

"I went to the ones that mattered."

"You mean, the one. The *one* that mattered to you," she corrected. "You showed up twenty minutes late to the cake tasting. And only because you were determined that it *had* to be carrot cake. Nobody likes carrot cake, Clark. Nobody."

"My mom does. And so does Molly-Leigh."

Ouch.

"I guess you found your perfect partner then," she whispered, raising her hand, her ring finger looking heartbreakingly bare.

Other people's choices are not a reflection on me, she reminded herself.

They were the words her childhood therapist had given her when she began to suffer panic attacks brought on when confronted with situations that left her feeling inadequate. Throughout her teens, she wore it like armor. As an adult, she liked to think it was more of a coping device when insecurities paid her an unwelcome visit.

"You still owe me half of the deposit," she reminded him.

"That's my Anh-Bon," he said softly, and once upon a time, the nickname would have given her heart a flutter. Today it made her want to throw up. "Always calling me on my shit. Without you, I never would have gotten through my selfish stage."

Annie laughed at the irony.

Growing up the adopted child of two renowned therapists, and the only rice cracker in a community of Saltines, Annie had acquired the unique ability to identify and soothe away people's fears. She could find a solution before most people realized they had a problem. It was what made her so good at her job. And so easy to open up to.

The nurses at the hospital had taken to calling her Dr. Phil.

Annie was a good girl with a good job who managed to attract good guys with the potential for greatness when it came to

love. Her life had been a nonstop revolving door of serial mo-
nogamists, each with a fatal flaw that kept him from finding *the
one*. For most of their time with Annie, the men were convinced
she was the one. Then, ultimately, she'd fix what was broken
and make some other woman enormously happy.

Annie had wife-in-training written all over her DNA. She
had a knack for helping her boyfriends overcome their issues.
Four of her last five met their wives within months of breaking it off with her. The fifth married his high school crush,
Robert.

Then came Clark. Her practical knight in surgical scrubs,
with an amazing family, a solid life plan, and an unshakable
foundation. He was the first guy to get down on one knee, tell
Annie that, for him, she was it.

Foolishly, she'd believed him.

And when he'd recanted, confessed he wasn't husband material, that it was him not her, she'd believed that too. Until mere
weeks after ending their engagement, when he and Molly-Leigh
had "put a ring on it."

"You have a lot to be called on. Let's start with the money for
the dress you now owe me."

He sighed, long and loud. "How much?"

"Four million dollars."

"Oh, for the love of God."

"No, Clark, for the love of my grandmother's dress. *My*
grandmother's dress." Her voice cracked, and so did her heart.

"Anh-Bon . . ." The sympathy in his voice was real. Sadly, so
was the pity, damn him.

"Five million dollars. Price just went up! And before you
Anh-Bon me one more time, don't forget you also owe me
half of the cost of the cake, the three hundred and fifty invita-
tions," of which only fifty were hers, "and the deposit I put
down to hold the venue." Being the mature bride-to-be, she
had insisted on covering. God forbid she appear incapable of
being a full partner in their union. "Since I haven't received
anything from the Hartford Club, I'm guessing the check was
mailed to you?"

It was the only reason she could gather for why her bank account was still short ten grand. Ten grand she desperately needed.

"You can forward me the check," she continued. "I assume you know how to break into my contacts and find my new address?"

"It's not breaking in if the owner grants you access," Clark teased. Annie didn't laugh. "Come on, Annie, don't be like that. I'll Venmo your half of the cake cost now, and I'll pay you back the deposit for the venue after the wedding."

"Pay me back?" Annie's hold on the dress slipped, the silk sliding nearly past her waist before she caught it. "What is there to pay back? The planner specifically told me that if the venue was rebooked by another party, she'd send a refund. The venue was rebooked over a month ago. Where's the refund, Clark?"

"Molls and I met my parents there for lunch, and I remembered what a great location it was." His tone was wistful. "Historical but with modern conveniences. Intimate but large enough to hold everyone. Classy but not too expensive."

Perfect but not for me. "Get to the refund."

"It checked off all our wedding wants and more. When Mom asked about availability, we were told they still had us booked for that weekend."

"Impossible. My mom told me she canceled it." Her statement was met with silence. "She never canceled it, did she? That's why my grandma's dress was still at Bliss."

"She said she was hoping we'd work it out." His words were followed by a long—that's not happening—pause that caused her insides to heat with embarrassment. A reaction that often accompanied her mother's matchmaking attempts. "I thought under the circumstances, it would be a shame to let such a beautiful venue go to waste."

That bad feeling had moved through her chest and worked its way up to twist around her throat. "What's a shame is that I spent two years waiting for that perfect venue. Half my wedding budget to reserve that venue." Her hand fisted in the silk at

her waist, the pressure wrinkling the silk. "Clark, please tell me that you didn't promise Molly-Leigh my venue."

"I didn't know what to do. She took one look at the giant windows and said the light from the afternoon sun illuminated the hall as if it were lit by a thousand candles. What was I supposed to say?"

"That you've been there, done that, dumped the bride, so that venue is off-limits."

"I tried, but she said after experiencing the magic of the Hartford Club, she couldn't think of a better place to get married."

Frustration bubbled up in her throat and the anger expanded, sealing off her airway until breathing became impossible and she feared she might pass out. Reaching behind her, she popped the top two eyehooks of her corset to let her lungs expand far enough to take in air.

It didn't help so she popped a third.

"Grab a pen and paper," she instructed, fury vibrating through her words. "Because I can think of a thousand other places to get married. Ready? Great. Now jot this down. 'Anyplace that isn't where you were going to walk down the aisle with another woman.' Or how about 'Find a place that won't hold my ex's money hostage.' That's my rainy-day money, Clark," she stressed. "I need it back."

"It's supposed to be a dry summer, but I promise I'll pay you back after the wedding. It will just be easier and less confusing that way."

"For who?" she asked.

Clark was silent, his devastating disregard for her situation sobering. "It's my grandparents' wedding date."

"I know," he said softly. "Which is the other reason I've been trying to get ahold of you. I wanted to get your thoughts before we committed to anything."

"The dress isn't up for discussion. Period." Realtering it again would be daunting, maybe even impossible, but there was no way in hell her grandmother's dress was going to be worn by any woman other than a Walsh.

"Of course not," he said, doing a piss-poor job of hiding his

disappointment. "I was referring more to the day of the wedding."

Annie had worked with Clark for six years, lived with him for three of those, so she knew his moods and quirks. Knew by the long, soft pauses between words that renowned surgeon Dr. Clark Atwood wasn't providing options. He was delivering a prognosis.

Whatever hopes Annie had about the possible outcome of this conversation were beside the point. Clark had weighed the possible scenarios, come to his decision, and nothing was going to get in the way of his wedding. It was moving forward regardless.

Any rational person would shout a resounding "Fuck off" to the universe, Clark, the inventor of carrot cake, and—she popped another eyehook—all of Victoria's rib-crushing secrets. But anger wasn't a luxury Annie had ever afforded herself.

"Clark, it doesn't matter what I think or even what I say. It's your wedding, you've made up your mind, and I'm no longer the bride."

Her heart gave an unexpected and painful bump, followed by enough erratic beats to cause concern. Not with resentment or jealousy. Not even anger. She'd learned long ago that resenting other people's happiness didn't lead to her own.

No, the familiar ache coiling its way around her bones and taking root was resignation. Resignation over losing someone who had never really been hers to lose.

Too tired to hold on any longer, Annie released her grip on the silk and the dress slid to her hips, leaving her with only a matching corset set, heels, and an overwhelming sense of acceptance, followed by acute loneliness.

"I know," he said gently. "But you're still my friend. When we broke up, we both promised to do whatever it took to keep our friendship. I don't want to lose that."

"You convinced me you weren't ready for marriage, and not even a month later you were Instagraming love sonnets about another woman."

"That was shitty timing on my part. I should have handled

it better." He released a breath, and she could almost picture him resting his forehead on the heel of his hand. "I don't even know how to explain what happened. Meeting Molly-Leigh was unexpected and exciting, and I know it seems completely insane but . . . suddenly everything made sense, the pieces all fell into place, and I couldn't wait another second to finally start my life."

Annie expelled a breath of disbelief, which sent Clark back-pedaling.

"God, Annie, I didn't mean that how it came out. But when it's the right one, when it's your person, you know it. And there's this urgency to grab on and hold tight. No matter what."

That's exactly how Grandma Hannah had described meeting Cleve. A single spin around the dance hall and—*bam*—they were in love.

"And when you said you loved me? Was that a lie?"

"No. I meant every word I said, and I still do. But over time it became clear that we were better as friends. You and I both know that."

Yeah, she did. But the rejection was still raw. Her best friend now belonged to someone else. And that hurt most of all.

"Good to know," she said. "Because I expect all my money to be Venmoed to me by tomorrow."

"I'll see what I can do," he said, then did the whole *hand over the mouthpiece while talking to a make-believe secretary.* "What? Okay, I'll be there in one second. Prep OR—"

"—Seven," Annie said in harmony with him, and he went silent. "Remember I was there when you invented OR seven to get off the phone with your ex?"

"Which is why I'd never be stupid enough to use it on you. I really am needed in the OR," he lied. "Gotta go."

"Don't you dare hang . . . up on me," she said the last few words to herself because he'd already hung up.

Annie dropped the phone on the couch and wondered, not for the first time, when it would finally be her time to belong. She wasn't greedy. One person would be enough.

Her grandparents had belonged to each other. Her parents,

to their patients. Which was why she'd been so understanding of Clark's late hours, his dedication to his career. Because in that world, she knew where she fit. Now she felt like she was in a free fall, spinning out of control, unsure where she was going to land.

Chapter 2

If Annie didn't come up with an escape plan—and STAT—she was going to be stuck in wedding hell. A ridiculous thought, since she was no longer even a bride. But the universe didn't seem to care.

Kicking off her shoes, Annie reached back for the next eyehook. Either her arms were too short, or the hook was too low, but she was willing to bet her last piece of pepperoni and green olive pizza that even Houdini couldn't liberate himself from this dress.

Gripping the cream silk and lacy cups with both hands, she pulled the bodice to the side. It didn't budge. She gave a hard tug while sucking in her belly, then again while jumping in the air.

"Shit!" The stupid thing had been so easy to put on and now she was afraid she'd have to cut herself out. "Shitshitshit!"

She'd relocated far away from everyone she loved and everything she knew to steer clear of Clark's wedding. Cut her long black hair—much to her mother's horror—into choppy layers that framed her face. Worked thirty-six-hour shifts to avoid answering the phone and reassuring her parents that she was fine—and her mother that she did not look like a boy. Which meant reassuring herself that she was fine.

And there she was, so *not* fine, stuck in some other person's wedding.

Even moving one hundred miles from her past hadn't changed

the trajectory of her future. It was as if she were still back in Hartford instead of making her fresh start in Rome—Rome, Rhode Island not Italy. Which explained the missing four thousand miles on her travel itinerary.

Sadly, when the temp agency e-mailed her a job offer in Rome, Annie had been head deep into a pity party for one—hosted by none other than Jose Cuervo. So she'd responded with a resounding yes. Which was how she'd arrived at this remote cabin on the banks of Buzzards Bay in historic Rome, Rhode Island, instead of a villa on the River Tiber.

Yup, Annie was living in the one state that was shockingly less diverse than Connecticut. Her ex-fiancé wanted her opinion on what lighting would make the first kiss most romantic. And her wedding was moving forward with a replacement bride.

"I guess if the medicine route doesn't work out, I could always start my own business," she said to the moose head that hung above the fireplace. "I'll trade in my PA for a PPA, Professional Practice Fiancée, and give men lessons on being a proper husband."

She'd make millions. She was already five for five in the happy-couples department.

Huffing her hair out of her face, she bent at the waist and tugged the fabric toward her head while making a shimmying motion with her torso. Finally! With a small tearing sound, which she'd feel for years to come, the dress fell to the floor.

Sweaty and overheated, she closed her eyes and let her hands dangle toward the floor. "What is up with my luck?"

"I've been asking myself the same question. In fact, I'll give you twenty bucks if you promise not to stop," an unexpected male voice said—from inside her house!

A lump of terror materialized in her throat as every horror movie Annie had ever watched came rushing back.

Telling herself it was still Clark on the phone, she opened her eyes and squeaked.

A big, broad figure loomed behind her—in her bedroom doorway. Even from her upside-down between-the-legs view, he looked mean and menacing, and very ax-murderer-esque.

Her heart pounding as if it were going to shake apart, she gripped her stiletto and whirled around. As a weapon, it wasn't quite as lethal as she'd like, but she leveled him with her most intimidating glare. A glare, Clark had said, that could scare small children, ward off vampires, and cause even the most impatient of patients to take a seat.

Clearly, ax murderers were immune. Or hers was, because he lifted a single brow and she swallowed—hard.

Huh. Simple, but effective.

"Who the hell are you?" She took in his bare chest, boxers, and bedhead—no sign of the ax. "And why are you sleeping in my bed?"

His eyes took in her attire while his lips kicked into a crooked smile. "I was about to ask you the same thing, Goldilocks."

Chapter 3

Emmitt Bradley was exactly two days out from a three-week stint in Shenzhen's finest ICU, and already he was experiencing some disturbing symptoms. Hallucinations being the most concerning.

She was certainly the sexiest little hallucination he'd ever conjured. He'd take it over the blinding headaches any day. Hell, maybe he was still overseas, and waking up to find nothing but cream lace and toned skin traipsing around his house could be some kind of medically induced wet dream.

No, he remembered the explosion, the crushing force of the blast that had leveled both him and the subbasement of the concrete factory he'd been covering. The ride to the hospital and following few weeks were a bit fuzzy, but the cold sweats and stabbing pain as the cabin pressurized on his flight home would be forever branded into his memory.

The doctor had warned him about flying before he was ready. Even gave him a strict list of things to avoid upon being discharged:

Work.

Whims.

Whisky.

Women.

Okay, the last had been his addition, because without bossy

women he wouldn't be sidelined while someone else covered his story. Something he didn't want to talk about just yet, which was why he'd kept his homecoming on the down-low.

Maybe he'd gone to the local bar and invited some barfly back to see if his bed was too big, too small, or just right. In his condition it was doubtful, but not out of the realm of possibility.

He sized her up with a single glance. Nah, a woman who looked like this one didn't hang around the Crow's Nest looking for one-night flings. And guys like Emmitt never offered more.

He was back to the coma theory. And if there was one thing Emmitt knew how to do better than anyone, it was testing a theory.

"Normally, I'd say the more the merrier." He ran a hand through his hair and—*damn*—even his follicles hurt. "But tonight's not good for me."

Her fear was immediately replaced with contempt. "I'm so sorry to intrude on your precious man-time," she said, then slung her heel at his head. "Now, get out!"

"Jesus." He ducked, because hallucination or not, that thing looked dangerous. Bright red, pointy toed, and sharp enough to pierce steel, or—he looked up at the spot on the wall where his head had been two seconds earlier—wedge itself into sheetrock.

"Seriously, who put you up to this?" he asked.

"What?"

"It was Levi, wasn't it? All self-righteous about dating, telling me my luck was bound to run out and I'd end up attracting one of those Crazy Cuties." He took his time giving her another once-over, paying extra-special attention to her panties—cheeky cut, if he were a betting man. "You don't look like one of those. But I've been wrong before."

"Crazy?" She snatched the remote control off the coffee table.

"See now, Goldilocks, you're missing the whole cutie part."

She stood there, straddling that threshold between retreat and retaliation, remote poised and aimed for complete castration, and contemplating her next move.

Emmitt stepped closer, dwarfing her with his size, then lev-

eled her with a *Come at me, I dare you* look that would scare most grown men shitless.

This woman was neither scared nor intimidated. Stubborn, narrowed eyes met his and made him wonder where the meek people-pleaser he'd heard on the phone had disappeared to. There was nothing meek about the woman standing in front of him. She looked like a genie who'd broken free from her lamp. Not that blond babe who granted wishes either. No, this genie looked as if she had a thousand years of anger stored up and ready to unleash on some poor SOB.

"My name is Anh Nhi Walsh. Or Annie if that's too cosmopolitan for you to manage."

He was about to inform her that his passport had more stamps than a philatelist when she decided *he* was the poor SOB.

Clutching the remote for all she was worth, she pulled back and smiled. Emmitt knew that smile well. He'd invented that smile.

In fact, he was the grand fucking master of smiles, with double-barreled dimples that he'd hated as a boy and exploited as a man.

Emmitt Bradley was a certified chameleon who could comfort, intimidate, or seduce with a simple twitch of the lip. But her particular smile promised war—painful and bloody.

So he took that smile and raised her a grin—Cheshire with a just enough *How you doing* to make her pause—and that was his window. Without giving her time to react, he did some quick maneuvering, pressing her against the adjacent wall, her hands pinned above her head.

With a startled gasp, she looked up at him with eyes that had to be the darkest shade of brown he'd ever seen.

"Let go," she shouted, her breath coming in erratic bursts. With every breath she took, the lace of her corset brushed his chest, reminding him that, between the two of them, they were barely wearing enough fabric to floss their teeth.

"You done?" he countered. When she narrowed her gaze, he took the remote from her hand, then tossed it on the chair. He gave her wrist one last warning squeeze. "We good?"

She nodded.

"I'm going to take your word for it." He studied the stubborn set of her chin, her full pouty lips, and those dangerously dark and tempting bedroom eyes that could make a man forget his good sense. She was trouble. And, *damn*, he loved trouble—almost as much as he loved women. "You break that trust and try to throw anything other than panties my way and I'll pin you to the floor. Got it, Anh Nhi Walsh?"

She froze the moment he spoke her name. And yeah, it had been good for him too. Kind of slid right off his tongue, coming out more a promise than the threat he'd intended. But hey, he'd go with it. Everything behind his boxers was demanding he rethink that no-women rule.

"Annie's fine. And my panties aren't going anywhere."

He stared her down for a long minute, then let her wrists go. He didn't back up though. He could pin her to the floor, but he was pretty sure he was sporting a woody and didn't want to bring any more attention to it.

She must have noticed, because her cheeks turned the sexiest tint of pink.

"Annie it is." He glanced at his home security panel. The light was blinking a steady red. It was armed. "Now, you want to tell me how you got past the security system?"

She opened her mouth to shout again—he could tell—so he put his fingers over her lips. His head was one word from the jackhammers breaking the rest of the way through his skull. "Quietly. Tell me quietly."

"I punched in the pass code," she said through her teeth. "Now you. How did you get in?"

"By unlocking the door I installed when I bought this house." He jerked his chin to the key ring hanging by the door, only then noticing the starlit sky beyond the windows. It was just as dark as when he'd closed his eyes earlier. "What time is it?"

"Eight-thirty."

He'd barely slept a few hours. No wonder he felt like crap. He was thirsty, tired, and needed to pee. Time to tell Goldilocks to start looking for a new bed, because even if his was just right, it was closed for the summer.

"Look, it's been fun," he said, running a hand down his face and coming to a hard stop when he reached his jaw. He touched it again and felt the days-old scruff against his palm. "What day is it?"

"Wednesday."

"Jesus." He'd slept twenty hours—not two—losing an entire day.

Slowly, he made his way to the kitchen, where he opened the fridge and grabbed a beer.

"*You're* Emmitt Bradley?"

"Never heard my name sound like an accusation before, but yeah." He popped the cap, took a long swallow, then contemplated spitting the liquid back in the bottle.

Whoever thought—he read the label—kiwi paired with hops should be fired. With a grimace, he lowered the bottle and found her standing in front of him, her earlier outfit covered by a blue scrub top.

"Emmitt of the 'Hey Emmitt, this is Tiffany,'" she said in a perfect barfly voice that was three parts helium, one part phone sex operator. "'You'd better call me when you get back in town. I had to hear it from Levi that you'd come and gone without so much as a kiss hello.'" She rolled her eyes and her voice went back to the deep, throaty one he preferred. "That's Tiffany with a Y. Not to be confused with Tiffani with an I, who won't be back until the leaves start to fall but wanted you to know she was thinking of you."

Fighting back a smile, he wiped the back of his mouth and set the bottle on the island. "And you know this how?"

Her bare feet shuffled over to the telephone. There was a stack of sticky notes posted next to it. She flipped through them, then held up exhibit one. "This is Tiffany with a Y." She walked over and smacked it on his bare chest. "This is Tiffani with an I." Another smack. "Then there's Shea, Lauren, and Jasmine."

Slap slap slap.

"Rachelle and Rochelle."

He grinned down at her. "That was only one slap. Which was it, Rachelle or Rochelle?"

"Both," she said dryly. "When your mailbox here filled up, they stopped by. Together." As his grin grew, her lips pressed together until they resembled a single line. "Then there's Chanelle, Amber, Ashley, Nicole, Sweet P, Diana"—she looked up—"who made me promise I'd write down 'Dirty Diana.' Said you'd know what that meant." That one got a big smack.

"Ow," he said, but she didn't look concerned.

"Here." She handed him what was left of the stack.

He pulled them off one by one, looking for the only message he cared about. He dropped them to the floor as quickly as he disqualified their importance. The further he went, the worse his head ached, until squinting only made things unbearable.

He held the notes back out to her. "Can you find the one from Sweet P?"

"I'm not your secretary."

"Now, there's another side of Annie I'd like to see. Glasses, pencil skirt." He gave a low whistle to which she responded by folding her arms over her chest.

The action didn't do much up top but gave him a hell of a lot of skin to admire down below. This getup was far less revealing than what she'd been sporting a minute ago, but he liked Hot Nurse Annie almost as much as Stripper Annie.

Almost.

"But just the message from Sweet P will do for now." He shoved the remaining sticky notes into her hands. When she didn't move to take them, he sighed. "Seriously, you've been squatting in my place for what?" He looked around at the cozy little nest she'd made for herself. "Six months?"

"Six weeks."

"You did all this in six weeks?"

His normally sparse cabin was decorated with minimal furniture, minimal fuss, and minimal effort. All he wanted was a quiet street with unobstructed views of nature. It was the one place on the planet he could decompress, find a sense of balance and peace.

There wasn't a shred of peace left. Every surface held a picture frame or stack of old books. His beer stein collection was

hidden behind sparkly wine flutes. And the usual scent of cedar was now masked by some kind of flowery candle. Probably the light purple ones burning on his mantle beneath his stuffed moose head.

He blinked—twice. "When did I get a mantle?"

She shrugged.

Then there was his couch. His very manly leather, made for watching hockey and Bear Grylls couch was barely visible beneath 137 throw pillows and a matching blue blanket.

And not a masculine dark blue either. Not even superhero blue. Nope, the big fuzzy atrocity was the same light blue as those jewelry boxes women go bonkers for. And don't even get him started on the twinkle lights dangling from Bull's antlers.

Emmitt had barely been upright when he'd arrived from the airport, so he hadn't noticed the changes. But now they intruded so violently, it was triggering a migraine.

"It's not permanent, so when I go, it goes."

At least she was honest about her crimes. Other people, he'd witnessed firsthand over the years, would go to great lengths to hide them.

"Then reading me one message is the least you can do for emasculating Bull"—he pointed to the moose—"and violating the privacy of my messages."

"Your voice mail is apparently full, so they started calling here. All hours of the night, ringing and ringing, so I began jotting down messages. And you emasculated him when you stuck his head on your wall as a trophy." She took the stack and flipped through it, huffing the entire time. Then handed a sticky note to him. "Here it is. Sweet P."

"Bull isn't real, and he was a gift. Now, could you read it aloud to me?" There went the stubborn set of her chin again. "I don't have my contacts in and I don't know where my glasses are," he lied.

With an exasperated sigh, Annie took the note.

"She's called a million times—her words, not mine—about this dress she's just got to have, again her words, not mine." To his relief, she didn't do some kind of sex operator imper-

sonation. "She's saving you the first dance. How sweet." She looked up. "Although, I bet Tiffani will have a problem coming in second."

Shit. He'd been looking forward to this dance for a long time, and he would be pissed if he missed it. "Did she say when the dance was?"

"No. Now, is that all, or do you want me to recite her number too?"

"I know it."

She considered that. "Do you know all of their numbers?"

"Nope." He smiled. "Just Sweet P's."

Paisley's was the only one that mattered.

"You might want to tell the others so they stop calling. It only leads to misunderstandings," she said, all kind of hoity-toity in her tone.

"So does pigeonholing," he said without further explanation, impressed by the way she managed to look both accusatory and apologetic.

It wasn't his fault Annie had jumped to conclusions. Emmitt worked hard to ensure that when it came to the most important person in his world there were zero misunderstandings—Paisley Rhodes-Bradley was his everything. His beautiful surprise of a daughter who owned his heart.

"Is the woman who's holding a bridal dress hostage judging me?"

"It's. My. Dress!" She stuck the message to his chest.

"So you said earlier. I don't think Clark got the memo." He pulled off a blank note and stuck it to her collarbone. "Maybe you should write it down for him."

She looked at the sticky note, then up at him through her raised brows. Neither gave an inch until the tension between them became murderous. Then she smiled, a *bite-me* smile that was surprisingly a turn-on.

"That's great advice, Emmitt." She grabbed a pen, scribbled something, then held it up.

"Fuck off?" He read with a chuckle. "Simple, straightfor-

ward, and leaves zero room for misinterpretation. I approve. Do you need an envelope and stamp?"

"It was meant for you." She tried to stick it to his forehead but she was too short, so she settled on his chin. His five o'clock shadow was too much for the glue, and they both watched it flutter to the floor. "I would never say that to a friend."

"Maybe you should try. Because from where I'm standing, he isn't a very good friend."

"Just because it turned out he's not my guy doesn't make him a bad guy," she said, trying to defend something that, in Emmitt's opinion, was not defendable. But he'd learned from experience, and she was going to have to come to that conclusion on her own.

"All I'm saying is, exes can't be friends."

"How about all of those." She pointed to the stack of sticky notes. "They seemed ready to get friendly."

"Those aren't exes. They're friends." He wiggled a brow and she smacked his hand, sending to the floor the notes he was holding.

"Then why don't you give one of them a call, see if they want to share a bed with you? Because I don't, and yours came as part of the rental agreement."

Emmitt choked on the residual bubbles stuck in his throat. "What?"

"Oh yeah," she purred. "If you want, I can write down the day my lease is up. That way you'll know how many friends you need to have lined up. I'll even read it to you."

Emmitt rarely spent more than a few weeks in Rome at any one time. In fact, since he'd purchased the house a decade ago, he'd spent more time overseas on assignment than in his cabin. So he'd sometimes rent it out as a rustic Airbnb, splitting the profits with his buddy Levi, who managed things while he was gone.

"How much time left on your vacation? Morning snuggles for a few days won't be so bad. I'll even let you be the big spoon."

She moved until she was practically shrink-wrapped to his

body. "I'm sure Tiffany wouldn't mind spooning. But be careful. She might turn into one of those Crazy Cuties."

"I'm leaving in a few weeks." As soon as he got a doctor to sign off so he could go back to work. His editor was intentionally following every rule to the letter. No doctor's clearance, no more assignments for her news desk. Including the one he'd been injured researching.

Carmen was a perfect example of why exes should never remain friends. Three years later, she was still holding his nuts to the fire because he'd moved on more quickly than the *Girlfriend's Guide to Breakups* thought respectful.

"Have a nice stay in Rome." Annie gently took the beer bottle from his fingers. "My lease lasts for another four months and I'm not leaving."

With that she swished her ass all the way into the bedroom.

"It's been fun," she said shortly before the door slammed, and he heard the lock engage.

Chapter 4

September was in a mood. The air was so thick that with one breath Emmitt choked on the humidity. He took it as a sign that Mother Nature was menopausal and his trip home was going to be a series of hot flashes with intermittent night sweats and unpredictable outbursts.

Emmitt shoved his hands in his pants pockets and took in the yellow and white house on the other side of the street. The large Cape Cod-style house was family ready with a charming front porch, matching bikes, a mini-me mailbox, and a Subaru that had just enough mom-mobile vibe to give any self-respecting bachelor hives. It was a far cry from the bungalow he'd grown up in a few blocks over.

It was the kind of place that had happy family written all over it.

Emmitt had never experienced that kind of family until the day he'd met Paisley.

One look at her and his entire world had changed. Emmitt had changed. Becoming an insta-dad had that kind of effect. And every day he was changing more and more. He only hoped he could change as fast as Paisley deserved.

But instead of knocking on the front door, he stood on the curb sweating his balls off in a hoodie and ballcap, looking like some kind of stalker casing the joint. By tomorrow his stealth

homecoming would likely make the front page of the morning paper, and he wanted Paisley to hear it from him first. Which was why, instead of picking the lock and climbing into bed with his smart-mouthed tenant, Emmitt had come here.

Ignoring the sweat on his brow, which had nothing to do with Mother Nature, Emmitt strode up the cobblestone pathway to the bright red door. There was a wreath of sunflowers hanging in the center, twinkle lights lining the porch rail and twisting up each of the columns, and a bronzed plaque on the wood shingled wall, reading THE TANNER FAMILY.

Emmitt let that sink in, and even after ten years it didn't sit right.

He pressed the heel of his hand to his eyes and, ignoring how gritty they were, entered the door code. The lock clicked open, and he let himself in. He considered hanging his jacket next to the others lined in a neat little row on their rightful hooks. Then he considered just how pissy Gray became over "outside" clothes lying on the upholstery and had a better idea.

Grinning, Emmitt tossed his jacket over the back of the couch. His ballcap went over the lamp, sneakers stayed on, and the loose leaf stuck to his right heel went squarely in the middle of the coffee table. Satisfied with his handiwork, he walked down the hallway toward the loud voices erupting from the kitchen, sure to squeak his shoes on the recently polished wood floor.

Sunday at the Tanner house was reserved for football, barbecuing, and—after Paisley went to bed—a few rounds of poker. And while he'd missed the feast part of the festivities, the four-letter tirade coming from the kitchen told him he'd arrived just in time for the cards.

In keeping with Tanner tradition, his buddies were engaged in a high-stakes game of car-pool poker where someone's man-card, it sounded, was in question.

"It's just a few hours out of your week," Gray said, cards in hand and working extra hard to maintain his poker face. For a guy whose career included delivering life-and-death news, he had more tells than an OCD patient in a public bathroom. "You know how important this dance committee thing is to Paisley."

"The science club was important to her, too, which was how I wound up spending a good chunk of last year knitting sweaters for penguins in New Zealand." This came from Grayson's brother-in-law, Levi Rhodes. A straight-shooter and retired sailing legend who now owned the Rome marina and attached bar and grill, he was also Emmitt's best friend—and the reason Emmitt had a half-naked woman sleeping in his bed. "I paid my time. You're up, pal."

"When she told me she'd signed me up to help with the dance decorations, I completely forgot that tomorrow is my only day off," Gray said and Emmitt might have stepped in to help a friend in need—had either one of his friends bothered to remind him that the dance in question was this month. Okay, so he'd been out of reach for a few weeks, but an e-mail would have been nice. So he stood quietly in the doorway and waited for them to notice his arrival.

"I have plans," Gray added.

Dr. Grayson Tanner was only a few years older than Emmitt but acted as if he were the grandpa of the group. He was stable, straitlaced, starched, and in the running for Stepdad of the Year. He liked long walks on the beach, shell collecting, and making detailed grocery lists color coded by category. He was a hometown freaking hero, and every single lady's real-life Dr. Dreamboat.

Not that Gray was all that interested in dating after losing the love of his life four months ago. Emmitt wouldn't be surprised if the guy never looked at another woman again.

"What? With a bottle of lotion?" Levi plucked two cards from his hand and placed them facedown, pulling two fresh ones from the deck.

"With your mom."

Levi met Gray's gaze over the top of his cards. "Everything all right?"

Gray shrugged. "Just catching up. We haven't seen each other much since Michelle's . . . uh . . . funeral."

"Want me to talk to her?"

"I don't need you holding my damn hand," Gray said, dis-

carding not a single card. "What I need is for you to find some-one to cover the bar so you can go with Paisley to the meeting, then take her home."

"No can do." Levi leaned back and cracked his neck from side to side. He was built like a bouncer; had more tattoos than fingers; and, with his buzzed head and badass attitude, was of-ten taken for a fighter rather than a boat builder who hand-carved high-end sailboats from wood boards.

"The Patriots are playing tomorrow, which means all hands on deck at the Crow's Nest. I know that's breaking news, since I have so many free nights," Levi patronized. "But I'll be working the bar and overseeing my new manager, which means you're doing decorations and babysitting."

"Can't someone fill in for you?" Gray tossed three flash cards into the pile—two COOK DINNER and one EMPTY DISHWASHER. "I call."

"Since when does a fifteen-year-old need a sitter?" Emmitt finally said, stepping into the room.

Both startled gazes swung toward him. Levi's accusatory. Gray's pissy.

Ah, home sweet home.

"What the hell are you doing home?" Levi asked at the same time Gray said, "Are you wearing shoes in my house? There's a shoe rack for a reason. I even put a sign above it so you'd re-member."

"Oh, I remembered." Emmitt opened the fridge, and the light caused a sharp pain to build behind his eyes. "I trampled through your flower bed on the way in. Lots of tread on these babies, wanted to make sure they were nice and dirty."

"You don't call, you don't write, you just show up and drink my beer," Gray said.

Water was more Emmitt's speed these days. Not that a cold beer didn't sound good after the shit in his fridge at home, but it wasn't all that compatible with the elephant-tranquilizer-sized painkiller he'd taken before leaving home. He popped the cap then tipped the bottle back, nearly emptying it in one swallow. He grabbed a second bottle before closing the fridge.

He was still in the throes of jet lag. "Jet lag" that, according to the doctors in China, could last another three to forever weeks, depending on how lucky he got. Recent history told him lady luck was one vindictive bitch.

"Seriously, what are you doing home?" Gray pressed.

"Nice to see you too." Emmitt flipped a kitchen chair around and, straddling it, took his seat at the table. "China was epic, by the way. The trip home was a little bumpy, but arrived safe and sound, thanks for asking." He turned to Levi. "Call him out. He's got a shit hand."

"Looking at my cards and then spilling isn't cool." Gray stood. "This is why I hate playing with you two."

"You love playing with us," Emmitt said. "For the record, don't look all smug when you have a shit hand. It tells everyone you have a shit hand."

"I fold." Gray tossed his cards on the table and stomped to the stove. When he came back, he held a big plate with a piece of chicken and—what smelled like—Michelle's mac-n-cheese recipe.

The delicious scent of the melted cheddar had Emmitt's stomach rumbling. He hadn't eaten more than a few bags of peanuts and a protein bar on his flight home. That was thirty-some-long-hours ago.

"Any more of that in the oven?" Emmitt asked.

"Nope."

"How about an extra fork?"

Gray looked up. Zero amusement on his face. "If you'd called to tell us you were home, I would've made more."

"Would you also have reminded me that the father-daughter dance is this month?" When the other two exchanged guilty looks, Emmitt added, "I got a note about needing a dress."

"Would it have mattered if I had told you?" Gray asked. "You're supposed to be on assignment for another few months."

Jesus, was the guy serious?

"Hell, yeah, it would have mattered," Emmitt said. "It's the *father*-daughter dance. I'm her father. Therefore, *I* should have been informed about the dance since I'll be the one taking her."

Her name was Paisley Rhodes-*Bradley*, for Christ's sake. Emmitt had first met Paisley's mom when he'd moved to Rome in middle school. He was twelve, Michelle sixteen, and she was his best friend's sister. But it wasn't until Emmitt had come home from college, when those four years didn't seem to make such a big difference anymore. Michelle was fresh out of a relationship and looking for a rebound, and Emmitt was looking to live out one of his childhood fantasies.

The timing seemed perfect.

All it took was one kiss and their fates were sealed. That kiss led to a sizzling-summer weekend spent together on a deserted strip of beach, sleeping in a tent and bathing in the Atlantic. They both knew it going in, the weekend was all they had, so they enjoyed every moment.

It wasn't until six years later, when he was covering a subway bombing in Berlin, that he heard from Michelle again. She'd had a baby. And she was pretty confident Paisley was his.

When Paisley had been born, Michelle thought the father was her current boyfriend, leaving no reason to notify Emmitt. But after some lab work had proven that Paisley's dad wasn't the guy on the birth certificate, she'd e-mailed Emmitt immediately. He was on the first flight home, ring in his pocket, ready to do the right thing.

Only, Michelle already had a steady man in her life. Dr. Dreamboat had come onto the scene a few years earlier with a heartfelt drop to a single knee.

Not that it mattered. One look at those big brown eyes and adorable dimples and Emmitt didn't need to wait for the test to come back. Without a doubt, that travel-sized pixie in soccer cleats and a grin that could heal the world was one hundred percent his.

Overnight, Emmitt had become daddy to a five-year-old little girl.

But Paisley was a package deal. She didn't go anywhere without her mom and the two men in her life—Uncle Levi and Stepdad Grayson, who'd already staked a solid claim in her little world.

Since Emmitt was the last one to the table, he was still fighting for his rightful place in the family, and in Paisley's life.

"If you're going by that logic," Gray explained, "then I'd like to go on record saying that since she introduces me as her father and you as her dad, I'm the most logical choice to take Paisley to the *father*-daughter dance."

"Go on record?" Emmitt laughed. "This isn't an autopsy, Doc. It's my kid's dance. And since my name's on the birth certificate now, it blows your logic right out of the water."

"So is mine," Levi interrupted. "She's a born-and-bred Rhodes. I'd also like to point out that I was around before any of you guys bothered to show up."

To say his family situation was complicated was an understatement.

"Raise your hand if you changed a single diaper," Levi went on.

Gray started to raise a hand, and Levi skewered him with a look. "Paisley's diapers? Your patients don't count."

Grayson folded his arms across his chest.

"Ever do a late-night drive through town until she fell asleep?" He looked around. His was the only hand up. "No? How about an early morning feeding where she puked your sister's breast milk all over your face? Snotted on your workshirt? Kicked you in the junk?"

All three hands went in the air at the last question.

Levi shook his head and gave an unimpressed huff. "She was already mobile by that point. That's on you guys." Levi put his hand down. "All I'm saying is that if anyone has a right to take Paisley to that dance, it's me."

"Like hell." Gray stood, getting on his self-righteous soapbox. "It's quality, not quantity. I'm the homework guy, the *hold my hand while I get a shot* guy, *wipe away the tears* guy, PTA guy, carpool guy—"

"Only because you're a shitty poker player," Levi pointed out.

"I'm the *everyday in the trenches* guy." Gray ended with so much superiority, Emmitt was surprised he didn't jump on the table and drop the mic.

"Sounds like you're the tight-ass guy who no one wants to take to a dance," Emmitt joked.

Gray didn't laugh. In fact, he looked more serious than usual. "I'm the guy who shows up every day, no matter what."

Emmitt didn't think Gray meant for his words to cut as deep as they did, but they'd definitely leave a mark.

When Emmitt was in Rome, he threw off the natural balance of things. He'd known that the moment he'd been accepted into the fold. It also wasn't a secret that when he was away on assignment, everyone else's life got a whole hell of a lot less complicated. Paisley didn't have to choose whose house she was going to sleep at. Didn't have to rush over before school because she'd left her homework at Gray's place. And she didn't have to divide her attention among her three dads.

Gray was always on his ass about cutting back on the number of assignments he took, being home more. Easy for someone whose job restricted him to a one-block radius to pass judgment.

Emmitt *had* cut back a lot over the past few years. With Michelle gone, he planned on cutting back even further. He'd even approached Paisley about moving in with him full time. To Emmitt's disappointment, her therapist had agreed with Gray that it was best to keep Paisley in the only home she'd ever known.

Emmitt had buried another dream that day. The full-time guy wasn't going to be him. That honor went to Gray. So Emmitt went back to being the cool dad, the one who interviewed the occasional star, gave outlandish and indulgent gifts, and came home on random weekends and holidays.

It sucked. Big time. But there wasn't much he wouldn't do to make his little girl happy, even if it meant co-parenting with a guy who was the poster child for Dad of the Year. And an uncle who fancied himself the father figure against which all other father figures should be measured.

Every girl should be so lucky as to have this much love surrounding her.

"I'd have an easier time showing up if you weren't always

keeping me out of the loop on things. Such as, I don't know? The father-daughter dance."

"I've been a little distracted. I buried the love of my life four months ago, and this is the first big event since Michelle's been gone," Gray whispered. "Let me have this. Michelle would have wanted it."

The table was silent for a long moment. Finally, Levi spoke, "Are you playing the widower card?"

Gray slowly smiled. "Did it work?"

"Hell no," Levi said, and they all burst out laughing.

"Michelle would have loved this," Emmitt said. "The three of us acting like a bunch of old biddies over a dance card."

"Yeah, she would have." Gray sobered, as did the rest of them.

The moment was suddenly swallowed by the grief that clung to each of them, weighing them down and making it hard to breathe.

Michelle had been Emmitt's last thought when the concrete factory he'd been covering in China exploded. She was the glue that held everyone together, the gentle strength of the family, and the one person who never gave Emmitt shit for being Emmitt and chasing a story.

Levi had lost his sister, Gray his soul mate, and Emmitt had lost the one person who never judged him.

And Paisley?

God, Paisley hadn't just lost her mom. She'd lost her best friend, her sounding board, and her advocate. The grounding love in her life that all other loves would be compared to. It was a soul-deep kind of loss Emmitt could relate to. So he'd vowed on his way to the hospital that Paisley wouldn't lose two parents in the same year.

He knew how isolating and painful it was to lose a parent. His mom had died when he'd been a little younger than Paisley. His dad became withdrawn, sullen, rarely putting the bottle down long enough to check in on Emmitt—let alone stock the kitchen or drive him to school. That day standing next to the

empty hole in the cemetery, Emmitt buried his childhood along with his mom.

So when they'd lost Michelle, he'd committed to doing whatever it took to make sure Paisley didn't grow up faster than she needed to.

"Does that gash on your arm there have anything to do with your unexpected arrival?" Gray pointed to the patch of raw skin, puckered from recent stitches, peeking from beneath Emmitt's shirt cuff.

Emmitt tugged down his sleeve. "There was a little mishap at the factory I was covering, and I got caught by a few pieces of stray concrete."

He resisted the urge to pull the bill of his ballcap lower. The last thing he wanted was to bring attention to the gash on his head. Not if he wanted the always cautious Dr. Grayson to clear him for duty, the last condition Emmitt had to meet before Carmen would put him back in the field. Emmitt didn't need Gray learning about the meteorite-sized chunk of concrete that had knocked him out cold.

"According to CNN, that *little mishap* leveled the entire factory," Gray corrected.

"You know how reporters exaggerate for ratings."

"That's what Carmen said." Gray's eyes never strayed from Emmitt's as he spoke. "When you didn't check in, I called your office. According to her, you'd finally got what was coming to you. According to Paisley, you were enjoying your trip."

"Aw, you do care," Emmitt joked, surprised at how moved he was to learn that Gray had checked up on him. He'd woken in the hospital to a few texts from Paisley but nothing from Levi or Gray. Not that Emmitt had contacted them. Paisley's mental well-being had precluded calling home.

His little girl had trouble sleeping as it was. She didn't need to see him bruised and battered in a hospital bed whenever she closed her eyes. So he'd kept a steady text thread going with her—funny memes, photos of China, the latest Maru the Cat videos—but not a word about how bad his injuries were.

"I told P that it was just a few—"

"Scrapes and bruises," the guys interrupted in unison. Then Gray said, "We heard."

"Scrape." He pointed to his arm, then showed his other elbow. "Bruise. As for the rest, I wanted to tell her in person. Is she asleep?"

"She's staying the night at Owen's," Levi said, referring to Paisley's best friend.

"On a school night?" Emmitt clarified, because here they were worried about a fifteen-year-old staying home alone for a few hours after school, but saw zero problems arising from her staying over at a boy's house—school night notwithstanding.

Was he seriously the only one unsure about his daughter's best friend being male. Yes, he was aware that Owen had been Paisley's bestie since they were in diapers. He was also aware that Owen's mom had been Michelle's best friend and would protect Paisley as if one of her own.

But a lot had changed between them. Most importantly the toxic level of hormones that could have even the most level-headed teens losing their good sense—and clothes. They were forced to sleep in different rooms now, so Emmitt was going along with it. But the second Owen started looking at Paisley as a girl, there was going to be some kind of come-to-Jesus meeting, with Owen in the hot seat.

"Tomorrow is a late start. Some kind of district meeting for the teachers," Gray said as if that were supposed to make everything better. "You want me to call her and tell her you're here?"

"No, if I wanted someone to call her, I'd call her myself," Emmitt said, wondering just how out of touch the guys thought he was when it came to his own daughter. "I'll surprise her tomorrow."

"She'll be bummed she missed you," Gray said. "But it's your call."

It was his call. And he was choosing to wait until he didn't feel as though his head were about to crack in half. And until he wasn't the reason for a fun "late start" sleepover to come to an early end. "It's been real, boys." Emmitt stood and went to stretch, cutting it short when a searing hot pain raced up his

right side. Masking a gasp with a yawn he added, "I'm going to head home and catch a few more Zzzs."

"Oh shit!" Levi stood too. "You're headed home. Like *home* home. When did you get in? Please tell me you came straight here."

Emmitt had to laugh. Thinking back to the feisty brown-eyed beauty sleeping in his bed, he had an idea why his friend was anxiously scrolling through the contacts in his phone.

"Nope. Met my new bunkmate first."

"Ah shit." Levi's head dropped into his hands, his fingers working the temples, pressing into the deep grooves of exhaustion in his face. "I kept meaning to e-mail you, but things have been crazy. Between trying to get the marina up and running and making sure the family bar stays open for business, I haven't had a spare second. So when Gray came to me with a preapproved tenant for your place, I jumped at it. I mean, I haven't even had time to work on my boat since, uh, Michelle."

A mix of complicated emotions, which had been knotting in Emmitt's stomach for the past few months, swelled and expanded until breathing became a painful reminder that the gaping holes left behind by Michelle's absence went further than just emotional. And everyone was struggling to fill the void in their own way.

"Tenant," Gray said firmly. "Unless you've bought a set of bunk beds, she's not your bunkmate, your bedmate, or even your roomie. And she sure as hell isn't a person you can ever see naked. Is that clear?"

Emmitt considered that, then smiled. "Can she see me naked?"

"No!" they said in unison.

"That will make things challenging." Emmitt tapped a finger against his chin, hoping to lighten the mood. "I do love a good challenge. It forces me to get creative."

"Oh no," Gray said. "Annie is strictly off-limits."

"Since when did you become the dating police? You gonna tell me where to piss next?"

"If it keeps you from pissing all over my plans," Gray said firmly. "Levi is, as you heard, busy and I've had my plate full

with new patients ever since Dr. Smith retired, not to mention helping out in the ER. Annie is my temp physician's assistant and, until Denise comes back from maternity leave, she's the only reason I'm able pick up Paisley after school."

"I can pick her up. What?" Emmitt said to their disbelieving faces. "She gets out at three—"

"Two."

"*Two*. I'm around. I can even get there a little early. Chat up some of the hot PTA moms while I wait. How hard can it be?"

"Hot PTA moms are a bad dad move," Levi said. "Trust me, you don't want to go there."

"Okay, so I avoid the moms and drive Paisley home. I mean, I'm here, I can do it and still have plenty of time to get better acquainted with Anh." Emmitt forced himself to appear more casual than he felt. He'd love to spend his afternoons helping Paisley with homework, making after-school snacks, kicking the soccer ball around. Getting to know Anh wouldn't be a hardship either, but he'd mainly added that part to piss off Gray.

"For how long?" When Emmitt started to argue, Gray held up a silencing hand. "You're here now, which is great. But in a few weeks, when you get bored or a new assignment comes in and you head off to Siberia, we're stuck without someone to hang with Paisley after school. Because you'll be gone, and Annie will have bailed even though you told her up-front you're only capable of casual. Because we all know, when it comes to you and women, they all think they will be the one to change you from globe-trotter to groom. But she won't. She'll be heart-broken and then quit. I'll be out a PA, and a sitter, and it'll be Paisley who suffers."

"Annie's had it rough," Levi added. "She came here to put her life back together. Not have her heart stomped on by some guy who's just passing through."

"Passing through?" Emmitt scoffed. "I own a fucking house."

"That I spend more time showing to potential tenants than you do sleeping in it," Levi pointed out. "To be safe, why don't you crash on my boat?"

"And listen to you snore all night?" Emmitt shook his head. "Thanks, but you're not my type."

"Neither is Annie and we both know it," Gray said, proving just how little he knew about Emmitt.

Annie was absolutely, positively, tight bod with a sharp tongue and soft lips, his type—which was why he tended to steer clear of women like her. It wasn't his fault fate had a twisted sense of humor.

He wasn't sure what was going on with Annie's love life, but based on what he'd heard, he had a pretty good idea. And it pissed him off that his two closest friends would lump him in with a guy like Clark. Emmitt had never once led a woman on. He was up-front and honest about what he was looking for and what he was capable of.

Women knew the score before he even ordered a second round.

"I know that what Annie and I do is none of your damn business," Emmitt said, loving to watch Gray squirm. "I also know she's a grown woman capable of making choices for herself, unless you think otherwise. I'd be happy to pass on your concerns about her ability to navigate the dating world, Doctor."

"Just leave her alone. You can have any other woman in town, just not Annie," Gray said, and Levi shook his head. "What?"

"Man, you just issued him a challenge," Levi said.

"Which I have accepted. And I'll pick Paisley up at two."

Chapter 5

Annie was in a bad mood. Any hope she'd had that her new roommate was just some terrible nightmare vanished when she was jarred awake at two in the morning by the front door slamming shut, signaling his return.

If his mother had taught him any manners, he'd long since forgotten them.

Emmitt flicked on every light in the house, including the hall light, which lit up her room like a solar flare. Then—as if to let her know it was intentional—he made himself a smoothie of metal bolts, glass shards, and the wails of small children.

Not even her noise-canceling headphones could block out the sound.

Whistling, he opened and closed some cupboards—seven to be exact—then slammed a few more before settling in for a long summer's snooze. Based on his sonic boom of a snore, evidently the hall light didn't bother him, because he'd left it burning bright.

And he'd been the one to make her feel guilty for waking him up at an hour when most people would be sitting down for dinner.

Beyond irritated by the hypocrisy of it all—another thing to add to her WORST ROOMMATE EVER list, right between HUMBLE-BRAGGING and STEALING MY BEER— she flung back the covers;

marched out the door; and came to a sudden, startled stop as the bottom of her stomach dropped out.

Sweet baby Jesus. Her lungs seized, unable to release any air because three feet in front of her was Rome's very own Romeo. Sprawled out on the recliner, with his ballcap pulled low, he and his Calvin Kleins were on full display. The man clearly had a thing against wearing pants.

Or he was marking his territory. Bringing out the big guns—the big *everything.*

She barely had time to register that he'd moved the recliner one hundred and eighty degrees, leaned it all the way back with the footrest fully extended, successfully blocking any escape come morning. Because her attention was drawn elsewhere.

With her blue fuzzy blanket only partially covering him, she was able to watch the hypnotic rise and fall of his chest—his very defined chest that had just the right amount of hair and just the right amount of muscle.

The peaceful way he slept irritated her. One arm flung over his eyes, a leg resting on the floor, and—*hello*—if that was his morning wood at two a.m., her body sighed a breathy *oh my* at the thought of how it would look come sunrise.

Placing a hand to her chest, Annie gave herself five seconds to gawk. Five seconds, then she'd retreat and he'd never know, because he'd clearly won this battle. As she saw it, her only other options were:

1. Hope that he'd wake up before she had to go to work and move the chair—not likely, because he was settled in for the long haul.

2. Nudge him awake and tell him he was a jerk—which meant admitting he was getting to her.

3. Come morning, crawl under the footrest—only, she was done shimmying for any man.

4. Crawl over him while he was half-naked—and wouldn't that just make his entire year to catch her on top of him, her heart going pitter-patter.

Which led her to another problem. When he was sleeping and not spewing man-speak, he almost looked human.

She could see how some women could find his strong, capable hands and washboard abs appealing. He was tall, fit, handsome in that worldly way that showed he'd lived a full life.

Oh, who was she kidding. The man was sex-tabulous.

"Reconsidering that spooning offer?" The deep rusty voice brought her attention to the fact that while she had been watching him, he'd been watching her. "There's room."

He patted his lap, mere inches from his mighty impressive package, and Annie's heart picked up pace as if it were racing in the Indy 500.

She pinned her guilty and embarrassed gaze on his, which was not embarrassed at all. His lack of pants didn't seem to affect him one iota, just brought a charming grin to his lips, and amusement—plus something a whole lot more dangerous—to his eyes.

"Nope. Merely reevaluating our public education system. Are you illiterate or just rude?"

Emmitt glanced at the empty carton on the ground with a big neon pink "*Anh's, Do Not Drink*" sticky note stuck to the front of it. "Rude would be putting it back with just a swallow left." He shifted in the chair, the movement starting a domino effect of ripples from his shoulder muscles all the way down past his abs.

His pecs danced mockingly, and Annie jerked her gaze north to find him smiling. "Now who's the one being rude?" He tsked. "Objectifying me when I'm in a vulnerable position."

She snorted. "Please, you knew exactly what you were doing when you decided to park yourself in a chair in the hallway in nothing but your boxers."

Picking up the blanket, he draped it over his belly as if making an effort, when really all he managed to cover was his right rib and flank, leaving his sirloin and all other loins completely on display. Then he reclined the chair even farther back, folding his hands behind his head in a pose that was so male, it had her lady parts tingling like champagne bubbles on the tongue. "What am I doing, Anh?"

"Trying to rattle me!"

"I have that effect on women." His voice was rough with sleep—as if he'd spent the earlier part of the night sharing long, hot, drugging kisses.

"Not this woman. I'm not rattled at all," she lied. "So sorry, your big plan to make me leave won't work."

"Actually, I—"

"May I finish?"

"Continue," he said, looking so unrattled it rattled her more.

"What you did was shitty. It's not as if my night hasn't already been crappy enough. You knew I was frustrated and tired and, well—hurt." The admission caught her off guard, but she decided to own it. "Yes, I was hurt and embarrassed, and to make it all worse, I discovered a stranger was, *rudely*, eavesdropping on a very difficult conversation. So I went to bed to lick my wounds in private and sleep because, well, because . . ."

"You are frustrated and tired and hurt," he prompted.

"Frustrated and tired, no longer hurt. Now I'm mad. At you!" She stabbed a finger in his direction.

"Me?" he asked as if finding this all incredibly entertaining.

"Yes, you! *I* am needed at the hospital very early, and *you* felt it necessary to come home and slam every cabinet in the kitchen. If you wanted to make a big enough ruckus to wake me, then well done, Emmitt Bradley, well done." She ended with a mocking slow clap.

"I didn't mean to wake you. And for that, I'm sorry. I also wasn't aware you had to work early, or I would have been quieter."

Admittedly, she was a little thrown by his sincere apology. "I don't actually have to work early. One of my patients is going in for gallbladder surgery tomorrow and she doesn't have any relatives on this coast, so I offered to be there when she woke up."

"Do you offer this kind of bedside service to all your patients?" he asked softly. No teasing, no goading, and absolutely no boyish innuendo. Just a tender look in his eye that she hadn't seen before.

"Just the special ones," she said, but didn't move, a sudden shyness taking over.

He let her comment hang in the air, then gave her the tiniest of smiles, which had her looking away.

"As for the cabinets, again I apologize. I came home with a splitting headache, and since all my things, including my pain-killers, were locked in the bedroom, I went in search of my back-ups, which used to be over the sink. Imagine my surprise when I found a small warehouse of scented candles in their place. It seems while I've been gone, someone's reorganized my kitchen."

"Oh," Annie said, now aware of how furrowed his forehead became when he spoke or moved, as if tensing it in anticipation of pain. Had she completely misjudged the situation? "I thought you were just being a jerk."

"I'm surprised, Goldilocks." He placed an affronted hand to his chest. "I took you for someone who looked beneath the cover before passing judgment."

It was the second time he'd said as much tonight, which had her reconsidering if, perhaps, she had been hasty in labeling him a self-absorbed playboy. The playboy part was true, but the other part? She wasn't so sure anymore.

"Seriously? Look at you, sitting here like the big bad wolf, blocking my exit and trying to intimidate me into getting your way."

"I think you're confusing fairy tales," he said, although his big, bad smile said he liked the comparison.

"I was afraid you were pissed from earlier," he went on, "and decided to play a game of hide-and-seek with my things. So I stationed myself outside the bedroom, in case you tried to sneak past me and lock the door before I could grab my things from inside."

She studied him for a good long moment and, even though her BS meter was going ballistic, she couldn't sense an ounce of deceit. And when he explained it like that, all sincere and ratio-nal, Annie felt like the jerk.

"Admittedly, I had a bad night and you may have caught some of the brunt, and for that I'm sorry. But I'm not actually one of those Crazy Cuties of yours who would do something

like that," she said, embarrassed that he'd think she'd stoop to such immature antics. "I did gather your personal things from the bedroom, though, and placed them next to the garage door so they'd be closest to your car when you left tomorrow. Even stuck a note on the pile."

"Bet I can guess what the note said." When she merely grinned, he laughed. "Then I guess it was worth it."

"I guess so," Annie said, and realized she was laughing as well. That was when Annie had another, more shocking, realization. She was no longer upset over her call with Clark. In fact, the apples of her cheeks felt bruised from her enormous grin.

"Imagine how good it will feel when you unleash on some guy who actually deserves it, like, I don't know, that asshat you were talking to earlier. A little suggestion though—you might want to consider cutting down the smile a bit and maybe lose the snickering, but I bet he'd drop that check in the mail A-sap."

She covered her face. "Just how much of the call did you overhear?"

"Enough to know that you clearly have a sweet side and that he's taking advantage of it." His tone was soft, his expression stone-cold, almost as if he were being defensive—of her.

"I'm as sweet as sweet comes. You just happen to bring out my—"

"Bad girl side?" He sounded hopeful.

"I was going to say my impatient side."

"Whatever it is, you might want to channel the girl who doesn't have a problem telling me to fuck off next time that idiot calls for wedding advice. Otherwise, you may as well kiss your ten grand goodbye."

"Just because I'm nice doesn't make me a pushover."

"Good." Emmitt scratched his chest like a bear settling in for the winter. "Then call him."

"What?"

"Go on," he goaded. "Call him and tell him that you aren't his Anh Bon and demand that he repay the ten grand immediately."

"Um . . . My phone is charging in the bedroom."

He lifted his cell from the armrest and offered it to her. "You can use mine."

"I don't need to call him in front of you to prove I'm not a pushover. I'll handle it."

"Good to know," he said, but it didn't look as if he believed her.

Even worse, Annie began to doubt whether she believed herself. Not only had she given Clark permission to steal her wedding venue and her grandparents' wedding date, the call ended before she could squeeze a concrete date as to when he'd return her money.

"Just don't come to me looking for a plus one when he asks you to be the best man. One look at me in a tux and you'll be elbowing ladies right and left to catch the bouquet."

"In your dreams."

"Seriously though, you need to say screw everyone else and just do you," Emmitt said without a hint of teasing in his tone. "I mean it. You don't owe him anything. Hell, the prick owes you—and not just the money. He owes you one hell of an apology for putting you in that situation. Then he needs to apologize to you in front of your friends and family about the dress and stealing your grandparents' wedding date."

Wow, not only had he heard nearly everything but he'd thought about it long enough to form a strong opinion. The whole situation turned Annie's stomach.

It wasn't what Emmitt had said or even how he'd said it that burned. It was the humiliating fact that he was the first person in her world to say those words, to tell her to stand up for herself. *What did it mean that a perfect stranger was able to understand what her closest friends and family had pushed aside in favor of civility? What did it say about her that she'd allowed them to?*

"Do you think all of that will fit on a sticky note?" she asked.

Emmitt's gaze lazily roamed over Annie's body and down, and Annie felt zips of awareness follow in its wake. "You strike me as the type of woman who, once she sets her mind to something, doesn't let anything stand in her way."

The confident way he said it sent a rush of tingles racing

through her body faster than her mom checking out a Black Friday sale.

"That's a bold statement to make about someone you've spoken to twice."

"What can I say—they've been insightful conversations. Plus, you're pretty easy to read."

Annie snorted—twice—because she was about as easy to read as a darkened street sign to a glaucoma patient.

Born Asian and raised by white parents, Annie came into the world a walking oxymoron. In fact, the more people came to know her, the more their initial assumptions were proved inaccurate. Annie was proof that you can't judge a book by its cover. So she was embarrassed she'd done the same to Emmitt.

If being mysterious was considered intriguing, being a never-ending surprise was off-putting. People liked to rely on their judgment, and Annie was often misjudged.

"You laugh, but I bet I know more about you than most guys would after six dates."

"This should be impressive, since I doubt you've been on six consecutive dates in the past six years." When he opened his mouth to argue, she added, "With the same woman?"

"I'm so observant, I don't need the same amount of time other people do to know if it's a forever kind of thing," he said, which surprised her because when he said "forever" he didn't look as if he wanted to gag or would break out in hives.

"Are you saying you're open to commitment?"

"If it's the right person who came along?" He shrugged. "Why not? But I don't need to string someone along to figure out if they're right for me. I don't play games with the people in my life, making them jump through hoops in order to figure out where they stand. Nah, that's childish and pretty shitty, if you ask me."

Annie saw a flash of fresh pain cross Emmitt's face and realized that beneath the confident swagger lingered an uncertainty that drew Annie in. Her gut said he'd been played by someone he trusted and cared for. Based on the new sadness lurking beneath his words, that someone had deeply hurt him. And recently.

The caretaker in Annie wanted to ask if he was okay, but the pragmatist in her understood better than to pry. The more she knew about him, the more human he'd become, and the harder it would be to kick him out of his own house.

After a night like tonight, a smart girl would cut her losses and go straight to bed. Only Annie was tired of playing things smart, because instead of wishing him good night, she said, "Okay, wow me with your observation skills."

If she was going to steer clear of charming players, then she might as well learn how to recognize the signs.

"Oh, you'll be wowed," he said and she rolled her eyes. "You don't believe me? Then let's make this a little more interesting. If I wow you with my superior observational skills, then tomorrow I get the bed."

As far as she was concerned, Emmitt wasn't going to be living here come tomorrow. So what was there to lose? "Wow me."

"This is going to be good." He rubbed his hands together like a kid in a candy store. "You have a thing for British mysteries, Shemar Moore, and reality dating shows."

"Knowing what's on my Hulu account doesn't make you observant, it makes you a snoop."

"No rules were stated at the beginning of the game as to how I come by my information. But I will lay off your horrific taste in television and get back to what a romantic you are."

"Of course I'm a romantic," she argued. "I was recently planning my own wedding. I'm sorry to say, Emmitt, you're just another man whose talents have left me wondering why I bother."

"You've clearly been hanging around the wrong men," he tsked. "I was going to say, your romanticism goes far deeper than dream weddings, Goldilocks. Most women would jump at the opportunity to blow a few grand on a new dress, yet you went in search of the perfect tailor to alter your grandma's. You also wanted to share her wedding date, which tells me she was not only the most important person in your life but that you never had to guess where you stood when you were with her."

He went silent, studying her in an intense way that kept Annie shifting on her feet.

She was practically bouncing on her toes when he finally said, "I imagine that without her, you've felt a little lost throughout this whole ordeal."

"Of course, I still miss her. It doesn't take a psychic to determine that."

"What was her name?" he asked, the question causing a wave of warm emotion to roll through her.

"Hannah," Annie said on a swallow, wondering why the simple exchange of sharing her grandmother's name felt so intimate. "And lots of women choose to wear their grandma's dress. It's a pretty common tradition."

"You didn't mention your mom wearing it, so I don't think it was a tradition thing. I think you did it because you wanted Hannah there with you and that was the closest you could come," he said, and her stomach did a little flip of uncertainty, because the guy was nailing it. "But clearly wedding talk isn't wowing you as much as it's upsetting you."

"I'm not upset," she lied, refusing to show him how hard it still was to talk about her grandmother. "I'm tired."

"Then I'll speed this up. You prefer baths but take showers to save on time. You have an appreciation for unexpected pairings, like pepperoni and green olives, dipping chocolate in jelly, oversized T-shirts and tiny panties. You're a neat freak, but I bet you have one place where you say screw it and throw order and tidiness out the door."

Her expression must have given away her surprise, because he laughed. "Is it the inside of your purse? Or maybe it's your car, littered with wrappers, empty water bottles, and probably even a few of those madeleine cookies floating around in case of emergency. Wherever it is, I bet it's a complete disaster. You are as much a romantic as a pleaser. You think nothing of sacrificing what you want in order to make things easier for other people, which is why you're okay with being called Annie when you prefer Anh."

A raw and familiar vulnerability swept through her, filling her heart before spilling over and burning like acid on metal everywhere it touched. Either he was incredibly intuitive or

everyone else in her life was blind. And she wasn't sure which upset her the most.

"You're staring," he said roughly.

"Just trying to figure you out is all, but since that would likely take longer than a PhD, and I have an early morning, I say we call it a night."

"I guess even bleeding hearts need their sleep."

"I guess they do." And before she did something stupid, like climb onto his lap and ask him to tell her a fairy tale, Annie flipped the switch, plunging the room into darkness.

Oh boy, was that ever a bad move.

She should have made Emmitt turn off the light after she locked the bedroom—with her safely on the other side. Then she wouldn't have noticed the way his Calvin Kleins seemed to grow brighter—and bigger—by the second. Perhaps her eyes were merely adjusting, still fully dilated to take in as much light as possible.

Or maybe her luck had finally hit rock bottom, because his undies were, without a doubt, glowing. The more her eyes became accustomed to the dark, the more confused she became, until she could hold back her laughter no longer. Emmitt of the "superior intuitiveness" Bradley wore a pair of glow-in-the-dark boxers.

She laughed as the shapes took form. "Are you serious? Kittens and rainbows."

His grin grew two sizes that day. "Tell me, Goldilocks. Is it too big or just right?"

Annie went through all the options she'd laid out before and decided on option five. A full, humiliating retreat.

She turned and ran, as if hellhounds were nipping at her butt, and made it to her room in two leaps, slamming the door before jumping into bed. Still feeling ridiculously embarrassed, she pulled the covers over her head and closed her eyes for extra protection.

"Was it the kittens?" he called through the door.

Chapter 6

Her mom often called her stubborn. Whereas Annie liked to think of herself as determined. But as determined as she was not to lose another second of sleep over the man in the glow-in-the-dark boxers, when the first hint of sun peeked through her window, she found herself wide awake.

Every time she'd closed her eyes, her breathing would become ridiculously erratic, her heart nearing stroke level.

"He's not all that," she said while she lay there until the combination of the comforter and her hot breath turned her bed into a sauna and she felt as if she'd suffocate.

"Damn him." She threw the covers back.

There was no way she could face him. She'd never be able to unsee all of . . . *that*. She'd never be able to look at a Calvin Klein ad and not have some kind of visceral experience. And she sure as hell couldn't, under any circumstances, let him know that he'd gotten to her.

Nope, no man had the power to derail her life. And the one outside her bedroom door was not going to steal another moment's peace from her.

She climbed out of bed and walked to the bathroom.

Feeling like a zombie, she took her time in the shower—letting the hot water run until she'd emptied the water heater. It didn't help much. Her eyes were still gritty, her brain sluggish, and

she ended up washing her hair with shaving cream. Which meant that every time she caught a whiff of her hair her nipples tightened.

Annie didn't know how she did it, but somehow she managed to talk herself out of crawling back into bed with trusty old B.O.B. Instead, she changed into jeans and a T-shirt, then, afraid he was still parked outside her door as he had been when she'd checked earlier, she did what any mature woman in her situation would do.

She quietly climbed out the window and ran for her car, sure to rev the engine a few times and wish him a long and loud good morning honk just in case he was still asleep. But as she peeled out of the driveway, an irritating thought jumped into her head.

Had she outsmarted him, or played right into his hand?

It was a new experience to go unrecognized at her place of work, and Annie relished her anonymity at Rome General. With her scrubs in her bag and a bouquet of wildflowers in hand, she wasn't dressed the part of physician's assistant.

In Connecticut, that wouldn't have mattered. She would have been spotted, and approached, by a dozen colleagues and patients before she'd even cleared the lobby. There would be questions—so many questions—about the wedding, her feelings, Clark, until eventually the inquisitors would arrive at the questions everyone wanted to ask: Why did *she* think Clark had called it quits?

If Annie knew the answer to that, then she wouldn't have had to relocate for perspective.

Here in Rome, Annie was an unknown. A fresh face, able to walk the halls of the ICU undetected. Able to focus on providing the kind of unconditional nurturing that had drawn Annie to medicine in the first place. She wanted to spend her days proving that every person deserved to be cared for.

Today, that person was Gloria, a retired school bus driver who needed a little extra in the care department. Could benefit in some support to help her overcome her fear of hospitals long enough to have her gallbladder removed. Annie wasn't there

to read Gloria's chart or take her pulse. She had come to the hospital hours before her shift began simply to hold the older woman's hand.

No one deserved to feel alone.

The ICU was uncharacteristically quiet as Annie made her way to Gloria's room. She lay in the bed closest to the window, her eyes closed, still coming out of the anesthesia. Annie silently walked over to the window.

Outside, the sun was radiant, shining through fluffy white clouds and blue skies. A slight breeze swayed the crape myrtles that lined Main Street, resembling dual rows of bright pink lollipops stretching all the way to the shoreline, where the whitecaps of the Atlantic kissed the sand.

"Are those forget-me-nots?" a sleep roughened voice asked.

Annie turned to find Gloria coming to, her cheeks warm with shy gratitude.

"And some lantana." Annie's hands brushed the brilliant red and orange umbrella-shaped blooms.

"My favorites," Gloria rasped, and Annie poured her a glass of water, then held a straw to Gloria's laugh-lined lips. "How did you know?"

"Delores at The Watering Can might have mentioned it."

"They're beautiful." Gloria's smile turned serious as she checked the door. "No one's looking, go check that chart there and tell me when it looks like I'll be going home. If it doesn't say today, then let's do a little fixing until it does."

"I am not looking at your chart, because I'm not your surgeon." Plus, they both already knew Gloria wasn't going home today. Gallbladder surgery was usually an outpatient procedure, but Gloria would be kept for two days because there was no one at home to care for her.

And if there was one thing being adopted had taught Annie, it was that traditional families didn't have a lock on from-the-heart caring.

Annie placed the vase of bright flowers on the empty table and took the seat next to the bed. She wasn't just the day's first visitor. She'd be the only visitor.

"How are you feeling?" Annie asked, taking Gloria's frail hand between her own.

The older woman gave a tentative smile, her fingers delivering a warm squeeze. "I'm better now."

Gloria silently watched Annie, as if wanting to cling to her company and enjoy the feeling of not waking alone, but her lashes soon began to slip lower until finally coming to rest on her cheeks.

Annie waited until she could hear even breathing, then headed into the hallway to call Gloria's sisters in Canada. Being the bearer of good news and giving loved ones peace of mind was a highlight of the job. Witnessing the love shared between family members was always so fascinating and Gloria's sisters did not disappoint. Even two thousand miles and an international border hadn't diminished the deep bond among the three older women.

The connection between siblings had always been as interesting to Annie as it had been isolating. She'd been born the youngest of three in Vietnam but raised as an only child in America. She had no recollection of her sisters, but even before Annie had heard her adoption story, she had always felt the absence of her siblings.

Every adoptee had their own story, retold around the family table every Adoption Day. In Annie's house, Adoption Day was as big a celebration as birthdays or Thanksgiving. And as her family cuddled up on the couch, and her mom opened the love-worn pages of her adoption album, Annie would find herself unable to breathe until they arrived at the part about her sisters.

She didn't know their names or their ages, only that there were three in total. All with shiny black hair and rich coffee-colored eyes, and all sharing the same dimples when they smiled. And for most of her life, the knowledge that they were out there brought some much-needed solace when the loneliness tucked her in to bed at night.

Was the love of a sibling more powerful than the love of another person because it was preordained from the moment of birth? If so, then what did it mean for someone such as Annie who was chosen by strangers to receive their love.

Annie had always thought that love, in any form, could be nurtured into the kind of unbreakable connection Gloria and her sisters shared. It was why she held so tightly to those in her life, because even when love changed forms, it was still love. Wasn't it?

After last night, when Emmitt had accused her of being a pushover, she began to wonder if maybe she was willing to hold on to love even when it was no longer healthy. Her talk with Clark had felt anything but healthy, leaving her feeling discounted and used.

And that wouldn't do. Not unless Annie was trading in her lab coat to become a Professional Practice Fiancée. So after ending the wellness call with Gloria's sisters, Annie gave herself a stern pep talk and made another pressing call—this one for her own peace of mind.

Clark was the one who said, above all else, he wanted to remain friends. Well, he was going to get his chance to prove himself. And Annie would get her chance to prove that remaining friends with an ex wasn't only doable, it could be healthy if done right.

Afraid she'd chicken out, Annie stepped into an empty exam room and immediately dialed. Her heart raced faster with each ring, until it stopped cold when he answered.

"I am so glad you called." His voice was bright and cheerful, as if he'd slept like a king last night. As if she were being silly and the past few months had changed nothing between them, leaving Annie painfully confused.

"You are?" She'd imagined this call going differently. In fact, she'd made a mental list of approximately ten thousand things to do *instead* of calling Clark—labeling sample tubes, buying doughnuts in desperate need of a home, fixing the leaky faucet in exam room nine—but it turned out she hadn't needed to.

Annie was about to set some boundaries and, it seemed, Clark was ready to acknowledge them.

"Of course. I wanted to apologize about last night. I got off the phone and felt like a dick. Emotions were high, and I wasn't

really thinking before I spoke. And you called it, there was no patient waiting. I was avoiding the inevitable."

"I think I have been too," she admitted. "Last night was an awkward situation, and we both could have handled it better." Annie thought back to what Emmitt had said. Make it simple, straightforward, and leave zero room for misunderstanding. "But the only way things will start to feel normal between us again is to clear the air."

Look at her go, confidently putting it out there. No softening or sugarcoating, just stating the facts and clarifying the game plan.

"You can't believe how happy that makes me," he said. "I not only felt like a dick, I felt as if I left you hanging. Afterward, I talked with Molly-Leigh, and she pointed out just how badly I'd blown it. I knew I needed to make things right. So I stopped by the post office this morning on my way in to work."

"Wow, Clark, that's great." And it had been so easy. "I thought you'd Venmo it along with the invitation money and cake deposit, which I got this morning by the way, so thanks for that. But if you'd prefer to settle the rest by check, that totally works too."

It would take a couple more days than she'd planned, and the bank might not clear a check of that size right away, but come Monday, she'd be cuddled on her own couch with a bottle of wine and a large pepperoni and green olive pizza all to herself.

"A check? What are you talking about?"

"The deposit for the venue. You dropped it in the mail, right?"

"What I put in the mail was an invitation to the wedding," he said as if she had somehow lost her mind. "We settled the venue issue last night."

"Actually, no. You said it would make things easier if you could wait until after the wedding to pay me back. I said that didn't work for me. It still doesn't. I need the money, this week."

"See, this is what I've been talking about. You and me, we're not the same as we used to be. You never used to freak about things like a deposit or a dress. It's like we're . . . I don't know . . ."

"Broken up?"

He ignored this. "Ever since you moved, it feels as if we're off somehow. And you know how much I hate it when we aren't on the same frequency. I mean, we vibe, that's what we do."

Surely, Annie misunderstood. She was talking about squaring up, paying off debts so she could move on—literally—and he was using words like *vibe* and *we* when there hadn't been a "we" in months.

"We don't have a frequency, Clark. When you changed the setting from KANW to KMLM, 'we' were no longer 'vibing,' which is why I have an issue with your keeping my money for another five weeks. *Five weeks.* I'm not freaking out, I'm moving on. So inviting me to your wedding is completely inappropriate."

"Inappropriate?" He, honest to God, sounded hurt by her words. "For the past six years, you have been the single most important relationship in my life. Nothing will change that."

"The ring on Molly-Leigh's finger says otherwise."

"So I'm getting married. So what? Molls knows how much I rely on you," he said, and Annie wondered how she'd ever considered him a sweet talker. "One day you'll get married too—that doesn't mean we can't be each other's rock."

"That's exactly what it means."

"Look, I didn't take your call to argue, I wanted to tell you that I blew it last night, not extending the invitation properly. Nothing would make me happier than for you to share in that special day with us," he said.

"You handed over your future happiness to another woman, Clark. I'm no longer responsible for your feelings."

"But you've put so much into this wedding, Annie," he went on as if she hadn't even spoken. "You deserve to enjoy the product of all the hard work. I invited your parents and assumed you'd know that invitation extends to your whole family, but I wanted to make sure I was clear. We want you at the wedding, Anh Bon."

She cringed. "You invited my parents?"

"Of course. How could I not? Maura's like a second mother to me."

Betrayal stuck to her ribs and pushed at her sternum. "Because she's *my* mom. And if you invite her, you know she'll feel obligated to say yes?"

"She should say yes and so should you. Even Molly-Leigh hopes that you'll come. She told me to pass along that she's saved you a seat at our table for the rehearsal dinner, so we can catch up. I've missed you."

Annie closed her eyes to keep the pain from spilling over. The only reason a woman wouldn't mind her man's very recent ex-fiancée coming to her retrofitted wedding was if she knew for certain the ex posed no threat. And while Annie had zero romantic interest in Clark now, it still stung to think his love for her had been so superficial that it was insignificant.

It was devastating that a single word summed up six years of her life. The most important romantic relationship she'd ever had was insignificant.

She tried to get angry, tried to picture Emmitt handing her that sticky note, but that one word seemed to take all the steam out of her. She wished she could be the woman to tell Clark to fuck off, but what was the point when her love was nothing more than a passing note in the life of the man she'd thought to marry.

This was why Annie subscribed to the head-down, pick-your-battles method of coping. She was about to turn the big three-oh and still hadn't found the right battle. But she knew in her heart, this wasn't it.

"I wish you well, Clark, I really do, but I won't be at your wedding. And I can't be your go-to person anymore. It hurts, and as long as you still have the power to hurt me, this won't work," she said, leaning forward and resting her forehead on the exam table. "I need some space. Some time away from you, the wedding, my parents, so I can figure things out."

Time away to figure out why she kept choosing people who didn't choose her back. To discover how she'd gone from blushing bride to Hartford's resident PPF.

More important, it was critical for her to understand what major life lesson she still had to learn to avoid ever finding herself in this situation again.

She thought back to her grandparents' house. To the wedding picture that hung above the fireplace in the living room.

As a child, Annie would wait until everyone was asleep before sneaking into the living room to stare at the photo in wonder. She used to believe it was her grandmother's dress that captivated her. As she grew older, Annie realized it was the way her grandparents looked at each other that made the risk of getting caught out of bed worth it.

Even through the photograph's patina of age, the unbreakable connection between the two had been visible. The love, mind-boggling. *They* were each other's person.

Clark had never looked at her that way. And, if she were being honest, she hadn't looked at him that way either. Annie feared she'd fallen victim to the fantasy of what marriage and happily ever after would mean for her.

She was too old to put stock in fantasy and fairy tales.

Especially after she'd accidentally come across Clark's Insta feed where he was looking at Molly-Leigh with the same adoration as her grandparents in that photo. It proved that a picture could be worth a thousand words.

Or at least as many as Annie needed to close all doors leading to Clark.

She'd closed a lot of doors over her lifetime. Just once, she wanted to be standing on the other side with someone holding her hand when the door slammed shut. Looking at her the way Grandpa Cleve always looked at Grandma Hannah.

Neither of them said anything for a long moment, just listened to the other breathe. The silence wasn't uncomfortable or weighted down with tension as Annie had imagined it would be. And the ache that was always wrapped around her like a leash, yanking her around at will, was gone. In fact, this was the lightest she'd felt since Clark had dropped to a knee and she'd said yes.

"Can you give me that?" she asked.

"Time? I can give you all the time you need," he said with sudden pep in his tone. "Just don't take too long. The wedding is right around the corner and—"

"I already said no."

"—the invite's already in the mail."

"Doesn't matter. You said you were waiting for my answer. Which, unless there's ten grand in that invite, is absolutely not."

"I'll see you at the wedding, Anh-Bon."

"It's not happening." Silence. "Clark?" But he'd hung up.

"Damn it!" She hung up, too, then immediately redialed his number. It went directly to voice mail. By the time his greeting ended she was fuming.

"Friends don't ask friends to go to stolen weddings, Clark. So, no, I'm not going to your wedding. And I need that deposit back now. Not next month, not at my stolen wedding, not even when the sun hits at the right moment and the hall looks like it's illuminated by a thousand candles. I need it back this week or—"

Her phone chimed that she had a new event on her calendar. She glanced down at the phone's screen and swore.

Clark and Molly-Leigh's Wedding

Pursing her lips, she opened tomorrow's calendar and her fingers punched a new event into the screen.

Send Annie $10,000. Or she'll call your mom.

Only moments after adding Clark to the event, it disappeared. Only to reappear on the day of the wedding—with her as the recipient. She didn't even have time to scream before a text appeared.

**And Mom would love to hear from U.
Tell her I say hi, Anh-Bon.**

"She's not my mom and stop calling me Anh-Bon!"

Chapter 7

Emmitt strolled through the leaded glass doors of Tanner and Tanner Family Practice, and the cool air chilled the sweat beaded on his forehead.

He wasn't sure whether it was walking ten blocks when the thermometer registered in the high eighties, with matching humidity, that had his chest spasming as if he was having a heart attack or if it was simply his body's reaction to the pain slicing through his head.

Bottom line, Emmitt needed a comfortable place out of the direct sun to sit—preferably with AC—before he embarrassed himself on the main strip in town.

Christ. What would his climbing friends say if they saw him now?

Two years ago, he'd climbed Everest with nothing but a rucksack, his camera bag, and ten days at base camp. Today, he'd made it a whole half a mile before oxygen deprivation made it feel as if his chest was about to explode.

If it exploded in Gray's clinic, Emmitt was SOL and would likely spend the next six weeks playing invalid on his couch. Then another scenario came to mind, one involving a sexy nurse-not-nurse who was—*lucky him*—into cheeky cut lace and possessed the softest hands he'd ever had the pleasure of being shoved with.

Would you look at that. Emmitt was suddenly all smiles. Teasing her last night had been fun. Better than fun, amusing. It was also one hell of a diversion from his other problems. Now, though, he needed to focus, get back into fighting shape. At least appear as if he wouldn't buckle under the force of a gentle summer's breeze.

Emmitt had one goal here: Convince Gray to clear him so he could get back to work.

Because, while Gray didn't approve of doctors who fudged on medical forms, Carmen made it clear that she wasn't going to risk sending an injured journalist on any kind of assignment, even the editorial variety—which was total bullshit—until a doctor cleared him. Neither his charm nor his Fear Nothing style of journalism was going to help him this time.

Emmitt had searched for a loophole that would allow him to keep working, without any luck. Carmen seemed fine being down one—take any assignment no matter how insane—journalist, and Emmitt was slowly going nuts being forced to sit stationary while stories were breaking somewhere in the world.

Maybe it was the thrill-seeker in him, or maybe it was that ten-year-old boy who needed answers to impossible questions, but photojournalism was in his blood. He didn't want to be so pretentious as to say it was his calling, but no matter how difficult the topic or how dangerous the landscape, something inside him refused to let it go.

Everyone deserved to have their story told. Emmitt sought out stories from the silenced, the ignored, and the so completely marginalized the rest of humanity was unaware of their struggles.

There wasn't enough time in the world to tell every person's story, but Emmitt was committed to shining the light on as many as possible. So every day he rode the bench over a stupid doctor's note was another missed opportunity to share someone's story.

There was no way Gray would clear Emmitt for work if he knew the extent of the accident and injuries. His co-parent

wasn't the kind of guy who could be bribed, bought, or charmed into looking the other way. Something that shouldn't piss off Emmitt the way it did.

When it came to his work, Emmitt had implemented his own strict code of ethics—and had never wavered. Didn't mean he was above misleading or manipulating a situation if it kept him from the truth. Unfortunately, the good doctor had but one kryptonite—and she was off limits.

Emmitt would bathe in BBQ chip dust and play punch-tag with a rabid grizzly before ever bringing Paisley into this. Which left him with just one option. He wasn't particularly proud of his game plan, but he was desperate. And desperate men did desperate things. Like lie to a man who could remove Emmitt's kidney while he slept.

Dragging in a few deep breaths, Emmitt wiped his brow and entered the waiting room of the clinic. The place was hopping with patients, ringing phones, and intercom pages. Behind the table sat Rosalie, who ran the front office with the efficiency of an air traffic controller.

Emmitt didn't know which was older, the town of Rome or Rosalie Kowalski. As far as he knew, she had been the office manager since before Dr. Tanner Senior hung out his shield sometime in the sixties.

Most people had assumed that when Gray graduated from med school he would come back to Rome and join the family practice. Anyone who knew Gray, like really *knew* him, would explain he was the kind of guy who liked to earn his accolades. Who always took the right path, even when it was the hardest.

Emmitt respected that. Respected him even more when, after his grandfather had a stroke, Gray gave up a lofty position in Boston to help his father with the practice until he could find another partner.

Then he'd met Michelle and decided Rome was where he wanted to be after all. Love was funny that way.

"Well, look who's here," Rosalie said, managing two phones at once. At first glance, the silver bun and perpetually nose-

perched glasses brought to mind a plumper Professor McGona-gall from Hogwarts. But while Rosalie had played Mrs. Claus in every Rome Christmas parade since the beginning of time, she was also the leader of Grannie Pack, a motorcycle club for people fifty-five and older. "Our own hometown hero."

"I don't know about that."

"I bet those women you pulled from the fire would disagree." Rosalie placed a pudgy hand to her chest. "Putting their lives before your own. We couldn't be prouder."

Emmitt itched the back of his neck. "The women?"

"Yes, the group of Future Female Engineers of the World who were visiting the plant the day of the explosion. I heard you saved them all in one fell swoop."

Emmitt cringed. The only way to keep his condition quiet was to say as little as possible. But instead of slowing the gossip, people took his silence as permission to fill in whatever holes were missing from his story.

In small town speak, people were flat-out lying.

"The lengths I'll go through to get a pretty lady's number." The only numbers he'd received were from his doctor. The num-ber of ribs fractured. Number of shrapnel pieces extracted. The number of days he'd been unresponsive. The number of months it would take to recover.

And the number of ways he was damned lucky to still be alive. Twenty-two women, eleven men, and nine children couldn't say the same.

Emmitt had reported on a lot of disasters over his career. One of the worst was a story he'd covered in Iraq when a truck bomb detonated three feet from the walls of a Marine base. It took seventy-three soldiers two weeks to locate all the genetic ma-terial belonging to the fourteen downed Marines, twenty-one civilian contractors, nine local workers, and six naval hospital corpsmen caught in the blast.

Soldiers go into a war zone trained to keep atrocities from happening, but equally trained in case the worst happens. In China, these were day laborers in a concrete plant. Moms and

dads who felt safe enough that many of them brought their young children to the day care located just outside the factory.

The knot in his stomach tightened and squeezed, which made his eyes burn with grit and his head pound double time.

Rosalie watched him with growing concern.

He was tempted to tell her it wasn't necessary. He was concerned enough for the two of them. And, before she got it in her head that he needed feeling sorry for, he flashed her enough pearly whites to thoroughly rattle her. It was one of those half-smile, half-grin deals that released a set of double-barreled dimples he'd hated as a kid but came to appreciate the moment he started *appreciating* women.

"I'm still waiting for your number, Rosalie," he said and, *would you look at that,* it worked like a charm.

He'd rather be home *rattling* his new roomie, but she'd snuck out of the house before he could see what color scrubs she had on today. And wasn't that a damn shame.

"Why are you sweet-talking me, Emmitt?"

"If you have to ask, then you're long overdue for some sweet talk and pampering. So why don't you call that uptight boss of yours out here. I'll set him straight."

"My boss treats me just fine. And he's too busy to be bothered by you."

"So the doc in, then?"

"Depends. You have an appointment?" Rosalie's smile vanished.

"No, but—"

"No appointment. No entry. You know the rules."

Emmitt liked to bend the rules whenever possible, and if he happened to screw with Gray's schedule in the process, all the better. "It will just take a minute."

"Dr. Tanner doesn't have a minute. You see this waiting room?" She pointed to the overly full room of patients. "He has a packed schedule, one of the nurses called in sick, and there's an outbreak of scabies going around the elementary school."

On second glance, Emmitt noticed that the room was filled

with moms and kids. Itching and scratching kids. "Trust me, I'll make it quick."

Emmitt had slept in some of the worst conditions humanity had to offer, dined on crickets before it was a delicacy, and covered every pandemic from malaria to Ebola and a recent outbreak of H1N1. But there was something about little bugs feasting on his skin that wigged him out.

Rosalie shook her head. "It's a no."

"I just need a minute."

"I heard you the first time." Rosalie crossed her arms and looked ready to take him down if necessary.

"Look, golden boy told me to stop by today."

"I have two PhDs," Gray said from the hallway. Glasses on, face buried in a file, he looked to be treating the scabies breakout singlehandedly. "I'm not a boy. And why are you here?" He paused. "Jesus, don't tell me it's because you can't pick up Paisley anymore? You can't bail thirty minutes before on me."

"I'm not bailing," Emmitt said, the *Fuck you, dickwad* clear in his tone. He might have lost a little track of time, but he'd never bail last minute on his kid. Especially not four months after losing her mom. "You told me to drop by. So here I am."

"I told you to drop by this morning." Gray pointed to his watch. "I don't know how time works in your world, but for the rest of us, morning comes after sunrise and before lunch. Come back tomorrow. *Morning.*"

Emmitt didn't have a big brother. Growing up, it was just him and his pops. If he'd had one, though, he imagined the guy would be as annoying as Gray.

"Can't. And I don't want to be late picking up Paisley. That would be . . . what did you guys call it the other day? Oh yeah, a bad dad move." Repeating the comment stung, almost as much as it had when the guys had uttered it last night. "So we'd better make this quick, Doc."

They exchanged glances. Neither one gave.

Gray crossed his arms. Emmitt followed suit. Same went for the glare. But when the boy with the ketchup stain on his upper

lip—who'd been scratching his junk a moment ago—dropped his Matchbox car and it started rolling toward Emmitt, he pointed to Gray's watch.

"Tick tock." He tapped with his middle finger.

"Fine." Gray handed a stack of files to Rosalie. "Could you push back Tommy Harper by five minutes. And if that five turns into six, buzz in and pretend I have a call so I can kick him out."

Offended, *Him* said, "I'm right here."

Gray ignored him and began walking back toward his office.

"Five minutes. I'll be watching my clock," Rosalie said to Emmitt.

He gave a respectful salute, then headed down the hallway, surprised to locate Gray in an exam room instead of his office.

Emmitt walked past the exam table, which was prepped for a thorough checkup, and plopped down on the chair usually reserved for the patient's plus one.

Sitting back, he leaned his head against the wall, sprawled his legs all the way out, sure to take up as much territory as possible. While the position helped with the dizziness and alleviated some of the soreness, he had to admit that the agitated way Gray moved around Emmitt's legs was even better.

Emmitt took great pleasure in ruffling the good doctor's lab coat every once in a while.

"So what brings you in?" Gray asked.

"Do I need a reason to visit my domestic partner?"

"We don't live together, so we aren't domestic partners." Gray took the Velcro thing from the wall and wrapped it around Emmitt's arm—tightly.

Emmitt opened his mouth to respond—and in went the thermometer.

Gray pressed his finger to Emmitt's wrist and silently checked his watch. He was grinning as if he found some kind of sick pleasure in making Emmitt follow the rules.

"How's my pulse?" he asked around the thermometer.

Gray lifted a single brow and struck his serious guy pose. "Did you swim back from China?"

"No."

"Then it's not good."

"The closer my proximity to assholes, the higher it gets."

The thermometer beeped. "It's 98.9." Gray coiled the stethoscope back around his neck and took a seat. "What happened in China? And before you give me some half-baked answer, like you did last night, remember I can order a whole panel of random tests if I think you're wasting my time."

Needles and being controlled were two big triggers for Emmitt. One came from watching a parent slowly die, the other from being on the receiving end of the remaining parent's coping techniques.

"I pretty much told you all of it," Emmitt began, choosing his words carefully. He needed to give enough info so Gray would clear him but not so much that he started asking more questions. "One of the silos failed, whatever warning system was in place failed, and kaboom." His hand became a bomb, his fingers sizzling fireworks.

"What I read online doesn't sound as benign as you're making it out to be."

"It wasn't. Over sixty people died," he said, unable to look anywhere but his lap. "It looked like a war zone, bro." He could still hear the screaming of the people stuck inside who—if they weren't lucky enough to pass out from the toxic smoke—were burned alive. He woke up every night to the lingering scent of smoldering ashes. "I was on the other side of the factory when it blew, so I was nowhere near the blast area. Most of my injuries were from flying shrapnel. I got off easy."

The sound Gray made said he strongly disagreed. "Are you talking to someone about it? These kinds of traumatic—"

"Yes, Dr. Phil. They brought in grief counselors and made all of us talk to someone at the hospital." Emmitt had been unconscious for the first part, and sweet-talked his way out of the last. Rehashing it wouldn't help. The only thing he could think about was getting home and hugging his kid. That hug would feel better than anything some shrink could have given him.

"Good to hear. I started seeing one after Michelle—" Gray cleared his throat. "It helped. A lot." Before Emmitt could ask

how he was doing, the good doctor was back to doctoring. "Did any of that flying shrapnel hit you in the head?"

Emmitt looked him directly in the eye and didn't waiver. A convincing technique he'd picked up while imbedded with a team of SEALs in Fallujah. When people lie, their gaze tended to shy away. Maintaining eye contact was an easy way to convince someone of your truthfulness—even when you're lying.

"Everyone was hit with little particles, but beside some lacerations from concrete and a few bruises, nothing major." Not a lie. It was the crumbling floor above him that did the real damage.

"Then you want to tell me why you couldn't sit still last night? Hell, you couldn't follow the card game."

Yup, Emmitt had been stupid enough to mention the embarrassing shrapnel he'd taken in the ass. Levi had asked him how badly he'd been injured, Emmitt had panicked, and out came the one part of the whole unlucky event that they'd never let him live down.

Better than spilling the truth though. Paisley was clearly having a tough time with her mom gone, and coming clean on all the details would have done nothing but unnecessarily worry her.

"Hard to concentrate on cards when the table is bitching like a bunch of biddies."

"That doesn't explain why you're so moody. Plus, you look like shit. How have you been sleeping?"

"As well as a man can when forced to sleep on his own recliner," Emmitt said, and the dickhead had the nerve to smile, as if finding Emmitt's current living situation hilarious. "Thanks for that, by the way."

"You have a problem, talk to your property manager."

"Levi may have agreed, but I know damn well it was because you pressed him," Emmitt said. "A heads-up would have been nice."

"If you'd kept in touch, I would have warned you." Gray picked up his pen and the little notebook he always carried, as if he hadn't been informed of the computer revolution. "Okay,

here's how this will work. You want me to clear you? You have to be up-front with me."

Emmitt gave a noncommittal shrug. "What more do you want to know?"

"Were there any complications from the blast that you're not telling me?"

"That would affect my ability to read and edit words?" When Gray waited for Emmitt to answer his own question, he sat up, and the sudden movement caused the throb in his head to settle behind his eyes. "No, Gray, I can read and write just fine."

"Doesn't matter. When you're hurt on the job, you need to be fully recovered before returning—you know this."

"You've been talking to Carmen."

He closed his notepad. "I took an oath, which is why I'll need to see the file from the hospital in China before we go any further."

"I don't have one." That was the truth. "They released me. I flew home. The only paperwork I got was a bill for my insurance company. Even if I did have my medical papers from the hospital stay, which I don't, they'd be in Mandarin."

"Then you'll need to call the hospital where you were treated. After they e-mail me their findings, we'll schedule an appointment for a proper checkup."

"Are you serious?" Emmitt scoffed. "Is this because I'm claiming my right to take Paisley to the father-daughter dance?"

Gray lifted a judgmental brow.

Okay, that came out a little angrier than he'd anticipated but, *Jesus effing Christ.* Why did Gray have to be such a Boy Scout all the time? Emmitt wasn't asking for clearance to drop into a hot zone from thirty thousand feet up. All he wanted was to finish the article he'd started, which required a few more interviews and pictures.

His camera and computer had made it back to Rome, but most of his notes and all the digital recordings Emmitt had compiled for the story were accidentally shipped to the home office in New York and were now being held hostage by Carmen.

"How about we make a deal?" The throb in his head had settled firmly behind his eyes. "You send Carmen an e-mail stating that I'm good to go and I promise not to take any new assignments until after the dance."

"Lie to Carmen Lowell?" Gray laughed. "That woman isn't going to let you off the hook until you apologize for every transgression since you met her."

"Which is why I need a doctor's note. Then it wouldn't be up to her. HR would step in and she'd have to let me finish the story."

"Did you ever stop to think that maybe the order came from HR and Carmen was just the messenger?"

No, Emmitt hadn't. He'd been so frustrated by the entire situation that he'd just assumed it was another one of her Carm-trums. "Remember when she sent me on a last-minute assignment to Moscow, booked me a flight that landed at three a.m. in the middle of January, only the person I was supposed to interview was in Moscow, Kansas?"

"And the story wasn't even yours to cover?" Gray had the nerve to laugh. "I warned you about mixing business and pleasure, Em. What can I say, you made your bed—not my problem that she's still pissed to no longer be in it. But backburning a story and having to redo the entire layout of the magazine seems a little extreme, even for Carmen."

"I'm not so sure." But if Carmen wasn't behind it, that meant the higher-ups made the call, and he needed to get Gray on board more than ever.

"Either way, you see why I have to do this by the book. If I clear you and then you're further injured on the job, I'm opening up myself and the hospital to a lawsuit."

"We both know I'd never sue you," Emmitt scoffed. "You're just making shit up because you get off controlling my life."

"Life isn't always about you and what you need, Em," Gray said in that calm zen way of his that pissed Emmitt off. "When my practice merged with Rome General, I had to adopt an entire binder of rules and a board I answer to. We can't all run around the world making up the rules as we go."

As far as direct hits went, that one sank his proverbial battle-ship.

Emmitt didn't globe-trot just for the hell of it. He had bills to pay, a college fund to contribute to. His job afforded him the opportunity to take Paisley on amazing trips around the world and explore places she'd never know of otherwise. She wasn't old enough to have a driver's license, but she had a stamp in her passport from four of the seven continents. Her upcoming graduation present—visiting the penguins of Antarctica—would bring that number to a whopping five.

From the moment Paisley had come into Emmitt's life, Gray had always managed to have the advantage. He had a say in what weekends and holidays Emmitt got to spend with his own kid, how Paisley was raised. He even had the nerve to school Emmitt on what kind of gift was considered "too extravagant."

Yes, Gray had been in Paisley's life since before she could remember. And yes, Emmitt was thankful every day that Michelle had someone to help her raise Paisley. But just because Gray had showed up first to the race—a race Emmitt didn't even know he'd been entered in until Paisley had turned five—that didn't make him a better dad.

"You're right, I don't play by the rules. Funny how if it benefits you, like when I didn't go after custody when Michelle died, it's the noble thing. But when there's nothing in it for you, I'm being selfish."

Gray went so very still he didn't even breathe. He just sat as if trying to register what Emmitt had said. When he spoke, it was barely a whisper, "You considered going for custody?"

"Damn right I did. She's my kid."

"She's mine too," Gray said, and Emmitt watched as the truth settled on the other man like a concrete slab. "Are you still? Thinking of going for custody?"

"I don't know." It was an honest answer to a difficult question he'd been struggling with since the day Paisley had called him in hysterical tears to tell him about Michelle's accident. At the time, he knew leaving her in her childhood home was the right call.

But a lot had happened since then, and Emmitt had started questioning his decision.

"Paisley is my life," Gray said. "The day I asked Michelle to marry me, I also asked Paisley if I could be her stepdad. And the day of the accident when I went to see Michelle, I promised I'd take care of Paisley."

"That's the thing, man," Emmitt said, standing so he could face Gray head-on. "You always assume you're the only one fit to take care of her. Did it ever cross your mind that she has a dad to keep her safe and wipe away the tears? That she has me?" Emmitt pressed his palm to his heart, as if the act alone would heal everything.

"How could I? You never let me forget," Gray accused. "But you always manage to forget that I'm the guy who's raised her since she was small."

"Not by my choice. If I'd known I had a kid, I would have been there from day one."

"I know." Gray sat down, resting his forehead in his palm. "Michelle said it was her biggest regret. But she also made it clear, she wanted Paisley to live with me."

Emmitt sat too. Or maybe his legs gave under the mounting insecurity that nugget of information had caused. "I know."

"Stability and routine are extremely important for a kid who is suffering loss. Mixing things up now could have horrible repercussions."

"I know. You don't need to lecture me."

"I mean, my house is the only home she knows."

"I know, Gray. Which is why I didn't sue." That and because Paisley had told him at the funeral that she wanted to stay with Gray. It wasn't a great conversation; in fact, it made Emmitt question what he was doing wrong. It seemed the longer he stayed in Rome, the more problematic his presence became, until every step forward with his family felt as if it complicated their routine—which was so vital to keeping Paisley's life on track.

After the funeral, tensions were at an all-time high, and Paisley struggled to keep it together, spending more and more time

away from home to avoid talking about her feelings. The last thing she needed was one more dad asking her how she was handling things.

In the end, Emmitt felt about as effective as a pinball machine flipper. All he wanted was to be her rock during that painful time. What he became was one more bumper for her to collide with, so he accepted an assignment where he felt useful—and Paisley had one less person to worry about.

"She's my world. Especially now with Michelle gone." Gray's voice hollowed out on the last word. "She's as much my kid as if she were biologically mine. Loving someone more would be virtually impossible."

And when he met Emmitt's gaze, a blast of raw agony hit him square in the chest. It was almost as humbling as the guy's love for Paisley. That was what always kept Emmitt in check. That another man in the world loved Paisley as fiercely as Emmitt.

Last night, Annie had implied he rattled people for amusement, and he'd quickly laughed it off. Listening now to Gray, Emmitt didn't feel much like laughing.

"Don't worry," he said. "She isn't going anywhere anytime soon. Where she wants to stay is her choice. I don't like that it's your place, but I'd never put her in a situation where she felt she had to choose between us. And I'd never stand in the way of her happiness."

"Same," Gray said with a rough chuckle, calling a truce.

Emmitt didn't mind ruffling the good doctor's lab cost occasionally, knocking him off his high horse. Michelle had always let the guys have their fun with each other—because they were all jackasses—but now they'd lost their buffer.

They'd lost the heart of their patchwork family. And they were all feeling her absence. The loss of her love.

"Paisley loves you, Em. She loves when you are around, and when you're gone she talks about you constantly. You're the fun dad, the one she brags about. Her love for me doesn't detract from the way she loves you."

The warm burst Emmitt usually experienced when talking about his daughter was slow to come. This time it was over-

shadowed by a dull longing that had slowly built over the past few months.

God, he was homesick. But for some unexplained reason, Emmitt didn't feel as if he'd made it home yet. In thirty minutes he was going to see his baby for the first time in months, and he felt about as uncertain as the first day he'd met her.

Chapter 8

For once, Annie wanted to know where she was going to land before she took off.

As Rome General's newest floater, her schedule was in constant flux. Besides the afternoons, when she filled in for Dr. Tanner, her shifts consisted of one surprise after another. Annie hated surprises, almost as much as infuriating landlords who dropped in unannounced.

Her new job was a lot like men: inconsistent and predictably unpredictable. Only on the hospital floor there was no window to crawl out of. No door to hide behind. And absolutely no room for error.

Annie had left Connecticut with the intent to shake things up a little, put some of the fun and excitement she'd been missing back into her life. But a little stability here and there would be nice. She missed the comfortable rhythm she'd mastered at her previous job. The friendships she'd fostered, the confident stride she'd adopted the moment she slid on that lab coat.

She was unflappable and unstoppable.

But here, every day seemed like a new opportunity for the universe to flip her the big one. It was as if she were trapped in a bizarre Groundhog Day loop that played the same twenty-four hours over and over. Only the obstacles were different, the learning curve steeper, and she was always the new kid on the ward.

While her morning had started out great, with Gloria laughing and telling stories about growing up as a triplet, by the time Annie was ready for her shift, she was still feeling a lingering ickiness from her call with Clark that she needed to shed.

Annie pulled on her lab coat and waited for Alicia Keys's song "Girl on Fire" to start playing in her head. Waited for the bass of life to kick in, the crackle of energy to thump against her chest.

All she felt was heartburn.

Resigned, she went to the nurses' station and checked the posted schedule: ER duty followed by a few hours in oncology and ending with the only constant in her day, family practice.

She started off strong, treating a set of siblings with strep throat, a sprained ankle, and three cases of the flu. Then the attending doctor asked her to take a patient to radiology to get an MRI, which the doctor assured her was scheduled.

It was not.

By the time she straightened things out, she was informed the MRI was no longer needed. From there, she spent the rest of her day playing catch-up. For a woman who listed "Accountability" as the second most important trait in a potential significant other—right beneath "Looks at me the way I look at pizza"—Annie's new life was about as predictable as a bouncy ball in a glass shower.

Every day brought a new department, new faces, and a whole new set of challenges. Even her patients were a complete mystery right up until the moment she walked through the exam room door.

The only thing she could count on lately was ending her day eating a large pepperoni pizza with green olives, drinking an extra-large glass of wine, while snuggling on the couch for some one-on-one time with good old Stephen Colbert, who managed to charm her with his wit and humor—numbers five and seven on her Boyfriend Checklist.

She couldn't cope with losing the comfort of that routine. Not after her chat with Clark. And not to some smooth-talking

playboy who needed a pack of sticky notes to keep his dates organized.

A strong motivator for Annie to spend her breaks trying to devise a solution to her living predicament. *Trying* being the operative word. A quick search online told her that without her ten thousand dollars, moving out wasn't an option. Late summer was still peak season for tourists, leaving rent prices and her pocketbook as incompatible as Annie and her new roommate.

She needed a plan.

By the time Annie had completed her stint in the ER and was headed over to the oncology department, she'd managed to eliminate every possible option except two: get Clark to return her ten thousand dollars or force Emmitt to move.

Option one hinged on going to her own wedding as a guest. There was no way Clark was going to give her the money beforehand, and hiring a lawyer would take too much time—and money. Even so, she was no-way no-how not-enough-wine-in-the-world going to that wedding. Which left option two.

Force Emmitt to move.

It wouldn't be an easy task. Emmitt was about as moveable as a cement truck with four flats and as sympathetic as the IRS. No, she'd have to get creative if she wanted Stephen and her pizza all to herself.

Her stomach rumbled at the thought. Oh wait, it was her cell phone vibrating in her shirt pocket. She fished it out, read the text, and—*oh my God*—closed her eyes. But that was a bad idea because the dark reminded her of things that glow, which brought to mind a particular pair of boxers that—

Oh no. This wouldn't do.

Annie's eyes snapped open, letting in all the light, but that didn't help one bit. Because in the light she could picture exactly who was wearing those boxers and what he looked like in them.

Pressing her phone to her chest, screen to skin, Annie glanced around the hallway and, when she was certain no one was looking, ducked into an empty exam room.

Deep breaths. Deep breaths.

Once inside, she reread the four words on the screen.

What are U wearing?

It was followed by a second text.

U act like white cotton but we both know U prefer silk & lace.

Annie paced the room, deciding exactly how to reply. She didn't need the phone to register anything other than Unknown Caller. The way her right eye twitched told her exactly who was annoying her.

How did you get my number?

She watched the three dots blink at the bottom of the screen. They blinked so long, she anticipated a lengthy reply. All she got was:

Rental agreement.

It was followed by a picture of her rental agreement. A bright pink "For a Good Time Call" was written above her number, and "Snores" was added to the disclaimer section at the bottom of the sheet.

That's for emergency use only.

This is an emergency.

The dots disappeared, then reappeared, only to disappear again, and Annie's hands began to sweat at the possibilities. The only person she'd given the house number to was her mom, and her mother would call there only if she couldn't reach Annie by cell. She was about to check her missed calls when his text came through.

> **We need to discuss what we're having for dinner . . .**

Was he serious? Of course he was. His black book was a collection of sticky notes. Stabbing the screen, she typed back.

> **There is no we! Discussion over.**

Releasing a tired breath, she rested her head against the far wall and closed her eyes. This time she didn't picture glow-in-the-dark boxers or their owner half naked. No, this time she pictured a brand-new deadbolt on the front door.

"That's a shame, because I was wondering if you wear silk and lace in other shades," an oh-so-smooth voice said from the doorway.

An unexpected—and unwelcome—warmth spread through her body, lighting up parts of her she'd forgotten had been extinguished. Bracing herself, she turned around and—*look out, trouble*—there stood her temporary roommate in the doorway, grinning like a big, bad decision ready to tempt some poor, unexpecting woman into throwing caution to the wind.

Annie might be poor, but she knew exactly what to expect when it came to men like him. "My lingerie is none of your business."

"Isn't that a shame." He flashed a smile that said *I'm yours— for tonight, anyway.*

"I was hoping for some light blue or maybe teal."

"Most men would say red," Annie said, wondering where the intuitive guy who'd called her Anh had disappeared to.

"I'm not most men."

Wasn't that the truth. Even fully clothed, and with the charm dialed down to panty melting, he made it hard for her to speak without her breath getting stuck in her throat.

Even in flip-flops and low-slung button-fly jeans, he looked delicious. Then there was the French blue button-up that hung loose and rolled at the sleeves, as if he couldn't be bothered to tuck it in. Up top he sported a well-loved ballcap, mirrored aviator glasses, and a cocky grin.

"What are you doing here?" she asked.

"I was next door chatting with Gray, then got distracted by a familiar pair of scrubs and came by to say good morning."

"Oh, you mean you were chatting with Gray about what's under the hat and glasses," she said.

"Want me to disrobe, Nurse Annie?" Emmitt hopped up on the exam table. "All you have to do is ask."

He shot her one of those smiles she was getting to know, but it was a little strained at the corners, and something about the way he was acting felt off. Curious, she played along.

"How about we start with the hat and glasses? I like to see my patients' eyes when they're bullshitting me."

"Didn't know I was your patient." He removed his glasses and set them on the exam table—the hat stayed on. It didn't matter; his golden-brown eyes locked on hers and something entirely inappropriate began to heat south of the border—not to mention in a few northern colonies.

"I was in the lab and heard that there's a poll going around about how you were injured," she said, watching him to see how he reacted. "The pot is up to three hundred and twenty dollars. Barb in phlebotomy is convinced you were hurt while rescuing a church full of virgins. Janice in urology said you helped a group of lost hikers climb down Everest."

Resting his palms next to his thighs, he leaned forward. "What do you think?"

She studied him for a good long minute, noting the way his

eyes dilated, the fine line that started at his temple and disappeared beneath his hat, and how his head was tilted so the bill of his cap shaded his face. Most of all, she noticed a flash of uncertainty that she could relate to.

"I think that whatever happened in China really shook you," Annie said quietly. "I think that your injuries are worse than you're letting on, and I think you sought me out because you're lonely and I'm the only person in your world who didn't know you before, so you don't have to worry that I'll notice the changes."

A slow smile spread across his face, but it never reached his eyes. "You didn't wow me, but you certainly haven't left me bored," he said. "As for your observation skills, a factory exploded, so half of China was shaken. Like I told Gray, flying concrete sucks but I've got nothing that won't heal. And I sought you out"—his smile turned genuine—"because I like talking to you and I didn't get the chance to wish you good luck with your special patient before you climbed out the window."

"Oh," she said, surprised that he'd remembered. It had been late, they'd both been tired, and he'd been in pain, yet he remembered. "Gloria is her name, and she's doing great. She should be ready to go home with part-time help in a couple of days. Thank you for asking."

"Thank you for sharing."

"I think I did wow you," she ventured, and his expression told her she was correct.

"I imagine you wow everyone you meet," he said, and her heart went a little gooey.

And then, because he was being so sweet and she had an ethical obligation to tell him, she confessed, "I saw your file this morning. I was taking a few patients off Gray's plate this afternoon and there it was, right on top. So I peeked."

He seemed to be amused at her confession. "And what did you learn?"

Uncomfortable with the formal way they were situated—him on the exam table, her facing him as if she were treating him—she stood next to him and rested a hip against the table. "That

you're home on a medical furlough. And employers don't like for their people to spend their days at home texting a roommate on the company dime."

"Roommate? I'm growing on you."

"Temporary roommate." It wasn't as if she could kick him out of his home now. Before, when he was just being sexy and irritating, he was fair game. "I'd look like a jerk now, kicking the hometown hero out of his own house and throwing him to the mercy of the single ladies of Rome."

"This hometown hero won't be home for long," he said. "This is more a case of 'exes can't be friends'—my boss is benching me for personal reasons, claiming HR won't let me work until I've been cleared."

"You slept with your boss?" Annie gasped.

"She wasn't my boss at the time." He laughed. "But yeah, we dated a few years back and it burned hot and fast. When she started talking about mingling families, I knew it was time to call it quits. I don't bring that part of my life home, ever. So I broke it off with her, left on good terms, and took an assignment overseas. When I came back, she'd been promoted to senior editor, and here we are."

"And here we are?" she repeated, sending him a disbelieving glance. "Clearly things weren't as clear-cut as you thought. *We want different things* doesn't make a woman hold a grudge for a *few* years."

He shrugged. "Shortly after I got back from the assignment, I ran into her at a bar. She was with her girlfriends. Bad timing, because I was making friends with a girl."

"Ah." Annie laughed. "And how long was this assignment?"

"Two weeks." At least he had the decency to sound sheepish. "I walked over and hugged her, asked about her dog, then bought them a round. I knew she was uncomfortable, so I left and went to a different bar."

"With the other girl?" Annie didn't even need to ask—she already knew the answer. "Seriously?"

Again with the shrug.

"Does your ex have a name? Because it would break my heart

if, when Clark talked about me, he referred to me as *she* or *her*. I'd hope that after sharing so much, he'd call me by name and not a pronoun."

"Carmen." He nodded gently. "Her name is Carmen. And you're right, I never thought of it that way."

"Can you see that maybe she did?" Annie asked, because *hello?* What was he thinking? "You knew she was upset seeing you and you left, but you took the girl you'd just met? That's shitty."

"Is this some kind of girl code thing?" he asked, and she caught a glitter of amusement in his eyes. "You stick up for each other even if you've never met?"

"I'm not sticking up for her," Annie said, thinking back to the day she'd found out about Molly-Leigh. The humiliation she'd felt after spending the entire day doing rounds, talking to colleagues, catching awkward glances from her peers, clueless that Clark had announced to the world that he'd finally found love. Meaning he'd never loved Annie in the forever kind of way. "I've been her and it sucks."

"I have always been straight with women, Ann." His words were spoken softly but delivered with conviction. "I've never cheated or lied, and I don't make promises I can't keep. I don't know what you went through, but I know it crushed you and that pisses me off."

She was so lost in what he was saying, she didn't even see his hand until it was resting on her upper arm. But there it was, palm flattened against her skin, his fingers gently brushing back and forth in a soothing pattern.

"You know what else gets to me?"

Annie swallowed and shook her head. A slow heat started at his fingers and wound its way up to the hairs that were brushing the back of her neck. Each follicle sparking with sexual awareness.

"The idea that you think I'm a bad guy. I'm not saying I'm a good guy, and maybe I could have handled it better, but the bottom line was that Carmen needed me to be someone I'm not, and pretending isn't my thing. I felt awful that our first time running into each other happened the way it did, but it wasn't intentional."

Deep down, Annie believed him. Trusted that he'd never intended to hurt Carmen. He wasn't callous or mean. In fact, in the short time she'd known him, he'd proven himself to be a warm and genuinely caring person. Yet his thoughtless decision had hurt Carmen in a way that had probably shaped the last few years of her life, and Emmitt wasn't seeing the big picture.

"When I saw a photo of Clark and Molly-Leigh on social media just weeks after our breakup—"

"I'm not Clark," he said sharply, a little defensive for someone who claimed to have "left things on good terms."

"I'm not saying you are," Annie said calmly, noticing that even though he was a little prickly, he hadn't moved his hand. In fact, it was now resting on the curve of her neck, his thumb sliding behind the curve of her jaw. "I'm only trying to explain how she might have felt. I knew Clark would move on quickly— he doesn't do single very well—but when he posted that he'd found *his person* so soon after our breakup, it was like I had to relive the breakup all over again. Friends called to console. My parents hovered. I saw Clark at work every day and he'd never told me he was seeing someone seriously. It hurt almost as bad as his breakup text."

"He broke up with you by text?" Emmitt's hand tightened. "Now that's shitty."

"It was." Annie laughed. It was easier to joke about it now, but at the time it had caused her to question everything about her life. "But so is leaving a bar with a virtual stranger in front of your very recent ex."

Emmitt leaned back against the wall and ran both hands down his face. "Jesus, I should've just called it a night and headed home alone. I really screwed that up, didn't I?"

"Maybe you should tell her that." Annie placed a hand on his arm. "It sounds like Carmen invested a lot of herself in you and your relationship. Maybe all she wants is for you to acknowledge what you both lost. I know it would have helped me."

"I'm not a good investment, Annie," he said quietly. "I've never hidden that from anyone."

Chapter 9

When someone stated who they were, Annie had learned it was best to listen. Which was why she made a mental sticky note and stuck it front and center in her memory.

> *"I'm not a good*
> *investment."*
> — *Emmitt Bradley,*
> *Rome's self-proclaimed*
> *heartbreaker*

As sad as his statement was, he clearly believed it and was determined to live his life as if it were the truth. So no matter how fiercely her heart argued that he was wrong, Annie's head was telling her to steer clear. Which left her with only one option: She had to find a way to get her wedding deposit back so she could rent a new place.

After a quick stop at Holy Cannoli—the best Italian bakery this side of the Vatican—where she picked up a piece of limoncello pie, Annie headed toward the nurses' break room. She'd

barely turned the corner when she became aware of excited chatter and energy in the air right outside the door.

Informally called the Fortress of Solitude, it was the only place nurses could go—besides their car or the bathrooms—to escape the noise, the headaches, and the doctors.

Surgeons, PAs, and doctors were persona non grata, with Annie being the exception. Sometimes being the exception came with perks.

The nurses took pity on the floater *and* new girl, awarding her temporary membership. Sometimes, Annie wondered if it was just because they needed someone to clean out the fridge every Friday. Either way, she was grateful.

Annie opened the door and was immediately waved over by Beckett Hayes, Rome's personal concierge who specialized in getting shit done. She also specialized in training emotional support companions and was a regular in the pediatric ward.

She had short choppy hair, a shorter temper, and the biggest heart of anyone Annie had ever met—one of the many reasons she was Annie's closest friend in Rome. She was also Team Ride or Pie's founding member.

Today Beckett was dressed in a superhero shirt, a frayed denim skirt, and Doc Martens. Today's hero of choice was Captain Marvel. Her boots were fire engine red with mismatched socks peeking out the top, and her chestnut hair was pinned into short pigtails.

At her feet was Diesel, a board-certified English bulldog and emotional support companion who was a favorite with the kids.

"Did you bring the necessities?" Beckett wanted to know.

Annie handed over the box, and Diesel didn't move an inch, but his eyes tracked the box's every move. "Did you text Lynn?"

"She's on her way." Beckett opened the pink pastry box and froze. Over the lid she said, "Limoncello pies with chocolate ganache? This must be some problem."

Annie slipped off her purse and hung it over the couch arm. "Do you think I'm a pushover?"

"What did Clark want this time?" Beckett guessed with a

startling confidence that had Annie wishing she'd told Clark to fuck off earlier.

"He invited me to the wedding," Annie said, and someone growled. Annie wasn't sure if it was Diesel or his owner. "He actually called to tell me he dropped, not the money he owes me, but an invitation to the Clark and Molly-Leigh dream wedding in the mail. Can you believe that?"

"That you seemed so surprised concerns me," Beckett said.

Well, damn, clearly the answer to her earlier question was a resounding *yes*, Annie was the queen of pushovers.

Beckett was about to go after the pie when Annie slapped the box shut—on Beckett's hand. "You know the rules. No nibbles until the meeting is called to order. Plus, I'm the one who's been pied, I get the first nibble."

"You already used Clark pieing you off, you can't use it again. Not when limoncello pie with chocolate ganache is in play," Beckett argued. "Double jeopardy, against the rules. Sorry."

Beckett went to open the lid again, and again Annie smacked it closed. "That is nowhere in the rules, and if you'd like to add it to the rules, then it will need to be voted on. When everyone is here."

"Fine." Beckett sighed and put the box in her lap, Diesel still tracking the package. "You might as well sit down then, because you look beat and Lynn was finishing up saying goodbye to her dreamboat. Plus, you look beat."

"I feel awful." Annie plopped down on the couch and leaned her head back against the pillows. Her eyes burned as she closed them. "I barely slept at all last night."

"Girl, if a man is keeping you up all night and you don't get your cookies, then I shouldn't have to tell you something's wrong."

Something was more than just wrong; it was broken. And Annie was afraid that something might just be her.

"The boutique screwed up the wedding dress," she said, her heart giving a painful squeeze at the reminder of just how fragile life plans could be.

"Oh, honey, your grandmother's dress?" Beckett said. "I know how much that dress meant to you."

"It's still in one piece—it just won't ever fit my pieces." Annie tried to shrug it off but just couldn't.

"We can fix it," Beckett assured her. "I am the MacGyver of broken possessions. Between my dad's clumsiness and my brother's outbursts, I have learned that there isn't anything duct tape, fishing line, and a pocketknife can't fix. Just this morning, I handed Thomas a piece of paper and asked him to write down what we needed at the market. When he said he didn't have anything to write on, I told him to use the wall."

Annie laughed into her hand. "Oh no, please tell me he didn't."

"Do exactly as I said? Yep." Beckett looked heavenward as if seeking divine intervention. It was a look Annie had come to know well whenever Beckett relayed her family's day-to-day dealings. "I now have 'tampon' written in marker on my kitchen wall."

Annie burst out laughing; she couldn't help it.

Thomas was Beckett's teenage brother and full-time responsibility. Diagnosed with Asperger's when he was six and Beckett was still a kid herself, Thomas had come to rely on her for a lot of things. Then, a year later, their mom left for work, and somewhere between dropping Thomas off at day care and her office, she decided to relocate to Las Vegas—alone.

They still lived with their dad, who also had Asperger's, although he was higher functioning than Thomas. A brilliant musician who scored a lot of television shows and movies, he could take care of himself. Taking care of his son, though, was often beyond his capacity.

Which left Beckett. She had forgone college to become a personal concierge, a job with enough flexibility to work around her brother's and dad's needs. Even with all that on her plate, she found time to be a good friend.

"Your stories make my life seem boring," Annie admitted.

"I'll trade you one night of boring for a night of Hayes family fun. *Jeopardy!* starts at seven if you want to feel unfit to hold a high school diploma."

"Or you can suffer through dinner with my mother-in-law, who comes in tonight for her end of summer stay," Lynn Vu said, plopping down between Annie and Beckett. "Tonight Ken and I get to tell her the good news, that we've decided to put the baby thing on hold so I can go back and finish grad school."

"Why take on more debt when you'll be home with the babies," Beckett said in her best mother-in-law impersonation.

Lynn snorted. "Exactly."

Lynn was a pediatric oncology nurse—making her a real-life superhero—who completed their Ride or Pie posse. She was petite, patient, and as fierce as a lioness when it came to her patients' recovery. She was also the mother hen of the group, who was never without her Mary Poppins of take-out bags.

"Then these are in order?" Beckett opened the bakery box, and Lynn sucked in a breath.

"Limoncello pie," she said, sighing. "Ken called earlier to say he had a late meeting, so I get his mother all to myself." Lynn pulled out three forks from her bag and passed them around. "I told him, while he's cleaning the house this weekend, I'll be getting pampered at the spa. Anyone want to join?"

"For a girl's day? I so need one of those," Beckett said with a sigh.

Annie sighed right alongside her friend. A day of pampering sounded heavenly. A day to not think about anything except herself would be a dream. The sudden silence said her friends were thinking the same thing. Annie had come into the lunchroom feeling as if life was picking on her. She needed this reminder that everyone's life was hard. Some more than others. And while she was, by no means, the one struggling with the biggest issues, her friends didn't have to go home and face them alone.

Crazy families or not, her friends both had people waiting for them after the workday finished. Annie had her pizza, her wine, and Stephen Colbert, but she didn't have anyone to share them with. Normally that didn't bother her, but for some reason, today it did.

"So when is this girls' day?" she asked. "Because I'm in."

"Not until you set things straight with this whole wedding BS," Beckett said. "No guilty piers allowed to ruin girl time."

"Wait, why are we still talking about Clark?" Lynn asked. "I thought we kicked him to the curb."

"We did," Beckett said. "But he's like that supergerm everyone is terrified of—once you catch him, he just won't go away."

Both of her friends knew the story of her breakup. Had heard it several times. But as Annie launched into the events of the last twenty-four hours, her friends sat speechless. The deeper Annie got into the retelling, the more doormat-like she sounded. By the time she reached the wedding blackmail part of the story, her girls looked ready to fly to Connecticut on Annie's behalf and do some pieing of their own—only Annie imagined they were leaning more toward the steaming kind of pie that one lit on fire and chucked at ex's front doors.

She hadn't had many girlfriends like them back in Connecticut, friends who didn't need to know all the sides and details in order to have Annie's back. They were squarely in her corner simply because they were friends.

It was refreshing to have that kind of person in her life.

"I should call his new fiancée," Beckett said, rubbing her hands together like an evil genius. "Warn her Clark is a habitual runaway groom."

"One time doesn't make it a habit," Annie said.

"If they run once, they'll run again," Lynn disagreed, placing a pie on a plate and handing it to Annie. "And girl code states that someone has to at least give the woman the facts. What she does with them is up to her."

Annie forked off a bite of pie and passed the plate around. "This meeting of the Ride or Pie club has officially begun."

Annie held up her fork and, after tinking with the others, slid it in her mouth. The mix of tart and sweet teased her tongue, and her eyes slid shut while she sighed in ecstasy.

"As for inviting your parents, that was a dick move," Beckett said around her second bite. "I haven't even met your mom and yet I know that she'd take one look at the invitation and be swayed by the card stock paper and embossed white doves."

"You need to call your mom before the invitation arrives and set her straight," Lynn said sternly. "They need to support you, no matter how badly your mom may want to go to the wedding."

"My mom loves to be the one to share news. If she went, it would be so she could tell the neighbors how much better the wedding would have been if she were still the mother of the bride," Annie said, feeling the need to defend her mom.

Even though her mom was nosy and opinionated, Annie never doubted how much her mother loved her. But where Annie was soft-spoken, her mother was like a freight train, and in emotional situations where Annie's instinct was to roll over, her mother often forgot to avoid Annie's tender spots.

Misunderstood? Absolutely.

Unloved? Never a day in her adopted life.

"I mean it's not a huge deal if she goes—"

"No," her friends said in unison.

"It is absolutely, categorically wrong on so many different levels," Lynn said. "You shouldn't even need to have this conversation. But from what you've said about your mom, even I know that this conversation is a must. And soon."

"You needed to be up-front with your mom from the moment the engagement ended," Beckett clarified. "Actually, you needed to be up-front the moment the engagement ended and your mom told Clark he was still welcome at Sunday brunches."

"And after that call, you need to do a wash and repeat with Dickless Wonder." Lynn covered her mouth. "Whoops, I meant Clark. Repeat after me, Anh, 'I am not a pushover.'"

Annie did, ignoring the way her gut hollowed at the thought of confronting her parents. Even though her mom was nosy and her dad easily distracted, Annie always felt cherished. But where Annie sought meaningful connection, her father favored his own company, and her mom tended to ride roughshod over Annie's opinions.

Growing up a tender spirit in a strident household had often caused a young, lonely Annie to look inside herself for ways to diminish the growing distance between family members. It

was a coping mechanism that spilled over into even her current relationships.

Not all relationships were meant to go the distance, but she'd be crushed if one ended because she hadn't tried hard enough.

"I think I'm going to have to do another few wash and repeats," Annie said with a sigh, silently begging the universe for a break. "And I need to get rid of my roommate."

"I didn't know you had a roommate," Lynn said.

"It was news to me too," Annie said, although she was so tired she wasn't all that sure she hadn't dreamed him up. He was more like a nightmare—one hell of an annoying and sexy nightmare. "The owner of the cabin came back early, didn't know the place had been rented out."

"Your roommate is Emmitt Bradley?" Lynn asked, and Annie slapped her hand over her friend's mouth.

"Not so loud," Annie whispered. "I don't want to be the object of the next break room gambling pool. He came home early, and no one told him about me or me about him. Trust me, he was as surprised to find me there as I was to find out he isn't planning on leaving anytime soon."

Lynn slapped Annie's hand away. "I'm still stuck on the part where you spent the night in the same house as Emmitt 'Big O' Bradley and you came in here talking about Clark. We need another piece of pie."

"We *need* to find a way to get rid of him," Annie said. "Both of them. I need a man-free zone."

"Easy, kick him out. If he comes back, throw his things on the lawn and light them on fire. He'll get the message," Beckett said, giving Diesel the empty plate. The dog licked every inch twice, then gave a grunt of pure bliss and lay back down.

"First I think I'll pull out my contract, see what rights I have." She would read it line by line. "The last thing I want is to live with a man right now."

"Especially one you aren't seeing naked on a regular basis," Beckett said. Not for the first time that day, Annie remembered just how good Emmitt had looked in nothing but his boxers. Glowy kitties or not, the man made David Beckham look flabby.

Even worse, he made her tingle.

Claiming it was nothing more than heartburn from having the first half of her cheesecake for breakfast, she said, "I may be in the market for a new place soon."

"You can always stay on my couch." Beckett was back into fix-it mode. "It's lumpy and you'll likely wake up with Thomas staring at you, but it's better than sitting on the toilet when both seats are left up."

"There's always my guest room," Lynn said. "You'd have to share it with Ken's mom for the next eight weeks, but then it's all yours," Lynn said.

Annie lolled her head to the side to look at her friends,

"Thanks for the offers," she whispered, her throat a little tight with emotion over the genuine show of kindness. "But I think I'll need something more permanent. I checked Craigslist and Zillow, but there's not a lot of availability right now. And of the little there is, nothing is in my price range."

"It's the tourists!" Beckett said, and Diesel released a startled fart. "They're like locusts. They come in swarms from New York and Boston, jacking up the prices on everything, crowding the beaches, eating up every reservation in town, stealing all the single men. It makes me wish for early snow."

"I thought you were done with men."

"I am. God, I'm so done with men I might as well burn my Spanx, donate all my sexy heels, and take up speedwalking," Beckett said. "I'm just saying that the only way to get anything in this town is to know someone who knows someone."

Annie gave a toothy grin. "I know you. Do you know someone?"

"If I did, do you think I'd be living in a six-hundred-square-foot studio above my dad's garage?"

"No." Annie flopped back down. "How do locals find affordable housing?"

"Usually someone has to die," Beckett said, one hundred percent serious. "I suggest keeping an eye on the obituaries."

"I think one of my auntie's friends has a summer cottage she might be willing to rent out," Lynn said. "I can also see if any-

one in my cooking group knows of one that might be coming on the market."

"Just like that?" Annie asked, skepticism in her tone.

"Yeah, my cousin might know someone who knows someone and, poof, you have a new place. That's how things work in my world."

Annie wasn't sure what to say. She'd watched how hard Lynn had advocated for a friend's niece who wanted a job at the hospital. Annie admired how close the Vietnamese community in Rome was. It was a small community, but everyone looked out for one another, even reaching down to pull others up with them. Jobs, cars, dating, services, and apparently even housing. Until today, Annie had only been an observer of the community.

Lynn wasn't just Annie's first friend in Rome. She was also Annie's first Vietnamese friend.

Oh sure, Annie kept in touch with the girls she'd met at Heritage Camp. When they were too old to be campers, they became camp counselors, and when they were too old for that, they started planning girls' trips every summer. But they were like her, born in Vietnam, raised by white parents.

They called themselves the In-Bees, in betweeners, with a foot grounded squarely in two separate worlds. Born with Vietnamese features and raised in white communities, In-Bees felt extreme pressure to represent both. And every July the In-Bees reunited for a week of girl bonding, which included drinks that came from a shaker, food that was prepared by someone other than them, and stories and struggles that only an inbetweener could ever understand.

Annie loved her parents for providing a group of friends she looked like and whom she could relate to, even if it was just for a week. Her parents had gone above and beyond to give Annie a taste of her heritage, but she always felt there was a piece missing.

Questions unanswered.

Important questions that she needed to explore before she could be whole. She knew a meaningful connection to her culture wasn't going to be achieved by going to Thet celebrations,

Vietnamese restaurants, or a summer camp. But while she was growing up, it was all that was available to her.

Since moving to Rome, Annie had learned more about what it meant to be Vietnamese from Lynn than she had in all her years in Connecticut. Rhode Island wasn't her dream destination, but it gave her the distance and freedom to explore who she was. And she was starting to find her place here. No way was she ready to leave.

Not yet.

"That would be great," Annie said. "Thanks for offering, and let me know if you hear of something." She shot Beckett a stern look. "That isn't a result of premature death."

"Your loss." With a shrug Beckett reached over to open Lynn's bag.

In seconds the break room filled with a warm, spicy smell that made Annie's lunch feel as if it belonged in her Backstreet Boys pail.

"What is that? It smells amazing."

"Wonton soup. *My mom's* wonton soup," Lynn clarified. Using her hands, she waved the heavenly air in Annie's direction. "I'm bringing the recipe to the next Pho Shizzle meeting." Her face became animated, and she clapped her hands. "You should totally come. You'd help bring the age average down, and you can ask around about rentals."

"I've asked you a dozen times for that recipe and you've never invited me," Beckett said, *after* she helped herself to some of Lynn's lunch.

"I invited you once. You chickened out."

"That's because Nurse Tran was there." Nurse Tran was Rome General's very own Nurse Ratched. Well, to the staff she was. To the patients she came off like everyone's favorite grandmother.

"Wait." Annie held her hands up. "Nurse Tran, who could scare Satan into wetting his pants, is part of a cooking group named Pho Shizzle?"

"She started the group," Lynn said, tilting the bowl and scooping rice into her mouth. "We meet once a month to share family recipes. It's a nice term for a bunch of competitive old

ladies who get together and argue about whose recipe is better. Slurs are thrown, egos are tested, and enemies are made. But everyone always leaves with a full belly. You should come."

"Sounds like a blast," Annie deadpanned.

"It's for serious cooks only," Nurse Tran said, suddenly standing in front of Annie. The woman was old enough to have been Buddha's first disciple, and the look of challenge on her face made Annie wonder if there could be truth to the rumors that Tran had made a murderous biker gang leader cower.

"We all make the same dish and compare—"

"Argue," Lynn corrected.

"—recipes. Then after the winner is chosen—"

"After the other participants are threatened into voting her way," Lynn interrupted again.

"We share secrets and useful tricks—"

"Steal, only to claim your family invented the trick during the Tang Dynasty."

Nurse Tran shushed Lynn before she continued. "This month's dish is *Mì Hoành Thánh*."

"I love dumpling soup." Annie smiled ridiculously big, as if she'd just proven she was fluent in the language rather than adept at reading a takeout menu.

"Good, then you have a family recipe to bring?" Tran said, launching into "Head Nurse" interrogator mode. "It has to be a family recipe, not something from the *Joy of Cooking* or *Martha and Snoop's Potluck* or whatever your generation uses."

Annie looked at her friends and, using every silent gesture from the Wing Girls handbook she knew, silently pleaded for someone to throw her a line. One line would be fine. Even just an encouraging smile of support while she faced the most feared person in the hospital would have helped.

In return, she got a giggle and a snort from Team Ride or Pie. Their message was clear: She'd awoken the beast—she was on her own.

"Yes, my mom's dumpling soup is amazing."

The older woman's eyes narrowed. "From a can?"

Annie stood, bringing herself to forehead level. Meaning her

eyes met the nurse's forehead. Annie had an inch and a half on the woman, easy. "Never."

"No bouillon allowed."

Her friends watched as if this were the final match at Wimbledon.

"From scratch. In fact, neighbors feign the flu just so my mom will bring them some of her soup."

Nurse Tran glowered. "My recipe is six generations old."

"My mom's dumpling soup has been in the family since, uh, the parting of the Red Sea."

She knew the response had thrown the woman slightly off-kilter but, to Annie's amazement, Nurse Tran rallied quickly. "Friday night. Six p.m. Hai Linh will give you the address."

"Hai Linh, that's me." Lynn waved her hand.

"See you then." And because Annie was raised with manners about speaking to her elders, she added, "Thanks, *Bác oi*."

The nurse stopped at the door and turned, piercing Annie with a look that had her shivering. "Hoan."

"Excuse me?" Annie asked, certain the woman had just told her to screw off or something.

"You should always know the name of the person who will annihilate you. Mine is Hoan." With that, Hoan Tran left the Fortress of Solitude.

No one said a word as her threat settled.

Lynn finally broke the silence. "I didn't know your mom cooks dumpling soup."

"Matzo balls are little dumplings floating in broth. How different can it be?"

Chapter 10

The sun was bright, the sky was blue, and Emmitt found himself humming as he strolled up to Rome High School. In a few minutes, the bell would sound and he would be reunited with his baby girl.

He couldn't wait to see the look on her face when she spotted him. Granted, as he walked past the line of cars, each waiting for its respective kid, he felt a little like the idiot who strolled up to the drive-through window on foot.

He'd considered going home to get his car, but since he was already near the high school, he didn't see the point. Plus, until his vision was a little more 20/20 and a little less water-in-the-goggles, Emmitt was going to be huffing it a lot more.

Today, being on foot would work to his benefit. What better way to catch up with his kiddo than a walk home on a sunny day? He'd ask her about school. She'd tell him first about the mischief she and Owen had gotten into on their late start morning, while it was still a fresh story.

The bell rang and kids spilled out the front doors and down the steps. Emmitt waited for Paisley at the edge of the lawn so she could easily spot him. But it was Emmitt who did the spotting. He had to do a double take to make sure it was his kid, but her long blond curls confirmed that the teen in the second-skin jeans and knee-high boots talking to a guy, who looked as if he

sweet-talked girls out of knee-high boots between passing periods, was indeed his daughter.

Emmitt knew approximately forty-eight ways to kill a man with knee-high boots, and he was about to demonstrate his top five when Paisley spotted him.

"Dad?" she asked, uncertain. Then her eyes went wide, lighting with something that warmed Emmitt all the way through. "Dad! You're home!"

Yes, I am, he thought, looking at her bright smile.

This, right here, was home. The moment Paisley walked down the steps, her bouncing curls coming his way, everything spun back to right. The explosion, the story, even the headache faded into the background.

Whenever he was gone, all he could think about was coming home to Paisley. And yet, whenever he was home, he worried that he was upsetting the delicate balance of her life. Emmitt never had many options growing up. Paisley had so many she worked hard keeping everyone happy—including him.

There were a lot of things he wanted to be for his daughter. A burden was never one.

When he felt the dynamics of their patchwork family begin to shift, he headed out on a new assignment.

"I wasn't expecting you," she said, and as if she suddenly remembered that she was standing on the front lawn of her high school, her smile flattening into boredom. No "I missed you" or "I'm so happy you're home." Just a simple "I wasn't expecting you."

Even the frosty greeting wasn't enough to distract him from the silk and lace top she wore. The shirt—if it could be labeled as such—was held together by a single strap that crisscrossed around her waist and secured in a bow right above her belly button.

"Come here," he said, searching for a clothed speck of body by which to hold her. When it became clear it was physically impossible, he considered giving her his T-shirt, the way he used to when she'd get too much sun at the public pool. But there was a strange vibe directed his way that made him reconsider.

Concluding the safest point of contact was her shoulders, he reeled her in. She came to him like a hesitant fish, arms flapping loosely at her sides, sucking in enough breath to last her until she made her escape. He'd thought about this moment, nonstop, for two months and she conveyed all the excitement of a wet noodle.

"God, I've missed you, kiddo." Thinking it was the height of her boots making the embrace awkward, he shifted slightly and tried again. But it was as if he'd never hugged anyone before and was doing it all wrong.

She didn't smile, didn't wrap her arms around him, didn't even pretend to return the hug. Nope, the only word that came to mind was *endure*. Which was so far from the complex mix of emotions filling Emmitt's chest.

It was as if he were a boy, standing in front of a girl, asking her to love him—and she was saying, "It's not me, it's you."

He wasn't sure what had transpired since he'd left for China, but he didn't like it.

Not one bit.

He was about to give up when he felt a brief shift in her posture, and the foundation of her walls wobbled; then everything changed. She tucked herself into him, her head resting against his shoulder, and she let out a shuddering exhale. Her breathing changed and her heartbeat synched to his as if she needed this hug as much as he did.

"I love you so much," he whispered.

Clearly it was a case of "too much too soon" because she immediately went rigid. Before he could tighten his hold and save the moment, she pretzeled herself sideways in one of those duck-and-twist moves she used to make when spotting anything green on her dinner plate. The result left them in a weird side hug before she pulled back entirely.

"How was school?"

"It was school," she said, casually studying a chip in her nail polish. It gave him time to casually study her and, *damn*, that was a lot of makeup, a little bit of shirt, and boots that might well have come with a do-it-yourself pole kit. And boobs! His

kid had sprouted boobs, side-hugged him—the fun dad—and was talking to boys who shaved. What the hell was happening?

"Why are you here?" Her tone said she was no longer irritated by his presence. She was pissed. At him.

This was new territory for Emmitt. He and Paisley didn't do pissy—not with each other. They joked and went on adventures and pulled outrageous pranks on the other "dads." They even shared the occasional tear over a bucket of ice cream and *Lilo & Stitch*.

But beneath the attitude, Emmitt sensed a deep sorrow that he couldn't fix with a joke or a trip to a tropical island. And the day he was no longer able to make her laugh was the day she no longer needed him.

Levi and Gray handled everything else.

"I thought we could walk home together. Catch up. Gray told me that you're thinking of trying out for varsity soccer. I want to hear all about it," he said, his excitement sounding a little forced even to him.

"This is high school, not middle. Only losers walk. Tryouts were last week. I made varsity. Yay me. And I have dance committee in an hour." She picked at her fingernail. "We all caught up? Great. Now, I have to go."

"Wait." He reached for her hand before she could make her escape. The second their fingers brushed, she jerked back as if he had cooties. "I came early so we could hang out. It's a nice day and I figured, instead of waiting here until dance committee starts, we could walk to Smoothie Social and share a Brazzleberry shake."

"Smoothie Social closed," she said, back to peeling the glittery blue goo on her nails. "You're two months too late."

"I didn't know," he said quietly, wondering if he could have screwed up this reunion more. Not likely.

Social Smoothie was their place. It had been the weekend drop-off spot. Every other Saturday after soccer, Michelle would bring Paisley to Smoothie Social and the three of them would have celebratory smoothies before he and Paisley started their weekend together.

There was no Levi, no Gray, no distractions. Just the three of them doing family their own special way. Now Smoothie Social was gone and, just as he'd been MIA when Michelle died, he hadn't been there for Paisley when it happened.

At moments like this, he questioned why he'd left home in the first place.

Not long ago, it had been all about the assignment. Back when he was looking for any adventure that would get his blood buzzing. Becoming an instant dad had changed a lot of that, but not the thrill of the assignment.

He'd just had the rush of a lifetime and walked away with his head still attached, but he wasn't sure it was screwed on the same. He should have come home feeling charged and invincible, excited to get his ducks in a row so he could head back out.

But now, looking at Paisley, he had to admit that navigating parenting without Michelle scared the shit out of him. He was five minutes into his big dad moment and he'd already struck out so bad, he was bound to ride the bench for a good long while.

"I'm sorry, kiddo."

She lifted a slim shoulder and let it drop. "Whatever. I'm more into lattes anyway."

They both stood there silently, and Emmitt wondered where the comfortable companionship that was so easy for them had gone.

He watched as the wind played with her curls, and when the sun caught her eyes, his chest tightened. She looked just like the photos of his mom when she'd been Paisley's age.

The sound of laughter and chatter circled around them as more students filed out of the buildings, saying their goodbyes before heading for home. He remembered what it felt like in those early days after losing his mom, knowing there was nothing but an empty house waiting for him. It felt a lot like the lonely confusion hiding beneath Paisley's couldn't-care-less posture.

He thought sadly back to the last time she'd looked this small and lost. It had been the day of Michelle's funeral, when Emmitt didn't think his heart could ache any more for his little girl.

He'd been wrong.

"You hungry?" he asked quietly. "We can grab a slice of pizza at Mangia Mia. I'll even splurge for a Piz-ookie."

Her forehead puckered. "Dad, I'm gluten intolerant."

"You are?" That was new, seeing as how he'd watched her down two helpings of lasagna with a couple pieces of garlic bread the night before he left for China. "I'm sure they have gluten-free crust."

She sighed. "I really need to get going. I'm supposed to work on a project with Owen before dance committee. This year's grades are really important. College is right around the corner."

"I doubt Harvard will reject you because you had a slice with your old man," he joked, but her eyes darted back to a group of kids standing at the entrance to the school.

"I have to go. Owen's waiting for me in the gym."

"Then I'll walk you there," he said, falling into step with her. "In fact, I'm headed to the gym myself. I called the school this morning to see if they needed any help with the dance, and I volunteered to help build the arches."

"You can't volunteer!"

"Already a done deal, kiddo."

"Why?" she accused. "Why now? You've never helped before!"

Wow, okay.

"I thought it would be a fun way to spend time together," he said, and thought that if Annie still needed help channeling her Fuck Off persona, then she could take lessons from his daughter, because the look Paisley shot him could reverse global warming.

"Oh my God, Dad! You're ruining my life."

"What the actual fuck?" Emmitt asked Levi, wondering if his daughter had been abducted and replaced by some kind of cyborg. "How worried should I be?"

"Assuming you just made that one infraction? She should be talking to you in a day or two," Levi said through the phone.

"I said hi. She lost her shit." Emmitt scanned the gym to see

if Paisley had come in yet, but he didn't find her in the crowd of gathering teens. She'd not only stormed off but gone into hiding. The dot on his phone pointed to her still being on campus, but it was a big campus and technology hadn't quite reached the *I never want to see you again* level of GPS. So he'd waited in the gym, with the sounds of the girls' basketball team practicing on the court, every bounce of the ball reverberated painfully around his brain.

"You didn't follow the rules, man," Levi said, and Emmitt pressed his cell closer to his ear so he could hear over the voices echoing through the gymnasium.

"I must have heard you incorrectly, because you are implying there are a set of rules. Rules, I'd like to point out, I was not given when Gray conned me into taking his place on the parent committee."

"I didn't con you." And there was Gray, pulling a total Gray move, his voice appearing out of nowhere to dispense some of his dad wisdom. "I was extending you an olive branch. Which I will happily take back."

Emmitt looked at the gymnasium, full of paper lanterns and glitter cannons and kids running around making more of a mess than progress. Then he spotted Paisley across the gym, working extra hard to let him know his presence wasn't welcome and everyone else know she wasn't with the weirdo in the corner.

"Know where I think you should shove that olive branch?" he said, wondering when his life had become one big episode of *Dr. Phil.* "And who invited you anyway? I called *Levi.*"

"And I patched in Gray because laughing at you alone just isn't as much fun as it is with a friend," Levi explained.

"Fuck you," Emmitt said a little too loud, because a fire hydrant of a woman in a maroon track suit and matching visor across the gymnasium, with sound amplifiers for ears, skewered him with a look.

He'd been on the receiving end of that look most of his life. Growing up, he wasn't a bad kid so much as curious to a fault. After his mom passed, that curiosity became an impulsive thirst

to challenge each line in the sand, find out how deeply they were drawn, and question how much disruption would result from crossing those lines.

Not much had changed over the years. Emmitt was just bigger now, and the lines he challenged came with far greater repercussions. The bigger the story, the higher the risk, the more alive he felt.

If someone had asked him six months ago, he'd have sworn it was enough. But something had shifted. Even before China, the rush that had fueled him was growing more fleeting, until half the time he felt as if he was running on empty.

The only way he was going to get his life back was to satisfy that thirst. First though, he needed to reflect on how he'd reached this point. Understand why all the things that used to come easy felt as if they were slipping away.

"What did I do wrong?" he asked, knowing he was announcing open season on himself.

"Let's start with you approaching Paisley in front of her friends," Levi said, his last few words dying beneath Gray's laughter.

"Levi told me you waited for her on the campus lawn, but I didn't know you approached her." Gray let out a low whistle. "Rookie move, man. Rookie move."

"Says the guy who didn't tell me about any fucking rules. How can I make a rookie move when I didn't even know the game had switched?" he asked, pressing a finger to his ear because someone's playlist was blaring through the gym's sound system.

"He's got a point, Gray. You didn't explain, so you can't blame," Levi said as if it were the theme to an after-school special. "But I'm still confused, and this is really why I called you, Gray. Approaching usually doesn't bring on a *You're Ruining My Life* episode."

"No," he agreed. "She's been prickly all week, but she seemed happy today when I dropped her off at school. What else did you do?"

"Why does it have to be something I did? I said hi, she was with some punk, I was excited to tell her we were working on the dance together, then I gave her a hug and—"

"Whoa, whoa, whoa," Levi interrupted.

"Never, ever initiate physical contact in public," Gray added, and Emmitt once again felt like the odd dad out. He also felt a headache coming on—and this one he couldn't blame on Gray's nagging.

"I hugged her because I haven't seen her in two months. Then I tried again because she looked upset. That's what dads do," he said. "She was smiling while chatting up that guy, but even from the lawn I could tell something was up. So I thought I'd do something to make that forced smile of hers real and offered to take her to get smoothies. And before you blame me for that, it was not my fault." Emmitt turned his head away from the gym door, but the movement made him wince. A normal reaction, his doctor had assured him, for someone who'd suffered extensive head trauma. "How was I not informed that Smoothie Social has closed down?"

The laughing and ribbing immediately stopped, and a tense silence vibrated through the phoneline. A silence that told Emmitt everything he needed to know. Paisley's reaction this afternoon wasn't about rules, and it wasn't about the hug.

He pressed his palm to his forehead. "Hasn't anybody talked to Paisley to see if she's upset by the closing?" he asked. "How she feels about her and her mom's favorite hangout being gone?"

"I totally blanked on the closing. I am so sorry," Levi said, and Emmitt could hear the regret in his friend's voice. "I've been so focused on getting her out of her room and interacting with people, I didn't even think . . . That's it. I didn't think."

"We've all been dealing with a lot, and you guys are juggling work, Paisley, and figuring out how to function without Michelle," Emmitt admitted, gratitude thick in his voice. "My intense travel schedule hasn't helped."

"It's your job," Gray said. "We all have to keep moving forward, but I'm just not moving as fast as you guys. And if someone else were telling me this sob story, I'd call bullshit. But the

last time I tried to talk to Paisley about Michelle, she holed up in her room for five days. Only came out to eat."

Gray released a breath big enough to hold all the problems of the world, and everything inside Emmitt stilled.

"The truth is, I'm scared," Gray said, emotion choking his words. Levi didn't say anything, but he didn't need to. The gravity of those two words weighed heavily on all of them.

The hell of it was, they were doing everything right, everything they had done before to make Paisley feel safe, happy, and loved. But now it clearly wasn't working and none of them knew why.

More concerning, none of them knew how to help.

Emmitt scanned the growing group of kids and parents in the gym and immediately zeroed in on his little girl. Only she wasn't so little, and she seemed to be as confused about that as he was. But what broke his heart was that the daughter who used to cuddle up in his lap and talk about anything and everything was doing her best to pretend he wasn't there.

"We have a dinner date tonight—I'll talk to her and fix it," he said, and the guys laughed.

"Let us know how that works out for you," Levi said. And the last thing Emmitt heard as he disconnected was loud, patronizing laughter—in stereo.

Chapter 11

It was official. Annie was in.

She'd never been "in" before, and she had to admit it felt good.

Three nurses from Lynn's Vietnamese-inspired cooking group had introduced themselves. One even told her about a relative's house coming up for rent next month. It was a sprawling two-bedroom with breathtaking views of the ocean and in walking distance to downtown. She was certain, on a photojournalist's salary, Emmitt could easily afford it.

But even if the place came through, that still left a few weeks of cohabitation—which was not going to happen. Annie knew she couldn't do many more ten-hour shifts on two hours' sleep before she hit a wall. Just as she knew she couldn't do many more half-naked, bump-in-the-night encounters before someone did something they regretted.

With new resolve, Annie picked up a yellow folder from the wall rack and walked in to meet her next patient, Leslie Jacobs.

"Hi, Leslie," she said, studying the chart. "I'm Annie Walsh. I'll be helping out Dr. Yates today."

"It's Les, and Dr. Yates is an idiot," Leslie said, his voice scratchy from a lifetime of smoking. In fact, everything about him was scratchy.

Mr. Jacobs was tall and wiry with squinty eyes and appeared as cuddly as a cactus. His skin was flaky and sallow from chemo,

and his clothes draped from his frame as if his body were nothing more than a hanger. And Annie's heart gave a hard tug.

Where most people would see a gruff old man, Annie saw a lonely and scared patient who needed someone to hold his hand. Luckily for Les, Annie specialized in hand-holding.

Even when she was well past hand-holding age, Annie still held her parents' hands while they walked to and from school, around the market, or even at home. In elementary school, her classmates teased her about it, but Annie was more afraid of letting go than she was of being called a baby.

Betty Everett got it wrong when she sang, "If you want to know if he loves you so, it's in his kiss." For Annie, it's in the way he holds hands.

Like kisses, there was an entire language built into the art of hand-holding. Sadly, most people took for granted just how intimate and expressive the gesture could be, and what had once been the greatest display of love and affection had, in modern times, been dismissed.

But since hand-holding wasn't a medical board–approved method of provider-patient interaction, Annie sat down on the chair and wheeled herself right into Les's personal space, then gentled her voice. "Dr. Yates is one of the best oncologists in the state."

"I've got hemorrhoids older than him."

"He has successfully treated more patients than years you've been alive." She clicked her pen and opened his chart. "Shall I add hemorrhoids to the issues we need to discuss today?"

One bushy brow lifted in reprimand, but then his lips slowly tilted up at the corners, transforming his face. "You're plucky. I want you to be my new doctor."

Annie grinned. "From you, I take that as a high compliment. Unfortunately, I'm not an oncologist or a surgeon."

"Doesn't bother me since I'm not having the surgery."

"But it's already scheduled. The operating room is reserved. The anesthesiologist is booked. I thought that was why you were here today. To discuss the removal of your—" She scanned the chart. "Ovaries?" She paused, reread the prognosis again, then looked up. "There must be some mistake."

"This is what I've been telling you. That doc wanted me to get a physical before the surgery. Blood tests, MRI, the whole shebang," he said. "I have more appointments than days in the week and usually see him more than I see my grandkid. But I agreed to the surgery. Why? Because he's the doctor. So there I am, missing out on my weekly bocce ball game, thinking the doctor's going to give me a simple checkup, make sure I'm not too sick to go under the knife.

"Isn't that a joke. Gotta be sick to get any real help but not too sick that they won't help you," he went on. "But there I am waiting for my checkup. Next thing I know the nurse hands me a pink gown and tells me to strip. Then I see these stirrups for my feet and I knew she wasn't going to ask me to cough. Damn idiot sent me to the lady doctor!"

Oh boy.

Annie turned her attention to the rest of his chart, trying to make sense of what was happening.

> Leslie F Jacobs. Five eleven, 173 pounds at 68 years of age. Suffers from heart disease, high blood pressure, and—*talk about typos*—ovarian cancer.

She closed the file and rested it on the counter. "Just give me a moment and let me find out what's going on. I'm sure it's a computer glitch."

"What's going on is, I'm leaving." Les slipped one foot into a shoe and started lacing. "I don't really know a whole lot about ovaries, except they make women nuts, but if I had some, I wouldn't want Dr. Yates anywhere near them." He laced up the other shoe and stood. "Just like he isn't messing with my boys."

"This is most likely a clerical mistake," Annie said, but Les wasn't listening. He was leaving. "I'm new and still learning the system and"—*and* a floater was the exact wrong person to handle this appointment. Les needed someone who was familiar with his diagnosis and his medical history—"and if you could have a seat, I'll call Dr. Yates and he can fix this in a jiffy."

Les gave a stern head shake. "Lady, if he can't tell by looking at me that I don't have ovaries, then this can't be fixed."

"Don't give up on Dr. Yates," Annie urged, walking behind him. "I've seen you in the chemo center. I know this is a scary time, even without the mix-up. You're clearly upset and need answers." Annie placed her arm on his shoulders. "Let me help you get them."

Les stopped at her touch. After a moment he slowly turned to face her, and Annie's chest ached for the man.

"All right." He held up a finger to make sure he was understood. "But only because you're a sweet girl and I don't want to get you in trouble with your boss. Idiot or not, he looks like a hard-ass. But if I come back and he requests a mammogram—"

"He won't," Annie said quickly. "I promise."

Les lifted a challenging brow.

"You have my word," she reassured him, but Les was already shuffling down the hallway, like a penguin with his egg between his feet. The moment he was out of sight, Annie burst out laughing.

It wasn't the most appropriate response to this mess, but it was better than crying.

Or quitting. Thankfully it was her lunch break, and she'd brought leftover pizza.

Annie researched the correct department to address Les's unusual situation and sent an e-mail detailing what had transpired. She was signing the e-mail when her phone buzzed.

She checked her phone's screen and her belly did a little flip—with excitement or nerves she wasn't sure.

> **Back 2 dinner. I was thinking steak & potatoes. Pick up some beer while U R at it. And none of that girly shit you have N the fridge.**

She refused to let herself smile as she texted back.

> **Sorry. Got plans.**

Plans that didn't include sharing her day over a beer with a man who wore glow-in-the-dark undies and warned women that he wasn't a good investment.

> **Why don't U text one of your "friends" to see if they R free.**

> **Not the kind of friend I'm looking for tonight.**

His words gave her pause. The downfall of texting was that there was no way to decipher the intent behind his words. On the upside, he couldn't see her blush. The emotion-free factor made texting the communication choice of men everywhere. But if she had to guess, she'd say those words were carefully chosen and loneliness was the reason behind his reaching out.

Not many people knew what it was like to be with company and feel completely alone. Nor did they know how isolating it was.

> **This "friend" is staring down a night on the couch. Too tired.**

> **The bed is big enough for 2 😉**

> **My mom warned me about men who rely on emojis 2 express themselves.**

> **Don't worry, Goldilocks, I have much more creative ways to express myself**

She'd barely finished texting when another one came through.

Annie's lips twitched; she couldn't help it. Three little emojis had erased all the ick from the day. By the time she texted back, she was laughing.

> **Not happening. Ever.**

> **I hope that's what U said 2 friendly ex.**

Annie paused, her fingers in mid text.

> **STILL working on that.**

> **I can help U work on it over dinner. U need inspiration & I need a friendly face.**

> **Is the commitment-phobe offering 2 give me dating advice?**

> **Not phobic. Picky.**

Was he trying to say that out of his limitless options for dinner companions, he'd picked her? Regardless, the last thing she needed was to play house with the sexy roomie who made her nervous. His smile made her nervous too. But not as much as the way her body reacted when he was near.

> **Like I said, have plans. Bye!**

Annie was about to power down her phone when the screen lit up.

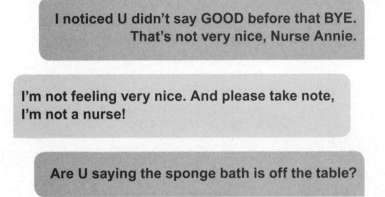

I noticed U didn't say GOOD before that BYE.
That's not very nice, Nurse Annie.

I'm not feeling very nice. And please take note,
I'm not a nurse!

Are U saying the sponge bath is off the table?

"You are so annoying," she shouted at the phone, ignoring the orderly who clearly thought she was crazy.

Emmitt made her crazy, in all the wrong ways—and some of the right ones.

While she'd been text-fighting with Emmitt, a speck of giddy anticipation had crept its way out of that deep, dark place she'd buried it and into her belly, making it tingle.

Tingling was bad. Tingling over an immature argument with her male roommate was very bad.

Afraid she might text back *"Sponge baths happen in bed, not the kitchen,"* Annie turned her phone to airplane mode, then zoomed in on the rental agreement photo. It was only the first page of the contract, and she read it twice, but it did zilch to calm her nerves.

All she could gather was that the house was officially listed as an Airbnb, so the agreement wasn't your standard lease. It did, however, contain a clause that allowed for the owner, or renter, to terminate the agreement seven days prior to stay. Did that mean if Emmitt gave her notice today, she'd have to find a new place by next week? Or that he'd had to have issued the notice seven days prior to the beginning of her stay?

She hadn't a clue. There was only one thing of which she was certain. Tingles or not, Annie was done with being the one to always pack up and move.

Chapter 12

As Annie circled the grocery store parking lot, she contemplated whether now was a good time to call her mother.

By good, she meant the best time for the call to go to voice mail.

She needed the Walsh family matzo ball soup recipe. Not a lecture on how Annie had let another good one slip through her fingers. She pulled up her mom's contact info, her palms going sweaty when it rang.

"Annie, honey? Is that you?" Her mother's voice filled the car. "Marty, Annie's on the phone."

In the background came a muffled, "Is that Annie?"

While her parents discussed the likelihood of it being Annie— even though her name must have appeared on her mom's phone the moment the call connected—Annie thunked her forehead on the steering wheel. Three times.

Her mouth opened, but all that came out was, "Mom?"

"Of course it's Mom. You called me, so why do you sound surprised?" Maura asked.

"I'm not. It's just, uh . . . ." *In thirty-five years, this is the first call you've ever answered during* Jeopardy!. "After I dialed, I realized what time it was. I didn't want to interrupt *Jeopardy!*. So I was just going to leave a message. In fact, I can still do that. Hang up and I'll call you back and leave a message."

"Why would I do that?" There was more muffling, as if her

mom was covering the receiver with her hand, then a distant "She wants me to hang up so she can leave a message. . . . No, she thought she was interrupting *Jeopardy!*."

When the hand was removed, it was her father on the line. "Remember Frank Shubert from the tennis club? His oldest just moved back home. What's his name?" The last part was directed at his wife.

"Jacob."

"Right. Jacob set us up with a new device that lets you watch shows anytime. It's really something. I just speak into the remote, and it plays what I want to watch. Next time you're over, I'll show it to you."

Her dad sounded so excited, Annie decided not to remind him about the Hulu subscription she'd given him last year for his birthday. And she most definitely did not remind him that he'd canceled it.

Other people's choices are not a reflection of me.

"But Mom likes to watch *Jeopardy!* live."

"There's no commercials, Annie," her mom said, as if she'd just been shown the eighth wonder of the world. "Can you believe that?"

"No, Mom. I can't," Annie deadpanned.

"Jacob got divorced—that's why he's home. What a shame. He's such a nice boy." One concerned sigh later, Maura perked up. " He's single, no kids, got a stable job now. He's lost a little of his hair around the front, you know, like your cousin Benjamin."

"Benjamin's bald." This from Marty. "I need a ten-letter word for *roused* that ends in *D*."

"*Receding* is the term they use nowadays," added Maura, the foremost expert on rousing. "Oh Annie, why don't you come home this weekend for dinner. I can invite the Shuberts. Wouldn't it be nice to catch up with Frank and Susan?"

"It would"—*not*—"but I can't this weekend."

Mom rolled on without a pause. "And of course Jacob would be invited. I'm sure spending time with old friends would be good for him right now."

"We were never friends," Annie pointed out.

"Isn't that just perfect?" Maura giggled with delight. "Making up for lost time and missed opportunities! He'd make a fine plus one to Clark's wedding, wouldn't he, Marty?"

"What?" Marty shouted.

"I said, 'wouldn't Jacob make a fine plus one to Clark's wedding?'"

"I thought you were taking me?" Marty asked. "And here I went and got my suit pressed."

"*I* got your suit pressed. And I was talking about Annie," Maura chided. "You could meet him this weekend."

"Sorry, Mom, but I'm working." Working on finding any excuse not to go home.

"Both days? That can't be healthy, now, can it? Maybe you should take a personal day. Shouldn't she, Marty."

"Personal day?" Her dad laughed. "We didn't have that in my day. We were thankful to have a job."

"Times are different now." Annie could almost hear her mom batting Marty's words away.

"Different or not, when has Annie ever called in sick? Never," Marty said, answering his own question. "Then why's she going to miss it for some balding divorced guy who lives above his parents' garage?"

Annie had to smile. Her dad was picking sides—and he'd picked Annie's. Something warm and familiar wove its way around Annie's heart.

She might not have much in common with her mom, but there were countless traits she shared with her dad. They were both bookworms, homebodies, people pleasers, and they tended to fall somewhere between structured and neurotic on the OCD scale, which drove Maura nuts. Her dad was also big on hugging, which worked out because Annie needed a lot of hugs. Top 5 things he was not big on:

1. Surprises.
2. Clutter.

3. Stuffed peppers.
4. Impulsiveness.
5. Parties—dinner, birthday, block, or any other variety that included more than three people and/or cloth napkins.

Once, Annie had overheard Maura describe Marty as dull. Whenever Annie thought of her dad, she felt warm and safe.

"Flapjack . . ." The use of her childhood nickname brought a sudden flood of emotion to her eyes. "How do you feel about missing a day of work to have dinner with two people old enough to be your grandparents and Alex Trebek?"

"Dad, you don't look a day over sixty." Impressive, since her dad had turned seventy-eight this past spring. A child of two professionals who'd decided to adopt at the height of their careers, she was often taken for her parents' grandchild. "And if I didn't have work . . ."

"There, she's been asked and she's answered," he said. "Now, let the girl be, Maura."

Her mother ignored him. "If you come down this weekend, we can go shopping and find you a nice dress for the wedding."

Annie's head shot up as the word finally registered. *Shitshitshit!* The invitation had beaten her to the punch. "I'm not coming home this weekend, and Mom, we are not going to the wedding." She made a big deal out of stressing the *we.*

"Don't be ridiculous, of course we are. When I ran into Clark's mom in speedwalking class, she was adamant that we were still on the list."

"Of course she said that." Likely after her mom interrogated Ms. Atwood about every detail of the wedding. "She was being nice and so was Clark by sending the invitation."

"Instigated!" her dad shouted. "Damn, it doesn't fit. Either that or I got nine across wrong."

"Nice or not, she told me herself that the wedding wouldn't be the same without her Annie."

"That's the point, Mom. I'm not her Annie anymore, so showing up would change everything. And not in a good way."

Had it not been for her friends, Annie would believe that she

was the crazy one. Because how could anyone think that her going to the wedding was a good idea? For her or Clark?

"Your father and I were talking, and we both think going to the wedding might be good for you. We will both be by your side the whole time in case you need us. We think you need closure, dear."

It was the same speech they'd given her on the first day of dance class. Her therapist had suggested that enrolling her in a group activity might help with her shyness. The last thing six-year-old Annie wanted was to join something that required her to perform in front of a crowd of strangers.

Her parents lived up to their word that day. And every day after, until Annie was comfortable enough to go to dance class on her own. For three years, one parent or the other sat on the studio floor during class. They never complained or made her compete and, as it turned out, dance was the ideal outlet for Annie to express herself without the pressure of being perfect.

But going with your parents to ballet and going with them to your ex's wedding were two wildly different things. She'd rather audition for Juilliard in a thong than sit at the table in the back of the ballroom, reserved for people whom the bride and groom are obligated to invite but hope don't show up. On the seating chart for Annie's wedding, it had been table nineteen.

Other people's choices are not a reflection of me. And Annie was nobody's table nineteen.

"I'm not going, Mom." *Be strong.* "And I don't want you or Dad to go either."

"But I already RSVPed. For the whole family. I ordered us all the vegetarian option. The chicken is always so dry at those things."

"Then un-RSVP."

There was a long pause during which Maura strategized her approach. Annie didn't need to strategize—she wasn't going. End of story. What her mother did now was out of Annie's hands. She'd expressed her opinion, even if it wasn't the loudest.

Feeling a touch of indigestion coming on, Annie said, "Actually, I've got to get going. I need to prep OR Seven," she lied,

hating herself for using Clark's trick. "I just called to ask if you could send me Grandma's matzo ball soup recipe."

"I didn't know you liked my matzo ball soup. You always looked like you thought it was bland."

Annie opened her mouth to say of course she liked it but paused. It was soup—what was not to like? But suddenly Annie found herself wondering about the soup her mother served every Passover. The soup her neighbors raved about, and her mother served so proudly.

"Of course it's not bland," she finally said. "Which is why I want to learn how to make it."

"You know Grandma never wrote it down," her mom said. "It's all by feel. She showed me. I'd have to show you."

Which meant Annie would have to go home. Not happening anytime soon. Or her mother would have to come to her. Annie thought about Emmitt and his glow-in-the-dark undies.

Never going to happen!

For a psychologist, her mother had extreme passive-aggressive tendencies. Probably why she never treated people, just studied them.

"Maybe you could guesstimate the amounts and e-mail me the recipe." She could figure out the rest. How hard could it be? "Thanks so much—gotta go. Love you both."

"We love you, Flapjack," her dad said, and then disconnected, most likely so that her mother couldn't invite herself and the Shuberts down for a fun cooking lesson at Annie's.

Silently, she sat there a moment, recalling the events that had brought her to this point in her life: being asked to be her parents' third wheel at her ex-fiancé's wedding while sitting in a parking lot in Rome, Rhode Island.

How had everything gotten so out of control? And when did Annie's opinion come to mean so little in her mother's eyes?

A loud tap on the passenger's-side window made her shriek and smack her head hard on the headrest. Cussing, she rubbed the smarting area and turned to see what had struck the glass. Only to find Emmitt, standing on the other side of the pane and laughing.

"Oh, come on. I give up." She sank down into the seat and closed her eyes.

"I can still see you," his gravelly—and extremely annoying—voice said from outside the car. "Who are you hiding from?"

Everyone, she thought. In fact, she was seriously considering moving to Siberia so she could get some privacy. Otherwise, this was how her time in Rome was going to play out. Until one of them found another place to live, they were going to be all up in each other's space.

Annie had left her own personal hell in Connecticut and wound up living with the devil. It explained why her body tingled with heat every time he was around.

This wasn't going to work. Someone had to give in, and it wasn't going to be her. Why should she be the one to move? *She* was most definitely not the problem. Everyone else was.

Straightening, she locked eyes on Emmitt and spoke loudly enough for her voice to carry through the closed window. "I'm not hiding."

His lips curled into a grin that slowly made its way up to his eyes. "As your friend, I should warn you to never play poker. Or if you do, make sure I'm there. The starting bet will be socks to get them out of the way up-front."

He didn't have to yell to be heard. His voice just slid through the glass and down her spine. The jerk.

She pulled out a slip of paper and a pen, then scribbled a note. She cracked the window just enough to slip it through.

He took his sweet-ass time reaching for the note, then slowly slid it from her fingers. Before he read it, he said, "I'm flattered, but I already have your number. It's on the rental agreement. Remember?"

Oh, she remembered. "Information that, going forward, will be used for business purposes only."

"I thought I made it clear when you were naked in my kitchen, I'd love for you to be my business."

And there he was, lightening the mood and making her giggle. Annie didn't realize how giggle deprived her life had been. "The note," she reminded him.

He unfolded the note, and a big grin spread across his face.

"What?" she asked with an offhanded shrug. But—*holy trouble*—his grin was as contagious as the measles, only a lot more fun. "As your roommate, I feel it's my duty to point out 'that the eighties called, and they want their mirrored aviators back,' " he read. Casually resting his forearm on the roof of the car, he leaned down and, even through the glasses, she could feel the intensity of his stare.

He'd cleaned up, she noticed. She also noticed that his scruff was trimmed, leaving a perfect five o'clock shadow that made his lips *oh-so* mesmerizing. He was wearing the heck out of a pair of jeans and a dark gray T-shirt that did little to hide the muscles beneath. He also had on a ballcap, turned backward, lending a boyish charm to the whole rugged ladies-man vibe he had going on.

Then, as if he were Magic Mike and this was some kind of *I'll show you mine* moment, he made a big deal of lazily lowering the sunglasses down his nose, then tilting his head just enough to give her a glimpse of those tempting brown eyes twinkling back.

A move, she was sure, he'd used on half the population in town. The female half. Well, Annie told herself, she wasn't going to be sucked in to whatever game he was playing. But as she told herself this, she felt herself being sucked in.

Not by his ridiculous grin, although it was a pretty powerful grin, but by the patch of raw skin splitting his left eyebrow. There was also the faint hint of yellow starting at his temple and disappearing into his hairline that was concerning. Together they hinted at a different story about why he'd come home unexpectedly.

As if sensing her interest, he straightened and pulled his cap around and down low. Annie knew when to press and when to back off. His body was flashing a big red *Do Not Push* button.

"Why are you following me?" she demanded.

"I was actually here first, so I think that means you were stalking me." Something across the parking lot caught his attention, and he froze.

"Shit," he mumbled and, without further warning, dropped to the ground, completely disappearing from view.

Unable to contain her curiosity, Annie unbuckled herself and maneuvered in the driver's seat until she could scramble onto her knees. Just in time to watch Emmitt perform some maneuvering of his own—an improv duck-and-cover routine that reminded her of a puppy trying to avoid crate time. He wasn't quite on all fours but was headed in that direction.

After one of the most entertaining thirty seconds of people-watching she had ever participated in, Annie saw Emmitt try to conceal himself from anyone exiting or entering the market. He was, however, in Annie's line of sight.

Unable to help herself, she reached for her phone to video the entire episode when he dropped down so far, he disappeared from her view.

She wasn't sure whom he was hiding from, but whoever it was, they had him taking ghosting to a whole new level—to the tune of sliding under her car.

Annie felt sorry for whoever this woman was and wanted to see just how far Emmitt would go to avoid a real conversation with one of his friendly friends with benefits.

Annie thought back to the men in her life and wondered why it was easier for them to run from conflict than talk it out.

Annie cracked her window and said, "Hey, whatcha doing down there?"

His reply was uttered though clenched teeth but still came through crystal clear. Four letters, rhymed with *duck*, and wasn't very neighborly of him.

Annie paused and, with a snort, picked up her phone. "Hey," she said out the window. "Guy hiding under my car. Do you know a ten-letter word for *roused* that isn't *instigated*?"

He was silent so long, she doubted he'd answer. Then a very annoyed, very loud whisper said, "*Aggravated*? Or, I don't know, how about, *Shutting Up*? *Zip it or Pay*? Oh, I know, *It's my House*."

"All good suggestions, but I don't think they match the spirit of the clue. Do you?"

She was met with silence, so she decided to see what had *roused* the bear. She scrambled across the center console, narrowly escaping an intimate moment with her parking brake, to get a closer look. And look she did.

Annie looked until her mouth went dry—which was the exact opposite of what was happening in her cheeky-cut panties. Because Emmitt was peering beneath her car to check whether the coast was clear, and the position forced his butt to stick up in the air, showcasing that grade A backside of his. It also did a lot to showcase just how worn and soft his jeans were.

Gravity did the rest.

The dark gray T-shirt that moments ago had clung to his chest with the day's humidity slid up to expose a slice of that work-honed body. He shifted slightly, gifting her with a profile view, which was equally impressive since it included some premium side coverage, starting from his upper ribs all the way down to the impressive V that must leave women drooling as it disappeared into his jeans.

You're becoming one of those women, she told herself, a little ashamed that she was objectifying him and a little breathless over the idea of just where that V ended.

Then she thought of *all* those women. The Tiffanys and Tiffanis of the world who had been led on and then left hanging by guys like Emmitt.

How one minute he would be dancing them into bed, the next ducking under cars to avoid talking.

Not this time, buddy. Not on her watch.

Annie cracked the window.

"Emmitt?" She spoke with a raised voice so it would easily be heard by whomever he was avoiding. "Is that you? I didn't know you were back."

Slowly he turned his head and looked directly up at her window. *Are you fucking kidding me* was written clearly across his face.

Annie shrugged a dramatic *Whoops*.

His brow rose in challenge. *Game on!*

It happened in slow-mo. She saw him reach for the door han-

dle, saw the intent in his eyes, and before she could hit the locks he had the door open and was diving across the seats. Well, diving as far as a six-foot-plus guy with a very impressive set of biceps and thighs could in her fuel-efficient compact.

There was a lot of grunting and elbows flying, and then next thing she knew, Annie was flat on her back, emergency break shanking her in the kidney, 180 pounds of solid man on top of her.

A grunt and three jabs to his ribs later, Emmitt lifted up enough for her to breathe.

"What are you doing?"

"Finding a new hiding spot, since you rudely blew mine."

"Get off me and then get out of my car!"

He considered her demand for a moment but didn't move. "Why don't you yell at Clark like that?"

"I don't yell. It's a waste of energy!"

"You're yelling at me right now. In fact, you yell at me a lot," he said, and she was embarrassed to realize she *was* yelling at him. And this wasn't the first time. Nearly every time she was around him, he managed to get under her skin and set her off— and not necessarily in a bad way. "Ah, you're into me."

"We aren't in grade school, and this isn't the playground," she said, careful not to raise her voice. "I'm not into you. I'm annoyed by you."

He smiled, his toothy grin glowing in the darkness. "It's a start. And a hell of a lot better than the pleasant *don't-want-to-upset-anyone* Annie who comes out when you're talking to Clark."

"Seriously, get off me." She shoved, taking in the intimacy of their bodies. She could feel every breath, every ripple, every, um—she wiggled and . . .

"I wouldn't do that," he warned.

Good thing it was dark, because there was a high probability that she was blushing. Wouldn't that just make his day.

She placed her hands on his chest, careful not to touch anything too intimate, and gave a shove. He didn't even budge. "Seriously, move."

"Not until the coast is clear." He lifted his head long enough to glance out the window. "You couldn't stay quiet, could you?"

"Probably one of your fans. Let me guess, one of your girl-friends wants to know why you're ghosting her." She was able to lift her head enough to peek out the window. But all she saw was an older couple with a shopping basket, an employee in a red vest collecting carts, and a group of teenage girls.

"Worse," he said, and dropped low again. "I think my daughter just caught me following her."

She laughed. And because of their position, she literally laughed in his face. "*You* have a daughter?"

He did not laugh. Not even a little. Nope, the confident and cocky, smooth-talking Emmitt was nowhere in sight. Even in the glow of the supermarket lights, she could see he'd become all prickly edges and defensive spikes.

And when he clenched his jaw tight and exhaled like a bull during a fight, she caught a glimpse of the raw power and cha-risma that drew people to him. *Like screws to a magnet*, she thought, a spark of sexual awareness sizzling through her.

Without a word, he lifted himself off her and into the passen-ger seat, careful to stay low enough that, with his ballcap and aviators on, he wasn't identifiable.

Not sure what had just happened, Annie shifted in her seat and straightened her clothes.

The jerk didn't need to straighten out anything. He looked perfectly imperfect, just like a man of the world should. "Gah!"

"What?" he finally said, his voice drained of any emotion. "You don't think I'd be a good dad?"

If he'd asked her that question five minutes ago, she would have kicked him out of her car. But now, seeing his emotional state, she didn't doubt for a minute that he was not only a father but a good one.

She glanced at the group of teens, now climbing into a mini-van, and caught a glimpse of her boss's stepdaughter.

"Paisley," she said. "Wait, Paisley is Sweet P! She's yours?"

"Yup."

Annie wasn't sure what was more shocking: that Emmitt had

a kid or that his kid was fifteen and female. She knew Paisley, knew Gray was her stepdad, even knew that Paisley's biological father was a photographer. But she'd never put two and two together and come up with Paisley was Emmitt's kid.

The single dads Annie knew didn't keep a dictionary-sized black book, nor did they scour the world's most dangerous places in search of injustice and suffering. And they most certainly did not look like a Range Rover dressed in North Face gear.

On one of the times Paisley had stopped by the hospital to see Gray, she'd mentioned that her "bio dad," as she called him, was stationed in China. Annie had assumed he was either military or an overseas contractor. She couldn't have been more wrong. Which made the tingling sensation swirling around in her belly all the more annoying.

"Then why are you hiding in my car instead of saying hi to her?" she asked.

He let out a breath. "I'm keeping an eye on her. Trying to figure out how she ticks."

Annie snorted. "She's fifteen. She doesn't tick, she explodes. Her goal is to be unpredictable and challenging and test every single limit to see how far she can push before one of you breaks."

With a shaky laugh, he tossed his glasses on the dash and leaned back. "Then she's doing a good job. She said a total of ten words to me today before she broke me. I don't know how she did it, but I'm broken." He turned to look at her and, *oh boy*, if this was him broken, she was in big trouble when he got back to his fighting weight.

His ballcap shadowed his face from the outside glow, but not so much that she couldn't see his eyes. A warm whisky color that reminded her of caramel. Annie loved caramel. She also loved the soft way he was watching her, his gaze gently searching hers, as if reaching out to create a connection. But there was also a sadness there, and a jumble of other intense emotions she didn't want to see.

"Is that why you wanted to hang out tonight?" she asked quietly.

"We were supposed to have dinner together, but she blew me off after dance committee. In the past, when there was a problem with Paisley, I'd go to Michelle and she'd help me see the female perspective, but Michelle's not here and . . ."

"And I'm a female?" She laughed.

"And sweet," he said. "Even when you're yelling at me, you can't hide it. I guess I needed a little sweet in my day."

Even through his dark lashes, Annie could see the flicker of humor in his eyes. She didn't know how to respond. It was probably one of the nicest things someone had ever said to her. But with Emmitt she could never decipher what was charm and what was real.

Thankfully her phone rang and an ABBA song played from her cell. She studiously ignored the call and groaned.

"Aren't you going to get that?" he asked.

"Just a telemarketer."

"Playing 'Mamma Mia'?"

The call went to voice mail, and Annie sighed in relief. "My mom and, before you ask, no, I'm not going to call her back."

"If she's anything like my dad, I get it."

"She's not so bad. I'm just having a day."

"My day started about three weeks ago and hasn't stopped."

She chuckled. "Having been a teenage girl once, I can tell you it is only going to get worse if she finds out you're spying."

"I'm not spying. I'm researching the subject. It's step one of a four-part plan to get to know my kid better."

"Give it whatever name you want, if she catches you breaking her trust, it's game over."

"Then she won't catch me." He took in her skirt and tank top, something she'd thrown on before leaving work, and whistled his appreciation. "Who are *you* hiding from?"

"Nobody." She exited her car and slammed the door. Shooting him a pissy glare over the hood, she said, "I need groceries. This is a grocery store. Have a good night."

Without waiting to see what dark shadow he'd slink into, she headed toward the supermarket. The doors opened, and she was hit with a cool blast of sweet strawberry and fresh-baked bread.

Annie took a moment to appreciate the slow rhythm and flow of the post-dinner-rush supermarket.

Annie picked the late hour precisely for this reason.

Leisurely shopping in a quiet store had become one of her favorite things. A great way to come down from a long day on the hospital floor. With no pressing matters to attend to, and no one waiting for her at home, she could drift up the produce aisle, past the butcher stand, and down the ice cream section, picking up nothing more than a basket of strawberries and vanilla ice cream.

The nurses at work had taken healthy to a whole new level. Annie didn't think she could ever look at a kale smoothie again and not gag a little. Grabbing a basket, she headed to aisle six—cookies and candy and wine, *oh my*!

"Great thinking," her shadow said, rolling up next to her with a shopping cart. "We can get food for dinner, then carpool home together. Good for the environment."

"What do you mean, home? You still plan on staying?" Annie grabbed a box of multigrain crackers, a bag of chips, and a jar of olives—then crossed all three off her list.

"It is my house." He picked up some cheese in a can and added it to her basket.

She took it out and placed it in his cart. "Which you rented to me."

"About that." He took her basket and emptied it into his cart, then set the basket on the top shelf, where she couldn't reach. "I looked at the lease and it seems pretty standard."

"You don't even know what kind of rental agreement you use?"

"Don't need to."

"This explains so much," she murmured.

"Anyway, it's a standard Airbnb agreement."

"When I saw Airbnb on the letterhead, I wasn't sure what it meant, so thank you for mansplaining. You have a good night now." She shoved the can of cheese into his chest, then, with a wiggle of the pinkie, took off with the cart.

She hooked a hard right, choosing produce instead of the al-

cohol aisle—which meant she would have to make do with the wine in her pantry. If it brought this fun grocery store adventure to a close, the sacrifice would be worth it.

"Look at that, Roomie." Back in went the aerosol cheese, along with some pudding cups. "Two days together and you read my mind. I'd kill for some baked potatoes."

"I also looked up the Airbnb legalese. Did you do that? No? Great. Then let me explain it to you." He stood in front of the cart, blocking it. And, in case she decided to back out in a bid for freedom, he put his foot on the under-rack of the cart. Then took his sweet time selecting the perfect potatoes, which meant holding and weighing each one as if he were twelve and they were boobs instead a starchy side dish. "It states that, as the owner, I can cancel up to seven days prior to the stay."

"I've been here a month!"

"Which means you know the town by now. And here I was worried I'd be a dick for kicking a lady out of my house."

They turned the corner, almost colliding with a tall blonde wearing heels and a high-end handbag with a white fluffy feline in it. The cat looked at Annie and hissed.

"Emmitt! I thought that was you. It's so good to see you," she said, wrapping her arms around his neck and climbing him as if he were made of catnip.

"Great to see you too." And there was something douchey about the way he said, "you too," dragging it out while patting her back, that told Annie if the world depended on his knowing the blonde's name, then Annie had better get moving on her BEFORE THE WORLD ENDS list.

When Emmitt managed to pry himself free, Annie gave him a friendly punch in the shoulder. "Emmitt, why don't you introduce me to your friend?"

Emmitt's *Fuck me* face was in full effect. It was followed by an uncomfortable chuckle, and finally a loud clearing of the throat, which did nothing—Annie was certain—to jog his memory.

"This is my roommate, Annie. Annie, this is Lena." He said the name so quickly, Annie almost missed it.

Lena was in the same boat, because she looked at him

strangely, but only for a moment. Then he winked. "Annie works for Gray, and since she is new to town, I offered up my place for a few weeks until she could find her own pad."

"Oh," the blonde said, her eyes darting back and forth as if trying to size up Annie and Emmitt's relationship. Annie gave him another slug to the arm, and Lena—whose name was not Lena—took that as a sign that Annie had been friend zoned. Therefore a nonthreat. "I was so sad you couldn't make our dinner. I heard you left to unearth some horrific world-shattering story."

"It was just a human-interest piece, but I had less than two hours to catch my flight."

"Human-interest piece?" Lena-not-Lena placed a finger on his chin, giving it a poke—complete with sound effects—before letting it run down his chest. "You make it sound like you're doing a puff piece on pandas in China instead of single-handedly rescuing a bus full of kids who were on a field trip when the factory blew up."

"Single-handedly?" Annie looked at Emmitt and held back a snort. "Sounds like a puff piece to me."

"I called to make sure you were okay. I heard you were, but not from you."

"Sorry about that. Only just back." With a wink, he gave the cat's tail a little ruffle, eliciting a purr—from them both.

"I guess I can let you make it up to me." Her shrug said she'd forgiven him before he'd even left for his last assignment. She stuck her card into his front pocket—the pocket of his jeans. "Call me. Nice meeting you, Annie."

"Bye, Lena," he said, and Annie plucked the card from his pocket—with two careful fingers.

She read the card and laughed. "Lena?"

"Was I even close?"

"Her name is Lana."

"Close enough." He picked up a handful of frozen pizzas.

"Have you had sex with her?"

"What kind of question is that?" He was aghast, as if she were the rude one.

Annie stared him down. He smiled—one of the most arrogant smiles in the history of mankind.

"Then not close enough." She flung the card in his face. "Give Lana a call. I'm sure she'd be more than happy to house you. If you need a reference, have her call me."

"No can do. Sets a bad precedent. If I sleep there, then she'd expect to sleep at my place. See the problem?"

He added a gallon of milk next to her almond milk, then gave a mischievous wink and added in a can of whipped cream.

This "peaceful" trip to the market had already blown past anything remotely relaxing. But, Annie had to admit, she was having fun. Her cheeks were sore from trying not to smile, her step lighter than it had been since Clark-2K struck. She imagined Emmitt could make going to the dentist fun.

"When diagnosing a problem, we look for contributing factors, things all the situations have in common. You're the only constant." She leaned in and whispered, "I'm afraid, Mr. Bradley, *you* might be the problem."

A flash of something almost human flickered before it was gone. Or maybe it was hiding behind the arrogant swagger he adopted as he leaned in to match her stance.

"I think your prognosis is wrong, Nurse Annie," he whispered, his lips so close to contact, she could taste the mint on his breath. *Knew*, beyond a shadow of a doubt, that he, Rome's Resident Sex Bandit, was going to kiss her, the Husband Whisperer.

And right there, clutching an ear of corn next to the peach and cantaloupe display, which read Juicy and ripe for the picking, Annie decided she just might let him. All he'd have to do was move a little closer and she'd know if his kiss lived up to the hype—it would be a first in Annie's world.

"I bet if we polled other women who have been in *any* kind of situation, position, or scenario with me, nine out of ten would say I'm not the problem. I'm the cure."

The way he said it, all smooth and full of innuendo, had her stomach fluttering—and her warning bells blaring.

"Well," she said on a breathy sigh, dropping the corn back in

the barrel and smiling, "I guess we'll never know who's right, since you left your sticky notes at home on the fridge."

With a carefree shrug, Annie grabbed some salad fixings, mushrooms, and a couple of pears, leaving Emmitt behind her—laughing.

"You know what the tenth would say?" And there he was again, right behind her, with an armload of ingredients that would never aspire to be anything more than game-day food.

"Don't care."

"She'd say it was a religious experience."

"Doesn't matter because, one, you're moving out soon." She ticked off a finger. Then another. "Two, we are just roommates and roommates don't care about each other's sexual score card. Nor do they point out that eighty percent of women fake 'Paying Witness' in order for the sermon to just be done. Three, until you move out, *no one* is to bring 'bed buddies' into the house."

"My house." He lowered one of her fingers. Then another. "If you want to keep it monogamous, that'd be new for me but I'm willing to give it a go." He left her with her extra special finger up. "And in seven days, depending on how this monogamy thing goes, I can invite over whoever I want."

With a kiss to her middle finger, he grabbed the cart and pushed it toward the butcher stand. "So what's for dinner?" He picked up a couple of T-bones and tossed them in. "I'm not all that picky. In fact I love just about everything except salmon, olives . . . oh, and I can't stand kale."

"Bummer, I was making a kale salad with broiled salmon and an olive tapenade."

"Huh. Did you know kale is food for people who don't know how to smile? It's scientifically proven."

"Liar." She was ordering that T-shirt for Clark. She'd send it anonymously in a box wired with a glitter bomb. Colors to coordinate with the wedding theme, of course.

"How about we go back to the steak idea? Two great big steaks with baked potatoes. We can grill them out back while drinking beer. What kind do you prefer? And don't tell me we're getting some passionfruit-flavored craft beer." He reached into

the chilled section and selected a six-pack from the back of the bottom shelf, making his rear look all kinds of amazing.

He set it in the cart.

Giving up, she moved it to the back of the cart, using a loaf of French bread to act as the wall of Jericho between their foods. "*We* won't be drinking beer."

"Ah, you're a wine lady." He looked her up and down, and Annie squirmed as she felt her face heat. She was tired, sore, and a mess. "I bet you drink one of those boring fruity, neutral white wines that are in the cabinet at home."

Hands on hips, she said, "Why? Because I'm boring?" Boring was synonymous with dull. And while most of the time she didn't mind being like her dad, today the word stung.

"My guess? Those bottles were gifts from someone who doesn't know a thing about you. And you're too nice to tell them, and too practical to buy a new bottle before you've finished those. And Anh"—his tone made her gooey inside—"I'd say you're the most interesting woman I've met in a long while."

This time when he looked at her, she didn't feel silly or embarrassed. She felt understood and, *oh boy*, was *that* sexy. And suddenly she was okay being boring—preferred it, in fact.

"So who bought them," he went on. "A boyfriend?"

That's all it took. One line and he was back to annoying. Oh, he was still sexy, just not to her. "My mom. She gives me a bottle for every holiday."

"The same mom you're avoiding?"

"I sound awful when you say it that way."

"Awful is a cabinet full of that wine. If she brought me that, I'd avoid her too."

"She really isn't that bad. She just likes what she likes," Annie said.

Emmitt studied her for a long moment, and Annie felt her face flush. "And because you're her kid, she thinks you should like it too?"

Annie shrugged. "The wine isn't horrible, and it gives her one more thing in common with me that she can tell her friends about. So that's the wine story. Moving on."

"Does your boyfriend like the wine?"

She laughed. "You don't give up. And no, you already know I don't have a boyfriend."

"Just double-checking. That would have been awkward. You living with me while having a boyfriend. Imagine the rumors *that* would start."

"I'm not living with you. We're roommates." She took the cart back and picked up her speed. "Temporary roommates. Nothing more."

"We're temporary roommates who know what the other looks like naked."

"I wasn't naked. I was in my undergarments."

"Undergarments are cotton and don't fall into the thong or cheeky cut category." Her speed did nothing to deter him. He merely sped up, tossing marshmallows in her cart. "Now for some graham crackers and chocolate. Then we can discuss the finer points of undergarments around the firepit while making s'mores."

"I hate marshmallows."

"Chocolate sauce is fine too."

"We are not making s'mores." In with the chocolate sauce. Milk chocolate—the jerk was playing dirty. "This is not a pajama party."

"So it's a PJs-optional kind of event." He shrugged and slid his sunglasses back on, as if he were big stuff and they were in Hollywood. "I can hang. Pillow fight later?"

Chapter 13

"Did you know in some cultures, putting groceries away with someone is a form of foreplay," Emmitt said, unlocking the front door and flicking on the lights.

"In my house, it was called being helpful," Annie said, not even sparing him a glance as she walked past him into the kitchen.

She set her bags on the counter and began emptying them in categories. Frozen foods first, then dairy, canned, dry. Even the produce was quickly divided into fruits and vegetables before going into the proper bins.

He plucked an apple out of Goldilocks's little hands, taking a big bite when she reached out to grab it back, intrigued when her lips went plump as she frowned.

"That's for the salad," she said, giving him a little shove. "If you plan on eating the ingredients, there won't be anything left to make a meal."

Sweet, bossy, and stubborn. Quite an unexpected pairing.

"Well, in my house"—he grabbed two stemmed glasses and a bottle of wine from the bag, then placed them on the table—"guests enjoy a glass of wine while I prepare the food."

She sent him an amused look. "You're going to cook? For me?"

"Some women find that romantic."

"Some women find it romantic when you remember their name."

Check. And mate. He was liking her more and more. "I must have missed that day in sex ed. I was more of a hands-on learner. Spent a good amount of time that year being tutored by Misty Callahan, the freshman next door, who liked my dimples."

"Exploring each other's dimples behind the bleachers isn't romantic, Emmitt. No wonder you're so—"

"Magnificent?"

"Cocky, arrogant, stunted." She broke off with a gasp. "Oh my God." Her face lit with an excitement that made her eyes sparkle and Emmitt's dimples man-up. "A ten-letter word for *roused. Challenged.*" She threw her head back and laughed. "You're romantically challenged."

Emmitt wasn't sure how to respond to that completely inaccurate summation of his character. He'd been on the receiving end of some pretty colorful criticism from women, but never when it came to his romantic prowess. And there he was pulling out all the stops—a little wine, top shelf banter, and his guaranteed-to-have-her-wanting-more pepper-crusted steak with pomegranate chutney that had a near-perfect proven success rate, and she was laughing at his game.

"Laugh all you want, Goldilocks. But I promise you that one night in my bed, with me, and you'll be changing your tune." He placed his hand a little lower on her back than was polite as he guided her to the island. With a wink, he gave the bar stool a pat.

She looked at it, and him, skeptically. And okay, maybe he did lean down to smell her hair as he pulled the stool closer. And in the process, he may have caught a hint of her scent, the same jasmine with a hint of amber that was all over his sheets.

Oh yeah, when Goldilocks left for work, Emmitt had crawled into his bed and crashed. Even with fresh sheets he couldn't escape the sexy scent of Annie. It fueled a few thoughts about how she looked in that soft gray pajama set, which was nothing more than drawstring shorts and a top with skinny straps,

but on her, *man oh man*, it was hot as hell. He sank into the mattress, buried beneath all dozen of her pillows and instantly he was dead to the world for a solid six hours with her smell to keep him company.

It was the best sleep he'd had in recent memory. There was something soothing about all the candles and little knick-knacks she had lying around. There was also something soothing about seeing her in his kitchen.

Annie sent him a sidelong glance. "I will take that glass of wine, but whatever game you're playing, it won't work. We both know I have the right to stay here, and you're morally obligated to find alternate housing. You're just trying to charm me into giving up the bed, and I paid for that bed. It's mine."

"You should have some guy charming you every day of the year, Anh. But tonight I don't want to talk about the housing situation. I just want to talk," he said. "To you."

Emmitt watched the way her lashes lowered to rest on her cheeks when she disappeared behind her shyness. He decided then and there, before this thing between them ended, she'd never feel shy around him again.

But since this was in the beginning stages, and she was closing up on him, he needed to lighten the mood. "I'm more of a *ring on my finger before shacking up* kind of guy."

"Turns out, I'm allergic to rings." She wiggled her fourth finger and they both laughed.

"How about we agree not to talk about our housing problem tonight," he said, then slid around to the other side, filling up his glass with water. "To a shitty day."

She paused for a moment, as though trying to figure out if there was a catch. There wasn't, but he didn't need to tell her that.

Emmitt had offered to cook her dinner to throw her off-balance, but one look at her in that frayed denim skirt and scoop neck tank and his brain had been scrambled. She must have changed from her scrubs into this piece of art before she arrived at the market.

His good fortune.

She had a smoking body and amazing legs, he decided when she kicked off her Converse and hopped up on the stool. Two powerful weapons he'd have to be diligently aware of.

Then she smiled and, *holy shit*, all the tension he'd been carrying since he landed stateside vanished.

"To a shitty day," she agreed and even toasted.

Before she charmed him beyond reason, Emmitt went to work making a stellar spinach and arugula salad while Annie eyed him tentatively over her wineglass.

"How did you leave it with your daughter today?"

"To be honest, I don't know. There was yelling, there was hugging, there were tears, there was avoidance, there were so many emotions. All the emotions all at once, it was terrifying."

"My dad says my teenage years are to blame for his premature graying. And I was a pretty easy kid," she said. Emmitt must have had a look of abject horror on his face, because Annie reached over and patted his hand. "You'll survive."

"Yesterday, I would have agreed with you. Today?" He gave a self-deprecating chuckle. "I don't know. She's blowing me off to have dinner with one of her friends, choosing to sleep at Gray's, and I'm stuck building the arbors for the dance's six selfie stations at a father-daughter dance, where I don't think I'll be welcomed."

She muffled a laugh. "What's a selfie station?"

"Hell if I know. I hate selfies on principle." But working with his hands sounded like fun. "Give me a nail gun and electric saw and I'm good. But what I was really hoping for was time with P, so I didn't give a shit what job they gave me. I'm there to initiate step two."

"Step two?" She laughed and, cupping her glass with both hands, rested her elbows on the counter. "Please enlighten me. What are these steps to decoding the mind of a teenager?"

"You laugh, but I've got this covered. I'm looking at this like an assignment."

"You already mentioned step one. Research."

"Yes." He was beyond pleased that she'd remembered. "And working with her will allow me to, step two, connect with the sub-

ject. Being on the committee allows me to, step three, watch her in her natural environment so I can, step four, show up prepared."

"I see," she said, but her smirk said all she saw was this plan blowing up in his face.

It was true, he knew jack shit about glitter and color themes, but Paisley asked him every few months to redecorate her room, so what better way to connect? Plus, how hard could it be to decorate a gym? Streamers, balloons, maybe a disco ball.

Piece of cake.

"Now, if I can just get her to wear clothes that aren't made of dental floss and lace—*oh,* keeping her away from guys who are too old to be looking her way, so I can sleep nights, would be nice."

"Wow, I never thought what it must be like for guys like *you* to have a daughter."

"Guys like *me* get offended when people like *you* lump us in with assholes," he said. "But I get your point. Today at the high school, most of the boys were huddled in groups talking about the girls, the girls were talking to their friends about the boys, and neither side had a clue as to how this dance is played out. But then there was this one guy who thought he was hot shit."

"I take it he was the 'too-old-for-my-daughter' guy you mentioned earlier?" She covered her mouth to hide her laugh. "I'm sorry, but this is just too good not to laugh. Plus, you never know, he might be a nice kid."

"Oh, he isn't, trust me. Nice guys don't look at nice girls the way he was looking at P, with me standing ten feet away." Emmitt didn't need to meet the guy to know what he was after, because Emmitt had been that guy. Hated to admit that, most of the time, he still was.

It had been in second grade when May Chen shared her rice crispy treat with him that he'd realized he had a way with girls. The next day she brought him one shaped like a heart, and every day after until her parents relocated to Idaho.

A flip was switched that day, and for Emmitt there was no going back.

His mother taught him to be respectful of women, to re-

member that they were all someone's sister or daughter. Emmitt didn't have a sister, but now he had a daughter and he wondered if this was karma playing at irony.

Paisley was hitting an age when she'd start dating guys—guys who thought like he did, charmed girls like he did, and broke hearts the way he did.

"God, I'm screwed." He looked at Annie, who was finding a hell of a lot of humor in his situation. "I'm serious. The way she acted today, the attitude and clothes. God, the lost look when talking about her mom. It gutted me."

The humor faded and her eyes grew tender and warm. Once again, she reached out to touch his hand, to comfort him. "She'll get through whatever this is. Losing her mom at such an important age is hard and will be a huge struggle for her. But a lot of what you're worried about is just Paisley being a normal, emotionally charged teenager."

"This is normal?" he choked out, and God help him, he hoped she was joking. Because if this was normal teenage behavior, then he still had a few years of it to struggle through.

"Yes, and I promise you'll survive," Annie said, showing him her sweet side, which was a nice treat.

"How did your dad do it?"

"He loved me for who I was in that exact moment. When you're loved like that, you don't have to worry about letting anyone down," she said, a warm glow lighting her face.

Emmitt pictured her as a little girl, all her dolls lined up in order, her quiet sweetness lighting her smile and imagined she would have been easy to love.

"That's what I want for Paisley."

His kid deserved that kind of love, but Emmitt had a thing about disappointing others. He'd been disillusioned so many times over the years, especially his younger years, that he went to great lengths to avoid being that guy to someone else.

Bottom line: He didn't want to be somebody's disappointment.

"I'm pretty sure she has it, she's just too emotional right now to realize it," Annie said.

"I hope you're right," he said, then he opened a cabinet, expecting to find his serving bowls and instead found pots and pans.

"It's more logical to put pots and pans on the bottom, because they're heavier." She bit her lower lip, then looked across the island at him, those dark brown eyes filled with a mix of guilt and sass. He wondered how they'd look if he leaned over and just kissed her.

Before he could answer that question, she slid off the stool and walked over to a cabinet to the right of the stove. "Serving bowls should go next to the stove so when you're ready to serve, you just lean over and grab."

She opened the door and, *voilà*, all his bowls, platters, and even some white modern-looking dishes he didn't recognize were stacked nice and neat. She did the game show girl thing with her hand, looking mighty proud of her handiwork.

"I'll grab a bowl." She went up on her tiptoes, causing her skirt to slide up, up, and even farther up. And he found himself thinking that sharing quarters with her for even a few weeks was going to be a hell of a long time to keep his hands to himself. Especially if she preferred skirts.

"Let me help," he said, knowing damn well she could reach the bowl on her own but, *come on*, he'd have to hand in his man card if he didn't take this opportunity.

Ignoring her protest, Emmitt slowly made his way toward her, sliding up right behind her and taking the bowl from her fingertips. She turned her head and, *again with the voilà*, her gaze went right to his lips.

"Did you know that's incredibly offensive to petite people?" she said, but he noticed her breath catch.

Interesting. She was as aware of the sexual heat that was blazing between them as he was.

His gaze slid down to the base of her neck, watching her pulse pound. It also afforded him a generous view of the black lace she had on beneath that tank.

"I didn't mean to offend you. I was just being helpful."

Not believing a bit of his BS—smart girl—Annie snuck un-

der his arm and headed back to her perch, placing the counter between them, but it didn't matter. It was clear Goldilocks thought he was just the right size.

And suddenly Emmitt knew that their living situation wasn't the problem. As long as they resided in the same town, this thing, whatever it was, wasn't going away anytime soon.

They both had a lot to prove, him even more so. And doing something as stupid as acting on this attraction would be crazy. But Emmitt also had a thing for crazy.

And Annie was proving to be just his kind of crazy.

Chapter 14

The only thing that pissed Annie off more than someone stealing her leftovers was if those leftovers were pizza.

She didn't have to look far to find the guilty party. And she had nobody to blame but herself.

After Emmitt cooked her a delicious dinner the other night, she'd decided to return the favor and order an extra-large pizza, which normally would have survived three days. But when feeding a man who ate like a bear after hibernation, the slices disappeared faster than she could say "Hands off my pizza."

Afraid it would be inhaled in one sitting, Annie had snatched up the last two pieces and tucked them safely away in her neon green PANGRY: A CRANKY STATE RESULTING FROM A LACK OF PIZZA lunch sack.

Only lunch break was here and instead of finding her pepperoni and green olive pizza, she found a sticky note.

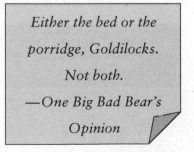

Either the bed or the

porridge, Goldilocks.

Not both.

—One Big Bad Bear's

Opinion

Annie wasn't sure what bothered her more: that he'd eaten her lunch—*after* complaining that green things didn't belong on a pizza—or that she was starting to look forward to these little blips of Emmitt in her everyday life.

Annie had uprooted her world in Hartford because it was easier than daily reminders of her past failures with men. So starting today, she was going to pick up as many shifts as she could: ER, pediatrics, urology—she wasn't choosy. The less time she was around Emmitt, engaging Emmitt, or whatever the blip was happening between them, the better it would be for her goal.

And her sanity.

Being forced to move would have been an easy solution. Only he hadn't threatened to enact the seven-day eviction clause yet, which was good, since the other place had fallen through and she hadn't located a single rental in her price range that wasn't a room-for-rent. If she wanted to stick to her man-free plan, then she wasn't sure how long she'd be able to stay.

But if she were being honest, she didn't want to move. She'd come to think of that cabin as her sanctuary and sparring with Emmitt as entertainment. Moving in with another roommate had all the appeal of steamed cabbage. Plus, it would feel like starting over again.

Been there, done that, had the Dolly Parton wedding dress to show for it.

Moving wasn't high on her list of how she wanted to spend her days. She'd come to Rome to move on, not move around from room to room. She had more entertaining ways to use her data plan than searching Craigslist.

With a grin, she picked up her phone and typed

> **Since I'm the paying customer it's only fair I get the bed.**

She stood there waiting for the reply and groaning over how ridiculous she was being. Dr. Tanner's office had been a drive-

through for strep throat and bronchitis patients today. There were enough cultures to label and paperwork to input that this would likely be her only downtime until she signed out. She shouldn't be wasting her break texting—especially with her pizza-thief of a roommate-not-roommate.

She set the phone on the table and pulled out the lone cup of applesauce that would make up her entire lunch while she stared at the phone.

The three little dots appeared on the screen, and anticipation danced in her chest.

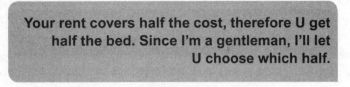

> Your rent covers half the cost, therefore U get half the bed. Since I'm a gentleman, I'll let U choose which half.

Lunch forgotten, her fingers glued themselves to the screen, and did a little click-a-dee-click dance of their own.

> Sorry, I don't play well with others.

> Maybe U aren't playing with the right people then.

> Sleep in the spare room.

> No can do. That's Paisley's room & I promised it would be hers any night she needs it.

Statements like that made it hard for her to dislike him. She'd been told when she rented the cabin that the locked room was

off-limits, so she'd never looked inside. She hadn't thought that rule applied to the owner, but now she knew it did.

He wanted Paisley to feel that she had her own space at his house, and he would rather sleep on a lumpy recliner than invade her privacy.

Enough had happened over the past couple days to have Annie reconsidering her earlier assessments. Either Emmitt wasn't as bad as she'd thought, or he was so good he had her conned. She was certain of one thing: He wasn't faking the little groan he tried to hide whenever she flicked on the lights or he moved his head too fast. Which made her feel guilty for taking the bed.

He didn't offer up any explanation for his injuries, and she didn't pry, but it was clear there was more going on than he was telling everyone. Her curiosity was further sparked when she overheard Gray ask Rosalie to contact the hospital in China—so that part was true, at least—and have Emmitt's medical records sent over.

Her phone vibrated. She wiggled in her seat.

> **What do U need 2night, Goldilocks?**

"Are you sexting?" Lynn asked from over Annie's shoulder. It wasn't both of her friends' sudden appearance at the table that had her dropping her phone, but the fact she'd been caught—sexting?

That was what she'd been doing, right? If not, then it would most definitely qualify as some kind of millennial foreplay.

Before she even registered Beckett was present, her friend had snatched up Annie's phone and was scrolling through the text history.

"Oh my God, she totally is!" Beckett waved the phone so Lynn could see. Annie reached for it, but Beckett held it above her head. And since Beckett was built like a runway model—well, a runway model in a Grumpy Cat shirt that read, THE PROBLEM WITH SOME PEOPLE IS THAT THEY EXIST—Annie gave up. "Oh girl, he so wants to play with you."

"Hand it over," Annie demanded, and Beckett complied. Before Lynn decided she wanted a look-see, which might lead to scrolling through the entire thread, Annie shoved it into her pocket. "And we were just having a roommate argument over the bed."

"If Emmitt 'Big O' Bradley was my roommate, I'd make it a rule that every argument happened *in* bed," Beckett said.

Annie shushed her and looked around the break room. Thankfully, it was busy on the floor, so the break room was almost empty. "I don't want any rumors to start, and Emmitt seems to be patient zero for half the town's gossip."

"Also for half the town's orgasms," Lynn said sweetly, while Beckett made a lewd gesture.

"Can you not?" Annie stuck her spoon in the applesauce and pushed it away, no longer hungry.

Beckett picked it up, sniffed it, and made a face as if she'd just sucked on a lemon. "Since when do you eat all healthy?"

Annie knew she'd met a kindred soul in Beckett when her friend had announced that a chocolate bar and a jar of peanut butter was a balanced meal.

"Since Emmitt stole my leftovers."

"He stole your pizza and you didn't kill him?" Her friends exchanged meaningful glances.

"He also picked off the olives."

"You sure he's just a roommate?" This from Lynn, who was setting out a lunch that looked Gordon Ramsay approved. Knowing Lynn, though, she'd likely made it as she dashed out the door. Lynn was awesome that way.

"Yes. Trust me, even that is too much of him." She tossed her applesauce in the trash. "I can't believe I'm asking this, but any new deaths this week?"

Lynn sliced her panini à la perfection in half and handed it to Annie—on a cute napkin of course. "Is he really that bad?"

"He's really that charming," she said around bits of bacon and avocado. "It was easier when I hated him. Only, the more I learn about him, the more I'm starting to like him."

"It's the lure of the unattainable lover syndrome," Beckett said. "It drives guys like Emmitt nuts."

"What do you mean?" Annie asked, because it was better than focusing on the way her belly dipped when she thought about being his lover.

"Guys like Emmitt never have to work hard for things, so when they meet a challenge like, say . . . a woman who expresses her lack of interest, they become invested in proving you wrong."

"He wants what he can't have," Lynn agreed.

Beckett sat back in her chair and propped her feet up on the empty seat between them. "You want to go back to thinking he's a tool? Go along with the flirting and pretend you're really into him. He'll disappear. Trust me, that's his MO."

"Are you saying sleep with him?" she asked, annoyed at the way her belly fluttered.

"Flirt, kiss, sleep." Beckett shrugged. "What's the worst that can happen?"

"I sleep with my roommate!"

"Who never stays in town for very long," Beckett pointed out. "If he doesn't follow his usual MO, then it's no biggie because your contract is up in a few months. And while I'd love for you to stay here forever and ever"—Beckett took her hand—"you have the world to see. Remember?"

She remembered. "What happened to 'Guys aren't worth the heartache? Man-Free Living'?"

"Who said anything about involving your heart? Man-Free Living doesn't mean orgasm-free, or I would have turned in my chip last night. It's about living your life on your terms," Beckett said, and it was as if she were speaking Swahili. Everything Annie did, she did wholeheartedly. Halfway wasn't in her genetic makeup.

Annie had learned firsthand that halfway led to regrets, and regrets wound up hurting the people you loved. Then again, maybe that was her problem. "You mean a fling?"

"He's been called the Male Wonder of the World. Supposedly

one night with him and it's like you've been reborn. I've even heard his dic—"

"Beckett!" Annie stopped her friend before she did the whole *I once caught a fish this big* routine.

"What? See if it's legend or legit. Either way, you have one hell of an awesome rebound sex story, and you close the door on Clark forever."

"He's marrying someone else. That pretty much closed, locked, and deadbolted the door."

"But this would be on your terms," Lynn said, and Annie's belly fluttered for a whole different reason.

Everything in Annie's life had always been on someone else's terms. From birth, all the way up until Clark, she'd never acted out or taken a risk for fear of disappointing someone.

"I've never had a fling," she admitted. "I've never had a one-night stand."

Even saying it made her feel as if she'd engineered her entire existence around exceeding external expectations. And maybe she had. Annie was so desperate to fit in, her life had been short on risk and adventure.

She'd learned early on that Asian women were placed in one of two stereotypes: the exotic dragon lady or the bookish curve setter. Annie didn't relate to either, but the older she became, the more determined people were to label her.

Her mother had once explained that when people struggle to understand someone different from themselves, they find comfort in labels. Annie had a few labels to overcome. She was a woman of color, raised by white parents in a predominantly white community. And she was adopted.

All things that made her different—not relatable.

She found, once labeled, people didn't bother trying to know *her*, and instead relied on the role they deemed the most fitting when making their assessments. To avoid awkward situations, she'd allowed herself to be cast, and even played the role to perfection because, like everything else in her life, Annie did it wholeheartedly. Which was how she'd become a grown woman

who didn't know what she'd find staring back at her in the mirror most mornings.

Damn, she was tired of wondering.

Annie slumped in her chair. "I'm almost thirty and I've never had a one-night stand. That's weird, isn't it?"

"It's not weird," Lynn said, but Beckett covered her mouth as if Annie had just confessed that she'd never licked the bottom of an ice-cream carton.

Emmitt was a lot like ice cream. Moose Tracks ice cream with its swirled caramel and fudge around chunks of cookie dough. One bite would lead to scarfing down an entire tub. Only to wake up the next morning, bloated and nauseous, vowing to never give in again. Until the next lonely night came along, and Moose Tracks was the only fix.

"I'm a binger," she said. "Work, junk food, Netflix. My control vanishes. Did you know I watched all three seasons of *This Is Us* in a single week? I got out of bed only to get tissues and pay the pizza delivery guy."

"So maybe you're just not a one-night-stand kind of girl," Beckett said, this time without an ounce of judgment in her tone. "Doesn't mean you can't have a fun summer fling."

Her heart raced at the very idea. "I've never had a casual anything. Not even friends."

Annie had never subscribed to the concept of a permanent ex. She kept in touch with every friend and boyfriend she'd ever had. In fact, she was the only reason the In-Bees were still so close. She took seriously the responsibility of fostering and nurturing relationships.

"And I wonder why I keep getting my heart tromped on." She laughed. "I've gone into every relationship I've ever had as if that person were the missing piece of me. And hoping I was theirs."

"Talk about pressure," Beckett said. "On you and the guy."

"I don't know how to do it any other way."

"Hey, as a fellow good girl, I get it," Lynn said. "Thinking long term, always doing the right thing, putting everyone else

first. It can make you nuts. Trust me, it gets to all of us at one point or another. For me it was spring break 2010. I have a tattoo of Zac Efron on my butt to prove it."

Beckett owl eyed Lynn. "Like *High School Musical* Efron? Or *The Greatest Showman* Efron?"

"*High School Musical.*"

Beckett laughed so hard, she snorted.

"Wait, I'm still stuck on you having a tattoo!" Annie gasped. "You are a bigger good girl than I could even aspire to."

"That's because I learned my lesson. Making stupid decisions when suffering from bad-girl envy is a decision you will come to regret."

"Maybe that's the problem," Annie said. "I've never done anything I regretted. I've never even attempted to do something a little wild for fear I'd regret it. Or disappoint someone. Or—"

"Been there, done that, got the tattoo. You aren't missing out." Lynn was trying really hard to prove a point. A point that clearly worked for Lynn, since she had a career she loved, a circle of friends who loved her back, and went home every night to a super great—not to mention incredibly hot—guy who adored her.

It was dangerous to get into a comparison game with someone like Lynn. Not that Annie didn't deserve the same kind of happiness, but Lynn wore happiness like a silk robe. She made it look sexy. She wore so many hats and wore them with ease.

Annie didn't even know what effortless and sexy looked like on her. And she wouldn't go so far as saying she was depressed, but finding happiness always seemed harder for her than everyone else. Whereas Lynn could make vegan cookies taste like the real thing, Annie wasn't even sure if her mom's soup made her happy.

She was tired of trusting everyone else. Wanted to experience things for herself. Wasn't that what this adventure of hers was about? Man-free didn't have to mean no flings. It just meant living her life for herself and not for a man.

"But how do I know if I don't even try? And look where caution has gotten me. My mom used to say, 'Good girls get good

husbands.' And here I am, single and childless with a wedding dress fit for another woman."

"You say that as if it's a bad thing." Beckett held up a hand. "Not the wedding-dress part, but the rest of it."

"It just seems like I've been playing by the rules and no one else has. Or maybe everyone's playing by a different set of rules and I was never given the playbook. Otherwise, how is it possible that every time I meet a good guy, he tells me I'm the best thing that's ever happened to him, and in the next breath he just wants to be friends? Well, I'm tired of being everyone's friend. I want to have some fun. You know what happens to women who spend their entire lives trying to do the right thing and thinking about consequences?" Annie stood. "You turn thirty never having had a one-night stand or a tattoo on your ass."

"And the biggest good girl award goes to you," Lynn deadpanned.

"Are you saying I shouldn't take a risk here and there? Because, serious confession time, I've never even kissed a stranger."

"Kiss away." Lynn laughed. "Just be careful you don't wind up with Zac Efron tattooed on your left ass cheek."

The sun was calling it, disappearing into the horizon and settling in for a good night's sleep. Something Annie would normally be doing, but tonight she had other plans.

Drinks with her girlfriends—on a work night! One couldn't go bad girl over a single serving of applesauce. There were steps to be taken, toes to be dipped, skills to be acquired before she took the plunge.

She wanted to splash around, identify dangerous waters so as not to get caught up in a current that pulled her out to sea.

Annie got out of her car and nearly melted in the humidity. Or maybe it was the anticipation of tonight. She was meeting Lynn and Beckett at the Crow's Nest, a bar and grill that jutted out over Lovers' Point beach, offering some of the best views in town—since it was located between the Coast Guard office and the firehouse.

The views of the Atlantic were nice too.

The former 150-year-old fish market had been repurposed into a place where Rome's locals could pull up a chair and throw back a few with friends while listening to live music. The two-story bar specialized in drinks served by the shot, shaker, or half shell and fancied itself a Rhode Island sourced, caught, and brewed kind of grill—making it a local hot spot.

Tonight was Tidepool Tuesday, so the billiards were on the house and anything that came in a barrel or a shell was half off. Half off meant double the drinks, double the laughs, and double the crowd.

Annie spotted her friends at the far end of the bar and waved before stepping down into the sway. As she pushed her way through the sea of tipsy patrons, barely able to see above the swell of the crowd, she quickly found herself disoriented.

"Excuse me," she yelled to be heard over the crowd. No one moved.

She patted a large man in front of her on the shoulder. "Excuse me, just trying to get past."

Being vertically challenged never really bothered her unless she was in a big crowd, and people used her petite stature as an excuse to ignore her. Like Paul Bunyan, who glanced down at her then, with a smile, went back to chatting up his bros.

"Jerk," she mumbled while searching for another way across the room. She backed up to retrace her steps when a hand slid around her waist and pulled her into a very big, very toned chest. She looked up to find a very smug Emmitt smiling down at her.

"If you wanted to dance, you could have just asked," he said, his voice having no trouble carrying over the crowd.

"I didn't even know you were here," she shouted.

"What?" He cupped his ear. "You want to buy me a beer? I'm flattered, but I have to be up-front. I'm not a *kiss on the first date* kind of guy."

"No, I think a date would be too much commitment for you."

That earned her a smile. "Need help out of here?"

"I'm good. Just going over there to meet my friends." She pointed toward the spot where she'd seen them, only Emmitt grabbed her finger and turned it in the opposite direction.

"Seriously?"

"Afraid so. The guys and I have been watching you walk around in circles for about ten minutes. There's even a betting pool on how long you'd last before you started throwing your shoes."

"I don't believe you."

"I'm not surprised." He looked down at her very high, very red, very sexy stilettos, and when he grinned, it was pure sin. "I see you came armed."

"I heard there were pizza thieves afoot." She batted his hand off her waist. "And I was not circling."

His hands went around her waist again with startling speed. She couldn't even protest before he lifted her off the ground as if she weighed twenty pounds and turned her to see his friends. A group of men waved back.

"You're a jerk."

Then he swiveled her to her friends, who were—farther away from her than when she'd started—giving her the A-OK on the hottie.

"Fine, I was a little lost. Can you put me down?" It was hard to appear tough when you were being carried like a child.

He set her down, ever so slowly, their bodies sliding against each other. By the time her feet were on the floor, her entire body was humming. "You did that on purpose."

"Did what?"

"That whole *slide me down your body* move. Is that how you get women? Pretend to save them, then get all handsy?"

Emmitt glanced down at her hands—which were pressed, fingers spread, across his pecs, her body leaning in to his. Even worse, his hands were in his pockets. "Who's getting handsy with who, Nurse Annie?"

She jerked her hands back and, well, she didn't know what to do with them. She was a little light-headed from all the touching and arguing, and she was hyperaware of her body.

"I didn't come here to argue," he went on, "but since you seem so bent on it, want to argue a little more over there, on the dance floor?"

Wanting to test Beckett's "Lure of Unrequited Love" theory, Annie said, "Maybe later. Tonight I'm hanging with my friends."

He gave a well-practiced pout, his hands sliding around her waist yet again. "I thought we were friends."

"Friends don't steal friends' leftovers. Now shoo." She was about to swat him away when the big guy behind her was shoved by an equally big guy, who nearly toppled over Annie. Had Emmitt not curved his body around hers like a cocoon—a warm, manly, yummy-smelling cocoon that was actively shielding her from the world—she would have landed on her butt.

Old-fashioned or not, there was something sexy about a man who placed himself between you and danger. Even if that danger was just a two hundred pound beer bottle with limbs. There was also something almost intimate about the way he held her. Not so much sexy, but as if there were a deeper connection forming between them.

He felt it, too, because that playboy grin faded and his eyes became warm and melty. Which was okay with her, because she was going warm and melty as well—in too many places to count.

"You okay?" he whispered, and he was so close she could hear. She nodded. "How about I help you to your friends, and we never have to speak of this again."

"Agreed. Whoa—" She clung to his neck as she was suddenly airborne. "What are you doing?"

With one arm behind her back, the other beneath her knees, he had her in his arms, as he did a convincing *An Officer and a Gentleman* reenactment through the bar. "Getting you safely to your friends."

"I didn't think you'd carry me. I thought you'd clear a path or something." She squirmed, but he only pulled her closer.

"Give up, Goldilocks," he said. "Clearing a path would have been easier, but then I wouldn't have had the chance to carry you. And I must admit, you look good in my arms."

"Enjoy it, because this is the last time it will ever happen." Damn, why did she have to sound so breathy? Bad girls definitely didn't do breathy.

"Oh, I intend to enjoy it. And Annie, it will happen again, only we'll be doing a hell of a lot more than crossing a dance floor." The intensity of his gaze made those caramel pools heat to melted milk chocolate—a close second in favorite midnight snacks—and Annie was glad she was in his arms, because she was certain her legs were like two wet noodles. "And I would put good money it will be instigated by you."

"You always this sure of yourself?"

"It's the first thing I've been sure of since the night you flashed me your panties." She shivered at his words. He grinned. "Yeah, that's how it will go down, because even though you would rather die than admit it, I get to you. I get to you bad."

Before she could reply, he was sitting her on the stool next to her friends, who were gawking at Annie. And Annie was gawking right back.

Seemed she'd missed the memo stating dump the little black dress and, instead, come as you are. To be fair, her dress was more navy blue than black, but it looked red carpet worthy next to Lynn's pink knit top with white collar.

And don't even get her started on Beckett, who was in her basic blue jeans, teal flip-flops, and a matching teal SAVING MANKIND. ONE MISSING SOCK AT A TIME tank. On her lap was a lop-eared bunny she was training for an autistic girl in town.

"Annie," Lynn said. "Introduce us to your friend."

"Roommate," Annie said.

"We're living together," Emmitt quickly corrected.

Lynn and Beckett exchanged a few looks. Which was okay, since Annie was exchanging a few looks of her own. *What the actual hell?* and *Way to leave a girl hanging* were the heart of her message, with some serious *You guys suck* undertones.

"Lynn, Beckett, this is my *roommate*, Emmitt." She leaned back so hands could be shaken. "Emmitt, these are my sneaky friends who punked me into dressing up for church."

"Sweetie, I've never seen a dress like that in church," Lynn said. "Plus, we didn't want to steal your thunder."

Annie felt her cheeks heat, because she had picked this dress for that exact reason. And while she'd never admit it aloud, she

wondered what Emmitt would think. She hadn't expected him to be here, but secretly she'd been hoping.

Beckett grinned. "No one could steal my thunder." She lifted up the bunny and kissed its nose. "This is Lord Hoppington. He decided to crash girls' night."

If Emmitt thought it was weird that her friend had brought a bunny into a bar, he didn't say anything.

"It's just a dress, and he's only my roommate for a few more days," Annie announced. "I'm looking for a new place to stay."

"That's not a dress. It's a statement." Emmitt scooted closer, sheltering her again from the crush of the crowd. Not a human shield so much as an exclamation point for anyone who might be thinking of bumping her chair. She didn't think he was aware of the gesture, but her nipples took notice. "As for the living arrangement, I think I have a solution."

"You're moving out? Wonderful, I'll bring the boxes and packing tape."

"While I do love me a good box party, admit it, you'd miss me." Before she could say something snarky, he added, "As of four hours ago, I'm Rome High School's official Decoration Chair for the father-daughter dance."

"I have no idea how that relates to your moving out—"

"I'm getting there."

"But you? On a decorating committee? Emmitt, that is the worst idea ever." *Like ever.* "I don't think faux taxidermy and stein collections are really what the committee is looking for."

"Let me restate, I am the committee. Me. Myself. And I. Crazy, right?"

"That's a word for it," Annie said.

"I admit, it's not the ideal position for a self-appointed bachelor, but that was the only way to work on the same committee as Paisley. The list came out today and while I was on the selfie-arbors, P was put in the decorations group. So I had to decide, nail gun and electric saw but never see Paisley or head up Team Glitter and Bling and spend every meeting right next to her."

"And you thought, 'How hard can glitter and bling be'?" Annie asked, not even bothering to hide her disbelief.

"Maybe at first. But then this lady hands me a tome full of color swatches, fabric pieces, and clippings of every formal high school dance from the past decade. These kids are expecting a royal wedding or something."

"What's the theme?" Lynn asked.

"Once Upon a Time," he said, and all the ladies laughed. Even Lord Hoppington twitched a whisker.

"Before you say it, the guys already gave me shit about how I'm going to ruin the dance and Paisley will never speak to me again." With a huge sigh, he sat down on the stool—her stool.

Scooting her over until she had but one butt cheek on the cushion, he slid in beside her. If it hadn't been for his arm around her waist—which was doing some sliding of its own—she would have fallen to the floor. "I was ready to call Rachel, the lady in charge, and admit I was in over my head, but Paisley already knows, so I can't bail."

"Are you breaking out in hives?" Annie turned to her friends. "Emmitt has adverse reactions to commitment, boring wine, and admitting he doesn't have the proper skill set to get the job done."

"Don't forget the green olives." He leaned down to whisper in her ear. "And you haven't seen my skills because, if you had, you'd know I always get the job done."

Goose bumps tingled over her exposed flesh while unadulterated thrills heated up everything else.

"It's a chromosome genetic disorder thing," Beckett was saying. "Ninety-nine percent of males suffer from it." She drained her martini in one swallow. "Imagine an X and one of the legs breaks off. What do you have? Oh, a Y. World's never been the same since. True story."

"Then it's a good thing I saw you," he said to Annie. "Here I am with my broken X, when I see you looking like a Roomba trying to map the room, and it hits me. That book. The one that's sitting on my patio? It was pretty extensive and detailed, leading me to think you have some serious planning skills."

Annie swallowed hard, lowering her voice so the conversation was just between the two of them. "You looked at my wedding planner?"

"Hard not to when it's wide open on my back porch. You've clearly got this event-planning thing down. I mean color schemes, napkin holders. Real thing, who knew napkins needed holders?"

"They're called rings. And it was for a *wedding*, not an event."

"Thanks for the clarification. You've planned four, right?"

Annie looked over her shoulder, relieved to see her friends were engaged in conversation with the bartender. "It was two."

"Two more than most."

"I was nine the first time. The groom was Ricky Martin."

"That explains the Copacabana theme."

Her eyes narrowed. "You snooping through my things?"

"One man's trash is another man's treasure. Tell me, did you intend to invite *all* your exes to the wedding?" he asked, seeming awfully satisfied with himself. "Before meeting you, I'd heard about women who stayed friends with their exes but, like most broken X's, I'd assumed they were an urban legend. Kind of like serial brides."

"Maintaining healthy relationships with one's exes doesn't make a woman a serial bride, it makes her mature," she said, not sounding mature at all.

Annie had always taken pride in the way she maintained close friendships with her exes. Yet talking about it now, considering her proclivity from a fresh perspective, she began to question what it really said about her. Was inviting people who'd disappointed her and broken her heart to share in her special day a sign of maturity, or did it just make her a pushover?

Annie knew which side of the argument Emmitt would fall on, and last week she'd been positive where she landed. But after the irritating situation Clark had put her in, uncaring how it inconvenienced her and complicated her life, Annie realized she needed to do some serious soul searching.

"Well then, mature Anh, what do you say to helping a friend in need? And before you say no again, hear me out. I have an offer you can't refuse."

"You're leaving Rome?"

"Better. I'm asking you to be my official roommate. You can

stay at my place, rent free, until your contract with the hospital is up."

"With you there?" She gave a dramatic sigh. "I don't know. Right now I need to focus on my job and myself. That was my whole reason for coming to Rome."

"Then moving should be out of the question," Beckett interrupted with a grin. "Think of all the time you'd waste checking out new places, applying, credit checks."

"Not to mention the deposit," Emmitt said. "Did Boy Wonder ever get your money back to you?"

"No." And since Clark hadn't returned any of her calls, except with a text saying she didn't need to bring a gift to the wedding because that might be awkward, she wasn't counting on seeing even a penny until after the wedding.

She looked at Emmitt and felt her resolve falter. "Fine. I will help plan, but I am not doing anything the day of."

"Does this mean you're staying?"

"It means I'll think about it."

"Now who's afraid of commitment?" He leaned in. "Come on, just say it, we're good together."

"You stole my pizza."

He waved a hand in surrender. "Won't happen again. I promise. Now, I think we should seal this deal with a kiss."

"If you want to kiss someone, any one of those ladies at the bar would say yes. Go ask one of them."

His gaze trailed down to her lips. "Seems I'm more of a one-woman kind of man lately. Plus I love it when you get all opinionated."

"I'm not in an arguing mood."

He leaned in. "What kind of mood are you in?"

"Are you flirting with me? Because that's not in the room-mate agreement."

"What roommate agreement? You haven't said yes. Are you saying yes?"

"*If* I do, we'll have a roommate agreement drawn up and it will state 'No Kissing' right at the top."

"We'll need to be clear," he said. "No kissing you? Or you can't kiss me? I'm unsure how I feel about that. It's not really fair if you can kiss me but I can't kiss you."

"I'm already regretting this." She put her face in her hands. "Don't you ever stop?"

"Not until I get what I want."

"That's all it is for guys like you."

"What do you mean *guys like me*?" He rested an elbow on the counter, then his cheek on his hands, leaning in as if all ears.

"If this went one flirt longer than you wanted it to go, you'd burn rubber out of here."

"Try me."

"I want to get married and have two kids by the time I'm thirty-five."

"And that's the problem with women like you." He tapped the tip of her nose with his pointer finger—twice. "The second a guy doesn't click off enough boxes in the Potential Husband category, you rule him out."

"I am not like that," she argued, but she so was like that and they both knew it. "And you'd never stay in one spot long enough to find out."

"I don't know, Goldilocks. Maybe I've just been searching for the right bed." He leaned down and rested his lips against the shell of her ear. "Think about it."

Chapter 15

Emmitt didn't have to be an arson investigator to know that if you played with enough fire, eventually someone would get burned.

As he sat on the other side of the bar, watching Annie and her friends, he decided that was reason enough for him to pack up his things and move onto the boat with Levi. The other reason was that barely legal blue number Annie had going on.

Short, sleek, and tied in place by two thin straps that disappeared over her shoulders, only to crisscross all the way down her back—from the curve of her neck to the gentle curve right above her panty line. Thong, he believed, a gut call he'd made while carrying her across the room.

There hadn't been much between his hand and her back because of the open nature of the dress. It must have been a bitch to get into. Getting out of it would be a whole other story.

A single tug of the string and the whole thing would come apart.

Then there was her body, slight and delicate with a waist his hands could span all the way around, and they did. While some might think her demure or fragile, Emmitt knew better.

What Annie had going on was a steely grace that was as rare as it was lethal. The main reason Emmitt had stationed himself on the opposite side of the bar, where a group of guys he often

hung with were shooting the shit. Not that he was tracking the conversation—he was too busy watching his roomie nursing a pink cocktail.

If she wound up like her friends, who were swigging their drinks as if they were punch, she might need help. And never one to leave a lady in need, he would offer. He was good with complicated dresses. He was real helpful that way.

Tonight, she'd worn her black layered hair sleek and straight, the glossy strands hitting right below her chin and inching shorter in the back, exposing her elegant neck.

There was something erotic about seeing the back of a woman's neck. It was as if he were getting a peek at something that should be covered. Viewing a silky patch of skin he'd love to gently bite.

He couldn't stop looking at her, and she knew it. Oh, she was pretending to be absorbed in conversation with her friends, but the way she kept fidgeting with her earlobe told him that he'd gotten to her.

Levi waved a hand in front of Emmitt's face. "You going to order?"

"What?"

"The bar is packed, and the dining room is a forty-minute wait." Levi pointed to the crowd clogging the entry to his bar, where local families and a few unfamiliar faces were waiting to be seated. "Dan called in sick, and so did my new hostess, which means they're probably taking each other's temperature with their tongues, so I don't have time for you to be eye-fucking my patrons. Either order or give up your bar stool."

"I'll have a burger and one of whatever you have on tap." It had been well over twelve hours since his last painkiller. "And for the record, I'm not eye-fucking your patrons."

Emmitt was only interested in one patron, and she'd throw her stilettos at him if he used that term.

Levi set a frosty mug under the spigot of a local IPA. "You know Gray will kick your ass if you screw around with his temp."

"I'm aware." And it wouldn't be nearly as bad as what Emmitt would do to himself if he hurt her. "And nothing's happened."

That wasn't entirely true. Nothing physical had happened, but a whole lot of other stuff was happening even as Annie pretended to ignore him. That she was pretending so hard confirmed it.

Being around her felt good. Watching her prance around his kitchen in her cotton pajamas while griping that he'd drunk all the milk was even better. Sitting at the kitchen table and sharing pizza and beer with her made him wish for things he shouldn't be wishing for.

Levi slid Emmitt his beer, and frothy foam spilled over the side and onto the bar top, which was made of planking stripped from an old boat. "You need to get laid by someone other than Annie before you do something stupid."

"Says the born-again virgin." Emmitt took a long swig. "Unless something happened since I was here last, you haven't been on a date with someone other than Paisley since Beth sailed away with that weekend warrior from Vermont."

"I've dated."

"Lotion and a sock don't count."

Levi rested his elbows on the bar top and leaned in. "You're just pissy because you've got a thing for Annie, and it scares the shit out of you."

"So, I think she's cute. So what?"

"Cute? I don't know if that is the pussiest thing you've ever said or the most refreshing."

"How else do I say that while, yes, I find her insanely attractive, I also like her, and not just in my bed. Not that I've had her in my bed. Okay I have, just not at the same time as me. But what I'm saying is I like her out of bed. It's weird."

"It's about to get weirder." Levi's grin was a little too big for Emmitt's comfort.

Someone slid up to the bar next to him. A very cute someone with pink glossy lips, who hip-checked him as she took half his chair. "Okay, deal."

"Seriously?" he asked, knowing he had a dopey grin on his face.

"Are you giving me a chance to reconsider?"

"Bartender, two glasses of your finest boring Pino Grigio." He held up two fingers.

Annie raised just one. "No more boring Pino for me." Then to Levi, "I'll have what he's having."

"Actually, she can have mine." He waved Levi off, then slid his mug her way.

She eyed the mug with suspicion. "Trying to pass off bad beer?"

"There are a couple things I'm not bad at. Picking a good beer is the other one."

After a skeptical look, she tilted her head back, making the delicate lines of her neck elongate, and took a sip. A tiny sip. Then her eyes twinkled with delight and she took a big gulp.

It was the freckles, he decided. The light sprinkling right across the bridge of her nose and cheeks was all kinds of cute. He'd never considered himself a freckles man. But she had him seriously reconsidering.

"So, what changed?" he asked.

She shrugged. "When I left Connecticut, my goal was to try new things. To throw caution to the wind and be open to experiences that come my way."

He picked up the mug and took a drink. "I've seen your aim. I wouldn't advise throwing anything."

"Then I will go over these one by one." She fanned a stack of bar napkins under his nose. "Now that it's official. Here."

"What are those?" There must have been fifteen napkins in the pile.

"Things any roommate should know, but since we weren't officially roommates, I won't hold it against you." She placed the first one down. "No kissing of any kind, as previously agreed upon."

"I don't remember agreeing to any such thing."

She ignored him and placed another napkin down, spinning it to face him.

"No leftover stealing," he read. "Whoever claims the leftover gets the leftover, unless said leftover is pizza; then it automatically belongs to Annie." He plucked the pen from her fingers and poised it on the napkin to make an addition. "May I?"

"Be my guest."

"You mean, be my roommate." As he scribbled on the napkin, he noticed she was reading over his shoulder, so he turned his body to block her view. She let out a huff that had him chuckling. When he was finished, he slid it to her.

She picked it up and laughed. The napkin now read, *Whoever claims the leftover gets the leftover, unless said leftover is pizza with green things on it. Then it automatically belongs to Annie. All other pizzas are up for grabs.*

"Next." He wiggled his fingers impatiently. She handed over the rule, which he read to himself, then tossed on the bar top. "Wait. You're bitching that I leave the toilet seat up in my own bathroom?"

"When the bathroom is connected to the bedroom I'm sleeping in, yes." She was indignant now, and for some reason that turned him on. "I don't like falling in the water at three in the morning."

"Who says you get the bed?"

She handed him the next napkin and he looked down, but focusing on the handwriting strained his eyes. "You read it."

The quirk of her brow was pretty much screaming bullshit. He quirked his back, and with a huff she reluctantly read it aloud. "Annie gets the bed, the whole bed, because she was there first and called dibs on it."

She gave him a sunny smile, and he laughed. That smile had him doing a whole lot more than laughing, but he was pretty sure *that* was against the rules too. But damn, her smiles were going to create problems. He already knew it. "How about we put up a wall of pillows and—"

"Nope," she interrupted. "The whole bed or it's a deal breaker."

"Fine, but I get to hold the remote control." He couldn't give two shits about the remote control. He just didn't want her to

think he was a pushover. Even though, when it came to her, he totally was.

"As long as it's understood that just because you hold the remote, doesn't make you boss."

"Don't I know it."

She pointed to the napkin, and he dutifully added that he didn't get to be the boss. They went through the remaining napkins, mostly rules about dishes and cooking and snooping. He added a few of his own, including that anything silk or lace had to be either in her drawer or on her body. If he found it hanging in the shower, she'd have to model for him.

When they were done, she stacked the napkins and handed them to him. He folded them in half and slid them into his front pocket. "Feel better?"

She bumped her shoulder with his. "A little. But there's one more."

Her eyes were filled with uncertainty as she handed him the last napkin. It was warm, the corners worried from being clutched in her hand. He wondered if it was separate from the others because she'd been considering holding it back.

He looked down, and his chest gave a hard thump. "Roommates have to be up-front and honest with each other. No fake promises or lies."

He met her gaze, but she was fiddling with the mug, tracing a line of foam down the side with her finger. Her eyes were hidden by a curtain of hair, her shoulders slumped forward like a protective barrier.

He hated that she felt the need to add the last two words, because it meant she'd had her fill of lies and disappointments, and that didn't sit right with him.

Annie dedicated her heart to everything she did and everyone she met. Her warmth filled the room even before she entered. What really astounded him was her amazing capacity to love. If she loved as openly and deeply as she did everything else, he could only imagine how many times she'd been let down over the years. How many Clarks had, intentionally or not, caused her pain?

Tucking her hair behind her ear, he tilted her head toward him. "No fake promises or lies."

She gave him a small smile. "Then we have a deal." She stuck out her hand, and the minute it slipped between his, something heated sparked between them. Rules or not, they were going to end up in bed.

True story.

She took a sip of beer, then passed him the mug. "Can I ask you something? Not because I'm snooping, but because now that I'm your roommate, if anything happens, I should know." This time she reached out, running a gentle finger from his temple to his eyebrow. "How bad is your head injury?"

Not what he was expecting. And not something he wanted to talk about in a noisy bar, if ever. So he leaned back until she was forced to drop her hand. "I'll tell you. Just not right now, okay?"

"Okay, but you're going to have to come clean soon. Your file is being sent from China, and I want to know what it says. But I'd rather hear it from you."

He didn't respond to her statement, only flagged down Levi to get a glass of water. But when Levi came over, he had his cell in hand.

"Where's Paisley?" Levi asked as if Emmitt had gotten her an after-school job at a strip club.

"She's at her friend's house working on some project."

"What project and what friend?" This was from Gray, who was on speaker phone. "Because Owen stopped by to work on their chemistry project. He said he swung by your place but you weren't there, so when she didn't answer his text, he came here. This is the second time Owen's come looking for her when she was supposed to be with him."

"I'm not sure what project," he said, feeling a little like a kid being called into the principal's office. "And she's at Sammy's."

"Sammy?" Levi sputtered. "You let her go home with Sammy?"

Gray said something similar except his question was much more colorful that Levi's. "Yeah, she seemed like a nice girl." From across the gym anyway.

Levi ran a hand down his face. "Sammy is Samuel Allen. The biggest player at the high school. Or as the teens would say, the biggest fuck boy in RHS history."

The same knot that had twisted around his chest when she'd told him he was ruining her life tightened two times harder. He told himself to breathe in and breathe out. "Fuck boy or not, Paisley wouldn't do anything."

"You mean like sneak a mini skirt and thigh-high boots to school in her backpack, sneak out, steal my beer?" Gray yelled. "Wake up and smell the estrogen."

"Dude," Levi said. "Sammy is you fifteen years ago. Just better looking."

"Shit." Emmitt stood and started searching his pockets for his keys, coming up empty. He looked at Levi. "I Ubered here."

"Of course you did. I'll get her," Gray said.

"No," Emmitt ground out. "I'm on duty tonight. I screwed up. I'll get her."

"You sure?" Gray sounded less than convinced, and Emmitt wanted to pull him through the phone. "You can't let this shit slide."

"I know how to parent."

"Says the guy who Ubered to a bar on his night," Gray spat out.

Emmitt was about to say something he couldn't take back when he felt a warm hand slide around his arm. And then there was Annie, with that big heart of hers right there in her eyes. "Actually, I'm headed home. We can pick up Paisley on the way."

Chapter 16

"I can't believe she lied to me!"

It was the first thing Emmitt said after folding himself into Annie's car. She'd barely had time to say goodbye to her friends before he started ushering her out the door. Beckett gave her the *Go for it* thumbs-up while Lynn was mouthing "Zac Efron tattoo."

At least she'd make one of them proud.

"In my experience, teen girls lie when they don't feel as if they have options," Annie said.

"That girl has more options than a drive-thru menu," he said. "I don't know about Curly or Moe back there, but I've made it clear she can come to me about anything."

She cut Emmitt a glance. "Even if it's about a cute boy?"

"Yes." He seemed absolute in his answer, but moments later added, "A cute boy? Absolutely. Some tool who's old enough to shave and is looking to 'Netflix and chill' with my kid? No conversation needed. It's a hard no."

Yikes! That was a pretty extreme answer to a very benign question. She could only hope he hadn't reacted this way with Paisley. If he had, it explained a lot.

"Let me guess, Sammy is the tool in question?"

"Fuck." He hit the dash. "I know I sound like some naive parent, and I know I said I had this handled, but I really

thought . . . no, I really believed she was being straight with me." Emmitt ran a hand down his face. "How could I have not put this together sooner?" He patted his pants pockets, front then back. "Crap. I can't remember where I put his address."

He rechecked the front again before pulling out all kinds of napkins. Their roommate agreement he put on the dash. A bunch of receipts and gum wrappers. Those went on her floor. A business card with lipstick on it balanced on this thigh. Last, he pulled out a wadded-up piece of crepe paper.

"Here it is." He punched the address into his phone and, lovely, they were being directed by what sounded like an Australian phone sex operator.

She motioned to a business card. "What's that?"

He picked it up and studied it before slipping it into his pocket. "It's from a woman I met at Paisley's school."

"Seriously, you're using your kid to meet hookups." Annie snatched the card and threw it out the window.

"First, I went to the school to be with my daughter. Second, Grace is on the dance committee and gave me her number. I didn't even know she stuck it in here. And last, even if I had been into her, which I am not, Gray warned me off sleeping with the PTA moms."

"You needed guidance in that?" Annie clicked on her blinker and turned toward the residential side of town, as the GPS instructed.

"God, that sounded awful," he admitted.

"I was just giving you a hard time," she said, and he chuckled. "So what exactly did Paisley say this afternoon?"

"We were at another dance committee meeting." He glanced her way. "She comes bounding up all smiles and *Please Dad*, asking if she could go to a friend's house. And if it weren't so dark in here you'd see the big fucking air quotes I put around the term 'friend.' So yeah . . . she sweetens the deal by giving me a hug, right there in front of God, Principal, and the student body, and I started thinking maybe I'm not the worst dad in the world."

"What would you have said if you knew Sammy was a guy?"

she asked quietly as she pulled off the main road into one of the newer developments.

"I would have told her no. Then I would have told her all the reasons why it was a no. And before you say it, I understand that is the exact wrong approach."

"I didn't say anything."

"You didn't have to. I can hear your judgment. But the bottom line is, she didn't ask, I didn't say no, she lied. End of story."

Extremely aware that the worried dad in her passenger seat was gripping the oh-shit handle as if it were "the tool's" neck, she ventured cautiously with her next question. "Did she lie? Or did you make an assumption that she didn't bother to correct?"

When his answer was to crack his neck from side to side, Annie pulled up to a red light and stopped before turning to face him. "Emmitt?"

Absolute silence.

"When you're done plotting this poor kid's death, you might want to think about that. Like when everyone in your family assumes you're doing fine and you don't correct them."

He turned to her and—*holy smokes*—he looked ready to blow. One wrong word from either Paisley or her friend who was a boy and Emmitt would go off like a roman candle.

"I know where you're going with this, and no, it's not the same as me hiding my medical issues."

And he was back to staring out the windshield.

"So you admit there's a problem?"

"The light is green."

"No one's behind me, so we can wait here all night."

He leaned back against the headrest and closed his eyes. "There's a problem."

His raw honesty cracked through her carefully constructed walls and wrapped around her heart.

"How bad?" she whispered. Annie reached across the seat and took off his ballcap. Instead of pulling away or swatting at her hand, he leaned into it while she gently traced the puckered skin above his brow. "You're what, four weeks out from the accident and still having light sensitivity issues, headaches when

you read, dizzy spells, or you wouldn't keep riding with me. How bad was the swelling?"

His eyes opened, but he didn't move. Except to take her hand with his and press it to his cheek as if he found her touch soothing. "I was unconscious for the better part of a week. Some of it medically induced, some of it not. Thank God I insisted on wearing my plate carrier that day, because I only wound up with a couple of bruised ribs."

"The plate carrier probably saved your life."

He finally looked at her. "The doctors said the same thing. It also limited the area of scarring but didn't do a damn thing to protect against a baseball-sized chunk of cement to the head."

Annie slid her fingers over the bruise, tracing until they disappeared into his hair. "Where is the scarring?"

"Most of it's on my back."

Which explained why she hadn't seen it that first night. Without having to ask, he tugged the hem of his shirt up and turned his body until she could see his back. She didn't need to flick on the overhead light. The traffic light had cycled back to red, casting enough of a glow for her to get a good look at the scars. They weren't from stitches. They were from pellet-sized pieces of concrete spraying his body at a close distance.

A galaxy of craters ran across the right side of his lower back, angry gouging wounds that told a story. Annie didn't have to try all that hard to fill in the details. She'd seen enough in the ER to piece it all together.

"Emmitt," she whispered, because he'd been shouldering this all by himself. Never once letting on how much pain she knew he had to be in. Walking to the market, working on the dance, even carrying her through the crowd at the bar must have caused him excruciating pain.

He whispered something back, maybe something sweet, she wasn't sure. She was too busy running her palm down his side and staring into his eyes. He was doing the staring thing, glancing at her from over his shoulder, his gaze tracing her lips.

It was starting to become inevitable, this thing between them.

She could feel it in the air whenever they were within touching distance, growing stronger the longer they were together.

A horn honked behind them and *poof*, the building intimacy became awkward, and Annie pulled through the intersection.

Clearing her throat, she said, "If your head took even half the force of your back, you need to tell Grayson."

"No way," he said, and out of the corner of her eye she watched as he stubbornly crossed his arms across his chest, making his biceps flex. The man was a driving hazard. "He'll tell Paisley and then she'll worry, and after Michelle . . ." He shook his head. "I can't tell them. Not right now. I need Gray to give me a clean bill of health so I can go back to work."

"You'll have to come clean soon. If Grayson gets your records from China before you tell him, he'll be hurt."

"He won't get them. I told the hospital not to release them. I need to be cleared by a doctor before I can finish my piece on the concrete factory. And Gray is too much of a Goody Two-shoes to sign off on me if he knew, so he can't know yet."

"Nothing wrong with having a Goody Two-shoes on your side," she said, wondering why she'd thought being a bad girl would be fun. "And loving someone means trusting them. It's hard to have one without the other. You've made a family with these guys, and family doesn't keep secrets."

"Is that your roundabout way of saying that Paisley's not straight with me because I'm not straight with her?"

"I'm not a parent, and I don't know the first thing about being one, so I don't know how much you should tell Paisley. You know her better than I do. But maybe try coming clean on smaller things." He was looking at her again with those golden brown eyes. "When she asked if she could go to Sammy's, you could have told her you'd been looking forward to spending tonight with her."

"I don't ever want her to feel obligated to hang out with me."

"Why not?" she asked. "I felt obligated to hang out with my dad every Saturday when he'd take me fishing."

"You fish?"

"With my dad I do. And stop grinning—it's our thing. Being obligated to do stuff with your parents is normal at her age. Her pretending to be all put out for having to spend time with you is normal as well, because inside she's secretly enjoying it."

"Fishing, huh?" he asked.

She squared her shoulders. "Yes, and I happen to be pretty good too." She placed her hand on his arm. "Emmitt, I know she loves your time together and probably even looks forward to it."

"Thank you for that, but I'm still not telling them."

"Men." She sighed. "Is this another symptom of male chromosome genetic disorder?"

"I don't know. Up until this week I thought I understood women, but clearly I have lost my touch, or that blast did more damage than I thought."

"Don't go blaming a poor piece of concrete for your being a stubborn ass."

He grinned. "You like my stubborn ass."

"What are the things you need to remember?" Annie said.

"Validate her feelings. Levelheadedness leads to listening. Don't be a dictator." Emmitt repeated the guidelines they'd talked about.

"And?"

"And remember, no matter what is going on inside that house, love her for exactly who she is in that moment." He sent her a sidelong glance. "That's a lot to ask of a dad whose kid is sneaking around with the school fuckboy." Annie raised a condemning brow, and Emmitt sighed. "Fine, but I don't have to like the moment."

Annie chuckled, but inside her heart went out to him. Giving the town playboy a daughter who was into playboys was payback for all the nights his dates' parents spent pacing the floor—awaiting their daughter's safe return. "Nope, but you do need to try to see it through her eyes. She knows she screwed up, is probably super disappointed with herself. And while she

needs to know that what she did was not okay, she also needs to know that you still love her."

"Right," Emmitt said, but he was too busy glaring out the window to be looking at Annie.

She followed his line of vision to the teenagers up ahead participating in some pretty PG-13 PDA. There was kissing, and then there was *kissing*, and the two high schoolers were quickly passing the first kind, racing toward the second.

"Not on my watch." Emmitt unfolded himself from the passenger seat, and before Annie could tell him to take a deep breath, he was already halfway up the walk, his chest puffed out, his arms pulled slightly from his body and swaying as he walked.

He looked like the Hulk coming to crash the party.

"Hey," he yelled as he disappeared into the night. "What are you doing to my daughter?"

"You're not my dad!" some girl said.

"Where's Paisley? Paisley Bradley-Rhodes, you better get your butt out here or I'm coming in!"

Not the levelheaded she was hoping for.

Annie strained to hear what was said next but could only make out the words "worst" and "nightmare," and she was certain it was Emmitt talking.

She told herself not to snoop. *This is none of your business.* Emmitt and Paisley were both going to be embarrassed by how tonight was going down. They didn't need some short-term tenant gawking at, what should be, a private family moment. That was what she told herself as she ducked her head to look out the passenger window.

The sun had set hours ago, and the moon was barely cutting through the thick fog that had blown in off the ocean. She could make out figures but no details, leaving her with two options: turn her car to face the house and flash the high beams, or press her nose to the passenger's side window and squint.

While the first choice was tempting, she decided to check out how good the view was from the other side of the car. After un-

buckling her seat belt, she climbed across the console and, knees on the seat, searched through the window for Emmitt.

She spotted him. He was standing on the front porch, with Paisley next to him while he towered over a boy who was likely Sammy. To the kid's credit, he didn't wet his pants or burst out crying. *If he came at me like that*, Annie thought, *I would have*.

"You. Car. Now!" Emmitt bellowed at Paisley, then turned back to Sam, and even through the fogged-up window, he looked lethal. "This is over. Understand?"

The kid stood silent as Emmitt marched Paisley—poor girl looked as if she were walking to her execution—straight to the car.

"Shit." They were headed her way.

In a panic, Annie lost her balance and tumbled backward, landing ass-first between the console and seat. She twisted and turned, used the steering wheel to get leverage, then cursed herself for not taking yoga more seriously. Wedging her heel into the seat, she pushed up and—thank God she was free—rolled into her seat.

She smoothed her hair out of her face and pretended to be watching the wind blowing through the trees.

Both doors opened at once, and she felt the car dip to the right a little before Emmitt settled in the passenger seat and then slammed the door. So hard the car rocked.

A little afraid of what she might find, she turned her head and saw one very pissed off father who was struggling with the reality that his daughter had conned him. It wouldn't be the last time Paisley pulled one over on Emmitt, but this time was hard because it was the first.

Her heart went out to him. Never had she wanted to hug someone as much as she wanted to hug Emmitt just then. His jaw was clenched, his muscles taut, and his body language screamed *failure*.

"My life is officially over," Paisley hissed as Annie pulled away from the curb and headed toward home. "I'm never going back to school again. Maybe I can homeschool or transfer

to Eastland High, but no way am I ever going to be able to face Sam or any of his friends!"

"You should have thought of that before you lied to me," Emmitt ground out.

"I didn't lie. I said I was going to my friend Sammy's house. Sam is my friend, and I was where? Oh, at his house! It's not my fault you don't know who Sam is. Daddy and Uncle Levi would have. And if they didn't, they would have asked before saying yes."

The comment was meant to hurt, but Annie didn't think Paisley realized just how much power she had over her dad— who didn't move, except for his hand tightening around the bill of his ballcap.

Annie knew Paisley's comment was spoken in anger, but the words hit Emmitt so hard he flinched. His face went blank and he stared blindly through the windshield. Annie's heart broke for him. Although Paisley would probably forget the whole incident in a month's time, for Emmitt her words were Sharpied into his heart. Every future decision he made as a parent would be impacted by this moment. Whenever he was confronted with a hard situation, he'd question himself.

"Are you seriously blaming this on me?" he finally said. "I know Levi and Gray would have asked—they made that fuc . . . *abundantly* clear when no one knew where you were."

"You could have texted to find out. Or called and I would have told you where I was. You didn't have to come barging in and threaten Sam or embarrass me in front of everyone!"

"You threatened a teenager?" Annie asked.

"He's eighteen and I didn't threaten him, just enlightened him on how things were going to be moving forward."

"No," Paisley argued. "You came in all President of the Cock Block Committee when nothing was happening. *Nothing!* And now nothing is ever going to happen."

Emmitt's grin said he wouldn't be losing any sleep over that.

"We were just hanging out," Paisley continued. "With his friends. And then his sister came out, and he introduced us, and

the minute we started talking, the guys acted like we weren't even there. I think Sam just invited me over because his sister's a freshman and doesn't have any friends and he thinks I'm nice or something. So all that 'This is over' BS only made me look stupid. He's just a friend, even though I thought maybe it was more. Basically he's never going to speak to me again, if that makes you happy."

Annie looked in the rearview mirror right as Paisley's lower lip began trembling. But no matter how hard she tried to keep her emotions at bay, she'd clearly hit her breaking point and burst into tears. She was no longer trying to hide her feelings or interested in talking to her father. In fact, she slid on a sweatshirt and pulled the hood over her head, cinching it around her face.

Annie was uncertain how to proceed. This was clearly a family situation and she wasn't family. Then again, Emmitt had come to her for help, not to mention her heart ached for Paisley. The poor girl had been caught, tarred, and feathered in front of half the varsity football team. She'd just experienced her first heartbreak—in a very public forum—and, more than anything, needed her dad's reassurance.

Annie reached over and gently squeezed Emmitt's hand, letting him know that she was here for him. His chest rose, then fell, and after a few breaths he gave her a little squeeze back.

"It doesn't make me happy, P," he finally said, his voice three octaves lower than it had been moments ago. "Seeing you upset would never make me happy."

Paisley didn't answer, just let his words hang in the air while she stared out the window and silently cried in the back seat. Emmitt looked as if he was debating between grounding her for life and buying her a convertible to get her to stop crying.

Annie let the silence go on for another few streets before she had to say something. She glanced again in the rearview mirror and saw Paisley curled into herself. Emmitt looked about as miserable, only he wasn't crying.

"What if he does talk to you again?" Annie asked, and before Paisley could answer, Emmitt was already shaking his head.

"Are you crazy?" Emmitt shot her a hard look. "He's eighteen. She's fifteen."

This time she shot him a look before returning her attention to the rearview mirror. She waited until Paisley met her gaze before saying, "What if he did talk to you again, and he wanted to be more than friends? Your being underage is a natural concern for your dad. Especially when you weren't up-front about today."

"If I was up-front, he would have said no," Paisley said with a sniffle.

"*He* is sitting right here. And *he* not only knows teenage boys, he knows the law. Sam is eighteen and you're a minor. End of story."

"I can only imagine how flattering it would be to have a senior guy ask you to hang out," Annie said gently. "How embarrassing it would have been to explain that your dad wouldn't let you come over. But if you love someone, you have to trust them. One doesn't work without the other. Do you love your dad?"

"Sometimes."

"Then you need to trust that he's doing what he thinks is the right thing for you."

"He thinks the right thing is for me to die a virgin." Paisley sat forward. "It's my body, my choice."

"Not until you're eighteen and living on your own," he said.

"Can't wait!"

Silence filled the car until it was thick enough to choke on. No one said a word, not even when Annie pulled into the driveway and put the car in Park. She undid her seat belt and turned to face Emmitt. He didn't turn her way, so she just waited until he finally looked back. When their eyes met, instead of being pissed, he took a deep breath and then gave a small, defeated smile.

"I'm trying my best to see why this is such a big deal," Paisley said.

Emmitt closed his eyes, and Annie could almost see him counting to ten.

"Seriously?" He turned in his seat to face his daughter for the first time since they'd gotten in the car. "That's your takeaway?"

Emmitt silently stared at his daughter and, as the seconds ticked by, he looked more and more overwhelmed by exhaustion. Finally he shook his head and said, "Then try harder, kiddo."

Annie gave Paisley a soft smile to let her know that while she had screwed up, she wasn't alone. Then she rested a hand on Emmitt's leg. "Or you could say, 'Loving someone means trusting them. And pushing boundaries is what kids are supposed to do. So starting now, I'll trust you enough to sit down and have an open and honest conversation about anything, as long as you promise to be honest back with me."

"Holy shit," Paisley said.

"Language," Emmitt scolded.

"You guys are totally dating," Paisley scolded back.

Annie jerked her hand off his leg as if it were on fire, her head rapidly shaking back and forth. "God, no. We're just roommates."

"Good." Paisley grabbed her backpack. "Because you deserve way better than my dad."

The slamming of the car door was like a gunshot right through Emmitt's chest. It did a pretty good job of rattling his skull too.

"I blew that." He closed his eyes to keep the overhead light from piercing his retina. "On a scale of *She'll get over it* to *Imminent emancipation*, how bad was it?"

"It was like you were walking through a minefield and decided to wear clown shoes," she said, and he laughed.

Even though he heard her shift closer and smelled the cool evening air on her skin, he was still surprised when her soft hands settled against his forehead, moving in slow circular sweeps.

"I'm sorry, I shouldn't have said anything." Her voice was as gentle as her hands. "I'm not a parent and challenging you in front of Paisley didn't help."

"So you'd wait to challenge my parenting skills until after she got out of the car?"

She gasped. "Somewhere between this afternoon and tonight

I became my mother. I won't ever challenge you again. That is a promise."

"Ever?"

She hesitated. "Well, about parenting stuff. As long as we're roommates, the rest of it's fair game."

Instead of being annoying, her insistence on calling him on his shit was a complete turn-on.

"I know your comments came from a good place. They just touched on a sore spot. I've never been the enforcer and it sucks. I suck at it, just like the guys said I would." He could already hear Gray's lecture coming. "I tried to be the fun dad, but that's Levi's job. Gray's had a lock on the live-in dad since before I was even in the picture. No matter what role I try to fill, someone else has been doing it longer or is better at it than me."

And then, because he couldn't keep his mouth shut, he added, "I catch grief from all sides now. But hearing it from you? Man, that rubbed me a little rawer than hearing it from them."

"You're a great dad, Emmitt. Even I can see that."

"I used to be the world's best dad. Even have the mug to prove it." He carried it with him everywhere he went. Even when he was limited to a single rucksack, that mug was never far from reach.

"You don't need a mug. The way she looked at you, even when she was mad, spoke loud and clear. You are her everything." The naked honesty in Annie's tone had him shifting in his seat. "Paisley is lucky to have as many people looking out for her and loving her as she does. My intention was to get her talking, not make you mad."

"You accomplished both. At first, it felt like you were taking her side, that it was me against the world again, and I was mad as hell. But it's hard to be mad at you when your hands are on me."

She paused, her tone light when she said, "I can take them off you."

"Tease," he whispered, meeting her dark, dreamy gaze. She was leaning so far over the console, it wouldn't take much to pull her into his lap. Which was exactly where he wanted her—

in his lap with her hands all over him. Because—Lord help him—he wanted his hands all over her.

And the wants didn't stop there. He could fill a book with all the things he wanted when it came to Annie.

"Concerned," she said, her fingers going back to his head.

He groaned because, *Christ*, his head was pounding. He wasn't so sure he'd make it to the couch if Paisley had left all the lights on inside the cabin.

"Here." She pressed a couple aspirin into his palm.

He looked down and laughed. "That's about as efficient as a bandage on a broken bone." He took a pain pill from his pocket and swallowed it dry. "If this concussion doesn't kill me, then my kid will."

"She's a great kid, Emmitt."

"It sounds like you have a *but* coming."

"No buts. You guys have raised a smart and loving daughter." Her palms cupped his cheeks, her thumbs gently massaging his temples. "Maybe let her explore how smart she is."

"That's the same as saying but."

She laughed, soft and husky. "When I was Paisley's age and my mom would forbid me to do something, it made me want to do it more. Not that I ever did—I was too much of a Goody Two-shoes, like Gray."

Wanting to get his hands on her for a moment, he ran his fingers through her hair, around to the back of her neck until the short, silky strands slid from his grasp and fell forward. "Trust me when I say, you are nothing like Gray."

"Why do you say that?" Her breath was unsteady as she spoke.

"I've never wanted to kiss Gray." Damn, her lips were right there, parted and ready. His part—oh, it was more than ready. "I've never wanted to kiss anyone this badly."

"Sounds like a but coming."

"I promised you that when this happened, you'd have to make the first move." Stupidest promise he'd ever made. "And I don't want to be some line that you want to push. I have enough of that in my life. When we kiss, I want it to be real."

"I wanted to take risks and be bold tonight, but being a bad girl is exhausting." The smile she gave him damn near severed his heart. It was full of resignation and disappointment, not at him but at herself.

"Bad girls are a dime a dozen. I like the cautious, caring, sweet Annie."

She rolled her eyes. "You forgot boring, pragmatic, and opinionated."

"Ah, Goldilocks." He clasped her hands in both of his and brought them to his lips. "You took a job in Rome. You were ready to fly to the other side of the world, but when you discovered it was Rhode Island, you still took the job. You didn't know anyone here, had never even been to this town, but you took a chance." He held her hands captive. "Do you regret it?"

"No," she breathed.

"You take risks, Anh. You take calculated ones. But maybe if you put aside some of the caution when the right opportunity comes your way, you'll find you have fun. You might be disappointed, or maybe you'll find what you've been looking for." He kissed the tips of each and every finger. "Isn't that worth the risk?"

Chapter 17

"At least you didn't get a tattoo," Lynn said, grabbing an armful of warm blankets.

Annie had been assigned to the infusion center today, working alongside Lynn to ensure that their patients were as comfortable as possible while undergoing various types of treatments.

"I also didn't get kissed. The whole point of the dress, the heels, the night was to take risks and get a kiss." Annie topped off mugs of hot cocoa with whipped cream.

"No, the point of last night was to dip your toes, not have . . ." Lynn looked over her shoulder at Penny, a six-year-old sporting a pixie dress and daisy-chain crown, and lowered her voice. "S. E. X. But you dipped, I saw."

"Not even my little piggy toe, and you know it. I wasn't expecting to have S.E.X. But a kiss would have been nice." She'd settle for a warm embrace from someone other than her mom at this point.

"The person you wanted to kiss would have left you with nothing but sweaty sheets and an 'It's Complicated' addendum to your roommate contract."

"Honestly, I don't know which would be a more awkward morning after. Seeing him in the kitchen this morning in nothing but pajama bottoms after he rejected my kiss"—Annie

looked up from dusting each mug with rainbow sprinkles—"or seeing him in my bed in nothing at all."

Lynn eyed her over an armful of blankets. "He didn't reject you. He said he didn't want a casual fling. Then you ran into the house and barricaded yourself in the bedroom."

"He's the king of casual—what was I supposed to do? Kiss the guy whose Patronus is an alley cat during mating season?"

"Who knows, maybe he isn't the alley cat everyone claims," Lynn said, and Annie had to admit that, after last night, she'd been wondering the same thing. "Harry Potter thought he was a doe, when it turns out he could change his Patronus at will. Maybe Emmitt wants to change his to a penguin."

"Or maybe it's just a bad case of unattainable lover syndrome." Stacking the mugs on a tray, she balanced it on one hand, leaving her other free to grab a couple of pillows. "And once it's requited, he'll be miraculously cured and I'll be sleeping a wall away from him and his glow-in-the-dark boxers, wondering what I did wrong. I've ridden that train too many times to believe I'm really last-stop material."

Annie turned around and nearly dropped the tray when she saw Nurse Tran in the doorway. "Behavioral Medicine is on the third floor. Now, if this therapy session is over, we have patients waiting."

Annie gave Lynn an apologetic look as her friend escaped into the main room. Annie tried some escaping of her own. She got as far as the door when the other nurse said, "*Cháu ơi!*" and while the term was usually a Vietnamese endearment, Nurse Tran did not look endeared with Annie right then.

Annie turned and Nurse Tran rapidly smacked the back of one hand against her other palm.

"No more dillydallying, got it." With a salute, Annie scurried out into the infusion room and took shelter behind the patients. Not even wanting to think about how awkward home would be tonight, she handed out the hot cocoas, then brought the pillows to the little redheaded girl.

"Here you go," she said, propping her up and making her as

cozy as possible. "How about I grab you one of the tablets that have movies. I think we even have *Tinker Bell*."

"I don't need one, but Rosetta might." Penny held up her doll, a red-haired fairy who had a bandage in the same place Penny's port would be, and Annie's chest squeezed.

Every week Penny came in for her platelet infusions, and every week she sat in a too-big chair, hooked up to more IV bags than years she'd been alive, and smiled at everyone who passed. Both of her parents always came and sat in the waiting room, holding hands, their love too strong to give up.

Not for the first time, Annie wondered about her birth parents, her birth mother mostly—and if she'd given Annie up out of love or rejection. She didn't know a lot about her birth family, only that Annie had been the third child of a married couple. She had two older sisters somewhere in the world whom she'd never met but thought about daily.

Not that she'd remember even if she had met them. Annie had been given up at birth, but she liked to think that if they'd been there when she was born, maybe her sisters thought about her every once in a while. She wondered if they were aware she'd been raised in America or that her favorite color was yellow, because that was the color of the blanket she'd left the hospital with.

She still had that blanket. It was in a keepsake box Annie brought with her everywhere she went. Lying between the adoption photo album her mom had made for her and her grandmother's quilt, it was one of her most valuable treasures.

She might never know the why, but every time a ladybug landed on her, she liked to think it was her birth mother sending her love.

"Would Rosetta like a hot cocoa too?" Annie asked.

Penny whispered something in her dolly's ear, then nodded. "Extra sprinkles?"

"Extra sprinkles it is."

After she got Penny and Rosetta settled in, Annie worked her way around to the other side of the room. She fluffed pillows,

started drips, and even gave Mr. Parson a little back rub. She had just grabbed a new supply of warm blankets—because the room was as frigid as an ice bar—when she saw Mr. Jacobs hobble past the window, his cane overhead like a pitchfork.

Annie set down the towels and dashed after him. She finally caught up with him at the welcome center where he was slumped low in a chair, with sweat beading his forehead, and his cane resting against his leg.

"Mr. Jacobs," she said. "Are you okay?"

"Mr. Jacobs was my dad. Call me Les," he said, managing to sound surly even though he was breathing like he'd just run a 10k. "And no, everything is not okay. I remembered I had an appointment today with my doctor, one I'd made a few months back, before all this ovary nonsense. So I came to face my impostor and tell her I want my identity back."

She bit back a smile. "They still haven't fixed the problem? Did you call the number I gave you?"

"Six times. Wasted a whole day being on hold, transferred, or hung up on. People in customer service don't know a thing about their customers or good service, so I came in person to handle things my way."

"With a cane?"

"If that's what it takes. Only I dozed off while sitting in the waiting room. I woke up to the nurse say my name. And that's when I saw her, my impostor. She was spitting mad, storming out of the office and making a ruckus. She was fast, but I did see she was a redhead, and you know how fiery they can get."

"I wouldn't lead with that if you ever meet her." Annie sat down and placed her fingers on his wrist to take his heart rate. "And as soon as you catch your breath, we'll get this taken care of."

"Waste of time, I tell you." He waved off the offer with his free hand. "They don't have more than three brain cells among the lot of them."

"I graduated top of my class, so I can assure you we will get to the bottom of this."

He considered this, then nodded. "But only if you hold my hand while we walk there. Cuz we can get Dottie—she's the only one old enough to vote over there—to take our picture and I can show the guys at bingo what a pretty lady my doctor is."

"Physician's assistant." She took his elbow and helped him up, holding his hand the whole way. And he wouldn't even give Dottie his insurance card until she took the picture.

"She was just in here," Dottie said. "Talk about a mix-up. What are the odds of two people with the same name, and insurance numbers one digit off?"

"Pretty good, it looks like," Les grumbled under his breath.

"I'll tell you the same thing I told her. I have to take this to my boss, but I promise it will be straightened out by Monday."

"Better be, or me and my you-know-what are going to find another hospital."

Dottie handed Les her card and scribbled her personal extension on it, which seemed to placate him.

He stuck the card in his shirt pocket and gave it a pat. "Got my picture taken and a number. Wait till I show the guys at bingo."

By the time Annie got him back to the welcome room, he was all worked up again. His skin was pale, and he looked ready to fall asleep—right there in his chair.

"I don't think you should drive right now," she said. "Is there someone I can call to pick you up?"

"Nope. Five minutes and I'll be good to go."

Five hours was more like it. So when he closed his eyes, Annie went to the closest terminal and opened his file. She scanned down to the emergency contact person, and Annie had to check her own heart rate.

Convinced it had to be either another clerical error or the universe's way of telling her she shouldn't walk outside in a thunderstorm, she double—then triple—checked.

Oh boy.

"Um, Les, why don't I give your son a call." *I have his number in my phone. It's the one with all the sexting under the name, Big Bad Wolf.*

Les was suddenly wide awake and standing next to her. "Don't bother. He doesn't have time to pick me up."

"What do you mean? Your son *Emmitt* has plenty of time for his dad." Annie waited for Les to correct her, to tell her his son was named Dale and lived in Alaska on a husky ranch. But Les didn't so much as blink.

"He's a big-shot photographer," Les said, and Annie couldn't help but notice the sadness under the pride when he spoke. "Travels the world and reports on things. Big stories. In fact, he's on assignment in Tasmania doing a story on those spinning devils."

The way his gaze kept darting around as he spoke told Annie that Emmitt wasn't some deadbeat son who wouldn't come get his dad if called. Les didn't want to call him for some other reason.

Emmitt never brought up his dad, even when Annie spoke of hers. He talked about Paisley, Levi, Gray, even Paisley's mom. Never once had he brought up Les. Which wouldn't be all that strange, since the two of them were just roommates—and new ones at that—except he knew she was a medical practitioner.

The moment people found out what she did for a living, they disclosed every ailment they or their family were suffering from. Questions about treatments, side effects, if their doctor's advice was sound.

Unless she was at work, Annie always redirected them back to their medical professional. She hadn't had to redirect Emmitt, because he'd never said a word.

"Les," she began softly. "Does he know you have cancer?"

Les looked as if his legs were going to give out, so she sat him down.

"Only Chip from my complex knows," he admitted. "And that's how I want it to stay."

"It's proven that patients who have their family's support have greater odds of beating it. They heal faster, they're happier, and"—she took his hand—"they don't have to go through it alone. Can't argue with science."

"It's my constitutional right to argue with anyone I want.

And I'm not alone." He took his hand away. "I have Chip. And I'll tell you what I told that doctor of mine. I'll sue anyone at this hospital who says boo to my family."

Great, one more secret to keep from Emmitt. Not only couldn't she kiss him for fear of falling in like with him, but now she couldn't tell him that his dad has stage three cancer.

"At least let me call Chip and have him pick you up," she asked.

"Only if you're holding my hand when he pulls in."

Like father, like son.

It was a matzo ball standoff. Annie on one side of the counter, whisk in hand. Maura on the other, her face bigger than life on Annie's tablet. No matter how many times Annie explained she didn't need to hold her iPad to her face, Maura seemed to think the closer she got to the screen, the closer she was to Annie.

It was either video call Maura or run the risk of her showing up on Annie's front porch, with a suitcase big enough for a two-week stay.

"Scooch me closer," Maura said, her squinting eyes filling the entire screen. When that didn't work, she put on her reading glasses. "Are those jars? There are no jars in my recipe."

Shoot. Annie had forgotten to move them out of sight when she emptied the groceries.

"It's stock, organic and locally made. The lady at the store guaranteed no one would be able to tell the difference."

"Then maybe you should ask the lady at the store for her recipe, because I guarantee mine doesn't use cans, boxes, or jars."

Annie sighed. "I don't want the lady at the store to help me, Mom. I want you to help me but I don't have six hours to make your stock."

"You don't need six hours, just use a pressure cooker," her mother explained as if everyone owned a pressure cooker.

"I don't have one." Annie regretted her admission immediately.

"No pressure cooker? Marty, Annie doesn't have a pressure cooker." Delight beamed off her mother's face before she

disappeared from the screen. A split-second later the clanking and rustling began. Then came, "I've got an extra you can borrow. Marty, get some pants on. Annie's borrowing our pressure cooker and I want to get on the road before it's dark."

"Mom, you don't need to drive over," Annie said, and Maura's head peeked up from the bottom of the screen. "I can pick one up at the cooking shop downtown after I get off work tomorrow."

"Why waste the money on a new one when we have an extra that will work just as well?" Her mom was already moving toward the front door. Annie had to look away from the screen because watching her childhood home whiz by was enough to make her seasick.

"Mom," she yelled, covering her eyes, but not in time. "Flip the screen back so I see you and not Dad." Who was sitting in his recliner in white boxers reading the day's paper.

"Oh, I must have hit the button. Hang on." It took her a good minute, and three flashes of her dad, up close and personal, lounging in his Fruit of the Looms, to swap views. "Oh, here we go."

Annnnnnd . . . Maura was back.

"Thanks for offering to come here, but I work the a.m. shift tomorrow and I'm scheduled for doubles this week. Maybe I can just pick up some soup at a takeaway place near the hospital."

"Oh," Maura said, completely deflated. "But then it won't be *your* mom's recipe."

The last thing she wanted was to disappoint her mom. Maura had canceled a Bunco game with her friends to teach Annie her recipe. The least Annie could do was serve her mom's soup at Pho Shizzle.

"You said I can freeze the cooked matzo balls, right?" Annie asked, noticing the spark was back in her mom's smile—well, what she could see of it at the bottom of the screen. "Why don't you and Dad mail me the pressure cooker? I'll pay for the shipping, and we can do the stock Friday afternoon."

It would be cutting it close, and the shipping would cost her more than buying her own pressure cooker, but if the appliance

would cut down the cooking time *and* make her mom smile like that, then it was worth every cent.

"And maybe you can throw in some of the Whole Food Plant Based muffins Dad was telling me about." Which would make her dad smile.

"I'll have your dad drop it in the mail first thing in the morning." Maura put a hand to her mouth, her eyes watering. "And I'll add the recipe with the muffins. You can't even tell there's no butter, sugar, or oil in it."

"I'll be sure to mention it to Dad," she said. "Then I'll Venmo you the cost of the shipping."

"Nonsense. You can pay me back when you come up for the wedding."

And just when Annie thought they were starting a new chapter in their relationship, Annie found herself right back at *Once upon a time there was a girl who couldn't keep a man* . . . "I e-mailed Clark's mom and said I wasn't going to be able to come," Annie lied, making a mental note to cancel with Ms. Atwood, since Maura would likely check the validity of Annie's story.

"Funny, I saw her at the dry cleaner and she assured me there was room for our family at the table."

Other people's choices are not a reflection of me. Other people's choices are not a reflection of me. OTHER PEOPLE'S CHOICES ARE NOT A REFLECTION OF ME!

"Hold on a sec, Mom." Annie muted the call and stepped out of view. "Are you kidding me? Your choice to make me look like some pathetic stalker of an ex *is* reflecting on me. And." She stomped. "That." She stomped again. "Reflection." A whole body stomp. "Is not looking good!"

"What you should be saying is, 'Loving someone means trusting them. It's hard to have one without the other.'" The amused whisper came from the bedroom. Annie didn't have to turn to know who was talking; her lips tingled their hello.

Emmitt wore faded jeans riding obscenely low on his hips, a wrinkled shirt, and bare feet. His hair was tousled, his eyes sleepy, as if he'd just woken up.

"You've been waiting to use that, haven't you?" she asked.

"If I say yes, will you throw that whisk at me?" he asked, and she laughed, deep from her belly until her eyes grew moist. Only partly from frustrated tears.

"Hey," he said, coming closer and pulling her into his arms. He was warm and strong and smelled like heaven. And she didn't want to ever let go.

His arms tightened around her as if he understood. The intensity of the emotion behind his embrace shook her. It was protective and real, and somehow pure.

Incredibly stupid move, she thought. Because one simple touch and her entire body registered just how amazing it felt to be in the safety of his arms. Tender and warm, he was holding her like he was a ninja master of hugs. Holding her as though he alone could make everything better.

A dangerous position for a woman who'd spent her entire life looking to belong, only to be replaced, time and again, by the people she loved.

"If you want, I can tell your mom Clark is an ass and nobody wants an ass for a son-in-law."

"No." She backed up and wiped her nose.

"Moms love me."

"That's the problem. She'd take one look at you, with the sleepy eyes and bed-tousled hair, and consider it as good as you asking for my hand. The wedding invites would be in the mail before you hung up."

"Hey, if we plan it on the same day as Clark's so it's impossible for you to go, I'm in."

He was joking, she knew he was joking. But her heart rolled over at his offer. It had been a while since someone had her back.

"That's okay. If I'm willing to dole out advice, I'd be a hypocrite not to take it in return. Especially when it's wise advice."

He grinned. "It's your wisdom."

She smiled. "I know." She blinked a few times. "Does it look like I've been crying?"

He wiped her face with the soft cotton hem of his shirt,

which smelled like sexy, sleepy man. He studied her, and the grin turned almost gentle. "You look beautiful."

She didn't know about beautiful. She was in cut-off jean shorts and an old college T-shirt bedazzled with wet matzo, and her hair was a mess. But when he looked at her like that, she felt beautiful.

"Thanks," she whispered. Her tablet started ringing and again and she released a huge sigh. "It's my mom."

"Who loves you no matter what," he reminded her softly.

After soaking in one last second of their closeness—okay, a few seconds—she walked around the counter and answered. "Sorry, Mom, I was, uh, thing is . . ." She looked at Emmitt, who gave her an encouraging thumbs-up. "I'm not going to the wedding. Not because I'm working or have other plans or can't find a date—"

"I'd date you," Emmitt whispered.

She shushed him with her eyes.

"I'm not going because Clark and I aren't together anymore, and it wouldn't bring me closure, it would bring me back to an unhappy time."

Her mom looked completely befuddled. "You two were incredibly happy. Everyone said so. Didn't they, Marty?" Then back to Annie. "Everyone said so."

"Everyone wasn't us, Mom. And we weren't happy together. But he's happy now and so I am," Annie said, feeling pretty darn proud that she got through that without a fresh stream of tears.

"Well, I . . ." Maura took a shaky breath. "I never meant to stick my nose where it didn't belong. I just thought . . . Apparently I thought wrong."

"We love you, Flapjack," Marty said, and his face appeared on half the screen. All puckered forehead and brows, just like her mom.

"I love you, too, Daddy," she said. "But why do you want to go to the wedding?"

"When he asked us for our permission, he became my son,"

Maura said. "Just because you broke up, that doesn't mean I can just walk away. He's family to me. But if it really makes you upset, I'll tell him I can't go."

Annie was floored. She'd never once considered what it was like for her parents when Annie's relationships didn't work out. It was the same fierce love that allowed Maura to love Annie as if she'd carried her nine months that kept her from missing Clark's big day.

Heart in her throat, Annie shoved away all the Clark-inspired frustration over the situation. "Go, Mom. It will be a beautiful wedding." *I should know.* "You can tell me if the floating peonies look as elegant as we pictured." Then quickly, "But don't feel obligated to share that picture."

"Are you sure?"

"This way you can get the ten grand Clark owes me."

They went through their five-minute routine of saying goodbye, which included Annie promising to eat three whole meals, Maura reminding her to floss, and blocking out time for the next video call—in pen.

"Love you guys," Annie said, finger poised to end the call.

"Maybe I'll find you a nice husband at the wedding," Maura said.

"What your mother means is, we love you," Marty said, then ended the call for her. He must have heard Annie request the rest of the muffins and wanted to return the favor.

She looked up at Emmitt, who was leaning against the counter, casual as can be, brows raised in question. "Flapjack?"

"Before you say anything more, remember Sweet P," Annie said. "Every kid gets an embarrassing nickname from their dad."

"Mine was Dump Shit," he said, and Annie was so stunned she jerked back.

"He"—she caught herself right before saying Les—"called you that?"

"And Sweet P is a great nickname," he said, ignoring her question.

The front door blasted open, and Emmitt and Annie sprang apart moments before Paisley came bursting into the kitchen. Backpack on the floor, bag of glitter and fabric on the counter, she jumped into her dad's arms.

"I passed out all the invites," she squealed. "And guess what?"

"What?"

"Everyone is coming." She gave him a big smack on the lips and then stepped out of his arms and skipped to the fridge. "Everyone! Even Kristan. She drove me home today. Don't worry. Daddy already knows her and she's driven me home from school before, and she's going to help me plan the most 'epic sleepover'"—she did dancing quotes with her fingers— "Kristan's words not mine. In fact, that's what she wants to refer to it as. She thinks it will help distract everyone from your 'No Boys policy,'" she said, not stopping to take a breath. "Oh, and I promised I'd talk to you about possibly removing the—"

"No boys. That was the deal."

"That's what I told her, but you know Kristan." She stopped and tilted her head sideways. "Wait, you do know who Kristan is, don't you?"

"Nope, but you seem excited. That's enough for me," he said, and it was Annie's turn to be amused.

"She's a junior who has her own car. Her own car!" Paisley's hands were in constant motion, grabbing a soda, a snack, putting her water bottle in the sink, bouncing around the kitchen like a pinball. Annie needed a nap just watching her. "It's super old, like a 2009 Nissan or something. Her grandma gave it to her, but who cares, she says we can go shopping for all the party stuff next week." And for the first time since she came home, she paused. "Is that okay?"

"Ah, yeah," he said. Paisley might never know just how much her simple question had affected Emmitt, but Annie could see the emotion in his eyes. "I can give you some cash."

"That's okay. Daddy gave me his credit card, and—" She turned. "Oh my God, I totally forgot to tell you, Sam told me what you did today."

Oh boy. Annie glanced at Emmitt, wondering what he could

have done to possibly top threatening the kid. Only instead of yelling, Paisley began squealing.

"I assume he talked to you about being on the decoration committee?" Emmitt was speaking to Paisley, but his *ye of little faith* tone was all for Annie.

"Yes! He joined! I'll tell you about it at dinner, I have homework to do, plus I have to Snap Kristan." Paisley slung her backpack over her shoulder; grabbed her soda; and, with a bag of chips between her teeth, said, "Hi, Annie. Bye, Annie."

Annie waited until she heard the bedroom door shut before she said, "A sleepover?"

He shrugged. "This morning at drop-off, one of the moms warned me of a rumor going around about a party at the Cliffs the weekend after the dance. It's a three-day weekend, and it's a 'go all-out' party. I know what those parties are like, so I figured that if I offered to have a party here, P and her friends will have a legit reason to be no-shows."

Annie rested against the counter next to him, their hips an inch apart. "That was very proactive of you. Your right eye didn't even start twitching when she brought up Gray paying for it."

"I get to be the hero and he picks up the tab?" He shrugged. "Fine with me. I'm more interested in you noticing I wasn't twitching." They were still a friendly distance apart, but his tone ate up any space between them. "Does that mean you were gazing into my eyes, Anh?"

She loved it when he said her name like that. "You have pretty eyes." Eyes that were fixed on her mouth as if she was the most erotic thing he'd ever seen. They were filled with promises of what was to come. "And they didn't burn with the flames of hell when she brought up Sam. You really asked him to be on the decorating committee?"

"Sam was already on the committee. I just convinced Gray that if they are properly supervised, it'll be okay for them to hang out."

She hip-checked him, but it wasn't playful like it had been the other night at the bar. Oh, there was a playful element to it,

but there was also a whole lot of heat sparking between them. "Wow, I'm very impressed."

"Before you go getting all sweet on me, you should know that I moved the decoration committee meetings to Gray's house. So he'll get to play the enforcer and I get to be the hero. Even if for just a minute."

Chapter 18

Annie should have stayed home, and that was the truth of it.

She hadn't even said her hellos and already she was dreaming up a list of excusable reasons for why she had to dish-and-dash.

It was Friday, and the monthly Pho Shizzle potluck was in full swing. When Lynn had invited her, Annie had imagined a dozen or so women in various stages of life sitting around the room sipping wine and talking about food.

Pho Shizzle was an ethnic cooking group that focused on homestyle Vietnamese dishes, so it was not unexpected to find a lot of dark-haired petites there. But looking around the room, Annie realized they were *all* dark-haired petite women. In fact, they were all Vietnamese.

A warm and unfamiliar emotion spread through her that she couldn't quite explain or describe, other than to say it's what she'd always imagined it felt like to belong.

It was ridiculous that Annie had been on the planet nearly thirty years and this was her first time being in a large group where everyone looked like her—and where she wasn't in the minority. For many, it wouldn't seem like a big deal, but to someone who had always been the odd girl out, it was huge.

Annie watched the women flutter back and forth in the kitchen, putting the final touches on their dishes, chattering away all at once. She could hear the conversations overlap-

ping, people talking over others to be heard—mainly the older women.

But as the night drew on, and women paused to look at all the dishes, that feeling began to chill, because Annie was beginning to see that, while no two dumpling soups were alike, hers was suffering from a serious case of "one of these things is not like the others."

Par for the course, she thought, watching the hustle and bustle around her.

Annie had managed to whip up a darn good replica of her mom's soup, fueling false hopes for the outcome of the night.

Her goal had never been to come into Nurse Tran's home and show her up, although she'd dreamed last night that Hoan was so taken by Annie's soup she'd asked Annie to host the next get-together. Now her goal was simply to make it through the night without crying.

Not sure how to slip seamlessly into the well-oiled machine that was Pho Shizzle, Annie turned out to be more of an obstacle than an extra hand. After mistaking ginger for galangal—a root vegetable that looked as if it had come through the wormhole with Dr. Who—and telling Lynn's grandmother her broth had too much fish sauce—because she'd said she used too much and Annie had agreed—Annie had given herself a culinary time-out.

So there she sat, on a bamboo and seagrass high-backed chair with a fragile smile on her face, as she watched not one, not two, but three generations of Vietnamese women laugh and learn and—the most beautiful part—love.

All in their native language. Menu Vietnamese wouldn't help Annie now.

Assigning herself to the role of Annie's advocate, Lynn seated herself right next to Annie and translated the conversations around them. Her efforts, as sweet as they were, only managed to make Annie feel more out of place. Instead of being the lone Asian girl in a Caucasian community, she'd become the lone Caucasian-raised girl in a tight-knit Asian cooking class.

And she wasn't sure which was more uncomfortable.

"I'll be right back," Lynn said, standing. "My grandma

knows she's supposed to ask for help when lifting heavy pots, and . . . *Bà ơi*, no! Let me get that." Lynn said something else in Vietnamese, but Annie didn't need to pull up her translating app, because Lynn's grandmother shuffled over to sit next to Annie.

Mai, her grandmother, was now Annie's assigned keeper.

When Annie had first arrived, Lynn had introduced her to everyone, and it quickly became apparent that the new "girl" didn't speak the language, so she wasn't surprised when the older woman spoke to her in English.

"Hai Linh tells me you're a Hanoi girl." The older woman smiled with her entire being, exposing a lifetime of crinkles and crannies and canyons of joy. "My family sent me from Hanoi to live with my aunt in New York when I was twenty-six." Which explained the thick accent that came through her words. "They wanted a better life for me, so I came to find a husband."

"Did you find him?" Annie asked, and Mai laughed.

"Yes, I found him and the next and the next."

"You've been married three times?" Annie asked, liking the idea that she wasn't the only one unlucky in love.

Mai shook her head. "Four grown kids, four grandkids, and four husbands. Four was my lucky number."

Annie wasn't sure what her lucky number was, but she hoped it was closer to two than ten.

"Do you miss your family in Hanoi?"

"Most have passed. But I miss the smells and sounds and commotion of the city. So much happening, so many things to do, but there wasn't a lot of opportunity for my generation." A frail hand came to rest on Annie's arm. "How old were you when you came to America?"

"I was five days old when my parents adopted me, but they had to wait for one more piece of paper to come through, so we didn't come home until I was a few months old." Her parents' three-week voyage turned into three months, but they'd refused to leave without her.

They had both taken a leave of absence from their practice to stay in Vietnam, going to the hospital every day during visiting

hours to hold Annie. Her mother would sing to her and her dad would read nursery rhymes.

There were photos of that time in Annie's adoption album, a present from her mother on Annie's eighteenth adoption day. Each one had a handwritten description, detailing the location and names of the people in the photo, and each one was accompanied with loving words from her parents about what that precise moment meant to the both of them.

At times, Annie struggled with how to be the person her parents saw when they adopted her.

Before Annie could ask Mai more about growing up in Vietnam, another woman sat in the chair across from her and pulled a brightly colored fan from her pocket. She fanned herself while speaking to Mai—about Annie.

Annie didn't need to know the language to understand she was the topic of their conversation. The puzzle they were trying to solve.

"You are a lucky girl that your parents picked you," the newcomer said.

"It's her ears," Mai stated, reaching out to pinch Annie's lobes. "They are small, which means lucky in Viet Nam."

"I've heard that," Annie said.

"Yes, lucky. You don't speak Vietnamese—how come?"

"Uh, I speak a little," Annie said. "The town I grew up in didn't have a big Vietnamese community, so there wasn't the opportunity to learn. But I can order some mean takeout."

Annie laughed. The newcomer did not.

"Hai Linh was born here in Rome and she learned how," the woman said, as if Annie was somehow lacking.

For women like Lynn it was so simple, growing up in a house that passed down all the cultural wealth to the younger generation. But for someone like Annie, who never fit into either community, it wasn't so simple.

The older woman eyed Annie calculatingly. "How much did you cost?"

Even though there was no harm intended by their questioning, they made it sound as if Annie had been one of many kids

locked in kennels while her parents strolled along saying, "Oh, she's too old. And this one's too fussy. But this one, right here, she has small, cute ears—we'll take one of her to go, please." Before handing over a cashier's check that amounted to their entire life savings to the "Baby Seller."

And while most of America would be shocked at the line of questioning, Annie took it in stride. She'd been asked it enough over the years to understand that the adoption process was a mystery to most, and every culture viewed it through a different lens.

But adoptive families came together the same way as biological ones. Annie was Maura and Marty's daughter. She just happened to have been carried by another woman, eight thousand miles away. And instead of being the product of two people's love, people like Annie were the sum of four people's.

In her book, that made her twice as loved and doubly special. At least that's what she told herself in moments of doubt. Moments like this.

"My mom says I'm worth every penny." It was the light-hearted answer that always got a laugh. And it didn't fail her tonight.

She fielded more painfully familiar questions that sparked even more painfully familiar emotions as she recited the recycled answers. Eventually, the questions slowed, leaving only awkward silence, marking the end of "Get to know Anh."

Only they didn't know *her* at all. They knew her story, where she came from, and how to properly say her name. But they didn't know the first thing about *who* she was, and that was as isolating as the conversation that continued in front of her, none of which she was included in or could understand.

The result: Annie had never felt so out of place in all her life—and that was saying a lot.

"*Cháu ơi*," Nurse Tran said to Annie. "There is something wrong with your *Mì Hoành Thánh*."

Yeah, about that.

Annie stood and smoothed her sweaty hands down her shirt. She'd taken care with her appearance, wearing a denim skirt

with a silky teal top. "It's not really Mi Hoanh Thanh. It's my mom's version of dumpling soup."

Nurse Tran sent her a leveling glare. "But I explained that this was *Mì Hoành Thánh* night."

"Mi Hoanh Thanh is a Vietnamese dumpling soup, right?" When no one moved, she added, "Well, I brought matzo ball soup. It's my mom's signature dish."

The ladies exchanged looks, but it was Nurse Tran who spoke. "You mean, your mom's American dish?"

"My parents are Irish, but it's a traditional Jewish dish that we make around . . . well, that doesn't matter. It's my family's recipe and it's quite good. In fact, my mom has won awards at the local temple cook-off."

"Hai Linh takes me to temple every week," Mai said gently, patting Annie's knee in support.

But Nurse Tran wasn't having any of it. She said something in Vietnamese, speaking for so long Annie thought maybe she was reciting the complete works of William Shakespeare just to screw with her.

Finally she finished, and all eyes were on Annie when Mai nodded and said, "Ah." A single sound that ricocheted off the chip Annie now had on her shoulder.

Time to get back to making that dish-and-dash list so she could get the heck out of there.

Emmitt walked up the steps of the Tanner house. It wasn't even six and the sun had taken shelter behind a cluster of clouds moving off the coast that had spread out to cover Rome and most of the neighboring towns. Summer had held on for longer than normal, so Emmitt had been surprised when the air became chilled, announcing that fall was about to make an appearance.

He looked up at the sky and squinted at the tiny molecules of rain flittering down. A drop landed on the tip of his nose and he smiled.

Tonight was his night. Steps one through three were coming together, and he was ready to implement step four.

In his line of work, being prepared could mean the difference between a couple of bruised ribs and coming home in a casket. If he'd thought there'd be any need for a helmet at that factory in China, he wouldn't have been caught with his pants down. Even though he was covering the work conditions of the factory, and not investigating the fact that the builders used inferior supplies to cut their bottom line, he should have known better.

Should have trusted his gut.

Well, he was listening now. As soon as he got the sign-off from Gray, Emmitt was turning this story into a two-part series, which he knew would be some of his best work.

Kind of like the chocolate cream pie he had in his arsenal this evening. No way was he walking in blind again. He had gone to great lengths to ensure he came out of tonight's family dinner with his World's Best Dad title reinstated.

Bypassing the knocker—because this was, after all, Family Friday and he was as family as family could get—he let himself inside the house. He was greeted with a warm blast of air, which smelled awfully close to Michelle's corn bread recipe, and a cacophony of laughter coming from the kitchen.

Frowning, he checked his watch. Ten to six. He held it to his ear to see if his grandfather's 1936 Elgin had finally given out, but according to the steady ticking, he was ten minutes early. Strange, since it sounded as if the fun was well underway.

Slipping off his shoes and placing them in the rack—*You're welcome, Gray*—Emmitt padded into the dining room where . . . *what the actual fuck?* Family Friday was in full swing.

Oh, they hadn't served dinner yet, but the table had been turned into a game center. Plates and glasses were shoved to the side, the Pokémon version of Monopoly he'd given Paisley for Christmas was spread out over the table, and Gray was purchasing Park Place as if the entire "family" was all well and accounted for.

And the part that was like a flaming arrow to the heart was the startling sight of his dad sitting in Emmitt's chair. Leslie Fucking Jacobs, the guy who hadn't bothered to show up at Emmitt's high school graduation, the guy he'd expressly forbid-

den to be a part of Paisley's life, was sitting in as Emmitt's replacement.

"Am I late?" he asked, because that possibility hurt a hell of a lot less than the idea that they'd started without him.

"Hey, Dad," Paisley said, picking up the die and rolling. No hug, no squeal, just a distracted *"Hey, Dad."*

Levi wasn't any better. He looked up from the table and said, "Dude, is that your mom's chocolate cream pie?"

Emmitt felt like holding it above his head the way he used to when he and Levi were kids and he didn't want Levi to play with his favorite toy. "I brought it for P."

"What's in it?" she asked without even looking up.

"Chocolate, cream cheese, crumbled Oreos for the crust. It's all homemade," he said proudly, even though his mind was flashing *Warning! Warning! Eject before it's too late.*

"Does it have sugar?" This from Paisley, who was staring at her phone, texting someone other than him.

"Well, yeah. It's pie." He chuckled. She texted. "But it's gluten free. I got special Oreo cookies from the health food store in town."

Her nose wrinkled as if he'd just said it was made from cooked cat shit and vomit. He didn't know what had happened between the last time he'd seen her—when he was the "best ever"—and now. But Emmitt was feeling like the ball in a foosball table.

"God, you don't know me at all," she said. "My friends are right."

He wasn't sure what her friends had to do with his mom's chocolate pie, but he was ready to call bullshit on the whole setup. Because that's what this had felt like from the get-go, one big setup. Just because Emmitt was the last dad to the party didn't mean he wasn't her dad. Didn't have Dad Rights.

Uncertainty crept in. Hell, it wrapped around Emmitt and started choking him. Not only was he unsure of what he'd done wrong, he hadn't a clue how to fix it.

Needing a wingman, he looked at Levi and Gray, who were all shrugs and bafflement—and dressed like twins in matching

jerseys, because *that's* normal. They were basically as helpful as a Q-tip in a gunfight.

When it came to women, Emmitt knew, when in doubt always apologize. "I'm sorry, P. When Gray asked me to bring a dessert, I immediately thought of my mom's chocolate pie." He held it up again, hoping she'd take a second look and her eyes would light up with the warm memories he associated with this pie. No such luck. "This was your favorite dessert when you were little. You used to ask if we could have it for breakfast."

"First off, in case you can't tell, I'm not little. Second, I'm on a strict no-sugar diet."

"When did that start?" He'd bet the second he said, "I brought pie," but she claimed her whole soccer team was doing a cleanse.

He looked at Levi for confirmation, since he was the soccer coach, and Levi lifted a confused hand, neither affirming nor denying that such a cleanse was going on within his team.

Emmitt scratched his eyebrow with a raised middle finger, leaving no confusion as to his response, then looked back at the only person in the room who mattered right then.

"You're right, you're not little and I feel like I'm playing a catch-up here." He considered what Annie would say in this situation and added, "Stick with me, and trust that I'm getting there, because there is nothing more important to me than you and your feelings." He just wished there weren't so many of them. "So if pie isn't your thing, maybe after dinner we can go to the store and pick up something you can eat. It will give me a better idea of what kind of snacks you want for the sleepover." Without waiting a beat, he turned to Les. "And what the hell are you doing here?"

"I was invited?" Les said, using the table to help him stand. Emmitt noticed the familiar grooves lining his father's face, which had become deeper and more pronounced since he'd seen Les last.

"By who?"

"By me," Paisley said, finally sparing him a glance. "And be-

fore you ask why, Grandpa's here because it's Friday, which is family dinner night. Do you have a problem with that?"

Fuck yeah, he did. Les was the walking, talking definition of a problem.

Emmitt met his old man's gaze. "This is a problem between me and him."

"We aren't talking about you and him. We're talking about *me* and *my* grandpa."

"He's right, sweetie," Les said in a soft tone Emmitt hadn't heard since his mom died, then walked over to place a comforting hand on Paisley's shoulder. "Why don't you let your dad and me talk about this. I don't want to ruin dinner."

"*You* aren't ruining anything, Grandpa," Paisley said, her tone neither soft nor comforting. In fact, she was shooting Emmitt an *eat shit and choke on it* look that implied *he* was the problem. "Anyone who thinks differently can leave, especially since my other dads don't have a problem with it." She turned to her "other dads," and asked, "Right?"

The Bobbsey Twins nodded, Paisley continued to glare, and Les—wanting to be the bigger fucking person for the first time since Nixon took office—said, "It's a little more complicated than that, sweetie. So, I think I'm going to check if there's any of those ice pops you bought still left in my freezer."

"Still the same old Les. Stir things up, then go on your merry way, completely oblivious to what you've done," Emmitt accused.

"I know what I've done, son," Les said. "But Michelle had a strict 'no swearing' policy in the house, so I think it's best I excuse myself. Thanks for the dinner."

"Grandpa . . ." Paisley jumped up, her voice animated and her face full of concern. Emmitt's heart tore in two when his daughter wrapped her arms about Les's neck and begged, "Don't go. We haven't even gotten to our game of chess."

"I know," Les said, giving her a kiss on the crown on her head. "But I'm a little tuckered out tonight. How about tomorrow? You and me, chess on the bluff?"

She gave a small nod and, just as she used to do to Emmitt

when she was six, Paisley went up on her tiptoes and kissed her grandpa's cheek. "Tomorrow. Promise?"

Les gave her a wink, then did what he did best, went on his merry way.

"Do you have a problem with that?" she asked, her hip popped out, challenging him to a showdown of who could walk the bad side better.

What she didn't know was, when it came to the bad side, Emmitt was the founder, mayor, and ruler supreme. "Actually I do. Not that you reached out to him but that you invited him and didn't give me a heads-up before I got here."

"If anyone deserved a heads-up, then it was Grandpa," Paisley said. "Because you're the new face at dinner, not him."

Everything inside Emmitt slowed down until every breath, every movement, every sound in the room faded away and all he was left with was the cold hard truth. He wasn't the third wheel in the trio of dads; he was the guy no one wanted at the party but felt obligated to invite. He was the guy who wasn't important enough to inform that his daughter was spending time with the man who'd made Emmitt's childhood one giant disappointment.

A man Emmitt was so desperate to escape that the day he turned eighteen, he went down to the courthouse and changed his last name to his mother's maiden name.

That—*that*—was who Levi and Gray had invited to dinner, and they hadn't even bothered to clear it with him. He didn't expect them to run everything by him. But this required his sign-off.

"You knew, man," he said to his supposed best friend, Levi. "You knew what he put me through, and you didn't think that, hey, maybe I should give Emmitt a call before we invite Les to all the family get-togethers?" He set the pie down for fear he'd chuck it at one of the idiots across from him. "Not all the family get-togethers, just the ones I'm not at."

"It's not like that," Levi tried to explain, but there was no explanation in the world that could justify what they'd done.

"Then tell me what it's like. Because I'm starting to connect the dots, and the picture it's making is pretty damn ugly."

"It isn't his fault," Paisley said, standing in front of Levi, as if he was her main concern. "I'm the one who reached out to Grandpa. I'm the one who invited him to dinner. I found a picture of him when I was at your house, and Mom told me he was my grandpa. So one night when Owen was sleeping over, we decided to look him up online. He was living like a mile away, so the next morning we jumped on our bikes and rode to his house."

And the blows kept coming.

"Michelle knew?" Emmitt staggered back a few steps. "How long has this been a thing?"

"Since sixth grade when I had to do a family crest."

"That was four years ago." Anger didn't even come close to what he was feeling when he turned to the Bobbsey Twins. "You two have been lying to me for four years? Jesus, you had Paisley lying to me."

"Michelle thought it would be better if this was about Les and Paisley, not you and your dad's relationship," Gray said.

"Les doesn't have relationships, Gray. He has burdens. And one mistake and it's game over."

"He's changed," Paisley said, her eyes a little too shiny for his liking. Then again, he was close to tears himself.

"He hasn't, sweetie," Emmitt said, his voice raw. "And I'm trying hard to understand why you didn't come to me when you started having questions about your family roots."

"Try harder, Dad," she said, throwing his words back at him. "And you know why I didn't come to you? You were gone, in South Africa, and the project was due in two weeks. I called, but you were somewhere without reception, so I went to Mom and she helped me find the pictures I needed, and I'm glad because I love Grandpa, and I love having him at family dinners."

Emmitt wanted to ask if she loved having *him* at family dinners but was afraid of the answer. Jesus, his kid had needed him and he hadn't answered her call. What kind of dad did that make him?

"I wish I'd been there, and I want you know that I'll always be here for you, but sometimes when I'm away—" He stopped

dead in his tracks because he sounded just like his dad. Even worse, Paisley was calling him on it.

"I wanted to tell you, but I didn't want you to freak out. You're not around much, so it didn't seem like a big deal for Grandpa to come over," she said. "And in case you go away between now and the dance, you should know that there is no sleepover. At least not at your house. My friends' parents won't let them sleep over at a house if they don't know the chaperone. So it's either no sleepover or I have it here with Daddy." She looked around the room at all three men. "Bet you wish you'd never offered. I know I do."

She didn't wait for a response, which cut deep because he didn't know how to respond. And she knew it. Here he'd come in thinking he had this whole dad thing figured out, that he was doing what needed to be done, and he'd missed every mark.

The screen door slammed, rocking on its hinges.

Emmitt ran a hand down his face, trying to collect himself enough so that he didn't embarrass himself in front of everyone.

"We never meant for you to find out this way," Levi said, and Emmitt lost it.

"When did you mean for me to find out? Graduation? Her wedding? And what does that even mean? Since when is it your choice when I find out that *my* kid is spending time with someone I've worked hard to keep her from? And in case you didn't hear me, she is my kid." He looked at Gray. "She might call you Daddy, but I'm her dad. Check the birth certificate." Then it was Levi's turn. "And you're her uncle. The only two people who had the right to make decisions about Paisley were me and Michelle. When she passed, her legal rights didn't transfer to either of you."

"Take it down a notch," Levi said, putting his hand against Gray's chest as if holding him back.

"Ah, I get it now. You're too busy watching his back to even notice the knife in mine," Emmitt scoffed. "And what the hell are you wearing?"

Emmitt knew he was coming off like an asshole, but it was better than breaking down in front of the two biggest traitors

in bro-code history. Never in his life had he felt so left out, so insignificant and alone. And with the childhood he'd had, that was saying a lot.

Levi looked at Emmitt as if he were the crazy one. "We play softball on Fridays."

"Since when?"

Levi and Gray looked at each other, sharing some secret glances Emmitt wasn't included in. Par for the course.

"Since four years ago," Levi said. "Michelle signed us up. She signed you up too, but when you didn't show up at the first few practices, they filled your spot."

"I swear to God, if you say with my dad, I will lose my shit." He didn't let them answer. "You both have my number—you could have texted or called or e-mailed. If you needed me, you knew how to get hold of me."

"That's just it, man," Gray said. "We're not your keeper. I work hard to make sure you're looped in as much as I can, but at some point you have to take the initiative."

"Here's the thing, *Gray*. You seem to think you're my daughter's keeper."

"E," Levi said cautiously. "It's a stupid weeknight league. It's not a big deal."

"It's a huge deal, because I'm trying to be a part of this family." He punched his chest with his fist, but it just felt empty. "And you both know that. I'm doing my best from five thousand freaking miles away. I thought you had my back."

"When was the last time you had ours?" Gray asked, and that's when Emmitt saw it.

The one thing that highlighted just what a joke of a dad he was. Sitting on the table next to Gray was the hit that brought him to his knees.

A World's Best Dad mug.

Chapter 19

Going with the whole "Early shift tomorrow" excuse, which Annie felt was far more believable than "My friend's toothless cat just gave birth and I have to cut the umbilical cords," she said her final goodbyes, then blew out of there as if her butt were on fire.

She didn't trust Nurse Tran not to check the schedule, so she called a coworker, who was a new mom, and offered to take her morning shift, then let the scheduling office know of the switch.

Annie turned onto the highway, her eyes straining to see the lanes through the sheets of water sliding down her front windshield. While she'd been inside, the drizzle had become a downpour, and the roads were overflowing with runoff.

Hands at ten and two, she drove at a snail's pace, listening to her Adele-inspired playlist, trying to come up with something to explain away her sudden departure to Lynn. It would have to be good enough to make her friend think everything was okay.

The last thing she wanted was for Lynn to bring out the kid gloves around Annie, the way her friends back in Connecticut had.

After what seemed like an eternity, she pulled into her neighborhood and loosened her hold on the wheel—and her emotions.

It was only then that Annie let herself cry. She had allowed

herself to believe that tonight would get her one step closer to a deeper understanding of who she was. Maybe it was the universe, karma, and the tooth fairy—who still had it in for Annie since she'd refused to hand over her teeth for a measly twenty-five cents a pop—all coming together to tell her, "Understand now?"

Maybe she had to grow up and face the facts that all this searching wasn't going to change a thing. And that hollowed-out feeling in her chest she felt at night when the house was quiet and the rest of the world was at peace? It was never going to go away.

And okay, some of the tears came from a severe lack of sleep. Annie was so tired that she was tired of being tired. Tired of hoping and wishing and winding up all alone. Just when she thought she couldn't be any more pathetic, Adele's song, "Someone Like You," filled her car.

The soul-crushing words slowly trickled through the night, sliding down her spine and into her heart, poking needle-size holes through her chest, as if it were the only way to let the pain drip out, tiny bits at a time because all at once would be too much.

Annie wasn't crying over Clark or her birth parents or even what had happened tonight. She was crying because she really, really loved this song. She loved it so much that when the chorus started, she cranked it up, belting out the lyrics with Adele, as if this was carpool karaoke and Adele was in the car singing with her.

After grabbing a take-out napkin stashed in her glove box, she dabbed at one eye and then the other before giving a quick blow. Just then, a shadowy figure emerged from the mist.

"What the hell?" Annie screamed, and jerked the wheel.

Heart hammering, she stomped on the brakes, sending up a quick prayer that she'd reacted fast enough. Her car slid across the slick road, stopping mere inches before she would have engaged in a very messy game of chicken with a pedestrian who, she noticed, was wearing a pair of low-hung jeans that encased one hell of an amazing butt. A very drenched butt she'd been

secretly admiring all too often lately had crossed the road right in front of her car.

She watched until he reached the sidewalk, then turned off the radio and took a few deep breaths to calm herself.

He had no umbrella, no raincoat, and absolutely no reason for walking in the middle of the road on this dark and stormy night. Not that he seemed to care.

Wiping her eyes on the sleeve of her coat, she slowly pulled alongside him. One last sniffle—God, she hoped it was dark enough outside that he would not be able to make out the tell-tale puffy eyes and red nose—and she rolled down the window.

"You know, there's a crosswalk ten yards ahead," she said out the window.

Silently, he stormed past her car without even sparing her a glance. Emmitt was in a mood—and working hard to ignore her.

Slowly, she crept forward until she was again by his side. "You okay?"

He stopped and turned to face her. Those usually warm brown eyes flickered with fire, but it was the way the soft planes of his face had folded in on themselves that had her worried. He was clearly in pain.

"Seriously, Emmitt, are you okay?" When he didn't answer, she added, "Hop in and let me give you a ride home."

He waved her off. "No thanks. I'm in a shitty mood and need to clear my head."

"In the rain?" The water was flowing across the street in sheets. "Why don't you clear your head in my car, where it's dry and warm. If you want, I can open the moonroof and it will be just like you're outside. Only you won't get wet."

"Already wet. Don't care," was all he said, and continued to head due north.

Annie took her foot off the brake and kept pace with him. Ignoring the rain pelting her in the face, she stuck her head out the window. "I care because you get grumpy when you're wet and I don't want to have to deal with Grumpy Emmitt." She gentled her voice. "Did something happen at the dinner?"

"What didn't happen?" He laughed, but there was zero humor in it.

"You want to talk about it?"

"So you can feel sorry for me? No thanks," he said, and considering the amount of water he had to trudge through, he was moving rather quickly.

"You want *me* to feel sorry for *you*? The guy with a booty-call list a hundred sticky notes long?" Hearing about someone else's shitty night might distract her from her own.

"Yeah, you know me," he said, tossing his arms in the air, then winced. He cracked his neck and went on—talking and walking. "The town stud, the *play it fast and loose* guy, the guy who gets to see his kid only on weekends, the guy who no one fucking thought to tell that his dad, who didn't give two shits about him growing up, now sits in his seat at family dinners."

Right, his dad. His stage-three cancer patient of a dad whose secrets she was legally bound to keep. Not that this would be the time to reveal them. The way Emmitt held his head every time he passed a streetlight was a good indication that if he didn't take his pain medicine and lie down, he was in for an unpleasant night of pain.

"How blurry is your vision?" she asked, and he came to a hard stop.

"Don't," he said. "Don't lecture me, don't diagnose me. And please, God, don't go all Nurse Annie on me. I don't want a ride. I want peace and quiet."

"You can kiss that ride home goodbye," she said, but she was talking to the air because he'd taken off again. This time when Annie pulled up alongside him, she made it clear she wasn't going anywhere. He glared at her. "And I'm a PA, not a nurse. I'm pretty much a doctor who can't do surgeries. Which means I am a badass in a white lab coat. It also means you can't tell me where to drive."

She thought she heard him chuckle, but he could have been mumbling for her to fuck off.

"It's your night," she continued. "Spend it how you want."

Clearly, he wanted to spend it walking home in the pouring

rain. And since he seemed set on this ridiculous plan, Annie followed right alongside him.

Him in the rain, her in her car, the entire way. Every so often, she'd flash her headlights at him and he'd flash her the bird in return. It wasn't until he reached the driveway that he finally stopped—keeping his back to her.

"They kept it from me," he said, his voice getting lost in the wind. "All of them. Even though they knew how strained my relationship with my dad is, *knew* I didn't want him around Paisley, they still went behind my back and let it happen. The people who I thought were my family put Paisley in a position to hide things from me."

With a shrug that spoke volumes on his emotional state, he turned and met her gaze. Annie felt the air leave her lungs in one long gasp, because he wasn't angry, as she'd previously thought. No, he was shell-shocked and devastated.

Absolutely, positively heartbroken.

"Oh, Emmitt. I don't even know what to say. That must have been hard for her to keep from you. And so incredibly hard for you to find out." Especially the way he did.

Emmitt was already uncertain about his role in Paisley's life, so desperate to do right by her, to be an active and meaningful presence in her life, that keeping something like this from him was cruel.

"This isn't a one-time thing either. He's been coming to dinners for more than four years. Four years! Can you believe that shit?"

"No. I can't." Annie knew how crushing it had been to learn that Clark wanted out of their relationship. She couldn't even imagine the anguish a secret this destructive could cause. "But I am sorry for how this all played out."

"Me too," he said, the defeat in his voice nearly tearing her heart in two.

A flash of light cut through the night's blackness, quickly followed by a booming rumble that had goose bumps dotting her arms. The temperature had fallen, making the drops of rain feel more like little pinpricks against her chilled flesh.

When lightning lit the sky again, he gripped his head and sucked in a few harsh breaths.

"If I were being PA Annie, I'd tell you I have some Excedrin in my purse, but I don't want to rouse Grumpy Emmitt."

That earned her a little smile, but she didn't imagine he'd be vertical longer than it took to stumble through the door and onto the couch.

With a few colorful words directed at Mother Nature, Emmitt made his way up the driveway but stopped short of the front porch, standing in the rain as if it were penance.

Annie parked the car and, grabbing her mom's pot, climbed out. By the time she reached him, her hair was plastered to her head, her clothes soaked through. The only dry part of Emmitt was the patch of forehead his ballcap protected.

The wind blew the rain sideways, and the streetlights flickered on and off before plunging the entire block into darkness. When Emmitt didn't move, Annie resigned herself to wait it out by his side until he told her differently. She knew what it was like to be on the outside, and maybe having her next to him would make it a little less painful.

Breathing deep through his nose, he cupped the rim of his cap over and over, tilting his head to the sky. Eyes closed, he let the rain wash down his face.

"Just once," he said, breaking the silence. "Just one damn time, I'd like to be in the know when it comes to my kid. She's my fucking kid." He dropped his head all the way to his chest. "Where do they get off keeping something like this from me?"

She hiked the pot against her hip and with her free hand touched his cheek. As he had the other day, he leaned into it and closed his eyes. "I wish I had been there so you wouldn't have felt alone in such an emotionally charged moment."

He looked up at her through rain-spiked lashes. "You can't help yourself, can you? Annie the Protector is on a mission," he teased warmly. "Were you born taking care of others or—"

He stopped short and, in a very manly fashion flipped his cap backward and got eye level with her. "What's wrong?"

"Nothing." She gave a bright smile, knowing she could fake anything with convincing success. She was a master.

Emmitt looked right past that smile and into her eyes, searching for what Annie hoped she'd buried deep enough to avoid detection. Hiding anything from a guy who read people for a living was harder than she'd first imagined. She knew the exact moment he realized her night hadn't gone all that stellar either.

"Nothing, my ass. Who made you cry?" he said as if he were vowing never to sleep again until he fixed whatever wrongs had been thrust upon her.

"No one." Which was the God's honest truth. No one person had made her cry.

"Who, Anh?"

And he'd teased her about being a protector? He looked ready to pummel whomever she blamed. His need to care for those around him—even at his own expense—made Florence Nightingale look apathetic.

"Seriously, it's allergies," she said, and this time she did lie. "Did Paisley want to spend time with her grandpa?"

"God, when you say it like that—'Spend time with her grandpa'—I feel like a dick." He looked up at the sky as if afraid of what *she'd* see. Now who was hiding? "She said she likes hanging with my dad. She was even the one to approach him."

"It's natural for her to be curious about her grandpa, especially with her unique family situation." She knew exactly how that felt, just like she knew how Paisley's curiosity caused Emmitt pain. It was this exact reason that Annie had waited so long to research her culture—and her birth parents.

She'd never wanted her parents to feel as if they weren't enough.

Right now, Emmitt was afraid he wasn't enough, and she wanted to tell him that he was more than enough. But he wasn't ready to hear that. Right now he needed someone to listen, so she took his hand, which was like holding melting ice, and without hesitation, his fingers laced with hers.

"She decided not to tell me because she was afraid it would

upset me and, get this, she said that because I'm not around much, it was no big deal. Jesus, my kid thought I was too busy to listen."

"Were you?"

He sent her a sidelong glance. "You said as much the first time you heard I was a father."

"I also didn't know you very well, and you've changed, which is what's important. Emmitt, you realized Paisley needed more so you stepped up and became the dad she needed. That's what love can do." She quickly debated whether to confess her recent connection. By not doing so, she'd be no better than his family. But he'd had all the *Funny thing happened* kinds of confessions he could take, so she said, "Maybe with age, your dad has changed too."

"No way." He spoke with absolute certainty that had Annie wondering exactly what had happened to break this family apart. "This is what my dad does. He's great at playing people. Then once he gets bored or busy or they disappoint, *poof*, he disappears. And trust me, when you realize you were nothing but a passing interest, you never fully come back from that."

Annie suddenly understood why Emmitt was the way he was. Why he was so against going all in when it came to relationships. And why he rarely let people see the deep, soft, and wonderful guy hidden beneath. If all he gave them was this easygoing, *everything slides right off me* persona, there was zero chance of building anything lasting and real—leaving zero chance of getting hurt.

"Emmitt—"

"Don't need to say it. I see the irony."

"I was going to say, 'People change,'" she said lightly. "Maybe your dad is trying to make up for how he parented you with Paisley. Maybe he wants to make it up to you but doesn't know how to reach out."

"My kid isn't the person he gets to use to feel better about himself."

"People who are given a second chance in life rarely waste it."

He looked at her as if she'd just confessed to sprinkling arsenic over Pediatrics' lollipop dish.

"I get that you're just trying to help. But you shouldn't talk about things you don't understand. His condescending tone was as confusing as it was hurtful. "Those studies you're always quoting are cute. But this is real life, Anh. And in real life, people disappoint. Beyond what a day of fishing can fix."

The remark was so below the belt, Annie dropped his hand and immediately stepped back. She'd only known him a few weeks, but that one comment cut deeper than anything she'd experienced tonight. He'd managed to humiliate her and discredit her in a single assessment. Even more upsetting, he'd gone about it by using personal and meaningful details from her life that she'd shared with him.

There were a few dozen hurtful things she could throw back at him. But Annie didn't do mean. She also didn't do confrontation, which was why she'd rather relocate to another state than continue this discussion.

"Noted," was all she said before turning toward the front door. Because she was one harsh word from embarrassing herself.

She sped up the driveway and wrestled with the door's lock, but her trembling hands and misty eyes weren't doing her any favors. Finally, after what seemed like eternity, the bolt clicked over. Not waiting to see if he was coming, she went to open the door when a large masculine hand appeared above her head, keeping her from budging it.

"Let go," she said, her voice unsteady.

"After I apologize." She could feel his breath against her ear, the warmth of his close proximity seeping through her clothes. "I was mad and took it out on you, and that's not fair."

"You did warn me. Next time I'll listen. In fact, next time, instead of offering you a ride, I'll drive by and splash mud all over you," she said, still not facing him.

"I deserve a drive-by mudding and a whole lot more." He moved closer, and she rested her head against the wood door.

"I'm sorry for what I said, Anh. Not only was it mean, it was uncalled for and you were the last one who deserved my wrath tonight."

"Apology heard. Now let go."

"After you tell me why you were crying." He rested a hand on her hip and pulled her back against him.

"It was just a really bad night?"

"Tell me what happened and how I can make it better?" he asked and for a brief moment Annie considered telling him about her night. Then his lips brushed her ear, and she felt his touch zing all the way down to her toes.

He felt it too, because he tugged her even farther into him, his hand sliding over her hip and—*oh my God*—he groaned. The kind of groan that had zero to do with Annie sharing her awful night, and everything to do with them sharing the bed all night long.

He whispered her name, and Annie jerked out of his grasp and yanked open the door.

"I cry when confronted by assholes." She stepped inside and whirled around. "Oh, and Emmitt, as your friendly neighborhood PA, I need to tell you that apologies aren't all roses and makeup sex."

With that, she slammed the front door in his face. And locked the deadbolt.

Chapter 20

Emmitt came awake with a start, clammy and shaking like a leaf, his head pounding louder than the thunder that had woken him.

He opened one eye to find it was still dark. The pink cotton sheets were tangled around his legs, the rest of the bedding had been shoved to the floor, and his heart was pounding out of his chest as if he'd spent the night playing a fun game of naked Twister with the sexy PA down the hall instead of crammed in Paisley's twin bed with Pookie the Cuddle Bunny and Mr. Big, the only two stuffed animals who had lived to tell the tale of the Great Paisley Purge of seventh grade.

Emmitt had waited for Annie to go to bed before turning in. Once the light under her door went out, he'd settled in his recliner for the night. It was a lumpy and impractical sleep space as it had always been, and after about an hour he gave up and crawled into Paisley's bed.

It wasn't his night with her—even if it had been, he doubted she'd have come home with him—so there was no sense twisting his body into a pretzel for another sleepless night when there was a spare bed available.

Not that a mattress and the ability to get completely horizontal helped. After spending the first three hours in bed rehashing the evening, he'd finally dozed off and managed to accomplish a whole forty-three minutes of sleep.

"Christ," he mumbled to himself, rubbing the sleep from his eyes.

Kicking off the last of the covers, he sat up and grabbed for his head, hoping to put enough pressure there to help with the spinning he had going on.

Too late. A blinding pain came at him hard from behind his skull, stabbing him through the left eye, making his stomach roil and the rest of him feel as if he were standing on a tilt-a-whirl. He'd forgone his pain pills tonight in an effort to prove something to himself.

All he'd managed to prove was that he was an ass, just like Annie accused.

Annie.

Man, he'd screwed that up. The look she'd given him there at the end, before she'd locked him out of his own house, pretty much gnawed at him all night. He'd have locked himself out too.

And he wouldn't have unlocked the back door for his sorry ass. Even when she was pissed, she couldn't help herself. Which was all she'd been trying to do earlier, protect him from his own stupidity.

And he'd pretty much told her to fuck off.

Taking a few deep breaths, he tugged on his sweats and padded to the kitchen to grab a bite to eat. Since he hadn't partaken in the family dinner, he was about ten hours out from his last meal. And his prescription came with a strict "take with meal" direction.

Forgoing the light switch, because he didn't need any more hurt right then, he opened the refrigerator door. Leaning his forearms against the top, he stared at his options, looking for anything that piqued his appetite.

"You really need to wear a bell around your neck. Or one of these times, I'll get lucky with my aim," Annie said.

He looked over his shoulder and knew what he was craving. Because one glance at her illuminated by the soft glow of the refrigerator light and he felt as if his luck was changing. He also

felt the bumbling idiot who always said the wrong thing around Annie waking up.

She was wearing a cotton T-shirt again—her sleepwear of choice, although it wasn't oversized or sporting her college logo. Tonight she'd gone for a plain white shirt with a low V neckline and an even higher hem that, had she been standing, would have come way up on her thighs.

But she wasn't standing. Oh no, Annie was sitting on the island, bringing that hem to barely legal levels, while going after a gallon of ice cream with the scooper—as if she'd decided mid-snacking that it was an out-of-the-tub kind of occasion.

Her normally silky straight hair was sticking up everywhere, making him think she'd crawled into bed without bothering to dry it off. But what had his heart rolling over was that her eyes were soft and half-lidded, as if she'd sleepwalked her way through the first half of the carton.

Then there were her bottoms—or serious lack thereof. Because peeking out from beneath that shirt was nothing but golden skin and teal-colored lace. Teal lace cheeky-cut undies, to be exact. Which had his bottom parts RSVPing for a pillow fight party of two.

"If I wear a bell, what will you be wearing?" he asked

"How's your head?"

"Rebelling against being upright, but at least I don't feel like puking anymore."

"Life goals," she said around a mouthful of ice cream. "You want some tea? Caffeine might help."

"More of a coffee guy, and already downed the pot left over from this morning." Which might be part of this whole sleep issue.

"Ice cream is always an option." She gestured to the abandoned spoon on the counter, which felt more like an olive branch. "It's just regular vanilla, but there's fudge and peanuts in the pantry if you need something a little more decadent."

"Decadence is overrated." Closing the fridge, he picked up the spoon and slowly made his way toward her, stopping only

when he was pressed against her knees. "Vanilla happens to be my favorite."

"And if it were chocolate, what would you have said?" She held the container hostage, like Gollum with the Ring.

"That vanilla is my favorite, but I'm an equal opportunity connoisseur when it comes to sharing ice cream with a beautiful woman."

She rolled her eyes but released her death grip on the container.

His gaze never leaving hers, he made a big to-do about dipping his spoon in and taking the biggest helping possible. The ice cream was half-melted but he made do.

"Is this the reason you're awake at three a.m.? An ice-cream craving?" he asked.

"Ice cream is best eaten at three a.m. But no." She worried her lip. "I had a hard time sleeping. Every time I closed my eyes, my brain would start processing everything you have going on right now. And all the stress you're under, all the new demands on you, and, well, if you want me to move out, I can call Beckett. She said I can crash on her couch until I find a place."

He'd been operating under the assumption that she'd been awake because she was mad at him. That the things he'd said had ruined any chance he had at repairing this *thing* growing between them.

She was still searching for solid ground after her world had fallen apart, and yet she was more concerned about his recovery than her own. Was even willing to uproot herself again and sleep on a couch if it made his life a little easier.

Annie was the only easy thing in his life, and he knew he'd have to work damn hard to make up for tonight. Even harder, if he wanted to stand a chance of keeping her. And he wanted. Good thing hard work had never scared Emmitt. Losing Annie? Now, that scared the shit out of him.

Emmitt had met a lot of women in his life, but he'd never known one as compassionate and selfless as Annie. He didn't think he'd ever meet another quite like her.

"Do you want to move out?" he asked.

Her response was to shove a scooper full of ice cream into her mouth and shrug. Most people would take that as indifference, but Emmitt knew better. Annie was preparing herself for another blow.

"I wouldn't blame you if you did," he began. "I was a complete dick earlier and there isn't enough pepperoni pizza in the world to make up for the things I said."

"You had a rough night and you were in a lot of pain. You still are."

"I'm still a dick? Or I'm still in pain?"

"Both," she said with a teasing smile. "But I know you're going to need time and privacy to work things out with Paisley, and I don't want to be in the way, which is why I'm offering to move."

He stuck the spoon in the ice cream and left it, freeing up his hands. Leaning forward, he rested his palms on the counter, bringing his eyes level with hers and his thigh flush with her bare legs. Her very sexy, very silky, very tempting bare legs.

"I'm really sorry about what I said. But I don't want you to move out."

"You don't?" she breathed.

"No. I don't. I like the arrangement. I like you being here. In fact, I like you." He parted her knees slightly, and she did the rest, relaxing so he could slip between them. Which he did. "A lot." But instead of going in for the kiss—which based on the way she was scoping out his mouth, he totally could have—he went for comfort and support, which was what he should have done earlier. "You want to tell me why you were crying earlier?"

"Not really."

"You sure?" he asked. "Because someone once told me that roommates need to be open and honest with each other, in case something happens. What happened, Goldilocks?"

"Is my being your roommate the only reason you want to know?"

"No. I want to know because I like you." He noticed her eyes were puffy from a recent cry, which gutted him. "A lot."

"I just spent the whole night being reminded that I don't fit

in." Her voice was soft and full of exasperated suffering, which he knew she'd never actually verbalize. "I went to the potluck so excited to find a deep connection, only to be smacked in the face with how different I am. I didn't connect. At all." She let out a laugh that was too close to a sob for his comfort. "I didn't even have the right words to begin to connect. Literally, they were all speaking Vietnamese, so I sat in the corner, acting like that shy little In-Bee I worked so hard to leave behind."

"In-Bee?"

She paused for a moment, as though trying to figure out if he was messing with her or being serious. "You know, someone who got stuck in between? Always battling people's expectations and my reality. Half the time, I feel like a big fake."

He shook his head. "You are as real as they come. That you care so much makes you uniquely Ann."

"Being unique is exhausting and always comes with disclaimers and explanations. Sometimes I just want to be like everyone else so when I walk into a room I don't have to play Twenty Questions before getting to the standard Get to Know You ones. Because no matter which side is asking, I'm never going to live up to their first impression."

"You exceeded mine in the first ten minutes, and you continue to amaze me," he said. Even in the limited light of the moon, he could see the tears pooling on her lashes, one blink from spilling over.

"When I walked into that room of women, they assumed I spoke Vietnamese, and when they realized I didn't, I explained that my parents didn't neglect their cultural duties; they're just white. Which led to the whole adopted part of the story, where they told me how lucky I was that I was picked, which made me think about all of the kids who weren't picked. And what it was that made me pickable so I keep doing that and not disappoint my parents. Maybe it was a onetime thing I happened to do, and Mom was like, 'Did you see that, Marty? She laughed just like my mom used to. She's the one!' But I don't really laugh like that, so maybe they feel conned, which ultimately leads me to

the reminder that in order to be picked someone had to discard me first."

She took a breath, jerky and trembling, and his heart clenched. Because when she'd said "discard" she looked embarrassed and a little lost and, the part that really slayed him, as if she believed she was truly discardable, when it couldn't be further from the truth. She had the kind of heart that, if one was lucky enough to receive even the smallest piece of, deserved to be protected and treasured forever.

"I know this all sounds crazy and I'm probably scaring you off," she said.

"You don't sound crazy, and if a stiletto torpedo didn't scare me off, nothing you do ever can," he whispered. "You mentioned the other side—what do they do when they meet you?"

"When I walk into a room of white people and they learn that I don't have fly chopstick skills or fall into some Asian stereotype, I have to explain that I was born in Vietnam but raised here in the states by white parents. The 'white bread upbringing' gives me enough cred that they take a chance getting to know me, but they should want to get to know me just because of me, not where I was born or what race my parents are. It's like, I have to straddle two worlds, knowing I'm never going to be fully accepted or fit into either one."

No wonder she worked so hard to please the people around her. Her life had been a nonstop battle to belong, where everyday encounters forced her to defend her own identity.

"You fit with me." Taking the ice cream out of her hands and setting it on the island, he took her into his arms. "See, a perfect fit."

She slid her arms around his neck and buried her face in his chest, holding on as if this was the most important hug of her life. Hell, it was for him. She fit so damn perfectly he never wanted to move, so he didn't. Just stood there, silently holding her while his heart pounded against his chest. Her heart was doing some pounding of its own, fast and erratic, the tempo radiating through him.

"You've never asked about any of that. Why?" she whispered.

"None of that matters to me," he murmured back, his voice a little huskier than before. "The moment you locked me out of my own room, I knew I wanted to learn everything there was to know about you."

"You said I was crazy."

"You always seem to leave out the cutie part," he said. "And while I do love a cutie, I was even more intrigued by the woman who tried to kill me in my own house, then lectured me and locked me out of my bedroom. Independent, real, honest, strong—and stubborn enough to call me on my shit even after you realized I was your landlord."

"You forgot smart." Her fingers, which had been laced around his neck, slowly slid up through his hair.

"And sexy." His fingers did some sliding too, down her back, lower and lower until he was reaching a line that, once crossed, could never be undone. "So incredibly sexy you have me stumbling over myself trying to impress you."

It was dark so he couldn't be certain, but he was pretty sure she was blushing—and staring at his mouth.

"For the record, you aren't my landlord, you're my roommate." She shimmied toward the edge of the counter—and him—making this a serious *run don't walk toward that finish line* kind of scenario, and he was just waiting for her to blow the whistle.

"We're a whole lot more than roommates, Anh."

"This would never work," she said—against the side of his neck. "You're all about grand gestures, and I'm into the little things."

He pulled back enough that she had to lift her head. "Only because you've never had a gesture grand enough to be worthy of you. And for the record, I think this will work just fine."

She seemed to have flipped to the same page as he, because she didn't take her gaze from his lips. "Are you going to kiss me now?"

"I believe this is a ladies-first kind of situation," he said,

knowing full well he didn't give a shit who kissed who first. All he cared was that it finally happened.

Actually, that wasn't true.

Emmitt knew Annie's life had been a revolving door of disappointment, and he cared about her too much to be one more person to take her for a spin.

"Which also means ladies set the rules. How far, how fast—this is on your terms," he whispered. "But if you're asking for my consent, then the big 'Fuck Yeah' in my pants is all the consent you need."

And luck of all that was lucky, she got the message.

One minute her lips weren't anywhere near his mouth; then she leaned forward and there they were and—Christ almighty—when Anh Nhi Walsh set her mind to something she was fully, completely, and mind-body-and-soulfully committed to the cause. And right now, she was proving that she was a kissing genius of the superhuman kind.

Emmitt had been kissed and he'd *been kissed*, but he'd never come close to being kissed like this. On a scale of scorching to molten lava, Annie was nearing surface-of-the-sun levels.

Not too hot that he'd be afraid of getting burned.

Not too cold that he'd have to wonder if she was going to ditch the shirt and teal lace.

Oh no, his Goldilocks' kiss was just right.

Teasing and languid, her mouth gently moved against his as if she'd been dreaming of this moment for as long as he had. And knowing her, his sweet and methodical Annie, she had a very detailed plan that, based on the sensation of her fingers gliding down his back and around to his bare chest, she'd worked out every detail. Not that he was complaining.

Nope, Emmitt was enjoying the hell out of every glide and touch.

Her kiss was finally going to shift the debate from *Who gets the bed* to *who's on top*. Although she seemed to be headed toward a *Heating up the kitchen* fantasy, which he was A-OK with.

As for her consent, that came when she smoothed her hands

down his stomach, making a brief visit right over, *bingo*, the front of his sweats. Talk about fantasies. This woman was checking off every box.

Never one to neglect his part of the work, Emmitt made his way out from her shirt and down to palm both cheeks of her ass—and what an outstanding ass it was—molding them until she was sitting on his hands instead of the counter.

"Emmitt," she said against his lips. Then her hand found its way under the hem of his sweats, going the extra millimeter just for him, and giving a startled laugh when she made contact. "I guess that answers my question about whether you normally sleep naked."

"I do a lot of things naked," he said, and then he was groaning because those elegant fingers of hers were exploring up and down and all around his consent.

"Big words for a guy who wears glow-in-the-dark boxers."

"Don't let the boxers fool you," he said, and in a move that was inspired, he had his hands under her ass, her legs around his waist, and she was pressed against the nearest wall while he kissed her with the power of a dozen restless nights spent playing out this exact moment.

Hundreds of hours to dream up hundreds of ways it could go down, and none of them could have prepared him for the real thing. Until Annie, he'd never had anything real with a woman. But she was as real as it got, so instead of one of his hot-and-heavy kisses, he delivered the kind of *whole-body, these cheeky cut panties are toast, real earth-shattering* kiss that a man gives a woman when he wanted to be clear about just how hard he's going to rock her world.

And rock it he did, kissing her until his arms were shaking and his head was spinning and one kiss melted into another. They were sharing the same breath, moving with the familiarity of two people who had known each other for years, decades even.

"Emmitt," she said between kisses, her hands tightening in his hair.

It was a few minutes longer before she spoke again. "Emmitt, wait. No fake promises, remember?"

"No fake promises." He leaned in to pick things back up, and she stuck a hand between their mouths and held it there until he pulled back.

"I need you to say it out loud so we both hear it, and nobody misunderstands."

Is she serious?

"I need you to promise you won't say anything you don't mean," she whispered, and he realized she was not only serious, she was completely terrified of his response.

Needing to give her question the consideration it deserved, the consideration she deserved, he walked over to set her on the counter opposite the spot where they'd begun.

Brushing her hair back so he could see her, he asked, "What do you think is going to happen? I make a promise to get you into bed and then tomorrow act like nothing's changed?"

She glanced down. "It's been known to happen."

Emmitt lowered his head so she was forced to look at him. She slammed her eyes shut.

"How are you going to know I'm being honest if you have your eyes closed?"

"Trust me, I've gone in eyes wide open before and it didn't work out so well for me. I figure if something goes wrong this time, I can blame it on my closed eyes."

"Or you can trust that I'm not the guy everyone seems to think I am, and when I tell you I won't ever lie to you, you can believe me," he said gently, and she opened one eye, then the other. "No fake promises."

"Thank you." She placed a tender whisper of a kiss on his lips. "And I believe you."

"Talk about a turn-on." He kissed her back.

"Me thanking you or trusting you?"

"Both. All of it. Everything about you is a turn-on, and that is as honest as it comes."

And they were finished with the discussion part of the eve-

ning, because Annie got down to the nonverbal communications section.

Emmitt had a PhD in nonverbal communication, so when she leaned back and lifted her arms he properly translated her invitation and, easing his thumbs under the hem of her shirt, slowly pushed it up. The higher the hem went, the harder he got, until he brushed the undersides of her breasts. When he tugged off the shirt, leaving her in nothing but teal, his breath lodged itself in his throat.

"Jesus." He ran a hand over his mouth. Toned core, elegant shape, and soft curves all there for him to catalogue and savor. And savor he did.

He started with letting his gaze roam her entire body, followed by his hands, which explored and worshiped every single inch of silky skin. And when he got to those cheeky cuts, he got up close and personal with her lace before continuing his trip all the way down until he was on his knees kissing each painted toe.

Annie wanted to rush him along, he could tell, but she patiently sat there, letting him look his fill. And to reward her for her thoughtfulness, he used his mouth on the way back up.

Gently taking her foot, he placing an opened-mouth kiss on the little divot above her ankle, and she let out this sexy noise that was the vocal equivalent of a hand job. Had he not promised her "big words," he would have gone right to the main course. But he was a man of his word, so he took his time to build the heat.

He placed another kiss, this one right below her knee. His mouth took a languid tour all the way up her leg, not stopping until he was inches from her pleasure button. Then he placed her foot on the edge of the counter and gave her a little pat, signaling for her to leave it there.

He did the same with her other leg, placing that foot in line with the first, and her in the right position for what would come next.

Specifically, her.

He watched her watching him as he kissed his way around

the edge of her panties, loving how her eyes got wider and wider as her breathing became shallower and shallower. He nipped the inside of her right thigh, deciding to lick the left, and then because she seemed to like that so much, he pressed her legs open even farther and licked her right up the middle of that teal lace.

"God, Emmitt," she moaned, leaning back on her hands.

"You can lose the God part. Emmitt's fine," he said, taking a moment to appreciate how the lace hugged her ass. Man, what a sight. The only thing he'd love to see more was for it to be gone.

This man of action was on the problem, hooking his finger under the scalloped edging by her leg and pulling it to the side so that when he licked a second time, there was no lace between them.

He nipped and teased, learning what she liked and memorizing what she loved. He'd always been a quick study, because with a few more strokes, he did this swirling thing with his tongue and she flew apart, screaming out his name. Not once, but over and over again until his name was nothing more than a sated whisper.

When she peeled herself off his chest, she looked up at him with a mischievous twinkle.

"These need to come off," she said.

"I couldn't agree more, Goldilocks."

And funny thing, he started tugging at her panties at the same time she went after his sweats, until they were a tangle of limbs and laughter.

"Not me," she said. His sweats lodged around his knees like a Hula-Hoop refusing to go down without a fight. She gave his ass a smack. "Your turn."

"Or." He kicked off his sweats and in a one-two action that even impressed him, Annie's panties joined his sweats on the floor, and she was over his shoulder. "Both our turns."

"Put me down." She smacked his ass again, so he gave her a little slap in return. Ignoring her laughs, he carried her over to the recliner after making a pitstop in the bathroom to grab a condom.

Taking a seat, he plopped her on his lap, noticing how her boobs gave a little jiggle. When he kicked the recliner back, they jiggled again.

"You're doing that on purpose." She scrambled upright, putting a leg on either side so she was straddling him, her wet, hot skin settling over his.

"You bet your sweet ass I did." He didn't smack it. Oh no, he planted his hands there as if claiming it for himself and gave a slight jerk that sent her falling forward and pressing those very naked body parts against his. "There, problem solved. No more jiggling."

"This problem is far from solved." She pressed against him in a lap-dance move that had his eyes rolling back into his head. "In fact, we have a very big problem on our hands." She sat back and smiled. "More correctly, in my hands."

Hands that she used to slowly drive him out of his mind and under her spell. A spell that was going to be broken in only a couple of ways. "One, you keep that up and this will end in quick and pleasurable fun for one. Or, two, you help me get this on"—he held up the condom—"and we can cross that finish line together."

"How about one, then two?"

"Yeah, one happens and it's going to take some serious recharge time before we get back to two. I made some pretty big promises and I intend to keep my word."

No longer able to wait for her to decide, Emmitt took charge, which had him bringing the chair upright so he could tear open the condom wrapper.

It was a little tricky, with her hands doing more stroking than helping, but together they managed to get him wrapped and inside her in a single thrust.

"Jesus," he moaned at the same time she groaned.

"So big."

Normally, he would have taken a moment to soak in the compliment, even thank her for it, but before he knew it, the chair tilted back, Annie tilted forward, and they were both fully hori-

zontal. Her hands were braced on either side of his head, those incredible breasts jiggling right in his face.

"I'm never getting rid of this recliner," he said, because all he had to do was lean up and—*sweet mercy*—he was appreciating her breasts the way they were intended to be appreciated.

Annie was done being patient, because she arched her back and sank down even further, pushing until he was all the way inside of her. They both stopped breathing, stopped moving, and for a long moment he swore he was going to cry at the rightness of it all.

But it was Annie to the rescue as she rose up only to sink deliciously back down. Taking her by the hips, he helped steady her while she moved faster and harder, their bodies becoming slick from the friction.

Sex with Annie was just like arguing with her: honest, real, and so damn unexpected he knew he'd never tire of it. Of her.

"Big promises," she challenged, and he was all in.

Lifting her by the hips, he guided her down at the same time that he rose up, and she choked on his name. Not that he was holding strong. A few more times and breathing seemed to do nothing but piss off his chest, so he gave up on it.

They found a frenzied but steady rhythm, and he was about to ask for mercy when she gasped, "Do that again."

"This?" he asked, lifting his hips. He knew when he hit the bull's-eye because she let out a throaty moan and closed her eyes. Then her body tightened, and all Emmitt could do was hold on while she exploded around him. But only a fraction of a second before him. Cutting it damn close, but not so close he couldn't technically claim he'd been true to his Ladies First oath. Then everything went black, and he collapsed against the chair, but not before he cradled her to him.

When he was finally able to breathe without danger of passing out, he noticed Annie was covering him like a blanket, her right hand intertwined with his left. She also had her eyes closed and was lightly snoring.

He brushed her hair away from her face and watched silently

as she slept, her lips gently parted, her lashes resting against her flushed face. Emmitt didn't think he'd ever seen anyone look so beautiful.

Or feel so perfectly right.

Now he just had to convince her that *he* was *her* perfectly right.

One minute, Annie was having *the* best orgasm of her life and the next she came awake drooling on Emmitt's chest.

It was still dark out, so she wouldn't have to do this walk of shame with the morning sun shining down on her. She listened to the steady rhythm of his breathing before she even dared to open one eye.

Whew. He was sound asleep.

Using the armrests for balance, she slowly lifted herself up and off Emmitt without disturbing him. Well, part of him was already wide awake.

Annie picked her panties up off the floor, then her shirt before using it to wipe her drool off Emmitt's chest. She didn't think a wet spot was what they had in mind when the term *drool-worthy abs* was coined.

A quick dab and—okay, she might have looked a little longer than was kosher for a smash-and-dash, but he had the kind of good looks usually reserved for the big screen.

He was clever, and tender, and felt things deeply. And the way he'd held her, as if he never wanted to let go—Annnnd . . . this was the reason she was pulling a smash-and-dash.

She believed him when he said no fake promises, but he'd never promised her anything resembling a relationship. So before she went and got herself all moony over the man, she needed to retreat to her own bed.

Her eyes had a mind of their own and lingered for another very long moment before she forced herself to turn and walk away. She made it to the bedroom and was just reaching for the handle when she heard him chuckle.

"You weren't going to invite me to share the bed?" he said, his voice all rough and sexy with sleep.

She turned around. "We're back to roommates, remember."

"Roommates who've seen each other naked." He appeared at the end of the hallway, hands on hips, everything else on display, as if proving his point.

"That doesn't imply morning cuddling or any other benefits. Remember?"

He laughed. "Then what the hell was that?"

Arousing amusement in a naked man didn't say a whole lot about her casual sex sophistication. Neither did gawking at him—all of him—as he snagged his sweats from the floor and stepped into them. With a smile that promised all kinds of things she was afraid to address, he stalked toward her.

Every step he took, she retreated backward—right into the door.

"Anh?" he whispered, closing the minuscule gap.

Sucking in a breath, she reached behind herself, blindly grabbing the doorknob with both hands—which was better than reaching for him because, blindly or not, she knew where her hands would end up.

He reached too—around her, capturing both her hands with one of his. "What was it?"

"Me taking a calculated risk," she whispered.

She expected him to get mad, but instead he grinned a boyish grin that did her in. "Was it worth it?"

She nodded, watching as he slowly lowered his head. With their gazes locked, his lips brushed hers, gently probing until the kiss became more of a conversation. A back and forth of emotions and questions they were too uncertain to voice.

But, *man oh man*, was she in trouble. If this was how he kissed when he was free and clear of any entanglements, she could only imagine how it would feel to be kissed by him when he was all in.

He pulled back, and it took Annie a moment to realize she was wrapped around him like a koala in a eucalyptus forest. "Good night, Goldilocks."

The door opened behind her and a rush of cool air rolled over her, causing her to break out in goose bumps.

"Good night," Annie said, but he'd already disappeared into the darkness of the house.

She backed into the bedroom and closed the door. Arms out to her sides, she fell backward on the bed and looked up at the ceiling with a goofy smile.

"Don't be stupid and fall for him." Then she told her heart, which was getting way ahead of itself, to slow its roll. Until further notice, it was on total lockdown—all perimeters were secured, and no unwanted emotions were permitted to enter or exit the premises.

Unfortunately, her heart was too busy rolling over and offering up its soft underbelly to get the memo.

Chapter 21

Feet propped up against the wall and her head hanging off the end of the mattress, Annie stared at the doorknob, willing it to turn.

There was no light filtering under the crack in the door, and she hadn't heard so much as a rustle since Emmitt kissed her good night. But she could sense that he was still awake.

She'd made the right call. Her heart was already becoming too involved with Emmitt, and her life was becoming intertwined with his family's. But as she lay there in his bed, all she could think about was how much more comfortable it would be with him in it.

Annie had never considered herself a cuddler, but she had a strong suspicion that if Emmitt slid in beside her and wrapped those strong arms around her, she'd be a convert.

Who was she kidding? After tonight she was already a convert.

Annie let out a frustrated sigh. She'd been lying there with the window open, listening to the rain dance against the wood deck for the past hour, recounting the steps that had led to her falling asleep on him in the chair. That wasn't normal, right? To be so comfortable with someone that seconds after shouting out her big O, she immediately fell asleep on him.

The part that really scared her, she realized in the middle of

a cold shower, was that when she was first coming awake, in that split second when dreams merge with reality, she'd had this overwhelming feeling of belonging.

She'd gone to Pho Shizzle tonight searching for a better understanding of who she was, where she came from. Yet she'd walked away feeling as if she were an interloper and worrying that she'd always be in transition. Her outsider status gave her the fluidity to move from one group to the next, one patient to another, make them all feel loved and cared for in the moments when their own people couldn't be by their side.

But when she'd been curled into Emmitt's side, their arms causally slung over one another, their bodies stuck together like magnets, she'd imagined that was what it felt like to be with "your person."

Here she was, no longer touching him, and that feeling hadn't disappeared in the slightest.

A gentle breeze lifted the curtain, and a few of the leftover sprinkles dotted the fabric. The storm had passed through, but Annie didn't want to risk getting the windowsill wet. She rolled off the bed and padded over to close it.

The night was still. The leaves on the maple tree hung heavy with rain, and the grass shimmered in the moonlight. She watched the runoff slide down the roof in a slow but steady drip into the swimming pool below, creating ripples on the surface and breathed in the fresh scent, which reminded her of wearing her dad's bright yellow galoshes and jumping through puddles.

She was about to close the window when something caught her eye at the far end of the pool. Two lean legs hung over the side, their bare feet dangling in the water. A closer look revealed Paisley, slouched on a cushion from the patio chair and dressed in jeans and a drenched hoodie, looking small and lost.

Annie checked the time even though she already knew that it was way past curfew.

She quickly ran through every option before deciding that there was no right way to handle this situation. The possibility that any of Paisley's dads would allow her to wander between

houses this early in the morning, was close to nil. Especially when it was cold and wet out. Nope, if anyone knew she wasn't safe in her bed, Emmitt would already be out searching for her.

His first stop would likely be Sam's house.

To add to Annie's conflict, Paisley had come here, to Emmitt's, for a reason. It seemed she was waiting for the courage to reveal that reason because she hadn't bothered to wake him. So while the adult thing to do would be to wake Emmitt and tell him his daughter was crying in the backyard, girl code demanded that Annie go out there and see if Paisley needed to talk.

When put like that, her choice was clear.

Grabbing a roll of chocolate doughnuts from her emergency stash—some people had Go Bags; she had doughnuts—and the blanket off the bed, Annie climbed through the window.

She wasn't even all the way out when Paisley spotted her. Without missing a beat, Annie confidently strode across the deck as if she were meeting up for a girl chat and plopped down next to Paisley.

Paisley watched, eyes wide like a cornered bobcat, as Annie wrapped herself in the blanket, then opened the roll of doughnuts and popped one in her mouth. She may have moaned just a little, then licked her fingers before grabbing another. This one, she nibbled at before setting the bag on the edge of the blanket nearest Paisley.

Paisley cautiously met Annie's gaze in question and Annie shrugged a shoulder, letting her know the doughnuts were fair game.

Paisley selected one, and the crinkle of the plastic was amplified by the stillness of the night. Neither said anything for a long while, just sat beside one another, watching the movement of the water. At one point Paisley pulled her feet out of the pool and hugged her knees to her chest. Annie took a corner of the blanket and draped it over her knees.

When the last doughnut was gone, Paisley asked, "You going to tell my dad?"

"Depends," Annie said. "Do you think he'd be worried if he found you weren't where you were supposed to be?"

"I guess." Paisley tilted her head slightly toward Annie. "But everyone else does it and no one freaks out. I mean, Dad One gets a call and the next day he's gone, or Bonus goes out sometimes for month-long sailing trips and no one says a word. But if I want just a quiet night to myself, or to go to the beach and just think, my dads think I'm depressed or that something's wrong."

Annie considered what Paisley had said, put two and two together, that Dad One was Emmitt and Bonus was her uncle. "What's Gray's nickname?"

"Dad Two."

"Do they know you call them that?"

She scoffed. "No. I don't do it to be mean. I do it because when I'm really upset, calling them Dad One or whatever takes some of the sting out of it."

"Makes sense," Annie said, looking back out at the pool. "My dad calls me Flapjack."

"Are you like a pancake freak?"

"I like them, but I'm really a *pastry for breakfast* kind of girl." Annie shook the empty bag, and Paisley gave a tiny laugh, not much more than a little breath pushing through her nose, but Annie could tell she was starting to relax.

"Then why did he call you that?"

"When I was six, my parents tried to enroll me in school, but they discovered one of the papers from my adoption had never been filed, so the adoption had never been finalized. My parents had to go through the whole adoption process again, prove they were good parents, that they had no criminal background, a ton of red tape kind of stuff. Then they had to go in front of a judge and petition to adopt the daughter they'd raised since birth," Annie said. "So for about two months my parents were terrified that they'd somehow lose me."

"They were your parents—how could someone just decide to take you away?" Paisley asked in a protective tone that was all Emmitt.

"My parents argued the same thing. But in the end, it all

worked out. The judge finalized the adoption, and I remember my dad saying that his love for me was so big he adopted me twice," Annie said, surprised that after all these years she still got emotional telling her adoption story. "On the way home we stopped at a diner to celebrate, and my dad asked what I wanted, and I said flapjacks, which made him laugh. He ordered flapjacks for the whole table, and somehow the name stuck."

"Does he still call you that?" Paisley asked.

"All the time," Annie said, and Paisley looked as if she'd just discovered where babies came from. "I know, it's silly, and when I was your age it embarrassed me, and once I told him to stop. Later that night he came into my room and said he called me Flapjack because it was a name between us, it wasn't on any official papers or court transcripts, it couldn't get misfiled or lost, and no matter what, it could never be taken away from us. The next day I told him I was okay with the name, but he could only use it at home."

Annie learned that day that her nickname represented an important part of her story. It was the day her parents stood up in front of a judge and fought to keep their family together. As she got older, she began to realize that her parents weren't just fighting for their family, they were fighting against society's views of what constitutes a family.

A piece of paper didn't make them family. It was their love.

"He uses it everywhere, by the way," Annie said. "But now I like it. And your dad—I mean Dad One—has a nickname for you. Sweet P, right? So it's only fair if he gets one too."

"I wasn't very sweet tonight," Paisley said with a shiver.

Annie scooted a little closer and shared more of the blanket. To someone looking on, they would appear to be a couple of friends chatting over doughnuts. But this was so much more.

"You don't always have to be sweet." Annie nudged Paisley with her shoulder. "You're figuring out who you are—that's hard."

"Does it get easier?" Paisley asked, and tears lined her lashes.

"I don't know if easier is the word," Annie said gently. "The

older you get, the better you'll become at figuring out who you are outside of other people's expectations and making choices that are right for you. When you get there, then I think it'll be easier."

At least that's what Annie was banking on, that by getting enough distance from all the noise and influences, her choices would suddenly become clear.

"What if no matter who you become, you're always going to make someone sad," Paisley whispered.

Annie took the time to choose her words before speaking. She didn't want to push too hard, but she also didn't want to wait too much longer before letting Emmitt know that Paisley had gone AWOL.

"Hypothetically, does this situation have to do with a daughter trapped between her many dads?" She slid Paisley an amused look. "Asking for a friend, of course."

"If I were to tell Dad One that I wanted to sleep at Dad Two's on his nights, he'd be so hurt. But if I don't ask, then Dad Two's at home all alone."

"Honey . . ." Annie wrapped her arm around Paisley's shoulders and tucked her in close. "Those guys have been taking care of themselves since before you were even a thought in your mom's head. And yes, for two guys who claim they aren't competitive, they can make the girls on *The Bachelor* look reserved. But when it comes to you and your happiness, from what I've seen, they're a team. They want you to be happy, even if it means they don't get exactly what they want."

"It's hard when everyone's telling you to be happy but you don't want to be," Paisley said, and Annie felt her own tears welling up. "Sometimes I just want to be, I don't know, nothing. Like, have everything inside just go still."

"I bet it's hard to be happy when the people around you are still so sad. It would be even hard to be sad when they're sad." Annie had seen Gray at the office. He was clearly drowning in grief. It was hard for Annie, as his friend, to watch. She could only imagine how painful it was for Paisley.

"Have you told your dads this?" Annie asked, and Paisley shook her head. "Do you think that's maybe why you came here? Even though you're mad at Emmitt, you don't have to feel so much here. You can just be?"

Paisley picked at a small tear in her jeans. "He's really pissed at me right now."

"I couldn't love you more for who you are at this exact moment," Emmitt said, and both Annie and Paisley turned to find him standing by the back door.

He had on the gray sweats from earlier, no shirt, and no ballcap to hide his injury.

"Dad." Paisley stood. "I was going to tell you I was here. I just needed—"

"Someplace quiet, where you feel safe," he said, walking toward them. "I get that. I needed the same thing earlier." His gaze locked on Annie, and "my person" was all she could think. *Which was so far from the truth.*

One romp didn't make him hers. One cuddle on the recliner didn't make him hers. And just because he was looking at her as if, he too thought, tonight was more than sex, that didn't make him "her person."

"And you know what helped?" he said, and Paisley, who was trembling with pent-up emotion, shook her head. "A really great hug. Want to see if it works for you?"

"Dad," Paisley whined, but walked right into his arms.

Emmitt pulled her so close, she almost disappeared in his embrace. Which was exactly what his daughter needed, because her body started shaking and Annie could hear sniffles.

It was exactly what her dad needed as well.

Paisley pulled back and frowned. She reached up and gently touched his head. "What happened? Are you okay? Oh my God, Dad, that looks serious."

"How about after we spend some time just being, you and I have a talk?"

Paisley buried her face back into Emmitt's chest and mumbled, "Okay."

Emmitt looked at her over Paisley's head and mouthed, "Thank you."

She just smiled, but her heart was beating double-time. She had completely misjudged him, and now that she saw who he really was, Annie knew she was in trouble.

The kind of trouble that could cost her her heart.

Chapter 22

Annie took pride in her ability to navigate a difficult situation with effortless grace. After working her first two years in a mental facility and the last four alongside her *It's not you, it's me* ex-fiancé, there wasn't much that shocked her.

Not that she was completely shocked. Annie had heard stories about the great and generous Dr. Widdle, from his renowned methods in the ER to his willingness to mentor younger practitioners. She had secretly hoped for a chance to work alongside the admired doctor ever since taking the job at Rome General. So when he asked her—out of all the amazing and talented practitioners working the ER that day—to consult on a difficult case he felt she was best equipped for, Annie could barely contain her excitement.

She'd worked hard her entire career for the chance to work under doctors such as Widdle—to learn from them. It was another reason why she embraced the idea of being a traveling PA. The only way to grow as a practitioner—and a woman—was to leave her comfort zone behind for the challenging experiences that came with working under exemplary figures in her field.

With a bright and ready smile, Annie strode through the ER toward exam room six to find her patient.

Annie pushed back the curtain and froze—her bright smile dimming a tad—when she saw an elderly woman embracing a

feverish and fussy toddler. The child was tugging at his ear and wailing to the gods; the woman was babbling on and on. But when she saw Annie, she went silent, as if she, too, understood Annie would be no help.

The woman looked at Dr. Widdle and back to Annie, her expression one of contemplation—as if she was thinking about shoving the child in Annie's direction and making a run for the nearest exit. Considering the volume and deafening dog-whistle pitch of the poor kid's screams, Annie withheld judgment.

"Thank God you're here," the great and generous Dr. Widdle said, looking expectantly at Annie. Had he really asked her to consult on what any first-year nursing student could tell was a standard ear infection?

"How can I help?" she asked, holding tight to her smile, even though her cheeks were giving under the strain.

"I need to know what medications Jun is allergic to," Dr. Widdle asked.

"Do you want me to check his file?" Annie prayed her assumption was wrong and Dr. Widdle was just one of those elitist doctors who was "too busy" to pull his own patient files.

"He's visiting his grandmother, so we don't have a file, which is part of the problem."

"The other part?"

"He's allergic to some kind of antibiotics." He shrugged. "That's all I was able to understand, so I called you."

Annie considered asking the good doctor to give *her* an ear exam to prove that she'd simply *mis*understood. Otherwise, no amount of hard work or hope was going to help Annie navigate this awkward moment gracefully.

"And you called me because?" She wanted to hear him say it.

"You speak Chinese, right?"

Right.

Shock wasn't quite the correct term. Disillusionment and anger were more accurate descriptions of what it felt like to know that a colleague, one she admired, considered her a translator instead of a talented practitioner.

Annie had endured situations like this before, so it shouldn't

have thrown her off-balance the way it did. But being stereo-typed in her place of work pissed her off.

Dr. Widdle had been too busy cataloguing her features to see her outstanding credentials. If his decision had been swayed by a nurse's breast size the way it had by Annie's Asian features, he'd be fired. Sexual harassment was illegal in all fifty states, but racial profiling was harder to prove.

"Chinese isn't a language, it's an ethnicity," Annie said in her most professional tone. "Your patient is speaking Mandarin. It wasn't offered at my high school, so I took Spanish because I heard it was easier than French. Even then, I was so bad, I had to retake Spanish 1 twice before I scraped by with a C minus. Man, was my mom ever PO'd. Grounded me for half the sum-mer." With a look of faux embarrassment, she gave a little shrug of the shoulders. "Google Translate would be more helpful than me."

There was nothing fake about Dr. Widdle's mortified expres-sion. Annie let him stew in it for a moment or three, then placed the file back in its holder. "Is there anything else?"

"No," Dr. Widdle said.

At the same time, Nurse Tran stepped into the room, getting nose-to-nose with Dr. Widdle. "Dr. Widdle called you to help. Looking at this patient, what would you say is the prognosis?"

"An ear infection," Annie said, thankful to be on this side of Nurse Tran's wrath for once.

"Spot-on diagnosis." Nurse Tran volleyed, "Wouldn't you agree, Dr. Widdle?"

The doctor cleared his throat uncomfortably. "Absolutely."

"Then we are all in agreement." Nurse Tran steepled her fin-gers, and Annie knew she was just warming up and was about to bring the heat. "As you can see, Miss Walsh is a gifted physi-cian's assistant whose talents are better used elsewhere than on a simple ear infection. She is not to be mistaken for a translator from patient relations. Understood?" Dr. Widdle nodded. "Not that this could have any bearing on her job performance, but she is Vietnamese, not Chinese. So you have not only offended her, you have offended Ms. Chin, who would never make the

mistake of mixing up you and Harvey Miller, the security officer who works the ER."

"I am so sorry for my ignorance," he said to Annie, the genuine embarrassment in his expression making it hard to hold anything against him. "It won't happen again."

"Good, because this hospital was lucky when Anh agreed to lend our small facility her expertise for the short time she can spare. I am sure there will be a case when her talents will be critical to your department, and I would hate for you to make a bad impression twice."

"Absolutely, Nurse Tran." He turned to Annie. "And I would love to consult with you at a later date."

Before Annie could answer, Nurse Tran said, "If we can spare her. She is an extremely valuable asset to our department. For the record, a plea of ignorance is beneath you, Dr. Widdle."

With that she ushered Annie out of the room and down the hallway. When they were out of the ER, and hearing range, Annie said, "Valuable asset?"

"You are," Nurse Tran said, then broke out into a laugh. "I shouldn't have been so hard on him. He's a nice man. But he asked you to come all the way over here to translate when we have an entire department for that and he was just too impatient to wait for them to fulfill his request."

"And the other part? About him and Harvey?"

She stopped and faced Annie. "Did I ever tell you about the time I was called in to assist with a craniectomy on a sixteen-year-old? It wasn't until I had scrubbed up and was told to stand aside that I realized they already had a full surgical team. Then I saw the photographer and knew having me in the photo would showcase the difficult surgery and that there was diversity here at Rome General."

Annie covered her mouth. "What did you do?"

"I made myself useful, then asked for a promotion because if I was talented enough to be on a surgical team who successfully pulled off a craniectomy on a teenager, then surely I deserved one." She gave Annie's cheek a maternal pat. "Just like you can

now use consulting on a difficult case with Dr. Widdle on your résumé."

"Thank you," Annie said. "You didn't have to step in on my behalf, but I am grateful you did."

"I'll have to tell you about Nurse Kramer, my boss when I first started here, and the time she ripped one of the thoracic surgeons a new one when he told me how he took his coffee." With another pat, Nurse Tran started walking toward the elevator.

"Aren't you going to tell me?" Annie called after her.

"I will, at the next Pho Shizzle."

Annie ran to catch up with her. "You want me to come to the next potluck?"

"Yes. You left so fast I didn't have a chance to tell you how much the ladies loved your mom's dumpling soup. It was the winner of the night." She gave Annie a warm smile. "We all decided you were just what the Pho Shizzles need, a breath of fresh air."

"Really?"

"Here." She handed Annie a slip of paper with a name and number.

"What's this?"

"That is my sister-in-law, Van. She is a retired schoolteacher who now runs a Vietnamese school out of her house. Tell her I sent you and she'll give you fifteen percent off the language package. She'll try to give you only ten percent—she's cheap— but barter until she gives you fifteen. Bartering is very Vietnamese. It will impress her."

"Why are you giving me this?" She'd never mentioned her desire to know more about where she came from or learn to speak her native language.

"So that when you come to my home, you don't come as a coworker or a student looking to learn about who you are. You come to my house as my friend."

Maybe Annie hadn't been the only one playing Twenty Inappropriate Questions the other night. "I'll call her tonight."

"Good. You can learn how to properly pronounce your

name." The doors opened and the nurse stepped inside, push-ing the button to her floor. "Oh, and we're continuing our soup theme for the fall, so the next dish is *Pho Ga*, and we are all anxious to try your mom's chicken noodle soup recipe, if she has one."

"It's actually my paternal grandmother's recipe and it's won a ton of awards," Annie teased.

"I'm counting on it."

When the doors slid closed, Annie shoved the card in her pocket, only to find it already filled. She pulled out the paper, and her heart leaped when she realized it was a folded-up sticky note. She unfolded it and read.

> *How about pizza,*
> *Netflix, and at least*
> *two Happy Endings*
> *tonight? No pressure, just*
> *throwing things out there.*
> *— Roommate with*
> *Benefits Looking*
> *for More*

Annie let out a laugh that started in her chest and radiated through her entire body. It was loud and unapologetic and came from a place of sheer happiness. And when she caught a glimpse of her reflection in the polished elevator doors, the joyful glow and big bright smile was one hundred percent real.

Chapter 23

"Do you feel like it had enough of, you know, the *Fuck off* vibe I was going for?" Annie asked, reading back over her e-mail.

"Read it one more time," Emmitt said, not even bothering to hide his smile.

"You just like to watch me swear."

"I like to watch you do a lot of things. But this doesn't even make my top ten list," he said, and a zing of heat shot through her, heading for the equator.

It could also be because his hands had been making lazy circles on her legs for the past twenty minutes while she crafted an e-mail to Clark.

They were sitting on opposite ends of the couch and he had her feet in his lap, rubbing his hands up and down her legs. With each stroke her flesh broke out in little bumps. What started as him trying to soothe her stress away had quickly turned into foreplay. And they both knew it.

"You have a list?" she teased.

"I have a list so long even Santa couldn't compete." He cupped both of her feet and tugged her closer, then ran his hands up and under the bottom of her skirt. "I can recite it to you."

"You've memorized it?"

"All of the important things I keep right here." He tapped his head with a finger.

"I'm surprised—most men would have pointed somewhere else."

"A few weeks ago I would have been one of those men," he said, and his tone was so sincere and convincing she wanted to believe him. But since the other night on the recliner, he hadn't asked once about the bed. Which left her confused.

"Okay, I'm going to send this before I chicken out." Her finger hovered over the Return key, and she let out a breath. "What if he calls my bluff and asks to speak to my lawyer?"

In the e-mail, Annie had clearly laid out that Clark had until Monday to deposit the money into her account. If he failed to comply, her lawyer would reach out to him. Only Annie didn't have a lawyer.

"Then you give my friend Judy his contact info, and she will reach out on your behalf."

"Emmitt, the whole point is that I'm broke, which is why I need the money. I can't afford to pay a lawyer to scare off my ex," she explained.

"Judy is a friend of mine who owes me a favor," he said, and Annie pulled her feet up under her.

"You're sending me to one of your *friends*? What kind of favor does she owe you?"

Emmitt grabbed her feet and pulled them back into his lap. "Judy was my mother's best friend, and when she and her husband renewed their vows on their fortieth, she asked me to photograph it for them."

Annie's cheeks heated. "That's sweet. But why would she help me for free?"

"Because I asked her to," he said. "I told her a very special friend of mine might need a lawyer to scare the crap out of a prick."

"You did not say that?"

"The part about the special friend I did." His fingers moved up the inside of her legs, then rubbed them down the outside.

"Your website says you don't do any kind of portrait or wedding photography."

"For Judy I do," he said, and there was a boyish look to him

whenever he spoke of anything having to do with his mom. "For special people in my life, I'd do almost anything."

Their gazes locked, and Annie's heart fell to her stomach. She believed every word. Emmitt would go to the end of the earth for his people.

He already had.

Her pulse quickened as she wondered what it would it be like to be on the receiving end of that kind of devotion.

"Have you been googling me, Goldilocks?"

Annie had to swallow before she could speak. "I needed to know I wasn't rooming with an ax murderer."

Emmitt laughed and leaned back against the armrest, but his hands never slowed.

"Tell me about the photographs on the wall," she asked. "There aren't many, which surprised me."

"Digital cameras have changed photography. People go on vacation and come home with three hundred pictures," he said. "The people I'm shooting deserve more than a bunch of random clicks of the finger. For me, it's about getting the shot."

When she'd first moved in, she'd remarked to Gray how odd it was that there weren't a lot of pictures on the wall. Gray had laughed and explained his friend didn't take pictures; he took photographs.

At the time, Annie had found it incredibly obnoxious. But now, after getting to know Emmitt, she thought the statement couldn't be more fitting.

At first glance, it would appear that Emmitt had never bothered to personalize his space by putting any of his belongings on display. There were no family pictures with Mickey Mouse, no Boy Scout camp photo of a grinning child holding a fish, not even a puff pic—like him climbing Kilimanjaro, which she knew from Gray that he had done. In the day and age of selfies, that was telling. Almost as much as the collection of photographs he had chosen.

She'd looked at them before, many times. There were nine in all, sitting in large, identical solid glass frames. Each photograph was of a different size, showing people she'd never meet

from places she'd never been, and each sparking an equally powerful but wildly different emotion.

Annie wondered what emotion she'd feel tonight when she looked at her favorite one with its artist in the room. Hanging near the fireplace, it had particularly drawn Annie.

She set her laptop on the coffee table and slid her legs out of Emmitt's embrace, then crossed the room.

The image was black and white, taken of a young girl, maybe four or five, standing barefoot in the dirt, eyes closed, face up-turned as someone off camera poured a bottle of water over her head. The shutter must have snapped the moment the first few drops hit the child's skin, because Annie could see tiny spots where the water had barely mixed with the hot dust before it slid over the girl's face.

The photo itself would barely fill out a four-by-six frame, but the look of wonder on the girl's face contained enough joy to erase the war-torn conditions around her. The contrast was as heartbreaking as it was breathtaking.

"That one was taken at a refugee camp right outside Afghanistan," Emmitt said from over her shoulder, and Annie realized that while she'd been studying his photos, he'd been studying her—from kissing range. "Madeena and her mother walked barefoot, nearly sixty miles through the mountains in hopes of finding her lost brother, whom they'd been separated from months earlier."

"Did they find him?" Annie asked past the tightness in her throat.

Emmitt's smile was light and warm, real and so completely unexpected that she took a step back, but there really wasn't anywhere to go, so she bumped into the wall. "Who do you think is holding the bottle?"

A pang of emotion had her clearing her throat. "How long ago was that taken?"

"Six years. She's now a fourth grader in Germany who loves science, kittens, and Pokémon. And pink. Last year she was all about bows. This year it's pink."

She laughed, and the release of emotion felt good. "How do you know?"

"Every year she sends me a first-day-of-school picture to show off her new dress," he said as if it was a normal thing to impact the life of a tiny girl on the other side of the world enough that she'd send him a photo. Every year.

"Did you buy those dresses as well?" She could tell he was shocked by her deductive reasoning, which, based on his shy smile, was spot-on.

His hands cupped her hips, and he turned her to face him completely, but he didn't let go. "I figure a girl whose smile can light up even the darkest corners of the world deserves a pretty dress now and again."

"But you don't keep the school pictures framed?" She moved a little closer.

"Nah, they're in a box in the garage," he said, and Annie knew there was only one box in the garage. It was big, metal, and fireproof. The kind of box where people kept their most precious items. But she also guessed there was another reason he didn't have those pictures lying about. Because then people would ask.

Emmitt didn't send Madeena dresses because he had a hero complex or wanted to impress. He did it because he cared. So deeply he didn't wish to share the feeling with just anyone. But he'd shared it with her.

"You're a very complex person, Emmitt Bradley," Annie said, placing her fingertips on his wrists, then slowly tracing his muscles all the way up his arms.

"Funny, with you I feel real," he whispered, tugging her closer.

Annie decided that today was the day to be bold. "Why haven't you tried to come in the bed?"

His expression was a mix of confusion and disappointment. "Because you haven't invited me."

Placing her hands on his shoulders, Annie went up on her tiptoes. "Emmitt, I'd like to go to bed now. And I'd like for you to come with me."

"I thought you'd never ask." And then they were kissing, and what a kiss it was.

Soft, tender, special. The kind of kiss someone shared with their person.

Emmitt was at his computer, working on one of the images he'd shot in China, when his vision started to blur.

Sitting back in the chair, he took off his glasses and rubbed his eyes. Maybe Gray wasn't being a Beaver Cleaver. Maybe he was right in advising him to take more time.

Emmitt couldn't stare at the screen for more than twenty minutes before the headache came back. That Gray was stuck with the decoration committee for the next two hours made him smile though. He was picturing the look on Gray's face as he realized the committee consisted of twenty teens, a few of whom smelled like saltines and BO, when the front door burst open.

"Dad?" he heard Paisley yell, and he could hear the tears in her voice a room away.

Before he could even stand, she came rushing into his office and flung herself into his arms. Her makeup was streaked, her face wet with tears, and Emmitt's heart stopped beating.

He wanted to ask her what had happened and who he needed to beat up, but she was making the quiet sobs she used to make when she was a kid and needed to let out her grief, so he just held her tight and said, "It's okay, baby. I got you."

When her sobs became little hiccups, he ventured, "You want to talk about it?" She wrapped her arms around his middle and buried herself into him. "Or we can just sit here in silence— whatever you need. Just know that if you want to talk about anything, today, tomorrow, next week, I'm here. No lectures, no judgment."

Lifting her eyes just high enough to meet his, she said, "About anything?"

"Anything, kiddo."

"You were right. Sam's a jerk." She paused, her expression said she was waiting to see if he was serious about the whole

no judging or lecturing promise. Emmitt bit his tongue. "I just caught him kissing my supposed friend in my bedroom."

"Do you want me to kick his ass?" he said, earning a giggle.

"That's not at all what I thought you were going to say." She laughed.

"I guess there are things we both need to learn about each other," he said.

"Yeah," she agreed. "And thank you for being on my side. Not telling me you told me so."

"How many times do you have to remind me that your mom's chili is too spicy for me?"

"Hundreds."

He wiped a tear away with his thumb. "We'll discuss how public education is failing you in simple math later. The point is, I still eat it even though I know how miserable I'll feel later. Why? Because the chili is too good to pass up."

"Are you saying Sam is my chili?"

"Do you feel bloated, gassy, and like your chest is on fire?"

"Yes," she said with a laugh, which made his chest swell. "Guys aren't worth it. I am totally over the whole boyfriend thing."

"Not all guys are Sams," he said. "And while I'd be perfectly happy with you being single until you're thirty-five, I also understand that's about as unlikely as you being 'totally over the boyfriend thing.' Someday, sooner than I'd like, a great guy is going to come into your life and figure out what a cool chick you are and just how lucky he'd be to have you on his arm."

"I don't know about that. But a nice guy who doesn't try to pawn me off on his sister would be nice."

"Man, did he ever Sam things up with you."

"Yeah." She laughed. "What a Samhole. At least his sister is nice. We're going to the movies next week."

"Do you want to stick with the story that all these tears are over some guy?" he asked, because Annie was right, the boy thing was normal teen stuff. But Paisley was also dealing with some pretty heavy issues that a girl her age shouldn't be forced to deal with. "Or do you maybe want to talk about your mom?"

She shook her head as she said, "It just feels like everything is upside down right now."

"How so?"

"I don't know. Mom's gone, if you haven't heard."

He took a napkin from the basket and dabbed her tears.

"I know," he said gently, brushing her hair out of her face. When he looked into those sad brown eyes, it nearly did him in right there.

"Do you? Because I don't. I don't feel like I know anything. Nothing makes sense, and the things that do don't matter." She let out a shaky breath and shifted sideways, resting her cheek against his chest. "I mean, Mom goes to the store to get me almond milk because I decided to be vegan and some guy keeps driving because of a missing stop sign. Neither one was speeding or drinking. There was no higher power in play, no destiny involved, just this freak occurrence that took her away."

"Gray told me that the stop sign had been stolen that day," he said. And the fact that he had to quote Gray because he hadn't been there to hold his kid like this when it happened made him feel as angry as it did selfish. There was no reason he had to take that assignment. He'd done it because life in Rome began to get complicated, so he'd bailed.

What kind of dad bails like that? Not the kind of dad that Emmitt wanted to be.

"The cops told us that a couple of guys thought it would be funny to hang it in their frat house above the bathroom door," Paisley went on. "If that's college fun, I don't want to go. I overheard Rosalie tell one of Daddy's patients, it was just a perfect storm, one of those things."

"Your mom's life was too meaningful to everyone she came in contact with, everyone she loved, to be summed up by 'Just one of those things.' You know that, right?"

"When she said it, I was so mad, but now . . . I don't know. My life is just one of those things. You came home for a weekend when Mom happened to have an ear infection, her doctor happened to give her antibiotics that canceled out her birth

control, you and Mom happened to, you know, and here I am. Some kids steal a stop sign and here we are."

"I don't buy into the whole *everything happens for a reason* crap, because if that were true, neither of us would have been forced to grow up without our moms. And your mom and I might not have been in love, but you came from the purest form of love," he said. "You are so loved, P. And just because your mom is gone doesn't take away from the fact that she loved you so fiercely when she was here, and it doesn't mean that her love for you vanished."

"Love hurts," she whispered.

"After I lost my mom, I promised myself I would never love again because losing her felt like losing my whole world. Nothing felt right after that. I was still me, but it was as if I was living in an alternate universe, where everything was the same except me."

"Did you ever love again?"

He kissed the top of her head. "The first day I met you, I learned just how much someone could love."

She looked up at him. "When did you start feeling at home again?"

"It took a while, but when my mom's sister told me it was okay to miss her, my life started to feel more normal. So I'm going to tell you the same thing she told me. You're allowed to not be over her. You're allowed to miss her."

"Am I allowed to be angry?"

"Oh, baby, anger is not only allowed, it's expected."

"Am I allowed to be angry at you?" she whispered.

Emmitt cupped her face in his hands, waited until she was really looking at him. "For as long as you need to."

"Because I am," she said, and he could tell she was trying her best not to cry, but it was a losing battle.

"I know, kiddo. I am too. I remember what it was like going through high school and not having my mom to talk to—it was hard. Worse than hard. It was the most difficult time of my life, and the one person who always loved me no matter what was gone."

"How old were you when she died?"

"Eleven."

"I've seen pictures of her at Grandpa's," Paisley said.

"She was pretty amazing." Man, he missed her. Didn't matter how much time had passed—he still missed her like it was yesterday. "Whenever I would have a bad day at school, which was often because I hated school, she'd bake me these cookies."

"Wait, you hated school?" She sounded shocked. "Listening to you and Uncle Levi talk, you made it sound like you two ran the school."

"That was when we were upper classmen. Before that I was a skinny kid with a camera attached to my face who worked on the school paper and wanted to be an Anderson Cooper. Yeah, school pretty much sucked. But then I'd get home and there they were, the cookies."

"Cookies?"

"Peanut butter chip oatmeal cookies. Man, they were good."

"Better than your mom's chocolate pie?"

"They were my chocolate pie," he said. "I never had to tell her it was bad day. She just knew. I'd come home and they'd be there sitting on the counter with milk. Chocolate milk. And she'd sit across from me and talk about my day. That was the best part, that I could say anything to her."

"Maybe we can make her cookies."

"I'd love that."

She looked him dead in the eye and said, "When does it stop hurting?"

"I wish I could tell you it does, because I'm your dad, and dads should be able to protect their kids from pain and disappointment, but you're not a kid anymore and we're doing this whole trust and honesty thing, so the truth is, it doesn't. But over time the sadness eases and the memories become a part of you."

"Do you still get sad when you talk about your mom?"

"Sometimes, but the good memories always outweigh the sad ones."

Paisley laid her head on his shoulder and closed her eyes.

They sat in silence, and he could feel she was thinking about Michelle.

"Did the sadness ever scare you?" she asked. "Like today was the best it would ever get?"

"Does it scare you?"

Because it sure as fuck scared him to hear her say that. But he remembered to love her for exactly who she was in this moment. And in this moment, she was a scared teen who had to face the loss of a parent way too soon. If he wanted her to keep the line of dialogue open, and be honest with him, then he needed to be honest with her.

"Sometimes," he said. "You know, it's okay to be sad and it's okay to admit that the sadness is too much to carry alone, and in those moments know that I'm here for whatever you need."

"Love you," she whispered.

"Love you, kiddo," he said, and she stood up. "How about we go find my mom's cookie recipe?"

"I'd like that," she said. "But first, I think I need to text Daddy and explain why there are a bunch of kids at his house making decorations and I'm here."

Emmitt smiled. "Maybe you should also let him know you're safe and with me, and that I can drive you home after we make cookies."

"Okay." She picked up her phone but hesitated. "Do you think maybe I can tell him I'm sleeping here for a while?"

"You are welcome here anytime. This is your house too," he clarified. "And as long as Gray is okay with it and you aren't staying here to get back at him for something, you can stay as long as you want."

"I want to stay with you because I miss you. And since we're working on the honesty thing, I also want to stay because it's not my home."

Talk about a hit to the chest. "I understand."

"No, I mean, this is my home with you, not my home with Mom. Everything over there reminds me of her."

"That's a good thing. When my mom died, Grandpa boxed up everything that was hers and pretended she never existed."

"Is that why you hate Grandpa?"

"God, P, I don't hate him," he said, feeling like a shitty parent for letting her think that. "We just have a lot to work through."

"When you're ready to talk about it, I'd like to hear more about Grandma and Grandpa and what happened."

He took both her hands. "When I'm ready, I'd love to tell you all about it. I even have an album my mom made with all kinds of embarrassing photos of me."

"Is that why you became a photojournalist? Because of that album?"

"I don't know," he said. "But I'm sure it had something to do with it."

"Maybe we can make one for me. With pictures of you, mom, me, all of us."

"It can be our thing," he said, and she looked confused. "You know, *our thing*." He wiggled his upper body in a total dad move. "You go to Gray for some things and Levi for others. Maybe this album can be something that we do together."

"If you say so, but I've always wanted to know how to take pictures like you do, so this will be fun." She gave him a kiss on the cheek, and Emmitt's world was back to normal.

"Oh, I had coffee with a couple of your friends' moms the other day," he said.

She clasped her hands and bounced on her toes. "And?"

"And it looks like they are all fine with the party being here if you still want it."

She covered her mouth. "Seriously?"

"Once they got to know me and learned that Annie is going to be here, they were okay with the whole thing."

"That's awesome. And Annie's okay with it?"

Play the honest card, buddy.

"I was thinking we could both ask her over pizza. Butter her up with pepperoni and green olives, then finish it off with vanilla ice cream—I'll get you a tub of sugar free."

"Regular vanilla is fine. I was just being a jerk," she admitted. "You said you guys aren't dating."

"We're not."

"But you want to?"

"Oh yeah," he said, shocked at how excited he was by the idea of a potential relationship. Usually, if a woman even said exclusive, he'd break out in a sweat.

"I didn't mean what I said in the car the other night, but I do know that she's different from anyone else I've ever seen you with, and it's clear she likes you, which is why—"

"Really? Go back. Define like. Like, she likes me, or she *likes* me?"

"If you're asking, you already know. And if you're asking, it means you know she's special, because you never ask me about girls. Ever. So here's my advice, Dad." She grabbed his cheeks and squished them together, making his lips pucker. "Don't Sam all over this and blow it with a cool chick."

"That's the plan."

"Good. Oh, I meant to ask you, would you be my date for the dance?"

He stood. "Absolutely. Yes and yes. All the cookies in the world yes. Do you have a dress? Can I buy you a dress?"

"First, I'm going dress shopping with Owen. Second, you're so lame."

He pointed to his smile. "This is called being honest. And speaking of honest, maybe I should text Gray and Levi while you're in the shower and let them know."

She rolled her eyes.

"Kidding. Kind of. Not really."

"Just so you know, I'm going to ask Gray and Levi too, since this is a father-daughter dance and all three of you are my dads."

"Of course." He pulled out the recipe box from the cabinet and set it on the island.

"But Dad, I asked you first."

"I know!" He high-fived the air, and once again she rolled her eyes. "Can I always be number one?"

"You are. Just ask Annie. You're Dad One and Gray's Dad Two."

Emmitt paused and his forehead crinkled. "Wait, like Thing One and Thing Two?"

Chapter 24

Emmitt was riding the bench—or the bleachers in this case.

It was the father-daughter dance, and this father had had exactly one dance with his daughter. More like a half of a dance.

He'd been right where he wanted to be, twirling his baby under the twinkle lights and holding back his tears as she looked up at him as if maybe, just for tonight, he was once again her prince who had ridden in and, with some epoxy, a blowtorch, and cascading glam lights strong-armed into the shape of giant stars, turned her life into a shimmering and glittery fairy tale.

Only instead of him playing the role of Prince Charming, that title belonged to some beanpole of a basketball player who was president of the junior class and therefore "working" the beverage stand. Emmitt wanted to point out that he needed to get his ass back behind the beverage table instead of "working" on Paisley. But Levi had yanked him back.

"A bottle of water," Emmitt said. "The little prick showed me up with a bottle of water."

"Being benched sucks, doesn't it," Gray said, still bitter that the sleepover was going down at Emmitt's place next weekend.

"You're more than welcome to come to the party," Emmitt offered, noticing that the strobe light wasn't making his head ache as much as he'd anticipated.

"Oh, to the party I'm paying for?" Gray folded his arms over his chest and glared. "Thanks."

"Hey, are that kid's hands on her butt, or is that a shadow," Levi asked, squinting into the crush of people on the dance floor and pointing in the general direction of where Emmitt had last seen Paisley.

"Definitely her butt. Good thing for that kid, he's not groping Paisley," Gray said, taking Levi's finger and repositioning it to the opposite side of the gym. "There's Paisley, behind the dad trying to foxtrot his daughter around the room."

"Ah, well then it's some other dad's problem." Levi relaxed back, resting his elbows on the bleacher row behind them. "It was the *way too short to be our kid's dress* that confused me."

"They're all wearing *too short to be kids' dresses*," Gray said. "And Paisley was right, the foxtrot does look lame."

"About the other girl," Levi began.

"Which one?" they both said.

"The one I thought was P. What if her dad isn't here or stepped out to take a call or something and he doesn't know that some punk is getting all handsy with his daughter?"

"Rookie move if he went to take a leak and left his daughter in that dress around this many horny boys," Emmitt said. "He should tough it out and stay dehydrated like the rest of us. I haven't had even a sip of liquid in seven hours, because I came prepared."

"Levi's right," Gray said. "If some guy was all over Paisley and one of us wasn't there to set the punk straight, I'd hope another dad would step in."

"I agree," Emmitt said. "But I already threatened one teenager this month—someone else will have to do it."

Levi sat forward. "I thought this was supposed to be a father-daughter dance. How did all these guys get in here?"

"According to the women in my Ladies Who Lunch group, the kids who didn't use the whole *my sister invited me because we're that close* excuse to get in volunteered to help out."

"Sneaky little shits," Levi said, sending Emmitt a sidelong glance. "Why didn't we think of that when we were kids?"

"They didn't have a father-daughter dance back in the day."

"Right, well, someone needs to fix this, because it creates a false sense of teen celibacy."

"We're meeting next week to discuss how to address it for next year," Emmitt said, and both guys exchanged amused looks. "What? I felt it was time to get to know the other moms, so they'd feel comfortable with their kids hanging out at my place."

"Just how well do you know these moms?" Gray asked in a tone that had Emmitt gritting his teeth.

"Well enough to know that they're nice ladies, some of whom have shitty exes and sometimes they need a dad's perspective on things."

"How many of them are single?" Levi asked.

"All but three," Emmitt said. "Most of them have kids who are friends of Paisley's, which makes sleeping with them a bad dad move."

"I told you not to start up with Annie, and you clearly didn't listen there," Gray snapped.

"She doesn't have kids, therefore not a bad dad move," Emmitt clarified. "And you said Annie was strictly hands-off. You never said anything about her hands on me."

"Always looking for the loophole," Gray said. "Annie's been through—"

Emmitt held a hand in front of Gray's face. "I know exactly what she's been through. She's told me everything, and we're both on the same page."

Gray batted at Emmitt until he lowered his arm. "What page is that?"

"A page that's between me and Anh."

"Anh," Gray said. "She prefers for everyone to call her Annie."

"Yeah, well, I'm not everyone," Emmitt said. "And I know exactly what she prefers, so why don't you shut the hell up?"

"What's crawled up your ass?" Levi asked.

"Nothing."

Levi chuckled, and then a slow grin spread across his face.

"Holy crap. You've got a smoking hot roommate sleeping in your bed, and you've been sleeping on the couch this whole time."

Actually, it was the recliner. Not that he'd admit that to these boneheads, because the truth of it was, now that he knew what it felt like to sleep with her in his arms, sleeping with a wall between them was driving him nuts.

"She's setting the pace."

Levi laughed. "That sounds like the title of some chick flick."

Gray rested his elbows on his knees and turned his head to Emmitt. "I take everything I said back. Annie's not the one in trouble, you are! And, man, I can't wait to see what happens next."

Neither could Emmitt.

Annie had said she needed a couple of days to think things through. And even though, by his calculations, a couple of days meant two, day six was coming to a close and he still hadn't resorted to sweet-talking her into going faster than she needed.

Oh, he'd been sweet, and they'd talked—nearly every night and about nearly everything. And on the nights they didn't talk, they snuggled up and watched movies. She favored rom-coms, and that was all right with him. Rom-coms led to kissing—okay, they kissed every night, rom-com or not—but he'd never pushed her for more.

Odd thing was, he didn't feel like anything was missing. Did he want to sleep with her again? Yes. Did he want to do more than just sleep? Hell, yes.

But he wasn't willing to do anything to screw up this relationship blossoming between them, and the fact that he used the word *blossoming* said just how far gone he was.

Annie was more than just a lover. She was a friend. If he played his cards right, she could be a whole lot more.

"I don't want to talk about it," he said, and the guys laughed.

"I haven't received your file from China," Gray began, and Emmitt swore. "Until you come back in so I can give you a complete evaluation, my recommendation is to avoid all forms of work and strenuous activity."

"Ohhhhh." Levi knocked knuckles with Gray, right in front of Emmitt's face. "You've been put on a sex hiatus by the good doctor here."

Emmitt was about to knock the smirks off their faces when the slow song ended and something more upbeat began to play. The partners separated, the dads took their designated seats— as far away from their kids as possible—and it became a big mosh pit of girls dancing.

"About time," Gray said.

"I slipped the DJ twenty bucks to play something that didn't sound like foreplay," Levi admitted.

Emmitt thought he saw Paisley looking his way. "Is she—?"

"Yup," Levi said, shifting to the edge of the bench, his back straight and his body language set to *You want to dance?*

"Hey, Dads," Paisley said, swishing up to them. "Anyone want to dance?"

"Me," all three guys said simultaneously.

There was a lot of jostling and elbow jabbing going on as they all stood at the same time. Emmitt's palms began to sweat as if he were fifteen again and the prettiest girl in the room had asked him to dance.

"Good thing it's a fast song," she said, kissing Levi on the cheek, then taking Gray and Emmitt by the hand. "I bet I'll be the only girl on the dance floor lucky enough to dance with three dads."

Standing at the counter covered in a light dusting of flour and a worn Boston University shirt she'd borrowed from Emmitt, Annie kneaded a batch of egg noodles for Grandma Hannah's farmhouse chicken soup recipe. It was her fifth batch and third change of clothes of the night.

Her mom had told her to buy the egg noodles, but Annie was determined to make it just like her grandma had when Annie was little. The next Pho Shizzle potluck was a little over a week away and, with some serious kitchen time, she actually had a shot at nailing this. Plus, the kneading brought up warm memories of the summers she'd spent in her grandparents' kitchen,

Grandma Hannah whisking up one of her many recipes with Annie standing on a wooden chair in pigtails and an oversized apron, with flour down her front, acting as sous chef.

She hadn't quite mastered the noodles, but she knew she was close to figuring out the perfect balance of working and resting time. It was more than she could say for her personal life.

She glanced at the sticky notes on the fridge that had been waiting for her when she came home from work, and her heart did a serious *baa boom* before rolling all the way over.

Off to the dance. Please ~~don't~~ wait up. I might be late. Prince Charming got it all wrong.

He fell for the ballgown and glam, when he should have gone for a girl in scrubs. They're way hotter.

— Much More Than a Roommate in Rome

She didn't know which part was sweeter—the big red line through the word "don't" or that he loved her scrubs.

Oh yes, she was in trouble. It was becoming more than apparent—no matter how much resting time she gave herself between kisses, she didn't think her need for Emmitt would ever go away. And it wasn't the physical need that frightened her.

She'd left home on a journey of self-discovery for one, vowing to figure out who she was on her own before inviting a man to the table. What she hadn't anticipated was just how long and lonely that journey could be. Nor had she imagined how much she would grow to like the person she was around Emmitt.

She'd never been around someone who affected her the way he did, but the changes he inspired didn't happen in a smoth-

ering or all-consuming way, like relationships of the past. His impact was gentle and nurturing and, when she let herself admit it, loving. He awakened parts of her personality she'd thought had taken a permanent sabbatical.

And she could see the subtle changes in him as well. Changes that were more a result of her shutting off what people said about him and seeing him for the man he really was. It was no surprise she'd fallen for him.

Which she had. Totally, completely, and irreversibly. She'd fallen hard for a guy who considered the world his home.

They had agreed—no fake promises and no secrets. While the good girl part demanded that she live up to the agreement and come clean, the other part of her, who remembered exactly how painful it was to be rejected, warned her that all being honest would do was effectively ruin the best thing that had ever happened to her.

Because being honest meant coming clean about everything. Love and trust were both vital parts of a relationship.

And if she were being honest with herself, it wasn't her fear of taking things too fast that had her stalling. She couldn't make love to Emmitt again—because they'd blown right past casual sex—until she came clean about Les's cancer.

Professionally, it wasn't her secret to share. But the feelings Annie had developed for Emmitt were anything but professional. So when she'd run into Les in the infusion center yesterday, she'd told him that he had to come clean with Emmitt. Or she would set up an accidental "run-in" for the two of them to get reacquainted. Which wasn't exactly breaking her medical oath, but in her heart she knew it would be breaking an ethical one.

She looked down at the tough and rubbery ball of dough and sighed. Another contribution to the garbage, she thought, as she chucked it into the trash bin she'd dragged to the end of the island. At least her shooting skills were improving.

She knocked the cutting board against the side of the sink to get the remaining flour and dough off, then set it back on the counter, swaying to the music coming from her phone. The ingredients were already lined up, so she added the flour and salt

to a clean bowl and was whisking them together when her cell vibrated.

She carefully picked the phone up between the palms of her hands, so as not to gum it up any further with dough. After blowing some stray hairs out of her face, she lifted the cell high enough to swipe right with the only part of her body not covered in flour—her nose. A text popped up.

> **How's the soup coming?**

Annie took in the disaster of a kitchen and laughed. Based on the mess, she should have a nine-course meal prepared. She used her knuckle to text back.

> **Well, the broth isn't too salty.**

> **That good, huh? Sounds like U need a break. How do U feel about dancing?**

And just like that, a million butterflies took flight in her stomach. She glanced at her reflection in the polished stainless-steel refrigerator door and gasped. Lord, was she ever a mess.

> **I'm about as cut out for public consumption as my soup.**

> **I can't wait to taste both. But first we dance.**

Only Emmitt could make her laugh and horny with a single text. It was another one of the many things she loved about being around him. She'd laughed more with him than she'd laughed in all her years with Clark.

I'm N an old t-shirt & covered N flour. I don't
think I'm dance material at the moment.

"You left out that it's my shirt and you're not wearing pants,"
a very amused and very masculine voice said from the general
direction of the front of the house.

Startled, Annie dropped the phone and it landed with a
muted thud, followed by a cloud of flour. Her heart was doing
some thudding of its own. The longer she looked at Emmitt,
dressed in a suit and tie fit for the red carpet with a leather
jacket that added a touch of bad boy to the GQ vibe he had going on, the louder the thumping became, until she was certain
he could hear it.

"My T-shirts and jeans are in the wash," she explained, then
reached into the bowl for her phone. But her hands were wet,
which caused the flour to stick to them.

"Lucky me," he said, coming up behind her until his front
was pressed against her back and his arms came around. "Let
me help."

He took her phone and set it on the dish towel next to the
cutting board, then brushed her hair to the side so he could kiss
the curve where her neck met her shoulder. And kiss and kiss,
until her head dropped back against his chest.

"As good as I remembered," he whispered.

"I didn't expect you home until later," she said. "How was
the dance?"

"Guess which dad got the first dance," he asked.

Smiling, she turned, expecting him to back up, which he did
not. She got an up-close-and-personal look at just how happy
he was. "You?"

"Me." He placed a hand on either side of her waist, then
brushed a tender kiss across her cheek, and her *baa booms* became louder, and closer together with an urgency that made her
dizzy. "And guess who got the last dance of the night?"

"You?"

"Technically all three of us dads shared the last dance, but

the last slow dance of the night went to me." He kissed the other cheek. "And guess who didn't threaten any teenagers, even when they danced with my daughter?"

"I'm so proud."

"Me too. It came close, but I managed to hold it together." This time when he spoke, it was barely a whisper. And when he kissed her, it was on the tip of her nose. "And guess whose house Paisley wants to spend more time at?"

"Yours?"

"Yeah." Another gentle kiss, this one against her lips, gentle and sweet and over way too quickly.

"I'm so happy for you, Emmitt," she whispered. "I know how hard you've worked to make tonight special for her and to show her how much you love her. The best part is she knows now. You deserved a night like this with her, and that you did it with Gray and Levi will only make the memory that much sweeter."

"Tonight was pretty perfect," he said. "Except for one thing."

"Gray was there?" she teased.

"No. You weren't. And I wish you had been," he said, and the bottom dropped out of her stomach, like it always did when he said things she wanted so badly to be true. "For the pictures, the dancing, the memories, all of it."

"Don't say it if you don't mean it," she warned, telling herself more than him.

"Look at me and tell me that I don't," he softly challenged, and she looked and—*fairy godmothers be true*—he meant every word. It was right there, staring back at her, everything she'd hoped to find but had been too afraid to acknowledge—love.

She wasn't saying it was the *forever and ever amen* kind of love. But what she saw was enough to make her breath stall out in her chest. And the longer she looked, the more apparent it became that along with the hunger and desire—was a vulnerable need to share his world with her.

As she realized how much she wanted to be on the giving *and* receiving end of that, her chest relaxed and all the air left her lungs in a whoosh.

"Yeah." He smiled. "It caught me off guard too. So much so

that tonight, when I saw people taking selfies under the arbors, I wanted to take one too. With you."

"Emmitt Bradley, award-winning photojournalist, taking a selfie?" she teased.

"What can I say, with you I want to try new things." He moved closer and lowered his voice. "All the things."

Annie had it all wrong. Emmitt wasn't romantically challenged. He was romantically choosy. And he'd chosen her.

"Let's start with the selfie." Because that was as far forward as her head would allow her to fantasize. Too bad her heart was one selfie away from forever. "What would we be doing in this selfie?"

"Dancing." He took one of her hands in one of his and slowly moved them to the center of the kitchen. "You would have been wearing that red dress that's hidden in the back of the closet, the one that still has the tags on it, and I would have taken you in my arms, and then as we started to move, I'd snap the camera to capture every single emotion I experienced when dancing with you for the first time."

She looked down. "I don't think the red dress is going to happen anytime soon."

"That's just it. When I came through the front door and caught you swaying in the kitchen, covered in flour and my shirt, I realized that even in the red dress you couldn't look any sexier."

Annie remembered singing a very bad, very embarrassing rendition of "Girl on Fire" by Alicia Keys while shaking her booty. "How long were you watching?"

"Long enough to make sure your dance card was open," he said, sliding an arm around her back, settling it low on the curve. "Put your arm around me, Anh."

"I'll get you all dirty."

"I like it when you get me dirty, but I love it when you hold me in your arms," he whispered, and she complied, because that was, quite possibly, the most romantic thing anyone had ever said to her.

She looked up at him through her lashes. "I can turn on some music."

"We can just sway all night for all I care." He pulled her close

and their bodies brushed as they moved together. So incredibly slow it was more like swaying while their feet took the tiniest of steps, and they barely moved at all.

But inside, Annie's heart was moving things around, making room for Emmitt, because she could no longer avoid the reality of this whole situation. Annie's journey of one had merged with his the moment she threw her shoe at him and he'd smiled.

She should have known then that she was going to fall, because he'd seen the irrational side of Annie come out in one of the most imperfect moments of her life, and instead of walking away or placating her—as so many other people had—he'd been intrigued. And the more of Annie she let out to play, the more interested he became. Now she was standing in front of him, covered in her many failed attempts at being a true Walsh woman, and all he wanted was to dance her around his kitchen.

So instead of just sliding her arms around his neck, she rested her cheek against his chest and finally, *finally*, gave in.

He groaned, and his embrace tightened. "And you slay me when you do that," he murmured against her ear, then slowly turned her in his arms.

"Then maybe I should do it more often." She pressed closer, tucking her body into his. He groaned again.

Around them the air felt magical. A gentle hum started at every point of contact they shared, softening her heart until it lifted a little white flag of surrender. No longer able to deny her feelings, Annie closed her eyes and gave her heart completely over to his care.

Unaware of how long they swayed in each other's arms, she felt tipsy on romance when he whispered, "I don't know how I will ever be able to thank you for everything you've done for me and Paisley."

"Thank me?" She looked up and, *pow*, he was the one who was doing the slaying. Stripping away her fears, her uncertainty, her insecurities until it was just Annie swaying in his arms. "Emmitt, everything that happened tonight was a result of your willingness to really hear what Paisley was saying and meet her on her terms."

"I never would have gotten there without your advice."

"Advice is easy to dole out. You were the one who put it into action."

And she couldn't have been prouder or happier for him.

"It wasn't just the advice, but for you being you. You didn't hold back when I was totally blowing it with Paisley, you helped me out with the dance when I was in over my head, and you even made my kid's year when you agreed to host and chaperone her party."

"Co-host," she clarified—against his lips. And since she was already there she figured she might as well steal a couple—dozen—kisses. "And how could I say no when she buttered me up with my very own extra-large pepperoni and green olive pizza? I wonder where she got that idea."

"Goldilocks, you had your own pizza because everyone else knows you don't put green olives on a pie," he said, their gazes locked as if magnetically charged. "Plus, I know a bunch of ways to butter you up, none of which include food."

Her body revved its engine, waiting for her to wave the white flag so they could do the damn thing. "It's just a party, and it will be fun. Although I wonder who's going to chaperone the chaperones?"

"We can take turns. You chaperone me while I try to seduce you, and then I'll chaperone you while you try to seduce me." He smiled. "Ah, I see the problem."

"I know." She stopped and, going up on her toes, planted one hell of a kiss on him. "How about we give up the whole pretense of a chaperone."

"Thank Christ," he growled against her mouth, and without breaking his hold he lifted her into his arms and carried her down the hallway.

"What are you doing?" She laughed.

"What I wanted to do the first night I met you. Make love to you in my bed, then wake up and do it all over again, until neither one of us can move." He tossed her onto the mattress, disposing of his tie and shirt before covering her with his body. "You have a problem with that?"

"No, but I, ah—" She tried to sit up, and he froze.

He came up on one elbow. "Don't shut me out," he whispered, dropping a tender kiss on her lips.

"What? No." She touched his face, and he leaned into it. "I'm not shutting you out. It's the opposite. I wanted to talk about something before we had sex again."

"Does it concern you and me and anything that is going to happen in this bed?"

She shook her head.

"Good." Pushing her hair back from her eyes, he traced the line of her lower lip. "Goldilocks, I have spent the past month talking it out with everyone in my life, dealing with more emotions than I knew existed, and worrying about everyone and everything to the point of exhaustion. But tonight, it all felt like it came together, and for the first time in a long time everything feels right and good and how it should be. And to make things even more perfect, I was able to come home and share it all with this amazing, sexy woman who gets me."

Annie's throat tightened and her eyes swelled with emotion.

"Usually, the problems I cover are either too big to solve or too small to matter, but with you, Goldilocks, it feels just right. So unless there is anything pressing that requires more talking or for you to leave this bed anytime soon, please just kiss me."

Afraid she was about to cry over the lovely and tender words he'd shared, she gripped the back of his neck and pulled him down for a kiss that reinforced what he'd said: The fit was just right.

When he lifted his head, she teased, "I should let you know that I do have work on Tuesday."

"Tuesday?" The sexy grin he gave her made everything tingle with anticipation. "That gives me seventy-two hours to convince you that you belong in my bed, with me, my arms wrapped around you, my heart pressed against yours."

Giving Annie seventy-two hours to convince herself that the guilt she was feeling was all for nothing.

Chapter 25

Normally, Emmitt would have ignored Gray's phone call to remind him of his appointment that day, but Annie had already left for work, after giving Emmitt one hell of a good morning, so he answered and agreed to be there at his scheduled time.

Their extended weekend hadn't offered up much in terms of sleep, but Emmitt wouldn't have had it any other way. They'd spent seventy of those hours in bed and the remaining two in the kitchen making egg noodles from scratch. It was an apron-only dress code with a hands-on approach to cooking.

There was more hands-on than cooking, but they'd managed to create some pretty amazing egg noodles. And the soup? He was never eating store-bought again.

He was in such a good mood, even Gray couldn't ruin his day. Which was why Emmitt arrived five minutes early for his appointment and, even when Gray took Emmitt to the exam room instead of his office—meaning this was a *turn your head and cough* kind of appointment—Emmitt didn't bring up the fact that Paisley had chosen him over Gray for the first dance.

"So, I hear Rosalie was able to get a copy of my chart from China," Emmitt said, hopping up on the exam table.

"Even from the distance of seven thousand miles, the woman can instill fear in her prey." Gray got busy with the pregame

warm-up, taking Emmitt's blood pressure and such. "It's why I pay her so much."

"I thought it was because you're scared of her."

"That too," Gray said, taking a seat and flipping the monitor around so Emmitt could see. "So we can skip over the whole *just a bit if shrapnel* BS you've been preaching."

"Like you believed it."

"When you walked to pick up Paisley I started to wonder, but when you Ubered everywhere, I knew it was bad."

Emmitt let out a breath and asked the question he wasn't sure he wanted the answer to. "How bad is it? I had a feeling a lot was lost in translation."

"It's a miracle you're alive. A millimeter to the right and you wouldn't have walked out of there, and that's not even considering the trauma to the head." Gray walked over and began to gently probe Emmitt's head, taking notes on the remaining sore spots. "Scale of one to passing out and puking, how are the headaches?"

"Today, I'd say a five, but there are times when the puking threatens. But not nearly as frequently as before." And since there was no point in hiding anything from Gray any longer, he took off his shirt.

Gray gave a low whistle. "That must have hurt like a bitch."

"Is that your official diagnosis?" he asked. Gray sent him a look. "And yes, it did and sometimes it still does."

"How often?"

Emmitt took a deep breath and thought of what Annie had said about how lucky he was to have a family to support him, if he'd just let them. And while he'd never admit it aloud for fear that Gray's ego would grow big enough to eclipse the sun, he loved the guy. He loved how Gray was with Paisley, respected the hell out of him for how seriously he took his role as her stepdad.

Oh, who was he kidding? Gray was as much Paisley's dad as Emmitt. He loved her with a ferocity that rivaled Emmitt's and would give his life if it meant saving Paisley's.

Bottom line, if Emmitt wanted this patchwork of a family to work, and he did, then he needed to start treating them all like family.

"More than it should," he admitted. "It's getting better, but if you were to accidently bump me in the ribs, it would knock the breath out of me."

"The soreness could last another four to six weeks, but that just means you're healing. That said, if you promise to take it slow and ease back into things, I'm comfortable clearing you for work."

"That's . . . I don't know what to say." Emmitt tugged on his shirt. "Thanks, man. This is great news." He could finally put this story to rest.

Gray's expression implied he wasn't so sure. Clearing his throat, he scooted to the computer, and the screen lit. "I can e-mail this to you, or if you can wait a few minutes, I'll have Rosalie get the paperwork together and your sentence in Rome will be over."

"I can wait," he said. "And for the record, I don't hate being home. And you can wipe the dumbfounded look off your face. Contrary to all the crap you guys give me, I love being home."

"Yet you keep hounding me about when you get to leave."

"And the second I'm gone, all I'll think about is coming home to Paisley. It happens every time." Emmitt shook his head. "When I'm working, I know where I stand and what my job entails. Then I come home and it's like I'm the idiot on *The Bachelorette* who thinks he's the one, then finds out he's only around because he got the pity rose."

"You watch *The Bachelorette*? *The Bachelor* I get, ton of babes, but *The Bachelorette*?"

Emmitt ignored this. "What I'm saying is, with Michelle gone, everything is uncertain and overwhelming. And if I'm feeling this way, I can't even imagine what it's been like for Paisley. I know that this man-off between us isn't helping, and I know she needs her family's support. All of her family."

"Wow."

"Seriously?" Emmitt stood. "I say all that and you come at me with *wow*?"

Gray raised a hand. "You dropped a lot right there, and *wow* was my first reaction. I needed to absorb it for a minute so that I could give you a response as honest and real as what you gave me. So take a seat."

Emmitt did—but in the chair this time.

"I agree with everything you said." Gray sat and rolled his chair closer. "And I'll admit I've been an ass lately."

"Lately," Emmitt deadpanned.

"Okay, ever since you stuck your hand out and said, 'Hi, I'm Paisley's dad, who the fuck are you?'"

Emmitt chuckled. "I did say that, didn't I? Guess it wasn't the best way to greet the man who'd raised my daughter. And before you whine that you're her dad too, I know. You're not some stand-in or temporary fix. You're her dad, and she loves you like a dad."

Gray nodded three or four times, not as if agreeing but as if the motion helped him pull himself together. "Thank you. It's hard, and I'm scared as shit that one day you'll decide I'm not relevant and take her away."

"I'd never take her away from someone who makes her so happy, and if we're sharing shit like we're on *Dr. Phil* or something, I'm scared to death that she comes to stay with me only because she feels obligated, not because she wants to. That when I come home, instead of making things better, I disrupt everyone's plans and I'm scared that at some point she'll come to resent me." He held up a hand. "And I see you itching to drop some serious medical knowledge on me, but before you go all doctor on my ass, I'm talking to my co-parent right now."

"Understood. Reeling it back in," Gray said. "First, as a co-parent, thanks for initiating this conversation. I'd like to think I'm man enough that eventually I would have broached it with you, but I'm not sure. Which takes me immediately into the second thing, because I don't want to give you a chance to ask me to repeat that you're the bigger man. Is this why you want to get back to work? Because you feel that there isn't room for you here?"

"I wouldn't have worded it like that, but yeah. The first time I walked in to meet my kid, I thought I'd find this little girl whom I was going to raise and love and who would need me to teach her how to ride a bike or throw a punch. Instead, I walked into a ready-made family, with Levi in the role of surrogate dad and you firmly entrenched as stepdad. With three already estab-

lished parents, Paisley wanted for nothing. There wasn't anything she needed that she couldn't get from you guys."

"No matter how hard we tried, we could never give Paisley the kind of love she gets from you. We all love her, but the love from each of us feels different to her, and she needs all of it to feel complete."

"If you really mean that, then after I lay this story to rest, I want to talk about the possibility of her spending more time at my house," Emmitt said. "That's why I want to get this story done. I admit, when I first got here, I just wanted to get back to China, because I hate leaving things open ended, especially with the promises I made to the families I met there. But after a while, I started to see what I was missing out on and began to fall into a rhythm with you guys and with Paisley—"

"And Annie?"

"Annie and I had a rhythm the second we met," he said, shocking not only Gray but himself. "And I don't want to lose the ground I've gained with anyone here. You were right—it's not your job to keep me in the know. I need to be in touch more. I don't ever want to come home and feel like I'm clueless about my kid and her life, or feel like I've been left out of the important stuff. I missed her first step, first word, hell, nearly all her firsts. I'm going to work hard not to miss any more."

"We never meant to leave you out," Gray said, and Emmitt let the reference to "we" slide off his back. "And if you're willing to keep in touch with me, then I'll do my best to keep you in the loop on what happens when you're on assignment."

"I'd love to be able to work locally like you and Levi, but that's not an option. So I've been thinking of a compromise. As soon as I finish this story, which I *can* do from here, I'm going to cut back on some of the travel and start taking assignments that are a little closer to home."

"Are you serious?"

"Talking to Paisley made me realize that the only way we're going to get through the next few years is to tackle it together.

"Hey—" Emmitt stuck out his hand. "I'm Paisley's dad, and

I want to thank you for everything you've done for her. I look forward to sharing this amazing kid with a guy like you."

Gray shook his hand, then pulled him in for a side hug. "No one I'd rather do it with."

"We better call Levi and tell him we love him too," Emmitt joked. "We don't need him whining like a little girl tonight during the ball game."

Emmitt headed toward the lobby with an extra skip in his step and an official letter from Gray's office in his back pocket. He wouldn't be diving out of planes or spending time on the front line anytime soon, but the more he thought about it, the more he warmed up to the idea of slowing things down a bit.

Make no mistake, Emmitt was itching to get back to work, but that didn't mean walking away from what he'd found in Rome. Something special was happening here, and he'd be damned if he didn't see where it led.

Gray offered to e-mail his company directly, but Emmitt told him to hold off for a couple hours. Carmen deserved to hear the news from Emmitt. And not some "Doctor is sending clearance. Please overnight my things" text. She deserved an apology. So he found a quiet cove off the lobby and dialed her direct line.

"Carmen Lowell," Carmen answered, her voice so bright it had Emmitt's chest pinching painfully. Not because he was about to say he was sorry, but because he'd been given a glimpse of the other side of goodbye through Annie and Paisley, and he was ashamed to admit that, when it came to Carmen, he'd acted no better than Clark or Sam.

He was sure there were quite a few other women over the years who would consider themselves part of that list.

"Hey Carmen, it's Emmitt."

There was a long pause and he could practically hear her deflate until, when she spoke, she had all the warmth of a cardboard box. "If you're calling to sweet-talk me into changing my mind, you're wasting your time."

"Actually, my doctor's office is sending over the letter today.

I've been cleared," he said. "And I wanted to tell you before you heard it from HR."

An exasperated laugh muddled through the earpiece. "Why am I not surprised? Emmitt Bradley always gets his way, no matter how it complicates everyone's life. How old was the nurse you sweet-talked?"

Okay, he deserved that one. "Actually, Gray's the one who cleared me, so you know there was no sweet-talking or shenanigans."

"Then you're okay?" she breathed.

"I have to take it easy—no extreme assignments for a few months—but I'm okay," he said. "I know I gave you shit for benching me, but it was the right call. I needed time to heal and decide my next steps."

"I'm happy to hear that, Emmitt, I really am." The sincere concern in her tone humbled him, made him uncomfortable because he didn't deserve her concern. "And it wasn't my call to bench you. That came from the top down. I admit, I enjoyed being the one to put a temporary hole in your sail. So I guess you're calling because you need your things?"

"Actually, I'm calling because I wanted to say sorry."

"For telling the other journalists I was throwing a Carmtrum," she accused. "Thanks for that, by the way. I don't think the junior journalists had heard that term before."

"I haven't talked to anyone since the explosion." But he hadn't squashed the term that one of the younger journalists, who felt Carmen wasn't giving him big-enough assignments, had coined. "But I'm sorry that I implied you were anything but professional. I'm also sorry for the way things ended."

"Seriously, Emmitt, it's okay, it was a long time ago and I've moved on." She waved it off, as he'd seen her do so many times when forced to deal with one of the hundred a-holes she managed or encountered while simply doing her job.

"It's not okay," he told her. "When I ran into you at Mahoney's I was too busy thinking how hard it was seeing you again. I didn't stop to consider how you were feeling. I should have, just like I should have handled the situation differently."

Carmen went silent, probably trying to figure out if he was BSing her. With their past interactions, he didn't blame her.

When she finally spoke, her voice was full of surprise and something warmer that he hadn't heard from her in years. "I'm actually at a loss for words, and you know how rare that is for me. I have a response to everything."

Emmitt leaned against the wall and smiled. Speaking with Carmen had been one of his favorite parts of their relationship. She was smart and funny and loved to talk, about anything and everything. "You don't have to say a word. I made a shit move that night. I was on a high because that assignment went amazing, but when I came home I realized I didn't have anyone to share it with. Paisley was on a family camping trip, you and I . . . well, we weren't that to each other anymore." And once he started talking, he decided to lay it all out there. "I knew breaking it off before it got more serious was the right call, but I didn't realize how much I'd miss you and how hard it would be to get over *us*. So I decided to head to Mahoney's and celebrate with a beer. I had no idea you would be there. If I did, the second the woman at the bar started chatting me up I would have shut it down."

"I could have left too," she admitted. "I knew you were home and, afraid I'd spend another weekend with Ben and Jerry, my girlfriends kidnapped me for a man-bashing night out. You were the man of the hour."

"I saw your roommate's T-shirt," he said, and Carmen laughed so loud it sounded muffled through the phone.

"I told all the girls to keep their jackets on until you left."

"Everyone wore one?" He smiled, thinking back to when her roommate yanked open her jacket, flashing him with her custom-made THE ONLY THING MY EX HASN'T FUCKED . . . IS OFF shirt with Emmitt's face front and center.

"I slept in mine for a long while after we broke up," she admitted.

"I'm not surprised." His voice turned somber. "I never cheated on you, Carmen. I may not have been the forever guy, but I never cheated."

"I know," she whispered. "But you let me fall in love with you, even when you knew you'd never commit."

"I wanted to. I just never got there," he admitted gently. "I knew your feelings were stronger than mine, but we had so much fun together that I let it go on longer than I should have. I just kept telling myself that because I'd been up-front with you, told you I'm not a long-term guy and I'd never change, it exonerated me from any wrongdoing. I was wrong. Out of respect for you and what we shared, I should have ended things sooner, and I should have left the bar that night alone. You deserved better, and I am sorry."

"Thank you," she whispered. "It wasn't all you though. You know that, right?" she asked, and Emmitt realized that, no, he hadn't.

For all the times he played it off that Carmen was just another Crazy Cutie, he carried a lot of blame for hurting her the way he did.

"Looking back," she continued, "all the signs were there. I was ignoring them. We both lied to ourselves, and we both made mistakes, but you're a good guy, Emmitt."

"A little slow on the uptake, but I'm working on that."

They both laughed at that, but eventually a comfortable silence grew between them as the past became lighter, creating space for a fuller future. A future that he could now picture. A future he wanted and was willing to work for.

With Paisley, the guys, and with Annie.

"I'll have your equipment and research overnighted to you," she said, her tone going more professional. "Do you want me to have it sent to your place in Rome? Or will you even be there long enough to sign for it?"

"Rome is fine." He wasn't planning on going anywhere anytime soon. How he saw it, there was enough in that small coastal town to keep him busy for a good long while—possibly forever. He'd still take assignments, still dedicate his time to finding the stories everyone else ignores, but they'd have to be pretty spectacular to drag him away from what he was building in Rome.

"I'll get it out today," she said. "Oh, and Emmitt, I wouldn't be so sure about the whole *I'll never change* number you've done on yourself. Because whoever she is, she looks nice on you."

Emmitt was still smiling when he disconnected and reached the lobby exit.

The sun was out, the sky blue, and he'd been given the all clear to roam at his pleasure. Yet all he could think about was making dinner with Annie.

There was a lot he couldn't wait to do with Annie. Between her working double shifts and him helping Paisley prep for the sleepover party, they'd barely seen each other since Tuesday. So yes, he couldn't wait to (fill in the blank) Annie.

Kiss.

Touch.

Talk.

Lick.

Cuddle.

Grinning like an idiot, he sent off one more text, this one to the woman who'd been his big spoon more than once. And even liked it.

> If U could fill in a blank with any action, what would it B?

Instead of heading to his car, he leaned against a column and waited for her reply. Before he knew it, those three little dots that created more anticipation than foreplay were blinking. Then came her reply.

> Are we playing Texting Mad Libs?

> Something like that. Action, go!

Is this one of those questions where I'm supposed to tell the truth? Like . . . what are U wearing? And I come back with "dirty scrubs & orthopedic shoes." Or would you rather it be a little more entertaining, like, "Black thong, red heels, matching lipstick & nothing else." Please advise on rules.

He barked out a laugh. Only Annie would ask for the rules in a made-up game. Man, she drove him crazy—in all the right ways. His fingers slid over the screen, tapping out his reply.

#1 has honesty going for it, and honesty is a complete turn-on I've recently learned. #2 creates an image that just flew to the top of my Lonely Nights Playlist. But I think I'll have to go with what's behind door #1, because I have a thing for a woman in scrubs. But U still haven't given me an action.

Thinking of a good one. Oh, hang on, Beckett's trying to read over my shoulder. Repositioning. Stay tuned.

BTW, Dr. cleared me for strenuous activities. In case that affects your reply

The dots disappeared and he settled in to wait for her reply, a big dopey grin on his face. The same kind of grin Emmitt used to give Gray heat for texting with Michelle.

His phone buzzed. The grin grew dopier.

Swallow.

Lord have mercy, he was no longer grinning or feeling dopey. He was alert and focused, and things were getting a little crowded in his jeans.

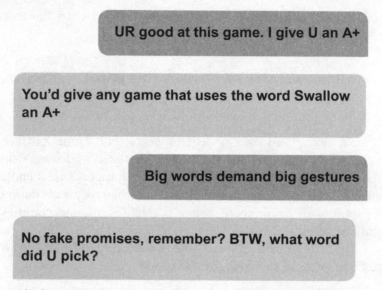

UR good at this game. I give U an A+

You'd give any game that uses the word Swallow an A+

Big words demand big gestures

No fake promises, remember? BTW, what word did U pick?

Oh, he remembered, all right. And every promise he'd made he was going to follow through on. Every. Single. One. Which was why his answer was more of a collection of words, each one requiring its own space.

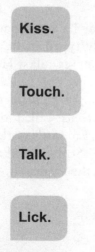

Kiss.

Touch.

Talk.

Lick.

> **Cuddle.**

He could imagine the expression she'd have when the texts came in one after the other.

> **Can I rearrange the order? How about . . . Kiss. Talk. Cuddle. Touch. Lick.**

He'd never been one for lists or notes, but Annie had him rethinking his stance. She knew what she liked and wasn't shy about letting him know. Which worked for him, because it ended the whole *feeling things out* BS people did when they were dating.

Nope, with Annie there were no pretenses, no uncertainties, and absolutely no games. She was, in a word, refreshing.

But a little spontaneity was always welcome, so he decided to add one more word to his list. He typed

> **I wasn't finished. My final word is . . . love**

then backspaced right over those last four letters because, WTF, he had really typed "love."

Well, his heart had, because there was no way his brain had anything to do with that snafu. He'd not only typed it, he'd almost sent it, and after all their No Fake Promises talks. He wouldn't have meant it.

Or maybe he would have. Wasn't that a thought he wanted to save for a rainy day. And just his luck, the forecast called for heavy showers tonight, because when it rained in Emmitt's world it poured down shrapnel and words like "love." So he added a very Emmitt-like "fuck" to the end of that text, then reread it.

> **I wasn't finished. My final word is . . . fuck.**

Send. He was replaying the last few seconds of his life, wondering how he was going to get back to the way things were before he prematurely typed the L-word, but no matter how hard he tried, he couldn't seem to take it back.

Even crazier, he hadn't tried all that hard before realizing he wasn't checking airlines for the next flight to Anywhere But Here or crafting a list of 192 reasons he couldn't feel the L-word after only a few weeks of knowing someone.

He'd had his emotional maturity compared to that of a twelve-year-old boy at a boob convention more times than he cared to remember. This might just be another case of his impairment confusing the situation.

Then again, loving someone meant trusting them, and one couldn't exist without the other. He trusted Annie implicitly. He trusted her more than he trusted himself, and that was saying a lot for a guy whose life often depended on following his instincts. And his instincts were telling him that in this case he didn't think it was a *trust before love* kind of situation.

If he trusted her, then he must also be feeling the other half of the equation.

His phone vibrated and he glanced down.

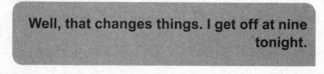

Well, that changes things. I get off at nine tonight.

He texted back the completely expected response.

Which means you'll be getting off with me by 9:15.

Emmitt wondered if she'd come back with another expected response when he noticed a man who looked suspiciously like his dad. He was dressed in white sweats that were held up by a belt around the waist, a polo and—*what the hell*—was he wearing house shoes?

Chapter 26

"Don't you run away from me, Leslie Jacobs. I know what you've been up to," he hollered, confirming Emmitt's suspicions that the man charging through the hospital lobby like a madman was, indeed, his father.

It wasn't so much his voice that gave him away, because he sounded winded, but the fact that he was wielding a cane like a sword and charging at some unsuspecting passerby.

Les hadn't noticed him yet, and Emmitt considered slipping out the back exit to avoid running into him, except his dad wasn't just winded, he was having a hard time keeping his balance. Emmitt looked around for a nurse, but the lobby was completely empty.

Except for Les, who was looking as if he was gasping for breath.

"Ah shit." Emmitt pocketed his phone and went over to make sure his old man wasn't going to stroke out. By the time he made it across the lobby, Les was leaning heavily against the wall, gasping for oxygen.

"You okay?" he asked.

"Fit as a fiddle," Les said, not able to lift his head to look Emmitt in the eyes, which told him just how bad off his dad was. Les had taught him that a self-respecting man always wore a belt and looked people in the eye when speaking.

His situation couldn't be too dire, Emmitt thought. He'd managed to get the belt part down.

"Let's take a seat over here," Emmitt said, taking his dad by the elbow, shocked at how frail Les felt. He didn't have time to consider much else, since Les jerked his arm away.

Not willing to go head-to-head with his father's stubbornness—he was still seeing stars from the last time—Emmitt stood back and, hands up in surrender, let Les work it out on his own.

Silently, Emmitt took the seat next to him and waited. And waited. A good five minutes passed before Les spoke.

"Did Annie send you here?" Les began. "I knew I couldn't trust that girl. She's too sweet on you."

"Why would Annie send me?" he asked, and Les closed his mouth so tight it looked as if he'd lost his teeth and forgot to put in his dentures. Then again, Emmitt hadn't a clue if his dad wore dentures.

Something he'd have to rectify since Les was now a part of Paisley's life, and Paisley seemed to care about him. If he was serious about the things he'd said to Gray, which he was, then he'd have to come to some kind of understanding with his dad.

For P's sake.

"And you can trust Annie," he assured Les, not sure how or why his dad knew Annie—he'd get to that question when Les didn't look like he was two heartbeats into cardiac arrest.

"I got to get going then," he said, using the armrests to stand as if they were an extension of his hands. "If I sit idle too long, I'll lose my namesake and they'll try to give me a hysterectomy. Bad enough they want to fiddle with the boys—they aren't giving me a hysterectomy!"

Les was on his feet before Emmitt could ask him a few simple questions: What year was it? Did he recognize Emmitt? Did Santa Claus visit him regularly? Les sure was spry for a man who'd lost his marbles. It took Emmitt some effort to catch up to him.

"Where you going?" Emmitt kept pace next to his dad.

"Chasing a pretty blonde."

"What's new?" Emmitt laughed. His dad had always had a thing for blondes. So had Emmitt until he'd met his new room-

mate. Now he had a thing for Annie. "Whoa, slow down. You're going to trample someone if you're not careful."

Actually, Emmitt had no such concern. Les running into a wall and knocking himself stupid? That was a different story.

"Last time I slowed down, she got away."

"Maybe she doesn't want to be caught." Then again, when it came to women, Les and Emmitt were cut from the same cloth. So his dad wouldn't be giving in until he found his lady.

Les barreled into the public relations office and walked right up to the counter. No one was manning the help desk, so Les started rapping his cane against the window.

"Dad, they can hear you in California," Emmitt said. "Let's take a seat and I'm sure someone will be out in a minute to help."

"Dottie said I could come anytime. Well, it's anytime." He rapped again.

Emmitt was about to take away his cane when a petite blonde in her early fifties came around the corner.

"Les," she said, opening the glass partition. "How nice of you to visit."

Les patted down his hair and straightened. "I saw her. She was walking out of the infusion room again, and I nearly caught up with her, but she's slippery, that one. Managed to get away again."

"Actually, that's what I was doing in the back," Dottie said. "I was able to figure out the problem, and it's an easy fix. All I need is for you both to fill out this form and you'll have your name back."

"Name back?" Emmitt asked, hoping that maybe there was a simple explanation for this whole situation that didn't end with learning his dad was losing his mind.

"It seems Mr. Leslie F. Jacobs here and a Mrs. Leslie E. Jacobs had their files mixed up."

"One little missing line and some lady's in charge of my life."

Emmitt laughed. "Seems to be going around a lot lately."

"Well, the buck stops here. She doesn't get to say what happens to my boys." Les used one hand to shield the other as it pointed to his crotch. "They're mine and I want them intact."

"I've been a widow for over a decade. I'm not sure I'd know

what to do with your boys," announced a petite blonde who'd been sitting unnoticed in the back of the room. She had likely been born in the same decade as Les and was dressed as if going to church. Her poise and honeyed accent made Emmitt think of a southern belle.

"You must be Mr. Leslie F. Jacobs." She stuck out her hand. "I'm Mrs. Leslie E. Jacobs."

And just like that, one pretty little soft-spoken Southerner took all the bluster out of the mighty Leslie F. Jacobs.

"Dad," Emmitt whispered. "Shake the lady's hand."

"What? Oh, right." He took her hand, but instead of shaking it, he brought it to his lips. "It's so nice to finally make your acquaintance. I was telling my son, here, that I couldn't wait to put a face to my name."

Les clearly needed some help on his game, but Leslie E. Jacobs didn't seem to mind. Nope, hand to her chest, she let out a musical laugh that left Les blushing.

"I just feel so awful about this mix-up," she began. "I'm new in town, and my penmanship isn't what it used to be. I reckon when I filled out my paperwork, the E for Elizabeth looked more like an F for, well, I guess I don't rightly know."

"Frank. Leslie Frank Jacobs." Resting on his cane, he took a bow. "I've lived in Rome my whole life, and it would be a pleasure to show you around."

"Why don't we sign these papers and then see about getting some iced tea. I don't know about you, but that treatment really takes the wind right out of my sails," she said, and Les did everything he could not to meet Emmitt's gaze. "Plus, I'd rather not wait until I've lost all my hair before our first date. Although, yours seems to be holding strong."

Les smoothed a hand over his hair and said, "It's a toupee."

Which explained the ridiculous color and style. But for every question that was answered, a dozen more sprang up in its place.

"Bless your heart for being honest. Mine's a wig too, but I didn't think it would be wise to lead with that."

"Mrs. Jacobs," Dottie said. "Would you mind coming to the window and filling this out?"

"Excuse me," the older woman said and waddled—the same waddle Emmitt had noticed Les using at the family dinner—to the counter.

When it was just the two of them, Emmitt asked, "Testicular cancer?"

"Afraid so," Les said, giving Emmitt the respect to meet his anger head-on.

Anger Emmitt had no right to be feeling. It wasn't as if he and Les had much contact, or the kind of relationship where Les would want to come to him with the scary truth. But he felt it all the same.

"Do Paisley and the guys know?"

"No, and I don't want you telling them either. I don't want her to be worrying about losing her granddad so soon after losing her mom." He held up a hand. "Not that I'm dying. The doctors give me fair odds, even at my age. Your mama would have said I was too stubborn for cancer to even stand a chance."

"Christ." Emmitt took a seat. It was either that or let his knees give out. "I won't tell anyone—that's your place." But he could already hear Gray giving him a lecture about how karma works. Because Emmitt was now starting to understand how painful it was to discover his own family hadn't come to him with something as serious as cancer.

Not that he'd gone to his dad after China.

And it wasn't just anger he was feeling. There was a lot of sadness mixed in there too. That they'd come to this place in their relationship. That his dad had suffered through this alone. That Emmitt had been so holier than thou at the family dinner he hadn't even noticed how frail and sickly his dad was.

"Does Levi know?" he asked, because he didn't like the idea of his dad being completely alone through this experience.

"Nope, just Chip and Annie."

Emmitt wasn't sure what had happened in his throat, but speaking was impossible. So was breathing and pretty much every other bodily function necessary to sustain life.

"Annie knows?" he got out finally. Then to be abso-fucking-lutely sure they were talking about his Annie—because look at

how many lives were sent into chaos over a simple E looking like an F—he added, "Annie Walsh?"

"I don't know her last name. She's my doctor. About this high, black hair, pretty eyes," Les said. "You know, the cute little thing renting your room."

Oh, Emmitt knew all right. Knew that he was a complete idiot. Twelve-year-old boy at a boob convention, that was him.

"She's a special one, that girl," Les went on as if Emmitt's world hadn't taken a nosedive. "Sweet as can be, never too busy to help me when I need it."

Just too busy to tell the guy she was sleeping with that his dad had testicular cancer. Annie, of the "No fake promises or lies," who'd given him shit for keeping his family in the dark about China, had been sitting on a secret so big that when it detonated Emmitt took a hit that made concrete shards feel like cotton balls.

Then there was this searing hot pain in his gut, like a knife cauterizing his insides. He wanted to double over in pain. Instead he sat down, memorizing exactly what it felt like to have his heart shredded to pieces so that he'd never, ever make this kind of mistake again.

"I know that stubborn look, son. And before you go blaming Annie, you need to know that I kept her quiet by using that doctor-patient privilege jargon."

Emmitt had used a similar tactic, only she'd given him a deadline to come clean or she'd spill his secret. Clearly, she took Les's secret a hell of a lot more seriously.

"She couldn't tell you," Les said, and wasn't this just the person he needed to hear the truth from. The guy who'd ruined the first part of Emmitt's life had teamed up with the woman who had effectively ruined the second part.

It was a one-two punch to the throat.

"Uh-huh," he heard himself say, but none of that mattered.

Sure, he got the whole confidentiality crap. What he didn't get was why, knowing about his dad's cancer, she'd made all those suggestions about his dad and Paisley, second chances, being honest with family, leading him to believe she was on his side. Period. Hard stop. End of story.

He thought she'd chosen him. That when push came to shove, she'd have his back every day of the damn week. Because that's what he'd been offering her.

He'd busted his ass proving to her that he was all in. He'd let his walls down, shared things with her he'd never shared with another living soul, let her so far into his heart that the marks she'd leave behind would be as good as branded. The scar tissue would harden over until the only love he'd have left to offer was for the people already inside his heart.

Love and trust can't exist without each other, my ass.

He was such a fool.

His phone buzzed and he felt a wash of anger and anxiety that made him light-headed. He glanced at the screen, wishing to hell that it was Annie with an excuse that would make everything okay. It was Carla.

> **How fast can you get the China piece done? I've got an assignment of a lifetime.**

Carla framed every assignment as the assignment of lifetime, especially the ones in some remote village afflicted with malaria and the avian flu. Both sounded less painful than the story he was living right now.

"I've got to get going." Emmitt stood. "You got a ride home?" he asked Les as if Emmitt himself had driven there instead of walked.

"Yeah, Chip's waiting for me outside." Les went to shove his hands into his pockets, only to remember he was wearing sweats. He rocked back on his heels instead.

"I hope you get this all straightened out without too much of a hassle," Emmitt said as if the cancer would go away once Les filed the right form.

Not sure what else to say in such a royally screwed-up situation, he turned to leave. He made it as far as the door when he paused, then blew out the mother of all breaths before turning back.

"When I'm in town, if you ever need a ride to the family din-ner, or an appointment or whatever, just call. I can always swing by and pick you up."

"That would be good, son." Les swallowed and got the same tightened expression he'd worn the day of his wife's funeral. "That would be good."

"Oh, you probably need my number."

Emmitt handed over his card. And how surreal was that, standing in a hospital helping his dad locate his missing identity, learning he had cancer, then offering him a ride, only to hand over a business card so his dad could contact him.

He was calling it. Day over. He was done.

Maybe Emmitt was the one who'd lost his mind. Either that or he was about to embark on locating his own identity—one that Annie wasn't part of.

And all these years later, Emmitt finally understood his dad's grim expression.

It was how the Jacobs men showed grief.

Annie finished her double shift and didn't see herself volun-teering to take on anymore. She was done hiding, from Emmitt, from her feelings, and from herself.

When she'd set off for her Roman holiday, she'd never imag-ined being grateful to have landed in Rhode Island and not Italy. Her contract was up in less than a month, and she was consider-ing applying for a full-time position at Rome General.

She was also hoping to land a full-time position in Emmitt's life. He hadn't mentioned there being an opening, but the way he'd looked at her this morning when she'd woken in his arms gave her hope that there would be one soon.

Which brought her to the other thing she'd been hiding from—telling Emmitt about his dad. Les still had a few days left to come clean, but Annie couldn't carry this secret any longer.

It wasn't just that she knew Les had a better chance of making it through his treatment with familial support; it was also that Les's family had become Annie's family. And while he might be okay keeping secrets from them, Annie wasn't.

Dropping her keys in the bowl by the front door, she walked into the kitchen to set her things on the table, next to the bags and bags of party supplies for Paisley's sleepover. She was surprised to find all the lights off.

It was already after nine and Emmitt was usually home by now. Or at least he'd text to let her know he was running late.

After the to-do list they'd come up with earlier, she wouldn't have been surprised to find him naked on the bed surrounded by a pool of rose petals.

Come to think of it, that was the last time she'd heard from him. She'd texted him but he hadn't responded. Concern pinched at her throat as she fished her phone out of her purse. She quickly scrolled through all the texts, looking for his thread.

Eleven texts from her mom, five from her dad telling her to check the texts from her mom, two from Gray, and one from Paisley about a cupcake recipe of her mom's that she wanted to make for the sleepover.

None from Emmitt.

She opened their thread and was about to ask where he was when a sticky note caught her attention.

Breathing a sigh of relief, she walked over and plucked it off the fridge. It was something he'd started doing a few weeks back. Leaving these cute sticky notes for her on the fridge. But by the time she was three words in, her smile felt as if it would shatter. By the sixth word she could barely see through the tears gathering, and by the time she got to the end, she was rubbing her chest.

"Emmitt," she called out.

No response.

She read the note again, waiting for it to make sense, then raced to the bedroom, which seemed like a better plan than sitting there crying. It was empty. He wasn't in the family room snoring away on his chair; she would have seen him.

The hits kept coming as she checked Paisley's room and the garage: both dark and heartbreakingly empty. By the time she found herself back in the bedroom, her heart was pounding against her chest so hard, she wished it would just break free so it wouldn't hurt this much.

"Emmitt?" she cried again.

She went to the dresser and jerked open each and every drawer he'd claimed. Empty. Empty. So completely empty. Kind of like what was going on in her chest.

Refusing to give up hope, she stumbled to the bathroom and pulled the top drawer all the way out, dumping it on the floor.

"No." She dropped to her knees, frantically sifting through the few things that remained.

No toothbrush. No razor. No aftershave that made him smell like a sex god. The only thing left was the Bubblicious-flavored toothpaste with laughing baby animals on the tube that she'd given him as a joke when he'd used hers without asking.

But no matter how long she looked, or how many times she told herself she was missing something, she couldn't locate a single toiletry or item of clothing.

"Emmitt?" she cried out, not expecting an answer this time. He'd summed up everything she needed to know in a single sticky note.

Swallowing past the pain, she leaned back against the wall and closed her eyes. The hurt cut so deep, it became impossible to think or breathe. Just when she thought she couldn't bear another moment of it, she looked down and found the note still in her hand.

> *Anh,*
> *Carla called with a new overseas assignment. I fly out on a redeye. The house is yours as long as you need it. It's been real.*
> *— E*

No quippy signature or comment about the future. She didn't even warrant his name at the bottom of the note. Just a single

letter that caused all the hope that had been growing inside her heart to well up and slowly slip down her cheeks to puddle on the cold tile floor.

They'd made no promises, there'd been no talk of what was to happen after her contract was up, but she'd let herself believe it would all work out. That was on her.

But to leave her with only a note, no explanation, nothing but a meme that was more suited for a high school yearbook than a goodbye after what they'd shared? After confiding in him about the ending of her last relationship? That was mean and spiteful.

Which was even more upsetting, because Emmitt was a lot of things, but she'd never imagined mean and spiteful were among them. So what did that say about her? Because her therapist was wrong; other people's choices were most definitely a reflection on her.

The wording in this note, or the lack thereof, told Annie exactly how important she'd been in Emmitt's life. The one person who, only moments ago, Annie couldn't imagine her life without had walked away with only a sticky note.

Maybe he thought ending it the way they had begun was poetic. She thought it was bullshit.

"Bullshit!" she sobbed, her words echoing off the tile walls. "You hear me? I call bullshit, Emmitt! On you, on us, on your stupid smile. But mostly I call bullshit on this sticky note."

She crumpled it up, then wadded it until it was nothing more than a glorified spitball. She threw it in the toilet and flushed. Then flushed again, making sure she never had to see it again.

Annie had experienced rejection. She'd lived through heartaches, big and small. She'd even managed to dust herself off after heartbreak. But Emmitt had accomplished in a single sticky note what no one else had ever come close to achieving.

He'd destroyed her desire to ever be loved.

Chapter 27

Annie needed to be more specific when it came to her wishes.

When she'd left Connecticut to go in search of a life-altering experience, she hadn't expected to wake up in the fetal position on a strange couch with her eyes swollen shut from crying. Nor had she expected to suffer through the lowest moment of her life with an audience.

"Are you awake?" Beckett asked.

Unable to stay in the cabin for even a night, Annie had called Beckett around two in the morning. Her friend caught on quickly that she was an emotional disaster and a danger to drivers at large, so Beckett's dad picked Annie up.

That had been two days ago.

"I'm awake," Annie said, pressing her hand to her eyes. Her head throbbed, her face was puffy, and when she blinked it felt as if she'd exfoliated her eyes. Then there was the cold emptiness that had settled so deep inside, her bones ached.

"You said that ten minutes ago, then went back to sleep," Beckett said. "I'm not falling for that trick twice."

"Eleven minutes and twenty-one seconds ago," put in a monotone voice that sounded a lot like Siri—had Siri been a pubescent boy.

Annie opened her eyes to see Thomas, Beckett's brother, curled up at the foot of the couch. Dressed in navy blue sweat-

pants, a navy blue shirt, and navy blue socks with a blanket draped over his lap and a book in his hand, Thomas looked as if he'd been there awhile. "Morning, Thomas."

"It's afternoon," he said. "I want to play Minecraft. I'd like you to get up now."

"Hey, buddy, can you give Annie and me a minute to talk in private?" Gray said from the entry to the kitchen, and Annie threw the covers over her head.

"My name is Thomas, not buddy, and I will give you one minute," Thomas said, and Annie heard the beep as he set his watch alarm.

"What Gray meant was he needs to talk to Annie," Beckett clarified. "He isn't sure how long he'll need, so why don't you and I go to your room and you can show me your baseball card collection."

"I don't want to go in my room. I want to play Minecraft, and I can't play that in the bedroom. I can only play that out here so they can have one minute."

"We going to do this today?" Beckett asked, and apparently, they were. Thomas started counting down the seconds until Gray's minute was up, Beckett started bartering, which turned to bribing, and before the clock struck zero, Gray promised to take him to the ballpark next time his local softball team played a game. Finally, he relented, leaving Annie and Gray alone.

Yippee.

"You okay?" he asked, and the gentle concern in his voice almost inspired the waterworks again.

"If you came to check on me as a friend, I'm fine. If you came as my boss, I'm still down with the smallpox."

"I can neither confirm nor deny anything you're telling me since you have a blanket over your head."

Annie took a moment to gather herself together, settled on no new tears, and shoved the blanket off her face. "See, I'm fine."

The look on Gray's face said she was nothing of the kind.

"You need to work on your poker face, Doctor," she said.

"You need to come up with a better lie than smallpox, since

that was eradicated in the eighties," he said. "I did go to medical school. I know things."

"What kind of things do you know?" she asked, sitting up. His lips thinned and she said, "I see you know all the things. Friend and doctor."

She anticipated how hard it was going to be to talk about Emmitt, but for Gray to be the first person she told made it so much worse. With Beckett or Lynn she could call Emmitt a bunch of crude names, and they'd call him even cruder names. But with Gray, she had to be mature about the whole thing. And she wasn't feeling very mature at the moment.

"I am sorry." He ran a hand through his hair. "You don't even know how sorry I am."

"You hunted me down and barged into my friend's house. I think I might have a good idea."

"I went by your place a few times to check on you when you didn't show up to work. When I called, it went to voice mail." He shrugged. "I was worried."

"It's Emmitt's place, and I left the night he did. As for my phone, I may have accidentally thrown it out the window and into oncoming traffic on my drive here." She glanced at the clock on the wall, and Thomas was right—she'd slept through the morning. "Shouldn't you be at work?"

His concern turned to serious concern. "It's Saturday."

"Oh? Really?" She counted on her fingers and grimaced. She'd been here four days not two. Then she remembered Paisley's party and shot up. "It's Saturday! Paisley's sleepover is tomorrow night, and since it's a long weekend, the kids plan on spending Monday in the pool."

Gray held up a hand. "That's not why I'm here. I just wanted to check in on you and let you know that you can take as much time as you need."

"Okay." Was that his way of letting her know her job had already been filled? Not that she'd blame him.

Gray arrived to work every morning at nine and left every night at six on the dot so he could have dinner with Paisley.

Some nights he came back to the office to finish up paperwork, after Paisley went to bed, but he never missed dinner. Rosalie said that was why Gray had merged his practice with Rome General, so that he could have more time with his family.

Then his wife had died, and he'd taken a two-month personal leave. He'd been back for less than a month when he'd hired Annie, so he could have the time he needed at home. With Annie calling in sick, he wouldn't have been able to get home in time for dinner.

"I'm sorry if I left you in the lurch the past few days. I planned to come back on Tuesday. If you still need me," she added, giving him an out.

And maybe giving herself one too. She wouldn't leave until she could train her replacement. But then she was gone. There was nothing for her here in Rome.

"I hadn't even thought that far." Gray squeezed the back of his neck. "I came to check on how you were and to give you this."

Gray pulled an envelope out of his pocket and handed it to her. She immediately recognized the writing. It was from Clark. It was also open. She looked up at Gray, and he shrugged.

"Rosalie intercepted it before I could. A lawyer came by the office this morning to drop the letter off. Rosalie said there's a note and a check inside." He held up a hand. "I didn't look."

Annie didn't want to look either. She wanted to cry over the irony. Clark had finally come through, right after Emmitt had left her behind. It was as if the universe were struggling to find balance.

He held out the envelope, and Annie jerked back as if he were handing over a petri dish of Ebola. "Yeah, I'll pass. I think I've read my fill of notes lately. I don't even want to touch it." With a scrunched nose, she waved it off. "Would you just tell me what it says?"

Gray's face softened as he took out the letter. "Annie, I'm sorry for the delay," he read, "but enclosed you'll find a cashier's check for the full amount of the deposit, plus interest. I'm sorry to hear you won't be attending the wedding, but know you'll

always have a little piece of my heart, and my world is brighter for loving you."

"Um, can you sum it up? This is too weird."

"Thank God," Gray said, wiping a hand across his brow. He scanned the note, then folded it and put it back in the envelope. Placing it on the coffee table, he said, "It seems your mom convinced the caterer, the florist, and someone named Molly-Leigh to withhold all future services until Clark, and this is in quotes, 'makes things right with you.'"

The idea that her mother had riled everyone up on Annie's behalf—including Molly-Leigh—was beyond touching. "I guess girl code works both ways." She glanced at the check. "Looks like I won't have a problem finding a new place."

"You shouldn't have to," Gray said. "If I'd had any idea Emmitt was coming back, I never would have offered you his place. And when he did come home, I should have found you different housing." He looked up at her. "I haven't been as attentive to details lately, and that's going to change."

"I'm a grown woman, Gray. If I needed a new place, I would have found one on my own or come to you. Honestly, I didn't want to move. I think, subconsciously, I knew that first night that I wanted to stay there. With him."

"He cares for you, Annie. I've never seen him care so much for anyone except Paisley."

"I've been on the receiving end of some pretty shitty variations of caring, but a complete disappearing act kind of takes the cake." She didn't get into the details. If Emmitt wanted to share that with his friends, it was his prerogative.

His gaze darted briefly away. "He's going to kill me for telling you this, but he knows about Les's cancer."

Annie felt herself nod, as if her head were no longer connected to her body. "That's good, for both of them. I'm glad Les came clean."

"Oh, he didn't come clean. Emmitt happened to stumble across him at the hospital and learned about it in a pretty sucky way. Les told me he also let it slip that you knew. That you'd known for a while."

It's been REAL.

"Oh my God." Annie's hands flew to her mouth to stop the guttural sound building up, but it slipped through her fingers. She'd done this. She'd set the ball in motion, and it had built so much momentum by the time it hit Emmitt, there was no going back.

"No wonder he left without a word. And no wonder he hates me so much that . . ." That he'd end things the way he had. "I'd hate me too."

"He doesn't hate you. In fact I'm pretty sure it's the opposite. And before you go defending him, understand that you found yourself between two stubborn men who have been battling for over twenty years. He's choosing to blame you because it's easier than blaming himself, which is pretty shitty in itself. But then to act like an idiot, tearing out of here without thinking of how it would affect the people he left behind. That's all on him."

"What did Paisley say? Is she upset?"

"She won't admit it, but I can tell she's devastated. I'll give him credit for coming to the house and talking with her. Explaining that he had an assignment that couldn't wait and no one else could handle. He assured her that if she didn't want him to go, he'd tell his editor it wasn't happening."

"Paisley told him to go," she guessed, wondering just how hard that must have been for her.

"She said she could just move the party to my place."

"Wow, I bet that hurt."

"Yeah, he brought her an adult problem so she gave an adult answer, but I know it wasn't the answer either of them was hoping for." He looked at her. "I've been so busy dealing with Paisley's emotions, I didn't think to come and check on you sooner."

Annie placed a hand on his shoulder. "Really, it's okay. You have enough on your plate without having to worry about your employees' dating lives."

"You aren't just an employee, Annie. You have become an important person in my life and Paisley's, one who would be impossible to replace. Which is why I'm hoping you'll stay on full time."

"You're offering me a job?"

"I hadn't planned on offering it like this, but yes." He laughed. "I was going to sit you down when your contract was coming up for renewal. In my office, where it would be professional. But when Emmitt left and you called in sick, I began to worry that if I waited any longer, we'd lose you."

"I don't know. I was thinking about moving on to San Francisco," she said. "One of my friends from medical school works at UCSF Medical Center and has been trying to get me to move there for years."

"They'd be lucky to have you," he said. "And if that's what you choose, I'll write you a stellar recommendation letter. But I hope you'll consider us when making your final decision. Maybe find it in your heart to give us a second chance."

"I'll think about it," she said, and he kissed her on the cheek and stood. "And Gray, they did so much work on the backyard for her party, I'd hate to see the party moved. My offer to chaperone still stands, that is, if Paisley's okay with it."

"She would love that," Gray said. "But you don't have to do this."

"I know, but I want to. I made her a promise and I'd like to see it through," she said. "Plus, I think I need to see it through."

Annie needed to spend one last night in the house, and she was too afraid to do it alone. It might be her only chance to find some sense of closure, and she desperately needed to find a way to close the door on her time in Rome.

Emmitt sat in a back office at the American embassy in India, waiting to interview a source who had proof that the Chinese concrete company had knowingly purchased faulty suspension preheaters that had the potential to explode if air quality caused overheating. The company was suspected of installing them at all seventeen of their plants, three of which were located in India.

The source made it clear that he'd speak only with Emmitt, and only in a specific room located in the underbelly of the embassy that didn't have windows, to eliminate the chance of being photographed speaking with a journalist.

So here he sat, for the third day, waiting for a guy who had yet to show his face. He was giving it another day, then packing it in. If the higher-ups took issue with his decision, then one of them could drag their sorry ass to India and spend their days in this stuffy, hot prison of a room.

Emmitt picked up his phone to check the time and saw he'd missed several calls from the Bobbsey Twins and one from Paisley. Moving to the one corner where his phone registered a single bar, he called Paisley back.

She picked up on the first ring.

"I was starting to think you were avoiding me." A very annoying, very Levi-esque voice came through the line, and Emmitt considered hanging up.

"I'd say don't take it personal, but I'd be lying," Emmitt said. "And using your niece's phone to trick me into answering is a new low. Even for you."

"I had to do something to save you from yourself. Annie called in sick again today."

Emmitt rested his head against the wall and rubbed his hand over his chest, trying to ease the raw ache that had been gnawing at him. It didn't help. Not even being seven thousand miles away helped.

In fact, the farther the plane flew, the deeper the ache got and the hollower his chest felt.

He hated hearing she was sick, almost as much as he hated that his first reaction had been to get on a plane and fly home to make her some of her grandmother's chicken noodle soup. Because if he went home, he'd forgive her.

As it was, he could barely eat, he wasn't sleeping at all, and every time he thought about how she must have looked when she'd seen his note, his eyes started doing this whole watering thing that most people would mistake for tears.

"I don't know what you want me to say, other than *she* lied to *me*." How many times was he going to have to repeat himself before his family got it? He was the injured party here.

"Says the pot about the kettle. Dude, she didn't do anything

you haven't done, and you know it. And what exactly did she lie about? Did you ask her how your dad was doing?"

"No."

"Did you ask her if any of your family members were suffering from a potentially terminal disease?"

"No, but—"

"But what? I threw in the disease part because the men in your family are suffering from a terminal case of stupidity," Levi said. "From what I understand, the moment she made the connection that Les was your dad, she encouraged him to come clean. But Les being Les, she had to give him an ultimatum. He had until the family dinner to come clean or she was going to tell you."

"I didn't know that," he said, not that it mattered. She'd had plenty of time to tell him and didn't.

"You hung up on me before I could get to that part," Levi said. "Only you could fall in love with a woman who actually didn't think you were an asshole, then blow it."

"I didn't say I loved her," he said, wondering again at the power of the L-word.

Not just the word, but the little flutter he got saying it. He'd told himself when he walked out of his kitchen, it was over. That it was better this way, to end it before they became too invested—even though he knew he was already a goner.

"You didn't have to, man." Levi laughed as if this was all so hilarious. "Only love could make you crazy enough to ruin what was an honest-to-God chance at what we're all hoping to find one day. You had it, right there in front of you, and you ran."

"I didn't run. I'm working."

"Working at being a miserable turd, like your old man."

"Well, maybe I finally understand him a little better."

"Are you kidding? Your mom died. Annie just kept her vow as a health practitioner. News flash, that's life, not some big slight against you." Levi lowered his voice. "And if anyone should understand the difficult position Annie was in, then it should

be you, man. The guy who went to jail rather than reveal his source. Hell, I've bailed you out of a ton of situations that had to do with your refusal to give up a source, and I'm still here."

"Those were sources, not family." Didn't Levi think he'd gone through the similarities a thousand times over, only to come to the same conclusion? "I didn't trust them with my kid or my secrets or my—"

"If you say love, I'm going to be the one hanging up on you. Because if you love her, then how could you punk out when all she was trying to do was give Les a chance to tell you, rather than give you another reason to hate him," Levi said. "And if you can't see that or admit just how badly you hurt the most honest and giving person you've ever been with, then don't come home. Because she deserves to be with someone who won't bail every time he gets his panties in a bunch."

"You done?" Emmitt asked.

"I don't know. Yeah, I guess I am."

"I did more than punk out. I hurt her," he said for the first time aloud and . . . "Jesus, I think I'm going to be sick." He sat down, or maybe his legs buckled under the ugly, staggering weight of what he'd done.

A rush of shame and regret choked him as he realized he'd left Annie alone to figure it out for herself. Made a decision when he was mad that would affect her for the rest of her life. What kind of man was he?

Not one his mom or daughter would be proud of.

"Breathe, man, you can fix this," Levi said, but Emmitt was already shaking his head.

"No, I can apologize and do everything in my power to make her realize I'm the ass, and I'm going to. But I don't know if I can fix what I did. To love someone is to trust them."

And Emmitt didn't deserve either from her.

Chapter 28

By the time Annie set out the last of the appetizers, she had batter dried to her shirt, shards of broken twinkle lights under her nails, and a thin dusting of glitter in every nook and cranny. She also had a heartache the size of the Grand Canyon and enough bags under her eyes to start her own airline.

"Why don't you go take a shower before everyone starts arriving," Levi said from atop the ladder. "I can finish this up on my own."

They were in the backyard, hanging the last few strands of lights, effectively turning Emmitt's backyard into a twinkling wonderland. The planter boxes were filled with colorful flowers, the deck around the pool resembled a tropical paradise, complete with a makeshift tiki bar stocked with all the virgin daiquiris the girls could drink.

"I'll make it quick."

"Take your time," he said. "Gray texted a few minutes ago to say Paisley is on her fifth change of clothes and it's not looking good for number six, seven, or eight."

Annie smiled at that as she reached up to grab the empty box Levi had placed on the roof. But when she went to take it from him, he held on until she was forced to meet his gaze. She felt her smile crumple.

"I can't, Levi." Her words trembled. "I just need to get through

tonight without crying, and when you look at me like that I want to cry, okay?"

"Okay," he said, and the sympathy in his voice was worse than the look.

He finally let go of the box, but she could tell it went against every manly fiber in him. Like Gray, Levi wanted to fix this mess, felt some kind of obligation to make right all of Emmitt's wrongs.

They didn't know what she knew. No amount of fixing would ever make her world right again. And it wasn't just Emmitt's wrongs. He'd left her at the first sign of rough waters, but he hadn't been solely to blame.

She'd betrayed his trust by keeping Les's condition from him. And he'd betrayed her love when he walked away without even a backward glance.

She tried not to think about that as she stripped and stepped under the hot spray. Just like she tried not to think about the last time she'd been in this shower, when Emmitt had been the one lathering her up.

Rather than using his shampoo and risk smelling like him, she used the body wash and wound up smelling like rosemary and lime. She'd match the tropical theme of the night.

And when the trying got too hard, she stood under the spray with her forehead against the tile wall and let the tears fall.

God, she was tired. The kind of tired that comes when the grief becomes larger than the soul. Annie had witnessed a lot of loss working in oncology and then the ER, but that kind of loss was different, and so was the grieving.

In oncology, the families were able to grieve in increments, experience the loss over time. There was the loss of future dreams, the loss of mobility, the loss of a full home, and finally the loss of the soul entirely.

In the ER, fatalities were often sudden and unexpected, leaving loved ones to overcome the shock of it all before they could even address what changes they were going to face. There were no last words, a lot of things left unsaid, the endless "what ifs"

that coincided with instantaneous death, and the guilt. The guilt in itself could be paralyzing.

Annie wasn't certain one loss was more painful than the other, but she did believe that the instantaneous loss had the most potential to shatter a person beyond repair.

That's where Annie was, still reeling from the shock of it all, afraid what had been done was beyond fixable.

She'd tried texting him, but he hadn't responded.

That was when she'd come to the decision that she didn't need a response. She wasn't reaching out so she could feel better about how things had gone down, but because he deserved to hear from her how truly sorry she was. He also deserved to hear from her how deeply he'd hurt her, not because he'd ended things—she'd given him more than enough reason—but because of the way he'd gone about it.

And while she spent every night staring at her phone, waiting for those blinking three dots to appear, wishing for him to open the lines of communication, she started to realize she'd have to find closure in her own way.

So she'd begun writing him a letter, on sticky notes, which was yet to be finished. It was more about his part in their breakup than hers at the present, but she was finding it therapeutic. And when she could say his name without wanting to cry, then maybe she'd be ready to write him a real letter.

But that day wasn't today, she decided, wiping angrily at her eyes.

Turning off the water, she stepped out of the shower and slowly began to dress. It was a one-leg-at-a-time pace, because that was all she could handle. She'd managed to get into her bra and panties, both brand-new with no sentimental ties, when she remembered she'd left her dress out on the bed.

Releasing a few more shuddering breaths, she walked into the bedroom and bent over to pick up her dress.

"Those are new," an unexpected but achingly familiar voice said from behind her.

A lump materialized in her throat as every memory they'd

created in this room came rushing back. Then she turned around. The real thing was way more painful than the memory.

Emmitt stood in the doorway dressed in slacks, a wrinkled button-up, his leather bomber jacket, and aviators. He looked handsome and worldly, the quintessential photojournalist for hire. He also looked sad, as if his heart were breaking too.

Hers was pounding hard, threatening to shake apart. "Does Paisley know you're here? She's going to be over the moon."

"It's a surprise," he said from across the room as if they were mere acquaintances.

"Oh, right. You probably want to shower first. I can, uh . . ." Holding her dress to her as if it had the power to keep her from breaking down, she grabbed her bag, then spun around looking for, "My shoe." She held it up. "I just need to find the other one, and I'll get out of your hair. There it is, under the bed." She looked up at him and gave a hysterical laugh. "Of course it's under the bed. Don't mind me."

She crouched down, her new panties and bra making a lasting memory she was sure, and retrieved the shoe. She was adding it to the pile of belongings when two big hands came into view.

"Anh," he murmured, taking everything but the dress from her, then helping her stand. "You don't have to leave. In fact, I've grown to love how you feel in my hair."

She looked up and met his gaze, and a seed of hope that she was certain had extinguished grew warm in her belly.

"Don't cry," he said, as if she had control over the matter. She looked at him like an idiot.

"I don't know what else to do," she admitted, then batted away his hand when he went to dry her face. "And you don't get to come in here and wipe away my tears just because they make you uncomfortable."

"They don't make me uncomfortable. They break my heart."

"Well, when you chase someone relentlessly until they give in, then charm them until the they fall for you, only to dump them via sticky note, tears happen, Emmitt," she sniffed, build-

ing up steam. "It was a really mean note, by the way. I would say it was some of your best work if I wasn't the subject. It evoked all kinds of emotions and epiphanies, like men suck."

She threw her shoe at him, but he ducked. "Men are cowards." The other shoe went flying, and he caught it. "Men are a waste of space."

Out of shoes, she went for her handbag, which landed to the right of him, dumping all its contents on the floor.

"Men are spineless jerks." Left with only her dress, she wadded it up and threw it as well. It fluttered through the air and landed, draped over his head. "You're a spineless jerk. And the worst epiphany," she whispered. "That I really am difficult to love."

He removed her dress from his face. "I'm all that and a whole lot of other colorful and unforgivable things. And you have every right to walk out that door and never give me a second thought. But I want to make sure that you know you were wrong about one thing."

"Really? You're going to point out that I'm wrong? I understand why you were mad. Had the roles been reversed, I'd be mad too, but I would have at least given you the chance to explain. What you did, that went beyond a mistake. It was intentional and purposeful and broke my heart, Emmitt. You broke my heart."

Feeling vulnerable and exposed, she crossed her arms.

"It was all those things, and also the biggest regret of my life." He handed her dress back, and she slipped it on. "But I am going to point out that one of your epiphanies was incorrect." He took a step closer. "Loving you is the easiest thing I've ever done. Getting out of my own way was the problem. You are everything that is right and good, and I was so lucky to experience being with you for even a moment. If you give me another chance, I'll prove to you just how easy you are to love."

"I don't believe you," she said, when—*dear Lord*—she wanted so badly to believe everything he was saying. But she was afraid to open herself up to that kind of pain again.

FOOL ME THRICE wasn't a T-shirt she wanted to own.

"Then I'm going to have to trust you," he whispered, closing the gap between them. "You once told me that if you love someone, you have to trust them. I love you, Anh, so damn much, and I'm putting my trust in you, believing that you meant every word you wrote."

He reached in his pocket and pulled out her Dear Diary sticky note collection. Annie stopped breathing. When she'd started that note it was with the idea of giving it to him, but the agonized words that she'd poured onto those sticky notes were her raw and unfiltered thoughts and fears, things about herself that she had a hard time admitting. It was everything she hated about herself in fifteen three-by-three notes. She'd never intended for anyone to read them.

Especially not him. And not with her in the room.

"You weren't supposed to see that. It's a work in progress." She reached for the notes, and he lifted them over his head. "I'll say whatever you want me to say, just please give them back."

"Did you mean what you wrote?"

"Please, Emmitt, give them back," she cried, her chest collapsing in on itself.

"As soon as you answer my question, because I read all fifteen notes, front and back, and I need to know if you meant it."

If she thought she'd reached her lowest point the other day, it was nothing compared to the humiliation and pain she felt now, burning so cold that her body felt as if it would crack into a million pieces.

"Yes," she said, sitting on the end of the bed.

He knelt in front of her. "Do you still mean it?"

She lifted her head so that he could see all the tears and embarrassment and pain. Everything she was feeling, stripped naked for him to see. "What do you want me to say?"

"The truth." This time when he went to wipe away her tears, she let him. "Just the truth."

"Yes, I meant every word and I still do," she whispered.

"Even this part?" He flipped to the last note and pointed to the last line.

I still love you and I always will.

"Even that part."

He took her hand in his and placed something in her palm. "Then I have a note for you. I didn't have access to any sticky notes, so I used this."

With trembling hand, and a terrified heart, she took the note.

Anh,

Love, once given, never goes away, nor can it be returned. Once you find the real thing, all you want to do is hold tight, because going on without it wouldn't be a life worth living. You have my heart and I hope in time you can trust me with yours.

— Just a Boy, Standing in Front of a Girl, Asking Her to Love Him in Rome

She was so stunned by the vastness swelling inside that she didn't realize he had pulled her onto his lap. Then he cupped her face between his hands and lifted her gaze to his. "I love you, Anh Nhi Walsh, and wherever you are is where I want to be. I don't want to be some chapter or footnote in your story. I want to be in every part of your story that you allow."

"I came to Rome looking for a new life, and I found you. And I don't want my life with you to end."

"Thank Christ." He brushed a kiss to her lips. "Otherwise this would have been an awkward moment. Flip it over."

She did, and in her hand on the back side of his note, were two tickets to Rome, Italy.

"You want to take me to Rome?" she asked.

"I want to take you a lot of places, but I figured I have a lot of groveling to do, so I picked one off your list first," he teased, and she wrapped her arms around him and kissed him. "With that reaction, I'm good going solely off your list."

"I love lists," she said, kissing him again. "And I love you."

And when they were done kissing, Annie asked, "Did you read the PS on the back of my last note?"

His expression said he had, in fact, not. She pressed her lips together while he flipped it over, then let out a laugh.

You're still an asshole!

"I guess I have a lot more groveling to do." He planted one on her that left them both breathless, and Annie was no longer afraid to be one of a kind, because with Emmitt she was perfectly happy to be exactly who she was—living and loving and thriving in the in-between.

Dear Reader,

This story began nineteen years ago in a hospital in Hanoi, when our family was brought together in the most unexpected of ways.

There I stood, staring down at my daughter, Thuy, with her gentle spirit and cute little ears—a sign of luck, I was told—and I thought, *What a miracle*. Among the billions of people on this planet, and separated by over seven thousand miles of ocean, we managed to find each other. Being a mother and raising Thuy has been the greatest experience of my life.

Her journey hasn't always been easy. I've watched with pride and sometimes anger as she's struggled and fought for her place, not just as a woman but as a woman of color, in today's society. Raised in a predominantly white community, she felt isolated as the only Asian girl with white parents. She felt trapped between two cultures, fearing she'd never be fully accepted by either. It was her courage and desire to see people like her in the pages of my books that inspired me to write *RomeAntically Challenged*, a story about a Vietnamese adoptee's journey toward self-discovery when her origins are seven thousand miles away.

I am thrilled to introduce Annie Walsh and Emmitt Bradley, two lost souls who come to Rome, Rhode Island, in hopes of finding that elusive thing they're missing—not knowing that the answer might be standing right in front of them. I truly hope you have loved reading their story as much as I loved writing it.

With love,
Marina Adair

Acknowledgments

When my husband and I met two strangers at the San Francisco International Airport, we had no idea it would end up here. I want to thank Rich and Hoan Sherwood for welcoming two complete unknowns into your family and, especially Hoan, my real-life Joan of Arc, for charging through every obstacle so we could bring our daughter home. And to the other gracious people whose kindness I could never even begin to repay: Aunti Thao and Brother-in-law Hai for treating us like family, Phuong Anh for ensuring Thuy was in my arms on Mother's Day, Thai and Van Nguyen for being our Ho Chi Minh City liaisons (and lifelong friends). And to Dr. Tsuong, Nurse Tran, and the entire nursing staff at Hanoi Obstetrics & Gynecology Hospital for the excellent care and compassion you showed our family. To Mr. Dat, Mrs. Thu from the Ministry of Health, the people from the passport and visa offices, and the many, many other people who were a part of this amazing journey. And to North Bay Adoption, on behalf of all the families you helped, thank you for your dedication to international adoption, uniting families, and believing that families come in all forms.

A special thank-you to my editor Alicia Condon for her enthusiasm and support for a story about a woman of color and about marginalized communities, Alex Nicolajsen for encouraging me to write Annie as I saw her and for your friendship, and the rest of the team at Kensington for all the support. And to my wonderful agent, Jill Marsal, who has become one of the most important women in my life, I treasure you.

And finally, to my husband, Rocco, a master of the art of handholding and unconditional love. And to my daughter, Thuy, the inspiration behind Annie, a character who represents all your sides. Being your mother has been the most rewarding and important part of my life, I couldn't be prouder of the woman you've become. The day you were placed in my arms was the day my heart became whole.

Connect with Us

Visit us online at
KensingtonBooks.com
to read more from your favorite authors, see books
by series, view reading group guides, and more.

for sneak peeks, chances to win books and prize packs,
and to share your thoughts with other readers.

facebook.com/kensingtonpublishing
twitter.com/kensingtonbooks

Tell us what you think!

To share your thoughts, submit a review,
or sign up for our eNewsletters, please visit:
KensingtonBooks.com/TellUs.